Directory of Dissertations in Accounting

Directory of Dissertations in Accounting

Second Edition

by

J. David Spiceland
University of Memphis

Kay E. Zekany
University of Memphis

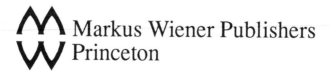 Markus Wiener Publishers
Princeton

Second updated and enlarged edition, 1996.
Copyright © 1996 by J. David Spiceland and Kay E. Zekany

For information write to: Markus Wiener Publishers
114 Jefferson Road, Princeton, NJ 08540

Library of Congress Cataloging-in-Publication Data

Zekany, Kay E.
        Directory of dissertations in accounting/by Kay E.Zekany,
    J. David Spiceland.—2nd ed.
    Includes index
    ISBN 1-55876-142-X
        1. Accounting—Bibliography.   2. Dissertations, Academic—
    United States—Bibliography.   I. Spiceland, J. David, 1949–   .
    II. Title.
Z7164.C81S77   1996
[HF5635]
016.657—dc20   96-26390
                                                     CIP

Printed in the United States of America

CONTENTS

Contents

Contents

Contents

PREFACE

The second edition of *The Directory of Accounting Dissertations* identifies and classifies accounting dissertations during the 1985 through 1995 academic years by functional area, topic and research method. The first edition lists dissertations through 1984. The purpose of this directory is to assist in the identification of relevant dissertation research by:

1. doctoral students developing a potential dissertation topic
2. faculty advisors of doctoral dissertations, and
3. accounting researchers approaching an area of research.

Many dissertations overlap more than one functional area of accounting, use multiple research methods, and may address multiple topics. In such cases, the classification is based on the dominant topic, functional area, and/or research method. In spite of the care taken in preparation of the data, some dissertations may be omitted or misclassified. Your comments are encouraged.

The second edition has adopted a revised Brown-Gardner-Vasarhelyi method [1987, *Accounting, Organizations & Society*] to classify dissertations by research method as follows:

Research Methods:

ANALYTICAL – INTERNAL LOGIC
  includes analytical papers as well as individual opinion type a priori papers

SURVEY
  uses a questionnaire and/or an interview approach asking for facts or opinions about certain issues

EXPERIMENTAL
  involves variable manipulation (also includes questionnaires containing hypothetical case(s)

ARCHIVAL – PRIMARY

uses large machine readable databases (i.e., COMPUSTAT, CRSP) as well as data compiled by others in non–magnetic form (i.e., 10–K reports)

ARCHIVAL – SECONDARY

consists primarily of literature reviews and reviews of legal decisions. It looks at issues generally comparing other studies

CASE

examines a particular issue by carefully observing a field situation but not interfering with it

ANALYTICAL – SIMULATION

involves computer–based simulation papers with random numbers

Dissertations Listed Alphabetically by Author

Author	Degree & Date / School / Advisor	Title	Functional Area / Research Method / Topic / pages
ABARBANELL, JEFFERY STEVEN	PHD 1989 UNIVERSITY OF PENNSYLVANIA LAMBERT, RICHARD A.	INFORMATION ACQUISITION BY FINANCIAL ANALYSTS IN RESPONSE TO SECURITY PRICE CHANGES	Financial Accounting Archival - Primary Financial Analysts 207
ABBASI, NISHAT ULHASAN	PHD 1987 UNIVERSITY OF COLORADO AT BOULDER TRACY, JOHN A.	IMPLEMENTATION OF DECISION SUPPORT SYSTEMS: A MODEL AND AN INVESTIGATION	Information Systems Survey Decision Support Systems 323
ABBOTT, HAROLD DON	PHD 1986 UNIVERSITY OF ARKANSAS	A COMPARISON OF ECONOMIC PERFORMANCE OF INVESTOR-OWNED CHAIN HOSPITALS AND NOT-FOR-PROFIT CHAIN HOSPITALS	General Archival - Primary Industry - Health Care 145
ABDEL-WAHAB, MOSTAFA AHMED	PHD 1988 THE UNIVERSITY OF NEBRASKA - LINCOLN JOHNSON, MARVIN M.	DIVISIONAL PERFORMANCE CONTROL: AN INTERDISCIPLINARY-BASED MANAGEMENT SCIENCE/OPERATIONS RESEARCH APPROACH	Cost/Managerial Management Control Systems 206
ABDELKARIM, NASER MOHAMMAD	DBA 1992 SOUTHERN ILLINOIS UNIVERSITY AT CARBONDALE STERNER-SOBERY, JULIE	AN EMPIRICAL EXAMINATION OF THE RELATIONSHIP BETWEEN ANNOUNCEMENT-PERIOD STOCK RETURNS AND THE POTENTIAL DILUTION EFFECT OF CONVERTIBLE BONDS ON EPS	Financial Accounting Archival - Primary Earnings Per Share 104
ABDUL-RAHIM, HASSAN MAHMOOD	PHD 1993 UNIVERSITY OF NORTH TEXAS MERINO, BARBARA D.	AN ANALYSIS OF CORPORATE ACCOUNTING AND REPORTING PRACTICES IN BAHRAIN	Financial Accounting Archival - Primary International/Global Issues 207
ABEKAH, JOSEPH YAW	PHD 1991 THE UNIVERSITY OF NEBRASKA - LINCOLN RAYMOND, ROBERT H.	USEFULNESS OF REQUIRED QUANTITATIVE DISCLOSURES UNDER FOREIGN CURRENCY TRANSLATION STANDARDS: AN EMPIRICAL EXAMINATION	Financial Accounting Archival - Primary Foreign Currency Translation 157
ABOUEL-ENIN, MOHAMED A.	DBA 1994 UNITED STATES INTERNATIONAL UNIVERSITY STAVENGA, MINK H.	AN EMPIRICAL STUDY OF FACTORS INFLUENCING THE SUCCESS OF EGYPT-UNITED STATES OF AMERICA JOINT VENTURES ENGAGING IN BUSINESSES IN EGYPT	General Survey International/Global Issues 302
ABRAHAM, REBECCA JACOB	DBA 1989 UNITED STATES INTERNATIONAL UNIVERSITY TRIPPI, ROBERT R.	COMPARISON OF COMPUTATIONAL METHODS AND INVESTIGATION OF THE TERM STRUCTURE OF INTEREST RATES IMPLIED IN OPTION PRICES	General Archival - Primary Capital Markets 209

Author	Degree & Date School Advisor	Title	Functional Area Research Method Topic pages
ABRAMOVITCH, RAFAEL	DBA 1991 UNITED STATES INTERNATIONAL UNIVERSITY MERRILL, GREGORY B.	A COST-BENEFIT ANALYSIS OF THE ALTERNATIVE FIVE-YEAR ACCOUNTING EDUCATION SYSTEM	Education Survey Curriculum Issues 175
ABRAMOWICZ, KENNETH FRANK	PHD 1991 UNIVERSITY OF MISSOURI - COLUMBIA PARKER, JAMES E.	AN EMPIRICAL INVESTIGATION OF TAX COMPLIANCE RELATED TO SCHOLARSHIP INCOME	Taxation Survey Tax Compliance 161
ACCOLA, WILTON LEE	PHD 1991 UNIVERSITY OF KENTUCKY KNOBLETT, JAMES A.	AN EMPIRICAL INVESTIGATION OF THE EFFECTS OF A CAPITAL BUDGETING COMPUTERIZED DECISION AID AND COGNITIVE STYLE DIFFERENCES ON INVESTMENT DECISIONS	Cost/Managerial Experimental Capital Budgeting 528
ACTON, DANIEL DICKSON	DBA 1986 KENT STATE UNIVERSITY	THE IMPACT ON DOMESTIC FINANCIAL STATEMENTS USERS OF DISCLOSING FOREIGN BUSINESS AND FINANCIAL PRACTICES: AN INVESTIGATION OF JAPANESE CORPORATIONS	Financial Accounting Experimental International/Global Issues 151
ADAMSON, IAN L.	PHD 1993 UNIVERSITY OF WATERLOO (CANADA)	AN OBJECT-ORIENTED FINANCIAL ACCOUNTING INFORMATION SYSTEM	Information Systems Analytical - Internal Systems Design &/or Development 338
ADAMSON, STANLEY RAY	PHD 1991 UNIVERSITY OF PENNSYLVANIA MCGILL, DAN M.	THE EFFECT OF ESOP IMPLEMENTATION ON THE VALUE OF LARGE PUBLICLY-HELD FIRMS	Financial Accounting Archival - Primary Incentive Compensation 266
ADDY, NOEL DOUGLAS, JR.	PHD 1985 UNIVERSITY OF FLORIDA	INTEREST RATE EXPECTATIONS FOR PENSION PLANS: INCENTIVES FOR DIVERGENT ACTUARIAL ASSUMPTIONS BETWEEN DOL AND FASB DISCLOSURES	Financial Accounting Archival - Primary Post Retirement Benefit Issues 134
ADEREMI, SYLVESTER OLUYEMISI	PHD 1985 GEORGIA STATE UNIVERSITY	AN EMPIRICAL STUDY OF THE IMPORTANCE OF CERTAIN ATTRIBUTES TO ACCOUNTING FIRMS' SELECTION OF NEW PARTNERS	General Survey CPA Firm Issues 185
ADHIKARI, AJAY	PHD 1990 VIRGINIA COMMONWEALTH UNIVERSITY TONDKAR, RASOUL H.	AN EMPIRICAL CROSS-NATIONAL STUDY OF ENVIRONMENTAL FACTORS INFLUENCING ACCOUNTING DISCLOSURE AND REPORTING REQUIREMENTS OF STOCK EXCHANGES	Financial Accounting Archival - Primary International/Global Issues 192

Author	Degree & Date School Advisor	Title	Functional Area Research Method Topic pages
ADIEL, RON	PHD 1994 UNIVERSITY OF PENNSYLVANIA HOLTHAUSEN, ROBERT W.	REINSURANCE AND THE MANAGEMENT OF EARNINGS IN THE PROPERTY-CASUALTY INSURANCE INDUSTRY	Financial Accounting Archival - Primary Industry - Insurance 173
ADLER, RALPH WILLIAM	PHD 1991 STATE UNIVERSITY OF NEW YORK AT ALBANY HALL, RICHARD	ACCOUNTING AND PERFORMANCE INDICATORS AS DETERMINANTS OF ORGANIZATIONAL DECLINE: THEORY AND EMPIRICAL EVIDENCE	Financial Accounting Experimental Performance Evaluation/Measurement 146
AGACER, GILDA MONTEAGUDO	PHD 1987 UNIVERSITY OF SOUTH CAROLINA	PERCEPTIONS OF THE AUDITOR'S INDEPENDENCE: A CROSS-CULTURAL STUDY	Auditing Survey Independence 98
AHLAWAT, SUNITA SINGH	PHD 1992 THE PENNSYLVANIA STATE UNIVERSITY MCKEOWN, JAMES C.	EXPLANATION EFFECTS IN SEQUENTIAL BELIEF-REVISION BY AUDIT GROUPS AND INDIVIDUALS	Auditing Experimental Judgment & Decision Making - Heuristics & Biases 174
AHMED, ANWER SHEHAB	PHD 1992 THE UNIVERSITY OF ROCHESTER WATTS, ROSS	ACCOUNTING EARNINGS, ECONOMIC RENTS AND STOCK RETURNS: AN EMPIRICAL ANALYSIS	Financial Accounting Archival - Primary Earnings 75
AHMED, ELTEGANI ABDELGADER	PHD 1990 UNIVERSITY OF HULL (UNITED KINGDOM)	ISLAMIC BANKING: DISTRIBUTION OF PROFIT	General Case Industry - Banking/Savings & Loan 511
AHN, BYUNGJUN	PHD 1990 PURDUE UNIVERSITY RO, BYUNG-TAK	THE INFORMATION CONTENT OF EARNINGS ANNOUNCEMENTS WITH VARYING RETURN PARAMETERS	Financial Accounting Archival - Primary Earnings Announcements 118
AHN, TAE SIK	PHD 1987 THE UNIVERSITY OF TEXAS AT AUSTIN CHARNES, ABRAHAM; COOPER, WILLIAM W.	EFFICIENCY AND RELATED ISSUES IN HIGHER EDUCATION: A DATA ENVELOPMENT ANALYSIS APPROACH	Not-for-Profit Archival - Primary College & University 193
AINSWORTH, PENNE LYN	PHD 1988 THE UNIVERSITY OF NEBRASKA - LINCOLN BALKE, THOMAS	THE INFORMATION CONTENT OF CASH FLOW DATA: AN EMPIRICAL INVESTIGATION	Financial Accounting Archival - Primary Cash Flows 201

Author	Degree & Date School Advisor	Title	Functional Area Research Method Topic pages
AKATHAPORN, PARPORN	DBA 1988 KENT STATE UNIVERSITY FETYKO, DAVID F.	INVENTORY METHODS AND THE PRICE EARNINGS ANOMALY: AN EMPIRICAL EXAMINATION	Financial Accounting Archival - Primary Inventory 187
AKERS, MICHAEL DEWAYNE	PHD 1988 THE UNIVERSITY OF MISSISSIPPI BRINER, RUSSELL F.	AN EMPIRICAL INVESTIGATION OF PRODUCT COST METHODS	Cost/Managerial Survey Cost Systems 208
AKSU, CELAL	PHD 1987 SYRACUSE UNIVERSITY	AN EMPIRICAL INVESTIGATION OF TIME SERIES PROPERTIES OF QUARTERLY CASH FLOWS AND USEFULNESS OF EARNINGS IN PREDICTING CASH FLOWS	Financial Accounting Archival - Primary Cash Flows 257
AKSU, MINE HATICE	PHD 1993 SYRACUSE UNIVERSITY ONSI, MOHAMED	MARKET RESPONSE TO TROUBLED DEBT RESTRUCTURING	Financial Accounting Archival - Primary Financial Distress or Bankruptcy 232
AL-DARAYSEH, MUSA M.	PHD 1990 THE UNIVERSITY OF NEBRASKA - LINCOLN BROWN, JAMES F. JR.	CORPORATE FAILURE FOR MANUFACTURING INDUSTRIES USING FINANCIAL RATIOS AND MACROECONOMIC VARIABLES WITH LOGIT ANALYSIS	Financial Accounting Archival - Primary Financial Distress or Bankruptcy 140
AL-ERYANI, MOHAMED FADL	DBA 1987 KENT STATE UNIVERSITY FETYKO, DAVID F.; MCMATH, H. KENT	POLICIES OF U.S. MULTINATIONAL CORPORATIONS ON PRICING INTRACOMPANY TRANSFERS WITH FOREIGN AFFILIATES IN MORE-DEVELOPED AND LESS-DEVELOPED COUNTRIES	Cost/Managerial Survey Transfer Pricing 341
AL-KAZEMI, ALI ABDUL-RAZZAQ	PHD 1993 UNIVERSITY OF PITTSBURGH	THE UTILIZATION OF MANAGEMENT ACCOUNTING TECHNIQUES WITH EMPHASIS ON QUANTITATIVE ANALYSIS IN THE PUBLIC SECTOR: BUILDING AN EFFECTIVE FINANCIAL MANAGEMENT SYSTEM	Not-for-Profit Survey Governmental 211
AL-NASRULLAH, ABDULAZIZ A.	DBA 1987 THE GEORGE WASHINGTON UNIVERSITY	AN EVALUATION OF INTERNAL CONTROLS OF COMMERCIAL LOANS IN SAUDI ARABIAN BANKS	General Survey International/Global Issues 246
AL-RASHED, WAEL E. R.	PHD 1989 UNIVERSITY OF HULL (UNITED KINGDOM)	KUWAIT'S TAX REFORMATION, ITS ALTERNATIVES AND IMPACT ON A DEVELOPING ACCOUNTING PROFESSION	Taxation Survey International/Global Issues 470

Author	Degree & Date School Advisor	Title	Functional Area Research Method Topic pages
AL-RWITA, SAAD SALEH	PHD 1993 UNIVERSITY OF COLORADO AT BOULDER SELTO, FRANK H.	OWNERSHIP, CONTROL, AND PERFORMANCE IN AN UNDERDEVELOPED MARKET ENVIRONMENT: THE CASE OF THE SAUDI BANKING INDUSTRY	General Case International/Global Issues 192
AL-SHIRAWI, BASHIR ISSA	PHD 1988 GOLDEN GATE UNIVERSITY SHOMALI, HAMID B.	PERFORMANCE OF COMMERCIAL BANKS OPERATING IN THE STATE OF QATAR: A MULTIVARIATE ANALYSIS OF FINANCIAL STATEMENTS	General Case Industry - Banking/Savings & Loan 269
AL-SUDAIRY, SALMAN ABDULRAHMAN	PHD 1991 THE UNIVERSITY OF TEXAS AT AUSTIN OLSEN, JOHN CHRISTIAN III	THE DETECTION AND DETECTABILITY OF MATERIAL MISSTATEMENTS IN INTERIM FINANCIAL REPORTS BY CAPITAL MARKET PARTICIPANTS	Financial Accounting Archival - Primary Interim Reporting 184
ALBRECHT, WILLIAM DAVID	PHD 1991 VIRGINIA POLYTECHNIC INSTITUTE AND STATE UNIVERSITY RICHARDSON, FREDERICK M.	THE DETERMINANTS OF THE MARKET REACTION TO AN ANNOUNCEMENT OF A CHANGE IN AUDITOR	Auditing Archival - Primary Agency Theory 272
ALBRIGHT, THOMAS LYNN	PHD 1990 THE UNIVERSITY OF TENNESSEE REEVE, JAMES M.	THE IMPACT OF PROCESS VARIATION ON UNIT MANUFACTURING COST	Cost/Managerial Case Activity Based Costing 121
ALCIATORE, MIMI LOUISE	PHD 1989 THE UNIVERSITY OF TEXAS AT AUSTIN DEITRICK, JAMES W.	THE INFORMATION CONTENT OF THE COMPONENTS OF THE CHANGE IN THE STANDARDIZED MEASURE	Financial Accounting Archival - Primary Accounting Change 276
ALDIAB, TAISIER FARES	PHD 1992 UNIVERSITY OF NORTH TEXAS	THE IMPACT OF THE CEILING TEST WRITE-OFF ON THE SECURITY RETURNS OF FULL COST OIL AND GAS FIRMS	Financial Accounting Archival - Primary Industry - Oil & Gas 135
ALEXANDER, JOHN C., JR.	PHD 1991 THE FLORIDA STATE UNIVERSITY PETERSON, PAMELA P.	EARNINGS EXPECTATIONS AND THE MARKET REACTION TO EARNINGS SURPRISE	Financial Accounting Archival - Primary Forecasting Financial Performance 200
ALI, ASHIQ	PHD 1987 COLUMBIA UNIVERSITY	PENSION ASSETS AND THE MARKET RISK OF EQUITY	Financial Accounting Archival - Primary Post Retirement Benefit Issues 104

Author	Degree & Date School Advisor	Title	Functional Area Research Method Topic pages
ALKHALIALEH, MAHMOUD ABDUL-HALEEM	PHD 1992 CITY UNIVERSITY OF NEW YORK LUSTGARTEN, STEVEN	NON-EARNINGS INFORMATION AND ANALYSTS' REVISIONS OF FUTURE EARNINGS FORECASTS	Financial Accounting Archival - Primary Financial Analysts 92
ALLEN, ARTHUR CONRAD, JR.	PHD 1989 THE UNIVERSITY OF ALABAMA INGRAM, ROBERT W.	EFFECTS OF LOCAL GOVERNMENT AUDIT QUALITY ON THE RELIABILITY OF ACCOUNTING NUMBERS AND INVESTOR DECISIONS	Auditing Archival - Primary Governmental 117
ALLEN, FRAN MARIE	PHD 1994 KENT STATE UNIVERSITY CURCIO, RICHARD J.	ENVIRONMENTAL RESPONSIBILITY, STAKEHOLDER THEORY AND THE VALUE OF THE FIRM	Financial Accounting Archival - Primary Social/Environmental Responsibility 220
ALLEN, GEORGE LOUIS	PHD 1985 UNIVERSITY OF NORTH TEXAS	AN EMPIRICAL INVESTIGATION OF THE COMPLEMENTARY VALUE OF A STATEMENT OF CASH FLOWS IN A SET OF PUBLISHED FINANCIAL STATEMENTS	Financial Accounting Experimental Cash Flows 178
ALLEN, PAUL WADE	DBA 1994 MISSISSIPPI STATE UNIVERSITY MCNAIR, FRANCES M.	EXPLAINING CPA PREFERENCES TOWARD ETHICAL ISSUES	General Survey Ethics 152
ALLEN, ROBERT DREW	PHD 1992 MICHIGAN STATE UNIVERSITY	STATISTICAL ANALYTICAL PROCEDURES USING INDUSTRY SPECIFIC INFORMATION: AN EMPIRICAL STUDY	Auditing Archival - Primary Analytical Review 193
ALLES, MICHAEL GAMINI	PHD 1991 STANFORD UNIVERSITY DATAR, SRIKANT	INCENTIVE ASPECTS OF COSTING	Cost/Managerial Analytical - Internal Cost Systems 92
ALLTIZER, RICHARD LEE	PHD 1994 THE UNIVERSITY OF OKLAHOMA AYRES, FRANCES L.	THE INTERACTION OF DIVIDEND POLICY AND TAXATION ON THE VALUE OF THE FIRM	Taxation Archival - Primary Dividends 115
ALRAWI, HIKMAT AHMAD ABDULGHAFOOR	PHD 1988 UNIVERSITY OF HULL (UNITED KINGDOM)	ACCOUNTING, RESOURCE ALLOCATION, PLANNING AND EFFICIENCY: CASE STUDIES OF THE UNITED KINGDOM AND IRAQI UNIVERSITIES	Not-for-Profit Case College & University 702

Author	Degree & Date School Advisor	Title	Functional Area Research Method Topic pages
ALY, IBRAHIM M. MOHAMED	PHD 1986 UNIVERSITY OF NORTH TEXAS	PREDICTION OF BUSINESS FAILURE AS A CRITERION FOR EVALUATING THE USEFULNESS OF ALTERNATIVE ACCOUNTING MEASURES	Financial Accounting Archival - Primary Financial Distress or Bankruptcy 119
AMEEN, ELSIE COKER	PHD 1989 UNIVERSITY OF SOUTH CAROLINA CHEWNING, EUGENE	THE EFFECTIVENESS AND EFFICIENCY OF STATISTICAL ANALYTICAL REVIEW IN AN AUDITING STRATEGY: A COMPARISON OF REGRESSION AND THE X-11 MODEL	Auditing Analytical Review 96
AMER, TAREK SAAD	PHD 1989 THE OHIO STATE UNIVERSITY BAILEY, ANDREW D. JR.	AN EXPERIMENTAL INVESTIGATION OF THE EFFECTS OF MULTI-CUE FINANCIAL INFORMATION DISPLAY AND TASK COMPLEXITY ON DECISION-MAKING	Financial Accounting Experimental Judgment & Decision Making 311
AMES, GARY ADNA	PHD 1988 UNIVERSITY OF GEORGIA EDWARDS, JAMES DON	EDP AUDITING OF MICROCOMPUTER SYSTEMS: AN EXPERIMENTAL ANALYSIS OF AUDITOR REACTION TO A CHANGED ENVIRONMENT	Auditing Survey Microcomputer Applications 129
AMIR, ELI	PHD 1991 UNIVERSITY OF CALIFORNIA, BERKELEY	ASSESSING ALTERNATIVE ACCOUNTING METHODS FOR POST-RETIREMENT BENEFITS OTHER THAN PENSIONS	Financial Accounting Archival - Primary Post Retirement Benefit Issues 116
AMMONS, JANICE LEE	PHD 1994 THE UNIVERSITY OF MICHIGAN DANOS, PAUL	THE IMPACT OF STATE CONTROL OF INDIRECT COST RECOVERIES ON AMERICAN RESEARCH UNIVERSITIES	Not-for-Profit Survey College & University 131
AMOBI, EMMANUEL NNABUIKE	PHD 1987 THE UNIVERSITY OF ALABAMA	THE DEVELOPMENT AND EMPIRICAL VERIFICATION OF A PREDICTIVE MODEL FOR ACCOUNTING STANDARD LOBBYING BEHAVIOR OF OIL AND GAS FIRMS	Financial Accounting Archival - Primary Standard Setting 136
ANCTIL, REGINA MARIE	PHD 1993 UNIVERSITY OF MINNESOTA JORDAN, JAMES S.	CAPITAL BUDGETING USING RESIDUAL INCOME MAXIMIZATION	Cost/Managerial Analytical - Internal Capital Budgeting 70
ANDERSON, ELLEN G.	PHD 1989 OKLAHOMA STATE UNIVERSITY BOATSMAN, JAMES R.	AGENCY THEORY AND CORPORATE ACQUISTIONS: EMPIRICAL TEST FOR A CERTAIN CLASS OF CORPORATE TAKEOVERS	Financial Accounting Archival - Primary Merger, Acquisition, Reorganization 63

Author	Degree & Date School Advisor	Title	Functional Area Research Method Topic pages
ANDERSON, JOHN CHARLES	PHD 1987 THE UNIVERSITY OF TENNESSEE	THE SELECTION DECISION FOR MICROCOMPUTER GENERAL LEDGER SOFTWARE: AN INVESTIGATION USING A KNOWLEDGE-BASED SYSTEM	Information Systems Survey Microcomputer Applications 124
ANDERSON, MARILYN TERESA	PHD 1987 QUEEN'S UNIVERSITY AT KINGSTON (CANADA)	ACCOUNTING EARNINGS ANNOUNCEMENTS AND DIFFERENTIAL PREDISCLOSURE INFORMATION	Financial Accounting Archival - Primary Earnings Announcements
ANDERSON, PHILIP NEIL	PHD 1985 UNIVERSITY OF SOUTH CAROLINA	AN EMPIRICAL STUDY OF RECENT CHANGES IN FEDERAL ESTATE TAXATION AND THEIR RELATED IMPACT ON THE FAMILY FARM	Taxation Archival - Primary Estate & Gift Taxation 93
ANDERSON, SHANNON WEEMS	PHD 1993 HARVARD UNIVERSITY WHEELWRIGHT, STEVEN C.	MEASURING MANUFACTURING FLEXIBILITY: THE IMPACT OF PRODUCT MIX COMPLEXITY ON OPERATING PERFORMANCE AND MANUFACTURING OVERHEAD COST	Cost/Managerial Case Performance Evaluation/Measurement 172
ANDERSON, SUSAN ELAINE G.	PHD 1991 THE UNIVERSITY OF TEXAS AT ARLINGTON HOPKINS, DEBRA W.	AN ANALYSIS OF THE EFFECT OF TAX LAW INSTABILITY AND PREFERENTIAL CAPITAL GAIN TREATMENT ON INVESTMENT IN RISKY ASSETS	Taxation Experimental Public Policy 146
ANDERSON, URTON LIGGETT	PHD 1985 UNIVERSITY OF MINNESOTA	THE AUDITOR'S ASSESSMENT OF CONTROL RISK: THE EXPLANATION PHENOMENON IN JUDGMENTS OF EVENT UNCERTAINTY	Auditing Experimental Judgment & Decision Making 219
ANELL, ANDERS LARS	FILDR 1991 LUNDS UNIVERSITET (SWEDEN)	FROM CENTRAL PLANNING TO LOCAL RESPONSIBILITIES: THE ROLE OF BUDGETING IN SWEDISH COUNTY COUNCIL HEALTH CARE [FRAN CENTRAL PLANERING TILL LOKALT ANSVAR: BUDGETERINGENS ROLL I LANDSTINGSKOMMUNAL SJUKVARD]	Not-for-Profit Analytical - Internal Budgeting 246
ANGELINI, JAMES PETER	PHD 1986 UNIVERSITY OF HOUSTON	AN INVESTIGATIVE ANALYSIS FOR THE DEVELOPMENT OF A FEDERAL TAX AMNESTY PROGRAM	Taxation Analytical - Internal Tax Compliance 212
ANGIMA, JACOB M.	PHD 1993 UNIVERSITY OF CALIFORNIA, LOS ANGELES MILLER, BRUCE	THE ASSOCIATION BETWEEN ALTERNATIVE EARNINGS AND PROFITABILITY MEASURES AND STOCK RETURN IN SELECTED INDUSTRIES	Financial Accounting Archival - Primary Earnings 122

Author	Degree & Date School Advisor	Title	Functional Area Research Method Topic pages
ANGRISANI, DAVID PETER	PHD 1994 GOLDEN GATE UNIVERSITY BEZABEH, ADMASSU	AN ACQUISITION MODEL FOR THE HOSPITAL INDUSTRY	Financial Accounting Archival - Primary Industry - Health Care 87
APOSTOLOU, BARBARA ANN	PHD 1988 THE LOUISIANA STATE UNIVERSITY AND AGRICULTURAL AND MECHANICAL COL. BRENNER, VINCENT C.	AN INVESTIGATION OF INTERNAL AUDITOR JUDGMENT ON THE IMPORTANCE OF INDICATORS OF POTENTIAL FINANCIAL FRAUD: AN ANALYTIC HIERARCHY PROCESS APPROACH	Auditing Experimental Fraud 134
ARCHAMBAULT, JEFFREY JAY	PHD 1992 MICHIGAN STATE UNIVERSITY	FINANCING AND INVESTING ACTIVITIES AND THE PREEMPTION OF EARNINGS	Financial Accounting Archival - Primary Earnings Announcements 100
ARCHAMBAULT, MARIE ELLEN EMMENDORFER	PHD 1992 MICHIGAN STATE UNIVERSITY BUZBY, STEPHEN	REACTION TO EARNINGS IN A TAKEOVER ENVIRONMENT	Financial Accounting Archival - Primary Earnings Announcements 144
ARMITAGE, JACK LONNIE	PHD 1988 THE UNIVERSITY OF NEBRASKA - LINCOLN RAYMOND, ROBERT H.	EFFECTIVENESS OF AUDIT CONFIRMATIONS FOR TRADE ACCOUNTS RECEIVABLE	Auditing Survey Confirmations 205
ARNESON, DEAN LEON	PHD 1991 THE UNIVERSITY OF NEBRASKA MEDICAL CENTER JACOBS, ELGENE W.	IMPACT OF MEDICAID DISCOUNTED AVERAGE WHOLESALE PRICE REIMBURSEMENT ON PHARMACISTS' DRUG PRODUCT SELECTION	General Archival - Primary Industry - Health Care 309
ARNOLD, PATRICIA JOSEPHINE	PHD 1987 THE UNIVERSITY OF WISCONSIN - MADISON	CAPITAL COSTS, ACCOUNTING CHOICE AND MULTIHOSPITAL SYSTEMS	General Industry - Health Care 151
ARTSBERG, KRISTINA ULRIKA	EKONDR 1992 LUNDS UNIVERSITET (SWEDEN)	POLICY MAKING AND ACCOUNTING CHANGE: INFLUENCES ON THE CHOICE OF MEASUREMENT PRINCIPLES IN SWEDISH ACCOUNTING [NORMBILDNING OCH REDOVISNINGSFOERAENDRING: VAERDERINGAR VID VAL AV MAETPRINCIPER INOM SVENSK REDOVISNING]	Financial Accounting Analytical - Internal International/Global Issues 252
ARUNACHALAM, VAIRAVAN	PHD 1991 UNIVERSITY OF ILLINOIS AT URBANA-CHAMPAIGN CHANDLER, JOHN S.	DECISION AIDING IN MULTI-PARTY TRANSFER PRICING NEGOTIATION: THE EFFECTS OF COMPUTER-MEDIATED COMMUNICATION AND STRUCTURED INTERACTION	Cost/Managerial Experimental Transfer Pricing 269

Author	Degree & Date School Advisor	Title	Functional Area Research Method Topic pages
ASARE, STEPHEN KWAKU	PHD 1989 THE UNIVERSITY OF ARIZONA WALLER, WILLIAM S.	THE AUDITORS' GOING CONCERN OPINION DECISION: INTERACTION OF TASK VARIABLES AND THE SEQUENTIAL PROCESSING OF EVIDENCE	Auditing Experimental Judgment & Decision Making - Heuristics & Biases 185
ASECHEMIE, DANIEL PELE SAMUEL	PHD 1987 UNIVERSITY OF ILLINOIS AT URBANA-CHAMPAIGN BECK, PAUL J.	AN EXPERIMENTAL STUDY OF TOURNAMENTS AND CONTRACTS: A PRINCIPAL'S PERSPECTIVE	Cost/Managerial Experimental Agency Theory 168
ASKREN, BARBARA J.	PHD 1991 OKLAHOMA STATE UNIVERSITY MEEK, GARY	MARKET VALUATION OF POSTEMPLOYMENT BENEFITS OTHER THAN PENSIONS	Financial Accounting Archival - Primary Post Retirement Benefit Issues 73
ATKINSON, MARYANNE	PHD 1990 DREXEL UNIVERSITY JAENICKE, HENRY R.	A STUDY OF POPULATION CHARACTERISTICS AFFECTING THE PERFORMANCE OF AUDIT SAMPLING TECHNIQUES IN SUBSTANTIVE TESTS	Auditing Simulation Audit Sampling 255
ATKINSON, SUE ANDREWS	PHD 1989 UNIVERSITY OF NORTH TEXAS KOCH, BRUCE	THE CONTRAST-INERTIA MODEL AND THE UPDATING OF ATTRIBUTIONS IN PERFORMANCE EVALUATION	Cost/Managerial Experimental Performance Evaluation/Measuremen t 211
AUSTIN, WALTER WADE	PHD 1989 UNIVERSITY OF GEORGIA CLARK, RONALD L.	A STUDY OF THE EFFECTS OF INTEGRATING MICROCOMPUTERS INTO THE INTRODUCTORY FINANCIAL ACCOUNTING COURSE	Education Experimental Instructional Methods 155
AVILA, MARCOS GONCALVES	PHD 1992 NEW YORK UNIVERSITY, GRADUATE SCHOOL OF BUSINESS ADMINISTRATION RONEN, JOSHUA	TRANSFER PRICING MECHANISMS: AN EXPERIMENTAL INVESTIGATION	Cost/Managerial Experimental Transfer Pricing 99
AWASTHI, VIDYA NIDHI	PHD 1988 UNIVERSITY OF WASHINGTON JIAMBALVO, JAMES	BUDGETARY SLACK AND PERFORMANCE UNDER PARTICIPATIVE BUDGETING: AN EXPERIMENTAL STUDY OF THE EFFECTS OF MONITORING, THE AGENT'S RISK PREFERENCE, AND THE QUALITY OF THE AGENT'S PRE-DECISION INFORMATION	Cost/Managerial Experimental Budgeting 106
BABA, ISLAHUDIN	PHD 1988 UNIVERSITY OF EAST ANGLIA (UNITED KINGDOM)	THE ROLE OF AUDITORS IN INFORMATION SYSTEMS DEVELOPMENT APPLIED TO THE MALAYSIAN PUBLIC SECTOR	Information Systems Survey Systems Design &/or Development 452

Listing by Author

Author	Degree & Date School Advisor	Title	Functional Area Research Method Topic pages
BACK, BARBRO CHRISTINA	FD 1991 ABO AKADEMI (FINLAND)	AN EXPERT SYSTEM FOR FINANCIAL STATEMENTS PLANNING	Information Systems Analytical - Internal Decision Support Systems 186
BAE, GIL SOO	PHD 1994 UNIVERSITY OF MINNESOTA	FURTHER INVESTIGATION OF POSTANNOUNCEMENT DRIFTS ASSOCIATED WITH EARNINGS, CASH FLOWS, AND ACCRUAL ADJUSTMENTS	Financial Accounting Archival - Primary Accruals 146
BAGINSKI, STEPHEN PAUL	PHD 1986 UNIVERSITY OF ILLINOIS AT URBANA-CHAMPAIGN	INTRA-INDUSTRY INFORMATION TRANSFERS ASSOCIATED WITH MANAGEMENT EARNINGS FORECASTS	Financial Accounting Archival - Primary Information Transfer 127
BAHNSON, PAUL RICHARD	PHD 1987 THE UNIVERSITY OF UTAH	AN ASSESSMENT OF THE CONTRIBUTION OF CASH FLOW AND THE OPERATING CASH FLOW COMPONENT IN CLASSIFYING FAILED COMPANIES	Financial Accounting Archival - Primary Financial Distress or Bankruptcy 158
BAILEY, JAMES ALMA	PHD 1992 THE UNIVERSITY OF NEBRASKA - LINCOLN CHEN, KUNG H.	AUDIT FEE EFFECTS ON AUDITOR INDEPENDENCE	Auditing Experimental Independence 116
BAIN, CRAIG EDGAR	PHD 1987 TEXAS A&M UNIVERSITY	EXPERTS' PERCEPTIONS OF SUBSTANTIAL AUTHORITY	Taxation Tax Professionals 128
BAKER, DONALD R.	DBA 1990 NOVA UNIVERSITY BECKER, EDWARD A.	RELATIONSHIPS OF INTERNAL ACCOUNTING CONTROLS AND OCCURRENCES OF COMPUTER FRAUD	General Survey Fraud 133
BAKER, JOHN HOWARD	PHD 1992 THE UNIVERSITY OF TEXAS AT ARLINGTON SCHKADE, LAWRENCE L.	A CONCEPTUAL DESIGN FOR SIMPLIFYING AND STRUCTURING ELECTRONIC DOCUMENTS: AN APPLICATION IN PROFESSIONAL CONDUCT STANDARDS	Information Systems Analytical - Internal Systems Design &/or Development 271
BAKER, WILLIAM MAURICE	PHD 1987 VIRGINIA POLYTECHNIC INSTITUTE AND STATE UNIVERSITY	THE EFFECTS OF ACCOUNTING REPORTS ON LOAN OFFICERS: AN EXPERIMENT	General Experimental Bank Loan Officers 184

Author	Degree & Date School Advisor	Title	Functional Area Research Method Topic pages
BAKKE, MARILYN	DBA 1991 MISSISSIPPI STATE UNIVERSITY DAUGHTREY, ZOEL	A STUDY OF THE DISCIPLINE OF CPAS BY STATE BOARDS OF ACCOUNTANCY	General Case Ethics 141
BALAKRISHNAN, RAMAMURTHY	PHD 1986 COLUMBIA UNIVERSITY	APPLICATIONS OF MULTIPERIOD AGENCY MODELS: AN ACCOUNTING CONTEXT	General Analytical - Internal Agency Theory 152
BALCOM, NORMA JEAN	PHD 1991 UNIVERSITY OF ARKANSAS FRIES, CLARENCE E.	AN INVESTIGATION OF PROSPECT THEORY'S EFFECTS ON DECISIONS OF MANAGEMENT ACCOUNTANTS	Cost/Managerial Experimental Judgment & Decision Making - Heuristics & Biases 123
BALDWIN, JANE NORA	PHD 1986 UNIVERSITY OF ARKANSAS	BANKRUPTCY PREDICTION USING QUARTERLY FINANCIAL STATEMENT DATA	Financial Accounting Archival - Primary Financial Distress or Bankruptcy 167
BALDWIN-MORGAN, AMELIA ANNETTE	PHD 1991 VIRGINIA POLYTECHNIC INSTITUTE AND STATE UNIVERSITY HICKS, JAMES O. JR.	THE IMPACT OF EXPERT SYSTEMS ON AUDITING FIRMS: AN INVESTIGATION USING THE DELPHI TECHNIQUE AND A CASE STUDY APPROACH	Auditing Case Decision Support Systems 255
BALSAM, STEVEN	PHD 1991 CITY UNIVERSITY OF NEW YORK LILIEN, STEVEN B.	EXECUTIVE COMPENSATION PACKAGES: A TOOL FOR RESOLVING THE OWNER-MANAGER CONFLICT	Cost/Managerial Archival - Primary Incentive Compensation 206
BANAFA, AHMED MOHAMMED	PHD 1991 UNIVERSITY OF COLORADO AT BOULDER FRANGOPOL, DAN M.	DESIGN RELIABILITY FOR ESTIMATING COSTS OF PILE FOUNDATIONS: FROM THEORY TO APPLICATION OF A PROBABILISTIC-FUZZY APPROACH	Cost/Managerial Case Cost Behaviors & Estimation 413
BANAS, EDWARD JOSEPH, JR.	PHD 1994 VIRGINIA POLYTECHNIC INSTITUTE AND STATE UNIVERSITY WHITE, ORION F. JR.	A DECONSTRUCTIONIST ANALYSIS OF ACCOUNTING METHODS FOR COMMUNITY COLLEGES IN THE STATE OF VIRGINIA	Not-for-Profit Case College & University 341
BANDYOPADHYAY, SATIPRASAD	PHD 1989 THE UNIVERSITY OF IOWA COLLINS, DANIEL W.	THE RELATIVE INFORMATIVENESS OF SUCCESSFUL EFFORTS AND FULL COST EARNINGS IN THE OIL AND GAS INDUSTRY	Financial Accounting Archival - Primary Earnings Response Coefficients 135

Listing by Author

12

Author	Degree & Date School Advisor	Title	Functional Area Research Method Topic pages
BANERJEE, AJEYO	PHD 1991 UNIVERSITY OF MASSACHUSETTS OWERS, JAMES	MANAGERIAL COMPENSATION AND SHAREHOLDER WEALTH CONSEQUENCES OF 'WHITE KNIGHT' BEHAVIOR	Financial Accounting Archival - Primary Merger, Acquisition, Reorganization 186
BANNISTER, JAMES W.	PHD 1988 THE UNIVERSITY OF NORTH CAROLINA AT CHAPEL HILL BLOCHER, EDWARD	EARNINGS SIGNALS AND INTER-FIRM INFORMATION TRANSFERS	Financial Accounting Archival - Primary Information Transfer 157
BARBEE, RONALD F.	PHD 1993 WASHINGTON STATE UNIVERSITY WONG-ON-WING, BERNARD	PARTICIPATION IN THE BUDGETARY PROCESS: AN ATTRIBUTIONAL ANALYSIS	Cost/Managerial Budgeting 349
BARCLAY, RODERICK STUART	PHD 1993 KENT STATE UNIVERSITY FETYKO, DAVID F.	COMPUTER CHARGEBACK SYSTEMS: A CRITICAL ANALYSIS AND NEW METHODOLOGY	Cost/Managerial Analytical - Internal Cost Allocation 218
BARDO, FREDERIC S.	PHD 1988 UNIVERSITY OF STIRLING (UNITED KINGDOM)	A NORMATIVE THEORY OF ACCOUNTING FOR ZIMBABWE: A THIRD WORLD COUNTRY	General Analytical - Internal International/Global Issues 445
BARIDWAN, ZAKI	DBA 1989 UNIVERSITY OF KENTUCKY TEARNEY, MICHAEL G.	FUNCTIONAL CURRENCY AND INFLATION RATE: AN ANALYSIS OF THE IMPACT ON FINANCIAL STATEMENTS: AN INDONESIAN CASE STUDY	Financial Accounting Case Inflation 133
BARIL, CHARLES PURDOM	PHD 1986 UNIVERSITY OF FLORIDA	LONG-TERM INCENTIVE COMPENSATION PLAN ADOPTION AND THE CAPITAL SPENDING DECISIONS OF MANAGERS	Cost/Managerial Archival - Primary Incentive Compensation 141
BARKMAN, BERYL V.	PHD 1988 UNIVERSITY OF SOUTH CAROLINA	INCOME SMOOTHING: A LABORATORY EXPERIMENT	Financial Accounting Experimental Earnings Management 98
BARNETT, DONALD JOSEPH	PHD 1989 UNIVERSITY OF CALIFORNIA, LOS ANGELES MCDONOUGH, JOHN J.	ATTRIBUTION BIASES, COMPETITIVE/COOPERATIVE WORK ENVIRONMENTS, AND THE MANAGEMENT CONTROL PROCESS	Cost/Managerial Survey Management Control Systems 220

Listing by Author

Author	Degree & Date School Advisor	Title	Functional Area Research Method Topic pages
BARNEY, DOUGLAS KEVIN	PHD 1993 THE UNIVERSITY OF MISSISSIPPI	MODELING FARM DEBT FAILURE: THE FARMERS HOME ADMINISTRATION	Financial Accounting Archival - Primary Industry - Agricultural 324
BARRETT, KEVIN STANTON	PHD 1991 VIRGINIA POLYTECHNIC INSTITUTE AND STATE UNIVERSITY O'NEIL, CHERIE J.	CHARITABLE GIVING AND FEDERAL INCOME TAX POLICY: ADDITIONAL EVIDENCE BASED ON PANEL-DATA ELASTICITY ESTIMATES	Taxation Archival - Primary Public Policy 193
BARRON, ORIE EDWIN	PHD 1993 UNIVERSITY OF OREGON MORSE, DALE	COSTLY TRADING: THE RELATION BETWEEN DISAGREEMENT (OR INFORMATION ASYMMETRIES) AND TRADING IN A WORLD WITH TRADING COSTS	Financial Accounting Archival - Primary Capital Markets 128
BARTH, MARY E.	PHD 1989 STANFORD UNIVERSITY BEAVER, WILLIAM H.	ASSESSING FINANCIAL ACCOUNTING MEASUREMENT ALTERNATIVES FOR ASSETS AND LIABILITIES	Financial Accounting Archival - Primary Post Retirement Benefit Issues 216
BARTON, THOMAS MICHAEL	PHD 1986 GEORGIA STATE UNIVERSITY - COLLEGE OF BUSINESS ADMINISTRATION	ON THE PREDICTION OF MERGERS AND BANKRUPTCIES WITH RATIOS FROM THE STATEMENT OF CHANGES IN FINANCIAL POSITION AND DIFFERENT FUNDS FLOW MEASURES	Financial Accounting Archival - Primary Financial Ratios 556
BARTOV, ELIAHU	PHD 1989 UNIVERSITY OF CALIFORNIA, BERKELEY LEV, BARUCH	CHANGES IN FIRM FINANCIAL POLICY AS SIGNALS FOR FUTURE EARNINGS: AN EMPIRICAL INVESTIGATION OF UNSYSTEMATIC STOCK REPURCHASES	Financial Accounting Archival - Primary Stock Transactions 85
BASAK, SULEYMAN	PHD 1993 CARNEGIE-MELLON UNIVERSITY	GENERAL EQUILIBRIUM CONTINUOUS-TIME ASSET PRICING OF: (1) PORTFOLIO INSURERS AND (2) NON-PRICE-TAKING INVESTORS	Financial Accounting Analytical - Internal Agency Theory 118
BASU, ONKER NATH	PHD 1992 THE PENNSYLVANIA STATE UNIVERSITY DIRSMITH, MARK W.	MANAGING THE ORGANIZATIONAL ENVIRONMENT: AN INTERPRETIVE FIELD STUDY OF THE UNITED STATES GENERAL ACCOUNTING OFFICE AND THE MAINTENANCE OF PROFESSIONAL INDEPENDENCE	Auditing Survey Governmental 271
BASU, PROGYAN	PHD 1992 THE UNIVERSITY OF NEBRASKA - LINCOLN BROWN, JAMES F. JR.	THE INFLUENCE OF CLIENT CONTROL ENVIRONMENT ATTRIBUTES ON EVALUATION OF INTERNAL CONTROL: AN EMPIRICAL INVESTIGATION OF AUDITOR JUDGMENT	Auditing Experimental Judgment & Decision Making 166

Author	Degree & Date School Advisor	Title	Functional Area Research Method Topic pages
BASU, SOMNATH	PHD 1990 THE UNIVERSITY OF ARIZONA CARLETON, WILLARD T.	INFORMATION, EXPECTATIONS AND EQUILIBRIUM: TRADING VOLUME HYPOTHESES	Financial Accounting Archival - Primary Information Content 194
BATCHELDER, WALTER IRVING	PHD 1988 VIRGINIA POLYTECHNIC INSTITUTE AND STATE UNIVERSITY	A STUDY OF THE LINK-CHAIN LIFO CONTROVERSY	Financial Accounting Experimental Inventory 176
BATTISTEL, GEORGE PETER	PHD 1992 UNIVERSITY OF OREGON KING, RAYMOND D.	AN EMPIRICAL ANALYSIS OF THE STOCK MARKET REACTION TO BONUS PLAN ADOPTIONS	Cost/Managerial Archival - Primary Incentive Compensation 110
BEALING, WILLIAM EARL, JR.	PHD 1991 THE PENNSYLVANIA STATE UNIVERSITY DIRSMITH, MARK W.	INSTITUTIONAL ASPECTS OF AUDITING REGULATION: THE BUDGETING RELATIONSHIPS AMONG THE SEC, CONGRESS AND THE PRESIDENT	Auditing Case Standard Setting 227
BEAN, DAVID FRANCIS	PHD 1994 TEMPLE UNIVERSITY LIPKA, ROLAND L.	THE FRAMING OF DECISION CHOICES BY INFORMATION PROVIDERS: AN EXPLORATORY STUDY	Cost/Managerial Experimental Judgment & Decision Making - Heuristics & Biases 103
BEAN, LUANN G.	PHD 1989 UNIVERSITY OF ARKANSAS COOK, DORIS M.	AN EXAMINATION OF STATUS-RISK AND PERSONALITY VARIABLES OF PRACTICING PUBLIC ACCOUNTANTS AND ACCOUNTING ACADEMICIANS AS EXPLANATIONS OF RECEPTIVITY/RESISTANCE TO INNOVATIONS	General Survey Accounting Career Issues 299
BEARD, DEBORAH F.	PHD 1987 UNIVERSITY OF ARKANSAS	THE IMPACT OF STATEMENT OF FINANCIAL ACCOUNTING STANDARDS NO. 13 ON SYSTEMATIC RISK AND ACCOUNTING VARIABLES	Financial Accounting Archival - Primary Leases 143
BEARD, VICTORIA KNAPP	PHD 1993 THE UNIVERSITY OF NORTH DAKOTA AHLER, JANET G.	REFLECTIONS OF PUBLIC ACCOUNTING INTERNS: A QUALITATIVE ANALYSIS OF EXPERIENTIAL LEARNING	Education Case Internships 139
BEAULIEU, PHILIP RAYMOND	PHD 1991 UNIVERSITY OF WASHINGTON JIAMBALVO, JAMES	COMMERCIAL LENDERS' USE OF ACCOUNTING INFORMATION: THE EFFECTS OF CHARACTER INFORMATION AND EXPERIENCE	General Experimental Industry - Banking/Savings & Loan 129

Listing by Author

15

Author	Degree & Date / School / Advisor	Title	Functional Area / Research Method / Topic / pages
BECKER, D'ARCY ANN	PHD 1992 THE UNIVERSITY OF WISCONSIN - MADISON RITTENBERG, LARRY E.	THE EFFECTS OF AUDIT DECISION AID DESIGN ON THE INTRINSIC MOTIVATION AND PERFORMANCE OF AUDITORS PREDICTING CORPORATE BANKRUPTCY	Auditing Experimental Decision Aids 180
BECKMAN, JUDY KAY	PHD 1991 TEXAS TECH UNIVERSITY	PREDICTING THE LEVEL OF MINORITY INTEREST FOLLOWING A TENDER OFFER	Financial Accounting Archival - Primary Merger, Acquisition, Reorganization 236
BECKMAN, RONALD JAMES	PHD 1988 UNIVERSITY OF NORTH TEXAS	AN EMPIRICAL INVESTIGATION OF THE LOBBYING INFLUENCE OF LARGE CORPORATIONS ON SELECTED FASB STANDARDS	Financial Accounting Standard Setting 149
BEDARD, JEAN	PHD 1986 UNIVERSITY OF SOUTHERN CALIFORNIA	INTERNAL CONTROL EVALUATION IN COMPUTERIZED SYSTEMS: EXPERTS VERSUS NOVICES	Auditing Experimental Judgment & Decision Making - Cognitive Processes
BEDARD, JEAN CATHERINE	PHD 1985 THE UNIVERSITY OF WISCONSIN - MADISON	USE OF DATA ENVELOPMENT ANALYSIS IN ACCOUNTING APPLICATIONS: EVALUATION AND ILLUSTRATION BY PROSPECTIVE HOSPITAL REIMBURSEMENT	General Industry - Health Care 248
BEEHLER, JOHN MICHAEL	PHD 1985 INDIANA UNIVERSITY	AN EMPIRICAL EXAMINATION OF THE EFFECT OF THE SECTION 465 AT-RISK RULES ON EQUIPMENT LEASING TAX SHELTERS	Taxation Archival - Primary Taxes 203
BEETS, STEPHEN DOUGLAS	PHD 1987 VIRGINIA POLYTECHNIC INSTITUTE AND STATE UNIVERSITY	EFFECTIVENESS OF THE COMPLAINT-BASED ENFORCEMENT SYSTEM OF THE AICPA CODE OF PROFESSIONAL ETHICS	General Survey Ethics 209
BEGLEY, JOY	PHD 1991 THE UNIVERSITY OF ROCHESTER WATTS, ROSS	THE USE OF DEBT CONVENANTS TO CONTROL AGENCY PROBLEMS	Financial Accounting Archival - Primary Long Term Debt 215
BEJAN, MARY RIORDAN	PHD 1985 UNIVERSITY OF CALIFORNIA, BERKELEY	THE DIFFERENTIAL IMPACT ON NOISY AND NOISELESS PUBLIC INFORMATION ON SOCIAL WELFARE	Financial Accounting Analytical - Internal Social/Environmental Responsibility 97

Author	Degree & Date School Advisor	Title	Functional Area Research Method Topic pages
BELL, ANGELA H.	DBA 1990 MISSISSIPPI STATE UNIVERSITY DAUGHTREY, ZOEL	AN EMPIRICAL STUDY OF THE TYPES AND FREQUENCIES OF ACCOUNTING PROBLEMS ENCOUNTERED DURING THE STAGES OF DEVELOPMENT OF SMALL BUSINESSES	General Archival - Secondary Small Business 158
BENARTZI, SHLOMO	PHD 1994 CORNELL UNIVERSITY LIBBY, ROBERT	WITHIN-SEGMENT DIVERSITY AND THE INFORMATION CONTENT OF LINE-OF-BUSINESS REPORTING: EVIDENCE THAT STOCK PRICES DO NOT FULLY REFLECT THE IMPLICATIONS OF DIVIDEND CHANGES FOR SUBSEQUENT EARNINGS	Financial Accounting Archival - Primary Segment Reporting 96
BENSON, VAUGHN LEON	PHD 1985 THE UNIVERSITY OF NEBRASKA - LINCOLN	A STUDY OF THE USEFULNESS OF SELECTED GAAP BASIS ACCOUNTING INFORMATION AND ITS ACTUAL USE IN THE SMALL PRIVATE COMPANY LOAN DECISION PROCESS	Financial Accounting Survey Small Business 365
BERG, GARY GENE	PHD 1987 TEXAS A&M UNIVERSITY	EARLY VERSUS LATE COMPLIANCE TO SFAS 52: AN EMPIRICAL INVESTIGATION OF FIRM CHARACTERISTICS AND THE MARKET RESPONSE	Financial Accounting Archival - Primary Accounting Choice 140
BERG, JOYCE ELLEN	PHD 1988 UNIVERSITY OF MINNESOTA	INFORMATIVENESS AND VALUE OF PUBLIC INFORMATION: AN EXPERIMENTAL TEST	Cost/Managerial Experimental Agency Theory 196
BERGER, HELMUT MAXIMILIAN	DRSOCOEC 1991 JOHANNES KEPLER UNIVERSITAET LINZ (AUSTRIA)	IMPROVEMENT AND IMPLEMENTATION OF A MODEL OF INTEGRATED ACCOUNTING [VERBESSERUNG UND IMPLEMENTIERUNG EINES MODELLES DER INTEGRIERTEN PLANUNGSRECHNUNG]	Information Systems Analytical - Internal Systems Design &/or Development 156
BERGER, PHILIP GARY	PHD 1992 THE UNIVERSITY OF CHICAGO	EXPLICIT AND IMPLICIT TAX EFFECTS OF THE RESEARCH AND DEVELOPMENT TAX CREDIT	Taxation Research & Development
BERGEVIN, PETER MICHAEL	PHD 1985 ARIZONA STATE UNIVERSITY	EQUITY VALUATION OF PETROLEUM EXPLORATION AND PRODUCTION FIRMS USING ALTERNATIVE ACCOUNTING METHODS	Financial Accounting Archival - Primary Industry - Oil & Gas 179
BERRY, DELANO HOWARD	PHD 1991 UNIVERSITY OF KENTUCKY VANDANIKER, RELMOND P.	AN EXTENSION OF MANAGERIAL ACCOUNTING AND OPERATIONAL AUDITING IN THE PUBLIC SECTOR: A CASE STUDY OF SCHOOL FOOD SERVICE PROGRAMS IN SELECTED LOCAL SCHOOL DISTRICTS IN THE COMMONWEALTH OF KENTUCKY	Not-for-Profit Case Not-for-Profit 199

Author	Degree & Date School Advisor	Title	Functional Area Research Method Topic pages
BERRY, LUCILLE M.	PHD 1987 SAINT LOUIS UNIVERSITY STANTON, CHARLES MICHAEL	THE CHANGES OF COMPUTER USAGE IN ACCOUNTING TEXTS FROM 1974-1984	Education Archival - Secondary Curriculum Issues 163
BETHEA, PRESTON, JR.	EDD 1992 NORTH CAROLINA STATE UNIVERSITY HARVEY, WILLIAM B.	A DESCRIPTIVE EXPLORATORY EXAMINATION OF THE ROLE AND RESPONSIBILITIES OF INTERNAL AUDITORS IN HIGHER EDUCATION	Not-for-Profit Survey Internal Auditing 217
BETTIS, J. C. CARR	PHD 1992 INDIANA UNIVERSITY SALAMON, GERALD L.	REVISITING THE PROFITABILITY OF INSIDER AND OUTSIDER TRADING	Financial Accounting Archival - Primary Insider Trading 131
BETTNER, MARK STEVEN	PHD 1988 TEXAS TECH UNIVERSITY CLANCY, DONALD K.	THE EFFECTS OF PERCEIVED ACCOUNTING COMPETENCE, MACHIAVELLIANISM, PAST BUDGETING BEHAVIOR, AND BELIEFS ABOUT THE EFFECTIVENESS OF PAST BUDGETING BEHAVIOR ON BUDGETARY ATTITUDE: AN EMPIRICAL ANALYSIS	Cost/Managerial Survey Budgeting 138
BETTS, NORMAN MURRAY	PHD 1992 QUEEN'S UNIVERSITY AT KINGSTON (CANADA)	AN EMPIRICAL EXAMINATION OF THE REPORTING PRACTICES AND DIFFERENTIAL INFORMATION CONTENT OF EARNINGS COMPONENTS	Financial Accounting Archival - Primary Information Content 106
BHATTACHARYA, SOMNATH	PHD 1994 UNIVERSITY OF SOUTH FLORIDA HOLSTRUM, GARY	THE USE OF RECALL AND RECOGNITION TECHNIQUES IN ELICITING EXPRIENCED-INEXPERIENCED AUDITOR DIFFERENCES IN THE DETECTION OF MANAGEMENT FRAUD	Auditing Experimental Fraud 330
BILBEISI, KHAMIS MOHAMAD	PHD 1989 THE UNIVERSITY OF MISSISSIPPI BURKETT, HOMER H.	CULTURAL EFFECTS ON THE RELATIONSHIPS BETWEEN BUDGETARY PARTICIPATION AND MANAGERIAL PERFORMANCE	Cost/Managerial Experimental Budgeting 237
BILLINGS, BOYSIE ANTHONY	PHD 1986 TEXAS A&M UNIVERSITY	BUSINESS COMBINATIONS: LITIGATION AND TAXPAYER STRATEGY	Taxation Merger, Acquisition, Reorganization 148
BILODEAU, JULIEN	PHD 1991 THE UNIVERSITY OF WESTERN ONTARIO (CANADA) LANFRANCONI, CLAUDE P.	THE USE OF ACCOUNTING NUMBERS IN DEBT AND PREFERRED SHARE COVENANTS: SOME CANADIAN EVIDENCE	Financial Accounting Archival - Primary International/Global Issues 244

Listing by Author

Author	Degree & Date School Advisor	Title	Functional Area Research Method Topic pages
BIRD, CYNTHIA ELIZABETH	PHD 1989 UNIVERSITY OF GEORGIA BARRACK, JOHN B.	AN EXAMINATION OF THE EFFECT OF THE TAX REFORM ACT OF 1986 ON INDIVIDUAL AND CORPORATE INVESTMENT IN RESIDENTIAL RENTAL REALTY	Taxation Simulation Industry - Real Estate 184
BISHOP, RACHEL ANN	PHD 1991 THE UNIVERSITY OF ARIZONA WALLER, WILLIAM S.	INCENTIVE SCHEMES, MORAL HAZARD, AND RISK AVERSION: INTRAFIRM RESOURCE ALLOCATION AND DETERMINANTS OF BUDGETARY SLACK	Cost/Managerial Experimental Incentive Compensation 297
BITNER, LARRY NEWELL	DBA 1985 THE GEORGE WASHINGTON UNIVERSITY	ACCOUNTING FOR CHANGING PRICES PER FASB 33 AND THE IMPACT ON INCOME SMOOTHING	Financial Accounting Analytical - Internal Inflation 116
BJORNSON, CHRIS E.	PHD 1993 UNIVERSITY OF ILLINOIS AT URBANA-CHAMPAIGN WILLIS, EUGENE	THE EFFECT OF INCOME TAX PREPAYMENTS ON TAXPAYER REPORTING BEHAVIOR: A BUSINESS SIMULATION	Taxation Experimental Tax Compliance 84
BLACCONIERE, WALTER GEORGE	PHD 1988 UNIVERSITY OF WASHINGTON BOWEN, ROBERT M.	ACCOUNTING REGULATIONS IN THE SAVINGS AND LOAN INDUSTRY: EVIDENCE OF MARKET REACTIONS AND IMPLICATIONS OF CONTRACTING THEORY	Financial Accounting Archival - Primary Industry - Banking/Savings & Loan 125
BLANKLEY, ALAN IRVING	PHD 1992 TEXAS A&M UNIVERSITY SWANSON, EDWARD P.	INCENTIVES IN PENSION ACCOUNTING: AN EMPIRICAL INVESTIGATION OF REPORTED RATE ESTIMATES	Financial Accounting Archival - Primary Post Retirement Benefit Issues 180
BLAZEK, MICHELE MCGLINCHY	PHD 1990 ARIZONA STATE UNIVERSITY RECKERS, PHILIP	AN EMPIRICAL STUDY OF BAYESIAN DECISION THEORY AND AUDITOR JUDGMENT UNDER UNCERTAINTY	Auditing Experimental Judgment & Decision Making 129
BLEDSOE, NANCY LLEWELLYN	PHD 1993 THE UNIVERSITY OF ALABAMA INGRAM, ROBERT W.	AN EMPIRICAL EXAMINATION OF THE EFFECTS OF PERFORMANCE EVALUATION ON GOAL CONGRUENCE WITHIN THE AUTOMOTIVE INDUSTRY	Cost/Managerial Survey Performance Evaluation/Measurement 102
BLESSING, LINDA JANE	DPA 1991 ARIZONA STATE UNIVERSITY WESCHLER, LOUIS F.	REPORTING OF GOVERNMENTAL PERFORMANCE INDICATORS FOR ASSESSMENT OF PUBLIC ACCOUNTABILITY	Not-for-Profit Survey Governmental 283

Author	Degree & Date School Advisor	Title	Functional Area Research Method Topic pages
BLOOMFIELD, ROBERT JAMES	PHD 1992 THE UNIVERSITY OF MICHIGAN NOEL, JAMES	EVOLUTIONARY MODELS IN LABORATORY AND AUDITING GAMES	Auditing Experimental Judgment & Decision Making - Heuristics & Biases 150
BLOUCH, WILLIAM EDWARD	DBA 1987 KENT STATE UNIVERSITY	EDP CONTROLS TO MAINTAIN DATA INTEGRITY IN DISTRIBUTED PROCESSING SYSTEMS	Auditing Survey EDP Controls 273
BOHAC, DARLENE MARIE	PHD 1986 UNIVERSITY OF HOUSTON	THE EFFECT OF MANAGEMENT BUDGETARY CONTROLS ON AUDIT PLANNING	Auditing Experimental Audit Planning 139
BONNER, SARAH ELIZABETH	PHD 1988 THE UNIVERSITY OF MICHIGAN LIBBY, ROBERT	EXPERIENCE EFFECTS IN THE COMPONENTS OF ANALYTICAL RISK ASSESSMENT	Auditing Experimental Judgment & Decision Making - Cognitive Processes 130
BOOYSEN, STEFANES FRANCOIS	DCOM 1993 UNIVERSITY OF PRETORIA (SOUTH AFRICA) KOEN, MARIUS	A FRAMEWORK FOR FINANCIAL REPORTING TO EMPLOYEES IN THE REPUBLIC OF SOUTH AFRICA	Cost/Managerial Survey International/Global Issues
BORDEN, JAMES PATRICK	PHD 1986 DREXEL UNIVERSITY	AN ASSESSMENT OF THE IMPACT OF DIAGNOSIS RELATED GROUP (DRG)-BASED REIMBURSEMENT ON THE TECHNICAL EFFICIENCY OF NEW JERSEY HOSPITALS	General Archival - Primary Industry - Health Care 136
BORKOWSKI, SUSAN CAROL	PHD 1988 TEMPLE UNIVERSITY SCHWEIKART, JAMES A.	AN INVESTIGATION INTO THE DIVERGENCE OF THEORY FROM PRACTICE REGARDING TRANSFER PRICING METHODS	Cost/Managerial Case Transfer Pricing 177
BOSCIA, MARIAN W. LARSON	PHD 1993 UNIVERSITY OF COLORADO AT BOULDER LEWIS, BARRY L.	THE RELATIONSHIP BETWEEN ESOP VOTING RIGHTS AND EMPLOYEES' JOB PERFORMANCE	Cost/Managerial Experimental Incentive Compensation 169
BOST, PATRICIA JAMES	PHD 1992 THE GEORGE WASHINGTON UNIVERSITY PAIK, CHEI-MIN	MOVEMENT TOWARD UNIFORMITY IN THE DESIGN OF ABC SYSTEMS	Information Systems Case Activity Based Costing 219

Author	Degree & Date School Advisor	Title	Functional Area Research Method Topic pages
BOUILLON, MARVIN L.	PHD 1986 UNIVERSITY OF KANSAS	ECONOMIC DETERMINANTS OF THE DECISION TO LIQUIDATE LIFO INVENTORY QUANTITIES	Financial Accounting Survey Inventory 128
BOULEY, JUDITH NOREEN	PHD 1991 THE UNIVERSITY OF ALABAMA BINDON, KATHLEEN R.	AN EMPIRICAL INVESTIGATION OF SFAS NO. 52 AND THE IMPLICATIONS FOR PERFORMANCE EVALUATION SYSTEMS	Financial Accounting Survey Foreign Currency Translation 197
BOWEN, PAUL LARRY	PHD 1992 THE UNIVERSITY OF TENNESSEE BORTHICK, A. FAYE	MANAGING DATA QUALITY IN ACCOUNTING INFORMATION SYSTEMS: A STOCHASTIC CLEARING SYSTEM APPROACH	Information Systems Analytical - Internal Quality Issues 106
BOYAS, ELISE A.	PHD 1991 RUTGERS THE STATE UNIVERSITY OF NEW JERSEY - NEW BRUNSWICK PALMON, DAN	IDENTIFICATION AND EXAMINATION OF FACTORS BEHIND CORPORATE IN-SUBSTANCE DEFEASANCE OF DEBT	Financial Accounting Archival - Primary Long Term Debt 198
BOYER, BENOI T NOEL	PHD 1987 UNIVERSITY OF CALIFORNIA, LOS ANGELES	THE IMPACT OF FINANCIAL ACCOUNTING STANDARDS BOARD STATEMENTS NUMBERS 8 AND 52 ON MULTINATIONAL CORPORATIONS	Financial Accounting Archival - Primary Foreign Currency Translation 137
BOYLE, EDMUND JOSEPH	PHD 1990 THE PENNSYLVANIA STATE UNIVERSITY JABLONSKY, STEPHEN F.	THE ROLE OF INTERNAL AUDITING IN THE DEFENSE INDUSTRY: AN EMPIRICAL STUDY	Auditing Case Internal Auditing 404
BOYNTON, CHARLES EDWARD	PHD 1985 UNIVERSITY OF ILLINOIS AT URBANA-CHAMPAIGN	TAX ACCOUNTING METHOD AND OFFSHORE PETROLEUM DEVELOPMENT: A POLICY EVALUATION MODEL EMPLOYING ROYALTY EQUIVALENTS AND EXCISE TAXES	Taxation Simulation Public Policy 286
BRACKNEY, KENNARD SAMUEL, JR.	PHD 1990 THE UNIVERSITY OF NORTH CAROLINA AT CHAPEL HILL RAMANAN, RAMACHANDRAN	EARNINGS ANNOUNCEMENT TIMELINESS AND INVESTOR WEALTH	Financial Accounting Archival - Primary Earnings Announcements 152
BRADLEY, CASSIE FRANCES	PHD 1994 THE UNIVERSITY OF ALABAMA ROBERTS, MICHAEL L.	AN EMPIRICAL INVESTIGATION OF FACTORS AFFECTING CORPORATE TAX COMPLIANCE BEHAVIOR	Taxation Survey Tax Compliance 139

Author	Degree & Date School Advisor	Title	Functional Area Research Method Topic pages
BRADLEY, LINDA JACOBSEN	PHD 1993 UNIVERSITY OF NORTH TEXAS BOYNTON, CHARLES	THE IMPACT OF THE 1986 AND 1987 QUALIFIED PLAN REGULATION ON FIRMS' DECISION TO SWITCH FROM DEFINED BENEFIT TO DEFINED CONTRIBUTION FOR PLANS LARGER THAN 100 PARTICIPANTS	Financial Accounting Archival - Primary Post Retirement Benefit Issues 174
BRADLEY, MICHAEL P.	PHD 1986 ARIZONA STATE UNIVERSITY	ACCOUNTING INFORMATION, INDIVIDUAL DIFFERENCES, AND ATTRIBUTIONS IN THE PERFORMANCE EVALUATION PROCESS	Cost/Managerial Experimental Performance Evaluation/Measurement 298
BRAMBLE, HULDAH ALETHA	PHD 1990 UNIVERSITY OF HOUSTON HOPWOOD, WILLIAM S.	THE USE OF ACCOUNTING RATIOS AS MEASURES OF RISK IN THE DETERMINATION OF THE BID-ASK SPREAD	Financial Accounting Archival - Primary Financial Ratios 108
BRAND, JOHN DAVID	PHD 1989 COUNCIL FOR NATIONAL ACADEMIC AWARDS (UNITED KINGDOM)	THE EXCHEQUER IN THE LATER TWELFTH CENTURY	General Archival - Secondary History 330
BRANNAN, RODGER LLOYD	PHD 1989 THE UNIVERSITY OF NEBRASKA - LINCOLN BROWN, JAMES F. JR.	THE SINGLE AUDIT ACT OF 1984: AN EXAMINATION OF THE AUDIT PROCESS IN THE GOVERNMENT SECTOR	Auditing Survey Governmental 222
BRANSON, BRUCE CLAYTON	PHD 1992 THE FLORIDA STATE UNIVERSITY LOREK, KENNETH S.	AN EMPIRICAL EXAMINATION OF FIRM-SPECIFIC CHARACTERISTICS ASSOCIATED WITH DIFFERENTIAL INFORMATION ENVIRONMENTS	Financial Accounting Archival - Primary Financial Analysts 162
BRANSON, LEONARD L.	PHD 1990 SAINT LOUIS UNIVERSITY JENNINGS, JAMES P.	ACCOUNTING INFORMATION, COGNITIVE PROCESSES, AND PERFORMANCE APPRAISAL	General Experimental Judgment & Decision Making - Cognitive Processes 157
BRAZELTON, JULIA K.	PHD 1985 UNIVERSITY OF SOUTH CAROLINA	TAX SIMPLIFICATION: THE IMPLICATIONS OF A CONSUMPTION TAX BASE ON THE INDIVIDUAL TAXPAYER	Taxation Archival - Primary Public Policy 194
BRICKER, ROBERT JAMES	PHD 1987 CASE WESTERN RESERVE UNIVERSITY PREVITS, GARY JOHN	AN EMPIRICAL INVESTIGATION OF THE INTELLECTUAL STRUCTURE OF THE ACCOUNTING DISCIPLINE: A CITATIONAL ANALYSIS OF SELECTED SCHOLARLY JOURNALS, 1983-1986	Education Archival - Secondary Academic Issues 392

Author	Degree & Date School Advisor	Title	Functional Area Research Method Topic pages
BRISCOE, NAT REEVE	PHD 1988 THE FLORIDA STATE UNIVERSITY HILLISON, WILLIAM	UNCERTAINTY, RISK, AND PROFESSIONAL LIABILITY: AN EMPIRICAL ANALYSIS USING THE IN-BASKET TEST	General Experimental Risk 118
BROCE, PATRICIA ANN	DBA 1991 UNIVERSITY OF KENTUCKY TEARNEY, MICHAEL G.; POE, C. DOUGLAS	THE USEFULNESS OF 'PRO FORMA' FINANCIAL STATEMENTS IN DECISION MAKING BY FINANCIAL ANALYSTS	Financial Accounting Survey Financial Analysts 274
BROCK, GLENDA CONERLY	PHD 1989 THE UNIVERSITY OF MISSISSIPPI WALLACE, WILLIAM	AN EMPIRICAL RESEARCH STUDY OF THE IMPACT UPON SMALL BUSINESS OF THE CHANGE IN THE INVESTMENT TAX CREDIT DICTATED BY THE TAX REFORM ACT OF 1986	Taxation Archival - Primary Small Business 208
BRODY, RICHARD GLEN	PHD 1993 ARIZONA STATE UNIVERSITY	ESCALATION OF COMMITMENT AS A THREAT TO INTERNAL AUDITOR OBJECTIVITY	Auditing Experimental Judgment & Decision Making 108
BROMAN, AMY J.	PHD 1987 THE UNIVERSITY OF MICHIGAN	THE IMPACT OF FEDERAL INCOME TAX POLICY ON THE CHARITABLE CONTRIBUTIONS BEHAVIOR OF HOUSEHOLDS	Taxation Archival - Primary Charitable Organizations 101
BROOKS, RAYMOND MICHAEL	PHD 1991 WASHINGTON UNIVERSITY LAMOUREUX, CHRISTOPHER G.	AN IMPLIED CASH DIVIDEND AND TRADING PATTERNS: VOLUME, SPREADS, SPREAD COMPONENTS AND ASYMMETRIC INFORMATION AROUND DIVIDEND AND EARNINGS ANNOUNCEMENTS	Financial Accounting Archival - Primary Dividends 206
BROOKS, RICHARD C.	PHD 1991 THE LOUISIANA STATE UNIVERSITY AND AGRICULTURAL AND MECHANICAL COL. APOSTOLOU, NICHOLAS G.	AN INVESTIGATION OF THE DETERMINANTS OF THE MUNICIPAL DECISION TO PRIVATIZE RESIDENTIAL SANITATION COLLECTION	Not-for-Profit Archival - Primary Governmental 171
BROWN, BETTY COFFEE	PHD 1985 VIRGINIA POLYTECHNIC INSTITUTE AND STATE UNIVERSITY	AN EMPIRICAL INVESTIGATION INTO DIFFERENCES BETWEEN COMPANIES THAT ELECTED AN EARLY COMPLIANCE WITH SFAS 52 AND COMPANIES NOT ELECTING AN EARLY COMPLIANCE	Financial Accounting Archival - Primary Accounting Choice 189
BROWN, DARRELL L.	PHD 1994 THE UNIVERSITY OF UTAH	THE INFLUENCE OF DECISION STYLE AND INFORMATION PRESENTATION FORMAT ON THE PERCEIVED USEFULNESS OF MANAGERIAL ACCOUNTING INFORMATION: AN EMPIRICAL INVESTIGATION	Cost/Managerial Experimental Presentation Format 158

Author	Degree & Date School Advisor	Title	Functional Area Research Method Topic pages
BROWN, KENNETH WAYNE	PHD 1992 UNIVERSITY OF ARKANSAS HAY, LEON E.	AN EXAMINATION OF DECISION-RELEVANT FINANCIAL AND NONFINANCIAL INDICATORS IN COLLEGES AND UNIVERSITIES	Not-for-Profit Survey College & University 289
BROWN, MATTHEW J.	PHD 1991 THE UNIVERSITY OF MICHIGAN LOHMANN, JACK R.	A MEAN-VARIANCE SERIAL REPLACEMENT DECISION MODEL	Cost/Managerial Capital Budgeting 134
BROWN, SARAH	DBA 1990 MISSISSIPPI STATE UNIVERSITY HERRING, DORA	AN INVESTIGATION INTO THE ASSOCIATION BETWEEN AUDIT FAILURES AND THE PRESENCE OR ABSENCE OF A CORPORATE AUDIT COMMITTEE	Auditing Archival - Primary Audit Committees 169
BROWN, WILLIAM P.	PHD 1985 THE UNIVERSITY OF NORTH CAROLINA AT CHAPEL HILL	SHARED AND DIFFERING PERCEPTIONS OF COSTS AND BENEFITS ASSOCIATED WITH INTERNAL/EXTERNAL AUDITOR SERVICES AND COOPERATION	Auditing Survey Internal Auditing 210
BROZOVSKY, JOHN ALLWIN	PHD 1990 UNIVERSITY OF COLORADO AT BOULDER SELTO, FRANK H.	THE EFFECT OF AUDITOR REPUTATION ON THE PRICING OF AUDIT SERVICES: AN EXPERIMENTAL STUDY	Auditing Experimental Audit Fees 271
BRUMETT, CLIFFORD	PHD 1993 KENT STATE UNIVERSITY BROWN, RICHARD E.; MCMATH, H. KENT	INVENTORY ADJUSTMENT AND ADVERSE INFORMATION MOTIVES IN SECURITY DEALER PRICING DECISIONS	Financial Accounting Archival - Primary Market Microstructure 107
BRYAN, BARRY JEROME	PHD 1994 TEXAS A&M UNIVERSITY STRAWSER, ROBERT H.	AN EMPIRICAL INVESTIGATION OF THE DETERMINANTS OF REPORTING QUALITY AND THE EFFECTIVENESS OF THE QUALITY REVIEW PROGRAM FOR SMALL ACCOUNTING FIRMS	Auditing Archival - Primary Audit Quality 106
BRYAN, STEPHEN HART	PHD 1994 NEW YORK UNIVERSITY, GRADUATE SCHOOL OF BUSINESS ADMINISTRATION SORTER, GEORGE	MANAGEMENT DISCUSSION AND ANALYSIS: FIRM COMPLIANCE AND INFORMATION CONTENT	Financial Accounting Archival - Primary Disclosures 93
BRYANT, JEFFREY JACK	PHD 1994 TEXAS TECH UNIVERSITY GATELY, MARY SUE	THE EFFECTS OF LOCAL TAXES ON ECONOMIC BEHAVIOR IN THE HOUSING MARKET	Taxation Archival - Primary Individual Taxation 145

Author	Degree & Date School Advisor	Title	Functional Area Research Method Topic pages
BUCKHOLD, J. W.	PHD 1986 ARIZONA STATE UNIVERSITY	ANALYSIS OF INDIVIDUAL TAXPAYER USE OF SELECTED TAX PREFERENCES--EMPIRICAL EVIDENCE	Taxation Archival - Primary Individual Taxation 150
BUKOVINSKY, DAVID MARTIN	PHD 1993 UNIVERSITY OF KENTUCKY TEARNEY, MICHAEL G.; CLARK, MYRTLE W.	CASH FLOW AND CASH POSITION MEASURES IN THE PREDICTION OF BUSINESS FAILURE: AN EMPIRICAL STUDY	Financial Accounting Archival - Primary Financial Ratios 224
BUKOWY, STEPHEN JOSEPH	PHD 1993 UNIVERSITY OF GEORGIA EDWARDS, JAMES DON	AN EMPIRICAL ANALYSIS OF THE USEFULNESS OF ACCOUNTING INFORMATION IN PREDICTING CLOSURES OF SMALL AND MEDIUM-SIZED HOSPITALS	Financial Accounting Archival - Primary Financial Distress or Bankruptcy 106
BULL, IVAN OLE	PHD 1987 UNIVERSITY OF ILLINOIS AT URBANA-CHAMPAIGN	MANAGEMENT PERFORMANCE IN LEVERAGED BUYOUTS: AN EMPIRICAL ANALYSIS	General Case Merger, Acquisition, Reorganization 106
BULLIS FRANSSON, DEBRA ALICE	PHD 1994 THE UNIVERSITY OF TEXAS AT AUSTIN ANDERSON, URTON L.	THE EFFECT OF INVESTMENT DECISION GOAL ON FINANCIAL ANALYSTS' USE OF INFORMATION IN JUDGMENTS ABOUT FIRMS	Financial Accounting Experimental Financial Analysts 156
BURCKEL, DARYL VINCENT	DBA 1986 MISSISSIPPI STATE UNIVERSITY	AN EMPIRICAL INVESTIGATION INTO DEVELOPING A FAILURE PREDICTION MODEL FOR FARMING ENTERPRISES: THE FIFTH FARM CREDIT DISTRICT	General Archival - Primary Industry - Agricultural 166
BURGESS, DEANNA OXENDER	PHD 1991 UNIVERSITY OF CENTRAL FLORIDA WELCH, JUDITH K.	THE EFFECTS OF GRAPHICAL DISTORTION OF ACCOUNTING INFORMATION ON FINANCIAL JUDGMENTS	Financial Accounting Experimental Presentation Format 166
BURILOVICH, LINDA JEAN SKANTZ	PHD 1990 THE UNIVERSITY OF MICHIGAN DANOS, PAUL; SLEMROD, JOEL	GAAP ELASTICITIES IN THE LIFE INSURANCE INDUSTRY: THE EFFECT OF TAX LAW CHANGES ON THE ACCOUNTING BEHAVIOR OF MUTUAL AND STOCK LIFE INSURANCE COMPANIES	General Archival - Primary Industry - Insurance 96
BURKETTE, GARY DALE	PHD 1994 VIRGINIA POLYTECHNIC INSTITUTE AND STATE UNIVERSITY LEININGER, WAYNE E.	A STUDY OF TASK UNCERTAINTY ASSOCIATED WITH PUBLIC ACCOUNTING FIRM SERVICES	Auditing Case Risk 130

Listing by Author

25

Author	Degree & Date School Advisor	Title	Functional Area Research Method Topic pages
BURKS, EDDY J.	DBA 1988 LOUISIANA TECH UNIVERSITY	STATEMENT OF FINANCIAL ACCOUNTING STANDARDS NO. 87 AND MARKET RISK ADJUSTMENT	Financial Accounting Archival - Primary Post Retirement Benefit Issues 154
BURROWES, ASHLEY WAYNE	PHD 1986 THE UNIVERSITY OF NEBRASKA - LINCOLN	A SURVEY OF SOPHISTICATED NEW ZEALAND USERS OF FINANCIAL STATEMENTS AND THEIR INTERIM REPORTING REQUIREMENTS	Financial Accounting Survey Interim Reporting 165
BUSH, HOWARD FRANCIS	PHD 1989 UNIVERSITY OF FLORIDA MESSIER, WILLIAM F.	THE USE OF REGRESSION MODELS IN ANALYTICAL REVIEW JUDGMENT: A LABORATORY EXPERIMENT	Auditing Experimental Analytical Review 145
BUSHMAN, ROBERT MICHAEL	PHD 1989 UNIVERSITY OF MINNESOTA	PUBLIC DISCLOSURE BY FIRMS IN THE PRESENCE OF A MONOPOLISTIC SELLER OF PRIVATE INFORMATION	Financial Accounting Experimental Voluntary Management Disclosures 71
BUSTA, BRUCE A.	PHD 1990 THE UNIVERSITY OF NEBRASKA - LINCOLN BALKE, THOMAS E.	A SIMULATION, REGRESSION ANALYSIS AND DELPHI SURVEY TO SEARCH FOR MATERIAL INEQUITIES RESULTING FROM THE REPEAL OF INCOME AVERAGING UNDER THE TAX REFORM ACT OF 1986	Taxation Public Policy 290
BUTLER, JANET ANN BASEMAN	PHD 1992 UNIVERSITY OF GEORGIA CLARK, RONALD L.	SELF-INTEREST IN ACCOUNTING: AN EXAMINATION OF DECISION-MAKING	Cost/Managerial Experimental Incentive Compensation 173
BUTT, JANE LOUISE	PHD 1986 THE UNIVERSITY OF MICHIGAN	FREQUENCY JUDGMENTS IN AUDITING	Auditing Experimental Judgment & Decision Making 146
BUTTARS, THOMAS ALAN	PHD 1988 THE UNIVERSITY OF WISCONSIN - MADISON WILLIAMS, THOMAS H.	A DISAGGREGATE APPROACH TO ACCOUNTING BASED MEASURES OF SYSTEMATIC RISK	Financial Accounting Archival - Primary Interim Reporting 146
BUTTROSS, THOMAS EDWARD	PHD 1991 THE UNIVERSITY OF MISSISSIPPI WALLACE, WILLIAM D.	THE EFFECT OF SELECTED PERSONALITY AND SITUATIONAL VARIABLES ON THE ETHICAL JUDGMENTS OF MANAGEMENT ACCOUNTANTS IN FEDERAL INCOME TAX COMPLIANCE	Taxation Experimental Ethics 200

Author	Degree & Date School Advisor	Title	Functional Area Research Method Topic pages
BYINGTON, JAMES RALPH	PHD 1985 UNIVERSITY OF ARKANSAS	ANALYSIS OF TIME SERIES PROPERTIES OF EARNINGS: COMPARISONS OF INDUSTRY MODELS AND BIVARIATE ANALYSIS FOR MODEL IMPROVEMENT	Financial Accounting Archival - Primary Forecasting Financial Performance 192
CAHAN, STEVEN F.	DBA 1988 UNIVERSITY OF COLORADO AT BOULDER SELTO, FRANK H.	LEGISLATIVE ACTION, POLITICAL COSTS, AND FIRM ACCOUNTING CHOICE	Financial Accounting Archival - Primary Earnings Management 190
CALDERON, DARRYL PATRICK	DBA 1987 NOVA UNIVERSITY	THE USE OF A FORMAL REVIEW PROCESS ON PROSPECTIVE FINANCIAL STATEMENTS BY NONPROFIT ORGANIZATIONS AS A PREDICTOR OF EFFECTIVENESS	Not-for-Profit Survey Forecasting Financial Performance 285
CALDERON, THOMAS GEORGE	PHD 1987 VIRGINIA POLYTECHNIC INSTITUTE AND STATE UNIVERSITY	BANKER NEEDS FOR ACCOUNTING INFORMATION	General Experimental Bank Loan Officers 989
CALLAGHAN, JOSEPH HENRY	PHD 1992 UNIVERSITY OF ILLINOIS AT URBANA-CHAMPAIGN MCKEOWN, JAMES C.	THE NATURE OF DEFERRED INCOME TAXES ARISING FROM DIFFERENCES IN DEPRECIATION METHODS	Financial Accounting Archival - Primary Taxes 109
CALLAHAN, CAROLYN MARGARET	PHD 1985 MICHIGAN STATE UNIVERSITY	A THEORETICAL AND EMPIRICAL EXAMINATION OF THE DETERMINANTS OF SYSTEMATIC RISK	Financial Accounting Archival - Primary Risk 135
CALLIHAN, DEBRA SALBADOR	PHD 1993 UNIVERSITY OF SOUTH CAROLINA WHITE, RICHARD A.	AN ANALYSIS OF THE RELATION BETWEEN IMPLICIT TAXES AND MARKET CONCENTRATION	Taxation Archival - Primary Corporate Taxation 95
CALVO SANCHEZ, JOSE ANTONIO	DR 1992 UNIVERSIDAD DEL PAIS VASCO/EUSKAL HERRIKO UNIBERTSITATEA (SPAIN)	THE RADICAL THINKING IN ACCOUNTING: FOUNDATIONS FOR ITS DEVELOPMENT [EL PENSAMIENTO RADICAL EN LA CONTABILIDAD: FUNDAMENTOS PARA SU DESARROLLO]	General History 451
CAMPBELL, ALAN DALE	PHD 1988 UNIVERSITY OF NORTH TEXAS BROCK, HORACE R.	AN ANALYSIS OF SMOOTHING OF PROVED OIL AND GAS RESERVE QUANTITIES AND AN ANALYSIS OF BIAS AND VARIABILITY IN REVISIONS OF PREVIOUS ESTIMATES OF PROVED OIL AND GAS RESERVE QUANTITIES	General Archival - Primary Industry - Oil & Gas 216

Author	Degree & Date School Advisor	Title	Functional Area Research Method Topic pages
CAMPBELL, ANNHENRIE	PHD 1991 UNIVERSITY OF COLORADO AT BOULDER	AUDIT CONTINUITY, CLIENT'S POLICY, AND THE INTERNAL AUDIT RELIANCE JUDGMENT	Auditing Experimental Internal Auditing 192
CAMPBELL, RONALD LOUIS	PHD 1989 TEXAS A&M UNIVERSITY WALLACE, WANDA A.	A CROSS-SECTIONAL AND TIME-SERIES INVESTIGATION OF MANAGERIAL DISCRETION REGARDING METHODS, RATES, PERIODS, AND DISCLOSURE: THE CASE OF EMPLOYERS' ACCOUNTING FOR PENSIONS	Financial Accounting Archival - Primary Accounting Choice 351
CAMPBELL, STEVEN VINCENT	PHD 1993 UNIVERSITY OF OREGON O'KEEFE, TERRENCE B.	THE SIGNIFICANCE OF DIRECT BANKRUPTCY COSTS IN DETERMINING THE OUTCOME OF BANKRUPTCY REORGANIZATION	Financial Accounting Archival - Primary Financial Distress or Bankruptcy 85
CAPOZZOLI, ERNEST ANTHONY	PHD 1991 THE UNIVERSITY OF MISSISSIPPI BARNES, JAMES H. JR.	AN EXPERIMENTAL INVESTIGATION OF THE EFFECTS OF A DECISION SUPPORT SYSTEM UTILIZING HYPERTEXT-BASED ACCOUNTING DATA ON INDIVIDUAL DECISION-MAKING BEHAVIOR	Information systems Experimental Decision Support Systems 148
CAPRIOTTI, KIM BOYLAN	PHD 1992 THE FLORIDA STATE UNIVERSITY ICERMAN, RHODA C.	AN INVESTIGATION OF THE USE OF VERBAL AND NUMERICAL PROBABILITY EXPRESSIONS IN BANK LENDING DECISIONS	Financial Accounting Experimental Disclosures 110
CARABALLO-ESTEB AN, TEODORO ANTONIO	DR 1992 UNIVERSIDAD DEL PAIS VASCO/EUSKAL HERRIKO UNIBERTSITATEA (SPAIN)	PROSPECTIVE FINANCIAL STATEMENTS: COMPARATIVE ANALYSIS AND DEVELOPMENT PROPOSAL [LOS DOCUMENTOS CONTABLES PREVISIONALES: ANALISIS COMPARADO Y PROPUESTA DE DESARROLLO]	Financial Accounting Forecasting Financial Performance 544
CARAYANNOPOULO S, PETER	PHD 1992 YORK UNIVERSITY (CANADA)	THE IMPACT OF STOCHASTIC INTEREST RATES ON THE PRICING OF CONVERTIBLE BONDS	Financial Accounting Archival - Primary Long Term Debt 138
CARCELLO, JOSEPH VINCENT	PHD 1990 GEORGIA STATE UNIVERSITY - COLLEGE OF BUSINESS ADMINISTRATION HERMANSON, ROGER H.	A COMPARATIVE STUDY OF AUDIT QUALITY AMONG THE BIG EIGHT ACCOUNTING FIRMS	Auditing Archival - Primary Audit Quality 154
CARDWELL, PAUL HERMAN, JR.	PHD 1991 THE UNIVERSITY OF TENNESSEE IZARD, CLIBURN DOUGLASS	THE EFFECT OF TAX REFORM ON THE EX ANTE VARIANCE OF SECURITY PRICES	Taxation Archival - Primary Public Policy 125

Author	Degree & Date School Advisor	Title	Functional Area Research Method Topic pages
CARGILL, WILLIE NEWTON	PHD 1986 UNIVERSITY OF MISSOURI - COLUMBIA	AN EQUITY RETENTION APPROACH TO ACCOUNTING FOR CHANGING PRICES	Financial Accounting Archival - Primary Inflation 230
CARLSON, STEVEN JAMES	PHD 1991 UNIVERSITY OF ARKANSAS GLEZEN, G. WILLIAM	AN EXAMINATION OF THE EFFECT OF A GOING CONCERN AUDIT REPORT ON SECURITY RETURNS AND TRADING VOLUME WHILE CONTROLLING FOR THE CONCURRENT RELEASE OF FINANCIAL STATEMENT INFORMATION	Financial Accounting Archival - Primary Audit Opinion 168
CARMENT, THOMAS MAXWELL	PHD 1991 OKLAHOMA STATE UNIVERSITY MEEK, GARY	THE MARKET EFFECT OF IN-SUBSTANCE DEFEASANCE ON BONDHOLDER DEFAULT RISK	Financial Accounting Archival - Primary Risk 72
CARNES, GREGORY ALVIN	PHD 1991 GEORGIA STATE UNIVERSITY - COLLEGE OF BUSINESS ADMINISTRATION ENGLEBRECHT, TED D.	AN EMPIRICAL INVESTIGATION OF THE RELATIONSHIP BETWEEN TAX INCENTIVES AND FINANCIAL REPORTING POLICY	Taxation Archival - Primary Earnings Management 189
CARNES, KAY C.	PHD 1990 SAINT LOUIS UNIVERSITY KEITHLEY, JOHN P.	THE EFFECTS OF CERTAIN PERSONAL AND ORGANIZATIONAL VARIABLES ON THE ATTITUDES OF INTERNAL AUDITORS TOWARD ETHICAL DILEMMAS	General Experimental Ethics 150
CARPENTER, BRIAN WELLS	PHD 1987 THE PENNSYLVANIA STATE UNIVERSITY	THE EFFECT OF NATURE OF TRANSACTION, RANK, EXPERIENCE, AND FAMILIARITY ON THE MATERIALITY JUDGMENTS OF AUDITORS: AN EMPIRICAL EXAMINATION	Auditing Experimental Materiality 229
CARPENTER, FRANCES HORVATH	PHD 1985 UNIVERSITY OF ILLINOIS AT URBANA-CHAMPAIGN	THE IMPACT OF MUNICIPAL REPORTING REQUIREMENTS ON MUNICIPAL OFFICIALS' FIXED ASSET ACQUISITION DECISIONS: A LABORATORY EXPERIMENT	Not-for-Profit Experimental Governmental 185
CARPENTER, JANICE LEE	PHD 1986 TEXAS A&M UNIVERSITY	AN AGENCY THEORY ANALYSIS OF CORPORATE LOBBYING IN RESPONSE TO THE DISCUSSION MEMORANDUM ON ACCOUNTING FOR INCOME TAXES	Financial Accounting Archival - Secondary Standard Setting 173
CARPENTER, VIVIAN LAVERNE	PHD 1985 THE UNIVERSITY OF MICHIGAN	THE INCENTIVES FOR THE EVOLUTION OF PERFORMANCE-ORIENTED ACCOUNTING INFORMATION SYSTEMS IN THE GOVERNMENTAL SETTING	Not-For-Profit Survey Governmental 297

Author	Degree & Date School Advisor	Title	Functional Area Research Method Topic pages
CARR, JANICE LYNN	DBA 1985 ARIZONA STATE UNIVERSITY	THE ACCELERATED COST RECOVERY SYSTEM: AN EXAMINATION OF ITS EFFECTS ON INCOME-PRODUCING PROPERTY	Taxation Simulation Public Policy 187
CARROLL, JAMES J.	DBA 1987 NOVA UNIVERSITY HODGETTS, RICHARD M.	CONTROL METHODOLOGIES FOR ACHIEVEMENT OF STRATEGIC OBJECTIVES	Cost/Managerial Survey Management Control Systems 179
CARROLL, THOMAS JOSEPH	PHD 1988 THE UNIVERSITY OF MICHIGAN IMHOFF, EUGENE A. JR.	THE NATURE OF THE DIVIDEND SIGNAL OF FUTURE EARNINGS	Financial Accounting Archival - Primary Dividends 67
CARSTENS, ROBERT HUGO KONRAD	PHD 1992 THE UNIVERSITY OF MISSISSIPPI GRAVES, O. FINLEY	AN ANALYSIS OF THE EXPERT OPINIONS AND EXPERIENCES OF AUDITORS ON THE TOPIC OF INCOME SMOOTHING	Financial Accounting Survey Earnings Management 163
CARTER, BEN DOUGLAS	PHD 1986 UNIVERSITY OF ARKANSAS	AN EMPIRICAL INVESTIGATION INTO THE PREDICTABILITY OF CHANGES IN CASH FLOW FROM OPERATIONS UNDER ALTERNATIVE METHODS OF ACCOUNTING FOR INCOME TAXES	Financial Accounting Archival - Primary Taxes 145
CARTER, GARY WILLIAM	PHD 1985 THE UNIVERSITY OF TEXAS AT AUSTIN	THE ACQUIESCENCE/NONACQUIESCENCE POLICY OF THE COMMISSIONER WITH RESPECT TO TAX COURT DECISIONS - AN EMPIRICAL ANALYSIS	Taxation Archival - Secondary Tax Court 212
CASCINI, KAREN T.	PHD 1988 THE UNIVERSITY OF CONNECTICUT BRAZZIEL, WILLIAM F.	A COMPARATIVE STUDY OF INVESTMENT STRATEGIES OF COLLEGES AND UNIVERSITIES AND COMMERCIAL CORPORATIONS	Not-for-Profit Survey College & University 167
CASLAN, DAVID FREDERICK	PHD 1992 SAINT LOUIS UNIVERSITY JENNINGS, JAMES	AN EXAMINATION OF THE DETERMINANTS OF DISCRETIONARY ACCOUNTING CHOICE BY MANAGEMENT	Financial Accounting Archival - Primary Accounting Choice 112
CASSIDY, JUDITH HELEN	PHD 1986 TEXAS TECH UNIVERSITY	A STUDY OF THE IMPACT OF MEDICARE PROSPECTIVE PAYMENT SYSTEM ON HOSPITAL COST CONTAINMENT ACTIVITIES	General Survey Industry - Health Care 169

Author	Degree & Date School Advisor	Title	Functional Area Research Method Topic pages
CASSILL, ARTHUR D.	PHD 1986 THE UNIVERSITY OF TENNESSEE	AN EMPIRICAL ANALYSIS OF THE INFLUENCE OF SELECTED POLITICAL PROCESS VARIABLES UPON INDUSTRY INCOME TAX BURDENS	Taxation Archival - Primary Public Policy 121
CASTER, ARTHUR BRUCE	PHD 1988 UNIVERSITY OF GEORGIA EDWARDS, JAMES DON	AN EMPIRICAL INVESTIGATION OF THE USEFULNESS OF FINANCIAL REPORTING INFORMATION IN PREDICTING FUTURE CASH FLOWS	Financial Accounting Archival - Primary Cash Flows 242
CASTER, PAUL	PHD 1987 UNIVERSITY OF NORTH TEXAS	THE EFFECTS OF MISSING DATA ON AUDIT INFERENCE AND AN INVESTIGATION INTO THE VALIDITY OF ACCOUNTS RECEIVABLE CONFIRMATIONS AS AUDIT EVIDENCE	Auditing Experimental Confirmations 127
CATANACH, ANTHONY HENRY, JR.	PHD 1994 ARIZONA STATE UNIVERSITY BOATSMAN, JAMES	A CAUSAL INVESTIGATION OF RISK, CASH FLOW, AND SOLVENCY IN THE SAVINGS AND LOAN INDUSTRY	Financial Accounting Archival - Primary Industry - Banking/Savings & Loan 152
CATHEY, JACK M.	PHD 1989 VIRGINIA POLYTECHNIC INSTITUTE AND STATE UNIVERSITY LEININGER, W. E.	CONTINGENT FACTORS AFFECTING BUDGET SYSTEM USEFULNESS: AN INFORMATION PROCESSING PERSPECTIVE	Cost/Managerial Survey Budgeting 229
CAVANAGH, WALTER FORBES	PHD 1985 STATE UNIVERSITY OF NEW YORK AT BUFFALO	THE ECONOMIC EFFECTS OF DEFINED BENEFIT PENSION FUNDING POLICY ON THE VALUE OF THE FIRM	Financial Accounting Archival - Primary Post Retirement Benefit Issues 144
CAVER, TROY VERNON	DSC 1990 THE GEORGE WASHINGTON UNIVERSITY SEWELL, HOMER B.	THE VALIDITY OF THE COST-IMPROVEMENT CURVE AS A COST PREDICTOR IN CHANGING PRODUCTION ENVIRONMENTS	Cost/Managerial Case Cost Behaviors & Estimation 159
CENKER, WILLIAM JOHN	PHD 1989 KENT STATE UNIVERSITY PEARSON, MICHAEL A.	AN EMPIRICAL ANALYSIS OF THE RESOLUTION OF CONFLICT AND THE PERCEPTIONS OF AUTONOMY AND RESPONSIBILITY OF INDEPENDENT AUDITORS	General Survey CPA Firm Issues 216
CERDA APARICIO, JOSE	PHD 1991 UNIVERSITAT DE VALENCIA (SPAIN)	COMPARATIVE ANALYSIS OF THE IMPLEMENTATION OF THE 4TH COMPANY LAW DIRECTIVE IN THE 12 MEMBER COUNTRIES OF THE EUROPEAN COMMUNITY [LA ADAPTACION DEL DERECHO DE SOCIEDADES A LA IV DIRECTIVA DE LA COMUNIDAD ECONOMICA EUROPEA: ANALISIS COMPARATIVO ENTRE LOS ESTADOS MIEMBROS]	Financial Accounting Analytical - Internal International/Global Issues 750

Author	Degree & Date School Advisor	Title	Functional Area Research Method Topic pages
CERF, DOUGLAS CLIFFORD	PHD 1991 UNIVERSITY OF CALIFORNIA, DAVIS	A STUDY OF INTERTEMPORAL VARIATION IN EARNINGS RESPONSE COEFFICIENTS: THE CASE OF THE MANDATED CHANGE IN ACCOUNTING RULES TO SFAS #87 ON PENSIONS	Financial Accounting Archival - Primary Post Retirement Benefit Issues 120
CERULLO, MARGARET VIRGINIA	PHD 1990 THE LOUISIANA STATE UNIVERSITY AND AGRICULTURAL AND MECHANICAL COL. SUMNERS, GLENN E.	A STUDY OF INTERNAL AUDITOR PERCEPTIONS OF SELECTED AUDIT ACTIVITIES PERFORMED DURING THE DESIGN PHASE OF SYSTEMS DEVELOPMENT	Information Systems Survey Systems Design &/or Development 311
CHAMBERLAIN, DARNLEY HUGH, JR.	DBA 1990 UNIVERSITY OF KENTUCKY VANDANIKER, RELMOND	FINANCIAL REPORTING IN THE HIGHER EDUCATION ENVIRONMENT: ASSESSING THE VIEWS OF SELECTED USERS ON THE USEFULNESS AND ACCESSIBILITY OF SPECIFIED OUTCOMES INFORMATION	Not-for-Profit Survey College & University 176
CHAN, CHRIS WAI-HONG	PHD 1993 UNIVERSITY OF MISSOURI - COLUMBIA WILSON, EARL R.; LAWRENCE, CAROL	EFFECTS OF NEGOTIATOR ACCOUNTABILITY, PERFORMANCE EVALUATION SYSTEM, AND PERCEPTION OF DIVISIONAL POWER ON TRANSFER PRICING NEGOTIATION OUTCOMES	Cost/Managerial Experimental Transfer Pricing 233
CHAN, KAM CHU	PHD 1991 UNIVERSITY OF SOUTH CAROLINA	A REEXAMINATION OF THE STOCK MARKET AND BOND MARKET REACTION TO LIFO ADOPTION	Financial Accounting Archival - Primary Inventory 94
CHANDRA, AKHILESH	PHD 1993 MEMPHIS STATE UNIVERSITY AGRAWAL, SURENDRA P.	FIRM SIZE, A SELF-ORGANIZED CRITICAL PHENOMENON: EVIDENCE FROM THE DYNAMICAL SYSTEMS THEORY	Financial Accounting Case Other 138
CHANDRA, RAMESH	PHD 1986 THE UNIVERSITY OF OKLAHOMA	AN EXAMINATION OF EVENT STUDY METHODOLOGY	General Simulation Capital Markets 202
CHANDRA, UDAY	PHD 1992 PURDUE UNIVERSITY RO, BYUNG-TAK	THE ASSOCIATION BETWEEN PREDISCLOSURE INDUSTRY INFORMATION AND THE INFORMATION CONTENT OF EARNINGS ANNOUNCEMENTS	Financial Accounting Archival - Primary Earnings Announcements 53
CHANG, CHUN SHYONG	PHD 1990 UNIVERSITY OF MARYLAND COLLEGE PARK LOEB, MARTIN	THE INFORMATION CONTENT OF TAIWANESE FINANCIAL STATEMENTS: THE CASE OF LOAN DEFAULT	Financial Accounting Archival - Primary International/Global Issues 270

Author	Degree & Date School Advisor	Title	Functional Area Research Method Topic pages
CHANG, CHUNG-YUEH C.	PHD 1993 UNIVERSITY OF HOUSTON	AN EXAMINATION OF TIME-VARYING EARNINGS GROWTH AND EARNINGS LEVELS AND THEIR IMPACTS ON SECURITY RETURNS	Financial Accounting Archival - Primary Earnings Response Coefficients 119
CHANG, HSI-HUI	PHD 1994 UNIVERSITY OF MINNESOTA BANKER, RAJIV D.	LINEARITY AND SEPARABILITY ASSUMPTIONS IN COST ACCOUNTING	Cost/Managerial Archival - Primary Cost Behaviors & Estimation 149
CHANG, JINNDER	DBA 1992 UNITED STATES INTERNATIONAL UNIVERSITY KHALIL, MOHAMAD A.	TRANSFER PRICING AND TAX STRATEGIES FOR MULTINATIONAL COMPANIES IN TAIWAN	Taxation Survey International/Global Issues 194
CHANG, STANLEY Y]	PHD 1987 TEXAS TECH UNIVERSITY	A STUDY OF THE BASIC CRITERIA AND STANDARDS BY INTERNAL SERVICE FUNDS	Not-for-Profit Survey Governmental 200
CHANG, YOUNG HANG	PHD 1988 VIRGINIA POLYTECHNIC INSTITUTE AND STATE UNIVERSITY LEININGER, W. E.	A COMPARATIVE STUDY OF THE ACCOUNTING SYSTEMS OF FIVE COUNTRIES IN EAST AND SOUTHEAST ASIA	General International/Global Issues 275
CHARITOU, ANDREAS G.	PHD 1986 THE PENNSYLVANIA STATE UNIVERSITY	THE INFORMATION CONTENT OF ACCRUAL AND CASH FLOW MEASURES: A CROSS-SECTIONAL VALUATION STUDY	Financial Accounting Archival - Primary Accruals 244
CHASE, BRUCE W.	PHD 1991 VIRGINIA COMMONWEALTH UNIVERSITY COFFMAN, EDWARD N.	AN EMPIRICAL INVESTIGATION OF A CHOICE OF ACCOUNTING METHOD FOR INVESTMENTS BY COLLEGES AND UNIVERSITIES: POSITIVE ACCOUNTING THEORY APPLIED IN A NOT-FOR-PROFIT ENVIRONMENT	Not-for-Profit Survey College & University 145
CHAU, CHAK-TONG	PHD 1992 THE FLORIDA STATE UNIVERSITY HILLISON, WILLIAM A.	COMPARING FORECASTING PERFORMANCE IN ANALYTICAL PROCEDURES: AN INTEGRATED STUDY USING STATE SPACE, EXPONENTIAL SMOOTHING AND REGRESSION MODELS	Auditing Simulation Analytical Review 107
CHAWLA, GURDEEP KUMAR	DBA 1994 GOLDEN GATE UNIVERSITY KALE, JIVENDRA K.	UNITED STATES GAAP VERSUS EUROPEAN COMMUNITY AND PACIFIC RIM COUNTRIES' ACCOUNTING STANDARDS: AN EMPIRICAL STUDY	Financial Accounting Archival - Primary International/Global Issues 239

Author	Degree & Date School Advisor	Title	Functional Area Research Method Topic pages
CHEH, JONGWOOK	PHD 1986 THE UNIVERSITY OF MICHIGAN	INCENTIVE EFFECTS OF INTER-AGENT MONITORING: IMPLICATIONS FOR RESPONSIBILITY ACCOUNTING AND AUDITOR-CONSULTANT INTERACTION	Auditing Analytical - Internal Agency Theory 112
CHEN, DAVID MING-DAU	PHD 1986 UNIVERSITY OF ILLINOIS AT URBANA-CHAMPAIGN	THE INFORMATION CONTENT OF QUARTERLY EARNINGS DATA AND THE MARKETS REVISION OF RISK PREDICTIONS IMPLIED IN OPTION PRICES	Financial Accounting Archival - Primary Earnings Announcements 153
CHEN, JIIN-FENG	PHD 1991 THE UNIVERSITY OF WISCONSIN - MADISON WEYGANDT, JERRY JOSEPH	AN EXPERT SYSTEM FOR THE IDENTIFICATION OF TROUBLED SAVINGS AND LOAN ASSOCIATIONS	Financial Accounting Case Financial Distress or Bankruptcy 227
CHEN, KEVIN CHIEN-WEN	PHD 1985 UNIVERSITY OF ILLINOIS AT URBANA-CHAMPAIGN	THE DETERMINANTS OF TOBIN'S Q RATIO AND AN EVALUATION OF SFAS 33 DATA	Financial Accounting Archival - Primary Inflation 155
CHEN, KUO-TAY	PHD 1992 THE UNIVERSITY OF TEXAS AT AUSTIN LEE, RONALD M.	SCHEMATIC EVALUATION OF INTERNAL ACCOUNTING CONTROL SYSTEMS	Auditing Analytical - Internal Internal Control 269
CHEN, RING DING	PHD 1985 UNIVERSITY OF FLORIDA	BUDGET-BASED CONTRACTS AND TOP-LEVEL EXECUTIVE COMPENSATION: AN EMPIRICAL EVALUATION	Cost/Managerial Archival - Primary Incentive Compensation 121
CHEN, SEAN SHAW-ZON	PHD 1992 UNIVERSITY OF PITTSBURGH	A MODEL OF BELIEF REVISION IN AUDIT RISK ASSESSMENT	Auditing Experimental Judgment & Decision Making - Heuristics & Biases 268
CHEN, SHIMIN	PHD 1992 UNIVERSITY OF GEORGIA CLARK, RONALD L.	AN EMPIRICAL INVESTIGATION OF THE USE OF PAYBACK METHOD IN CAPITAL BUDGETING: EFFICIENT VIEW VS OPPORTUNISTIC VIEW	Cost/Managerial Archival - Primary Capital Budgeting 141
CHEN, YI-NING	PHD 1993 UNIVERSITY OF SOUTH CAROLINA LEITCH, ROBERT A.	THE ERROR DETECTION OF STRUCTURAL ANALYTICAL REVIEW PROCEDURES: A SIMULATION STUDY	Auditing Simulation Analytical Review 147

Author	Degree & Date School Advisor	Title	Functional Area Research Method Topic pages
CHEN, YUANG-SUNG AL	PHD 1989 GEORGIA INSTITUTE OF TECHNOLOGY COMISKEY, EUGENE E.	FINANCIAL ANALYST FORECAST DISPERSION: DETERMINANTS AND USEFULNESS AS AN EXANTE MEASURE OF RISK	Financial Accounting Archival - Primary Financial Analysts 170
CHENG, PAYYU	PHD 1990 THE UNIVERSITY OF NEBRASKA - LINCOLN CHEN, KUNG H.	THE INCREMENTAL INFORMATION CONTENT OF FUND FLOW STATEMENTS: A QUARTERLY APPROACH	Financial Accounting Archival - Primary Cash Flows 203
CHENG, RITA HARTUNG	PHD 1988 TEMPLE UNIVERSITY GAFFNEY, MARY ANNE	TOWARD A POSITIVE THEORY OF STATE GOVERNMENT ACCOUNTING DISCLOSURE	Not-for-Profit Governmental 267
CHEONG, INBUM	PHD 1991 GEORGIA STATE UNIVERSITY - COLLEGE OF BUSINESS ADMINISTRATION SKIPPER, HAROLD D. JR.	AN ANALYSIS OF SOLVENCY REGULATION AND FAILURE PREDICTION IN THE UNITED STATES LIFE INSURANCE INDUSTRY	Financial Accounting Archival - Primary Financial Distress or Bankruptcy 272
CHESTER, MICHAEL CARTER, JR.	PHD 1991 VIRGINIA COMMONWEALTH UNIVERSITY SPEDE, EDWARD CHARLES	AN EMPIRICAL STUDY OF CORPORATE MANAGEMENT SUPPORT FOR PUSH DOWN ACCOUNTING	Financial Accounting Archival - Survey Accounting Choice 169
CHEW, ANDREW SWEE-CHUNG	PHD 1993 UNIVERSITY OF NEW SOUTH WALES (AUSTRALIA)	A STRUCTURATIONAL ANALYSIS OF MANAGEMENT ACCOUNTING PRACTICE IN ITS ORGANISATIONAL CONTEXTS: A SOCIAL SCIENCE PERSPECTIVE	Cost/Managerial Accounting Career Issues
CHI, CHARLES CHI-WEI	PHD 1989 UNIVERSITY OF FLORIDA ABDEL-KHALIK, A. RASHAD	THE INFORMATION CONTENT AND HEDGING PERFORMANCE OF FOREIGN CURRENCY TRANSLATIONS: AN EVALUATION OF SFAS NO. 8 VS NO 52	Financial Accounting Archival - Primary Foreign Currency Translation 118
CHI, SUNG-KUON	PHD 1989 UNIVERSITY OF WASHINGTON SUNDEM, GARY L.	ETHICS AND AGENCY THEORY	General Analytical - Internal Ethics 113
CHIASSON, MICHAEL ANTHONY	DBA 1994 LOUISIANA TECH UNIVERSITY JOHNSON, GENE	ORGANIZATIONAL-PROFESSIONAL CONFLICT AND THE WHISTLEBLOWING INTENTIONS OF PROFESSIONAL ACCOUNTANTS	General Survey Ethics 149

Author	Degree & Date School Advisor	Title	Functional Area Research Method Topic pages
CHIEN, CHIN-CHEN	PHD 1992 RUTGERS THE STATE UNIVERSITY OF NEW JERSEY - NEWARK LEE, CHENG-FEW	ALTERNATIVE METHODS FOR THE ESTIMATION OF EARNINGS AND DIVIDENDS ANNOUNCEMENT EFFECTS: REVIEW, INTEGRATION, AND EXTENSION	Financial Accounting Archival - Primary Earnings Announcements 298
CHILTON, ROBERT CARTER	DBA 1992 BOSTON UNIVERSITY PRESTON, ALISTAIR M.	THE AMERICAN ACCOUNTING PROFESSION AND ITS CODE OF ETHICS: 1887-1933	General Analytical - Internal Ethics 236
CHIPALKATTI, NIRANJAN H.	PHD 1993 UNIVERSITY OF MASSACHUSETTS CALLAHAN, CAROLYN	ADVERSE SELECTION COSTS AND THE DEALERS' BID-ASK SPREAD AROUND EARNINGS ANNOUNCEMENTS: DIFFERENTIAL INFORMATION AND SIGNAL QUALITY	Financial Accounting Archival - Primary Agency Theory 341
CHIU, CHUI-YU	PHD 1992 AUBURN UNIVERSITY PARK, CHAN S.	ARTIFICIAL INTELLIGENCE AND ITS APPLICATIONS TO CAPITAL BUDGETING DECISIONS UNDER UNCERTAINTY	Information Systems Analytical - Internal Decision Support Systems 165
CHO, JANG YOUN	PHD 1987 UNIVERSITY OF FLORIDA ABDEL-KHALIK, A. RASHAD	TIMELINESS OF EARNINGS REPORTS: A SIGNALLING APPROACH	Financial Accounting Archival - Primary Earnings Announcements 105
CHO, WHAJOON	PHD 1992 INDIANA UNIVERSITY OGAN, PEKIN	THE RELATIONSHIP BETWEEN EVIDENCE SEQUENCE AND TIME PRESSURE ON AUDITORS' CONTROL RISK ASSESSMENTS	Auditing Experimental Judgment & Decision Making - Heuristics & Biases 126
CHOE, YONG SUN	PHD 1990 UNIVERSITY OF FLORIDA KRAMER, JOHN L.	THE EFFECT OF A TAX DEDUCTION ON CHARITABLE CONTRIBUTIONS BY LOW- AND MIDDLE-INCOME TAXPAYERS	Taxation Archival - Primary Tax Compliance 125
CHOI, BYEONGHEE	PHD 1994 THE UNIVERSITY OF IOWA COLLINS, DANIEL W.; JOHNSON, W. BRUCE	MARKET VALUATION OF POSTRETIREMENT OBLIGATIONS: A TEST OF HOW DIFFERENCES IN RELIABILITY AFFECT THE VALUATION IMPLICATIONS	Financial Accounting Archival - Primary Post Retirement Benefit Issues 94
CHOI, JONG UK	PHD 1988 UNIVERSITY OF SOUTH CAROLINA MARKLAND, ROBERT	A CONSTRUCTIVE APPROACH TO BUILDING A KNOWLEDGE-BASED INTERNAL CONTROL EVALUATION REVIEW SYSTEM	Auditing Analytical - Internal Decision Support Systems 317

Author	Degree & Date School Advisor	Title	Functional Area Research Method Topic pages
CHOI, JUNG HO	PHD 1987 UNIVERSITY OF HOUSTON KHUMAWALA, SALEHA B.	MANAGEMENT EARNINGS EXPECTATIONS, EARNINGS UNCERTAINTY, AND VOLUNTARY DISCLOSURE OF EARNINGS FORECASTS BY MANAGEMENT: AN EMPIRICAL EVALUATION OF CURRENT DISCLOSURE PRACTICES UNDER THE VOLUNTARY RULES	Financial Accounting Archival - Primary Voluntary Management Disclosures 140
CHOI, KWAN	PHD 1991 SYRACUSE UNIVERSITY ISMAIL, BADR E.	DETERMINANTS OF TIME SERIES PROPERTIES OF ANNUAL EARNINGS AND CASH FLOWS	Financial Accounting Archival - Primary Accruals 146
CHOI, MUN SOO	PHD 1993 UNIVERSITY OF KANSAS SALATKA, WILLIAM	THE EFFECT OF DISPERSION OF ANALYSTS' FORECASTS ON STOCK AND BOND PRICES	Financial Accounting Archival - Primary Financial Analysts 130
CHOI, NAHNHEE J.	PHD 1990 THE UNIVERSITY OF NORTH CAROLINA AT CHAPEL HILL BLOCHER, ED	THE MANAGER-AUDITOR GAME REVISITED: ON THE EFFECT OF INCOMPLETE INFORMATION, THE DUE CARE LEVEL, AND THE MATERIALITY LEVEL IMPOSED BY THE STANDARD-SETTING BOARDS	Auditing Analytical - Internal Materiality 205
CHOI, SOONJAE	PHD 1992 NEW YORK UNIVERSITY, GRADUATE SCHOOL OF BUSINESS ADMINISTRATION ROUEN, JOSHUA	THE INFORMATION CONTENT OF ACCOUNTING NUMBERS: USING A BELIEF REVISION MEASURE OF STOCK PRICES	Financial Accounting Archival - Primary Information Content 90
CHOI, SUNG KYU	PHD 1985 THE UNIVERSITY OF IOWA	DIFFERENTIAL INFORMATION CONTENT OF PUBLICLY ANNOUNCED EARNINGS: THEORETICAL AND EMPIRICAL ANALYSIS	Financial Accounting Archival - Primary Earnings Announcements 142
CHOI, WON WOOK	PHD 1993 COLUMBIA UNIVERSITY OHLSON, JAMES	FINANCIAL STATEMENT ANALYSIS: THE STUDY OF RETURN ON COMMON EQUITY AND INTANGIBLE ASSETS	Financial Accounting Archival - Primary Capital Markets 109
CHOI, YEONG CHAN	PHD 1989 DREXEL UNIVERSITY JAIN, ROHIT	EARLY ADOPTION OF SFAS NO. 87 AND THE DEFENSIVE ACTION HYPOTHESIS: A POSITIVE THEORY ANALYSIS	Financial Accounting Archival - Primary Accounting Choice 132
CHOO, TECKMIN	PHD 1993 UNIVERSITY OF PITTSBURGH BIRNBERG, JACOB G.	AUDITORS' INFORMATION SEARCH AND EVALUATION IN HYPOTHESIS-TESTING: POSITIVITY, EXTREMITY, PSEUDODIAGNOSTICITY AND CONFIRMATION EFFECTS	Auditing Experimental Judgment & Decision Making - Heuristics & Biases 167

Author	Degree & Date School Advisor	Title	Functional Area Research Method Topic pages
CHOU, LING-TAI LYNETTE	PHD 1985 UNIVERSITY OF HOUSTON	A SURVEY EXAMINATION OF THE OBJECTIVE OF ACCOUNTS RECEIVABLE CONFIRMATION AND THE BEHAVIOR PATTERN OF CONFIRMATION RESPONDENTS	Auditing Survey Confirmations 190
CHRISMAN, HEIDI HADLICH	PHD 1990 UNIVERSITY OF WASHINGTON SUNDEM, GARY L.	THE EFFECTS OF THE MATURITY STRUCTURE OF NOMINAL CONTRACTS ON EQUITY RETURNS IN AN INFLATIONARY ENVIRONMENT	Financial Accounting Archival - Primary Inflation 126
CHRIST, LEROY FREDERICK	PHD 1991 THE UNIVERSITY OF TEXAS AT AUSTIN MARCHANT, GARRY A.; ROBINSON, JOHN R.	A COMPARISON OF INSTRUCTIONAL STRATEGIES IN THE DEVELOPMENT OF CATEGORICAL TAX KNOWLEDGE WITH AN EXAMINATION OF THE EFFECT OF INCONSISTENT PRE-EXISTING KNOWLEDGE	Taxation Experimental Judgment & Decision Making - Cognitive Processes 104
CHRIST, MARY YORK	PHD 1988 THE UNIVERSITY OF TEXAS AT AUSTIN TOMASSINI, LAWRENCE A.; ANDERSON, URTON L.	ATTENTION AND ENCODING DURING AUDIT PLANNING: AN EXPERIMENTAL STUDY USING A SCHEMATIC FRAMEWORK	Auditing Experimental Judgment & Decision Making - Cognitive Processes 211
CHRISTENSEN, ANNE LESLIE KEENEY	PHD 1989 THE UNIVERSITY OF UTAH EINING, N. LAVAR	TAX RETURN QUALITY: A CLIENT AND PREPARER PERSPECTIVE	Taxation Survey Tax Professionals 184
CHRISTENSEN, DAVID SCOTT	PHD 1987 THE UNIVERSITY OF NEBRASKA - LINCOLN	THE APPLICATION OF MATHEMATICAL PROGRAMMING TO THE PRODUCTIVITY INVESTMENT FUND PROGRAM: A CAPITAL RATIONING PROBLEM	Not-for-Profit Archival - Primary Capital Budgeting 205
CHRISTENSEN, JO ANN	DBA 1993 LOUISIANA TECH UNIVERSITY	AUDITOR SWITCHING AND WHITE COLLAR CRIME	Auditing Case Auditor Changes 125
CHRISTENSEN, LINDA FAY	PHD 1989 UNIVERSITY OF SOUTH CAROLINA DOUPNIK, TIMOTHY S.	SUBSIDIARY MANAGEMENT ACCOUNTING SYSTEMS OF U.S.-BASED MULTINATIONAL ENTERPRISES	Cost/Managerial International/Global Issues 172
CHRISTIAN, CHARLES WILLIAM	PHD 1985 UNIVERSITY OF GEORGIA	AN EMPIRICAL TEST OF THE EFFECTS OF INTERNAL REVENUE CODE SECTION 465 ON RISK-TAKING BY INVESTORS IN OIL AND GAS DRILLING PROGRAMS	Taxation Archival - Primary Industry - Oil & Gas 118

Author	Degree & Date School Advisor	Title	Functional Area Research Method Topic pages
CHU, LILUAN ERIC	PHD 1991 NEW YORK UNIVERSITY, GRADUATE SCHOOL OF BUSINESS ADMINISTRATION	MARKET-BASED ACCOUNTING RESEARCH: AN INTERNATIONAL COMPARISON AND NEW EVIDENCE	Financial Accounting Archival - Primary International/Global Issues 202
CHUNG, DENNIS Y.	PHD 1991 UNIVERSITY OF ALBERTA (CANADA)	THE INFORMATIONAL EFFECT OF MANAGEMENT'S DECISION TO LOBBY AGAINST PROPOSED ACCOUNTING STANDARDS	Financial Accounting Archival - Primary Standard Setting 209
CHUNG, HAY YOUNG	PHD 1987 UNIVERSITY OF CALIFORNIA, BERKELEY	EMPIRICAL INVESTIGATION INTO THE STOCK MARKET REACTIONS TO CORPORATE EARNINGS REPORTS	Financial Accounting Archival - Primary Earnings Announcements 190
CHUNG, KEE-YOUNG	PHD 1985 THE UNIVERSITY OF TEXAS AT AUSTIN	AN INVESTIGATION OF THE EFFECTS OF INFLATION-ADJUSTED ACCOUNTING DATA ON EQUITY VALUE	Financial Accounting Archival - Primary Inflation 185
CHUNG, KI-YOUNG	PHD 1986 UNIVERSITY OF CALIFORNIA, BERKELEY	AN ESSAY ON THE INTERTEMPORAL GENERAL EQUILIBRIUM MODEL OF EXCHANGE RATES IN A CONTINUOUS-TIME VERSION	General Analytical - Internal International/Global Issues 146
CHUNG, KUN YOUNG	PHD 1988 THE UNIVERSITY OF WISCONSIN - MADISON WILLIAMS, THOMAS H.	FIRM SIZE, INDUSTRY ACCOUNTING NORMS, AND THE INFORMATION CONTENT OF ACCOUNTING CHANGE ANNOUNCEMENTS	Financial Accounting Archival - Primary Accounting Change 145
CHUNG, KWANG-HYUN	PHD 1990 CITY UNIVERSITY OF NEW YORK PASTENA, VICTOR	CORPORATE LOBBYING AND MARKET REACTION TO PROPOSED ACCOUNTING RULES: THE CASE OF POSTRETIREMENT BENEFITS OTHER THAN PENSIONS	Financial Accounting Archival - Primary Standard Setting 143
CHUNG, LAI HONG	PHD 1992 UNIVERSITY OF PITTSBURGH BIRNBERG, JACOB G.	THE JOINT EFFECTS OF PRIOR OUTCOME AND PRESENTATION FORMAT ON INDIVIDUAL AND GROUP RESOURCE ALLOCATION DECISIONS: THE ROLE OF MENTAL ACCOUNTS	General Experimental Judgment & Decision Making - Heuristics & Biases 187
CHUNG, MOON-CHONG	PHD 1992 UNIVERSITY OF ILLINOIS AT URBANA-CHAMPAIGN KWON, Y.	AN INVESTMENT CENTER VS. A PROFIT CENTER: CAPITAL INVESTMENT UNDER INFORMATIONAL ASYMMETRY	Cost/Managerial Analytical - Internal Agency Theory 98

Author	Degree & Date School Advisor	Title	Functional Area Research Method Topic pages
CHUNG, TSAI-YEN	DBA 1985 TEXAS TECH UNIVERSITY	MANAGEMENT MOTIVATION FOR SELECTING ACCOUNTING PRINCIPLES: A MARKET-BASED EMPIRICAL INVESTIGATION	Financial Accounting Archival - Primary Accounting Choice 193
CHURCH, BRYAN KEVIN	PHD 1986 UNIVERSITY OF FLORIDA	AN INVESTIGATION OF CONFIRMATORY BIAS IN AN AUDIT SETTING: A CONCEPTUALIZATION AND LABORATORY EXPERIMENT	Auditing Experimental Judgment & Decision Making - Heuristics & Biases 156
CHURCH, PAMELA HARMON	PHD 1986 UNIVERSITY OF HOUSTON	ENVIRONMENTAL VOLATILITY AND CAPITAL BUDGETING PRACTICES	Cost/Managerial Capital Budgeting 154
CHWASTIAK, MICHELE EILEEN	PHD 1990 UNIVERSITY OF PITTSBURGH EVANS, JOHN H.	AN EMPIRICAL INVESTIGATION INTO THE DOD'S CHOICE OF CONTRACT TYPE	General Archival - Primary Governmental 149
CLARK, COROLYN ELIZABETH	PHD 1985 TEMPLE UNIVERSITY	AN EXPERIMENT TO DETERMINE THE EFFECTS OF A BEHAVIOR MODIFICATION INTERVENTION PROGRAM ON ANXIETY LEVELS AND ACHIEVEMENT OF STUDENTS IN PRINCIPLES OF ACCOUNTING CLASSES	Education Experimental Curriculum Issues 147
CLARK, STANLEY J.	PHD 1991 UNIVERSITY OF KENTUCKY TEARNEY, MICHAEL G.	AN EMPIRICAL EXAMINATION OF FIRMS' MOTIVATIONS FOR EARLY ADOPTION OF SFAS 96 AND THE INFORMATION CONTENT OF FIRMS' DECISION TO EARLY ADOPT SFAS 96	Financial Accounting Archival - Primary Taxes 143
CLARKE, DOUGLAS A.	PHD 1987 THE UNIVERSITY OF WISCONSIN - MADISON	AN EXAMINATION OF THE IMPACT OF INDIVIDUAL RISK ATTITUDES AND PERCEPTIONS ON AUDIT RISK ASSESSMENT	Auditing Risk 346
CLAYPOOL, GREGORY ALLEN	PHD 1988 KENT STATE UNIVERSITY FETYKO, DAVID F.	AN EXPLORATORY STUDY OF THE COGNITIVE FRAMEWORKS USED BY CPAS AND THEOLOGIANS WHEN CONFRONTED WITH ETHICAL DILEMMAS	General Survey Ethics 202
CLAYTON, HOWARD ROBERTSON	PHD 1991 UNIVERSITY OF GEORGIA NETER, JOHN	CONFIDENCE BOUNDS BASED ON THE BOOTSTRAP AND HOEFFDING'S INEQUALITY FOR DOLLAR UNIT SAMPLING IN AUDITING	Auditing Simulation Audit Sampling 513

Author	Degree & Date School Advisor	Title	Functional Area Research Method Topic pages
CLAYTON, PENNY RENEE	PHD 1990 OKLAHOMA STATE UNIVERSITY	AUDITOR DECISION PROCESSING AND THE IMPLICATIONS OF BRAIN DOMINANCE: A PREDECISIONAL BEHAVIOR STUDY	Auditing Experimental Judgment & Decision Making - Cognitive Processes 193
CLEMENT, ROBIN PAULA	PHD 1994 MICHIGAN STATE UNIVERSITY ANTHONY, JOSEPH H.	ACCOUNTING CHANGES AND THE DETERMINANTS OF SYSTEMATIC RISK: THE CASE OF FAS NO. 36: DISCLOSURE OF PENSION INFORMATION	Financial Accounting Archival - Primary Post Retirement Benefit issues 107
CLEMENTS, ALAN BRUCE	PHD 1989 UNIVERSITY OF FLORIDA KRAMER, JOHN L.	AN EMPIRICAL ANALYSIS OF LOW-INCOME HOUSING TAX INCENTIVES	Taxation Archival - Primary Public Policy 173
CLEVENGER, THOMAS BENTON	DBA 1987 MEMPHIS STATE UNIVERSITY	THE DEVELOPMENT OF GUIDELINES FOR INTEGRATING MICROCOMPUTERS INTO THE ACCOUNTING CURRICULUM	Education Survey Curriculum Issues 320
CLINCH, GREGORY JOHN	PHD 1988 STANFORD UNIVERSITY FOSTER, GEORGE	INFORMATION AND MOTIVATION ISSUES IN COMPENSATION DESIGN: AN APPLICATION TO HIGH TECHNOLOGY COMPANIES	Cost/Managerial Case Incentive Compensation 131
CLOYD, C. BRYAN	PHD 1992 INDIANA UNIVERSITY PRATT, JAMIE H.	THE EFFECTS OF KNOWLEDGE AND INCENTIVES ON INFORMATION SEARCH IN TAX RESEARCH TASKS	Taxation Experimental Judgment & Decision Making - Cognitive Processes 148
COATE, CHARLES JOSEPH	PHD 1992 UNIVERSITY OF MARYLAND COLLEGE PARK LOEB, MARTIN	A TWO PERIOD BIDDING MODEL OF THE AUDIT MARKET	Auditing Analytical - Internal Auditor Changes 179
COBB, LAUREL GORDON	PHD 1993 UNIVERSITY OF SOUTH FLORIDA HOLSTRUM, GARY L.	AN INVESTIGATION INTO THE EFFECT OF SELECTED AUDIT COMMITTEE CHARACTERISTICS ON FRAUDULENT FINANCIAL REPORTING	Auditing Archival - Primary Fraud 138
COBERLY, JANET WOOD	PHD 1989 UNIVERSITY OF HOUSTON	AN ANALYSIS OF THE EFFECTIVENESS OF THE RESEARCH AND EXPERIMENTATION TAX CREDIT WITHIN A Q MODEL OF VALUATION	Taxation Archival - Primary Research & Development 204

Listing by Author

41

Author	Degree & Date School Advisor	Title	Functional Area Research Method Topic pages
COCCO, ANTHONY F.	PHD 1991 THE FLORIDA STATE UNIVERSITY BAILEY, CHARLES	THE EFFECTS OF STANDARD DIFFICULTY AND COMPENSATION METHOD ON THE PARAMETERS OF THE INDUSTRIAL LEARNING CURVE AND OVERALL PERFORMANCE OF MANUAL ASSEMBLY AND DISASSEMBLY TASKS	Cost/Managerial Experimental Standard Costs & Variance Analysis 218
COCKRELL, SUSAN ROBERTA	PHD 1993 THE UNIVERSITY OF ALABAMA ROBBINS, WALTER	TESTING THE DETERMINANTS OF DISCLOSURE COMPLIANCE BY MUNICIPALITIES USING CONFIRMATION FACTOR ANALYSIS	Not-for-Profit Case Governmental 184
COFF, RUSSELL W.	PHD 1993 UNIVERSITY OF CALIFORNIA, LOS ANGELES FLAMHOLTZ, ERIC G.; MITCHELL, DANIEL J. B.	CORPORATE ACQUISITIONS OF HUMAN-ASSET-INTENSIVE FIRMS: LET THE BUYER BEWARE	General Archival - Primary Merger, Acquisition, Reorganization 255
COFFER, CURTIS ALAN	PHD 1991 THE UNIVERSITY OF MICHIGAN IMHOFF, EUGENE A.; LIPE, ROBERT C.	THE EFFECTS OF UNCERTAINTY AND THE INFORMATION ENVIRONMENT ON THE RELATION BETWEEN ACCOUNTING EARNINGS AND STOCK RETURNS FOR NEWLY PUBLIC FIRMS	Financial Accounting Archival - Primary Earnings Response Coefficients 142
COHEN, JEFFREY R.	PHD 1987 UNIVERSITY OF MASSACHUSETTS	THE IMPACT OF CONSERVATISM, INTERNAL CONTROL RELIABILITY, AND EXPERIENCE ON THE USE OF ANALYTICAL REVIEW	Auditing Experimental Analytical Review 186
COKER, DIANNA ROSS	PHD 1993 VIRGINIA POLYTECHNIC INSTITUTE AND STATE UNIVERSITY BROWN, ROBERT M.	THE ROLE OF VISUAL-SPATIAL APTITUDE IN ACCOUNTING COURSEWORK	Education Case Academic Achievement 193
COKER, JOHN WILLIAM	PHD 1990 THE UNIVERSITY OF MISSISSIPPI FLESHER, DALE L.	AN EMPIRICAL ANALYSIS OF THE USE OF THE INCOME TAX BASIS OF ACCOUNTING ON THE LENDING DECISIONS OF BANKERS: AN EXPERIMENT	General Experimental Bank Loan Officers 209
COLBERT, GARY J.	PHD 1991 UNIVERSITY OF OREGON O'KEEFE, TERRENCE B.	AN EMPIRICAL INVESTIGATION OF THE TRANSFER PROCESS AND TRANSFER PRICING: A MULTI-CASE RESEARCH DESIGN	Cost/Managerial Survey Transfer Pricing 233
COLBERT, PAUL JOSEPH	PHD 1993 BOSTON COLLEGE PULA, FRED JOHN	THE INFLUENCE OF WORK CONTEXT PERCEPTIONS AND EXPERIENCES ON THE ORGANIZATIONAL COMMITMENT OF FIRST-YEAR EMPLOYEES: A LONGITUDINAL STUDY	General Survey Job Performance, Satisfaction &/or Turnover 343

Author	Degree & Date School Advisor	Title	Functional Area Research Method Topic pages
COLBURN, STEVEN CHARLES	PHD 1989 UNIVERSITY OF GEORGIA DAVIS, EARL F.	AN EMPIRICAL ANALYSIS OF THE IMPACT OF THE TAX REFORM ACT OF 1986 ON INVESTMENTS IN REAL ESTATE LIMITED PARTNERSHIPS	Taxation Archival - Primary Industry - Real Estate 167
COLDWELL, SUSAN GAIL	PHD 1986 UNIVERSITY OF HOUSTON	ERTA AS AN INVESTMENT STIMULUS: A MICRO BASED ANALYSIS OF FIRM INVESTMENT BEHAVIOR	Taxation Archival - Primary Investments 140
COLE, CHARLES STEVEN	PHD 1989 UNIVERSITY OF ARKANSAS SMITH, STANLEY D.	THE IMPACT OF PRIVATE DEFAULT RISK INSURANCE ON THE YIELDS OF SEASONED TAX-EXEMPT BONDS	General Archival - Primary Capital Markets 307
COLEMAN, CLARENCE, JR.	PHD 1990 UNIVERSITY OF SOUTH CAROLINA	DEFERRED INCOME TAX CREDITS: AN EMPIRICAL ANALYSIS OF PERCEIVED MARKET RISK	Financial Accounting Archival - Primary Taxes 113
COLLEY, JAMES RONALD	PHD 1986 GEORGIA STATE UNIVERSITY - COLLEGE OF BUSINESS ADMINISTRATION	AN INVESTIGATION OF PERCEPTIONAL DIFFERENCES REGARDING MICROCOMPUTER USE BY CPA FIRMS	Information Systems Survey Microcomputer Applications 186
COLLINS, ALLISON BENNETT	PHD 1987 UNIVERSITY OF HOUSTON	A COMPARISON OF HISTORICAL COST DATA AND FASB STATEMENT NO. 33 CURRENT COST DATA IN THE PREDICTION OF CORPORATE BOND RATING	Financial Accounting Archival - Primary Inflation 145
COLLINS, DAVID THOMAS	PHD 1993 GEORGIA STATE UNIVERSITY BHADA, YEZDI	AN EMPIRICAL INVESTIGATION INTO GEOGRAPHIC SEGMENT DISCLOSURE AND ITS ASSOCIATION WITH SYSTEMATIC RISK	Financial Accounting Archival - Primary Segment Reporting 153
COLLINS, KAREN MARIE	PHD 1988 VIRGINIA POLYTECHNIC INSTITUTE AND STATE UNIVERSITY KILLOUGH, LARRY N.	A COMPREHENSIVE STUDY OF STRESS ON INDIVIDUALS IN MIDDLE-MANAGEMENT POSITIONS IN PUBLIC ACCOUNTING	General Survey Accounting Career Issues 194
COLLINS, MARY KATHERINE	PHD 1991 SYRACUSE UNIVERSITY ISMAIL, BADR	THE BUDGETARY PROCESS: A BEHAVIORAL PERSPECTIVE	Cost/Managerial Survey Budgeting 226

Author	Degree & Date School Advisor	Title	Functional Area Research Method Topic pages
COLLURA RAPACCIOLI, DONNA	PHD 1989 NEW YORK UNIVERSITY, GRADUATE SCHOOL OF BUSINESS ADMINISTRATION BILDERSEE, JOHN	WEALTH REDISTRIBUTIONS OR CHANGES IN FIRM VALUE: AN ANALYSIS OF THE RETURNS TO BONDHOLDERS AND STOCKHOLDERS AROUND INSIDE TRADE EVENTS	Financial Accounting Archival - Primary Insider Trading 133
COMSTOCK, S. MARK	PHD 1991 THE UNIVERSITY OF OKLAHOMA BUTLER, STEPHEN A.	THE COGNITIVE PROCESS UNDERLYING THE ACQUISITION OF ACCOUNTING EXPERTISE	General Experimental Judgment & Decision Making - Cognitive Processes 166
CONNELL, JAMES ALLEN, JR.	DBA 1992 LOUISIANA TECH UNIVERSITY	INFORMATION SYSTEMS INVESTMENT EVALUATION	Information Systems Archival - Primary Investments 142
CONOVER, TERESA LYNN	PHD 1988 TEXAS A&M UNIVERSITY WALLACE, WANDA A.	AN EMPIRICAL INVESTIGATION OF THE EFFECTS OF THE ACCOUNTING TREATMENT OF FOREIGN CURRENCY TRANSLATION ON MANAGEMENT ACTIONS IN MULTINATIONAL FIRMS	Financial Accounting Archival - Primary Foreign Currency Translation 147
CONRAD, EDWARD JOHN	PHD 1991 THE FLORIDA STATE UNIVERSITY	ENVIRONMENTAL AND FIRM CHARACTERISTICS AS DETERMINANTS OF TRADING VOLUME REACTION TO EARNINGS ANNOUNCEMENTS	Financial Accounting Archival - Primary Earnings Announcements 229
CONWAY, ROBERT C.	PHD 1992 THE UNIVERSITY OF WISCONSIN - MADISON EICHENSEHER, JOHN	THE EFFECT OF ALTERNATE DECISION FRAMES ON DECISIONS THAT USE ACCOUNTING INFORMATION	General Experimental Judgment & Decision Making - Heuristics & Biases 264
COOK, GAIL LYNN	PHD 1990 THE UNIVERSITY OF UTAH	A SYSTEMIC STUDY OF COORDINATED DECISION-MAKING ACROSS FUNCTIONAL AREAS	Information Systems Experimental Decision Support Systems 244
COOK, HAROLD BARTLEY	PHD 1986 THE UNIVERSITY OF MICHIGAN	THE RELATIONSHIP BETWEEN MANAGERIAL OWNERSHIP AND THE USE OF ACCOUNTING-BASED BUDGETING SYSTEMS TO MONITOR SUBORDINATES	Cost/Managerial Survey Budgeting 133
COOKE, T. E.	PHD 1989 UNIVERSITY OF EXETER (UNITED KINGDOM)	AN EMPIRICAL STUDY OF FINANCIAL DISCLOSURE BY SWEDISH COMPANIES	General Survey International/Global Issues 402

Author	Degree & Date School Advisor	Title	Functional Area Research Method Topic pages
COOMER, SUSAN DARLENE	PHD 1993 THE UNIVERSITY OF TENNESSEE	THE EFFECT OF PRIOR YEAR'S ERRORS AND IRREGULARITIES AND MANAGEMENT'S CHARACTERISTICS ON AUDIT PLANNING: AN EMPIRICAL INVESTIGATION	Auditing Survey Audit Planning 204
COOPER, JEAN CLAIRE	PHD 1985 THE UNIVERSITY OF NORTH CAROLINA AT CHAPEL HILL	COMPENSATION CONTRACT SELF-SELECTION, PARTICIPATIVE STANDARD SETTING AND JOB PERFORMANCE	General Experimental Job Performance, Satisfaction &/or Turnover 275
COOPER-FEDLER, PAMELA ANN	EDD 1991 TEXAS TECH UNIVERSITY HENSLEY, OLIVER D.	A CHARACTERIZATION AND ANALYSIS OF FACULTY ACTIVITY AND PRODUCTIVITY REPORTING SYSTEMS IN RESEARCH UNIVERSITIES	Education Survey Academic Issues 219
COPLEY, PAUL ANDREW	PHD 1987 THE UNIVERSITY OF ALABAMA INGRAM, ROBERT W.	AN EMPIRICAL INVESTIGATION OF THE DETERMINANTS OF LOCAL GOVERNMENT AUDIT FEES	Not-for-Profit Archival - Primary Governmental 167
COPP, CYNTHIA ANN	PHD 1991 UNIVERSITY OF FLORIDA KRAMER, JOHN L.	THE EFFECT OF TAX STRUCTURE VARIABLES ON THE DECISION FRAME ADOPTED AND THE TAX REPORTING CHOICE: TAXABLE INCOME COMPONENTS AND TAX PAYMENT TIMING	Taxation Experimental Tax Compliance 166
COPPAGE, RICHARD EDWARD	DBA 1985 UNIVERSITY OF KENTUCKY	AN EMPIRICAL DEFINITION OF ETHICS FOR MANAGEMENT ACCOUNTANTS	General Survey Ethics 337
CORBIN, DONNA PHILLIPS	PHD 1991 TEXAS A&M UNIVERSITY ADDY, NOEL D.	AN INVESTIGATION OF THE PREDICTABILITY OF THE AUDITOR'S OPINION IN A MULTINOMIAL LOGISTIC REGRESSION FRAMEWORK	Auditing Archival - Primary Audit Opinion 126
CORY, SUZANNE NELLIE	PHD 1988 UNIVERSITY OF MARYLAND COLLEGE PARK LOEB, STEPHEN E.	AN INVESTIGATION OF AUDIT PRACTICE QUALITY	Auditing Survey Audit Quality 271
COSTIGAN, MICHAEL LAWRENCE	PHD 1985 SAINT LOUIS UNIVERSITY	THE MARGINAL PREDICTIVE ABILITY OF ACCRUAL ACCOUNTING INFORMATION WITH RESPECT TO FUTURE CASH FLOWS FROM OPERATIONS	Financial Accounting Archival - Primary Accruals 156

Listing by Author

45

Author	Degree & Date School Advisor	Title	Functional Area Research Method Topic pages
COTTRELL, DAVID MARK	PHD 1992 THE OHIO STATE UNIVERSITY JENSEN, DANIEL L.	MARKET-BASED AUDITING STANDARDS: EXPERIMENTAL TESTS OF MARKET DISCLOSURES AS SUBSTITUTES FOR EXTERNAL REGULATION	Auditing Experimental Audit Quality 182
COULMAS, NANCY ELLEN	PHD 1989 THE PENNSYLVANIA STATE UNIVERSITY FERRARA, WILLIAM L.	AN INTENSIVE CASE STUDY OF COST BEHAVIOR ANALYSIS IN AN INDUSTRIAL SETTING	Cost/Managerial Case Cost Behaviors & Estimation 181
COULTER, JOHN MICHAEL	PHD 1994 UNIVERSITY OF MASSACHUSETTS SMITH, JAMES F.	THE EFFECTS OF AUDIT EXPERIENCE AND PROBABILITY KNOWLEDGE ON AUDITORS' USE OF HEURISTICS IN JUDGMENTS UNDER UNCERTAINTY	Auditing Experimental Judgment & Decision Making - Heuristics & Biases 228
COWAN, ARNOLD RICHARD	PHD 1988 THE UNIVERSITY OF IOWA LINN, SCOTT C.	TWO-TIER TENDER OFFERS: COERCION, HUBRIS OR IMPROVED MANAGEMENT?	General Archival - Primary Merger, Acquisition, Reorganization 172
COWLING, JOHN FREDERICK	PHD 1989 INDIANA UNIVERSITY SALAMON, GERALD L.	THE VARIATION OF ACCOUNTING INFORMATION FOR SEASONAL FIRMS ACROSS ALTERNATIVE FISCAL YEAR ENDS	Financial Accounting Archival - Primary Accounting Choice 207
COYLE, WILLIAM HENRY	PHD 1993 TEXAS A&M UNIVERSITY WIGGINS, CASPER E. JR.	THE DIFFERENTIAL EFFECTS OF INCENTIVES AND MONITORING ON EARNINGS MANAGEMENT AT THE TIME OF A CEO CHANGE	Financial Accounting Archival - Primary Earnings Management 138
COZORT, LARRY ALVIN	PHD 1985 VIRGINIA POLYTECHNIC INSTITUTE AND STATE UNIVERSITY	THE EFFECT OF ACCRUED PENSION BENEFIT PRESERVATION ON WORKER MOBILITY IN MULTIEMPLOYER PLANS	Taxation Post Retirement Benefit Issues 129
CRAIG, CAROLINE KERN	PHD 1987 UNIVERSITY OF ILLINOIS AT URBANA-CHAMPAIGN	THE SHIFTING OF CORPORATE CAPITAL ACQUISITION TAX SUBSIDIES: AN EMPIRICAL ANALYSIS	Taxation Archival - Primary Corporate Taxation 151
CRAIN, JOHN L.	PHD 1988 THE UNIVERSITY OF MISSISSIPPI WALLACE, WILLIAM D.	AN INVESTIGATION OF THE USEFULNESS OF RESERVE QUANTITY DISCLOSURES FOR PETROLEUM ENTITIES	General Archival - Primary Industry - Oil & Gas 151

Author	Degree & Date School Advisor	Title	Functional Area Research Method Topic pages
CRAIN, TERRY LYNN	PHD 1989 TEXAS TECH UNIVERSITY BURNS, JANE O.	AN EMPIRICAL ANALYSIS OF THE EFFECT OF ALTERNATIVE CAPITAL GAIN TAX PROVISIONS ON HORIZONTAL AND VERTICAL EQUITY	Taxation Archival - Primary Corporate Taxation 207
CRAMER, LOWELL JAMES	PHD 1994 FLORIDA INTERNATIONAL UNIVERSITY DAVIDSON, LEWIS F.	AN AFTER TAX ECONOMIC ANALYSIS OF HOME EQUITY CONVERSION FOR THE ELDERLY	Taxation Simulation Individual Taxation 188
CRAVENS, KAREN SUE	PHD 1992 TEXAS A&M UNIVERSITY SHEARON, WINSTON T. JR.	A COMPARATIVE INVESTIGATION OF TRANSFER PRICING PRACTICES IN AN INTERNATIONAL ENVIRONMENT	Cost/Managerial Survey Transfer Pricing 166
CRAWFORD, DEAN	PHD 1988 THE UNIVERSITY OF ROCHESTER ZIMMERMAN, JEROLD L.	THE STRUCTURE OF CORPORATE MERGERS: ACCOUNTING, TAX, AND FORM-OF-PAYMENT CHOICES	General Archival - Primary Merger, Acquisition, Reorganization 157
CRAWFORD, JEAN GREENE	PHD 1987 THE UNIVERSITY OF ALABAMA	AN EMPIRICAL INVESTIGATION OF THE CHARACTERISTICS OF COMPANIES WITH AUDIT COMMITTEES	Auditing Archival - Primary Audit Committees 114
CRAYCRAFT, CATHERINE ANN	PHD 1991 THE OHIO STATE UNIVERSITY BURNS, THOMAS J.	THE RELEVANCE OF SOCIOECONOMIC INFORMATION IN EXPLAINING BOND RATINGS OF QUASI-CORPORATIONS	Financial Accounting Archival - Primary Industry - Health Care 100
CREADY, WILLIAM MONTGOMERY	PHD 1985 THE OHIO STATE UNIVERSITY	AN EMPIRICAL INVESTIGATION INTO THE RELATIONSHIP BETWEEN THE VALUE OF ACCOUNTING EARNINGS ANNOUNCEMENTS AND EQUITY INVESTOR ENDOWMENT SIZES	Financial Accounting Archival - Primary Earnings Announcements 185
CREDLE, SID HOWARD	PHD 1989 THE UNIVERSITY OF TEXAS AT AUSTIN DIETRICH, J. RICHARD	THE MARKET REACTION TO THE FORGIVENESS OF DEFERRED TAXES OF THE DOMESTIC INTERNATIONAL SALES CORPORATION (DISC): EMPIRICAL EVIDENCE REGARDING THE 'INDEFINITE REVERSAL CRITERION'	Taxation Archival - Primary International/Global Issues 174
CRIPPS, JEREMY	PHD 1992 THE UNION INSTITUTE	ON ACCOUNTING	General Archival - Secondary History 203

Author	Degree & Date School Advisor	Title	Functional Area Research Method Topic pages
CROSBY, WILLIAM MORRIS	PHD 1985 UNIVERSITY OF GEORGIA	AN EXAMINATION OF THE EFFECTS WHICH A CHANGE IN THE INTEREST RATE HAS ON PENSION COSTS AND LIABILITIES INCOMPANIES WITH DEFINED-BENEFIT PENSION PLANS	Financial Accounting Case Post Retirement Benefit Issues 159
CROSSER, RICK LYNN	PHD 1987 OKLAHOMA STATE UNIVERSITY USRY, MILTON F.	THE RELATIVE EFFECT OF PENALTY MAGNITUDES ON COMPLIANCE: AN EXPERIMENTAL EXAMINATION OF DETERRENCE	Taxation Experimental Tax Compliance 109
CROWELL, STEVEN JUDSON	PHD 1987 UNIVERSITY OF GEORGIA	AN EMPIRICAL ANALYSIS OF THE DIFFERENTIAL IMPACT OF THE RESEARCH AND EXPERIMENTATION TAX CREDIT ON U.S. CORPORATE RESEARCH EXPENDITURES	Taxation Archival - Primary Research & Development 154
CUCCIA, ANDREW DANIEL	PHD 1990 UNIVERSITY OF FLORIDA KRAMER, SANDRA S.	AN EXAMINATION OF THE EFFORT AND AGGRESSIVENESS OF PROFESSIONAL TAX PREPARERS: THE EFFECTS OF ECONOMIC SANCTIONS AND ROLE PERCEPTIONS	Taxation Experimental Tax Professionals 238
CULLINAN, CHARLES P.	PHD 1991 UNIVERSITY OF KENTUCKY KNOBLETT, JAMES A.	LABOR ORGANIZATION AND ACCOUNTING POLICY CHOICE: AN EMPIRICAL STUDY	Financial Accounting Archival - Primary Accounting Choice 202
CULPEPPER, DAVID HUNT	PHD 1991 THE UNIVERSITY OF ALABAMA STONE, MARY S.	EXECUTIVE COMPENSATION PLANS: EMPIRICAL ANALYSIS OF THE TAX EXPLANATION OF COMPENSATION PLAN CHOICE	Taxation Archival - Primary Incentive Compensation 72
CUMMINGS, CHARLES WILLIAM	PHD 1986 UNIVERSITY OF MISSOURI - COLUMBIA	BUDGET SLACK AND PREDICTION PERFORMANCE IN AN UNCERTAIN ENVIRONMENT: AN EXPERIMENTAL INVESTIGATION	Cost/Managerial Experimental Budgeting 203
CUNNINGHAM, REBA LOVE	PHD 1991 UNIVERSITY OF NORTH TEXAS KLAMMER, THOMAS	AN EMPIRICAL INVESTIGATION OF COMMON CHARACTERISTICS OF COMMERCIAL BANKS USING STANDBY LETTERS OF CREDIT, LETTERS OF CREDIT, INTEREST RATE SWAPS, AND LOAN SALES	Financial Accounting Archival - Primary Industry - Banking/Savings & Loan 224
CZYZEWSKI, ALAN BENJAMIN	PHD 1985 UNIVERSITY OF SOUTHERN CALIFORNIA	THE PRODUCT LIFE CYCLE AND BUDGETING FUNCTIONS: PLANNING, CONTROL, AND MOTIVATION	Cost/Managerial Survey Budgeting

Author	Degree & Date / School / Advisor	Title	Functional Area / Research Method / Topic / pages
DAHER, AHMAD HASAN ABDEL-RAHIM	PHD 1988 THE UNIVERSITY OF WISCONSIN - MADISON FRANK, WERNER	GAP MANAGEMENT, SIZE AND RISK OF COMMERCIAL BANKS	General Archival - Primary Industry - Banking/Savings & Loan 164
DALTON, THOMAS M.	PHD 1992 UNIVERSITY OF HOUSTON	AN EMPIRICAL INVESTIGATION OF THE RELATIONSHIP BETWEEN TAX-LOSS SELLING AND THE JANUARY EFFECT	Taxation Archival - Primary Capital Markets 104
DANCER, WELDON TERRY	PHD 1988 THE UNIVERSITY OF MISSISSIPPI DAVIS, JAMES	A STUDY OF THE ATTITUDES AND PERCEPTIONS OF MASTER'S LEVEL ACCOUNTING STUDENTS TOWARD A CAREER IN ACCOUNTING EDUCATION	Education Survey Academic Issues 208
DANIEL, SHIRLEY JUNE	PHD 1985 OKLAHOMA STATE UNIVERSITY	AUDITOR JUDGMENTS: A DESCRIPTIVE STUDY OF THE ASSESSMENT OF AUDIT RISK	Auditing Experimental Judgment & Decision Making 140
DANIELS, DEANNA KAY	PHD 1985 UNIVERSITY OF SOUTHERN CALIFORNIA	EVALUATING THE QUALITATIVE CHARACTERISTICS OF ACCOUNTING INFORMATION: A DESCRIPTIVE STUDY OF IMPORTANCE WEIGHTS AND LOCATION MEASURES	Financial Accounting Survey Methodology
DANIELS, JANET DELUCA	DBA 1988 BOSTON UNIVERSITY YOUNG, DAVID	AN INVESTIGATION OF MUNICIPAL FINANCIAL REPORT FORMAT, USER PREFERENCE, AND DECISION-MAKING	Not-for-Profit Survey Governmental 282
DANIELS, ROGER B.	PHD 1991 THE UNIVERSITY OF MISSISSIPPI TAYLOR, CHARLES W.	AN EMPIRICAL INVESTIGATION OF THE EFFECTS OF THE ADOPTION OF A SECURED PROCESS ON THE UNIFORM CERTIFIED PUBLIC ACCOUNTANT EXAMINATION	General CPA &/or CMA Examination 196
DAS, SOMNATH	PHD 1988 CARNEGIE-MELLON UNIVERSITY	DIFFERENTIAL INFORMATION CONTENT OF STOCK DIVIDEND ANNOUNCEMENTS	Financial Accounting Archival - Primary Dividends 133
DATAR, SRIKANT MADHAV	PHD 1985 STANFORD UNIVERSITY	THE EFFECTS OF AUDITOR REPUTATION IN MORAL HAZARD AND ADVERSE SELECTION SETTINGS	Auditing Analytical - Internal CPA Firm Issues 174

Author	Degree & Date School Advisor	Title	Functional Area Research Method Topic pages
DAVID, JEANNE MARIE	PHD 1988 TEXAS A&M UNIVERSITY BENJAMIN, JAMES J.	THE EFFECT OF DEFINED BENEFIT PENSION PLANS ON CORPORATE VALUATION: AN EMPIRICAL INVESTIGATION	Financial Accounting Archival - Primary Post Retirement Benefit Issues 213
DAVIDSON, RONALD ALLAN	PHD 1988 THE UNIVERSITY OF ARIZONA FELIX, WILLIAM L.	SELECTION-SOCIALIZATION CONTROL IN AUDITING FIRMS: A TEST OF OUCHI'S MODEL OF CONTROL	General Survey CPA Firm Issues 225
DAVIS, CHARLES ELLIOT	PHD 1991 THE UNIVERSITY OF NORTH CAROLINA AT CHAPEL HILL BLOCHER, EDWARD	THE EFFECTS OF AUDITOR KNOWLEDGE STRUCTURES AND EXPERIENCE ON PROBLEM IDENTIFICATION AND HYPOTHESIS GENERATION IN ANALYTICAL REVIEW	Auditing Experimental Judgment & Decision Making - Cognitive Processes 307
DAVIS, DOROTHY A.	DBA 1989 MISSISSIPPI STATE UNIVERSITY HERRING, DORA ROSE	AN EMPIRICAL INVESTIGATION INTO EXISTING BUDGETING PRACTICES TO DETERMINE DIVERSITY IN INTERPRETATIONS OF THE LAW ON BUDGETING AT THE MUNICIPAL LEVEL IN MISSISSIPPI	Not-for-Profit Archival - Primary Budgeting 231
DAVIS, ELIZABETH BOOZER	PHD 1992 DUKE UNIVERSITY ASHTON, ROBERT H.	AIDING GOING CONCERN JUDGMENTS: THE INFLUENCE OF DECISION AID TYPE AND ACCOUNTABILITY	Auditing Experimental Decision Aids 160
DAVIS, JEFFERSON TORONTO	PHD 1993 THE UNIVERSITY OF TENNESSEE SCHEINER, JAMES H.	AUDITOR EXPERIENCE IN PRELIMINARY CONTROL RISK ASSESSMENTS: NEURAL NETWORK MODELS OF AUDITORS' KNOWLEDGE STRUCTURES	Auditing Experimental Judgment & Decision Making - Cognitive Processes 159
DAVIS, JON STUART	PHD 1987 THE UNIVERSITY OF ARIZONA	AUDITOR BIDDING AND INDEPENDENCE: A LABORATORY MARKETS INVESTIGATION	Auditing Experimental Independence 192
DAVIS, KAREL ANN	PHD 1987 PURDUE UNIVERSITY	AN EMPIRICAL INVESTIGATION OF THE STOCK MARKET'S RESPONSE TO CHANGES IN INVENTORY AND DEPRECIATION METHODS	Financial Accounting Archival - Primary Accounting Change 126
DAVIS, LARRY R.	PHD 1986 INDIANA UNIVERSITY	THE EFFECTS OF QUESTION COMPLEXITY AND FORM OF PRESENTATION ON THE EXTRACTION OF QUESTION-ANSWERS FROM AN INFORMATION PRESENTATION	General Experimental Presentation Format 216

Author	Degree & Date School Advisor	Title	Functional Area Research Method Topic pages
DAVIS, MICHAEL LEE	PHD 1986 UNIVERSITY OF MASSACHUSETTS	AN EMPIRICAL ANALYSIS OF THE IMPACT OF MERGER ACCOUNTING METHOD ON STOCK PRICES	Financial Accounting Archival - Primary Merger, Acquisition, Reorganization 173
DAY, MARY MARLENE	PHD 1993 UNIVERSITY OF WOLLONGONG (AUSTRALIA)	CRITICAL ACCOUNTING PEDAGOGY IN PRACTICE: (RE)CONSTRUCTIONS OF 'A TRUE AND FAIR VIEW'	Education Analytical - Internal Instructional Methods
DE MELLO-E-SOUZA, CARLOS ALBERTO	PHD 1989 CORNELL UNIVERSITY	OPTIMAL CONTRACTING BETWEEN AGENTS WITH DIFFERENT PLANNING HORIZONS IN THE PRESENCE OF INFORMATION ASYMMETRIES	Cost/Managerial Analytical - Internal Agency Theory 148
DEAN, DONALD C.	PHD 1991 RENSSELAER POLYTECHNIC INSTITUTE DIWAN, ROMESH	DECAPITALIZATION AND THE THEORY OF REPLACEMENT: ECONOMETRIC ANALYSIS OF SFAS 33	Financial Accounting Archival - Primary Inflation 399
DEBERG, CURTIS LYNN	PHD 1985 OKLAHOMA STATE UNIVERSITY	STRUCTURAL CHANGES IN SYSTEMATIC RISK AND INFLATION ACCOUNTING: A THEORETICAL AND EMPIRICAL EXAMINATION OF ASR190 AND FAS33	Financial Accounting Archival - Primary Inflation 112
DEBRUINE, MARINUS	PHD 1991 THE OHIO STATE UNIVERSITY MURDOCK, RICHARD J.	AN AGENCY-THEORETIC ANALYSIS OF THE EXTERNAL AUDITOR'S USE OF THE INTERNAL AUDITOR IN CONDUCTING THE FINANCIAL AUDIT	Auditing Analytical - Internal Internal Auditing 108
DECHOW, PATRICIA MARY	PHD 1993 THE UNIVERSITY OF ROCHESTER WATTS, ROSS L.	ACCOUNTING EARNINGS AND CASH FLOWS AS MEASURES OF FIRM PERFORMANCE: THE ROLE OF ACCOUNTING ACCRUALS	Financial Accounting Archival - Primary Accruals 120
DECKER, LARITA MARIE	PHD 1992 INDIANA UNIVERSITY HILL, JOHN W.	INFORMATION AND INCENTIVE MECHANISMS FOR ALIGNING PRINCIPAL AND AGENT INTERESTS IN ESCALATION SITUATIONS	Cost/Managerial Experimental Agency Theory 116
DEFLORIA, JAMES DALE	PHD 1988 UNIVERSITY OF PITTSBURGH	THE PERCEPTIONS OF ACCOUNTING STUDENTS AS TO THE IMPORTANCE OF WRITTEN COMMUNICATION SKILLS FOR SUCCESS IN ACCOUNTING CAREERS	Education Survey Curriculum Issues 93

Author	Degree & Date School Advisor	Title	Functional Area Research Method Topic pages
DEFOND, MARK LEROY	PHD 1987 UNIVERSITY OF WASHINGTON	AN EMPIRICAL TEST OF THE ASSOCIATION BETWEEN CLIENT FIRM AGENCY COSTS AND AUDIT FIRM CHARACTERISTICS	Auditing Archival - Primary Auditor Changes 118
DEGG, MARTIN ROBERT	PHD 1988 UNIVERSITY OF NOTTINGHAM (UNITED KINGDOM)	EARTHQUAKE HAZARD IN THE MIDDLE EAST: AN EVALUATION FOR INSURANCE AND REINSURANCE PURPOSES	General Industry - Insurance 624
DEINES, DAN STUART	PHD 1985 THE UNIVERSITY OF NEBRASKA - LINCOLN	A TEST FOR THE SIMILARITY OF ANALYSTS' AND INVESTORS' EXPECTATIONS SUBJECT TO THE RELEASE OF MANDATED ACCOUNTING DISCLOSURES	Financial Accounting Archival - Primary Disclosures 94
DEIS, DONALD RAY, JR.	PHD 1988 TEXAS A&M UNIVERSITY GIROUX, GARY A.	TOWARDS A THEORY OF THE ROLE OF THE PUBLIC SECTOR AUDIT AS A MONITORING DEVICE: A TEST USING TEXAS INDEPENDENT SCHOOL DISTRICTS	Auditing Not-for-Profit 98
DEL VECCHIO, STEPHEN CARL	DBA 1991 SOUTHERN ILLINOIS UNIVERSITY AT CARBONDALE WELKER, ROBERT B.	AN EMPIRICAL STUDY OF THE FORGETTING OF AUDIT TASK EXPERTISE	Auditing Experimental Judgment & Decision Making - Cognitive Processes 166
DELANEY, JOHN EDWARD	PHD 1989 THE UNIVERSITY OF TEXAS AT AUSTIN COOPER, WILLIAM W.	A DELPHI STUDY OF REVENUE CYCLE AUDITS	Auditing Experimental Judgment & Decision Making 237
DELEO, WANDA IRVIN	PHD 1985 GEORGIA STATE UNIVERSITY - COLLEGE OF BUSINESS ADMINISTRATION	AN ANALYSIS OF FINANCIAL INFORMATION AS IT RELATES TO FAILED COMMERCIAL BANKS: A MULTIVARIATE APPROACH	Auditing Archival - Primary Financial Distress or Bankruptcy 175
DEMIRAG, ISTEMIHAN SEFIK	PHD 1985 UNIVERSITY OF GLASGOW (UNITED KINGDOM)	FOREIGN CURRENCY ACCOUNTING AND MANAGEMENT EVALUATION OF FOREIGN SUBSIDIARY PERFORMANCE	Cost/Managerial Survey International/Global Issues 519
DEMPSEY, STEPHEN JEFFREY	PHD 1985 VIRGINIA POLYTECHNIC INSTITUTE AND STATE UNIVERSITY	PARTITIONING MARKET EFFICIENCIES BY ANALYST ATTENTION: THE CASE OF ANNUAL EARNINGS ANNOUNCEMENTS	Financial Accounting Archival - Primary Earnings Announcements 208

Author	Degree & Date School Advisor	Title	Functional Area Research Method Topic pages
DENNA, ERIC LEROY	PHD 1989 MICHIGAN STATE UNIVERSITY	TOWARD A REPRESENTATION OF AUDITOR KNOWLEDGE: EVIDENCE AGGREGATION AND EVALUATION	Auditing Analytical - Internal Decision Support Systems 151
DENNIS, PAMELA ERICKSON	PHD 1989 UNIVERSITY OF FLORIDA ABDEL-KHALIK, A. RASHAD	THE EFFECTS OF BANNING DIRECT UNINVITED SOLICITATION ON PRICING, BIDDING, SEARCH AND SWITCHING DECISIONS IN THE MARKET FOR AUDIT SERVICES	Auditing Analytical - Internal Auditor Changes 242
DENT D'ALMUANO, ROSELINE	PHD 1991 ARIZONA STATE UNIVERSITY	TRANSFER STUDENTS' ACHIEVEMENT IN INTERMEDIATE ACCOUNTING: AN EMPIRICAL STUDY OF ARIZONA STATE UNIVERSITY STUDENTS	Education Case Academic Achievement 97
DEPPE, LARRY ARTHUR	PHD 1968 THE UNIVERSITY OF UTAH BARTLEY, JON W.	AN EMPIRICAL INVESTIGATION OF THE IN-SUBSTANCE DEFEASANCE OF DEBT	Financial Accounting Archival - Primary Long Term Debt 116
DEPREE, CHAUNCEY MARCELLOUS, JR.	DBA 1987 UNIVERSITY OF KENTUCKY	TESTING THE CONCEPTUAL FRAMEWORK OF ACCOUNTING THROUGH AN APPLICATION OF A FORMAL STRUCTURE	Financial Accounting Analytical - Internal Standard Setting 259
DERESHIWSKY, MARY IRENE	PHD 1985 UNIVERSITY OF MASSACHUSETTS	ALIGNMENT OF SPECIAL-INTEREST SUBJECTS IN THE ACCOUNTING STANDARD-SETTING PROCESS: AN INVESTIGATION	Financial Accounting Case Standard Setting 364
DESAI, ARUN RAMADHAR	PHD 1992 KENT STATE UNIVERSITY ALAM, PERVAIZ; CURCIO, RICHARD	AN EMPIRICAL STUDY OF POST MERGER PERFORMANCE OF ACQUIRING FIRMS	financial Accounting Archival - Primary Merger, Acquisition, Reorganization 115
DESAI, SURYAKANT T.	EDD 1989 EAST TEXAS STATE UNIVERSITY TUNNELL, JAMES W.	DESIRABLE NON-CONTENT ATTRIBUTES IN PRINCIPLES OF ACCOUNTING MICROCOMPUTER TEST BANKS AMONG TWO-YEAR AND FOUR-YEAR COLLEGE ACCOUNTING INSTRUCTORS: A DELPHI STUDY	Education Survey Curriculum Issues 177
DESHMUKH, ASHUTOSH VASANT	PHD 1993 MEMPHIS STATE UNIVERSITY AUSTIN, KENNETH R.	THE ROLE OF AUDIT TECHNOLOGY AND EXTENSION OF AUDIT PROCEDURES IN STRATEGIC AUDITING	Auditing Analytical - Internal Audit Technology 137

Listing by Author

Author	Degree & Date School Advisor	Title	Functional Area Research Method Topic pages
DEUTSCH, ROBERT ALLEN	PHD 1991 UNIVERSITY OF KENTUCKY MADDEN, DONALD L.; VIATOR, RALPH E.	RECRUITING DECISIONS BY SELECTED BIG SIX CPA FIRMS: AN INVESTIGATION OF CHARACTERISTICS THAT INFLUENCE DECISIONS TO SELECT ACCOUNTING STUDENTS FOR OFFICE VISITS	General Survey Accounting Career Issues 167
DEVANEY, SHARON ANN LOHR	PHD 1993 THE OHIO STATE UNIVERSITY HANNA, SHERMAN	AN EMPIRICAL ANALYSIS OF THE PREDICTIVE VALUE OF HOUSEHOLD FINANCIAL RATIOS	Financial Accounting Archival - Primary Financial Ratios 176
DEVIDAL, DOUGLAS PAUL	PHD 1991 THE UNIVERSITY OF TEXAS AT AUSTIN MAY, ROBERT G.; ROBINSON, JOHN R.	THE ROLE OF PRIVATE LETTER RULINGS IN TAX-FREE REORGANIZATIONS	Taxation Archival - Primary Merger, Acquisition, Reorganization 98
DEVINE, KEVIN MARK	PHD 1990 THE UNIVERSITY OF NEBRASKA - LINCOLN BROWN, JAMES F. JR.	THE EFFECTS OF INFORMATION FRAMING ON DECISION-MAKING BEHAVIOR RELATED TO RESOURCE ALLOCATIONS	Cost/Managerial Experimental Judgment & Decision Making - Heuristics & Biases 209
DEVINE, WILFRED FRANCIS	PHD 1985 TEMPLE UNIVERSITY	THE INFLUENCE OF CONSTITUENCY INPUT IN SETTING ACCOUNTING STANDARDS	Financial Accounting Case Foreign Currency Translation 232
DEXTER, LEE	PHD 1986 THE UNIVERSITY OF NEBRASKA - LINCOLN	USAGE OF PROCEDURES AND CONTROLS IN INNOVATIVE MANUFACTURING COMPANIES	Cost/Managerial Survey Management Control Systems 202
DHANANI, KARIM A.	DBA 1986 LOUISIANA TECH UNIVERSITY	AN EMPIRICAL STUDY OF FINANCIALLY DISTRESSED COMMERCIAL BANKS: A DISCRIMINANT MODEL FOR PREDICTING FUTURE BANK FAILURES	Financial Accounting Archival - Primary Financial Distress or Bankruptcy 156
DICKEY, HAZEL VIRGINIA COLEMAN	EDD 1992 UNIVERSITY OF ARKANSAS CLAYTON, DEAN	RELATIONSHIP OF STUDENTS' PREPARATION AND PERCEPTIONS WITH FINAL GRADES IN PRINCIPLES OF ACCOUNTING I IN PUBLIC TWO-YEAR COLLEGES IN ARKANSAS	Education Case Academic Achievement 112
DIETZ, DONNA K.	PHD 1989 THE UNIVERSITY OF NORTH DAKOTA BLOOMQUIST, ROGER	INFORMATION SYSTEMS CONTENT IN UNDERGRADUATE ACCOUNTING PROGRAMS	Education Survey Curriculum Issues 162

Listing by Author 54

Author	Degree & Date School Advisor	Title	Functional Area Research Method Topic pages
DILLA, WILLIAM NOEL	PHD 1987 THE UNIVERSITY OF TEXAS AT AUSTIN	TESTS OF INFORMATION EVALUATION BEHAVIOR IN A COMPETITIVE ENVIRONMENT	General Experimental Judgment & Decision Making 206
DIMITRY, KENNETH ELIA	PHD 1990 THE FLORIDA STATE UNIVERSITY LOREK, KENNETH S.	AN EMPIRICAL EXAMINATION OF THE TIME-SERIES PROPERTIES OF EARNINGS-PER-SHARE USING TRANSFER FUNCTION ANALYSIS AT THE INDUSTRY LEVEL	Financial Accounting Archival - Primary Earnings Per Share 272
DIPIETRO, JANICE DIANE	DBA 1989 BOSTON UNIVERSITY GOSMAN, MARTIN	AN EMPIRICAL INVESTIGATION OF THE IMPACT OF AUDIT EXPERIENCE AND TASK ON THE UTILIZATION OF DECISION HEURISTICS	Auditing Experimental Judgment & Decision Making - Heuristics & Biases 260
DO, SANGHO	PHD 1992 UNIVERSITY OF PITTSBURGH BIRNBERG, JACOB G.	THE EFFECT OF OUTCOME FEEDBACK AND EXPERIENCE ON THE PREDICTION OF CORPORATE FAILURE: PERFORMANCE OF HUMAN VS. MODEL	General Experimental Judgment & Decision Making - Cognitive Processes 191
DOBITZ, CAROL S.	PHD 1989 THE UNIVERSITY OF NORTH DAKOTA BLOOMQUIST, ROGER	FUND ACCOUNTING PRINCIPLES ADVOCATED BY ACCOUNTING EDUCATORS AND HOSPITAL/MUNICIPAL/COLLEGE CHIEF ACCOUNTANTS	Education Survey Curriculum Issues 299
DOBY, VICTORIA JEAN	DBA 1992 THE GEORGE WASHINGTON UNIVERSITY SEGEL, FRANK WILLIAM	THE RELATIONSHIP OF JOB STRAIN TO STAFF TURNOVER IN PUBLIC ACCOUNTING FIRMS	General Survey Job Performance, Satisfaction &/or Turnover 216
DODD, JAMES LEE	PHD 1992 UNIVERSITY OF GEORGIA CLARK, RONALD L.	ACCOUNTING INFORMATION TIMELINESS: AN EXPLORATORY STUDY OF INTERNAL DELAY	Financial Accounting Survey Other 137
DONABEDIAN, BAIRJ	PHD 1989 COLUMBIA UNIVERSITY	STANDARD-SETTING IN CPA LICENSURE: A STUDY IN PROFESSIONAL SELF-REGULATION	General Accounting Career Issues 82
DONADIO, JANETTE MARIE	PHD 1992 UNIVERSITY OF COLORADO AT BOULDER LEWIS, BARRY L.	AN EMPIRICAL STUDY OF THE JOINT EFFECTS OF KNOWLEDGE, INTELLECTUAL SKILL, AND TASK STRUCTURE ON THE ACCURACY OF AUDITORS' PERFORMANCE OF DIAGNOSTIC AUDIT TASKS	Auditing Experimental Judgment & Decision Making - Cognitive Processes 206

Author	Degree & Date School Advisor	Title	Functional Area Research Method Topic pages
DONADIO, PAUL JOSEPH	PHD 1991 UNIVERSITY OF COLORADO AT BOULDER BUCHMAN, THOMAS A.	MANAGEMENT DEFECTS AS A CAUSE OF CORPORATE FAILURE: AN INVESTIGATION OF ARGENTI'S THEORY OF CORPORATE COLLAPSE	Financial Accounting Archival - Primary Financial Distress or Bankruptcy 158
DONELAN, JOSEPH G.	PHD 1989 SAINT LOUIS UNIVERSITY BANKS, DOYLE W.	THE RELATIONSHIP BETWEEN PENSION ACCOUNTING INTEREST RATE ASSUMPTIONS AND FIRM RISK	Financial Accounting Archival - Primary Post Retirement Benefit Issues 229
DONNELLY, WILLIAM JAMES, JR.	PHD 1987 GOLDEN GATE UNIVERSITY	THE CPA'S LIABILITY IN TAX PRACTICE: HISTORY, TRENDS, PROBLEMS, POSSIBLE SOLUTIONS	Taxation Archival - Secondary Legal Liability 297
DOOGAR, RAJIB KUMAR	PHD 1994 THE PENNSYLVANIA STATE UNIVERSITY CUSHING, BARRY E.	THREE ANALYTICAL ESSAYS IN ACCOUNTING: INDUSTRY EQUILIBRIUM IN THE AUDIT MARKET AND PROCESS LEARNING IN AGENCIES	General Analytical - Internal Agency Theory 98
DORAN, DAVID THOMAS	PHD 1985 UNIVERSITY OF PITTSBURGH	STOCK DIVIDENDS, STOCK SPLITS, AND FUTURE EARNINGS: ACCOUNTING RELEVANCE AND EQUITY MARKET RESPONSE	Financial Accounting Archival - Primary Stock Transactions 115
DORIGAN, MICHAEL P.	PHD 1991 UNIVERSITY OF MISSOURI - COLUMBIA STOWE, JOHN D.	CORPORATE DEFINED BENEFIT PENSION POLICIES: AN EMPIRICAL ANALYSIS OF ALTERNATIVE STRATEGIES	Financial Accounting Archival - Primary Post Retirement Benefit Issues 247
DOUCET, THOMAS ARTHUR	PHD 1992 UNIVERSITY OF GEORGIA BAREFIELD, RUSSELL	THE DETERMINATION OF THE USEFUL LIFE OF A CLIENT BASE: AN EMPIRICAL STUDY	General Survey CPA Firm Issues 101
DOW, KATHY J.	DBA 1989 BOSTON UNIVERSITY MEYER, PHILIP	AN EXAMINATION OF MATERIALITY FROM THE USER-DECISION PERSPECTIVE	General Experimental Materiality 227
DRAKE, PHILIP D.	PHD 1990 THE OHIO STATE UNIVERSITY BURNS, THOMAS J.	AN ANALYSIS OF THE AUDIT SERVICES MARKET: THE EFFECT OF AUDIT STRUCTURE ON AUDITOR EFFICIENCY, A DATA ENVELOPMENT ANALYSIS APPROACH	General Archival - Primary Audit Structure 202

Listing by Author

Author	Degree & Date School Advisor	Title	Functional Area Research Method Topic pages
DREWS-BRYAN, ALISON LUEDTKE	PHD 1991 UNIVERSITY OF GEORGIA CLARK, RONALD L.	THE PERCEIVED USEFULNESS OF SELECTED INFORMATION CHARACTERISTICS FOR MUNICIPAL BUDGETING	Information Systems Survey Governmental 173
DRUKER, MOSHE	DRSOCOEC 1990 UNIVERSITY OF VIENNA (AUSTRIA)	ACCOUNTING (INCLUDING TAXATION AND COMPANY LAW) IN AN INFLATIONARY PERIOD--INVESTIGATED ON ISRAELI MODEL	Financial Accounting Case Inflation 269
DUCHAC, JONATHAN EHRLICH	PHD 1993 UNIVERSITY OF GEORGIA BAREFIELD, RUSSELL M.	EARNINGS MANAGEMENT AND THE PRECISION OF EARNINGS SIGNALS IN THE BANKING INDUSTRY	Financial Accounting Archival - Primary Earnings Management 115
DUCHARME, LARRY L.	PHD 1994 UNIVERSITY OF WASHINGTON SEFCIK, STEPHEN E.	IPOS: PRIVATE INFORMATION AND EARNINGS MANAGEMENT	Financial Accounting Archival - Primary Initial Public Offerings 138
DUFFY, WENDY ANN	PHD 1989 UNIVERSITY OF ILLINOIS AT URBANA-CHAMPAIGN MCKEOWN, JAMES C.	FINANCIAL REPORTING STANDARDS FOR PENSIONS: THE RELATIONSHIP BETWEEN FINANCIAL REPORTING AND CASH FLOW VARIABLES AND CHANGES IN THE INTEREST RATE ASSUMPTION	Financial Accounting Archival - Primary Post Retirement Benefit Issues 109
DUGAR, AMITABH	PHD 1989 NORTHWESTERN UNIVERSITY	THE INFORMATION CONTENT OF THE STATEMENT OF CHANGES IN FINANCIAL POSITION	Financial Accounting Archival - Primary Information Content 131
DUH, RONG RUEY	PHD 1986 UNIVERSITY OF MINNESOTA	ECONOMIC MAN AS AN INTUITIVE BAYESIAN: AN EXPERIMENTAL STUDY	General Experimental Capital Markets 156
DUHALA, KAREN	PHD 1987 THE PENNSYLVANIA STATE UNIVERSITY CURLEY, ANTHONY J.	A GENERAL MODEL FOR BOND REFINANCING	General Simulation Long Term Debt 300
DUKE, JOANNE CHRISTINE	PHD 1987 THE PENNSYLVANIA STATE UNIVERSITY	DEBT COVENANT RESTRICTIONS AND ACCOUNTING TECHNIQUE CHOICE: AN EMPIRICAL STUDY	Financial Accounting Archival - Primary Accounting Choice 161

Listing by Author

Author	Degree & Date School Advisor	Title	Functional Area Research Method Topic pages
DUNBAR, AMY ELINOR	PHD 1989 THE UNIVERSITY OF TEXAS AT AUSTIN FOWLER, ANNA C.	AN EMPIRICAL INVESTIGATION OF THE ASSOCIATION OF PRODUCTIVITY WITH EMPLOYEE STOCK OWNERSHIP PLANS OF PUBLICLY HELD CORPORATIONS	Cost/Managerial Archival - Primary Incentive Compensation 215
DUNN, CHERYL LYNN	PHD 1994 MICHIGAN STATE UNIVERSITY MCCARTHY, WILLIAM E.	AN INVESTIGATION OF ABSTRACTION IN EVENTS-BASED ACCOUNTING SYSTEMS	Information Systems Experimental Judgment & Decision Making 115
DUNN, SARAH ANNE	PHD 1993 THE FLORIDA STATE UNIVERSITY HILLISON, WILLIAM A.	A DESCRIPTIVE ANALYSIS AND EMPIRICAL INVESTIGATION OF CORPORATE ENVIRONMENTAL DISCLOSURES	Financial Accounting Archival - Primary Social/Environmental Responsibility 208
DUNNE, KATHLEEN M.	PHD 1988 TEMPLE UNIVERSITY GAFFNEY, MARY ANNE	DETERMINANTS OF THE CHOICE OF ACCOUNTING TREATMENT FOR BUSINESS COMBINATIONS: A POSITIVE THEORY APPROACH	Financial Accounting Case Merger, Acquisition, Reorganization 167
DURKEE, DAVID ALLEN	PHD 1987 OKLAHOMA STATE UNIVERSITY	THE EFFECT OF COSTLY VS. COSTLESS PENSION DISCLOSURE ON COMMON SHARE PRICES	Financial Accounting Archival - Primary Post Retirement Benefit Issues 78
DUSENBURY, RICHARD BENNETT	PHD 1989 UNIVERSITY OF FLORIDA KRAMER, SANDRA	TAX COMPLIANCE: THE EFFECT OF THE TIMING OF PAYMENTS	Taxation Experimental Tax Compliance 170
DUTTA, SAURAV KUMAR	PHD 1991 UNIVERSITY OF KANSAS	EVIDENCE AGGREGATION FOR PLANNING AND EVALUATION OF AUDIT: A THEORETICAL STUDY	Auditing Analytical - Internal Audit Planning 229
DUVALL, LINDA GRIFFITH	PHD 1993 UNIVERSITY OF MARYLAND COLLEGE PARK BEDINGFIELD, JAMES P.	REGULATORY VALUE OF UNREALIZED SECURITY GAINS AND LOSSES IN THE BANKING INDUSTRY	Financial Accounting Archival - Primary Industry - Banking/Savings & Loan 124
DWYER, MARGARET MARY DEVINE	PHD 1992 THE UNIVERSITY OF WISCONSIN - MADISON WILLIAMS, THOMAS H.	A COMPARISON OF STATISTICAL TECHNIQUES AND ARTIFICIAL NEURAL NETWORK MODELS IN CORPORATE BANKRUPTCY PREDICTION	Financial Accounting Archival - Primary Financial Distress or Bankruptcy 212

Author	Degree & Date School Advisor	Title	Functional Area Research Method Topic pages
DWYER, PEGGY DIANE	PHD 1988 UNIVERSITY OF MISSOURI - COLUMBIA LAMPE, JAMES C.	AN EMPIRICAL INVESTIGATION OF THE EFFECTS OF CERTAIN CLIENT CHARACTERISTICS ON AUDITORS' EVALUATIONS OF ACCOUNTING ESTIMATES	Auditing Experimental Judgment & Decision Making 271
DZENG, SIMON C.	PHD 1991 DREXEL UNIVERSITY JAENICKE, HENRY R.	A COMPARISON OF VECTOR AUTOREGRESSION MODELS AND ORDINARY LEAST SQUARES MULTIPLE REGRESSION MODELS FOR ANALYTICAL PROCEDURES PERFORMED AS SUBSTANTIVE TEST	Auditing Simulation Analytical Review 165
EAKIN, CYNTHIA FIREY	PHD 1993 THE FLORIDA STATE UNIVERSITY SCHAEFER, THOMAS	ACCOUNTING CHANGES AND EARNINGS MANAGEMENT: EVIDENCE FROM THE EARLY ADOPTION OF SFAS NO. 96 'ACCOUNTING FOR INCOME	Financial Accounting Archival - Primary Accounting Change 127
EASON, PATRICIA LEE	PHD 1994 TEXAS TECH UNIVERSITY GATELY, MARY SUE	AN EMPIRICAL ANALYSIS OF CONSUMPTION SENSITIVITY TO TAX POLICY UNCERTAINTY	Taxation Survey Individual Taxation 213
EASTERGARD, ALF MOODY	PHD 1988 THE UNIVERSITY OF NEBRASKA - LINCOLN HUBBARD, THOMAS D.	THE COMPATIBILITY OF MARKET RETURNS AND INCOME NUMBERS OBSERVED AFTER ADJUSTMENTS TO RETAINED EARNINGS	Financial Accounting Archival - Primary Earnings 151
EASTERWOOD, CINTIA MENDEZ	PHD 1993 UNIVERSITY OF HOUSTON	HOSTILE TAKEOVERS AND INCENTIVES FOR EARNINGS MANIPULATION: AN EMPIRICAL ANALYSIS	Financial Accounting Archival - Primary Earnings Management 123
ECKSTEIN, CLAIRE	PHD 1988 NEW YORK UNIVERSITY, GRADUATE SCHOOL OF BUSINESS ADMINISTRATION BILDERSEE, JOHN	TIME-SERIES PROPERTIES AND FORECASTING OF FINANCIAL RATIOS	Financial Accounting Archival - Primary Financial Ratios 57
EDMONDS, CYNTHIA D.	PHD 1991 THE UNIVERSITY OF ALABAMA DUGAN, MICHAEL T.	AGENCY COST EXPLANATIONS FOR THE DEMAND FOR AUDIT QUALITY: AN EMPIRICAL INQUIRY INTO THE REASONS FOR THE PRESENCE OF AUDIT COMMITTEES OF THE BOARD OF DIRECTORS	Auditing Archival - Primary Audit Committees 148
EDWARDS, RANDAL KEITH	PHD 1988 THE UNIVERSITY OF TENNESSEE REEVE, JAMES M.	GROWTH COMPANIES AND CHANGES TO LARGER AUDIT FIRMS: AN EXAMINATION	Auditing Case Auditor Changes 131

Author	Degree & Date School Advisor	Title	Functional Area Research Method Topic pages
EINING, MARTHA MCDONALD	PHD 1987 OKLAHOMA STATE UNIVERSITY DORR, PATRICK B.	THE IMPACT OF AN EXPERT SYSTEM AS A DECISION AID ON LEARNING DURING THE AUDIT PROCESS: AN EMPIRICAL TEST	Auditing Experimental Decision Aids 189
EL FEKEY, MAHMOUD ELSYED	PHD 1989 THE UNIVERSITY OF MISSISSIPPI GRAVES, FINELY	AN EMPIRICAL INVESTIGATION OF THE ROLE OF ALTERNATIVE ACCOUNTING VARIABLES IN ASSESSING A FIRM'S ABILITY TO PAY INCREASED WAGES	Financial Accounting Archival - Primary Financial Ratios 166
EL HOSSADE, SALEM ISMAIL	PHD 1987 UNIVERSITY OF HULL (UNITED KINGDOM)	MANAGEMENT OF ANNUAL REPORTED INCOME IN THE U.K.: THE SEARCH FOR INDICATORS	Financial Accounting Archival - Primary Earnings Management 228
EL SHAMY, MOSTAFA AHMED	PHD 1989 NEW YORK UNIVERSITY, GRADUATE SCHOOL OF BUSINESS ADMINISTRATION	THE PREDICTIVE ABILITY OF FINANCIAL RATIOS: A TEST OF ALTERNATIVE MODELS	Financial Accounting Archival - Primary Financial Ratios 83
EL-HASHASH, HADEYA A.	PHD 1993 RUTGERS THE STATE UNIVERSITY OF NEW JERSEY - NEWARK PALMON, DAN	THE ASSOCIATION BETWEEN FIRM CHARACTERISTICS AND EXECUTIVE COMPENSATION SCHEMES AND THE EFFECT OF ADOPTION OF SUCH SCHEMES ON FIRM PERFORMANCE	Cost/Managerial Incentive Compensation 148
EL-ISSA, YASIN AHMAD MOUSA	PHD 1988 UNIVERSITY OF LANCASTER (UNITED KINGDOM)	THE USEFULNESS OF CORPORATE FINANCIAL DISCLOSURE TO INVESTORS IN THE AMMAN FINANCIAL MARKET	Financial Accounting Archival - Primary International/Global Issues 369
EL-RAJABI, MD-TAYSIR A	PHD 1986 THE UNIVERSITY OF WISCONSIN - MADISON	THE INFORMATION CONTENT OF ANNOUNCING THE CAPITAL INVESTMENT DECISIONS AND THE ACTUAL INVESTMENT NUMBERS	Financial Accounting Archival - Primary Voluntary Management Disclosures 140
EL-REFADI, IDRIS ABDULSALAM	PHD 1986 UNIVERSITY OF NORTH TEXAS	FOREIGN EXCHANGE RISK MANAGEMENT IN U.S. MULTINATIONALS UNDER SFAS NO. 52: CHANGE IN MANAGEMENT DECISION-MAKING IN RESPONSE TO ACCOUNTING POLICY CHANGE	Financial Accounting Survey Foreign Currency Translation 200
EL-SABBAGH, AMAL	PHD 1993 CITY UNIVERSITY OF NEW YORK LUSTGARTEN, STEVEN	MARKET EVALUATION OF DISCOVERY OF DISTORTED EARNINGS SIGNALS: EMPIRICAL TESTS OF CHANGES IN CASH FLOW EXPECTATIONS, RISKINESS, AND EARNINGS QUALITY HYPOTHESES	Financial Accounting Archival - Primary Earnings Management 174

Author	Degree & Date School Advisor	Title	Functional Area Research Method Topic pages
EL-ZAYATY, AHMED ISMAIL	PHD 1986 CITY UNIVERSITY OF NEW YORK	BUSINESS FAILURE PREDICTION: AN ANALYSIS OF TYPE II PREDICTION ERRORS	Financial Accounting Archival - Primary Financial Distress or Bankruptcy 129
ELDAHRAWY, KAMAL M.	PHD 1985 UNIVERSITY OF NORTH TEXAS	AN EMPIRICAL INVESTIGATION OF THE DISCRIMINANT AND PREDICTIVE ABILITY OF THE SFAS NO. 69 SIGNALS FOR BUSINESS FAILURE IN THE OIL AND GAS INDUSTRY	Financial Accounting Archival - Primary Financial Distress or Bankruptcy 100
ELDENBURG, LESLIE GAY	PHD 1991 UNIVERSITY OF WASHINGTON SUNDEM, GARY	THE USE OF INFORMATION IN A COST CONTAINMENT ENVIRONMENT: AN ANALYSIS OF THE AGENCY RELATIONSHIP BETWEEN HOSPITALS AND PHYSICIANS	General Archival - Primary Industry - Health Care 125
ELDER, RANDAL JEFFREY	PHD 1993 MICHIGAN STATE UNIVERSITY ARENS, ALVIN A.	AUDITOR INDUSTRY EXPERIENCE AND INITIAL PUBLIC OFFERINGS	Auditing Archival - Primary Initial Public Offerings 172
ELECHIGUERRA ARRIZABALAGA, CRISANTA	DR 1991 UNIVERSIDAD DEL PAIS VASCO/EUSKAL HERRIKO UNIBERTSITATEA (SPAIN)	ACCOUNTING INFORMATION DURING PERIODS OF ECONOMIC INSTABILITY [LA INFORMACION CONTABLE EN LOS PERIODOS DE INESTABILIDAD ECONOMICA]	Financial Accounting International/Global Issues 592
ELETR, AMR	DBA 1992 MISSISSIPPI STATE UNIVERSITY HERRING, DORA	A COMPARISON BETWEEN CONTROLLERS AND PRODUCTION MANAGERS IN THE ELECTRONICS MANUFACTURING INDUSTRY OF THE PERCEIVED RELEVANCE AND USE OF MANAGEMENT ACCOUNTING SYSTEMS' CHARACTERISTICS AND PROFITABILITY AS PRODUCTION TECHNOLOGIES/METHODS CHANGE	Cost/Managerial Survey Management Control Systems 175
ELFRINK, JOHN ALBERT	PHD 1987 SAINT LOUIS UNIVERSITY	AN EMPIRICAL INVESTIGATION INTO THE UTILITY OF THE UNIFORM CERTIFIED PUBLIC ACCOUNTANT EXAMINATION AS AN ENTRY REQUIREMENT FOR THE ACCOUNTING PROFESSION	General Survey CPA &/or CMA Examination 208
ELHOSSEINY, MOHAMED AHMED	PHD 1988 CITY UNIVERSITY OF NEW YORK CARMICHAEL, DOUGLAS	PROSPECTIVE INFORMATION IN SEC FILINGS: AN ANALYSIS OF MANAGEMENT CHOICE AND THE EFFECT OF AUDITOR INVOLVEMENT--A SIGNALING APPROACH	Auditing Archival - Primary Forecasting Financial Performance 157
ELITZUR, RACHAMIM RAMY	PHD 1988 NEW YORK UNIVERSITY, GRADUATE SCHOOL OF BUSINESS ADMINISTRATION	FINANCIAL REPORTING AND MARKET DATA--A SIGNALLING EQUILIBRIUM PERSPECTIVE	Financial Accounting Archival - Primary Capital Structure 129

Author	Degree & Date School Advisor	Title	Functional Area Research Method Topic pages
ELKHATIB, SOBHY MAHMOUD	PHD 1991 THE UNIVERSITY OF TEXAS AT ARLINGTON HALL, THOMAS	AN EMPIRICAL TEST OF THE BERG PROCEDURE FOR INDUCING RISK PREFERENCES	General Experimental Risk 114
ELMORE, ROBERT CLINTON	PHD 1986 THE UNIVERSITY OF MISSISSIPPI	A CONTINGENCY THEORY APPROACH TO AN EMPIRICAL CLASSIFICATION OF MANAGEMENT ACCOUNTING INFORMATION SYSTEMS	Cost/Managerial Survey Management Control Systems 246
ELNATHAN, DAN	PHD 1989 UNIVERSITY OF PENNSYLVANIA LARCKER, DAVID F.	ANALYSIS OF ISSUES CONCERNING OTHER POST EMPLOYMENT BENEFITS	Financial Accounting Archival - Primary Post Retirement Benefit Issues 141
ELSAYED-AHMED, SAMEH METWALLY	PHD 1986 UNIVERSITY OF NORTH TEXAS	AN EMPIRICAL EXAMINATION OF THE EFFECTS OF FASB STATEMENT NO. 52 ON SECURITY RETURNS AND REPORTED EARNINGS OF U.S.-BASED MULTINATIONAL CORPORATIONS	Financial Accounting Archival - Primary Foreign Currency Translation 231
EMIG, JAMES MATTHEW	PHD 1987 TEXAS A&M UNIVERSITY	THE RELATIONSHIP BETWEEN LEADER BEHAVIOR AND SUBORDINATE SATISFACTION IN AN AUDIT ENVIRONMENT: AN EMPIRICAL INVESTIGATION	General Survey Job Performance, Satisfaction &/or Turnover 191
ENGELBRET, WILLIAM G.	PHD 1990 THE PENNSYLVANIA STATE UNIVERSITY MALCOM, ROBERT E.	ASSESSING PARTICIPATION BY CERTIFIED PUBLIC ACCOUNTANTS IN CONTINUING PROFESSIONAL EDUCATION AND THE RELATIONSHIP BETWEEN EDUCATION AND CAREER PERFORMANCE	Education Survey Continuing Education 233
ENGLISH, DENISE MAY	PHD 1989 INDIANA UNIVERSITY HEINTZ, JAMES A.	THE INFLUENCE OF TIME PRESSURE, FIRM METHODOLOGY, AND CLIENT SIZE ON AUDITORS' MATERIALITY JUDGMENTS: AN INFORMATION ACQUISITION APPROACH	Auditing Experimental Materiality 160
ENGLISH, THOMAS JAMES	PHD 1988 ARIZONA STATE UNIVERSITY KAPLAN, STEVEN	AN EXAMINATION OF THE EFFECT OF SOCIAL INFLUENCE ON AUDITORS' MATERIALITY JUDGMENTS	Auditing Experimental Independence 96
EPELLE, CHUKUEMERIE TAMUNOTONYE	PHD 1992 UNIVERSITY OF SOUTH CAROLINA	THE IMPACT OF ORGANIZATIONAL GOALS UPON BANK LOAN OFFICERS' CREDIT WORTHINESS DECISIONS	Financial Accounting Experimental Bank Loan Officers 265

Author	Degree & Date School Advisor	Title	Functional Area Research Method Topic pages
EPPS, RUTH WILLIAMS	PHD 1987 VIRGINIA COMMONWEALTH UNIVERSITY HOLLEY, C. L.	AN EMPIRICAL INVESTIGATION OF THE EFFECTS OF THE QUALITY OF SEGMENTAL DISCLOSURE ON THE BEHAVIOR OF SYSTEMATIC RISK OF DIVERSIFIED FIRMS	Financial Accounting Archival - Primary Segment Reporting 149
ERIKSEN, SCOTT DOUGLAS	PHD 1987 UNIVERSITY OF NORTH TEXAS	A CRITICAL INVESTIGATION OF POSITIVISM: ITS ADEQUACY AS AN APPROACH FOR ACCOUNTING RESEARCH	Education Archival - Secondary Academic Issues 268
ESSEX, PATRICIA ANN	PHD 1993 MICHIGAN STATE UNIVERSITY	SYSTEMS DEVELOPMENT FRICTION: A CAUSAL MODEL BASED ON EQUITY CONSIDERATIONS	Information Systems Experimental Systems Design &/or Development 182
ETHERIDGE, HARLAN LYNN	PHD 1991 THE LOUISIANA STATE UNIVERSITY AND AGRICULTURAL AND MECHANICAL COL. HARTMAN, BART P.	AN EXAMINATION OF SEMIOTIC THEORIES OF ACCOUNTING ACCRUALS	Financial Accounting Archival - Primary Accruals 164
ETHRIDGE, JACK R., JR.	PHD 1986 UNIVERSITY OF ARKANSAS	OPERATIONAL AUDITING AND ORGANIZATIONAL PERFORMANCE: SOME PERCEPTIONS OF EXECUTIVES AND INTERNAL AUDITORS	Auditing Survey Performance Evaluation/Measurement 298
ETTER, EDWIN ROGER, JR.	PHD 1992 THE OHIO STATE UNIVERSITY JENSEN, DANIEL L.	THE INFORMATION CONTENT OF BRITISH AND JAPANESE EARNINGS ANNOUNCEMENTS: A PRICE AND TRADING VOLUME APPROACH	Financial Accounting Archival - Primary Earnings Announcements 120
ETZIONI, RUTH	PHD 1990 CARNEGIE-MELLON UNIVERSITY	BAYESIAN GROUP SEQUENTIAL SAMPLING WITH APPLICATION TO TAX AUDITING	Auditing Analytical - Internal Audit Sampling 175
EWER, SID ROY	PHD 1989 THE UNIVERSITY OF MISSISSIPPI BRINER, RUSSELL F.; WALLACE, WILLIAM D.	A STUDY OF THE EFFECT OF TRANSBORDER DATA FLOW RESTRICTIONS ON U.S. MULTINATIONAL CORPORATE ACCOUNTING CONTROL SYSTEMS	General Survey International/Global Issues 238
EWING, PER	EKONDR 1992 HANDELSHOGSKOLAN I STOCKHOLM (SWEDEN)	MANAGEMENT CONTROL OF INTERDEPENDENT UNITS [EKONOMISK STYRNING AV ENHETER MED INBORDE VERKSAMHETSSAMBAND]	Cost/Managerial Case Management Control Systems 202

Author	Degree & Date School Advisor	Title	Functional Area Research Method Topic pages
EYLER, KEL-ANN SHELDON	PHD 1990 GEORGIA STATE UNIVERSITY - COLLEGE OF BUSINESS ADMINISTRATION JACOBS, FRED A.	AN EXAMINATION OF THE EFFECTS OF AUDIT STRUCTURE AND GROUP TASK SETTINGS ON THE MATERIALITY JUDGMENTS OF AUDITORS	Auditing Experimental Materiality 191
FAIRFIELD, PATRICIA MARIE	PHD 1986 COLUMBIA UNIVERSITY	THE INFORMATION CONTENT OF LEVERAGE: A TIME-SERIES ANALYSIS	Financial Accounting Archival - Primary Risk 152
FANG, CHIH-CHIANG	PHD 1993 SAINT LOUIS UNIVERSITY PHILIPICH, KIRK L.	THREE EMPIRICAL INVESTIGATIONS INTO EARNINGS AND DIVIDENDS	Financial Accounting Archival - Primary Dividends 101
FARGHER, NEIL LAWRENCE	PHD 1992 THE UNIVERSITY OF ARIZONA DHALIWAL, DAN S.	THE ASSOCIATION BETWEEN UNEXPECTED EARNINGS AND CAPITAL EXPENDITURE	Financial Accounting Archival - Primary Investments 118
FARRELL, BARBARA R.	EDD 1993 COLUMBIA UNIVERSITY TEACHERS COLLEGE HUGHES, JONATHAN	ELEMENTS INFLUENCING SUCCESS ON THE CPA EXAMINATION	General Case CPA &/or CMA Examination 191
FEDHILA, HASSOUNA	PHD 1990 UNIVERSITY OF COLORADO AT BOULDER REED, RONALD	THE CONSTRUCTION OF AN EXPERT SYSTEM TO MAKE COMMERCIAL LOAN CLASSIFICATIONS	Information Systems Case Decision Support Systems 177
FEENEY, P. W.	PHD 1989 UNIVERSITY COLLEGE OF NORTH WALES, BANGOR (UNITED KINGDOM)	EURONOTES: RISK AND PRICING	General International/Global Issues 533
FELDMANN, DOROTHY A.	DBA 1992 BOSTON UNIVERSITY MENON, KRISHNAGOPAL	THE MARKET REACTION TO UNEXPECTED EARNINGS: THE CASE OF INDIVIDUAL AND INSTITUTIONAL INVESTORS	Financial Accounting Archival - Primary Earnings Response Coefficients 132
FELTON, SANDRA	PHD 1988 STATE UNIVERSITY OF NEW YORK AT BUFFALO	THE IMPACT OF LEASE ACCOUNTING REGULATION ON THE SHARE PRICES OF FIRMS WHICH LOBBIED ON SFAS NO. 13	Financial Accounting Archival - Primary Standard Setting 232

Author	Degree & Date School Advisor	Title	Functional Area Research Method Topic pages
FELTUS, OLIVER LEONARD	PHD 1986 THE UNIVERSITY OF ALABAMA	THE INFORMATION CONTENT OF FINANCIAL STATEMENTS: PREDICTING EARNINGS PER SHARE USING FINANCIAL RATIOS	Financial Accounting Archival - Primary Financial Ratios 152
FENNEMA, MARTIN GENE	PHD 1993 UNIVERSITY OF ILLINOIS AT URBANA-CHAMPAIGN KLEINMUNTZ, DON N.	ANTICIPATIONS OF EFFORT AND ACCURACY IN MULTIATTRIBUTE CHOICE	General Experimental Judgment & Decision Making 91
FENTON, EDMUND DAVID, JR.	DBA 1986 UNIVERSITY OF KENTUCKY	AN EMPIRICAL INVESTIGATION INTO THE TAX COURT ASSESSMENT OF THE ECONOMIC INTEREST CONCEPT IN NATURAL RESOURCE TAXATION	Taxation Archival - Secondary Tax Court 157
FERN, RICHARD HULL	DBA 1986 UNIVERSITY OF KENTUCKY	AN INQUIRY INTO THE ROLE OF THE CORPORATE CONTROLLER IN STRATEGIC PLANNING	Cost/Managerial Survey Accounting Career Issues 175
FERREIRA, LOURDES DALTRO	DBA 1989 HARVARD UNIVERSITY KAPLAN, ROBERT S.	LINKAGES BETWEEN EXECUTIVE COMPENSATION PROVISIONS AND THE DIVIDEND DECISION	Financial Accounting Archival - Primary Dividends 101
FERRERI, LINDA BARLOW	PHD 1986 CASE WESTERN RESERVE UNIVERSITY	UNIVERSITY BUDGET SYSTEMS: A TEST OF CONTINGENCY THEORY AT PRIVATE INSTITUTIONS	Cost/Managerial Survey Budgeting 189
FESLER, ROBERT DANIEL	DBA 1986 MISSISSIPPI STATE UNIVERSITY	LITIGATION REPORTING UNDER SFAS NO. 5: AN EMPIRICAL INVESTIGATION OF COMPARABILITY	Financial Accounting Archival - Primary Legal Liability 178
FIEDERLEIN, KATHLEEN J.	PHD 1992 INDIANA UNIVERSITY STERN, JERROLD J.	AN EQUITY ANALYSIS OF SOCIAL SECURITY TAXING AND FINANCING SCHEMES: SIMULATIONS OF ALTERNATIVE TAX PROVISIONS	Taxation Archival - Primary Public Policy 320
FIGLEWICZ, RAYMOND E.	DBA 1988 SOUTHERN ILLINOIS UNIVERSITY AT CARBONDALE TUCKER, MARVIN W.	AN EXAMINATION INTO THE FEASIBILITY OF USING MEASURES OF SYSTEMATIC RISK VARIABILITY AS PREDICTORS OF CORPORATE FAILURE	Financial Accounting Archival - Primary Financial Distress or Bankruptcy 367

Author	Degree & Date School Advisor	Title	Functional Area Research Method Topic pages
FILTER, WILLIAM VIGGO	PHD 1990 THE UNIVERSITY OF NEBRASKA - LINCOLN RAYMOND, ROBERT H.	A STUDY OF THE MARKET BEHAVIOR IN RESPONSE TO THE LIQUIDATION OF LIFO LAYERS	Financial Accounting Archival - Primary Inventory 131
FINDORFF, PAUL CURTIS	DBA 1992 UNITED STATES INTERNATIONAL UNIVERSITY BECKER, TIM A.	ACQUISITIONS AND ECONOMIC PERFORMANCE IN THE AIRLINE INDUSTRY SINCE THE AIRLINE DEREGULATION ACT OF 1978	Financial Accounting Archival - Primary Industry - Airline 221
FINGER, CATHERINE ANNE	PHD 1991 UNIVERSITY OF CALIFORNIA, BERKELEY LEV, BARUCH	THE RELATION BETWEEN FINANCIAL INFORMATION AND FUTURE CASH FLOWS	Financial Accounting Archival - Primary Cash Flows 157
FINN, PHILIP MORTON	PHD 1990 CITY UNIVERSITY OF NEW YORK PASTENA, VICTOR	AN EXAMINATION OF THE MARKET REACTION TO A MANDATED ACCOUNTING CHANGE: THE CASE FOR THE COSTS OF COMPUTER SOFTWARE	Financial Accounting Archival - Primary Accounting Change 110
FINNEGAN, THOMAS ROBERT	PHD 1993 UNIVERSITY OF ILLINOIS AT URBANA-CHAMPAIGN DIETRICH, J. RICHARD	THE EFFECT OF THE 1986 TAX REFORM ACT AND FINANCIAL ACCOUNTING CHANGES ON UTILITY RETURNS AND RATE SETTING	Financial Accounting, Archival - Primary Industry - Utilities 200
FINNEY, SHARON GARY	PHD 1989 GEORGIA STATE UNIVERSITY - COLLEGE OF BUSINESS ADMINISTRATION ENGLEBRECHT, TED D.	AN EMPIRICAL INVESTIGATION INTO THE PREDICTABILITY OF FAILURE IN INSURED SAVINGS INSTITUTIONS	Financial Accounting Archival - Primary Financial Distress or Bankruptcy 229
FISCHER, CAROL M.	PHD 1993 THE PENNSYLVANIA STATE UNIVERSITY DIRSMITH, MARK W.	PERCEIVED DETECTION PROBABILITY AND TAXPAYER COMPLIANCE: A CONCEPTUAL AND EMPIRICAL EXAMINATION	Taxation Survey Tax Compliance 335
FISCHER, MICHAEL J.	PHD 1992 THE PENNSYLVANIA STATE UNIVERSITY DIRSMITH, MARK W.	'REAL-IZING' THE BENEFITS OF NEW TECHNOLOGIES AS A SOURCE OF AUDIT EVIDENCE: AN INTERPRETIVE FIELD STUDY	Auditing Survey Audit Technology 350
FISHER, DANN G.	PHD 1992 UNIVERSITY OF MISSOURI - COLUMBIA PARKER, JAMES E.	ASSESSING TAXPAYER MORAL REASONING: THE DEVELOPMENT OF AN OBJECTIVE MEASURE	Taxation Survey Tax Compliance 334

Author	Degree & Date School Advisor	Title	Functional Area Research Method Topic pages
FISHER, JOSEPH GERALD	PHD 1987 THE OHIO STATE UNIVERSITY	THE ALLOCATION MECHANISM OF AUDITS: AN EXPERIMENTAL APPROACH	Auditing Experimental Auditor Changes 204
FISHER, STEVEN ALLEN	DBA 1985 KENT STATE UNIVERSITY	AN EMPIRICAL INVESTIGATION OF EXPERT JUDGMENTS CONCERNING THE SELECTION STATEMENT OF FINANCIAL ACCOUNTING STANDARDS NUMBER 52'S FUNCTIONAL CURRENCY	Financial Accounting Experimental Foreign Currency Translation 202
FLAGG, JAMES CALVIN	PHD 1988 TEXAS A&M UNIVERSITY GIROUX, GARY A.	A DESCRIPTION AND ANALYSIS OF THE CORPORATE FAILURE PROCESS USING AN EVENTS-BASED LOGIT MODEL	Financial Accounting Archival - Primary Financial Distress or Bankruptcy 133
FLEAK, SANDRA KREISEL	PHD 1988 UNIVERSITY OF MISSOURI - COLUMBIA WILSON, EARL R.	THE GOING-CONCERN AUDIT OPINION AND SHARE PRICE BEHAVIOR	Auditing Archival - Primary Audit Opinion 173
FLETCHER, LESLIE B.	PHD 1993 THE LOUISIANA STATE UNIVERSITY AND AGRICULTURAL AND MECHANICAL COL. BRENNER, VINCENT C.	THE PREDICTION OF FINANCIAL TURNAROUND OF FINANCIALLY DISTRESSED FIRMS	Financial Accounting Archival - Primary Financial Distress or Bankruptcy 118
FLINN, RONALD EARL	DBA 1989 UNIVERSITY OF KENTUCKY POPE, THOMAS R.	AN INVESTIGATION OF PROPOSED CHANGES IN THE FEDERAL INCOME TAXATION OF ACQUISITIVE REORGANIZATIONS	Taxation Analytical - Internal Merger, Acquisition, Reorganization 597
FLYNN, RICHARD STEVEN	PHD 1987 UNIVERSITY OF CINCINNATI SALE, TIMOTHY	AN EMPIRICAL INVESTIGATION OF THE EFFECTS OF ALTERNATIVE PERFORMANCE MEASUREMENT SCHEMES ON THE AGENT'S DISCLOSURE OF PRIVATE INFORMATION	Cost/Managerial Experimental Agency Theory 144
FOGARTY, TIMOTHY JOSEPH	PHD 1989 THE PENNSYLVANIA STATE UNIVERSITY DIRSMITH, MARK W.	AUDIT PERFORMANCE: AN EMPIRICAL SYNTHESIS OF THREE THEORETICAL EXPLANATIONS	Auditing Survey Job Performance, Satisfaction &/or Turnover 595
FORAN, NANCY JOYCE HOFFMAN	PHD 1985 OKLAHOMA STATE UNIVERSITY	THE EFFECT OF THE ECONOMIC RECOVERY TAX ACT OF 1981 AND THE TAX EQUITY AND FISCAL RESPONSIBILITY ACT OF 1982 ON THE FORM OF DISPOSITION BY INDIVIDUALS OF NONRESIDENTIAL REAL PROPERTY	Taxation Simulation Individual Taxation 175

Listing by Author

Author	Degree & Date School Advisor	Title	Functional Area Research Method Topic pages
FORDHAM, DAVID RONALD	PHD 1993 THE FLORIDA STATE UNIVERSITY HILLISON, WILLIAM	A COMMUNICATIONS-BASED TYPOLOGY OF COLLABORATION IN DECISION-MAKING	General Experimental Judgment & Decision Making 154
FORGIONE, DANA ANTHONY	PHD 1987 UNIVERSITY OF MASSACHUSETTS MANNINO, RONALD C.	INCENTIVES AND PERFORMANCE IN THE HEALTH CARE INDUSTRY: THE CASE OF FOR/NON PROFIT MULTIHOSPITAL SYSTEMS	Cost/Managerial Archival - Primary Industry - Health Care 175
FORNEY, CHARLES T.	DBA 1992 NOVA UNIVERSITY CARLSON, CHRISTOPHER K.	AN INVESTIGATION INTO THE TIME-SERIES NATURE OF FOREIGN SUBSIDIARY EARNINGS AND MANAGEMENT'S ABILITY TO FORECAST THEM	Financial Accounting Archival - Primary Forecasting Financial Performance 117
FORSYTH, TIMOTHY BUSH	PHD 1991 THE UNIVERSITY OF ALABAMA DUGAN, MICHAEL T.	A STUDY OF THE ABILITY OF FINANCIAL RATIOS TO PREDICT CORPORATE FAILURE AND THE RELATIONSHIP BETWEEN BANKRUPTCY MODEL PROBABILITY ASSESSMENTS AND STOCK MARKET BEHAVIOR	Financial Accounting Archival - Primary Financial Distress or Bankruptcy 174
FORT, CHARLES PATRICK	PHD 1993 UNIVERSITY OF COLORADO AT BOULDER BUCHMAN, THOMAS A.	ANALYSTS' FORECAST ACCURACY AND THE PRESENTATION OF MANDATED ACCOUNTING CHANGES	Financial Accounting Archival - Primary Accounting Change 93
FORTIN, ANNE	PHD 1986 UNIVERSITY OF ILLINOIS AT URBANA-CHAMPAIGN	THE EVOLUTION OF FRENCH ACCOUNTING THOUGHT AS REFLECTED BY THE SUCCESSIVE UNIFORM SYSTEMS (PLANS COMPTABLES GENERAUX)	General Archival - Secondary History 815
FOSHEE, KENNETH HAROLD	PHD 1990 MISSISSIPPI STATE UNIVERSITY PHILLIPS, TRAVIS D.	ESTIMATING THE COSTS OF PRODUCING CONTAINER GROWN PLANTS WITH THE ASSISTANCE OF COMPUTER ACCOUNTING SOFTWARE	General Case Industry - Agricultural 136
FOSS, HELGA BERTA	PHD 1987 UNIVERSITY OF CINCINNATI	THE EFFECT OF ACCOUNTING CHANGES AND TAX CONSEQUENCES ON INVESTOR BEHAVIOR	Financial Accounting Experimental Accounting Change 104
FOSTER, BENJAMIN PATRICK	PHD 1991 THE UNIVERSITY OF TENNESSEE ANDERSON, KENNETH E.	TESTING THE APPROPRIATENESS OF NONPROFIT HOSPITALS' TAX EXEMPTIONS WITH LOGISTIC REGRESSION ANALYSES OF HOSPITAL FINANCIAL DATA	General Archival - Primary Industry - Health Care 154

Author	Degree & Date / School / Advisor	Title	Functional Area / Research Method / Topic / pages
FOUCH, SCOTT RANDALL	PHD 1990 OKLAHOMA STATE UNIVERSITY KIMBRELL, JANET	EMPIRICAL RESEARCH INTO THE SHIFTING OF THE CORPORATE INCOME TAX OF LIFE INSURANCE COMPANIES	Taxation Archival - Primary Industry - Insurance 121
FOUST, KAREN MCLAFFERTY	PHD 1994 TULANE UNIVERSITY LEE, CHI-WEN JEVONS	INTERNAL STRUCTURE AND THE TRANSITION FROM A TWO-TIER TO A THREE-TIER HIERARCHY	Cost/Managerial Case Agency Theory 153
FOWLER, CALVIN D.	DBA 1991 NOVA UNIVERSITY KELLEY, JAMES A.	AN EMPIRICAL STUDY OF LEARNING CURVES AMONG NON-REPETITIVE JOB SHOP OPERATIONS	Cost/Managerial Case Cost Behaviors & Estimation 203
FRANCIS, JENNIFER	PHD 1987 CORNELL UNIVERSITY	CORPORATE COMPLIANCE WITH DEBT COVENANTS	Financial Accounting Archival - Primary Long Term Debt 165
FRANKEL, MICAH PAUL	PHD 1991 THE UNIVERSITY OF ARIZONA DHALIWAL, DAN S.	THE DETERMINANTS OF LIFO LAYER LIQUIDATIONS: TAX MINIMIZATION AND AGENCY COST FACTORS	Taxation Archival - Primary Inventory 106
FRANKEL, RICHARD MOSES	PHD 1993 STANFORD UNIVERSITY MCNICHOLS, MAUREEN	ACCOUNTING INFORMATION AND FIRMS WITH LOW-GRADE BONDS	Financial Accounting Archival - Primary Cash Flows 124
FRANZ, DAVID PAUL	PHD 1986 THE PENNSYLVANIA STATE UNIVERSITY	THE INFORMATION CONTENT OF CASH FLOW MEASURES: AN EMPIRICAL ANALYSIS	financial Accounting Archival - Primary Cash Flows 138
FRANZ, DIANA RUTH	PHD 1993 TEXAS TECH UNIVERSITY LAMPE, JAMES C.	AN ANALYSIS OF THE EFFECT OF THE EXPECTATION GAP STATEMENTS ON AUDITING STANDARDS ON THE REPORTING OF GOING CONCERN	Auditing Archival - Primary Audit Opinion 201
FRAZER, JOHN DOUGLAS	PHD 1987 TEMPLE UNIVERSITY	PERFORMANCE EVALUATION OF AUDITORS: THE IMPORTANCE OF TIME-BUDGET PRESSURE THROUGH A FOCUS ON THE EVALUATOR	Auditing Experimental Job Performance, Satisfaction &/or Turnover 143

Listing by Author

Author	Degree & Date School Advisor	Title	Functional Area Research Method Topic pages
FRAZIER, JESSICA JOHNSON	DBA 1990 UNIVERSITY OF KENTUCKY FULKS, DANIEL L.	AN ANALYSIS OF THE EFFECT OF THE PROPOSED AD VALOREM PROPERTY TAXATION OF UNMINED COAL PROPERTY IN KENTUCKY	Taxation Archival - Primary Public Policy 221
FREDERICK, DAVID MICHAEL	PHD 1986 THE UNIVERSITY OF MICHIGAN	AUDITORS' REPRESENTATION AND RETRIEVAL OF KNOWLEDGE IN INTERNAL CONTROL EVALUATION	Auditing Experimental Judgment & Decision Making - Cognitive Processes 111
FREDERICKSON, JAMES RAY	PHD 1990 UNIVERSITY OF WASHINGTON JIAMBALVO, JAMES	RELATIVE PERFORMANCE INFORMATION: THE EFFECTS OF COMMON UNCERTAINTY AND CONTRACT TYPE ON AGENTS' GOALS AND EFFORT	Cost/Managerial Experimental Performance Evaluation/Measurement 153
FREEMAN, GARY ROSS	PHD 1988 GEORGIA STATE UNIVERSITY - COLLEGE OF BUSINESS ADMINISTRATION HERMANSON, ROGER	AN INVESTIGATION OF THE USEFULNESS OF CURRENT COST INCOME TO CAPITAL MARKET PARTICIPANTS	Financial Accounting Archival - Primary Inflation 184
FRENCH, GEORGE RICHARD	PHD 1990 THE UNIVERSITY OF MISSISSIPPI WALLACE, WILLIAM D.	AN ANALYSIS OF THE INTERPERSONAL STYLE OF PERSONAL FINANCIAL PLANNERS (CPAS AND NONACCOUNTANTS) AND TRADITIONAL ACCOUNTANTS WITH IMPLICATIONS FOR THE ACCOUNTING PROFESSION	General Experimental Accounting Career Issues 267
FRESE, PHILLIP BRUCE	PHD 1993 DREXEL UNIVERSITY	THE EFFECT OF CHANGES IN TAX STRUCTURE ON THE BEHAVIOR OF RATIONAL INVESTORS IN MARKETS FOR RISKY ASSETS: AN EMPIRICAL STUDY OF THE IMPACT OF THE OMNIBUS BUDGET RECONCILIATION ACT OF 1987 ON THE INVESTORS IN PUBLICLY TRADED PARTNERSHIPS	Taxation Archival - Primary Business Form 196
FRIAR, SHIRLEY ANNE	PHD 1986 THE UNIVERSITY OF TEXAS AT AUSTIN	DECISION MAKING UNDER RISK: AN EXPERIMENTAL STUDY WITHIN A BUSINESS CONTEXT	General Experimental Judgment & Decision Making 264
FRIEDLAN, JOHN MICHAEL	PHD 1990 UNIVERSITY OF WASHINGTON DUKES, ROLAND E.	ACCOUNTING INFORMATION AND THE PRICING OF INITIAL PUBLIC OFFERINGS	Financial Accounting Archival - Primary Initial Public Offerings 187
FRIEDLANDER, PHILIP HOWARD	DBA 1993 NOVA UNIVERSITY	INFORMATION TECHNOLOGY AND STRATEGIC ATTITUDES IN THE PUBLIC ACCOUNTING PROFESSION: A STRATEGIC GROUP ANALYSIS	General Survey CPA Firm Issues 385

Author	Degree & Date School Advisor	Title	Functional Area Research Method Topic pages
FRISCHMANN, PETER JAMES	PHD 1992 ARIZONA STATE UNIVERSITY	TAXPAYER RESPONSE TO KINKED BUDGET CONSTRAINTS: NEW EMPIRICAL EVIDENCE OF TAX PRICE AWARENESS	Taxation Archival - Primary Tax Compliance 84
FRISKE, KARYN ANNE BYBEE	PHD 1994 TEXAS A&M UNIVERSITY CRUMBLEY, LARRY	AN EXAMINATION OF THE EFFECTS OF STANDARD SETTING AND EARNINGS MANAGEMENT IN THE OIL AND GAS INDUSTRY: THE LESSON OF SFAS NO. 96	Financial Accounting Archival - Primary Industry - Oil & Gas 124
FRITSCHE, STEVEN RODNEY	PHD 1991 THE UNIVERSITY OF ALABAMA DUGAN, MICHAEL T.	ACCOUNTING RATE OF RETURN AND CONDITIONAL ESTIMATE OF INTERNAL RATE OF RETURN: AN INVESTIGATION OF TWO SURROGATES FOR INTERNAL RATE OF RETURN	Cost/Managerial Simulation Capital Budgeting 118
FROWNFELTER, CYNTHIA ANN	PHD 1993 DREXEL UNIVERSITY CURATOLA, ANTHONY P.	THE EFFECTS OF DIFFERING INFORMATION PRESENTATIONS OF GENERAL PURPOSE FINANCIAL STATEMENTS ON USERS' DECISIONS	Financial Accounting Experimental Presentation Format 242
FUGLISTER, JAYNE	DBA 1985 THE GEORGE WASHINGTON UNIVERSITY	CORPORATE CAPITAL STRUCTURE AND TAXES: SOME EVIDENCE	General Survey Capital Structure 212
FUHRMANN, JOHN STANLEY	PHD 1991 THE UNIVERSITY OF TEXAS AT AUSTIN NEWMAN, DONALD PAUL	THE ASSOCIATION BETWEEN SECURITY RETURNS AND FIRMS' LOBBYING POSITIONS ON ACCOUNTING STANDARDS	Financial Accounting Archival - Primary Standard Setting 158
FULKERSON, CHERYL LINTHICUM	PHD 1993 OKLAHOMA STATE UNIVERSITY	EARNINGS EXPECTATIONS, FIRM VALUATION AND RISK ASSESSMENT USING FOREIGN AND RESTATED ACCOUNTING DATA	Financial Accounting Archival - Primary International/Global Issues 87
FULTS, GAIL JOHNSON	PHD 1987 CLAREMONT GRADUATE SCHOOL	HOW PARTICIPATORY EVALUATION RESEARCH AFFECTS THE MANAGEMENT CONTROL PROCESS OF A MULTINATIONAL NON-PROFIT ORGANIZATION	Not-for-Profit Survey Charitable Organizations 453
FULTZ, M. ELAINE	PHD 1991 NEW YORK UNIVERSITY ALTSHULER, ALAN	DELEGATED REGULATION: A STUDY OF THE NATIONAL FUTURES ASSOCIATION	General Case Other 305

Author	Degree & Date School Advisor	Title	Functional Area Research Method Topic pages
FURZE, SALLY	PHD 1993 UNIVERSITY OF OREGON MORSE, DALE	SFAS 94 AND NOISY EARNINGS SIGNALS	Financial Accounting Archival - Primary Earnings Response Coefficients 86
GABALLA, MAHMOUD A.	PHD 1990 NEW YORK UNIVERSITY ARGYRIADES, DEMETRIOS	PERFORMANCE AND CONTROL OF PUBLIC ENTERPRISE IN EGYPT	General Survey International/Global Issues 489
GABBIN, ALEXANDER L.	PHD 1986 TEMPLE UNIVERSITY	AN EMPIRICAL INVESTIGATION OF CANDIDATE ATTRIBUTES SIGNIFICANTLY AFFECTING RECRUITING OF ACCOUNTING GRADUATES BY A NATIONAL CPA FIRM	General Case Accounting Career Issues 159
GABER, MOHAMED KHAIRAT ABDEL-GELIL	PHD 1985 CITY UNIVERSITY OF NEW YORK	MANAGEMENT INCENTIVES TO REPORT FORECASTS OF CORPORATE EARNINGS	Financial Accounting Archival - Primary Voluntary Management Disclosures 151
GABRIEL, ELIZABETH ANN	PHD 1993 THE OHIO STATE UNIVERSITY JENSEN, DANIEL L.	MARKET COMPETITION AND THE INCENTIVE TO INVEST IN PRODUCT COST INFORMATION: AN EXPERIMENTAL INVESTIGATION	Cost/Managerial Experimental Cost Systems 175
GADDIS, MARCUS DAMON	PHD 1993 UNIVERSITY OF KENTUCKY MADDEN, DONALD L.	INVESTIGATING THE INFLUENCE OF ASSERTIONS BY ACCOUNTING AND APPRAISAL PROFESSIONALS ON REAL ESTATE LENDING DECISIONS	General Experimental Bank Loan Officers 224
GAGNE, MARGARET LEE	PHD 1989 INDIANA UNIVERSITY SPILLER, EARL JR.	THE IMPACT OF FIRM SIZE ON THE PRICE AND VOLUME REACTIONS TO ANALYSTS' EARNINGS FORECAST REVISIONS	Financial Accounting Archival - Primary Financial Analysts 116
GAHARAN, CATHERINE INNES GREEN	PHD 1988 THE LOUISIANA STATE UNIVERSITY AND AGRICULTURAL AND MECHANICAL COL. MISTER, WILLIAM G.	A COMPARISON OF THE EFFECTIVENESS OF THE OPERATING FUNDS FLOW MEASURES OF CASH, NET QUICK ASSETS, AND WORKING CAPITAL IN PREDICTING FUTURE CASH FLOW	Financial Accounting Archival - Primary Cash Flows 135
GALANTINE, CAROLYN ANN	PHD 1994 UNIVERSITY OF SOUTHERN CALIFORNIA SWENSON, CHARLES	PRINCIPAL-AGENT THEORY WITH APPLICATIONS TO THE THREE-PARTY PROBLEM BETWEEN TAXPAYERS, EXAMINERS AND THE GOVERNMENT	Taxation Analytical - Internal Agency Theory

Author	Degree & Date School Advisor	Title	Functional Area Research Method Topic pages
GARCIA DELGADO, SONIA M.	DR 1994 UNIVERSIDAD DEL PAIS VASCO/EUSKAL HERRIKO UNIBERTSITATEA (SPAIN)	MATERIALITY IN AUDITING	Auditing Materiality 685
GARLICK, JOHN RICHARD, SR.	PHD 1989 UNIVERSITY OF SOUTH CAROLINA	CUMULATIVE ABNORMAL RETURNS; INTERVENTION ANALYSIS: A METHODOLOGICAL COMPARISON	Financial Accounting Archival - Primary Capital Markets 213
GARNER, ROBERT MICHAEL	PHD 1986 UNIVERSITY OF ARKANSAS	S. PAUL GARNER: A STUDY OF SELECTED CONTRIBUTIONS TO THE ACCOUNTING PROFESSION	General Archival - Secondary History 215
GARRISON, LARRY RICHARD	PHD 1986 THE UNIVERSITY OF NEBRASKA - LINCOLN	THE EXCLUSION FROM INCOME OF SCHOLARSHIPS AND FELLOWSHIP GRANTS: AN EMPIRICAL INVESTIGATION OF TAX COURT DETERMINATIONS	Taxation Archival - Secondary Tax Court 152
GATIAN, AMY ELIZABETH WILLIAMS	PHD 1989 VIRGINIA POLYTECHNIC INSTITUTE AND STATE UNIVERSITY HICKS, JAMES O. JR.	USER INFORMATION SATISFACTION (UIS) AND USER PRODUCTIVITY: AN EMPIRICAL EXAMINATION	Not-for-Profit Survey College & University 252
GAUMNITZ, CAROL BOTHAMLEY	PHD 1985 THE UNIVERSITY OF WISCONSIN - MADISON	AN ANALYSIS OF THE INTERNAL REVENUE SERVICE'S DECISION PROCESS WITH RESPECT TO THE UNRELATED BUSINESS INCOME TAXPROVISIONS CONTAINED IN CODE SECTIONS 511-513	Taxation Archival - Primary Not-for-Profit 413
GAUNTT, JAMES EDWARD, JR.	PHD 1986 THE JUILLIARD SCHOOL	A SIMULATION STUDY OF STATISTICAL ESTIMATORS USED IN VARIABLES SAMPLING	Auditing Simulation Audit Sampling 255
GAVER, JENNIFER JANE	PHD 1987 THE UNIVERSITY OF ARIZONA	INCENTIVE EFFECTS AND MANAGERIAL COMPENSATION CONTRACTS: A STUDY OF PERFORMANCE PLAN ADOPTIONS	Cost/Managerial Incentive Compensation 131
GEIGER, DALE RAIMONDE	DBA 1993 HARVARD UNIVERSITY KAPLAN, ROBERT S.	FEDERAL MANAGEMENT ACCOUNTING: DETERMINANTS, MOTIVATING CONTINGENCIES, AND DECISION MAKING RELEVANCE	Cost/Managerial Governmental 219

Author	Degree & Date School Advisor	Title	Functional Area Research Method Topic pages
GEIGER, MARSHALL ALLEN	PHD 1988 THE PENNSYLVANIA STATE UNIVERSITY THIES, JAMES B.	SETTING THE STANDARD FOR A NEW AUDITOR'S REPORT: AN ANALYSIS OF ATTEMPTS TO INFLUENCE THE AUDITING STANDARDS BOARD	Auditing Archival - Secondary Audit Opinion 356
GEKAS, GEORGE ANDREW	PHD 1989 UNIVERSITY OF HULL (UNITED KINGDOM)	ACCOUNTING EDUCATION AT DOCTORAL LEVEL: A CANADIAN PERSPECTIVE WITH SPECIAL REFERENCE TO THE DEMAND AND SUPPLY OF ACADEMIC ACCOUNTANTS	Education Academic Issues 591
GELARDI, ALEXANDER MARIA GEORGE	PHD 1991 ARIZONA STATE UNIVERSITY RENEAU, J. HAL	THE EFFECT OF QUANTITY AND ORDER OF CUES ON SEQUENTIAL BELIEF REVISION IN TAX JUDGMENTS	Taxation Experimental Judgment & Decision Making - Heuristics & Biases 140
GEORGE, CAROLYN R.	DBA 1991 MEMPHIS STATE UNIVERSITY SPICELAND, J. DAVID	THE EFFECT OF THE GOING-CONCERN AUDIT DECISION ON SURVIVAL	Auditing Archival - Primary Audit Opinion 124
GEORGE, NASHWA ELGALLAB	PHD 1988 CITY UNIVERSITY OF NEW YORK RULAND, WILLIAM	MANAGEMENT EARNINGS FORECAST DISCLOSURE: AN EMPIRICAL STUDY OF FACTORS INFLUENCING THE DECISION	Financial Accounting Archival - Primary Voluntary Management Disclosures 147
GERBING, MONICA DIANE	PHD 1988 THE UNIVERSITY OF TEXAS AT AUSTIN JONES, SALLY M.	AN EMPIRICAL STUDY OF TAXPAYER PERCEPTIONS OF FAIRNESS	Taxation Survey Tax Compliance 185
GERSICH, FRANK, III	EDD 1993 NORTHERN ILLINOIS UNIVERSITY SCHROEDER, BETTY L.	AN INVESTIGATION OF THE IMPORTANCE OF SELECTED KNOWLEDGE AREAS AND SKILLS FOR A PUBLIC ACCOUNTING AUDITING CAREER AND THE EXTENT OF ACADEMIC PREPARATION AS PERCEIVED BY AUDIT SENIORS AND AUDIT MANAGERS	Auditing Survey Accounting Career Issues 248
GHANI, WAQAR I.	PHD 1993 DREXEL UNIVERSITY NDUBIZU, GORDIAN	THE ECONOMIC IMPACT OF ACCOUNTING INFORMATION AGGREGATION AND DISAGGREGATION ON INFORMEDNESS AND CONSENSUS: THE CASE OF CONSOLIDATED NONHOMOGENEOUS SUBSIDIARIES	Financial Accounting Archival - Primary Merger, Acquisition, Reorganization 242
GHICAS, DIMITRIOS CHRISTOS	PHD 1985 UNIVERSITY OF FLORIDA	AN ANALYSIS OF THE CHANGE OF ACTUARIAL COST METHODS FOR PENSION ACCOUNTING AND FUNDING	Financial Accounting Archival - Primary Post Retirement Benefit Issues 127

Author	Degree & Date School Advisor	Title	Functional Area Research Method Topic pages
GHOSH, ALOKE	PHD 1994 TULANE UNIVERSITY LEE, CHI-WEN JEVONS	VALUATION OF GAINS FROM MERGERS: SOURCES AND ESTIMATION OF THESE GAINS FROM DISCIPLINARY TAKEOVERS AND DIFFERENT TAX-RELATED ISSUES	General Archival - Primary Merger, Acquisition, Reorganization 151
GHOSH, DIPANKAR	PHD 1991 THE PENNSYLVANIA STATE UNIVERSITY CUSHING, BARRY E.	AN EXPERIMENT COMPARING NEGOTIATED AND CENTRALLY ADMINISTERED TRANSFER PRICES	Cost/Managerial Experimental Transfer Pricing 230
GIBSON, ANNETTA MAE	PHD 1992 WASHINGTON STATE UNIVERSITY FRAKES, ALBERT H.	AN EMPIRICAL INVESTIGATION INTO ETHICAL DECISION-MAKING IN ACCOUNTING	General Survey Ethics 307
GIBSON, DANA L.	PHD 1993 THE UNIVERSITY OF TEXAS AT ARLINGTON HALL, THOMAS	THE EFFECTS OF ALTERNATIVE SCREEN LAYOUTS AND FEEDBACK TYPES ON OCCASIONAL USER PRODUCTIVITY AND SATISFACTION IN A GENERAL LEDGER ENVIRONMENT	Information systems Experimental Presentation Format 122
GIBSON, THOMAS HARRISON, JR.	EDD 1992 MONTANA STATE UNIVERSITY STROHMEYER, ERIC	THE 1985 NCAA FINANCIAL AUDIT LEGISLATION: IS IT WORKING, FROM COLLEGE AND UNIVERSITY PRESIDENTS' PERSPECTIVE?	Not-for-Profit Survey College & University 150
GIGLER, FRANK BARRY	PHD 1992 UNIVERSITY OF MINNESOTA KANODIA, CHANDRA	SELF-ENFORCING VOLUNTARY DISCLOSURES	Financial Accounting Analytical - Internal Voluntary Management Disclosures 95
GILBERT, LISA R.	DBA 1989 BOSTON UNIVERSITY MENON, KRISHNAGOPAL	ACCOUNTING STANDARDS, EARNINGS EXPECTATIONS, AND MARKET PRICES: THE CASE OF SFAS 52	Financial Accounting Archival - Primary Foreign Currency Translation 171
GILL, JOHN WAITS	PHD 1992 THE UNIVERSITY OF MISSISSIPPI FLESHER, DALE L.	THE EFFECTS OF A RED FLAGS QUESTIONNAIRE AND SELECTED ELEMENTS OF COGNITIVE STYLE ON THE AUDIT PLANNING TASK OF ASSESSING THE PROBABILITY OF MATERIAL MANAGEMENT FRAUD	Auditing Experimental Fraud 261
GILL, SUSAN	PHD 1994 MICHIGAN STATE UNIVERSITY ANTHONY, JOSEPH	MOTIVATIONS FOR AND REACTIONS TO VOLUNTARY MANAGEMENT DISCLOSURES	Financial Accounting Archival - Primary Voluntary Management Disclosures 141

Author	Degree & Date School Advisor	Title	Functional Area Research Method Topic pages
GIRARD, ALINE CHANTAL	PHD 1990 THE UNIVERSITY OF TENNESSEE STANGA, KEITH G.	THE EFFECTS OF CONTEXT, TERMINOLOGY, AND EXPERTISE ON THE UNDERSTANDABILITY OF ACCOUNTING CONCEPTS: A LABORATORY EXPERIMENT	General Experimental Other 218
GIST, WILLIE EARL	PHD 1988 TEXAS A&M UNIVERSITY STRAWSER, ROBERT	AN EXPLORATORY STUDY OF THE EFFECTS OF PRODUCT DIFFERENTIATION AND ECONOMIES OF SCALE ON EXTERNAL AUDIT FEES	Auditing Archival - Primary Audit Fees 129
GLOECK, JUERGEN DIETER	DCOM 1993 UNIVERSITY OF PRETORIA (SOUTH AFRICA) DE JAGER, H.	THE EXPECTATION GAP WITH REGARD TO THE AUDITING PROFESSION IN THE REPUBLIC OF SOUTH AFRICA	Auditing Survey International/Global Issues
GLOVER, HUBERT DARNELL	PHD 1992 TEXAS A&M UNIVERSITY GIROUX, GARY	MEASURING AUDIT STRUCTURE AND DETERMINING THE SOURCES OF VARIATION: AN APPLICATION OF ORGANIZATIONAL SCIENCE	Auditing Survey Audit Structure 182
GLOVER, JONATHAN CHARLES	PHD 1992 THE OHIO STATE UNIVERSITY JENSEN, DANIEL L.; YOUNG, RICHARD A.	IMPLEMENTATION USING SIMPLE MECHANISMS: SOME THEORETICAL RESULTS AND APPLICATIONS TO ACCOUNTING	General Analytical - Internal Agency Theory 106
GNIZAK, CHARLES JAMES	PHD 1993 KENT STATE UNIVERSITY BARNIV, RAN; ZUCCA, LINDA J.	INTEREST CAPITALIZATION TAX LAW: ITS EFFECT ON CAPITAL STRUCTURE AND MARKET VALUE	Taxation Archival - Primary Capital Structure 154
GOBER, JERALD ROBERT	PHD 1994 TEXAS TECH UNIVERSITY BURNS, JANE O.	THE BLEND OF TAXES USED TO FUND NATIONAL, STATE, AND LOCAL GOVERNMENTAL BODIES: A FACTOR IN THE ECONOMIES OF THE WORLD?	Taxation Archival - Primary International/Global Issues 229
GODWIN, JOSEPH HUDSON	PHD 1988 THE UNIVERSITY OF WISCONSIN - MADISON WEYGANDT, JERRY J.	THE ECONOMIC DETERMINANTS OF ACCOUNTING CHOICE: THE CASE OF ACCOUNTING FOR PENSIONS	Financial Accounting Archival - Primary Accounting Choice 160
GOEDDE, HAROLD	DBA 1988 UNIVERSITY OF KENTUCKY POPE, THOMAS	AN EMPIRICAL STUDY OF TAX PRACTITIONERS PERCEPTIONS OF THE EFFECT OF THE 1986 TAX REFORM ACT ON SIMPLIFICATION AND FAIRNESS OF THE FEDERAL INCOME TAX	Taxation Survey Tax Professionals 172

Author	Degree & Date School Advisor	Title	Functional Area Research Method Topic pages
GOLDBERG, STEPHEN RICHARD	PHD 1988 THE UNIVERSITY OF WISCONSIN - MADISON WILLIAMS, THOMAS H.	THE IMPACT OF EXCHANGE RATE CHANGES ON SECURITY RETURNS AND FINANCIAL REPORTING: THEORY AND EMPIRICAL FINDINGS	Financial Accounting Archival - Primary International/Global Issues 186
GOMA, AHMED TAWFIK	PHD 1985 CITY UNIVERSITY OF NEW YORK	EMPIRICAL INVESTIGATION OF THE INFORMATION CONTENT OF SPECIFIC PRICE CHANGE DISCLOSURES	Financial Accounting Archival - Primary Inflation 209
GONZALEZ CABAN, ARMANDO	PHD 1993 CORNELL UNIVERSITY SALTZMAN, SIDNEY	FIRE MANAGEMENT COSTS AND SOURCES OF VARIABILITY IN PRESCRIBED BURNING COSTS IN THE FOREST SERVICE'S NORTHERN, INTERMOUNTAIN, AND PACIFIC NORTHWEST REGIONS	Cost/Managerial Survey Industry - Agricultural 238
GONZALEZ, LUIS	PHD 1994 NEW YORK UNIVERSITY O'CONNOR, BRIDGET N.	LEVELS OF INFORMATION TECHNOLOGIES INTEGRATION AS FACTORS AFFECTING PERCEPTIONS OF JOB CHARACTERISTICS AND PROFESSIONALISM OF MANAGEMENT ACCOUNTANTS	Cost/Managerial Survey Accounting Career Issues 143
GONZALEZ, PEDRO	PHD 1993 LEHIGH UNIVERSITY	FINANCIAL CHARACTERISTICS OF COMPANIES INVOLVED IN CROSS-BORDER MERGERS AND ACQUISITIONS	Financial Accounting Archival - Primary Merger, Acquisition, Reorganization 142
GOPALAKRISHNAN, VENKATARAMAN	PHD 1986 UNIVERSITY OF NORTH TEXAS	MARKET REACTIONS TO ACCOUNTING POLICY DELIBERATIONS: THE CASE OF PENSIONS	Financial Accounting Archival - Primary Standard Setting 140
GORDON, GUS ALLEN	DBA 1988 LOUISIANA TECH UNIVERSITY	A DISCRIMINANT MODEL TO PREDICT FINANCIAL DISTRESS IN OIL AND GAS COMPANIES	Financial Accounting Financial Distress or Bankruptcy 137
GORDON, TERESA PEALE	PHD 1986 UNIVERSITY OF HOUSTON	BOUNDED RATIONALITY AND BUDGETING: RESOURCE DEPENDENCE, AGENCY POWER, INDIVIDUAL MOTIVATION AND INCREMENTALISM IN BUDGETARY DECISION-MAKING	Cost/Managerial Survey Budgeting 251
GOSS, BETSY CATON	PHD 1991 THE UNIVERSITY OF WISCONSIN - MADISON WILLIAMS, THOMAS H.	ACCOUNTING QUALITY AND DISPERSION OF FINANCIAL ANALYSTS' FORECASTS: AN EMPIRICAL INVESTIGATION	Financial Accounting Archival - Primary Financial Analysts 227

Author	Degree & Date School Advisor	Title	Functional Area Research Method Topic pages
GOSSE, DARREL IRVIN	PHD 1989 MICHIGAN STATE UNIVERSITY	AN EMPIRICAL FIELD STUDY OF THE ROLE OF COST ACCOUNTING IN A COMPUTER-INTEGRATED MANUFACTURING ENVIRONMENT	Cost/Managerial Survey Cost Systems 276
GOSSELIN, DAVID J.	PHD 1986 UNIVERSITY OF ARKANSAS	AN EMPIRICAL INVESTIGATION OF CORPORATE INCOME SMOOTHING: A FACTOR ANALYTIC AND DISCRIMINANT APPROACH TO FIRM IDENTIFICATION	Financial Accounting Archival - Primary Earnings Management 180
GOTLOB, DAVID	PHD 1985 UNIVERSITY OF MISSOURI - COLUMBIA	INVESTOR AND CREDITOR PERCEPTIONS OF CORPORATE PERFORMANCE: A MULTIDIMENSIONAL SCALING APPROACH	Financial Accounting Survey Disclosures 303
GOULD, JOHN FRANKLIN	PHD 1991 UNIVERSITY OF CALIFORNIA, LOS ANGELES CORNELL, BRADFORD	ESSAYS ON THE RELATION BETWEEN THE ACCOUNTING SYSTEM AND THE CAPITAL MARKET	Financial Accounting Archival - Primary Risk 122
GOVINDARAJ, SURESH	PHD 1990 COLUMBIA UNIVERSITY	ESSAYS ON FINANCIAL MARKETS WITH APPLICATIONS TO ACCOUNTING	Financial Accounting Analytical - Internal Capital Markets 81
GRAFF, LOIS MARIE	PHD 1989 MASSEY UNIVERSITY (NEW ZEALAND)	COMPUTERIZED FINANCIAL PLANNING FOR SCHOOL DISTRICTS IN THE UNITED STATES	Not-for-Profit Budgeting 309
GRAHAM, LISE NEWMAN	PHD 1993 MICHIGAN STATE UNIVERSITY BUTLER, KIRT C.	THE MAGNITUDE AND TIMING OF ANALYST FORECAST RESPONSE TO QUARTERLY EARNINGS ANNOUNCEMENTS	Financial Accounting Archival - Primary Financial Analysts 158
GRAHAM, ROGER CHARLTON, JR.	PHD 1990 UNIVERSITY OF OREGON KING, RAYMOND D.	THE ASSOCIATION BETWEEN ORDER OF ANNOUNCEMENT AND SECURITY PRICE REACTIONS TO AN EARNINGS RELEASE	Financial Accounting Archival - Primary Earnings Announcements 139
GRAMLICH, JEFFREY DOUGLAS	PHD 1988 UNIVERSITY OF MISSOURI - COLUMBIA PARKER, JAMES E.	AN EMPIRICAL ANALYSIS OF THE EFFECT OF THE ALTERNATIVE MINIMUM TAX BOOK INCOME ADJUSTMENT ON THE EXTENT OF DISCRETIONARY ACCOUNTING ACCRUALS	Taxation Archival - Primary Earnings Management 209

Author	Degree & Date School Advisor	Title	Functional Area Research Method Topic pages
GRANGE, EDWARD VANCE, JR.	PHD 1987 THE UNIVERSITY OF TEXAS AT AUSTIN	AN EXAMINATION OF THE IMPACT OF SELECTED FEDERAL INCOME TAX CHANGES ON BIOTECHNOLOGY COMPANIES IN THE UNITED STATES	Taxation Survey Corporate Taxation 272
GRANT, CHARLES TERRELL	PHD 1992 THE FLORIDA STATE UNIVERSITY SCHAEFER, THOMAS F.	FINANCIAL DISTRESS PREDICTION WITH AN EXPANDED INFORMATION SET	Financial Accounting Archival - Primary Financial Distress or Bankruptcy 160
GRANT, JULIA ELIZABETH STUART	PHD 1989 CORNELL UNIVERSITY	NON-PENSION RETIREMENT BENEFITS	Financial Accounting Archival - Primary Post Retirement Benefit Issues 140
GRASSO, LAWRENCE PETER	DBA 1989 BOSTON UNIVERSITY MENON, KRISH	THE ORGANIZATIONAL DETERMINANTS OF THE USE OF INCENTIVES IN COMPENSATING BUSINESS UNIT MANAGERS	Cost/Managerial Survey Incentive Compensation 272
GRAVES, OLIVER FINLEY	PHD 1985 THE UNIVERSITY OF ALABAMA	ACCOUNTING FOR INFLATION: GERMAN THEORY OF THE 1920S	Financial Accounting Archival - Secondary Inflation 204
GREEN, BRIAN PATRICK	PHD 1991 KENT STATE UNIVERSITY BROWN, RICHARD	IDENTIFYING MANAGEMENT IRREGULARITIES THROUGH PRELIMINARY ANALYTICAL PROCEDURES	Auditing Archival - Primary Analytical Review 153
GREEN, SHARON L.	PHD 1989 UNIVERSITY OF PITTSBURGH	A BEHAVIORAL INVESTIGATION OF THE EFFECTS OF ALTERNATIVE GOVERNMENTAL FINANCIAL REPORTING FORMATS ON ANALYSTS' PREDICTIONS OF BOND RATINGS	Financial Accounting Experimental Presentation Format 334
GREENAWALT, MARY BRADY	PHD 1986 UNIVERSITY OF GEORGIA	AN EMPIRICAL INVESTIGATION OF THE ACCOUNTING ESTIMATES OF LOAN LOSSES IN THE BANKING INDUSTRY	Financial Accounting Archival - Primary Industry - Banking/Savings & Loan 123
GREENLEE, JANET STELLE	PHD 1993 UNIVERSITY OF KENTUCKY KNOBLETT, JAMES A.	THE USE OF ACCOUNTING AND OTHER INFORMATION IN DETERMINING THE ALLOCATION OF RESOURCES TO VOLUNTARY HEALTH AND WELFARE ORGANIZATIONS: AN EMPIRICAL ANALYSIS	Not-for-Profit Survey Charitable Organizations 156

Author	Degree & Date School Advisor	Title	Functional Area Research Method Topic pages
GREENSPAN, JAMES WILLIAM	PHD 1986 TEXAS A&M UNIVERSITY	DISTINGUISHING A PURCHASE FROM A POOLING THROUGH THE USE OF HOSTILE AND FRIENDLY TENDER OFFERS	General Archival - Primary Merger, Acquisition, Reorganization 96
GREENSTEIN, BRIAN RICHARD	PHD 1987 UNIVERSITY OF HOUSTON	AN EMPIRICAL ANALYSIS OF THE QUALIFIED TERMINABLE INTEREST PROPERTY ELECTION AND RELATED PROVISIONS	Taxation Archival - Secondary Estate & Gift Taxation 238
GREENSTEIN, MARILYN E. MAGEE	PHD 1991 TEMPLE UNIVERSITY SAMI, HEIBATOLLAH	AN EMPIRICAL INVESTIGATION OF THE EFFECTS OF SEGMENT REPORTING ON THE BID-ASK SPREAD AND VOLUME OF TRADE	Financial Accounting Archival - Primary Segment Reporting 227
GREENWOOD, THOMAS G.	PHD 1991 THE UNIVERSITY OF TENNESSEE KIRBY, KENNETH E.	AN ACTIVITY-BASED CONCEPTUAL MODEL FOR EVALUATING PROCESS COST INFORMATION	Cost/Managerial Analytical - Internal Activity Based Costing 552
GREGSON, TERRY	PHD 1987 UNIVERSITY OF ARKANSAS	AN EMPIRICAL INVESTIGATION OF THE RELATIONSHIP BETWEEN COMMUNICATION SATISFACTION, JOB SATISFACTION, TURNOVER, AND PERFORMANCE FOR PUBLIC ACCOUNTANTS	General Survey Job Performance, Satisfaction &/or Turnover 126
GREIG, ANTHONY CHARLTON	PHD 1992 THE UNIVERSITY OF ROCHESTER BALL, RAY	FUNDAMENTAL ANALYSIS AND SUBSEQUENT STOCK RETURNS	Financial Accounting Archival - Primary Financial Ratios 51
GRIBBIN, DONALD WAYNE	PHD 1989 OKLAHOMA STATE UNIVERSITY LAU, AMY	ANALYSIS OF THE DISTRIBUTION PROPERTIES OF COST VARIANCES AND THEIR EFFECTS ON THE COST VARIANCE INVESTIGATION DECISION	Cost/Managerial Simulation Standard Costs & Variance Analysis 113
GRIFFIN, LYNN DRAGER	PHD 1986 UNIVERSITY OF SOUTH CAROLINA	AN EXPECTANCY THEORY EXAMINATION OF MANAGERIAL MOTIVATION TO IMPLEMENT JUST-IN-TIME	Cost/Managerial Experimental Inventory 135
GRINER, EMMETT HAMILTON	PHD 1991 UNIVERSITY OF MARYLAND COLLEGE PARK GORDON, LAWRENCE	INSIDER OWNERSHIP AND THE LEVEL OF CAPITAL EXPENDITURES IN THE LARGE INDUSTRIAL FIRM: AN EMPIRICAL INVESTIGATION	Cost/Managerial Archival - Primary Incentive Compensation 201

Author	Degree & Date / School / Advisor	Title	Functional Area / Research Method / Topic / pages
GROSS, NORMA JEAN	PHD 1986 SAINT LOUIS UNIVERSITY	CASH FLOW CONCEPTS IN THE FINANCIAL PERFORMANCE EVALUATION OF FOREIGN SUBSIDIARY MANAGERS	Cost/Managerial Survey Management Control Systems 335
GRUBE, NANCY WEATHERHOLT	PHD 1988 UNIVERSITY OF KANSAS	EXAMINATION OF INITIATING DIVIDEND EFFECTS	Financial Accounting Archival - Primary Dividends 136
GRUBER, ROBERT ALLEN	PHD 1990 THE UNIVERSITY OF WISCONSIN - MADISON	AN EMPIRICAL INVESTIGATION INTO THE COGNITIVE LEVEL OF THE UNIFORM CPA EXAMINATION	General Case CPA &/or CMA Examination 509
GRUCA, STANLEY P.	DBA 1990 NOVA UNIVERSITY GAST, MICHAEL F.	ADVERTISING BY CPA FIRMS IN THE STATE OF ILLINOIS: AN ANALYSIS OF INCIDENCE, ATTITUDES, AND EFFICACY	General Survey CPA Firm Issues 235
GUENTHER, DAVID A.	PHD 1990 UNIVERSITY OF WASHINGTON KELLY, LAUREN	THE EFFECT OF INCOME TAXES ON THE FORM OF BUSINESS ENTITY	Taxation Archival - Primary Business Form 268
GUESS, AUNDREA KAY	PHD 1993 UNIVERSITY OF NORTH TEXAS KOCH, BRUCE	THE IMPACT OF AMBIGUITY AND RISK ON THE AUDITOR'S ASSESSMENT OF INHERENT RISK AND CONTROL RISK	Auditing Experimental Risk 159
GUFFEY, DARYL MAX	PHD 1989 UNIVERSITY OF SOUTH CAROLINA	BANKRUPTCY COSTS: ADDITIONAL EVIDENCE FROM THE TRANSPORTATION INDUSTRY	General Financial Distress or Bankruptcy 112
GUIDRY, FLORA GAIL	PHD 1992 THE UNIVERSITY OF ARIZONA MUTCHLER, J.	A TEST OF THE DETERMINANTS OF AUDITOR TENDENCY TO ISSUE GOING-CONCERN AUDIT REPORTS TO NONFAILING COMPANIES	Auditing Archival - Primary Financial Distress or Bankruptcy 121
GULLEDGE, DEXTER EUGENE	DBA 1991 MISSISSIPPI STATE UNIVERSITY HERRING, DORA	AN INVESTIGATION OF MARKET REACTION TO RELATIVE CHANGES IN REPORTED AMOUNTS FOR BUSINESS SEGMENTS UNDER FASB NO. 14: AN APPLICATION OF SHANNON'S ENTROPY MEASURE	Financial Accounting Archival - Primary Segment Reporting 371

Author	Degree & Date School Advisor	Title	Functional Area Research Method Topic pages
GULLEY, LAWRENCE	PHD 1986 TEXAS A&M UNIVERSITY	A DETERMINATION OF THE EFFECTS OF A CHANGE IN INFORMATION-PROCESSING CAUSED BY A CHANGE IN ACCOUNTING METHODS	Cost/Managerial Experimental Pricing 270
GUMENIK, ARTHUR JEFFREY	PHD 1993 VIRGINIA COMMONWEALTH UNIVERSITY OLDS, PHILIP R.	THE ASSOCIATION OF DISCRETIONARY CASH FLOW WITH SECURITY RETURNS	Financial Accounting Archival - Primary Cash Flows 138
GUNDERSON, ELIZABETH ANN WEISS	PHD 1991 THE UNION INSTITUTE	EXPERTISE IN SECURITY VALUATION: OPERATIONALIZING THE VALUATION PROCESS	Financial Accounting Experimental Financial Analysts 277
GUNDERSON, KONRAD ERIK	PHD 1992 THE UNIVERSITY OF NEBRASKA - LINCOLN BALKE, THOMAS E.	DISPERSION OF FINANCIAL ANALYSTS' EARNINGS FORECASTS AS A RISK MEASURE: ARGUMENT AND EVIDENCE	Financial Accounting Archival - Primary Financial Analysts 107
GUO, MIIN HONG	PHD 1989 THE UNIVERSITY OF ARIZONA DHALIWAL, DAN S.	DIFFERENTIAL EARNINGS RESPONSE COEFFICIENTS TO ACCOUNTING INFORMATION: THE CASE OF REVISIONS OF FINANCIAL ANALYSTS' FORECASTS	Financial Accounting Archival - Primary Earnings Response Coefficients 97
GUPTA, MAHENDRA R.	PHD 1990 STANFORD UNIVERSITY FOSTER, GEORGE	AGGREGATION ISSUES IN PRODUCT COSTING	Cost/Managerial Case Cost Allocation 202
GUPTA, MANOJ	PHD 1990 UNIVERSITY OF ILLINOIS AT URBANA-CHAMPAIGN FINNERTY, J.	THE CURRENCY RISK FACTOR IN INTERNATIONAL EQUITY PRICING	Financial Accounting Archival - Primary International/Global Issues 100
GUPTA, PARVEEN PARKASH	PHD 1987 THE PENNSYLVANIA STATE UNIVERSITY	THE AUDIT PROCESS AS A FUNCTION OF DIFFERENTIATED ENVIRONMENT: AN EMPIRICAL STUDY	Auditing Survey Audit Planning 339
GUPTA, RAMESHWAR DASS	PHD 1985 UNIVERSITY OF ARKANSAS	AN INQUIRY INTO THE ACCOUNTING PRINCIPLES AND REPORTING PRACTICES FOLLOWED BY SELECTED STATE UNIVERSITY HOSPITALS	Not-for-Profit Case Industry - Health Care 333

Author	Degree & Date School Advisor	Title	Functional Area Research Method Topic pages
GUPTA, SANJAY	PHD 1990 MICHIGAN STATE UNIVERSITY	DETERMINANTS OF THE CHOICE BETWEEN COMPREHENSIVE AND PARTIAL INCOME TAX ALLOCATION: THE CASE OF THE DOMESTIC INTERNATIONAL SALES CORPORATION	Financial Accounting Archival - Primary Accounting Choice
			220
GUPTA, SANTOSH PRABHA	PHD 1993 DREXEL UNIVERSITY CHAKRABARTI, ALOK K.	R&D INTENSITY, SIZE, RELATEDNESS, TAKEOVER PROCESS AND POST-MERGER CHANGE IN R&D	Financial Accounting Archival - Primary Research & Development
			154
GURGANUS, FRANKIE EDWARDS	PHD 1991 VIRGINIA COMMONWEALTH UNIVERSITY EVERETT, JOHN O.	A STUDY OF THE UTILITY OF REPORTING POSTRETIREMENT HEALTH CARE BENEFITS	Financial Accounting Experimental Post Retirement Benefit Issues
			155
GURKA, GEOFFREY J.	PHD 1992 MICHIGAN STATE UNIVERSITY OUTSLAY, EDMUND	THE ROLE OF NEUTRALIZATION STRATEGIES IN THE TRADEOFF BETWEEN PRACTITIONER RESPONSIBILITIES	Taxation Analytical - Internal Tax Professionals
			133
GUSTAFSON, LYAL VAL	PHD 1989 GEORGIA STATE UNIVERSITY - COLLEGE OF BUSINESS ADMINISTRATION HERMANSON, ROGER H.	AN EMPIRICAL INVESTIGATION OF THE USEFULNESS OF MANAGEMENT EARNINGS FORECASTS AS EVIDENCED BY THEIR EFFECT ON ANALYSTS' PREDICTIONS	Financial Accounting Archival - Primary Voluntary Management Disclosures
			171
GUTIERREZ, THERESA KAY	PHD 1992 UNIVERSITY OF NORTH TEXAS MICHAELSEN, ROBERT	THE EFFECTS OF INTERACTIONS WITH IRS EMPLOYEES ON TAX PRACTITIONERS' ATTITUDES TOWARD THE IRS	Taxation Survey Tax Professionals
			153
HA, GOOKLAK	PHD 1993 PURDUE UNIVERSITY RO, BYUNG T.	THE INFORMATION CONTENT OF AUDITOR SWITCHES	Auditor Changes
			84
HABEGGER, JERRELL WAYNE	PHD 1988 VIRGINIA POLYTECHNIC INSTITUTE AND STATE UNIVERSITY BEAMS, FLOYD A.	AN INTERNAL AUDITING INNOVATION DECISION: STATISTICAL SAMPLING	Auditing Survey Internal Auditing
			235
HACKENBRACK, KARL EDWARD	PHD 1988 THE OHIO STATE UNIVERSITY BAILEY, ANDREW	ASSESSING A COMPANY'S EXPOSURE TO FRAUDULENT FINANCIAL REPORTING: IMPLICATIONS OF SEEMINGLY IRRELEVANT EVIDENCE	Auditing Experimental Fraud
			168

Author	Degree & Date School Advisor	Title	Functional Area Research Method Topic pages
HADDAD, AMIN MOHAMMED	DBA 1989 SOUTHERN ILLINOIS UNIVERSITY AT CARBONDALE WELKER, ROBERT B.	THE MARKET REACTION TO FOREIGN CURRENCY TRANSLATION POLICY-SETTING PROCESS: A NEW APPROACH	Financial Accounting Archival - Primary Foreign Currency Translation 88
HAGAN, JOSEPH MARTIN	PHD 1990 GEORGIA STATE UNIVERSITY - COLLEGE OF BUSINESS ADMINISTRATION LARKINS, ERNEST R.	AN EMPIRICAL STUDY OF THE EFFECT OF THE TAX REFORM ACT OF 1986 ON ECONOMIC EFFICIENCY AS MEASURED BY AVERAGE EFFECTIVE TAX RATES	Taxation Archival - Primary Public Policy 236
HALL, BETHANE JO PIERCE	PHD 1987 UNIVERSITY OF NORTH TEXAS	AN ANALYSIS OF THE EQUITY AND REVENUE EFFECTS OF THE ELIMINATION OR REDUCTION OF HOMEOWNER PREFERENCES	Taxation Archival - Primary Individual Taxation 291
HALL, SHEILA HUNTLEY	PHD 1991 UNIVERSITY OF SOUTH CAROLINA HARRELL, ADRIAN	AN EXPERIMENTAL INVESTIGATION OF FINANCIAL STATEMENT USERS' SELF-INSIGHT IN REPORTING DECISION-MAKING PROCESSES	General Experimental Judgment & Decision Making - Heuristics & Biases 72
HALL, STEVEN C.	PHD 1990 THE UNIVERSITY OF UTAH LOEBBECKE, JAMES K.	ECONOMIC MOTIVATIONS FOR ACCOUNTING STRATEGY CHOICES	Financial Accounting Archival - Primary Accounting Choice 209
HAM, CHANGYONG	PHD 1988 UNIVERSITY OF CALIFORNIA, BERKELEY SEN, PRADYOT K.	ESSAYS ON VALUE OF INFORMATION, COMMUNICATION, AND DELEGATION IN PRINCIPAL AND AGENT RELATIONSHIPS	Cost/Managerial Analytical - Internal Agency Theory 188
HAMBY, WILLIAM LYLE, JR.	PHD 1992 THE UNIVERSITY OF ALABAMA MASON, JOHN O. JR.; LEITCH, ROBERT A.	AN INVESTIGATION OF INTERNAL ACCOUNTING CONTROL IN MICROCOMPUTER-BASED SMALL BUSINESS ACCOUNTING SYSTEMS	Information Systems Survey Small Business 177
HAMDALLAH, AHMED EL-SAYED	PHD 1985 CITY UNIVERSITY OF NEW YORK	AN INVESTIGATION OF MOTIVATION FOR VOLUNTARILY TERMINATING OVERFUNDED PENSION PLANS	Financial Accounting Archival - Primary Post Retirement Benefit Issues 123
HAMILL, JAMES ROBERT	PHD 1987 ARIZONA STATE UNIVERSITY	AN EXPERIMENTAL ANALYSIS OF THE IMPACT OF INCOME TAXES ON NOMINAL INTEREST RATES	Taxation Experimental Taxes 187

Listing by Author

Author	Degree & Date School Advisor	Title	Functional Area Research Method Topic pages
HAMILTON, CHARLES THOMAS	PHD 1987 UNIVERSITY OF ILLINOIS AT URBANA-CHAMPAIGN	INDIVIDUAL JUDGMENT IN ANALYTICAL REVIEW PERFORMANCE	Auditing Experimental Judgment & Decision Making 234
HAMMER, SETH	PHD 1993 UNIVERSITY OF PITTSBURGH BIRNBERG, JACOB	THE CPA'S ROLE AS RISK ADVISER	Taxation Survey Tax Compliance 166
HAMMOND, JOSEPH ANDREW	DBA 1994 UNITED STATES INTERNATIONAL UNIVERSITY KHALIL, MOHAMED A.	RISK EXPOSURE AND MANAGEMENT PRACTICES IN RESPONSE TO FLOATING EXCHANGE RATE VOLATILITY IN GHANA	General Survey International/Global Issues 422
HAMMOND, THERESA ANNE	PHD 1990 THE UNIVERSITY OF WISCONSIN - MADISON COVALESKI, MARK	THE MINORITY RECRUITMENT EFFORTS OF THE MAJOR PUBLIC ACCOUNTING FIRMS IN NEW YORK: A SOCIOLOGICAL ANALYSIS	General Survey Accounting Career Issues 249
HAN, BONG-HEUI	PHD 1991 THE UNIVERSITY OF TEXAS AT AUSTIN JENNINGS, ROSS	DISPERSION IN FINANCIAL ANALYSTS' EARNINGS FORECASTS: IMPLICATIONS ON RISK AND EARNINGS	Financial Accounting Archival - Primary Financial Analysts 115
HAN, CHI-YING	PHD 1986 STATE UNIVERSITY OF NEW YORK AT BUFFALO	MANAGEMENT FORECASTS: INCENTIVES AND EFFECTS	Financial Accounting Archival - Primary Voluntary Management Disclosures 249
HAN, INGOO	PHD 1990 UNIVERSITY OF ILLINOIS AT URBANA-CHAMPAIGN CHANDLER, JOHN	THE IMPACT OF MEASUREMENT SCALE ON CLASSIFICATION PERFORMANCE OF INDUCTIVE LEARNING AND STATISTICAL APPROACHES	General Simulation Methodology 185
HAN, JIN-SOO	PHD 1986 INDIANA UNIVERSITY	INTERNAL CONTROL EVALUATION AND AUDIT PROGRAM PLANNING JUDGMENTS BY INDIVIDUAL AUDITORS AND AUDIT TEAMS: A STUDY OF SOUTH KOREAN CPA'S	Auditing Experimental International/Global Issues 190
HAN, KI CHOONG	PHD 1990 MICHIGAN STATE UNIVERSITY BUTLER, KIRT C.	MARKET RESPONSE TO EARNINGS ANNOUNCEMENTS: THE EFFECTS OF FIRM CHARACTERISTICS	Financial Accounting Archival - Primary Earnings Announcements 154

Author	Degree & Date School Advisor	Title	Functional Area Research Method Topic pages
HAN, KYEONG SEOK	PHD 1989 PURDUE UNIVERSITY WHINSTON, ANDREW B.	A FORMAL ALGORITHMIC MODEL COMPATIBLE WITH ACCOUNTING INFORMATION SYSTEMS	Information Systems Analytical - Internal Systems Design &/or Development 220
HAN, MAN-HO	PHD 1992 GEORGIA STATE UNIVERSITY SRIVASTAVA, ALOK	A KNOWLEDGE-BASED DECISION SUPPORT SYSTEM (KBDSS) FOR CORPORATE PORTFOLIO ANALYSIS: AN INTEGRATIVE MODEL APPROACH	Information systems Analytical - Internal Decision Support Systems 201
HANDLANG, ALICE MAY	DBA 1991 UNIVERSITY OF KENTUCKY KNOBLETT, JAMES A.	A CRITICAL ANALYSIS OF RESPONSES TO SELECTED FINANCIAL ACCOUNTING STANDARDS BOARD EXPOSURE DRAFTS TO DETERMINE THE IMPORTANT FACTORS RELEVANT TO ITS CONSTITUENCY	Financial Accounting Case Standard Setting 242
HANNA, JOHN DOUGLAS	PHD 1991 CORNELL UNIVERSITY DYCKMAN, THOMAS R.	A FURTHER EXAMINATION OF THE INCREMENTAL INFORMATION CONTENT OF CASH-FLOW ANNOUNCEMENTS	Financial Accounting Archival - Primary Cash Flows 130
HANNO, DENNIS MICHAEL	PHD 1990 UNIVERSITY OF MASSACHUSETTS KIDA, THOMAS	THE USE OF INFORMATION IN THE SEQUENTIAL EVALUATION OF AUDIT EVIDENCE	Auditing Experimental Judgment & Decision Making - Heuristics & Biases 192
HANSEN, JAMES DAVID	PHD 1993 THE UNIVERSITY OF NEBRASKA - LINCOLN HUBBARD, THOMAS D.	THE EFFECT OF INFORMATION LOAD AND COGNITIVE STYLE ON DECISION QUALITY IN A FINANCIAL DISTRESS DECISION TASK	Auditing Experimental Judgment & Decision Making - Cognitive Processes 148
HARGADON, JOSEPH MICHAEL	PHD 1993 DREXEL UNIVERSITY NDUBIZU, GORDIAN	ADOPTION CHOICE OF MANDATED ACCOUNTING CHANGES: A JOINT DECISION APPROACH	Financial Accounting Archival - Primary Accounting Choice 127
HARPER, RICHARD ROBERT	PHD 1989 UNIVERSITY OF MANCHESTER (UNITED KINGDOM)	AN ETHNOGRAPHIC EXAMINATION OF ACCOUNTANCY	General Analytical - Internal Accounting in Society 213
HARRINGTON, ROBERT PICKENS	PHD 1985 VIRGINIA POLYTECHNIC INSTITUTE AND STATE UNIVERSITY	FORECASTING CORPORATE PERFORMANCE	Financial Accounting Experimental Forecasting Financial Performance 259

Author	Degree & Date School Advisor	Title	Functional Area Research Method Topic pages
HARRIS, CAROLYN REBECCA	PHD 1989 THE UNIVERSITY OF TEXAS AT ARLINGTON SCHKADE, LAWRENCE L.	AN EXPERT DECISION SUPPORT SYSTEM FOR AUDITOR GOING CONCERN EVALUATION	Information Systems Decision Support Systems 282
HARRIS, DAVID GARLAND	PHD 1994 THE UNIVERSITY OF MICHIGAN BERNARD, VICTOR; SLEMROD, JOEL	THE IMPACT OF UNITED STATES TAX LAW REVISION ON MULTINATIONAL CORPORATIONS' CAPITAL LOCATION AND INCOME SHIFTING DECISIONS	Taxation Archival - Primary International/Global Issues 85
HARRIS, ELLEN KAY	PHD 1991 THE UNIVERSITY OF UTAH FAERBER, LEROY G.	FACTORS THAT INFLUENCE PRODUCT COSTING INFORMATION SYSTEM CHANGES	Information Systems Case Systems Design &/or Development 271
HARRIS, JEANNIE E.	PHD 1990 VIRGINIA POLYTECHNIC INSTITUTE AND STATE UNIVERSITY HICKS, SAM A.	TAX EXPENDITURES: REPORT UTILIZATION BY STATE POLICY MAKERS	Taxation Case State Taxation 309
HARRIS, JUDITH ANN BERMAN	DBA 1988 BOSTON UNIVERSITY NANNI, ALFRED J.	A FIELD STUDY EXAMINING THE STRUCTURE AND SUBSTANCE OF COST ACCOUNTING SYSTEMS	Cost/Managerial Survey Cost Systems 241
HARRIS, MARY ALICE STANFORD	PHD 1994 THE UNIVERSITY OF MICHIGAN BERNARD, VICTOR	THE IMPACT OF COMPETITION ON MANAGER'S REPORTING POLICIES FOR BUSINESS SEGMENTS	Financial Accounting Archival - Primary Segment Reporting 120
HARRIS, THOMAS DONALD	PHD 1989 UNIVERSITY OF SOUTH CAROLINA WHITE, RICHARD	THE EFFECT OF TYPE OF TAX KNOWLEDGE ON INDIVIDUALS' PERCEPTIONS OF FAIRNESS AND COMPLIANCE WITH THE FEDERAL INCOME TAX SYSTEM: AN EMPIRICAL STUDY	Taxation Survey Tax Compliance 144
HARRISON, PATRICIA MACKEL	PHD 1991 UNIVERSITY OF NEW ORLEANS	INVESTMENT, ENTRY, AND PERFORMANCE OF SAVINGS AND LOAN ASSOCIATIONS IN THE 1980S	Financial Accounting Archival - Primary Industry - Banking/Savings & Loan 247
HARSH, MARY FRANCES	PHD 1993 VIRGINIA POLYTECHNIC INSTITUTE AND STATE UNIVERSITY KILLOUGH, LARRY N.	THE IMPACT OF ACTIVITY-BASED COSTING ON MANAGERIAL DECISIONS: AN EMPIRICAL ANALYSIS	Cost/Managerial Experimental Activity Based Costing 255

Listing by Author

Author	Degree & Date School Advisor	Title	Functional Area Research Method Topic pages
HARSTON, MARY ELIZABETH	PHD 1991 UNIVERSITY OF NORTH TEXAS MERINO, BARBARA D.	A COMPARISON OF THE EVOLUTION OF ACCOUNTING INSTITUTIONS IN GERMANY AND THE UNITED STATES	General Analytical - Internal History 316
HARTER, CHARLES IVES	PHD 1991 THE UNIVERSITY OF NEBRASKA - LINCOLN RAYMOND, ROBERT H.	AN ANALYSIS OF THE EFFECT OF DISCRETIONARY CASH ON THE EARNINGS RESPONSE COEFFICIENT	Financial Accounting Archival - Primary Cash Flows 118
HARTWELL, CAROLYN L.	PHD 1992 UNIVERSITY OF CINCINNATI BURNS, DAVID C.	THE EFFECT OF PRIOR YEAR'S AUDIT INFORMATION AND PERFORMANCE FEEDBACK ON STAFF AUDITORS' PERFORMANCE	Auditing Experimental Job Performance, Satisfaction &/or Turnover 284
HARVEY, PATRICK JAMES	PHD 1994 UNIVERSITY OF SOUTHERN CALIFORNIA SWENSON, CHARLES W.	ENHANCING TAX BENEFITS VIA PURCHASE OF LEGISLATIVE AUTHORITY: AN EXPERIMENTAL APPROACH	Taxation Experimental Public Policy
HARWOOD, ELAINE MARIE	PHD 1993 UNIVERSITY OF SOUTHERN CALIFORNIA MANEGOLD, JAMES G.	ADOPTION OF REGULATORY ACCOUNTING PRINCIPLES BY STOCKHELD SAVINGS AND LOAN ASSOCIATIONS: AN EVENT STUDY OF DISCRETIONARY ACCOUNTING CHOICE	Financial Accounting Archival - Primary Accounting Choice
HASLAM, JIM	PHD 1991 UNIVERSITY OF ESSEX (UNITED KINGDOM)	ON THE PRESCRIBING OF ACCOUNTING AND ACCOUNTING PUBLICITY BY THE STATE IN EARLY TO MID-NINETEENTH CENTURY BRITAIN: ACCOUNTING HISTORY AS CRITIQUE	General Analytical - Internal History 486
HAWKINS, KYLEEN WHITEHEAD	DBA 1992 LOUISIANA TECH UNIVERSITY BYINGTON, J. RALPH	AN EMPIRICAL ANALYSIS OF FACTORS USED BY COURTS WHEN DECIDING MOTIONS TO DISMISS RULE 10B-5 LITIGATION AGAINST ACCOUNTANTS	Financial Accounting Case Legal Liability 130
HAYES, ROBERT D.	PHD 1987 UNIVERSITY OF ARKANSAS	THE CONSTANT - INPUT - PROPORTION ASSUMPTION IN THE BUDGETARY PROCESS	Cost/Managerial Case Budgeting 126
HAYN, CARLA K.	PHD 1987 THE UNIVERSITY OF MICHIGAN	THE ROLE OF TAX ATTRIBUTES IN CORPORATE ACQUISITIONS	Taxation Archival - Primary Merger, Acquisition, Reorganization 176

Author	Degree & Date School Advisor	Title	Functional Area Research Method Topic pages
HAYNES, CHRISTINE MILLER	PHD 1993 THE UNIVERSITY OF TEXAS AT AUSTIN KACHELMEIER, STEVEN J.	AN EXAMINATION INTO THE EFFECTS OF CONTEXT AND EXPERIENCE ON AUDITORS' BELIEF REVISIONS IN CASCADED-INFERENCE TASKS	Auditing Experimental Judgment & Decision Making - Heuristics & Biases 193
HAZERA, ALEJANDRO	DBA 1989 UNIVERSITY OF KENTUCKY TIPGOS, MANUEL A.	A NORMATIVE MODEL FOR ASSESSING THE COMPETENCE OF EVIDENTIAL MATTER IN AUDITING	Auditing Archival - Primary Audit Quality 341
HE, XIAOHONG	PHD 1991 THE UNIVERSITY OF TEXAS AT DALLAS GUISINGER, STEPHEN E.	INTERNATIONAL TAX TRENDS AND COMPETITION: TAX SENSITIVITY OF U.S. FOREIGN INVESTMENT ABROAD	Taxation Archival - Primary International/Global Issues 138
HE, XIN XIN	PHD 1991 THE PENNSYLVANIA STATE UNIVERSITY HAYYA, JACK C.; ORDER, J. KEITH; XU, SUSAN H.	STOCHASTIC INVENTORY SYSTEMS WITH ORDER CROSSOVER	Information Systems Simulation Inventory 148
HEAGY, CYNTHIA DONNELL	DBA 1987 MEMPHIS STATE UNIVERSITY	A NATIONAL STUDY AND EMPIRICAL INVESTIGATION OF THE ACCOUNTING SYSTEMS COURSE: ACADEMIC PRACTICE VERSUS PROFESSIONAL NEEDS	Education Survey Curriculum Issues 394
HEBBLE, ANNETTE	PHD 1989 UNIVERSITY OF HOUSTON PRATT, JAMES W.	THE EFFECT OF ALTERNATIVE SYSTEMS OF TAXATION ON INDIVIDUAL SAVINGS: AN EXPERIMENTAL APPROACH	Taxation Experimental Individual Taxation 120
HEBERT, MARCEL G.	PHD 1987 TEXAS TECH UNIVERSITY FREEMAN, ROBERT J.	AN INVESTIGATION OF THE EFFECT OF ALTERNATIVE PRESENTATION FORMATS ON PREPARERS AND USERS OF CITY FINANCIAL REPORTS	Not-for-Profit Survey Governmental 325
HEFLIN, FRANK LEE	PHD 1992 PURDUE UNIVERSITY KROSS, WILLIAM	SECURITIES MARKET RESPONSE TO LEGISLATED CHANGES IN THE PENSION PLAN REVERSION EXCISE TAX	Taxation Archival - Primary Post Retirement Benefit Issues 199
HEFZI, HASSAN	PHD 1988 ARIZONA STATE UNIVERSITY	ECONOMIC INCENTIVES OF MANAGEMENT FOR INSUBSTANCE DEFEASANCE OF DEBT: AN EMPIRICAL INVESTIGATION	Financial Accounting Analytical - Internal Long Term Debt 112

Author	Degree & Date School Advisor	Title	Functional Area Research Method Topic pages
HEIAN, JAMES BERNARD	PHD 1985 THE UNIVERSITY OF UTAH	A STUDY OF THE DETERMINANTS OF SENIOR CERTIFIED PUBLIC ACCOUNTANT LEADERSHIP EFFECTIVENESS	General Case Accounting Career Issues 338
HEIER, JAN RICHARD	DBA 1986 MISSISSIPPI STATE UNIVERSITY	A QUANTITATIVE STUDY OF ACCOUNTING METHODS AND USAGE IN MID - NINETEENTH-CENTURY ALABAMA AND MISSISSIPPI	General Archival - Secondary History 193
HEIMAN, VICKY BETH	PHD 1988 THE UNIVERSITY OF MICHIGAN LIBBY, ROBERT	AUDITORS' ASSESSMENTS OF THE LIKELIHOOD OF ANALYTICAL REVIEW EXPLANATIONS	Auditing Experimental Judgment & Decision Making - Cognitive Processes 117
HELLELOID, RICHARD TRYGVE	PHD 1985 UNIVERSITY OF MINNESOTA	HINDSIGHT BIAS AND JUDGMENTS BY TAX PROFESSIONALS	Taxation Experimental Judgment & Decision Making - Heuristics & Biases 218
HENNING, STEVEN LYLE	PHD 1994 THE UNIVERSITY OF WISCONSIN - MADISON WARFIELD, TERRY D.	ACCOUNTING FOR GOODWILL: CURRENT PRACTICES, VARIATION IN SOURCE AND COMPONENTS, AND MARKET VALUATION	Financial Accounting Archival - Primary Other 125
HENRY, LAURIE JANE	PHD 1993 THE UNIVERSITY OF MISSISSIPPI GRAVES, O. FINLEY	A PERSISTENCE-PERFORMANCE MODEL: AN OPERATIONAL MODEL TO ASSIST IN PREDICTING AN INDIVIDUAL'S FUTURE SUCCESS IN ACCOUNTING	General Survey Job Performance, Satisfaction &/or Turnover 406
HERMANSON, DANA ROGER	PHD 1993 THE UNIVERSITY OF WISCONSIN - MADISON RITTENBERG, LARRY E.	THE ASSOCIATION BETWEEN AUDIT FIRM CHARACTERISTICS AND THE AUDITOR'S PROPENSITY TO QUALIFY BANKRUPTCY-RELATED OPINIONS	Auditing Archival - Primary Financial Distress or Bankruptcy 118
HERMANSON, HEATHER MARIE	PHD 1993 THE UNIVERSITY OF WISCONSIN - MADISON RITTENBERG, LARRY E.	THE IMPACT OF CONTROL RISK AND BUSINESS RISK ON SAMPLE EVIDENCE EVALUATION	Auditing Experimental Audit Sampling 146
HERREMANS, IRENE M.	PHD 1989 KENT STATE UNIVERSITY PEARSON, MICHAEL	AN INVESTIGATION OF THE TRIADIC RELATIONSHIP OF SOCIAL PERFORMANCE, SOCIAL DISCLOSURE, AND ECONOMIC PERFORMANCE	Financial Accounting Archival - Primary Social/Environmental Responsibility 645

Author	Degree & Date School Advisor	Title	Functional Area Research Method Topic pages
HERRING, CLYDE EDSEL	PHD 1988 THE UNIVERSITY OF ALABAMA INGRAM, ROBERT W.	AN EMPIRICAL ANALYSIS OF THE SELECTION OF FINANCIAL ACCOUNTING PRACTICES BY COLLEGES AND UNIVERSITIES	Not-for-Profit College & University 174
HERZ, PAUL JOSEPH	PHD 1994 THE UNIVERSITY OF UTAH	AN INVESTIGATION OF PROCEDURAL MEMORY AS AN INGREDIENT OF TASK PERFORMANCE IN ACCOUNTING	General Experimental Judgment & Decision Making - Cognitive Processes 205
HESLOP, GORDON B.	DBA 1986 MISSISSIPPI STATE UNIVERSITY	AN ANALYSIS OF THE TAXATION TREATMENT UNDER SECTION 280A OF THE INTERNAL REVENUE CODE OF 1954 OF EXPENSES INCURRED IN CONNECTION WITH THE BUSINESS USE OF A DWELLING UNIT	Taxation Archival - Secondary Individual Taxation 210
HETHCOX, KATHLEEN BLACKBURN	PHD 1993 THE UNIVERSITY OF OKLAHOMA AYRES, FRANCES L.	BUSINESS COMBINATIONS ACCOUNTED FOR BY THE PURCHASE METHOD: AN EMPIRICAL ANALYSIS OF THE MAGNITUDE OF GOODWILL AND ACQUIRING FIRMS' STOCK RETURNS	Financial Accounting Archival - Primary Merger, Acquisition, Reorganization 146
HIGGINS, MARK MATTHEW	PHD 1989 THE UNIVERSITY OF TENNESSEE IZARD, C. DOUGLASS	AN EMPIRICAL ANALYSIS OF THE RELATIONSHIP BETWEEN CORPORATE EFFECTIVE TAX RATES AND BOOK EFFECTIVE TAX RATES WITH AN ANALYSIS OF THE FINANCIAL CHARACTERISTICS THAT INFLUENCE CORPORATE EFFECTIVE TAX RATES	Taxation Archival - Primary Corporate Taxation 257
HIGHSMITH, GWENDOLYN JANNETT	PHD 1988 UNIVERSITY OF HOUSTON BOOCKHOLDT, JAMES	AN EMPIRICAL INVESTIGATION OF THE PERFORMANCE OF THE EDP QUALITY ASSURANCE FUNCTION ON THE INDEPENDENT AUDITOR'S EVALUATION OF INTERNAL CONTROL	Auditing Experimental Internal Control 341
HIGSON, ANDREW WILLIAM	PHD 1987 UNIVERSITY OF BRADFORD (UNITED KINGDOM)	AN EMPIRICAL INVESTIGATION OF THE EXTERNAL AUDIT PROCESS: A STUDY OF THE REACTION OF PROFESSIONAL AUDITORS TO RECENT CHANGES IN THE AUDIT ENVIRONMENT	Auditing International/Global Issues 431
HILL, JOHN WARREN	PHD 1986 THE UNIVERSITY OF IOWA	THE ECONOMIC CONSEQUENCES OF ACCOUNTING CHOICE: DEFERRAL OF LOAN SALE LOSSES IN THE SAVINGS AND LOAN INDUSTRY	General Archival - Primary Industry - Banking/Savings & Loan 158
HILL, MARY CALLAHAN	PHD 1993 UNIVERSITY OF GEORGIA BAMBER, E. MICHAEL	THE AVAILABILITY AND USE OF FEEDBACK IN AUDIT PLANNING	Auditing Experimental Audit Planning 149

Author	Degree & Date School Advisor	Title	Functional Area Research Method Topic pages
HILL, NANCY THORLEY	PHD 1990 THE UNIVERSITY OF WISCONSIN - MADISON FRANK, WERNER G.	THE ADOPTION OF COSTING SYSTEMS IN THE HOSPITAL INDUSTRY	Cost/Managerial Survey Industry - Health Care 240
HILLEBRAND, ANDREAS WILHELM	DRSOCOEC 1990 UNIVERSITAET INNSBRUCK (AUSTRIA)	A CONCEPT FOR A PERSONAL-COMPUTER-AIDED FINANCIAL STATEMENT ANALYSIS WITH REGARD TO THE GERMAN ACCOUNTING DIRECTIVES LAW [ENTWICKLUNG EINES KONZEPTS ZUR PERSONAL-COMPUTER-GESTUETZTEN ANALYSE PUBLIZIERTER JAHRESABSCHLUESSE UNTER BERUECKSICHTIGUNG DER RECHNUNGSLEGUNGSAENDERUNGEN DURCH	Financial Accounting Analytical - Internal International/global Issues 411
HILTEBEITEL, KENNETH MERRILL	PHD 1985 DREXEL UNIVERSITY	THE ACCOUNTING STANDARDS OVERLOAD ISSUE: AN EMPIRICAL TEST OF THE EFFECT OF FOUR SELECTED FINANCIAL ACCOUNTING STANDARDS ON THE LENDING DECISIONS OF BANKERS	Financial Accounting Experimental Bank Loan Officers 262
HINDI, NITHAM MOHD	DBA 1991 MISSISSIPPI STATE UNIVERSITY HERRING, DORA	AN EMPIRICAL INVESTIGATION INTO THE IMPACT OF OFF-BALANCE SHEET ACTIVITIES ON THE RISKINESS OF COMMERCIAL BANKS: A MARKET-BASED ANALYSIS	Financial Accounting Archival - Primary Industry - Banking/Savings & Loan 253
HIRST, DAVID ERIC	PHD 1992 UNIVERSITY OF MINNESOTA JOYCE, EDWARD J.	AUDITORS' SENSITIVITY TO FACTORS AFFECTING THE RELIABILITY OF EVIDENCE SOURCES IN BELIEF REVISION	Auditing Experimental Judgment & Decision Making - Heuristics & Biases 215
HITE, PEGGY SULLIVAN	PHD 1986 UNIVERSITY OF COLORADO AT BOULDER	AN EXPERIMENTAL INVESTIGATION OF TWO POSSIBLE EXPLANATIONS FOR TAXPAYER NONCOMPLIANCE: TAX SHELTERS AND NONCOMPLIANT PEERS	Taxation Experimental Tax Compliance 111
HITZIG, NEAL B.	PHD 1985 CITY UNIVERSITY OF NEW YORK	SUBSTANTIVE AUDIT TESTS OF DETAILS AND THE ESTIMATION OF RARE ERRORS BY DOUBLE SAMPLING WITH PROBABILITY PROPORTIONAL TO SIZE	Auditing Experimental Audit Sampling 119
HO, JOANNA LEE-YUN	PHD 1986 THE UNIVERSITY OF TEXAS AT AUSTIN	CONJUNCTION FALLACY IN AUDITORS' PROBABILITY JUDGMENT PROCESSES	Auditing Experimental Analytical Review 167
HO, LI-CHIN	PHD 1990 THE UNIVERSITY OF TEXAS AT AUSTIN MAY, ROBERT G.	THE EFFECTS OF OPTION TRADING ON THE INFORMATION CONTENT OF EARNINGS DISCLOSURES: AN EMPIRICAL ANALYSIS	Financial Accounting Archival - Primary Earnings Announcements 157

Author	Degree & Date School Advisor	Title	Functional Area Research Method Topic pages
HO, SHIH-JEN KATHY	PHD 1988 SYRACUSE UNIVERSITY	THE USEFULNESS OF CASH FLOWS RELATIVE TO ACCRUAL EARNINGS: A SECURITY VALUATION STUDY	Financial Accounting Archival - Primary Cash Flows 158
HODGE, THOMAS GLEN	PHD 1991 THE UNIVERSITY OF MISSISSIPPI FLESHER, DALE L.	THE EMPIRICAL DEVELOPMENT OF ETHICS DECISION MODELS FOR MANAGEMENT ACCOUNTANTS	General Survey Ethics 399
HOFFMANS, SHARRON RAE DYE	PHD 1991 OKLAHOMA STATE UNIVERSITY KIMBRELL, JANET	THE CHANGE FROM FINANCIAL ACCOUNTING STANDARD NO. 8 TO FINANCIAL ACCOUNTING STANDARD NO. 52 AND MANAGEMENT FINANCING DECISIONS	Financial Accounting Archival - Primary Foreign Currency Translation 79
HOGAN, THOMAS JEFFERY	PHD 1985 UNIVERSITY OF MASSACHUSETTS	MANAGEMENT DECISIONS REGARDING CHOICES OF ACCOUNTING METHODS AND SUBMISSIONS TO THE FASB: AN EMPIRICAL STUDY OF FIRM CHARACTERISTICS	Financial Accounting Archival - Primary Accounting Choice 350
HOLLANDER, ANITA SAWYER	PHD 1987 THE UNIVERSITY OF TENNESSEE SCHEINER, JAMES H.	A RULE-BASED APPROACH TO VARIANCE ANALYSIS	Cost/Managerial Standard Costs & Variance Analysis 254
HOLLEY, JOYCE MARIE HIGGINS	PHD 1986 UNIVERSITY OF HOUSTON	AN INVESTIGATION OF INTERNAL INTERIM REPORTING BY MUNICIPALITIES	Not-for-Profit Archival - Primary Governmental 246
HOLLINGSWORTH, DANNY P.	DBA 1988 MEMPHIS STATE UNIVERSITY SPICELAND, J. DAVID	AN EMPIRICAL INVESTIGATION INTO THE CHANGE IN TAX EQUITY WITHIN THE FINANCIAL SERVICES INDUSTRY AS A RESULT OF THE 1986 TAX REFORM ACT	Taxation Archival - Primary Industry - Banking/Savings & Loan 169
HOLMES, RICHARD LAWRENCE	PHD 1993 THE UNIVERSITY OF NORTH CAROLINA AT CHAPEL HILL ZELMAN, WILLIAM N.	ON THE DETERMINATION AND REIMBURSEMENT OF COSTS IN THE PROVISION OF MEDICAID SERVICES BY LOCAL HEALTH DEPARTMENTS	General Case Industry - Health Care 792
HOLT, PAUL EDWIN	PHD 1992 OKLAHOMA STATE UNIVERSITY PATZ, DENNIS H.	A COMPARATIVE EXAMINATION OF THE EARNINGS EFFECTS OF ALTERNATIVE TRANSLATION METHODS	Financial Accounting Archival - Primary Foreign Currency Translation 192

Author	Degree & Date School Advisor	Title	Functional Area Research Method Topic pages
HOLTER, NORMA C.	PHD 1992 THE GEORGE WASHINGTON UNIVERSITY VAILL, PETER B.	AUDITOR-FIRM CONFLICT IN THE DEFENSE CONTRACTING INDUSTRY: AN EMPIRICAL STUDY OF THE CONTRIBUTING FACTORS TO THE PERCEIVED IMBALANCE OF POWER	Auditing Survey CPA Firm Issues 244
HONG, CHANGMOK	PHD 1990 THE UNIVERSITY OF TEXAS AT AUSTIN NEWMAN, DONALD PAUL	AUDITORS' LEGAL LIABILITY AND REPUTATION: A GAME-THEORETIC ANALYSIS OF THE DEMAND FOR AUDITING IN AN ADVERSE SELECTION SETTING	Auditing Analytical - Internal Legal Liability 179
HONG, YONG-SIK	PHD 1989 MICHIGAN STATE UNIVERSITY	A GAME-THEORETIC ANALYSIS OF TRANSFER PRICE NEGOTIATION UNDER INCOMPLETE INFORMATION CONDITIONS	Cost/Managerial Analytical - Internal Transfer Pricing 119
HOOKS, JON ALLAN	PHD 1989 MICHIGAN STATE UNIVERSITY	INFLATION, INFLATION ACCOUNTING, AND REAL STOCK RETURNS: AN ALTERNATIVE TEST OF THE PROXY HYPOTHESIS	Financial Accounting Archival - Primary Inflation 149
HOPE, NORMAN PHILLIP	PHD 1994 KANSAS STATE UNIVERSITY MEISNER, ROBERT	MODES OF CONTINUING PROFESSIONAL EDUCATION: A FACTOR ANALYTIC TEST OF HOULE'S MODES OF LEARNING WITH CERTIFIED PUBLIC ACCOUNTANTS	Education Survey Continuing Education 170
HOPPE, PAUL PETER, III	PHD 1993 NEW YORK UNIVERSITY, GRADUATE SCHOOL OF BUSINESS ADMINISTRATION	ACCIDENTAL DATA IN A STATISTICAL AUDITING PLAN	Auditing Simulation Audit Planning 93
HORN, BETTY C.	PHD 1987 GEORGIA STATE UNIVERSITY - COLLEGE OF BUSINESS ADMINISTRATION WINKLE, GARY M.	AN EXPERT SYSTEM MODEL TO EVALUATE MANAGEMENT'S ASSERTION OF VALUATION FOR AN ACCOUNTING ESTIMATE: AN APPLICATION TO PROPERTY/CASUALTY INSURANCE LOSS RESERVES	General Industry - Insurance 195
HOSKINS, MARGARET ANN	PHD 1992 THE UNIVERSITY OF MISSISSIPPI FLESHER, DALE L.	THE MURPHY MODELS FOR ACCOUNTING: A TEST OF RELEVANCE	General Analytical - Internal History 424
HOTCHKISS, EDITH HARRIET SHWALB	PHD 1994 NEW YORK UNIVERSITY, GRADUATE SCHOOL OF BUSINESS ADMINISTRATION	INVESTMENT DECISIONS UNDER CHAPTER 11 BANKRUPTCY	General Archival - Primary Financial Distress or Bankruptcy 117

Author	Degree & Date School Advisor	Title	Functional Area Research Method Topic pages
HOUSTON, CAROL OLSON	PHD 1986 UNIVERSITY OF WASHINGTON	U.S. MANAGEMENT HEDGING PRACTICES SUBSEQUENT TO THE ADOPTION OF SFAS NO. 52 'FOREIGN CURRENCY TRANSLATION'	Financial Accounting Survey Foreign Currency Translation 244
HOWARD, ARLEY ANN	PHD 1985 THE UNIVERSITY OF NEBRASKA - LINCOLN	COST ANALYSIS OF DISTRIBUTION CHANNELS: AN EMPIRICAL DETERMINATION OF THE OPTIMAL CHANNEL STRATEGY	Cost/Managerial Case Other 181
HRNCIR, THERESA JUNE	PHD 1994 THE UNIVERSITY OF OKLAHOMA FOX, ROBERT D.	ACCOUNTANTS IN BUSINESS AND INDUSTRY: DIFFUSION OF INNOVATION WITH REGULATED CHANGE	Education Survey Continuing Education 104
HSIEH, SU-JANE	PHD 1985 PURDUE UNIVERSITY	THE ECONOMIC VALUE OF FINANCIAL DISTRESS INFORMATION: AN EMPIRICAL ASSESSMENT	Financial Accounting Archival - Primary Financial Distress or Bankruptcy 100
HSU, KO-CHENG	PHD 1993 MEMPHIS STATE UNIVERSITY STEINBART, PAUL J.	THE EFFECTS OF COGNITIVE STYLES AND INTERFACE DESIGNS ON EXPERT SYSTEMS USAGE: AN ASSESSMENT OF KNOWLEDGE TRANSFER	General Experimental Judgment & Decision Making - Cognitive Processes 177
HUANG-TSAI, CHUNGHUEY	PHD 1993 STATE UNIVERSITY OF NEW YORK AT BUFFALO HAN, JERRY C. Y.	THE ASSOCIATION BETWEEN FINANCIAL STATEMENT INFORMATION AND STOCK PRICES	Financial Accounting Archival - Primary Information Content 135
HUBBARD, DANIEL JULIAN	PHD 1992 VIRGINIA POLYTECHNIC INSTITUTE AND STATE UNIVERSITY BEAMS, FLOYD A.	AN ACCOUNTING STUDY OF AMERICAN DEPOSITARY RECEIPTS	Financial Accounting Archival - Primary Industry - Banking/Savings & Loan 336
HUDACK, LAWRENCE RALPH	PHD 1989 UNIVERSITY OF NORTH TEXAS MERINO, BARBARA D.	AN EXPLORATORY INVESTIGATION OF SOCIO-ECONOMIC PHENOMENA THAT MAY INFLUENCE ACCOUNTING DIFFERENCES IN THREE DIVERSE COUNTRIES	Financial Accounting Case International/Global Issues 381
HUDSON, CARL DEERING	PHD 1988 ARIZONA STATE UNIVERSITY	EXTERNAL MONITORING AND SECURITY OFFERING ANNOUNCEMENTS	General Archival - Primary Capital Markets 133

Author	Degree & Date School Advisor	Title	Functional Area Research Method Topic pages
HUDSON, DENNIS HERSCHEL	PHD 1986 UNIVERSITY OF ARKANSAS	AN INQUIRY INTO THE ACCOUNTING PRACTICES AND ATTITUDES OF SELECTED SMALL BUSINESSES: THE IMPACT OF RELEVANCE	General Survey Small Business 184
HUFFMAN, STEPHEN PHILLIP	PHD 1990 THE FLORIDA STATE UNIVERSITY PETERSON, PAMELA P.	TESTS OF THE FREE CASH FLOW THEORY OF TAKEOVERS	Financial Accounting Archival - Primary Merger, Acquisition, Reorganization 274
HUFNAGEL, ELLEN M.	PHD 1988 UNIVERSITY OF PITTSBURGH	SOME DETERMINANTS OF PERCEIVED FAIRNESS IN CHARGEBACK SYSTEMS AND THE EFFECTS OF PERCEIVED FAIRNESS ON USER DECISION MAKING	Cost/Managerial Experimental Cost Allocation 122
HUGHES, SUSAN BOEDEKER	PHD 1990 UNIVERSITY OF CINCINNATI SALE, J. TIMOTHY	THE IMPACT OF PRIVATE ACCOUNTING INFORMATION DISCLOSURE WITHIN THE CONTEXT OF COLLECTIVE BARGAINING: AN EMPIRICAL STUDY	General Experimental Other 292
HUH, SUNG-KYOO	DBA 1988 KENT STATE UNIVERSITY MCMATH, H. KENT	THE IMPACT OF PERCEIVED ENVIRONMENTAL UNCERTAINTY, COMPENSATION PLANS, AND SIZE ON THE CHOICE OF COST VARIANCE INVESTIGATION SYSTEMS IN LARGE MANUFACTURING FIRMS: AN EMPIRICAL STUDY	Cost/Managerial Survey Standard Costs & Variance Analysis 159
HUH, SUNGKWAN	PHD 1986 STATE UNIVERSITY OF NEW YORK AT BUFFALO	ON THE DETERMINANTS OF PERFORMANCE-DEPENDENT MANAGEMENT COMPENSATION: A THEORETICAL AND EMPIRICAL INVESTIGATION	Cost/Managerial Incentive Compensation 138
HULME, RICHARD DOUGLAS	PHD 1991 WASHINGTON STATE UNIVERSITY WONG-ON-WING, BERNARD	AN EMPIRICAL INVESTIGATION OF THE EFFECTS OF ORDER AND SAMPLE EVIDENCE REPRESENTATIONS ON AUDITORS' USE OF BASE RATES	Auditing Experimental Judgment & Decision Making - Heuristics & Biases 138
HULSE, DAVID STEWART	PHD 1992 THE PENNSYLVANIA STATE UNIVERSITY MCKEOWN, JAMES C.; CRUM, ROBERT P.	THE TIMING OF THE STOCK MARKET REACTION TO RIFLE-SHOT TRANSITION RULES IN THE TAX REFORM ACT OF 1986	Taxation Archival - Primary Public Policy 149
HUMAN, WILLEM ADRIAAN FRANS	DCOM 1993 UNIVERSITY OF PRETORIA (SOUTH AFRICA) DU RANDT, S. L.	THE ABILITY OF THE SOUTH AFRICAN AUDIT PROFESSION TO AUDIT IN THE ELECTRONIC DATA INTERCHANGE ERA	Auditing Survey International/Global Issues

Author	Degree & Date School Advisor	Title	Functional Area Research Method Topic pages
HUME, EVELYN C.	PHD 1988 THE LOUISIANA STATE UNIVERSITY AND AGRICULTURAL AND MECHANICAL COL. ORBACH, KENNETH N.	THE EFFECTS OF THE TAX REFORM ACT OF 1986 ON THE REAL ESTATE CAPITAL MARKETS AND ITS DIFFERENTIAL EFFECTS ON ENTITY AND FUNCTIONAL FORMS: AN EMPIRICAL INVESTIGATION	Taxation Archival - Primary Industry - Real Estate 142
HUNT, STEVEN CRAIG	PHD 1991 UNIVERSITY OF FLORIDA MESSIER, WILLIAM F. JR.	CERTAIN COGNITIVE FACTORS AFFECTING PERFORMANCE EVALUATION IN CPA FIRMS	General Experimental Job Performance, Satisfaction &/or Turnover 213
HURT, ROBERT LEE	PHD 1991 CLAREMONT GRADUATE SCHOOL OLFMAN, LORNE	THE EFFECTS OF COMPUTER-ASSISTED INSTRUCTION ON MOTIVATION AND ANXIETY IN FIRST-YEAR UNDERGRADUATE ACCOUNTING STUDENTS	Education Experimental Instructional Methods 169
HUSSAEN, NIDHAM MOHAMMED ALI	PHD 1988 UNIVERSITY OF HULL (UNITED KINGDOM)	THE EVOLUTION OF ACCOUNTING FOR INFLATION IN GERMANY, 1920-1923	Financial Accounting Archival - Secondary Inflation 467
HUTCHINSON, PATRICK JOHN	PHD 1987 UNIVERSITY OF BATH (UNITED KINGDOM)	THE FINANCIAL PROFILE OF GROWTH SMALL FIRMS: AN ANALYSIS OF THE ACCOUNTING RATIOS OF AUSTRALIAN COMPANIES AT AND AFTER FLOTATION, 1964/5-1983/4	Financial Accounting Archival - Primary International/Global Issues 309
HUTTON, MARGUERITE ROACH	PHD 1985 UNIVERSITY OF HOUSTON	PERCEPTUAL DIFFERENTIATION WITH REGARD TO PENALTIES IN PROFESSIONAL TAX PRACTICE	Taxation Survey Tax Professionals 207
HWANG, HO-CHAN	PHD 1992 GEORGIA INSTITUTE OF TECHNOLOGY SCHNEIDER, A.	PROFESSIONAL ACCOUNTANTS' ETHICAL BEHAVIOR: A POSITIVE APPROACH	General Survey Ethics 146
HWANG, IN TAE	PHD 1993 STATE UNIVERSITY OF NEW YORK AT BUFFALO HAMLEN, SUSAN	THE DETERMINANTS OF EXECUTIVE INCENTIVE CONTRACTS	Cost/Managerial Archival - Primary Incentive Compensation 167
HWANG, NEN-CHEN	PHD 1991 SAINT LOUIS UNIVERSITY JENNINGS, JAMES P.	FINANCIAL CHARACTERISTICS OF CORPORATIONS CHANGING COMMON STOCK LISTING FROM THE OVER-THE-COUNTER MARKET TO THE NEW YORK STOCK EXCHANGE	Financial Accounting Archival - Primary Capital Markets 124

Author	Degree & Date / School / Advisor	Title	Functional Area / Research Method / Topic / pages
IBRAHIM, MOHAMED EL HADY M.	PHD 1985 UNIVERSITY OF NORTH TEXAS	AN EXAMINATION OF AN INTEGRATIVE EXPECTANCY MODEL FOR AUDITORS' PERFORMANCE BEHAVIORS UNDER TIME BUDGET PRESSURE	Auditing Survey Auditor Behavior 187
IGWE, VICTOR IHEUKWU	DBA 1991 NOVA UNIVERSITY BLACKWELL, CHARLES	THE IMPACT OF AUDITORS' PERCEPTION OF PERFORMANCE APPRAISAL ON THE EFFORTS EXERTED TOWARDS JOB PERFORMANCE: A STUDY OF AUDITORS THAT AUDIT GOVERNMENTAL ENTITIES, COLLEGES AND UNIVERSITIES IN THE STATE OF FLORIDA	Auditing Survey Job Performance, Satisfaction &/or Turnover 146
IKEOKWU, FRANCIS AHAMEFULE	PHD 1994 THE UNION INSTITUTE JORDAN, JOSEPH F.	FLORIDA SALES TAX REVENUE: A COMPARATIVE STUDY TO DETERMINE THE RELATIONSHIP BETWEEN SALES TAX RATE AND SALES TAX REVENUE IN FLORIDA	Taxation Archival - Primary State Taxation 119
ILDERTON, ROBERT BLAIR	PHD 1987 MEMPHIS STATE UNIVERSITY DENG, L. Y.	EVALUATION OF SAMPLES WITH FEW NON-ZERO ITEMS	Auditing Simulation Audit Sampling 165
IM, JONG-GEOL	PHD 1989 UNIVERSITY OF PENNSYLVANIA STICKEL, SCOTT E.	DIFFERENTIAL INFORMATION ENVIRONMENT AND THE MAGNITUDE OF CAPITAL MARKET RESPONSES TO EARNINGS ANNOUNCEMENTS	Financial Accounting Archival - Primary Earnings Announcements 100
IMOISILI, OLUMHENSE ANTHONY	PHD 1985 UNIVERSITY OF PITTSBURGH	TASK COMPLEXITY, BUDGET STYLE OF EVALUATING PERFORMANCE AND MANAGERIAL STRESS: AN EMPIRICAL INVESTIGATION	Cost/Managerial Survey Budgeting 201
INDJEJIKIAN, RAFFI J.	PHD 1989 UNIVERSITY OF PENNSYLVANIA VERRECCHIA, ROBERT E	THE IMPACT OF INFORMATION ON THE EXTENT OF AGREEMENT AMONG INVESTORS: A NEW PERSPECTIVE ON FIRM DISCLOSURES	Financial Accounting Analytical - Internal Disclosures 112
INDRIANTORO, NUR	PHD 1993 UNIVERSITY OF KENTUCKY MADDEN, DONALD L.; HOLMES, JAMES R.	THE EFFECT OF PARTICIPATIVE BUDGETING ON JOB PERFORMANCE AND JOB SATISFACTION WITH LOCUS-OF-CONTROL AND CULTURAL DIMENSIONS AS MODERATING VARIABLES	Cost/Managerial Survey Budgeting 221
IRELAND, ALICE MARIE	PHD 1990 DALHOUSIE UNIVERSITY (CANADA)	AN INTELLIGENT DECISION SUPPORT SYSTEM FOR DEBT MANAGEMENT	Information Systems Decision Support Systems 336

Author	Degree & Date School Advisor	Title	Functional Area Research Method Topic pages
ISAACS, PATRICIA COLE	PHD 1994 UNIVERSITY OF KENTUCKY	IMA'S CODE OF ETHICS: AN EMPIRICAL EXAMINATION OF VIEWPOINTS OF CERTIFIED MANAGEMENT ACCOUNTANTS	General Survey Ethics
	HOLMES, JAMES R.; MADDEN, DONALD L.		476
ISMAIL, ZUBAIDAH BINTE	PHD 1993 UNIVERSITY OF NEW SOUTH WALES (AUSTRALIA)	THE IMPACT OF THE REVIEW PROCESS IN HYPOTHESIS GENERATION TASKS	Auditing Experimental Judgment & Decision Making
ISSA, HUSSEIN MOHAMED AHMED	DBA 1992 UNITED STATES INTERNATIONAL UNIVERSITY	A PROPOSED MODEL FOR CAPITAL BUDGETARY CONTROL IN THE AMERICAN FOOD PRODUCT CORPORATION SECTOR	Cost/Managerial Simulation Capital Budgeting
	KHALIL, MOHAMED A.		449
ITTNER, CHRISTOPHER DEAN	DBA 1992 HARVARD UNIVERSITY	THE ECONOMICS AND MEASUREMENT OF QUALITY COSTS: AN EMPIRICAL INVESTIGATION	Cost/Managerial Survey Quality Issues
	KAPLAN, ROBERT S.		177
IVANCEVICH, DANIEL MICHAEL	PHD 1991 TEXAS A&M UNIVERSITY	AN EMPIRICAL INVESTIGATION OF THE ACCOUNTING DIFFERENCES FOR GOODWILL IN THE UNITED STATES AND UNITED KINGDOM	Financial Accounting Archival - Primary International/Global Issues
	STRAWSER, ROBERT		144
IYER, VENKATARAMAN MOHAN	PHD 1994 UNIVERSITY OF GEORGIA	FACTORS RELATED TO INCLINATION AND CAPACITY OF CPA FIRM ALUMNI TO BENEFIT THEIR FORMER FIRM: AN EMPIRICAL STUDY	Auditing Survey CPA Firm Issues
	BAREFIELD, RUSSELL		127
JACKSON, ANTHONY WAYNE	PHD 1985 UNIVERSITY OF CINCINNATI	THE INFLUENCE OF BUDGET RELATED PERFORMANCE EVALUATION MEASURES ON DECISION MAKING BEHAVIOR UNDER UNCERTAINTY	Cost/Managerial Experimental Performance Evaluation/Measurement
			122
JACKSON, CYNTHIA MAPP	PHD 1992 UNIVERSITY OF SOUTH CAROLINA	THE INFLUENCE OF USER INVOLVEMENT AND OTHER VARIABLES ON BEHAVIORAL INTENTION TO USE AN INFORMATION SYSTEM	Information Systems Survey Systems Design &/or Development
	LEITCH, ROBERT A.		171
JACKSON, PAMELA GAIL ZIEMER	PHD 1990 UNIVERSITY OF GEORGIA	AN INVESTIGATION OF THE EFFECT OF CONTINGENCY THEORY VARIABLES ON THE DESIGN OF COST ACCOUNTING SYSTEMS IN SERVICE FIRMS	Cost/Managerial Survey Management Control Systems
	CLARK, RONALD L.		155

Author	Degree & Date School Advisor	Title	Functional Area Research Method Topic pages
JACKSON, STEVEN ROY	PHD 1993 ARIZONA STATE UNIVERSITY BOATSMAN, JAMES R.	AN EMPIRICAL ASSESSMENT OF MEASUREMENT ERROR IN HISTORICAL COST AND SELECTED CHANGING PRICES INCOME NUMBERS	Financial Accounting Archival - Primary Inflation 60
JACKSON-HEARD, MARY FRANCES	PHD 1987 NEW YORK UNIVERSITY, GRADUATE SCHOOL OF BUSINESS ADMINISTRATION	THE EFFECT OF THE AUDIT COMMITTEE AND OTHER SELECTED FACTORS ON THE PERCEPTION OF AUDITORS' INDEPENDENCE	Auditing Survey Audit Committees 142
JACOB, RUDOLPH AUBREY	PHD 1987 NEW YORK UNIVERSITY, GRADUATE SCHOOL OF BUSINESS ADMINISTRATION	THE TIME-SERIES BEHAVIOR AND INFORMATIONAL CONTENT OF SELECTED CASH FLOW VARIABLES	Financial Accounting Archival - Primary Cash Flows 133
JAGANNATHAN, JAYASHRI V.	PHD 1993 THE UNIVERSITY OF IOWA GRIMLUND, RICHARD A.; JAGANNATHAN, RAJ	SEQUENTIAL STOPPING RULES FOR ESTIMATING THE TOTAL ERROR IN ACCOUNTING POPULATIONS USING MONETARY UNIT SAMPLING	Auditing Simulation Errors 252
JAKUBOWSKI, STEPHEN THOMAS	PHD 1988 KENT STATE UNIVERSITY BROWN, RICHARD E.	THE EFFECT OF THE SINGLE AUDIT ACT OF 1984 ON THE INTERNAL CONTROL SYSTEMS OF LOCAL GOVERNMENTAL UNITS	Not-for-Profit Archival - Primary Governmental 191
JAMAL, KARIM	PHD 1991 UNIVERSITY OF MINNESOTA JOHNSON, PAUL E.; BERRYMAN, R. GLEN	DETECTING FRAMING EFFECTS IN AUDIT JUDGMENT	Auditing Experimental Judgment & Decision Making - Heuristics & Biases 399
JAN, CHING-LIH	PHD 1988 UNIVERSITY OF CALIFORNIA, BERKELEY OHLSON, JAMES	THE MARKET'S EVALUATION OF FOOTNOTE DISCLOSURES FOR FIRMS USING LIFO INVENTORY ACCOUNTING	Financial Accounting Archival - Primary Inventory 109
JANAKIRAMAN, SURYA N.	PHD 1994 UNIVERSITY OF PENNSYLVANIA LARCKER, DAVID F.	STRATEGIC CHOICE OF CHIEF EXECUTIVE OFFICERS' COMPENSATION: AN EMPIRICAL ANALYSIS	Cost/Managerial Archival - Primary Incentive Compensation 163
JANG, HWEE-YONG	PHD 1987 PURDUE UNIVERSITY RO, BYUNG T.	TRADING VOLUME AND ACCOUNTING RESEARCH: THEORY, IMPLICATION, AND EVIDENCE	Financial Accounting Archival - Primary Earnings Announcements 123

Author	Degree & Date School Advisor	Title	Functional Area Research Method Topic pages
JANG, JEE IN	PHD 1989 STATE UNIVERSITY OF NEW YORK AT BUFFALO	FINANCIAL ANALYST EARNINGS FORECAST REVISIONS: FORMATION PROCESS AND INFORMATION VALUE	Financial Accounting Archival - Primary Financial Analysts 149
JANG, YEONG MIN	DBA 1991 MISSISSIPPI STATE UNIVERSITY HERRING, DORA R.	AN EMPIRICAL EVALUATION OF THE CURRENT ACCOUNTING COMMON STOCK EQUIVALENCY TEST AND AN ALTERNATIVE MARKET MODEL	Financial Accounting Archival - Primary Earnings Per Share 148
JEFFREY, CYNTHIA GEISLER	PHD 1989 UNIVERSITY OF MINNESOTA	THE IMPACT OF ESCALATION OF COMMITMENT ON LOAN EVALUATION JUDGMENTS OF INDEPENDENT AUDITORS AND BANK LOAN OFFICERS	General Experimental Judgment & Decision Making 276
JENKINS, ELIZABETH KLAFF	PHD 1986 UNIVERSITY OF HOUSTON	EXECUTIVE COMPENSATION SCHEMES AND SHORT-RUN DECISION-MAKING: AN EMPIRICAL EXAMINATION	Cost/Managerial Archival - Primary Incentive Compensation 130
JENNINGS, ROSS GRANT	PHD 1987 UNIVERSITY OF CALIFORNIA, BERKELEY	A STUDY OF THE CROSS-SECTIONAL HOMOGENEITY OF THE INFORMATION CONTENT OF ACCOUNTING INCOME AND ITS COMPONENTS	Financial Accounting Archival - Primary Earnings 165
JENSEN, DAVID EDWARD	PHD 1987 THE PENNSYLVANIA STATE UNIVERSITY	THE INFORMATION CONTENT OF CASH FLOW MEASURES IN REGARD TO ENTERPRISE DIVIDEND POLICY	Financial Accounting Archival - Primary Cash Flows 165
JENSON, RICHARD L.	PHD 1988 THE UNIVERSITY OF UTAH BARTLEY, JON W.	PARAMETRIC ESTIMATION OF PROGRAMMING EFFORT IN A MANUFACTURING DATABASE ENVIRONMENT	Information Systems Case Systems Design &/or Development 180
JERRIS, SCOTT I.	PHD 1987 PURDUE UNIVERSITY	THE ASSOCIATION BETWEEN STOCK RETURNS AND ALTERNATIVE EARNINGS PER SHARE NUMBERS	Financial Accounting Archival - Primary Earnings per Share 116
JETER, DEBRA COLEMAN	PHD 1990 VANDERBILT UNIVERSITY CHANEY, PAUL K.	ACCOUNTING EARNINGS AND SECURITY RETURNS: STUDIES ON EARNINGS RESPONSE COEFFICIENTS, AUDIT REPORTS, AND DEFERRED TAXES	Financial Accounting Archival - Primary Taxes 120

Author	Degree & Date School Advisor	Title	Functional Area Research Method Topic pages
JIN, JONG-DAE	PHD 1989 THE UNIVERSITY OF ARIZONA DHALIWAL, DAN S.	THE IMPACT OF EARNINGS ANNOUNCEMENT ON BOND PRICE	Financial Accounting Archival - Primary Earnings Announcements 119
JOH, GUN-HO	PHD 1988 UNIVERSITY OF PENNSYLVANIA LEE, CHI-WEN JEVONS	INTERFIRM INFORMATION TRANSFER AND DISCLOSURE TIMING	Financial Accounting Archival - Primary Information Transfer 139
JOHN, TERESA ANNE	PHD 1986 NEW YORK UNIVERSITY, GRADUATE SCHOOL OF BUSINESS ADMINISTRATION	CORPORATE MERGERS, INVESTMENT INCENTIVES AND FIRM VALUE: AN AGENCY THEORETIC ANALYSIS	General Analytical - Internal Merger, Acquisition, Reorganization 171
JOHNSON, BRAD ROY	PHD 1993 UNIVERSITY OF HOUSTON	THE EXISTENCE AND NATURE OF DISPARATE VOLUME CAP CONSTRAINING EFFECTS ACROSS RURAL AND NONRURAL COMMUNITIES: AN EMPIRICAL ANALYSIS	Not-for-Profit Other 446
JOHNSON, CAROL BAUMAN	PHD 1993 ARIZONA STATE UNIVERSITY BOATSMAN, JIM	THE IMPACT OF CURRENCY CHANGES ON THE PERSISTENCE AND PRICING OF MULTINATIONAL CORPORATION EARNINGS	Financial Accounting Archival - Primary Foreign Currency Translation 66
JOHNSON, DAVID MARK	PHD 1989 UNIVERSITY OF CINCINNATI	INSIDER OWNERSHIP AND SIGNALS: A STUDY OF STOCK AND BOND ISSUE ANNOUNCEMENT EFFECTS	Financial Accounting Archival - Primary Agency Theory 98
JOHNSON, ERIC NOEL	PHD 1989 ARIZONA STATE UNIVERSITY RECKERS, PHILIP M. J.	EFFECTS OF EXPERIENCE, TASK VARIABLES, AND PRIOR BELIEFS ON AUDITORS' SEQUENTIAL JUDGMENTS	Auditing Experimental Judgment & Decision Making - Heuristics & Biases 181
JOHNSON, GARY GENE	PHD 1989 UNIVERSITY OF ARKANSAS HAY, LEON E.	COMPLIANCE AUDITING IN THE PUBLIC SECTOR: AN EMPIRICAL INVESTIGATION INTO THE EXTENT OF NONCOMPLIANCE WITH STATE LAWS BY COUNTY GOVERNMENTS	Not-for-Profit Survey Governmental 171
JOHNSON, GENE HERBERT	PHD 1986 TEXAS TECH UNIVERSITY	THE RELATIVE USE OF FORMAL AND INFORMAL INFORMATION IN THE EVALUATION OF INDIVIDUAL PERFORMANCE	Cost/Managerial Survey Performance Evaluation/Measuremen t 168

Author	Degree & Date School Advisor	Title	Functional Area Research Method Topic pages
JOHNSON, GEORGE ALFRED	PHD 1990 VIRGINIA POLYTECHNIC INSTITUTE AND STATE UNIVERSITY BROWN, ROBERT M.	THE INFORMATION VALUE OF NEW DISAGGREGATED ACCOUNTING INFORMATION: THE CASE OF VOLUNTARY CORPORATE SPINOFFS	Financial Accounting Archival - Primary Information Content 134
JOHNSON, JOYCE MARIE	PHD 1992 UNIVERSITY OF GEORGIA DAVIS, EARL F.	AN EVALUATION OF THE FEDERAL CIVIL TAX PENALTY FOR THE FAILURE TO TIMELY DEPOSIT PAYROLL TAXES: A SURVEY OF GEORGIA TAX PRACTITIONERS	Taxation Survey Tax Compliance 170
JOHNSON, KENNETH HAROLD	PHD 1989 GEORGIA STATE UNIVERSITY - COLLEGE OF BUSINESS ADMINISTRATION GIOVINAZZO, VINCENT J.	OWNERSHIP STRUCTURE AND THE INFORMATION CONTENT OF EARNINGS ANNOUNCEMENTS: AN EMPIRICAL INVESTIGATION	Financial Accounting Archival - Primary Earnings Announcements 240
JOHNSON, LAURENCE ERNEST	PHD 1991 TEXAS TECH UNIVERSITY FREEMAN, ROBERT J.	AN INVESTIGATION OF CITY FINANCIAL STATEMENT READERS' REACTION TO DUAL-BASIS REPORTING OF GENERAL FUND OPERATING RESULTS: INTEGRATION OR EMPHASIS?	Not-for-Profit Experimental Governmental 214
JOHNSON, LINDA MARIE	PHD 1990 ARIZONA STATE UNIVERSITY O'DELL, MICHAEL A.	AN EMPIRICAL INVESTIGATION OF THE EFFECTS OF ADVOCACY ON PREPARERS' EVALUATIONS OF EVIDENCE	Taxation Experimental Judgment & Decision Making - Heuristics & Biases 93
JOHNSON, MARILYN FRANCES	PHD 1992 UNIVERSITY OF WASHINGTON BOWEN, ROBERT M.	BUSINESS CYCLES AND THE RELATION BETWEEN SECURITY RETURNS AND EARNINGS	Financial Accounting Archival - Primary Earnings Response Coefficients 156
JOHNSON, RICHARD ALAN	PHD 1989 UNIVERSITY OF GEORGIA JOHNSON, JOHNNY R.	AN EMPIRICAL INVESTIGATION OF THE ASSOCIATION OF ACCOUNTING-BASED PERFORMANCE MEASURES WITH THE AUDITOR REPLACEMENT DECISION	Auditing Archival - Primary Auditor Changes 146
JOHNSON, ROXANNE THERESE	PHD 1987 THE PENNSYLVANIA STATE UNIVERSITY	AN ANALYSIS OF THE EARLY RECORD-KEEPING IN THE DUPONT COMPANY--1800-1818	General Case History 129
JOHNSON, STEVEN D.	PHD 1991 VIRGINIA POLYTECHNIC INSTITUTE AND STATE UNIVERSITY KILLOUGH, L. N.	AN EMPIRICAL STUDY OF THE FIDELITY OF ORGANIZATIONAL ACCOUNTING COMMUNICATION AND THE IMPACT OF ORGANIZATIONAL CULTURE	Cost/Managerial Survey Other 283

Author	Degree & Date School Advisor	Title	Functional Area Research Method Topic pages
JOHNSON, VAN EDWARD	PHD 1992 ARIZONA STATE UNIVERSITY KAPLAN, STEVEN E.	AN EXAMINATION OF THE EFFECTS OF ACCOUNTABILITY ON AUDITOR JUDGMENTS	Auditing Experimental Judgment & Decision Making 175
JOHNSTON, HOLLY HANSON	PHD 1990 CARNEGIE-MELLON UNIVERSITY BANKER, RAJIV	EMPIRICAL STUDIES IN MANAGEMENT ACCOUNTING: THREE ESSAYS ON THE U.S. AIRLINE INDUSTRY, 1981-1985	Cost/Managerial Archival - Primary Industry - Airline 244
JONES, FREDERICK LAWSON	DBA 1991 BOSTON UNIVERSITY MENON, KRISHNAGOPAL	THE MARKET REACTION TO THE AUDITOR'S GOING CONCERN EVALUATION	Auditing Audit Opinion 193
JONES, JENNIFER JEAN	PHD 1988 THE UNIVERSITY OF MICHIGAN BRADLEY, MICHAEL MICHAEL W. MAHER	THE EFFECT OF FOREIGN TRADE REGULATION ON ACCOUNTING CHOICES, AND PRODUCTION AND INVESTMENT DECISIONS	Financial Accounting Archival - Primary Accounting Choice 106
JONES, SCOTT KENNETH	PHD 1988 DREXEL UNIVERSITY JAENICKE, HENRY R.	THE RISK PROPERTIES OF ANALYTICAL PROCEDURES THAT USE ORTHOGONAL POLYNOMIAL REGRESSIONS	Auditing Simulation Analytical Review 165
JONNERGARD, KARIN	FILDR 1988 LUNDS UNIVERSITET (SWEDEN) (0899)	FEDERATIVE PROCESSES AND ADMINISTRATIVE DEVELOPMENT--A STUDY OF FEDERATIVE COOPERATIVE ORGANIZATIONS (SWEDEN, CANADA) [FEDERATIVA PROCESSER OCH ADMINISTRATIV UTVECKLING--EN STUDIE AV FEDERATIVA KOOPERATIVA ORGANISATIONER]	General Case International/Global Issues 366
JOO, HYUNGHWAN	PHD 1991 UNIVERSITY OF ILLINOIS AT URBANA-CHAMPAIGN KWON, YOUNG K.	INCOME SMOOTHING: AN ASYMMETRIC INFORMATION APPROACH	Financial Accounting Analytical - Internal Earnings Management 97
JOO, INKI	PHD 1986 NEW YORK UNIVERSITY, GRADUATE SCHOOL OF BUSINESS ADMINISTRATION	INFORMATION CONTENT OF STOCK SPLITS IN RELATION WITH PRIOR YEAR'S EARNINGS' GROWTH, FIRM SIZE, SPLIT SIZE, AND REPUTATION: AN EMPIRICAL ANALYSIS	Financial Accounting Archival - Primary Information Content 231
JOO, JIN-KYU	PHD 1988 UNIVERSITY OF CALIFORNIA, BERKELEY PENMAN, STEPHEN	EARNINGS SURPRISE AND EX-ANTE PRICE EFFECTS IN OPTIONS MARKETS	Financial Accounting Archival - Primary Earnings Announcements 97

Listing by Author

Author	Degree & Date School Advisor	Title	Functional Area Research Method Topic pages
JORDAN, CHARLES EDWARD	DBA 1986 LOUISIANA TECH UNIVERSITY	THE DEVELOPMENT OF A STATISTICAL ANALYTICAL REVIEW MODEL FOR USE BY EXTERNAL AUDITORS IN EVALUATING BANKS' LOAN-LOSS RESERVES	Auditing Archival - Primary Industry - Banking/Savings & Loan 165
JORDAN, LELAND GONCE	DBA 1985 THE GEORGE WASHINGTON UNIVERSITY	ARE THE INTERIM FINANCIAL STATEMENTS OF FAILING FIRMS BIASED?	Financial Accounting Archival - Primary Financial Distress or Bankruptcy 163
JORDAN, ROBERT EARL	PHD 1992 THE UNIVERSITY OF MISSISSIPPI FLESHER, DALE L.	THE INSTITUTE OF MANAGEMENT ACCOUNTANTS' CONTRIBUTION TO ACCOUNTING THOUGHT: A DESCRIPTIVE AND EVALUATIVE STUDY	General Survey History 329
JOSEPH, GILBERT WILLIAM	PHD 1992 UNIVERSITY OF SOUTH FLORIDA HOLSTRUM, GARY L.	DESIGNING DECISION AIDS TO OVERCOME BELIEF REVISION BIASES: AN EMPIRICAL INVESTIGATION USING INTERNAL CONTROL RISK ASSESSMENTS IN A DATABASE ENVIRONMENT	Auditing Experimental Decision Aids 176
JOY, ARTHUR C., JR.	PHD 1985 UNIVERSITY OF ILLINOIS AT URBANA-CHAMPAIGN	AN EMPIRICAL INVESTIGATION INTO TRANSFER PRICING PRACTICES	Cost/Managerial Survey Transfer Pricing 470
JUDD, ANDREW JACKSON	PHD 1985 UNIVERSITY OF FLORIDA	AN EXAMINATION OF SIGNIFICANT VARIABLES USED BY COURTS IN WORTHLESS STOCK CASES	Taxation Archival - Secondary Tax Court 186
JUNG, KOOYUL	PHD 1987 UNIVERSITY OF FLORIDA	THE RELATIONSHIP BETWEEN CHANGES IN CERTAIN FIRM CHARACTERISTICS AND THE CHANGES IN THE STRUCTURE OF TOP MANAGEMENT COMPENSATION PLANS	Cost/Managerial Incentive Compensation 135
JUNG, WOON-OH	PHD 1986 UNIVERSITY OF CALIFORNIA, LOS ANGELES	ACCOUNTING DECISIONS UNDER ASYMMETRIC INFORMATION	Financial Accounting Analytical - Internal Accounting Choice 125
JURAS, PAUL EDWARD	PHD 1991 SYRACUSE UNIVERSITY	ANALYSIS OF RELATIVE EFFICIENCY MEASURES OF MEDICAL NURSING UNITS FOR MANAGERIAL DIAGNOSIS AND CONTROL	Cost/Managerial Case Industry - Health Care 227

Listing by Author

Author	Degree & Date School Advisor	Title	Functional Area Research Method Topic pages
KACHELMEIER, STEVEN JOHN	PHD 1988 UNIVERSITY OF FLORIDA ABDEL-KHALIK, A. RASHAD	A LABORATORY MARKET INVESTIGATION OF THE DEMAND FOR AUDITING IN AN ENVIRONMENT OF MORAL HAZARD	Auditing Experimental Agency Theory 289
KAENZIG, REBECCA	PHD 1987 UNIVERSITY OF SOUTH CAROLINA	THE INDIVIDUAL VERSUS THE FAMILY: AN EMPIRICAL ANALYSIS OF HORIZONTAL EQUITY AND TAX-PAYER FILING STATUS	Taxation Archival - Primary Individual Taxation 160
KALBERS, LAWRENCE PACKARD	PHD 1989 THE PENNSYLVANIA STATE UNIVERSITY DIRSMITH, MARK W.	THE AUDIT COMMITTEE: A POWER NEXUS FOR FINANCIAL REPORTING AND CORPORATE ACCOUNTABILITY	Auditing Survey Audit Committees 461
KALLAPUR, SANJAY GOKULDAS	PHD 1990 HARVARD UNIVERSITY KAPLAN, ROBERT	DETERMINANTS OF THE STOCK PRICE RESPONSE TO EARNINGS	Financial Accounting Archival - Primary Earnings Response Coefficients 101
KANDIEL, EL-SAYED HUSSEIN AHMED	PHD 1985 CITY UNIVERSITY OF NEW YORK	ACCOUNTING FOR INTERNALLY DEVELOPED SOFTWARE COSTS: A POSITIVE APPROACH	Financial Accounting Archival - Primary Accounting Choice 239
KANE, GREGORY DALE	PHD 1992 VIRGINIA POLYTECHNIC INSTITUTE AND STATE UNIVERSITY BROWN, ROBERT M.	ACCOUNTING DATA AND STOCK RETURNS ACROSS BUSINESS-CYCLE ASSOCIATED VALUATION CHANGE PERIODS	Financial Accounting Archival - Primary Financial Ratios 301
KANG, JUNGPAO	PHD 1991 NEW YORK UNIVERSITY, GRADUATE SCHOOL OF BUSINESS ADMINISTRATION BRIEF, RICHARD P.	GENERALIZED PROFITABILITY MEASURES UNDER STEADY-STATE CONDITIONS	Cost/Managerial Simulation Performance Evaluation/Measurement 183
KANNAN, RAMU S.	PHD 1991 SYRACUSE UNIVERSITY	A KNOWLEDGE-BASED APPROACH FOR CONTROL DESIGN: A CASE STUDY IN THE PURCHASING CYCLE	Information Systems Case Internal Control 202
KARAYAN, JOHN EDWARD	PHD 1994 THE CLAREMONT GRADUATE SCHOOL	THE ECONOMIC IMPACT OF A TAX LAW CHANGE: PUBLICLY TRADED PARTNERSHIPS UNDER THE REVENUE ACT OF 1987	Taxation Archival - Primary Partnership Taxation 302

Author	Degree & Date School Advisor	Title	Functional Area Research Method Topic pages
KARCHER, JULIA NANCY	PHD 1992 THE FLORIDA STATE UNIVERSITY BAILEY, CHARLES D.	AUDITORS' ABILITY TO DISCERN THE PRESENCE OF ETHICAL PROBLEMS	General Experimental Ethics 139
KASURINEN, VEIKKO ANTERO	DSC 1991 TAMPEREEN YLIOPISTO (FINLAND)	CORPORATE SOCIAL ACCOUNTING: A MEASURING EXPERIMENT APPLIED TO THE PRODUCTION, TRADE AND CONSUMPTION OF ALCOHOL IN FINLAND [YRITYKSEN YHTEISKUNNALLISEN LASKENTATOIMEN MITTAAMISKOKEILU: SOVELLUS ALKOHOLITALOUTEEN SUOMESSA]	Financial Accounting Experimental Social/Environmental Responsibility 238
KATTELUS, SUSAN CONVERY	PHD 1990 MICHIGAN STATE UNIVERSITY	PRIVATE NONOPERATING FOUNDATIONS: AN EMPIRICAL INVESTIGATION OF PAYOUT RATES AND FOUNDATION CHARACTERISTICS BEFORE AND AFTER THE ECONOMIC RECOVERY TAX ACT OF 1981	Taxation Archival - Primary Public Policy 149
KAUFFMAN, NORMAN LEROY	PHD 1988 THE OHIO STATE UNIVERSITY DILLARD, JESSE F.	PERFORMANCE EVALUATION AND JOB-DIRECTED EFFORT IN THE CPA FIRM: AN INTEGRATION OF EXPECTANCY THEORY, ATTRIBUTION THEORY, AND NEED THEORY	General Survey Job Performance, Satisfaction &/or Turnover 188
KAYE, GERALDINE DELLA	PHD 1991 THE CITY UNIVERSITY (LONDON) (UNITED KINGDOM)	EXPENSES OF UNITED KINGDOM LIFE INSURERS WITH SPECIAL REFERENCE TO 1980-1986 DATA PROVIDED BY THE ASSOCIATION OF BRITISH INSURERS	General Analytical - Internal Industry - Insurance 291
KAZENSKI, PAUL M.	PHD 1991 GEORGIA STATE UNIVERSITY - COLLEGE OF BUSINESS ADMINISTRATION STABLER, H. F.	A NON-LINEAR APPROACH TO DETECTING ESTIMATION AND VALUATION ERRORS IN THE REPORTED RESERVES OF PROPERTY-LIABILITY INSURERS	Financial Accounting Archival - Primary Errors 155
KEARNS, FRANCIS E., JR.	PHD 1986 STATE UNIVERSITY OF NEW YORK AT BUFFALO	AN INVESTIGATION OF THE RELATIVE PREDICTIVE VALIDITY OF QUARTERLY REPORTS BEFORE AND AFTER AUDITOR INVOLVEMENT UNDER ASR #177	Financial Accounting Archival - Primary Forecasting Financial Performance 197
KEASLER, HUBERT LEVERT, JR.	DBA 1991 MISSISSIPPI STATE UNIVERSITY HERRING, DORA R.	A COMPOSITE PROFILE OF PROPOSED INDIRECT COST RATES APPLICABLE TO ORGANIZED RESEARCH AND DEVELOPMENT AT COLLEGES AND UNIVERSITIES THAT USE MODIFIED TOTAL DIRECT COSTS BASIS FOR FEDERAL IC RATE NEGOTIATIONS	Not-for-Profit Survey College & University 271
KEATING, PATRICK J.	PHD 1990 THE PENNSYLVANIA STATE UNIVERSITY JABLONSKY, STEPHEN F.	'MANAGING BY THE NUMBERS': AN EMPIRICALLY INFORMED THEORETICAL STUDY OF CORPORATE FINANCIAL WORK	Cost/Managerial Case Capital Budgeting 409

Author	Degree & Date School Advisor	Title	Functional Area Research Method Topic pages
KEDSLIE, MOYRA JEAN MCINTYRE	PHD 1987 UNIVERSITY OF HULL (UNITED KINGDOM)	AN ANALYSIS OF THE FACTORS INFLUENCING THE FORMATION AND POLICIES OF PROFESSIONAL ACCOUNTING BODIES IN SCOTLAND, 1850-1900	General Archival - Primary History 502
KEINATH, ANNEMARIE KATHARINA	PHD 1989 MICHIGAN STATE UNIVERSITY	IMPACT OF ACCOUNTING INFORMATION ON ATTRIBUTIONAL CONFLICTS AND EMPLOYEE EFFORT IN A PERFORMANCE APPRAISAL SETTING	Cost/Managerial Experimental Performance Evaluation/Measuremen t 232
KELLEY, CLAUDIA LU	PHD 1991 THE UNIVERSITY OF ALABAMA SCHNEE, EDWARD J.	A STUDY OF THE STOCK MARKET REACTION TO SECTION 382 OF THE TAX REFORM ACT OF 1986 AND THE CHARACTERISTICS OF TARGETS WITH LOSS CARRYOVERS	Taxation Archival - Primary Merger, Acquisition, Reorganization 181
KELLIHER, CHARLES FRANCIS, JR.	PHD 1990 TEXAS A&M UNIVERSITY STRAWSER, ROBERT H.	AN EMPIRICAL INVESTIGATION OF THE EFFECTS OF PERSONALITY TYPE AND VARIATION IN INFORMATION LOAD ON THE INFORMATION SEARCH STRATEGIES EMPLOYED BY DECISION-MAKERS	General Experimental Judgment & Decision Making - Cognitive Processes 256
KELLY, ANNE SULLIVAN	PHD 1986 UNIVERSITY OF CINCINNATI	THE COMPARISON OF SEVERAL INTERNAL CONTROL EVALUATION METHODOLOGIES ON THE ASSESSMENT OF RISK AND OTHER AUDIT PLANNING DECISIONS: AN EMPIRICAL INVESTIGATION	Auditing Experimental Decision Aids 264
KELLY, KIRK PATRICK	PHD 1985 UNIVERSITY OF PITTSBURGH	EXPERT PROBLEM SOLVING SYSTEM FOR THE AUDIT PLANNING PROCESS	Auditing Case Decision Aids 311
KELTING, WILLIAM ROBERT	PHD 1988 UNIVERSITY OF ARKANSAS GLEZEN, G. WILLIAM	AUDIT PLANNING: AN EMPIRICAL INVESTIGATION INTO THE TIMING OF PRINCIPAL SUBSTANTIVE TESTS	Auditing Experimental Audit Planning 186
KEMERER, KEVIN L.	PHD 1990 VIRGINIA POLYTECHNIC INSTITUTE AND STATE UNIVERSITY BEAMS, FLOYD A.	ACCOUNTING VARIABLES, STOCK SPLITS AND WHEN-ISSUED TRADING	Financial Accounting Archival - Primary Capital Markets 196
KEMPTON, PETER A.	PHD 1987 UNIVERSITY OF BATH (UNITED KINGDOM)	THE CONTROL OF TAX EVASION--QUESTIONS FOR PRACTISING ACCOUNTANTS	Taxation Survey Tax Compliance 435

Author	Degree & Date School Advisor	Title	Functional Area Research Method Topic pages
KENNEDY, DUANE BRIAN	PHD 1987 CORNELL UNIVERSITY	CLASSIFICATION TECHNIQUES IN ACCOUNTING RESEARCH: EMPIRICAL EVIDENCE OF COMPARATIVE PERFORMANCE	Education Simulation Academic Issues 298
KENNEDY, JEFFREY LEE	PHD 1987 TEXAS A&M UNIVERSITY	A COMPARISON OF GENERALLY ACCEPTED ACCOUNTING PRACTICE AND STATEMENT OF FINANCIAL ACCOUNTING STANDARDS NO. 33 INCOME MEASUREMENT	Financial Accounting Archival - Primary Inflation 134
KENNEDY, SUSAN JANE	PHD 1992 DUKE UNIVERSITY ASHTON, ROBERT H.	DEBIASING AUDIT JUDGMENT WITH ACCOUNTABILITY: A FRAMEWORK AND EXPERIMENTAL RESULTS	Auditing Experimental Judgment & Decision Making - Heuristics & Biases 155
KENNY, SARA YORK	PHD 1989 UNIVERSITY OF NORTH TEXAS DEAKIN, EDWARD	PREDICTING FAILURE IN THE SAVINGS AND LOAN INDUSTRY: A COMPARISON OF RAP AND GAAP ACCOUNTING	Financial Accounting Archival - Primary Financial Distress or Bankruptcy 141
KENYON, PETER B.	PHD 1985 SANTA CLARA UNIVERSITY	AN INVESTIGATION OF THE EFFECT OF ANNUAL ACCOUNTING REPORTS ON MUNICIPAL BOND INTEREST COST	Not-for-Profit Archival - Primary Governmental 104
KERBY, DEBRA K.	PHD 1989 THE UNIVERSITY OF NEBRASKA - LINCOLN BALKE, THOMAS	CORPORATE LOBBYING AGAINST PROPOSED ACCOUNTING STANDARDS: EVIDENCE FROM THE FASB'S PENSION ACCOUNTING PROJECT	Financial Accounting Archival - Primary Standard Setting 163
KERCSMAR, JOHN	PHD 1985 UNIVERSITY OF HOUSTON	INDIVIDUAL INVESTORS' INFORMATION CHOICE, INFORMATION PROCESSING, AND JUDGMENT BEHAVIOR: A PROCESS-TRACING STUDY OF THE VERBAL PROTOCOLS ASSOCIATED WITH STOCK SELECTION	Financial Accounting Survey Capital Markets 269
KERN, BETH BURCHFIELD	PHD 1986 INDIANA UNIVERSITY	THE IMPACT OF THE ECONOMIC RECOVERY TAX ACT OF 1981 ON CORPORATE INVESTMENT IN PLANT AND EQUIPMENT	Taxation Archival - Primary Investments 185
KERR, DAVID SAMUEL	PHD 1989 MICHIGAN STATE UNIVERSITY	INFORMATION INTEGRATION IN AUDIT PLANNING	Auditing Experimental Audit Planning 226

Listing by Author

Author	Degree & Date School Advisor	Title	Functional Area Research Method Topic pages
KHALIFA, ZAKAA MOHAMED	PHD 1992 RUTGERS THE STATE UNIVERSITY OF NEW JERSEY - NEWARK VASARHELYI, MIKLOS A.	THE IMPACT OF THE FINANCIAL CONDITION OF THE FIRM ON AUDITORS' MATERIALITY/DISCLOSURE JUDGMENTS: AN EXPERIMENTAL STUDY	Auditing Experimental Materiality 168
KHALSA, JODHA SINGH	PHD 1987 ARIZONA STATE UNIVERSITY	CONTEXT EFFECTS IN CERTIFIED PUBLIC ACCOUNTING FIRM SELECTION DECISIONS: THE SMALL BUSINESS ENVIRONMENT	General Survey Small Business 116
KHAN, ZAFAR ULLAH	PHD 1987 THE LOUISIANA STATE UNIVERSITY AND AGRICULTURAL AND MECHANICAL COL. APOSTOLOU, NICHOLAS G.	THE IMPACT OF COMPREHENSIVE ALLOCATION AND FLOW-THROUGH METHOD OF ACCOUNTING FOR THE INCOME TAXES ON THE INVESTMENT DECISION: A FIELD EXPERIMENT	Financial Accounting Experimental Taxes 197
KHURANA, INDER KRISHAN	PHD 1989 ARIZONA STATE UNIVERSITY BOATSMAN, JAMES R.	AN EMPIRICAL INVESTIGATION INTO THE SECURITY MARKET EFFECTS OF FASB STATEMENT NUMBER 94	Financial Accounting Archival - Primary Accounting Change 80
KIANG, YIHWA	PHD 1991 THE UNIVERSITY OF TEXAS AT AUSTIN WHINSTON, ANDREW B.	EXPLORATION OF QUALITATIVE REASONING AND ITS APPLICATIONS TO MANAGEMENT	Auditing Analytical - Internal Decision Support Systems 173
KIDWELL, LINDA ACHEY	PHD 1993 THE LOUISIANA STATE UNIVERSITY AND AGRICULTURAL AND MECHANICAL COL. HARTMAN, BART P.	THE IMPACT OF BUDGET VARIANCE, FISCAL STRESS, POLITICAL TURNOVER, AND EMPLOYMENT SECTOR ON COMPLIANCE REPORTING DECISIONS	Not-for-Profit Case Governmental 154
KILANI, KILANI ABDULKERIM	PHD 1988 UNIVERSITY OF HULL (UNITED KINGDOM)	THE EVOLUTION AND STATUS OF ACCOUNTING IN LIBYA. (VOLUMES I AND II)	General Analytical - Internal International/Global Issues 877
KILE, CHARLES OWEN, JR.	PHD 1993 WASHINGTON UNIVERSITY POWNALL, GRACE	AN ANALYSIS OF THE IMPACT OF OMITTED EVALUATIVE INFORMATION ON FINANCIAL REPORTING: EVIDENCE FROM DISCLOSURES TO AMEND MANAGEMENT'S DISCUSSION AND ANALYSIS	Financial Accounting Archival - Primary Disclosures 63
KILLINGSWORTH, BRENDA LOU	PHD 1987 UNIVERSITY OF SOUTH CAROLINA MARKLAND, ROBERT E.	THE DESIGN OF A KNOWLEDGE-BASED DECISION SUPPORT SYSTEM ENHANCING AUDIT PROGRAM PLANNING	Auditing Analytical - Internal Decision Support Systems 426

Author	Degree & Date School Advisor	Title	Functional Area Research Method Topic pages
KIM, BYOUNG HO	PHD 1991 NORTHWESTERN UNIVERSITY MAGEE, ROBERT	THE ASSOCIATION BETWEEN UNEXPECTED CHANGES IN INVENTORY AND RECEIVABLE BALANCES AND SECURITY PRICE CHANGES: CROSS-SECTIONAL ANALYSES	Financial Accounting Archival - Primary Accruals 171
KIM, CHANGSOO	PHD 1993 FLORIDA INTERNATIONAL UNIVERSITY HENDRICKSON, HARVEY S.	A STUDY OF INVESTMENT IN INFORMATION TECHNOLOGY: FINANCIAL PERFORMANCE EFFECT AND FUTURE ECONOMIC BENEFIT TO THE FIRM	Information Systems Archival - Primary Investments 142
KIM, DONG CHULL	PHD 1989 THE UNIVERSITY OF IOWA SCHEPANSKI, ALBERT	RISK PREFERENCES IN PARTICIPATIVE BUDGETING	Cost/Managerial Experimental Budgeting 104
KIM, DONG HOON	PHD 1987 THE UNIVERSITY OF TEXAS AT AUSTIN	TWO ESSAYS ON ECONOMIC AND FINANCIAL THEORIES OF INSURANCE	General Industry - Insurance 94
KIM, GWON HEE	PHD 1990 THE UNIVERSITY OF WISCONSIN - MADISON NAIR, RAGHAVAN D.	LAG STRUCTURE, AMORTIZATION, AND PRODUCTIVITY CONTRIBUTION OF RESEARCH AND DEVELOPMENT COSTS	Financial Accounting Archival - Primary Research & Development 298
KIM, GYUTAI	PHD 1994 AUBURN UNIVERSITY PARK, CHAN S.	AN ECONOMIC ANALYSIS OF AN ADVANCED MANUFACTURING SYSTEM WITH ACTIVITY-BASED COSTING SYSTEMS	Cost/Managerial Analytical - Internal Activity Based Costing 178
KIM, HOJOONG	PHD 1993 GEORGIA STATE UNIVERSITY PARK, MANYONG	AN INVESTIGATION INTO FACTORS DETERMINING THE CASH FLOWS/STOCK RETURNS RELATIONSHIP	Financial Accounting Archival - Primary Cash Flows 169
KIM, HWAN	PHD 1990 UNIVERSITY OF ILLINOIS AT URBANA-CHAMPAIGN MCKEOWN, JAMES C.	THE SPEED OF SECURITY MARKET REACTION AND THE LEVEL OF UNCERTAINTY ASSOCIATED WITH ANNUAL EARNINGS INFORMATION: ANALYSIS AND EVIDENCE	Financial Accounting Archival - Primary Earnings 92
KIM, HYUK	PHD 1985 INDIANA UNIVERSITY	AN EMPIRICAL STUDY OF THE MARKET REACTION TO STATEMENT OF FINANCIAL ACCOUNTING STANDARDS NO. 52: 'FOREIGN CURRENCYTRANSLATION'	Financial Accounting Archival - Primary Foreign Currency Translation 201

Listing by Author

111

Author	Degree & Date School Advisor	Title	Functional Area Research Method Topic pages
KIM, IL-WOON	PHD 1985 THE UNIVERSITY OF NEBRASKA - LINCOLN	AN EMPIRICAL STUDY ON THE INFORMATION CONTENT OF FINANCIAL LEVERAGE TO STOCKHOLDERS	Financial Accounting Archival - Primary Capital Structure 180
KIM, JAE-OH	PHD 1987 THE UNIVERSITY OF IOWA	SEGMENTAL DISCLOSURES AND INFORMATION CONTENT OF EARNINGS ANNOUNCEMENTS: THEORETICAL AND EMPIRICAL ANALYSIS	Financial Accounting Archival - Primary Segment Reporting 114
KIM, JEEHONG	PHD 1987 UNIVERSITY OF CALIFORNIA, BERKELEY PENMAN, STEPHEN	THE E/P EFFECT AND THE EARNINGS FORECAST ERROR EFFECT: A COMPARISON OF TWO STOCK MARKET ANOMALIES	Financial Accounting Archival - Primary Forecasting Financial Performance 187
KIM, JEONG BON	PHD 1986 TEMPLE UNIVERSITY	EMPIRICAL EVALUATION OF THE VALUES OF ACCOUNTING ALTERNATIVES IN THE OIL AND GAS INDUSTRY IN THE CONTEXT OF RISK ASSESSMENT	Financial Accounting Archival - Primary Industry - Oil & Gas 186
KIM, JEONG YOUN	PHD 1989 WASHINGTON STATE UNIVERSITY ETTREDGE, MICHAEL	AN EMPIRICAL INVESTIGATION OF THE EFFECT OF LIFO ADOPTION ON DIVIDEND POLICIES	Financial Accounting Archival - Primary Dividends 168
KIM, JEONG-JAE	PHD 1992 GEORGIA STATE UNIVERSITY JACOBS, FRED A.	PRICE AND VOLUME REACTION TO THE ANNOUNCEMENT OF QUALIFIED AUDIT OPINIONS	Financial Accounting Archival - Primary Audit Opinion 185
KIM, JEONGKUK	PHD 1991 THE UNIVERSITY OF NEBRASKA - LINCOLN RAYMOND, ROBERT H.	THE EFFECT OF SFAS NO. 52 ON THE SECURITY ANALYSTS' PERCEPTION OF THE PREDICTIVE USEFULNESS OF REPORTED EARNINGS	Financial Accounting Archival - Primary Foreign Currency Translation 91
KIM, JINSUN	PHD 1990 THE UNIVERSITY OF TEXAS AT AUSTIN MAY, ROBERT G.	AN EMPIRICAL ANALYSIS OF CHANGES IN INVENTORY ACCOUNTING METHODS IN 1974	Financial Accounting Archival - Primary Inventory 182
KIM, JONG HO	PHD 1988 UNIVERSITY OF MISSOURI - COLUMBIA HOWARD, THOMAS; STEWART, JENICE	A BETTER SURROGATE FOR MARKET EXPECTATION OF QUARTERLY EARNINGS	Financial Accounting Archival - Primary Forecasting Financial Performance 126

Author	Degree & Date School Advisor	Title	Functional Area Research Method Topic pages
KIM, JOOHO	PHD 1986 UNIVERSITY OF COLORADO AT BOULDER	TOBIN'S Q VERSUS MODIFIED Q: AN INVESTIGATION OF SHAREHOLDERS' WEALTH MAXIMIZATION VERSUS FIRM VALUE MAXIMIZATION	General Archival - Primary Investments 124
KIM, JUN	PHD 1993 MEMPHIS STATE UNIVERSITY LUKAWITZ, JAMES M.	PRIOR AND POSTERIOR BELIEFS, DIVERGENCE OF ANALYSTS' FORECASTS, AND TRADING ACTIVITY	Financial Accounting Archival - Primary Financial Analysts 109
KIM, KWON-JUNG	PHD 1991 STATE UNIVERSITY OF NEW YORK AT BUFFALO BROWN, LAWRENCE D.	INFORMATION RELEASES, STOCK RETURNS, AND FIRM SIZE	Financial Accounting Archival - Primary Earnings Announcements 107
KIM, KYUNGHO	PHD 1987 PURDUE UNIVERSITY SCHROEDER, DOUGLAS A	THE EFFECT OF ACCOUNTING BASED BONUS PLAN INCENTIVES ON MANAGERS' FINANCIAL REPORTING BEHAVIOR AND ANALYSTS' FORECAST ACCURACY	Financial Accounting Archival - Primary Accounting Choice 94
KIM, MOON KYUM	PHD 1991 UNIVERSITY OF ILLINOIS AT URBANA-CHAMPAIGN LINKE, CHARLES M.	INCREMENTAL INFORMATION CONTENT OF CASH FLOW VARIABLES: A SPANNING APPROACH	Financial Accounting Archival - Primary Cash Flows 129
KIM, MOONCHUL	PHD 1993 UNIVERSITY OF ILLINOIS AT URBANA-CHAMPAIGN RITTER, JAY R.	THE ROLE OF ACCOUNTING INFORMATION IN THE PRICING OF IPOS	Financial Accounting Archival - Primary Initial Public Offerings 184
KIM, NEUNG JIP	PHD 1988 TEMPLE UNIVERSITY HYON, YONG HA	THE ASSOCIATION OF PERFORMANCE ATTAINMENT PLANS WITH CORPORATE PERFORMANCE	Cost/Managerial Case Incentive Compensation 83
KIM, OLIVER	PHD 1990 UNIVERSITY OF PENNSYLVANIA VERRECCHIA, ROBERT E	PRICE AND VOLUME REACTIONS TO PUBLIC ANNOUNCEMENTS AND ENDOGENOUS PRE-ANNOUNCEMENT INFORMATION	Financial Accounting Archival - Primary Information Content 74
KIM, SUNGSOO	PHD 1993 CITY UNIVERSITY OF NEW YORK LILIEN, STEVEN B.	INTEREST RATE SWAPS: FIRM CHARACTERISTICS, MOTIVATIONS AND DIFFERENTIAL MARKET REACTIONS	Financial Accounting Archival - Primary Long Term Debt 140

Listing by Author

Author	Degree & Date School Advisor	Title	Functional Area Research Method Topic pages
KIM, TAE-YONG	PHD 1990 CITY UNIVERSITY OF NEW YORK LILIEN, STEVEN B.	EARLY DEBT-REDEMPTION: AN EMPIRICAL INVESTIGATION OF MOTIVATION AND IMPACT	Financial Accounting Archival - Primary Long Term Debt 345
KIM, TONG HUN	PHD 1987 UNIVERSITY OF WASHINGTON SUNDEM, GARY L.	THE VALUE OF COMMUNICATION IN A MULTIPLE AGENT FRAMEWORK	Cost/Managerial Analytical - Internal Agency Theory 110
KIM, YONG HWAN	PHD 1993 THE PENNSYLVANIA STATE UNIVERSITY MCKEOWN, JAMES C.	LIQUIDITY, INFORMED TRADING, AND PUBLIC INFORMATION: THEORY AND EVIDENCE--A MARKET MICROSTRUCTURE ANALYSIS	Financial Accounting Archival - Primary Market Microstructure 107
KIMMEL, PAUL DAVID	PHD 1989 THE UNIVERSITY OF WISCONSIN - MADISON NAIR, R. D.	AN INVESTIGATION OF THE USE OF ACCOUNTING NUMBERS IN THE REGULATION OF BANK CAPITAL	Financial Accounting Archival - Primary Industry - Banking/Savings & Loan 182
KIMMELL, SHARON LEE	DBA 1986 KENT STATE UNIVERSITY	AN EXAMINATION OF MANAGEMENT MOTIVATION AND STOCK DISTRIBUTION SIZE	Financial Accounting Stock Transactions 138
KING, JAMES B., II	PHD 1988 INDIANA UNIVERSITY HEINTZ, JAMES	INDIVIDUAL AND TEAM PLANNING MATERIALITY JUDGMENTS IN STRUCTURED AND UNSTRUCTURED ACCOUNTING FIRMS	Auditing Experimental Materiality 229
KING, JOHN WILLIAM	PHD 1986 THE FLORIDA STATE UNIVERSITY	INFORMATION EFFECTS OF TRANSLATION ADJUSTMENTS UNDER SFAS 52 AND SFAS 70	Financial Accounting Archival - Primary Foreign Currency Translation 384
KING, RONALD RAYMOND	PHD 1986 THE UNIVERSITY OF ARIZONA	EFFECTS OF CHANGES IN THE LEVEL OF PUBLIC DISCLOSURE ON THE ACQUISITION OF PRIVATE INFORMATION: AN EXPERIMENTAL MARKETS INVESTIGATION	Financial Accounting Experimental Disclosures 134
KING, TERESA ANN TYSON	PHD 1989 GEORGIA STATE UNIVERSITY - COLLEGE OF BUSINESS ADMINISTRATION STABLER, HENRY	AN ANALYTIC STUDY OF SELECTED CONTRIBUTIONS OF PAUL F. GRADY TO THE DEVELOPMENT OF ACCOUNTANCY	General Archival - Secondary History 160

Author	Degree & Date School Advisor	Title	Functional Area Research Method Topic pages
KING, VICKY ARNOLD	PHD 1989 UNIVERSITY OF ARKANSAS	AUDITOR DECISION-MAKING; AN ANALYSIS OF THE EFFECTS OF ORDERING AND TESTS OF THE PREDICTIVE VALIDITY OF THE CONTRAST/SURPRISE MODEL	Auditing Experimental Judgment & Decision Making - Heuristics & Biases 167
KINNEY, MICHAEL RICHARD	PHD 1990 THE UNIVERSITY OF ARIZONA DAHLIWAL, DAN S.	CHANGES IN CORPORATE CAPITAL STRUCTURES AND INVESTMENT IN RESPONSE TO TAX INCENTIVES IN THE ECONOMIC RECOVERY TAX ACT OF 1981	Taxation Archival - Primary Capital Structure 178
KIRK, FLORENCE REARDON	PHD 1988 CORNELL UNIVERSITY	THE ROLE OF TAXES IN ACQUISITIONS	Taxation Archival - Primary Merger, Acquisition, Reorganization 199
KIRSCH, ROBERT JOHN	PHD 1986 UNIVERSITY OF SOUTH CAROLINA	SFAS NO 52, AN ACCOUNTING POLICY INTERVENTION: U.S.-BASED MULTINATIONAL CORPORATE PRE-ENACTMENT LOBBYING BEHAVIOR AND POST-ENACTMENT REACTION	Financial Accounting Archival - Primary Foreign Currency Translation 147
KITE, DEVAUN MARIE	PHD 1992 UNIVERSITY OF FLORIDA SNOWBALL, DOUG	THE IMPACT OF THE FREQUENCY OF ACCOUNTING-BASED PERFORMANCE REPORTS ON CAPITAL BUDGETING DECISIONS	Cost/Managerial Experimental Capital Budgeting 150
KLEIN, LINDA SCHMID	PHD 1987 THE FLORIDA STATE UNIVERSITY PETERSON, DAVID R.	EARNINGS INFORMATION CONTENT OF STOCK DIVIDEND AND SPLIT ANNOUNCEMENTS	Financial Accounting Archival - Primary Dividends 216
KLEINMAN, GARY BRUCE	PHD 1992 RUTGERS THE STATE UNIVERSITY OF NEW JERSEY - NEWARK HOFFMAN, L. RICHARD	CONSTRUCTING THE AUDITOR AND ACCOUNTANT	General Survey Ethics 252
KLEINSORGE, ILENE K.	PHD 1988 UNIVERSITY OF KANSAS KARNEY, DENNIS	INCORPORATION OF QUALITY CONSIDERATIONS IN MEASURING RELATIVE TECHNICAL EFFICIENCY OF NURSING HOMES	General Archival - Primary Industry - Health Care 152
KLEMSTINE, CHARLES FREDERICK	PHD 1991 THE UNIVERSITY OF MICHIGAN DANOS, PAUL; IMHOFF, EUGENE A. JR.	INTERNAL AND EXTERNAL AUDIT SUBSTITUTION	Auditing Survey Internal Auditing 89

Author	Degree & Date School Advisor	Title	Functional Area Research Method Topic pages
KO, CHEN-EN	PHD 1987 UNIVERSITY OF MINNESOTA	MODEL-BASED SAMPLING IN AUDITING	Auditing Simulation Audit Sampling 174
KO, WANSUK MATTHEW	PHD 1985 THE OHIO STATE UNIVERSITY	AUDITOR'S INCENTIVE, LEGAL LIABILITY AND REPUTATION UNDER INFORMATION ASYMMETRY	Auditing Analytical - Internal Legal Liability 107
KOCH, PAULA LOUISE	PHD 1989 NORTHWESTERN UNIVERSITY MAGEE, ROBERT P.	THE EFFECTS OF FINANCIAL DISTRESS ON ACCOUNTING METHOD CHOICE	Financial Accounting Archival - Primary Accounting Choice 141
KOCHER, CLAUDIA SUE	PHD 1993 MICHIGAN STATE UNIVERSITY GILSTER, JOHN	COSTLY CONTRACTING: THE CASE OF EVENT RISK COVENANTS	Financial Accounting Archival - Primary Long Term Debt 141
KOEN, MARIUS	DCOM 1992 UNIVERSITY OF PRETORIA (SOUTH AFRICA) VILJOEN, G. VAN N.	UTILISING THE COMPUTER AS AN AID FOR TEACHING ACCOUNTING	Education Instructional Methods
KOFMAN, ALFREDO MARCOS	PHD 1990 UNIVERSITY OF CALIFORNIA, BERKELEY	COLLUSION, REPUTATION AND COMMUNICATION: THREE ESSAYS IN ECONOMIC THEORY	General Analytical - Internal Other 230
KOH, HIAN CHYE	PHD 1987 VIRGINIA POLYTECHNIC INSTITUTE AND STATE UNIVERSITY	PREDICTION OF GOING-CONCERN STATUS: A PROBIT MODEL FOR THE AUDITORS	Auditing Archival - Primary Financial Distress or Bankruptcy 171
KOH, SEUNGHEE	PHD 1992 THE UNIVERSITY OF OKLAHOMA MORIARITY, SHANE R.	RATIONAL ACCOUNTING CHOICE UNDER INFORMATION ASYMMETRY: THE CASE OF INVENTORY ACCOUNTING	Financial Accounting Archival - Primary Accounting Choice 94
KOONCE, LISA LYNN	PHD 1990 UNIVERSITY OF ILLINOIS AT URBANA-CHAMPAIGN SOLOMON, I.	BELIEF PERSEVERANCE IN AUDIT ANALYTICAL REVIEW	Auditing Experimental Judgment & Decision Making - Heuristics & Biases 242

Author	Degree & Date School Advisor	Title	Functional Area Research Method Topic pages
KOPCZYNSKI, FRANK JOSEPH	PHD 1993 THE UNION INSTITUTE	THE SYSTEMS PARADIGM IN THE ANALYSIS OF PROSPECTIVE FINANCIAL INFORMATION: A PRAXIS BASED MODEL REFLECTING THE SYSTEMS VIEW OF THE FIRM	Financial Accounting Case Forecasting Financial Performance 427
KOPEL, ROANN RAE	PHD 1986 THE UNIVERSITY OF NORTH CAROLINA AT CHAPEL HILL	VOLUNTARY CHANGES IN ACCOUNTING POLICIES: AN APPLICATION OF THE POSITIVE THEORY OF ACCOUNTING	Financial Accounting Archival - Primary Accounting Change 164
KORTE, LEON	PHD 1992 THE UNIVERSITY OF NEBRASKA - LINCOLN BALKE, THOMAS E.	SYSTEMATIC BIAS EFFECTS AND REGULATOR INTERVENTION: THE SAVINGS AND LOAN INDUSTRY	Financial Accounting Archival - Primary Industry - Banking/Savings & Loan 244
KOTHARI, SRIPRAKASH	PHD 1986 THE UNIVERSITY OF IOWA	A COMPARISON OF ALTERNATIVE PROXIES FOR THE MARKET'S EXPECTATION OF QUARTERLY EARNINGS	Financial Accounting Archival - Primary Earnings 136
KRAWCZYK, KATHERINE ANN	PHD 1992 THE UNIVERSITY OF TEXAS AT AUSTIN ROBINSON, JOHN; MARCHANT, GARRY	REASONING WITHIN TAX RESEARCH: THE EFFECT OF TAX LAW FORM AND ORDER OF FACT PRESENTATION ON PROBLEM REPRESENTATIONS	Taxation Experimental Judgment & Decision Making - Cognitive Processes 140
KREN, LESLIE	PHD 1988 UNIVERSITY OF HOUSTON LIAO, WOODY M.	EFFECTS OF INCENTIVE EMPLOYMENT CONTRACTS ON PERFORMANCE AND INFORMATION REVELATION: EMPIRICAL EVIDENCE	Cost/Managerial Experimental Management Control Systems 176
KRIPPEL, GREGORY LEE	PHD 1991 THE FLORIDA STATE UNIVERSITY LOREK, KENNETH S.	THE ECONOMIC DETERMINANTS OF THE TIME-SERIES PROPERTIES OF EARNINGS, SALES, AND CASH FLOWS FROM OPERATIONS	Financial Accounting Archival - Primary Earnings 230
KRISHNAN, JAGANNATHAN	PHD 1991 THE OHIO STATE UNIVERSITY STEPHENS, RAY G.	AUDITOR SWITCHING, OPINION SHOPPING AND CLIENT SIZE	Auditing Archival - Primary Auditor Changes 124
KROPP, KARL V.	PHD 1992 LEHIGH UNIVERSITY MCALLISTER, GREGORY T.	ASYMPTOTICS OF A FREE BOUNDARY PROBLEM RESULTING FROM THE DETERMINATION OF AN AMORTIZING LOAN'S REFINANCE OPTION	Financial Accounting Analytical - Internal Long Term Debt 84

Listing by Author

Author	Degree & Date School Advisor	Title	Functional Area Research Method Topic pages
KRUEGER, THOMAS MICHAEL	DBA 1987 UNIVERSITY OF KENTUCKY	AN EMPIRICAL ANALYSIS OF THE EFFICIENT MARKET HYPOTHESIS BASED ON WIDELY DISSEMINATED ANOMALY INFORMATION	Financial Accounting Archival - Primary Capital Markets 382
KRUMWIEDE, TIMOTHY GERARD	PHD 1993 TEXAS TECH UNIVERSITY GATELY, MARY SUE	THE EFFECT OF TAXATION ON RESIDENTIAL REAL ESTATE: AN EMPIRICAL ANALYSIS OF REAL ESTATE CONSTRUCTION	Taxation Archival - Primary Industry - Real Estate 176
KUMAR, AKHIL	PHD 1986 UNIVERSITY OF NORTH TEXAS	BUDGET-RELATED PREDICTION MODELS IN THE BUSINESS ENVIRONMENT WITH SPECIAL REFERENCE TO SPOT PRICEPREDICTIONS	General Experimental Industry - Oil & Gas 172
KUMAR, KRISHNA RADHAKRISHNAN	PHD 1988 COLUMBIA UNIVERSITY HARRIS, TREVOR	THE DETERMINANTS OF PERFORMANCE PLAN ADOPTION: AN EMPIRICAL STUDY	Cost/Managerial Archival - Primary Incentive Compensation 295
KURTENBACH, JAMES MATTHEW	PHD 1992 UNIVERSITY OF MISSOURI - COLUMBIA WILSON, EARL R.	ENTITY RELATIONSHIPS: MARKET IMPACT AND MANAGEMENT INCENTIVES	Not-for-Profit Analytical - Internal Governmental 187
KWAK, SU KEUN	PHD 1987 THE UNIVERSITY OF NORTH CAROLINA AT CHAPEL HILL	AN EMPIRICAL EVALUATION OF THE PREDICTIVE ABILITY OF SEGMENT DATA DISCLOSED IN ACCORDANCE WITH FASB STATEMENT NO. 14	Financial Accounting Archival - Primary Segment Reporting 175
KWAK, WIKIL	PHD 1990 THE UNIVERSITY OF NEBRASKA - LINCOLN CHEN, KUNG H.	EARNINGS RESPONSE COEFFICIENTS AND THE QUALITY OF EARNINGS: THE CASE OF AUDITOR CHANGE	Financial Accounting Archival - Primary Earnings Response Coefficients 112
KWIATKOWSKI, VERNON EVERETT	DBA 1986 UNIVERSITY OF KENTUCKY	INFRASTRUCTURE ASSETS: AN ASSESSMENT OF USER NEEDS AND RECOMMENDATIONS FOR FINANCIAL REPORTING	Not-for-Profit Survey Governmental 232
KWON, SOON-YONG	PHD 1990 THE UNIVERSITY OF OKLAHOMA MORIARITY, SHANE R.	INCOME STRATEGY AND EARNINGS RESPONSE COEFFICIENTS	Financial Accounting Archival - Primary Accounting Choice 118

Author	Degree & Date School Advisor	Title	Functional Area Research Method Topic pages
KWON, SOOYOUNG	PHD 1991 WASHINGTON UNIVERSITY POWNALL, GRACE	CHOICE OF CONSOLIDATION POLICY AND PARENT FIRMS' RESPONSES TO SFAS NO. 94: CONSOLIDATION OF ALL MAJORITY-OWNED SUBSIDIARIES	Financial Accounting Archival - Primary Standard Setting 106
KWON, SUNG SOO	PHD 1989 MICHIGAN STATE UNIVERSITY	FINENESS OF INFLATION-ADJUSTED ACCOUNTING DISCLOSURES AND STOCK PRICE VARIABILITY	Financial Accounting Archival - Primary Inflation 125
KWON, SUNKOOK	PHD 1989 THE UNIVERSITY OF OKLAHOMA AYRES, FRANCES L.	ECONOMIC DETERMINANTS OF THE ASSUMED INTEREST RATE IN PENSION ACCOUNTING	Financial Accounting Archival - Primary Post Retirement Benefit Issues 126
LA GRANGE, JOHANNES FREDERICK	DCOM 1992 UNIVERSITY OF PRETORIA (SOUTH AFRICA) DEKKER, G. M.	RESPONSIBILITY ACCOUNTING WITH THE RESTRUCTURING OF CERTAIN INSTITUTIONS	Cost/Managerial Analytical - Internal Management Control Systems
LADNER, ROBERT	DRSOCOEC 1990 UNIVERSITAET INNSBRUCK (AUSTRIA)	BALANCE SHEET ANALYSIS: OLD LEGAL SITUATION [BILANZANALYSE NACH NEUEM RECHT]	Financial Accounting Analytical - Internal International/Global Issues 359
LAGRONE, R. MICHAEL	PHD 1990 UNIVERSITY OF SOUTH CAROLINA	AN EVALUATION OF MULTIVARIATE EARNINGS FORECASTING	Financial Accounting Archival - Primary Forecasting Financial Performance 216
LAI, SYOUCHING	DBA 1992 SOUTHERN ILLINOIS UNIVERSITY AT CARBONDALE STERNER-SOBERY, JULIE	AN ANALYTICAL ANALYSIS OF EPS RULES FOR CONVERTIBLE SECURITIES, WARRANTS, AND OPTIONS	Financial Accounting Archival - Primary Earnings Per Share 142
LANDER, JOEL MARTIN	PHD 1990 UNIVERSITY OF CALIFORNIA, LOS ANGELES HIRSHLEIFER, JACK	ESSAYS ON THE CORPORATE TAX POLICY EFFECTS ON INVESTMENT AND FINANCING CHOICES	Taxation Archival - Primary Public Policy 136
LANDOE, GENE ARLAN	PHD 1992 GOLDEN GATE UNIVERSITY HOMAN, A. GERLOF	THE IMPACT OF MICROCOMPUTER TECHNOLOGY ON NORTHERN CALIFORNIA CERTIFIED PUBLIC ACCOUNTING FIRMS	General Survey Microcomputer Applications 287

Author	Degree & Date School Advisor	Title	Functional Area Research Method Topic pages
LANDRY, RAYMOND MAURICE, JR.	PHD 1987 UNIVERSITY OF ARKANSAS LETZKUS, WILLIAM C.	AN EMPIRICAL INVESTIGATION OF EDP AUDIT JUDGMENTS AND CONSENSUS BETWEEN EXTERNAL AND INTERNAL AUDIT EXPERTS	Auditing Survey EDP Controls 168
LANDRY, STEVEN PAUL	PHD 1992 UNIVERSITY OF COLORADO AT BOULDER SELTO, FRANK H.	ACCOUNTING INFORMATION IN THE BUDGETING DECISION-MAKING PROCESS IN A UNITED STATES GOVERNMENT ASSET INFRASTRUCTURE ENVIRONMENT	Not-for-Profit Case Governmental 194
LANESE, KAREN BENNETT	PHD 1993 UNIVERSITY OF SOUTH FLORIDA O'NEIL, CHERIE J.	VISIBILITY OF INCOME: A MODEL TO PREDICT USE OF THE CHILD CARE CREDIT	Taxation Archival - Primary Individual Taxation 187
LANGEMEIER, BRIAN LEON	PHD 1987 THE UNIVERSITY OF NEBRASKA - LINCOLN	A MODEL OF CHOICE OF BUSINESS ENTITY USING DISCRIMINANT ANALYSIS	General Survey Business Form 319
LANGSAM, SHELDON ALLEN	PHD 1989 UNIVERSITY OF ARKANSAS HAY, LEON E.	THE EFFECT OF MANDATORY INCLUSION OF COMPONENT UNITS ON THE REPORTED FINANCIAL CONDITION OF SELECTED LOCAL GOVERNMENTAL UNITS	Not-for-Profit Archival - Primary Governmental 193
LANGSTON, CAROLYN ANN PATTI	DBA 1987 LOUISIANA TECH UNIVERSITY	AN EVALUATION OF THE COST ACCOUNTING PROCEDURES FOR OUTPATIENT CARE AT A VA MEDICAL CENTER	Cost/Managerial Case Industry - Health Care 229
LARKIN, JOSEPH MICHAEL	PHD 1988 TEMPLE UNIVERSITY SCHWEIKART, JAMES A.	A PERFORMANCE MODEL FOR STAFF AUDITORS IN AN INTERNAL AUDIT ENVIRONMENT	General Case Job Performance, Satisfaction &/or Turnover 161
LARSON, ROBERT KEITH	PHD 1993 THE UNIVERSITY OF UTAH	AN EMPIRICAL INVESTIGATION OF THE RELATIONSHIPS BETWEEN INTERNATIONAL ACCOUNTING STANDARDS, EQUITY MARKETS AND ECONOMIC GROWTH IN DEVELOPING COUNTRIES	Financial Accounting Archival - Primary International/Global Issues 233
LASALLE, RANDALL EUGENE	PHD 1991 DREXEL UNIVERSITY JAIN, ROHIT	THE EFFECT OF CEO TENURE ON EARNINGS MANAGEMENT	Financial Accounting Archival - Primary Earnings Management 299

Listing by Author

120

Author	Degree & Date School Advisor	Title	Functional Area Research Method Topic pages
LAUX, JUDITH ANN	DBA 1990 UNIVERSITY OF COLORADO AT BOULDER MELICHER, RONALD W.	CONTENT ANALYSIS AND CORPORATE BANKRUPTCY	Financial Accounting Archival - Primary Financial Distress or Bankruptcy 179
LAWRENCE, CAROL MARTIN	PHD 1989 INDIANA UNIVERSITY PARRY, ROBERT W. JR.	THE EFFECT OF ACCOUNTING SYSTEM TYPE AND OWNERSHIP STRUCTURE ON HOSPITAL COSTS	General Archival - Primary Industry - Health Care 197
LAWRENCE, JANICE ELIZABETH	PHD 1992 TEXAS A&M UNIVERSITY STRAWSER, ROBERT H.	AUDITS OF A FEDERAL LOAN PROGRAM: A CLASSIFICATION MODEL OF REPORTED IRREGULARITIES	Auditing Case Audit Opinion 150
LAWRENCE, ROBYN	PHD 1988 UNIVERSITY OF HOUSTON KHUMAWALA, SALEHA B.	IN-SUBSTANCE DEFEASANCE: AN EMPIRICAL EXAMINATION OF THE FACTORS AFFECTING THE MARKET REACTION AND THE DECISION	Financial Accounting Archival - Primary Long Term Debt 162
LAZAR, LAURA KRISTEN	PHD 1986 INDIANA UNIVERSITY	EFFECTS OF PENSION INFORMATION ON CREDIT QUALITY JUDGMENTS OF MUNICIPAL BOND ANALYSTS	Not-for-Profit Experimental Post Retirement Benefit Issues 127
LEAUBY, BRUCE ALAN	PHD 1990 DREXEL UNIVERSITY	DETERMINANTS OF CORPORATE TAX AVOIDANCE STRATEGY: AN EMPIRICAL ANALYSIS	Taxation Archival - Primary Tax Compliance 140
LEAVINS, JOHN R.	PHD 1987 UNIVERSITY OF HOUSTON LIAO, WOODY	AN EXAMINATION OF BUDGET SLACK WITHIN AN EXPECTANCY THEORY FRAMEWORK	Cost/Managerial Budgeting 144
LECLERE, MARC JOSEPH	PHD 1989 THE PENNSYLVANIA STATE UNIVERSITY KETZ, J. EDWARD	THE MEASUREMENT AND INTERPRETATION OF A CASHFLOW AVERAGE EFFECTIVE TAX RATE	Taxation Public Policy 278
LEE, ANDREW TONG KIN	PHD 1993 NEW YORK UNIVERSITY, GRADUATE SCHOOL OF BUSINESS ADMINISTRATION RONEN, JOSHUA	ON DELAYED RESPONSES TO EARNINGS ANNOUNCEMENTS	Financial Accounting Archival - Primary Earnings Announcements 112

Author	Degree & Date School Advisor	Title	Functional Area Research Method Topic pages
LEE, BYUNG-CHULL	PHD 1993 UNIVERSITY OF KANSAS BUBLITZ, BRUCE O.	ECONOMIC CONSEQUENCES OF THE ACCOUNTING RULE FOR SOFTWARE COSTS	Financial Accounting Archival - Primary Standard Setting 155
LEE, CHANGWOO	PHD 1987 UNIVERSITY OF CALIFORNIA, BERKELEY OHLSON, JAMES	MARKET REACTIONS TO LEASE LIABILITIES AND REPORTING ENVIRONMENT CHANGES	Financial Accounting Archival - Primary Leases 163
LEE, CHARLES M. C.	PHD 1990 CORNELL UNIVERSITY	INFORMATION DISSEMINATION AND THE SMALL TRADER: AN INTRADAY ANALYSIS OF THE SMALL TRADER RESPONSE TO ANNOUNCEMENTS OF CORPORATE EARNINGS AND CHANGES IN DIVIDEND POLICY	Financial Accounting Archival - Primary Earnings Announcements 139
LEE, DAISUN	PHD 1987 THE UNIVERSITY OF NEBRASKA - LINCOLN RAYMOND, ROBERT H.	INFORMATION CONTENT AND ECONOMIC CONSEQUENCES OF INTERIM SEGMENT REPORTING: AN EMPIRICAL TEST	Financial Accounting Archival - Primary Segment Reporting 94
LEE, EUNSANG	PHD 1990 STANFORD UNIVERSITY WOLFSON, MARK A.	TAX TREATMENT UNCERTAINTY AND THE IRS INDIVIDUAL RULINGS PROGRAM--A COMPREHENSIVE ANALYSIS	Taxation Analytical - Internal Individual Taxation 111
LEE, HYUN-SOO	PHD 1992 THE UNIVERSITY OF MICHIGAN CARR, ROBERT I.; IOANNOU, PHOTIOS G.	AUTOMATED INTERACTIVE COST ESTIMATING SYSTEM FOR REINFORCED CONCRETE BUILDING STRUCTURES	Information Systems Analytical - Internal Cost Systems 232
LEE, IHNSHIK	PHD 1992 UNIVERSITY OF NORTH TEXAS KUANLI, AL	A SIMULATION STUDY COMPARING VARIOUS CONFIDENCE INTERVALS FOR THE MEAN OF VOUCHER POPULATIONS IN ACCOUNTING	Auditing Simulation Audit Sampling 119
LEE, JONG-CHEON	PHD 1989 UNIVERSITY OF ILLINOIS AT URBANA-CHAMPAIGN MCKEOWN, JAMES C.	OPTIMAL CONTRACTING WITH PREDECISION INFORMATION: COMMUNICATION PROBLEMS UNDER PURE ASYMMETRY OF INFORMATION	General Analytical - Internal Agency Theory 126
LEE, KYUNG JOO	PHD 1990 THE UNIVERSITY OF ARIZONA DHALIWAL, DAN S.	THE EFFECT OF TIME-SERIES PROPERTIES ON THE PREDICTIVE VALUE OF QUARTERLY EARNINGS FOR FORECASTING ANNUAL EARNINGS	Financial Accounting Archival - Primary Forecasting Financial Performance 119

Author	Degree & Date School Advisor	Title	Functional Area Research Method Topic pages
LEE, KYUNG TAE	PHD 1992 UNIVERSITY OF CALIFORNIA, LOS ANGELES MILLER, BRUCE; SUH, YOON	OPTIMAL CONTROL SYSTEMS IN MANAGERIAL ACCOUNTING	Cost/Managerial Analytical - Internal Transfer Pricing 98
LEE, MANWOO	PHD 1987 UNIVERSITY OF GEORGIA	IMPACT OF UTILIZING LONG-TERM EXECUTIVE COMPENSATION PLANS ON CAPITAL INVESTMENT DECISIONS	Cost/Managerial Archival - Primary Incentive Compensation 198
LEE, MINWOO	PHD 1993 UNIVERSITY OF PITTSBURGH PRAKASH, PREM	THE ROLES OF AUDITORS AND INVESTMENT BANKERS IN SIGNALLING PRIVATE INFORMATION AND INSURING LITIGATION RISK IN THE NEW EQUITY ISSUES MARKET	Financial Accounting Archival - Primary Initial Public Offerings 129
LEE, MYUNG GON	PHD 1990 UNIVERSITY OF MISSOURI - COLUMBIA WILSON, EARL	THE DIFFERENTIAL PREDICTIVE INFORMATION CONTENT OF EARNINGS ON ANALYSTS' FORECAST REVISIONS	Financial Accounting Archival - Primary Financial Analysts 122
LEE, NAM JOO	PHD 1988 THE UNIVERSITY OF TEXAS AT AUSTIN MAY, ROBERT G.	AN EMPIRICAL EVALUATION OF OUTLIER ADJUSTED QUARTERLY EARNINGS	Financial Accounting Archival - Primary Forecasting Financial Performance 149
LEE, SANGSOO	PHD 1986 THE UNIVERSITY OF TEXAS AT AUSTIN	DECENTRALIZATION, INFORMATIONAL ASYMMETRY, AND THE VALUE OF COMMUNICATION AND DELEGATION	Cost/Managerial Analytical - Internal Other 105
LEE, SEOK-YOUNG	PHD 1992 UNIVERSITY OF MINNESOTA BANKER, RAJIV D.	ESSAYS ON MANAGEMENT ACCOUNTING AND INCENTIVE CONTRACTS FOR SOME NEW PRODUCTION AND SELLING STRATEGIES	Cost/Managerial Case Incentive Compensation 135
LEE, SUK JUN	PHD 1993 WASHINGTON UNIVERSITY POWNALL, GRACE	THE EFFECT OF GAAP DIFFERENCES ON PRICE VARIABILITY AND DISPERSION OF BELIEFS	Financial Accounting Archival - Primary International/Global Issues 85
LEFANOWICZ, CRAIG EDWARD	PHD 1990 THE UNIVERSITY OF TEXAS AT AUSTIN OLSEN, JOHN CHRISTIAN III	IMPLICATIONS OF CHANGES IN EQUITY VALUES ASSOCIATED WITH SIGNIFICANT EQUITY INVESTMENTS FOR INVESTEE AND INVESTOR FIRMS	Financial Accounting Archival - Primary Investments 165

Author	Degree & Date School Advisor	Title	Functional Area Research Method Topic pages
LEGGE, REBECCA SUE SCRUGGS	PHD 1988 THE UNIVERSITY OF MISSISSIPPI TAYLOR, CHARLES W.	A HISTORY OF WOMEN CERTIFIED PUBLIC ACCOUNTANTS IN THE UNITED STATES	General Archival - Secondary History 325
LEGGETT, CARL LEE	PHD 1990 THE UNIVERSITY OF MISSISSIPPI THOMPSON, JAMES H.	AN EMPIRICAL INVESTIGATION OF THE MARKET REACTION TO SELECTED CATEGORIES OF DISCRETIONARY CHARGES	Financial Accounting Archival - Primary Earnings Management 169
LEHMAN, CHERYL R.	PHD 1985 NEW YORK UNIVERSITY, GRADUATE SCHOOL OF BUSINESS ADMINISTRATION	DISCOURSE ANALYSIS AND ACCOUNTING LITERATURE: TRANSFORMATION OF STATE HEGEMONY, 1960 - 1973	General Archival - Secondary History 264
LEINICKE, LINDA M.	PHD 1987 THE UNIVERSITY OF MISSISSIPPI	AN ANALYSIS OF THE BUSINESS ADVISORY SERVICE ACCOUNTANT VERSUS THE TRADITIONAL ACCOUNTING SERVICE ACCOUNTANT, WITH IMPLICATIONS FOR THE ACCOUNTING PROFESSION	General Survey CPA Firm Issues 238
LEMLER, BRADLEY K.	PHD 1990 INDIANA UNIVERSITY KULSRUD, WILLIAM N.	TAXPAYER EXPECTATIONS, TAX INVESTMENT INCENTIVES AND TAXPAYER ECONOMIC BEHAVIOR: AN ANALYSIS OF INVESTMENT BEHAVIOR IN MANUFACTURING FIRMS FROM 1954 TO 1985	Taxation Archival - Primary Tax Compliance 173
LENK, MARGARITA MARIA	PHD 1991 UNIVERSITY OF SOUTH CAROLINA HARRELL, ADRIAN	PRIVATE INFORMATION AND A MANAGER'S MOTIVATION: AN EXPECTANCY THEORY TEST OF AGENCY THEORY'S EFFORT-AVERSION ASSUMPTION IN A PARTICIPATIVE BUDGETING SETTING	Cost/Managerial Experimental Budgeting 161
LEONG, KENNETH KIN ON	DBA 1985 UNIVERSITY OF COLORADO AT BOULDER	THE EXISTENCE OF BONUS COMPENSATION PLANS AND THE RELATED EFFECT ON THE SIZE OF REPORTED ACCOUNTING EARNINGS	Cost/Managerial Archival - Primary Incentive Compensation 131
LETOURNEAU, CLAIRE ANGELA	DBA 1987 LOUISIANA TECH UNIVERSITY	FINANCIAL DISCLOSURE AND THE ACCOUNTANT'S RESPONSIBILITY TO SHAREHOLDERS: THE CASE OF INSIDER TRADING	Financial Accounting Archival - Primary Insider Trading 111
LEUNG, VICTOR KWAN LAP	PHD 1991 UNIVERSITY OF ARKANSAS MILLAR, JAMES A.	BUDGETING IN RESPECT TO INFORMATION ASYMMETRY, PARTICIPATION AND EVALUATION FROM PERSPECTIVES OF AGENCY THEORY AND SOCIAL BEHAVIOR THEORY	Cost/Managerial Survey Budgeting 185

Author	Degree & Date School Advisor	Title	Functional Area Research Method Topic pages
LEVENSTEIN, MARGARET CATHERINE	PHD 1991 YALE UNIVERSITY PARKER, WILLIAM N.	INFORMATION SYSTEMS AND INTERNAL ORGANIZATION: A STUDY OF THE DOW CHEMICAL COMPANY, 1890-1914	Information Systems Case Systems Design &/or Development 410
LEWELLYN, PATSY ANN GRANGER	DBA 1987 LOUISIANA TECH UNIVERSITY	AN INVESTIGATION OF FACTORS RELATED TO TERMINATION IN THE PUBLIC ACCOUNTING PROFESSION AND THE QUALITY OF LIFE OF CERTIFIED PUBLIC ACCOUNTANTS	General Survey Job Performance, Satisfaction &/or Turnover 124
LEWIS, MERRILL TIM	PHD 1985 UNIVERSITY OF SOUTHERN CALIFORNIA	EX ANTE EVALUATION OF AUDIT EVIDENCE	Auditing Analytical - Internal Audit Planning
LI, JUNE FANG	PHD 1992 UNIVERSITY OF KENTUCKY KNOBLETT, JAMES A.; CLARK, MYRTLE W.	AN EMPIRICAL STUDY OF THE PERCEPTIONS OF FINANCIAL EXECUTIVES AND FINANCIAL ANALYSTS REGARDING SELECTEDASPECTS OF FOREIGN CURRENCY TRANSLATION AS CURRENTLY PROMULGATED BY THE FINANCIAL ACCOUNTING STANDARDS BOARD	Financial Accounting Survey Foreign Currency Translation 183
LI, SHU-HSING	PHD 1990 NEW YORK UNIVERSITY, GRADUATE SCHOOL OF BUSINESS ADMINISTRATION BALACHANDRAN, KASHI R.	TRANSFER PRICING UNDER INFORMATION ASYMMETRY IN MULTIAGENT SETTINGS	Cost/Managerial Analytical - Internal Transfer Pricing 140
LIGHTLE, SUSAN SANTALUCIA	PHD 1992 UNIVERSITY OF CINCINNATI RICKETTS, JERI B.	AN EMPIRICAL INVESTIGATION OF THE EFFECT OF THE USE OF INTERNAL CONTROL CHECKLISTS ON AUDITORS' INTERNAL CONTROL EVALUATIONS	Auditing Experimental Decision Aids 179
LILLIE, RICHARD EUGENE	EDD 1990 NORTHERN ILLINOIS UNIVERSITY	AN ANALYSIS OF LEARNING STYLES OF PROFESSIONAL PERSONNEL BY LEVEL AND BY FUNCTION WITHIN A NATIONAL PUBLIC ACCOUNTING FIRM (ACCOUNTING EDUCATION)	General Survey Accounting Career Issues 117
LIM, SUK SIG	PHD 1990 UNIVERSITY OF MINNESOTA	ACCURACY OF PARTIAL VALUATION RULES AND OPTIMAL USE OF PRICE INDEXES	Financial Accounting Archival - Primary Inflation 152
LIM, TAYSEOP	PHD 1993 THE UNIVERSITY OF NORTH CAROLINA AT CHAPEL HILL LANDSMAN, WAYNE R.	THE EFFECT OF INFORMATION ASYMMETRY AROUND EARNINGS ANNOUNCEMENTS	Financial Accounting Archival - Primary Earnings Announcements 184

Listing by Author

Author	Degree & Date School Advisor	Title	Functional Area Research Method Topic pages
LIN, HSIOU-WEI WILLIAM	PHD 1994 STANFORD UNIVERSITY MCNICHOLS, MAUREEN F.	SECURITY ANALYSTS' INVESTMENT RECOMMENDATIONS	Financial Accounting Archival - Primary Financial Analysts 151
LIN, LIANGQI	DRECON 1993 KATHOLIEKE UNIVERSITEIT LEUVEN (BELGIUM)	ECONOMIC DETERMINANTS OF VOLUNTARY ACCOUNTING CHOICES FOR R&D EXPENDITURES IN BELGIUM	Financial Accounting Archival - Primary International/Global Issues 200
LIN, MEI-HWA	PHD 1987 DREXEL UNIVERSITY	AN EMPIRICAL STUDY OF INFORMATION TRANSFER FROM A LEADING FIRM TO LARGE FIRMS AND SMALL FIRMS IN THE SAME INDUSTRY	Financial Accounting Archival - Primary Information Transfer 129
LIN, PAO-CHUAN	PHD 1988 THE LOUISIANA STATE UNIVERSITY AND AGRICULTURAL AND MECHANICAL COL. HARTMAN, BART P.	INFORMATION ACQUISITION AND DECISION MAKING IN CREDITORS' DECISION ENVIRONMENT	Financial Accounting Experimental Bank Loan Officers 156
LIN, SUMING	PHD 1993 ARIZONA STATE UNIVERSITY CHRISTIAN, CHARLES W.	INCOME TAX RETURN PREPARATION FEES AND TAX SAVINGS OF USING TAX RETURN PREPARERS	Taxation Archival - Primary Tax Professionals 86
LIN, WENSHAN	PHD 1994 UNIVERSITY OF NORTH TEXAS RAMAN, K. K.	ACCOUNTING REGULATION AND INFORMATION ASYMMETRY IN THE CAPITAL MARKETS: AN EMPIRICAL STUDY OF ACCOUNTING STANDARD SFAS NO 87	Financial Accounting Archival - Primary Post Retirement Benefit Issues 165
LIN, YOU-AN ROBERT	PHD 1989 UNIVERSITY OF CALIFORNIA, LOS ANGELES LANDSMAN, WAYNE R.	THE USE OF SUPPLEMENTARY ACCOUNTING DISCLOSURES FOR CORPORATE TAKEOVER TARGETS PREDICTION	Financial Accounting Archival - Primary Inflation 86
LINDAHL, FREDERICK WILLIAM	PHD 1985 THE UNIVERSITY OF CHICAGO	QUANTAL CHOICE MODELS AND ACCOUNTING CHANGE	Financial Accounting Archival - Primary Accounting Change
LINDQUIST, TIMOTHY MARK	PHD 1991 UNIVERSITY OF COLORADO AT BOULDER YOUNG, S. MARK	DISTRIBUTIVE AND PROCEDURAL JUSTICE: IMPLICATIONS FOR MANAGEMENT CONTROLS AND INCENTIVE SYSTEMS	Cost/Managerial Experimental Incentive Compensation 171

Author	Degree & Date School Advisor	Title	Functional Area Research Method Topic pages
LINDSAY, DAVID HENDERSON	PHD 1992 KENT STATE UNIVERSITY ALAM, PERVAIZ; FETYKO, DAVID F.	A TEST OF CONTRACTING COST THEORY ON STATEMENT OF FINANCIAL ACCOUNTING STANDARDS NO. 2: ACCOUNTING FOR RESEARCH AND DEVELOPMENT COSTS	Financial Accounting Archival - Primary Research & Development 162
LINDSAY, ROGER MURRAY	PHD 1988 UNIVERSITY OF LANCASTER (UNITED KINGDOM)	THE USE OF TESTS OF SIGNIFICANCE IN ACCOUNTING RESEARCH: A METHODOLOGICAL, PHILOSOPHICAL AND EMPIRICAL INQUIRY	Cost/Managerial Archival - Secondary Methodology 440
LINNEGAR, GARY JOHN	DBA 1988 MISSISSIPPI STATE UNIVERSITY HERRING, DORA R.	AN INVESTIGATION INTO THE MANAGEMENT OF CHANGE IN COST ACCOUNTING INFORMATION SYSTEM REQUIREMENTS DURING THE TRANSITION FROM TRADITIONAL MANUFACTURING TO JUST IN TIME CONCEPTS	Cost/Managerial Case Inventory 190
LINSMEIER, THOMAS J.	PHD 1985 THE UNIVERSITY OF WISCONSIN - MADISON	A DEBT COVENANT RATIONALE FOR A MARKET REACTION TO A MANDATED ACCOUNTING CHANGE: THE CASE OF THE INVESTMENT TAX CREDIT	Financial Accounting Archival - Primary Accounting Change 129
LINTON, FRANK BRUCE	PHD 1992 UNIVERSITY OF HOUSTON HORVITZ, JEROME S.	FEDERAL INCOME TAXING SYSTEM AND ITS EFFECT ON STATE INCOME TAX STRUCTURES	Taxation Archival - Primary State Taxation 327
LIPE, ROBERT CALVIN	PHD 1985 THE UNIVERSITY OF CHICAGO	THE INFORMATION CONTAINED IN THE COMPONENTS OF EARNINGS	Financial Accounting Archival - Primary Earnings
LIPPMAN, ELLEN J.	PHD 1991 UNIVERSITY OF OREGON GERNON, HELEN	AN INVESTIGATION OF THE EFFECTS OF LOAD, FORMAT, AND EXPERTISE ON DECISION QUALITY AND DECISION PROCESSING STRATEGIES	General Experimental Judgment & Decision Making 254
LITTLE, PHILIP LEE	DBA 1986 LOUISIANA TECH UNIVERSITY	AN EXAMINATION OF FACTORS RELEVANT TO THE PREDICTION OF GOING CONCERN SUBJECT-TO QUALIFICATIONS OR DISCLAIMERS OF OPINION IN THE OIL AND GAS INDUSTRY	Auditing Archival - Primary Financial Distress or Bankruptcy 143
LIU, CHAO-SHIN	PHD 1992 UNIVERSITY OF ILLINOIS AT URBANA-CHAMPAIGN ZIEBART, DAVID. A.	MANAGEMENT EARNINGS FORECASTS, SECURITY PRICE VARIABILITY, AND THE MARGINAL INFORMATION CONTENT OF EARNINGS ANNOUNCEMENTS	Financial Accounting Archival - Primary Voluntary Management Disclosures 123

Listing by Author

Author	Degree & Date School Advisor	Title	Functional Area Research Method Topic pages
LIU, CHI-CHUN	PHD 1994 NEW YORK UNIVERSITY, GRADUATE SCHOOL OF BUSINESS ADMINISTRATION RONEN, JOSHUA	TRADERS' MULTIPLE INFORMATION ACQUISITION AND ITS IMPACT ON MARKET BEHAVIOR: A RATIONAL EXPECTATIONS ANALYSIS	Financial Accounting Analytical - Internal Agency Theory 168
LIU, SHUEN-ZEN	PHD 1993 UNIVERSITY OF PITTSBURGH PATTON, JAMES M.	SIGNALING, CAPITAL ADEQUACY RATIO REGULATIONS, AND THE RECOGNITION OF LOAN IMPAIRMENT BY COMMERCIAL BANKS	Financial Accounting Archival - Primary Industry - Banking/Savings & Loan 185
LIU, SUPING	PHD 1994 FLORIDA INTERNATIONAL UNIVERSITY DAVIDSON, LEWIS F.	SFAS 94: AN EXAMINATION OF THE ASSOCIATION BETWEEN MARKET AND ACCOUNTING RISK MEASUREMENTS	Financial Accounting Archival - Primary Risk 131
LO, MAY HWA	PHD 1992 DREXEL UNIVERSITY JAIN, ROHIT	DIFFERENTIAL CAPITAL MARKET VALUATIONS OF FUNCTIONAL COMPONENTS OF EARNINGS: AN EMPIRICAL ANALYSIS	Financial Accounting Archival - Primary Earnings 224
LOPEZ GRACIA, JOSE	PHD 1991 UNIVERSITAT DE VALENCIA (SPAIN)	ACCOUNTING INFORMATION AND STOCK EXCHANGE: EMPIRICAL ANALYSIS OF THE INTERIM REPORTS AND THEIR RELEVANCE IN DECISION-MAKING [LA INFORMACION CONTABLE Y EL MERCADO DE VALORES: ANALISIS EMPIRICO DE LOS INFORMES INTERMEDIOS Y SU RELEVANCIA EN LA TOMA DE DECISIONES]	Financial Accounting Archival - Primary Interim Reporting 700
LORD, ALAN TUNIS	PHD 1989 CASE WESTERN RESERVE UNIVERSITY PREVITS, GARY JOHN	THE EFFECTS OF CONTEXTUAL FACTORS ON AUDITORS' DECISION BEHAVIOR UNDER PRESSURE	Auditing Experimental Judgment & Decision Making 213
LOUDDER, MARTHA LYNN	PHD 1990 ARIZONA STATE UNIVERSITY BOATSMAN, JIM	AN EMPIRICAL INVESTIGATION OF THE ECONOMIC EFFECTS OF SFAS 90 AND 92 IN THE ELECTRIC UTILITY INDUSTRY	Financial Accounting Archival - Primary Industry - Utilities 82
LOUWERS, TIMOTHY JAMES	PHD 1993 THE FLORIDA STATE UNIVERSITY WHEELER, STEPHEN W.	AN EMPIRICAL INVESTIGATION OF THE RELATIONSHIP BETWEEN FINANCIAL DISTRESS, EXTERNAL FACTORS, AND THE AUDITOR'S GOING CONCERN OPINION MODIFICATION	Auditing Survey Audit Opinion 110
LOVE, WILLIAM H.	PHD 1986 UNIVERSITY OF ARKANSAS	SIMULATED PENSION SCENARIOS WITH STOCHASTIC DEMOGRAPHIC AND INVESTMENT EXPERIENCE UTILIZING ALTERNATIVE ACTUARIAL COST METHODS AND ACCOUNTING PRINCIPLES	Financial Accounting Simulation Post Retirement Benefit Issues 355

Author	Degree & Date School Advisor	Title	Functional Area Research Method Topic pages
LOWE, DANA R.	PHD 1993 THE GEORGE WASHINGTON UNIVERSITY PAIK, CHEI-MIN	THE RELATIONSHIP BETWEEN STRATEGY CHANGE AND THE DESIGN OF MANAGEMENT ACCOUNTING SYSTEMS: A MULTIPLE CASE STUDY	Cost/Managerial Case Management Control Systems 330
LOWE, DAVID JORDAN	PHD 1992 ARIZONA STATE UNIVERSITY	AN EMPIRICAL EXAMINATION OF THE HINDSIGHT BIAS PHENOMENON IN EVALUATION OF AUDITOR DECISIONS	Auditing Experimental Judgment & Decision Making - Heuristics & Biases 133
LOYLAND, MARY JENNIFER OLSON	PHD 1989 THE UNIVERSITY OF NEBRASKA - LINCOLN BALKE, THOMAS	AN EMPIRICAL INVESTIGATION OF CPA FIRM ATTRIBUTES AND PROFESSIONAL LIABILITY COVERAGE	General CPA Firm Issues 173
LUBICH, BRUCE HOWARD	PHD 1991 THE PENNSYLVANIA STATE UNIVERSITY MCKEOWN, JAMES C.	THE IMPACT OF TAX NONCOMPLIANCE ON HORIZONTAL AND VERTICAL DISTRIBUTIONS OF INCOME	Taxation Archival - Primary Tax Compliance 259
LUCAS, MARCIA J.	PHD 1991 SAINT LOUIS UNIVERSITY JENNINGS, JAMES P.	EARNINGS PER SHARE: A STUDY OF CURRENT REPORTING	Financial Accounting Archival - Primary Earnings Per Share 136
LUEHLFING, MICHAEL STEVEN	PHD 1990 UNIVERSITY OF GEORGIA SHOCKLEY, RANDOLPH A. (SKIP)	THE IMPACT OF CLIENT RISK CHARACTERISTICS AND AUDIT PARTNER EXPERIENCE ON THE EXTENT OF THE SECOND PARTNER REVIEW IN AUDIT ENGAGEMENTS	Auditing Case Risk 156
LUFT, JOAN LUISE	PHD 1992 CORNELL UNIVERSITY LIBBY, ROBERT	BONUS AND PENALTY INCENTIVES: CONTRACT CHOICE BY EMPLOYEES	Cost/Managerial Experimental Incentive Compensation 136
LUKAWITZ, JAMES MARTIN	PHD 1989 THE FLORIDA STATE UNIVERSITY LOREK, KENNETH S.	THE EFFECT OF PARTIAL EQUITY ISSUES ON THE MEASUREMENT OF FINANCIAL LEVERAGE	Financial Accounting Archival - Primary Capital Structure 187
LUNDBLAD, HEIDEMARIE	PHD 1986 UNIVERSITY OF WASHINGTON	VOLUNTARY FINANCIAL DISCLOSURE: AN INTERNATIONAL COMPARISON OF MANAGERIAL POLICIES	Financial Accounting Survey International/Global Issues 563

Author	Degree & Date School Advisor	Title	Functional Area Research Method Topic pages
LUTTMAN, SUZANNE MARIE	PHD 1988 UNIVERSITY OF ILLINOIS AT URBANA-CHAMPAIGN	THE DISTRIBUTIONAL AND LABOR SUPPLY EFFECTS OF ALTERNATIVE INDIVIDUAL INCOME TAX PROPOSALS	Taxation Archival - Primary Public Policy 90
LYNCH, HOWELL JACKSON, JR.	PHD 1991 TEXAS A&M UNIVERSITY CRUMBLEY, LARRY	EFFECTIVE CORPORATE INCOME TAX RATES AND THEIR RELATIONSHIP TO CORPORATE ATTRIBUTES: A MULTIDEFINITIONAL, MULTIPERIOD VIEW	Taxation Archival - Primary Corporate Taxation 104
LYON, JOHN DOUGLAS	PHD 1991 THE OHIO STATE UNIVERSITY BAILEY, ANDREW D. JR.	THE VALUATION INFORMATION ASSOCIATED WITH THE SEQUENCE OF ACCOUNTING EARNINGS	Financial Accounting Archival - Primary Earnings 108
MA, SHEREE SHIOW-RU	PHD 1989 THE UNIVERSITY OF ALABAMA STONE, MARY S.	AN EMPIRICAL EXAMINATION OF THE STOCK MARKET'S REACTION TO THE PENSION ACCOUNTING DELIBERATIONS OF THE FINANCIAL ACCOUNTING STANDARDS BOARD	Financial Accounting Archival - Primary Post Retirement Benefit Issues 200
MACKIE, JAMES JAY	PHD 1986 TEXAS A&M UNIVERSITY	AN EMPIRICAL INVESTIGATION OF THE IMPACT OF PERSONALITY TYPE ON SUPERVISOR-SUBORDINATE RELATIONSHIPS IN A BUDGETARY SETTING	Cost/Managerial Case Budgeting 135
MACQUARRIE, ALLAN JAMES	PHD 1989 THE PENNSYLVANIA STATE UNIVERSITY FERRARA, WILLIAM L.	HEALTH CARE COST CONTAINMENT IN THE NEW ENVIRONMENT OF PROSPECTIVE PRICING OF SERVICES: THE IMPLICATIONS FOR THE ACCOUNTING AND FINANCIAL FUNCTION	Cost/Managerial Survey Industry - Health Care 292
MACUR, KENNETH MICHAEL	PHD 1988 UNIVERSITY OF ILLINOIS AT URBANA-CHAMPAIGN	THE EFFECTS OF CLUSTERING AND RESPONSE MODE CORRESPONDENCE ON THE EVALUATION OF INTERNAL ACCOUNTING CONTROLS	Auditing Experimental Internal Control 307
MADDOCKS, PAULINE MERLE	PHD 1989 UNIVERSITY OF FLORIDA ABDEL-KHALIK, A. RASHAD	OUTCOME KNOWLEDGE AND AUDITOR JUDGMENT	Auditing Experimental Judgment & Decision Making - Heuristics & Biases 228
MAGNAN, MICHEL LOUIS	PHD 1989 UNIVERSITY OF WASHINGTON NOREEN, ERIC	THE RELATION BETWEEN INDUSTRY-SPECIFIC VARIABLES AND COMPENSATION: THE CASE OF COMMERCIAL BANKS	Cost/Managerial Archival - Primary Incentive Compensation 126

Author	Degree & Date School Advisor	Title	Functional Area Research Method Topic pages
MAGNER, NACE RICHARD	DBA 1990 SOUTHERN ILLINOIS UNIVERSITY AT CARBONDALE WELKER, ROBERT	A FIELD STUDY OF PROCEDURAL JUSTICE AS AN INTERVENING VARIABLE BETWEEN PARTICIPATION IN BUDGETING AND ORGANIZATIONAL OUTCOMES	Cost/Managerial Survey Budgeting 160
MAHENTHIRAN, SAKTHIHARAN	PHD 1991 TEMPLE UNIVERSITY GREENBERG, RALPH H.	NEGOTIATED TRANSFER PRICING: AN INTEGRATED EMPIRICAL EXAMINATION	Cost/Managerial Experimental Transfer Pricing 131
MAHER, JOHN JOSEPH	PHD 1985 THE PENNSYLVANIA STATE UNIVERSITY	PENSION OBLIGATIONS AND THE BOND CREDIT MARKET: AN EMPIRICAL ANALYSIS OF ACCOUNTING NUMBERS	Financial Accounting Archival - Primary Post Retirement Benefit Issues 168
MAHMOUD, AMAL ABDEL WAKIL	PHD 1985 THE UNIVERSITY OF WISCONSIN - MADISON	THE EFFECT OF DIFFERENTIAL AMOUNTS OF INTERIM INFORMATION ON STOCK PRICES VARIABILITY: THE CASE OF ANALYSTS' FORECASTS AND FIRM SIZE	Financial Accounting Archival - Primary Financial Analysts 126
MAHONEY, DANIEL PAUL	PHD 1990 SYRACUSE UNIVERSITY ANDERSON, JOHN C.	PENNSYLVANIA'S MUNICIPAL LABOR MARKET BEFORE AND AFTER THE ENACTMENT OF THE MUNICIPAL PENSION PLAN FUNDING STANDARD AND RECOVERY ACT: AN EMPIRICAL STUDY	General Case Post Retirement Benefit Issues 216
MAIN, DAPHNE	PHD 1990 THE OHIO STATE UNIVERSITY BAILEY, ANDREW D. JR.	AUDITOR DECISION-MAKING UNDER AMBIGUITY: A TEST OF THE EINHORN AND HOGARTH AMBIGUITY MODEL	Auditing Experimental Judgment & Decision Making 110
MAKAR, STEPHEN DOUGLAS	PHD 1994 KENT STATE UNIVERSITY ALAM, PERVAIZ	POLITICAL COSTS OVER THE BUSINESS CYCLE: THE INCENTIVES FOR THE MANAGEMENT OF ACCOUNTING ACCRUALS	Financial Accounting Archival - Primary Earnings Management 279
MAKRIGEORGIS, CHRISTOS N.	PHD 1991 TEXAS A&M UNIVERSITY GARCIA-DIAZ, ALBERTO	DEVELOPMENT OF AN OPTIMAL DURABILITY-BASED HIGHWAY COST ALLOCATION MODEL	Cost/Managerial Analytical - Internal Cost Allocation 216
MALLADO RODRIGUEZ, JOSE ANTONIO	PHD 1990 UNIVERSIDAD DE SEVILLA (SPAIN)	THE MEASURE OF EFFECTIVENESS AND EFFICACY IN PUBLIC EXPENSES: AN EMPIRICAL APPLICATION [LE MEDIDA DE LA EFICACIA Y DE LA EFICIENCIA DEL GASTO PUBLICO: UNA APLICACION EMPIRICA]	Not-for-Profit Case International/Global Issues 531

Author	Degree & Date School Advisor	Title	Functional Area Research Method Topic pages
MALLEK, JAMES RANDOLPH	PHD 1986 THE UNIVERSITY OF TEXAS AT AUSTIN	PROBLEM RECOGNITION IN PROFESSIONAL TAX ACCOUNTING	Taxation Experimental Tax Professionals 843
MALONE, CHARLES FRANCIS	PHD 1992 UNIVERSITY OF MISSOURI - COLUMBIA ROBERTS, ROBIN	AN EMPIRICAL INVESTIGATION OF THE RELATIONSHIPS BETWEEN INDIVIDUAL AND FIRM CHARACTERISTICS AND REDUCED AUDIT QUALITY	Auditing Survey Audit Quality 275
MALONE, JOHN DAVID, JR.	PHD 1987 UNIVERSITY OF ARKANSAS FRIES, CLARENCE	AN EMPIRICAL INVESTIGATION OF THE EXTENT OF CORPORATE FINANCIAL DISCLOSURE IN THE OIL AND GAS INDUSTRY	Financial Accounting Survey Industry - Oil & Gas 147
MANDE, VIVEK GOPAL	PHD 1991 UNIVERSITY OF CALIFORNIA, LOS ANGELES ELY, KIRSTEN	THE INFORMATION CONTENT OF EARNINGS AND DIVIDENDS: THE SUBSTITUTION HYPOTHESIS	Financial Accounting Archival - Primary Dividends 113
MANKO, KENNETH MICHAEL	EDD 1988 AUBURN UNIVERSITY WILSON, RUSSELL C.	THE RELATIONSHIP OF MEASURES OF SELF-CONCEPT AND ANXIETY TO ACADEMIC ACHIEVEMENT IN ACCOUNTING	Education Survey Academic Achievement 118
MANN, GARY J.	PHD 1986 TEXAS TECH UNIVERSITY	EFFECTS OF HUMAN NEEDS, GROUP INFLUENCE, AND MANAGEMENT STYLE ON CHANGE-RELATED BEHAVIORAL INTENTIONS IN INFORMATION SYSTEMS	Information Systems Survey Systems Design &/or Development 213
MANRY, DAVID LEE	PHD 1992 THE UNIVERSITY OF TEXAS AT AUSTIN DIETRICH, J. RICHARD; ROBINSON, JOHN R.	TARGET FIRM EARNINGS, GREENMAIL, AND SHAREHOLDERS' INTERESTS	Financial Accounting Archival - Primary Merger, Acquisition, Reorganization 177
MANSFIELD, JON L.	PHD 1992 GEORGIA STATE UNIVERSITY KLEIN, JOHN J.	THE EFFECTS OF SFAS NO. 8 AND NO. 52 ON MULTINATIONAL COMPANY STOCK RETURNS: 1973-1982	Financial Accounting Archival - Primary Foreign Currency Translation 199
MANZON, GIL B., JR.	DBA 1990 BOSTON UNIVERSITY MENON, KRISHNAGOPAL	AN INVESTIGATION OF FACTORS AFFECTING THE INCOME STRATEGIES OF FIRMS SUBJECT TO THE ALTERNATIVE MINIMUM TAX	Taxation Archival - Primary Earnings Management 132

Listing by Author

Author	Degree & Date School Advisor	Title	Functional Area Research Method Topic pages
MANZONI, JEAN-FRANCOIS	DBA 1993 HARVARD UNIVERSITY KAPLAN, ROBERT S.	USE OF QUANTITATIVE FEEDBACK BY SUPERIORS: CAUSES AND CONSEQUENCES	Cost/Managerial Case Performance Evaluation/Measurement 572
MARABELLO, CARMINE F., JR.	DBA 1991 NOVA UNIVERSITY GREENWOOD, RONALD G.	A STUDY OF PUBLIC ACCOUNTING INTERNSHIPS IN NEW ENGLAND: AN EVALUATION FROM THE VIEWPOINT OF CPA FIRMS	Education Survey Internships 137
MARAIS, MARTHINUS LAURENTIUS	PHD 1985 STANFORD UNIVERSITY	SOME APPLICATIONS OF COMPUTER INTENSIVE STATISTICAL METHODS TO EMPIRICAL RESEARCH IN ACCOUNTING	General Archival - Secondary Methodology 367
MARCHANT, GARRY ALLEN	PHD 1987 THE UNIVERSITY OF MICHIGAN	ANALOGICAL REASONING AND ERROR DETECTION	Auditing Experimental Errors 184
MARGAVIO, GEANIE WADGE	PHD 1990 THE UNIVERSITY OF ALABAMA	PORTFOLIO RESPONSES OF SAVINGS AND LOANS TO THE TAX REFORM ACT OF 1986	Taxation Archival - Primary Industry - Banking/Savings & Loan 338
MARONEY, JAMES JOSEPH	PHD 1994 THE UNIVERSITY OF CONNECTICUT BIGGS, S. F.	THE IMPACT OF KNOWLEDGE CONTENT AND STRUCTURE ON AUDITORS' HYPOTHESIS TESTING BEHAVIOR IN ANALYTICAL PROCEDURES	Auditing Experimental Judgment & Decision Making - Cognitive Processes 140
MARSHALL, LEISA LYNN	DBA 1993 MISSISSIPPI STATE UNIVERSITY DAUGHTREY, ZOEL W.	AN EMPIRICAL INVESTIGATION OF FINANCIAL MEASURES' ABILITY TO PREDICT FINANCIAL DISTRESS LEVELS OF AGRICULTURAL PRODUCERS	Financial Accounting Archival - Primary Financial Distress or Bankruptcy 228
MARTIN, LISA CLINE	PHD 1985 GEORGIA STATE UNIVERSITY - COLLEGE OF BUSINESS ADMINISTRATION	AN EMPIRICAL INVESTIGATION OF THE JOB MOBILITY OF CERTIFIED PUBLIC ACCOUNTANTS WORKING IN INDUSTRY	General Survey Accounting Career Issues 277
MARTIN, LOUISA ANN	PHD 1993 UNIVERSITY OF MINNESOTA DALEY, LANE A.	PRIVATE INFORMATION AND BLOCK TRADING	Financial Accounting Archival - Primary Agency Theory 91

Author	Degree & Date School Advisor	Title	Functional Area Research Method Topic pages
MARTIN, SUSAN WORK	PHD 1988 MICHIGAN STATE UNIVERSITY	MODELING THE LOCAL GOVERNMENT GENERAL FUND DEFICIT	Not-for-Profit Archival - Primary Governmental 132
MARTINDALE, BOBBIE COOK	PHD 1989 UNIVERSITY OF NORTH TEXAS MICHAELSON, ROBERT	IMPACT OF TAX COMPLEXITY ON TAXPAYER UNDERSTANDING	Taxation Experimental Tax Compliance 127
MARTINEZ-MORALES, MANUEL	PHD 1991 TEXAS TECH UNIVERSITY DURAN, BENJAMIN S.	ADAPTIVE PREMIUM CONTROL IN AN INSURANCE RISK PROCESS	General Simulation Industry - Insurance 72
MARXEN, DALE EDWIN	PHD 1988 UNIVERSITY OF COLORADO AT BOULDER TRACY, JOHN A.	GROUP POLARIZATION IN THE SETTING OF AUDIT TIME BUDGETS	Auditing Experimental Audit Planning 129
MASEDA GARCIA, AMAIA	1994 Universidad Del Pais Vasco/euskal Herrko Unbertsitatea (Spain)	INNOVATION IN CASH FLOW STATEMENTS [INNOVACION EN ESTADOS DE FLUJOS: UN MODELO DE TESORERIA]	Financial Accounting Cash Flows 540
MASIMBA, RODERICK DAVID	PHD 1990 UNIVERSITY OF COLORADO AT BOULDER SELTO, FRANK H.	THE AGENCY PROBLEM: AN EMPIRICAL INVESTIGATION OF MANAGERIAL BEHAVIOR UNDER EXOGENOUSLY IMPOSED PRINCIPAL-AGENT RELATIONSHIPS IN TANZANIA	Cost/Managerial Case Agency Theory 178
MASON, J. DAVID	PHD 1993 UNIVERSITY OF COLORADO AT BOULDER DAVIS, JON S.	A BEHAVIORAL MODEL OF SIMILARITY JUDGMENTS BY TAX PROFESSIONALS	Taxation Case Tax Professionals 106
MASTRACCHIO, NICHOLAS JAMES, JR.	PHD 1993 UNION COLLEGE (NEW YORK) LIPPITT, JEFFREY	AN EXAMINATION OF THE THEORETICAL BASIS AND THE APPLICATION OF THE CAPITALIZATION OF EARNINGS METHOD AND THE EXCESS EARNINGS METHOD TO CLOSELY HELD BUSINESSES	Financial Accounting Archival - Primary Earnings 227
MATHEWS, MARTIN REGINALD	EDD 1993 UNIVERSITY OF MONTANA EVANS, R. D.	THE REACTIONS OF ACADEMIC ADMINISTRATORS TO THE ACCOUNTING EDUCATION CHANGE COMMISSION, 1989-1992	Education Survey Curriculum Issues 205

Author	Degree & Date School Advisor	Title	Functional Area Research Method Topic pages
MATIKA, LAWRENCE A.	PHD 1988 KENT STATE UNIVERSITY FETYKO, DAVID F.	THE CONTRIBUTIONS OF FREDERICK ALBERT CLEVELAND TO THE DEVELOPMENT OF A SYSTEM OF MUNICIPAL ACCOUNTING IN THE PROGRESSIVE ERA	Not-for-Profit Archival - Secondary History 146
MATSUNAGA, STEVEN ROY	PHD 1992 UNIVERSITY OF WASHINGTON BURGSTAHLER, DAVID	THE EFFECTS OF FINANCIAL REPORTING AND TAX COSTS ON THE RELATIVE USE OF EMPLOYEE STOCK OPTIONS	Taxation Archival - Primary Incentive Compensation 173
MATTISON, DOROTHY MCCALL	PHD 1990 THE GEORGE WASHINGTON UNIVERSITY VAILL, PETER B.	THE INFLUENCE OF SELECTED VARIABLES ON THE FINANCIAL PERFORMANCE OF NOT-FOR-PROFIT AND FOR-PROFIT HOSPITALS: A COMPARATIVE ANALYSIS	General Archival - Primary Industry - Health Care 188
MAUTZ, RICHARD DAVID, JR.	PHD 1987 THE UNIVERSITY OF TENNESSEE	THE IMPACT OF SUPPLEMENTARY, INFLATION-ADJUSTED FINANCIAL STATEMENT INFORMATION ON LABOR'S ASSESSMENT OF CORPORATE ABILITY TO PAY	Financial Accounting Experimental Inflation 174
MAYDEW, EDWARD LYLE	PHD 1993 THE UNIVERSITY OF IOWA COLLINS, DANIEL W.	INCENTIVES TO MAGNIFY NET OPERATING LOSSES FOLLOWING THE TAX REFORM ACT OF 1986	Taxation Experimental Earnings Management 134
MAZACHEK, JULIANN	PHD 1993 UNIVERSITY OF KANSAS SHAFTEL, TIMOTHY	THE IMPACT OF ACCOUNTING PERFORMANCE MEASURES ON MANAGERIAL BEHAVIOR: A MODEL AND SURVEY	Cost/Managerial Performance Evaluation/Measurement 163
MAZHAR, NAHEED	DBA 1991 UNITED STATES INTERNATIONAL UNIVERSITY HARRIFF, RICHARD B.	FACTORS RELATED TO CORPORATE CAPITAL STRUCTURE	Financial Accounting Archival - Primary Capital Structure 193
MCBETH, KEVIN H.	PHD 1989 THE UNIVERSITY OF UTAH STERLING, ROBERT R.	REDEFINING THE FEDERAL INCOME TAX BASE FOR INCREASED EQUITY, NEUTRALITY, AND SIMPLICITY	Taxation Analytical - Internal Public Policy 250
MCCARRON, KAREN ELIZABETH BRADSHAW	PHD 1988 THE UNIVERSITY OF ALABAMA KEE, ROBERT C.	AN EMPIRICAL INVESTIGATION OF THE USEFULNESS OF FINANCIAL ACCOUNTING RATIOS IN PREDICTING THE EFFECTS OF A TROUBLED DEBT RESTRUCTURING	Financial Accounting Archival - Primary Financial Ratios 136

Listing by Author

Author	Degree & Date School Advisor	Title	Functional Area Research Method Topic pages
MCCARTHY, IRENE N.	PHD 1993 NEW YORK UNIVERSITY BRONNER, MICHAEL	PROFESSIONAL ETHICS CODE CONFLICT SITUATIONS: ETHICAL AND VALUE ORIENTATION OF COLLEGIATE ACCOUNTING STUDENTS	General Survey Ethics 171
MCCARTHY, MARK GOODWIN	PHD 1992 UNIVERSITY OF SOUTH CAROLINA CHEWNING, EUGENE G. JR.	THE INFORMATION CONTENT OF THE FORM 10-K AND ANNUAL REPORT TO SHAREHOLDERS: A TRADING VOLUME AND PRICE APPROACH	Financial Accounting Archival - Primary Earnings Announcements 76
MCCLENNY, RUTH LORRAINE	PHD 1992 VIRGINIA POLYTECHNIC INSTITUTE AND STATE UNIVERSITY KILLOUGH, LARRY N.	CHANGING TAXPAYER ATTITUDES AND INCREASING TAXPAYER COMPLIANCE: THE ROLE OF INDIVIDUAL DIFFERENCES IN TAXPAYERS	Taxation Experimental Tax Compliance 196
MCCLURE, RONNIE CLYDE	PHD 1987 UNIVERSITY OF NORTH TEXAS	THE IMPACT ON CHARITABLE CLASSES IN DALLAS COUNTY, TEXAS, RESULTING FROM CHANGES IN THE TAX ECONOMICS OF PRIVATE PHILANTHROPY	Taxation Archival - Primary Charitable Organizations 246
MCCOY, TIMOTHY LYNN	PHD 1994 THE UNIVERSITY OF MISSISSIPPI TAYLOR, CHARLES W.	AN ANALYSIS OF MORAL JUDGMENTS AND OTHER FACTORS AFFECTING BEHAVIORAL INTENTIONS OF CERTIFIED PUBLIC ACCOUNTANTS	General Experimental Ethics 196
MCCRAW, JOSEPH HARRISON, JR.	PHD 1986 UNIVERSITY OF GEORGIA	A STUDY OF THE FEASIBILITY OF USING LINEAR REGRESSION IN THE MANAGEMENT OF THE INDIVIDUAL TAX RETURN PREPARATION PROCESS	Taxation Case Tax Professionals 307
MCDANIEL, LINDA SUE	PHD 1988 THE UNIVERSITY OF MICHIGAN KINNEY, WILLIAM R. JR.	THE EFFECTS OF TIME PRESSURE AND AUDIT PROGRAM STRUCTURE ON AUDIT EFFECTIVENESS AND EFFICIENCY	Auditing Experimental Audit Quality 121
MCDERMOTT, EUGENE WILLIS	PHD 1994 UNIVERSITY OF SOUTH CAROLINA SPILLER, EARL A. JR.	THE IMPACT OF TASK COMPLEXITY AND SELECTED COGNITIONS ON THE MOTIVATING ASPECTS OF BUDGETING	Cost/Managerial Experimental Budgeting 145
MCDERMOTT, NANCY ANN	DBA 1986 THE GEORGE WASHINGTON UNIVERSITY	THE INTERNAL ACCOUNTING CONTROL SYSTEM IN A MICROCOMPUTER ENVIRONMENT: AN ANALYTIC HIERARCHY PROCESS APPROACH	Auditing Microcomputer Applications 187

Author	Degree & Date School Advisor	Title	Functional Area Research Method Topic pages
MCDUFFIE, ROBERT STEPHEN	DBA 1990 LOUISIANA TECH UNIVERSITY	CONSTRUCTION AND VALIDATION OF AN EXPERT SYSTEM PROTOTYPE TO DETERMINE THE ACCOUNTING TREATMENT FOR BUSINESS COMBINATIONS	Information Systems Decision Support Systems 296
MCEACHARN, ELIZABETH MICHELLE	DBA 1994 LOUISIANA TECH UNIVERSITY	A FUZZY REASONING EXPERT SYSTEM FOR PLANNING-STAGE MATERIALITY JUDGEMENTS	Auditing Analytical - Internal Materiality 216
MCEWEN, RUTH ANN	PHD 1986 GEORGIA INSTITUTE OF TECHNOLOGY	AN EMPIRICAL ASSESSMENT OF ERROR METRICS APPLIED TO ANALYSTS' FORECASTS OF EARNINGS	Financial Accounting Archival - Primary Financial Analysts 134
MCGEE, ROBERT WILLIAM	PHD 1986 THE UNION FOR EXPERIMENTING COLLEGES AND UNIVERSITIES	A MODEL PROGRAM FOR SCHOOLS OF PROFESSIONAL ACCOUNTANCY	Education Analytical - Internal Curriculum Issues 356
MCGHEE, THOMAS MITCHELL	PHD 1989 UNIVERSITY OF SOUTH CAROLINA	A COMPARISON OF THE STATUTORY AND ECONOMIC INCIDENCE AMONG THE TAX REFORM ACT OF 1986, PRIOR LAW AND THREE TAX PROPOSALS	Taxation Archival - Primary Individual Taxation 188
MCGILL, GARY ANDERSON	PHD 1988 TEXAS TECH UNIVERSITY GATELY, MARY SUE	THE CPA'S ROLE IN INCOME TAX COMPLIANCE: AN EMPIRICAL STUDY OF VARIABILITY IN RECOMMENDING AGGRESSIVE TAX POSITIONS	Taxation Experimental Tax Compliance 177
MCGILSKY, DEBRA ERTEL	PHD 1986 MICHIGAN STATE UNIVERSITY	AN EMPIRICAL STUDY OF A RATEMAKING ISSUE: DETERMINING THE FEDERAL INCOME TAX ALLOWANCE OF AN AFFILIATED UTILITY	General Industry - Utilities 446
MCGOVERN, THOMAS WILLIAM	PHD 1988 UNIVERSITY OF WARWICK (UNITED KINGDOM)	ACCOUNTING AND TRADE UNIONS: THE INCOMPATIBLES? A CASE STUDY OF CLOSURES AT DUNLOP	General Case Other 548
MCGOWAN, ANNIE SMITH	PHD 1994 UNIVERSITY OF NORTH TEXAS KLAMMER, THOMAS	AN INVESTIGATION OF THE BEHAVIORAL IMPLICATIONS OF ADOPTING ACTIVITY-BASED COST MANAGEMENT SYSTEMS: AN EXPLORATORY STUDY	Cost/Managerial Survey Activity Based Costing 194

Listing by Author

137

Author	Degree & Date School Advisor	Title	Functional Area Research Method Topic pages
MCGOWAN, JOHN R.	PHD 1988 SOUTHERN ILLINOIS UNIVERSITY AT CARBONDALE TRESCOTT, PAUL B.	AN ANALYSIS OF THE EFFECT OF THE TAX REFORM ACT OF 1986 ON STOCK PRICES: A MARKET STUDY	Taxation Archival - Primary Capital Markets 253
MCGREGOR, CALVERT, JR.	PHD 1987 VIRGINIA POLYTECHNIC INSTITUTE AND STATE UNIVERSITY KILLOUGH, LARRY N.	AN INVESTIGATION OF ORGANIZATIONAL - PROFESSIONAL CONFLICT IN MANAGEMENT ACCOUNTING	General Survey Job Performance, Satisfaction &/or Turnover 187
MCINNES, WILLIAM MCKENZIE	PHD 1987 UNIVERSITY OF GLASGOW (UNITED KINGDOM)	ACCOUNTING CHOICES AND REPORTED FINANCIAL PERFORMANCE: THE UNITED KINGDOM GAS INDUSTRY, 1970-1980. (VOLUMES I AND II)	Financial Accounting Case Accounting Choice 500
MCKEAN, GERALD WILLIAM	PHD 1985 ILLINOIS STATE UNIVERSITY	CONGRUENCIES OF COMPUTER COMPETENCIES AS VIEWED BY ACCOUNTING PRACTITIONERS AND ACCOUNTING EDUCATORS	Education Survey Curriculum Issues 233
MCKENNA, JOHN N.	PHD 1993 NEW YORK UNIVERSITY BRONNER, MICHAEL	ETHICAL DILEMMAS IN FINANCIAL REPORTING SITUATIONS AND THE PREFERRED MODE OF RESOLUTION OF ETHICAL CONFLICTS AS TAKEN BY CERTIFIED AND NONCERTIFIED MANAGEMENT ACCOUNTANTS IN ORGANIZATIONS WITH PERCEIVED DIFFERENT ETHICAL WORK CLIMATES	General Survey Ethics 365
MCLANAHAN, JAMES CRAIG	PHD 1992 UNIVERSITY OF MASSACHUSETTS KETCHAM, MICHAEL	COST AND ERROR CHARACTERISTICS OF THREE COST ACCOUNTING SYSTEM TYPES: FULL COSTING, MARGINAL COSTING, AND ACTIVITY BASED COSTING	Cost/Managerial Experimental Cost Systems 128
MCLAUGHLIN, THOMAS DAVID	DBA 1990 MISSISSIPPI STATE UNIVERSITY HERRING, DORA R.	GOING CONCERN DETERMINATIONS UNDER SAS NO. 59 AND THE RESULTING IMPACT ON AUDIT OPINIONS: THE CASE OF THE SAVINGS AND LOAN INDUSTRY	Auditing Archival - Primary Financial Distress or Bankruptcy 146
MCMATH, HERBERT KENT	PHD 1985 UNIVERSITY OF SOUTH CAROLINA	THE IMPACT OF MANDATED ACCOUNTING CHANGES ON MANAGEMENT DECISIONS: THE STATEMENT NO. 8 EPISODE	Financial Accounting Case Foreign Currency Translation 232
MCMILLAN, JEFFREY JOSEPH	PHD 1990 UNIVERSITY OF SOUTH CAROLINA	THE ROLE OF CONFIRMATION BIAS, EXPERIENCE, AND MODE OF INFORMATION PROCESSING IN AUDIT JUDGMENT	Auditing Experimental Judgment & Decision Making - Heuristics & Biases 162

Listing by Author

Author	Degree & Date School Advisor	Title	Functional Area Research Method Topic pages
MCMULLEN, DOROTHY ANN	PHD 1992 DREXEL UNIVERSITY	AUDIT COMMITTEE STRUCTURE AND PERFORMANCE: AN EMPIRICAL INVESTIGATION OF THE CONSEQUENCES AND ATTRIBUTES OF AUDIT COMMITTEES	Auditing Experimental Audit Committees 178
MCNAIR, CAROL JEAN	PHD 1987 COLUMBIA UNIVERSITY	THE EFFECTS OF BUDGET PRESSURE ON AUDIT FIRMS: AN EMPIRICAL EXAMINATION OF THE UNDERREPORTING OF CHARGEABLE TIME	Auditing Survey Audit Planning 194
MCNAIR, FRANCES ELIZABETH	PHD 1987 THE UNIVERSITY OF MISSISSIPPI	AN EMPIRICAL INVESTIGATION OF THE PERCEIVED EFFECTS OF TAX REFORM ON TAXPAYER COMPLIANCE	Taxation Experimental Tax Compliance 174
MCNAMEE, ALAN HOWARD	PHD 1988 THE UNIVERSITY OF NORTH CAROLINA AT CHAPEL HILL ROCKNESS, HOWARD	THE CONTINGENT EFFECT OF PERFORMANCE EVALUATION CRITERIA ON BUSINESS UNIT PERFORMANCE	Cost/Managerial Survey Performance Evaluation/Measurement 134
MCNETT, STEPHEN ALLEN	PHD 1987 UNIVERSITY OF MISSOURI - COLUMBIA	AN EXAMINATION OF THE IMPACT OF SECTION 911 ON ENTRY-LEVEL JOB SELECTION DECISIONS IN SELECTED SITUATIONS	Taxation Experimental Individual Taxation 281
MCQUEEN, PATRICIA DORAN	PHD 1993 NEW YORK UNIVERSITY, GRADUATE SCHOOL OF BUSINESS ADMINISTRATION	THE INFORMATION CONTENT OF FOREIGN GAAP EARNINGS AND SHAREOWNERS' EQUITY AND THE UNITED STATES GAAP RECONCILIATION DISCLOSURES IN SEC FORM 20-F	Financial Accounting Archival - Primary International/Global Issues 210
MEADE, JANET ALICE	PHD 1987 ARIZONA STATE UNIVERSITY	THE LOCK-IN EFFECT OF CAPITAL GAINS TAXATION AND THE WILLINGNESS TO UNDERTAKE RISKY NEW INVESTMENT	Taxation Experimental Individual Taxation 191
MEADE, NANCY MARGARET LOWMAN	PHD 1990 VIRGINIA POLYTECHNIC INSTITUTE AND STATE UNIVERSITY BROWN, ROBERT M.	ANTITAKEOVER DEVICES AND FIRM PERFORMANCE: AN EMPIRICAL STUDY USING ACCOUNTING MEASURES	General Archival - Primary Other 205
MEHAFDI, MESSAOUD	PHD 1990 COUNCIL FOR NATIONAL ACADEMIC AWARDS (UNITED KINGDOM)	BEHAVIOURAL ASPECTS OF TRANSFER PRICING IN UNITED KINGDOM DECENTRALISED COMPANIES	Cost/Managerial Survey Transfer Pricing 414

Listing by Author

Author	Degree & Date School Advisor	Title	Functional Area Research Method Topic pages
MEIER, HEIDI HYLTON	DBA 1987 KENT STATE UNIVERSITY	AUDITOR INDEPENDENCE: AN EXAMINATION OF AUDITOR LOBBYING BEFORE THE FINANCIAL ACCOUNTING STANDARDS BOARD ON FINANCIAL ACCOUNTING STANDARDS PERTAINING TO THE BANKING AND THRIFT INDUSTRIES	Financial Accounting Standard Setting 254
MEIXNER, WILDA FURR	PHD 1985 TEXAS A&M UNIVERSITY	THE EFFECT OF THE ORGANIZATIONAL ENVIRONMENT ON JUDGMENT CONSENSUS: THE CASE FOR PROFESSIONAL GOVERNMENT AUDITORS IN THE STATE OF TEXAS	Auditing Experimental Judgment & Decision Making 130
MENSAH, MICHAEL OFOSU	PHD 1990 UNIVERSITY OF HOUSTON	THE INCREMENTAL INFORMATION CONTENT OF CASH FLOW FROM OPERATIONS--AN EXPLORATORY STUDY OF INTERTEMPORAL AND FIRM-SPECIFIC EFFECTS	Financial Accounting Archival - Primary Cash Flows 119
MEREDITH, VICKI BANET	DBA 1985 UNIVERSITY OF KENTUCKY	AN EMPIRICAL EXAMINATION OF BANKERS' PERCEPTIONS OF PROCEDURES PERFORMED BY CPAS IN LIMITED ASSURANCE ENGAGEMENTS	Auditing Survey Bank Loan Officers 143
MESERVY, RAYMAN DAVID	PHD 1985 UNIVERSITY OF MINNESOTA	AUDITING INTERNAL CONTROLS: A COMPUTATIONAL MODEL OF THE REVIEW PROCESS	Auditing Internal Control 364
MESSINA, FRANK MICHAEL	DBA 1993 MISSISSIPPI STATE UNIVERSITY DAUGHTREY, ZOEL W.	PREDICTION MODELS FOR DEBT COVENANT VIOLATIONS OF AGRICULTURAL COOPERATIVES	Financial Accounting Archival - Primary Industry - Agricultural 148
METH, BRACHA NAOMI	PHD 1989 UNIVERSITY OF PENNSYLVANIA LAMBERT, RICHARD A.	REDUCTION OF INCOME VARIANCE--OPTIMALITY AND INCENTIVES	Cost/Managerial Analytical - Internal Agency Theory 109
MEYER, DAN WESLEY	PHD 1988 UNIVERSITY OF MISSOURI - COLUMBIA PARKER, JAMES	SOME CHARACTERISTICS AND ENVIRONMENTAL SENSITIVITIES OF TAXPAYERS TAKING THE UNITED STATES POLITICAL CONTRIBUTION TAX CREDIT DURING 1979-1982	Taxation Archival - Primary Individual Taxation 131
MEYERMANS, ERIC AUGUST	DRECON 1992 KATHOLIEKE UNIVERSITEIT LEUVEN (BELGIUM)	ECONOMETRIC ALLOCATION SYSTEMS FOR THE FOREIGN EXCHANGE MARKET: SPECIFICATION, ESTIMATION AND TESTING OF TRANSMISSION MECHANISMS UNDER CURRENCY SUBSTITUTION	General Archival - Primary International/Global Issues 361

Author	Degree & Date School Advisor	Title	Functional Area Research Method Topic pages
MICHAEL, RODNEY RICHARD	PHD 1992 UNIVERSITY OF NORTH TEXAS MERINO, BARBARA	AN ANALYSIS OF THE ACCOUNTING SYSTEM OF THE QUINCY MINING COMPANY: 1846-1900	Information Systems Case History 292
MICHELMAN, JEFFREY ELIOT	PHD 1987 THE UNIVERSITY OF WISCONSIN - MADISON	THE DEVELOPMENT AND USES OF ACCOUNTING INFORMATION FOR MANAGERIAL REPORTING AND CONTROL IN A HEALTHCARE SETTING	General Industry - Health Care 408
MICHELSON, STUART EDWARD	PHD 1991 UNIVERSITY OF KANSAS PINCHES, GEORGE E.	CORPORATE CAPITAL EXPENDITURES, TAX LAWS, ASSETS-IN-PLACE, AND THE MARKET VALUE OF THE FIRM	Financial Accounting Archival - Primary Investments 112
MIDDLEMIST, MELANIE R.	PHD 1986 OKLAHOMA STATE UNIVERSITY	THE RELATIONSHIP BETWEEN OUTCOME MEASURABILITY AND PRINCIPAL'S PREFERENCE FOR CONTRACT TYPE: A LABORATORY EXPERIMENT	Cost/Managerial Experimental Incentive Compensation 121
MIDDLETON, MARY MARTIN	PHD 1988 UNIVERSITY OF GEORGIA EDWARDS, JAMES DON	THE INFORMATIONAL IMPACT OF PENSION LIABILITIES ON CORPORATE RISK	Financial Accounting Archival - Primary Post Retirement Benefit Issues 146
MILACEK, EMIL CRAIG, JR.	PHD 1986 UNIVERSITY OF NORTH TEXAS	AN ASSESSMENT OF THE EFFECT OF THE INVESTMENT TAX CREDIT ON CAPITAL INVESTMENT IN FARM SUPPLY COOPERATIVES IN MICHIGAN, MINNESOTA, NORTH DAKOTA, AND WISCONSIN	Taxation Archival - Primary Investments 105
MILLER, CHARLES ROBERT, II	PHD 1987 THE UNIVERSITY OF ARIZONA FELIX, WILLIAM L.	ASSESSING AUDITORS' BUSINESS RISK	Auditing Risk 129
MILLER, GARY ARTHUR	PHD 1985 SANTA CLARA UNIVERSITY	THE COSTS AND BENEFITS OF INTERPERIOD INCOME TAX ALLOCATION	Financial Accounting Survey Taxes 107
MILLER, GERALD JOHN	PHD 1994 UNIVERSITY OF KENTUCKY VANDANIKER, RELMOND P.	AN EMPIRICAL STUDY OF THE IMPROVEMENT IN FINANCIAL MANAGEMENT PRACTICES OF STATE AND LOCAL GOVERNMENTS IN RESPONSE TO THE SINGLE AUDIT ACT	Not-for-Profit Survey Governmental 186

Author	Degree & Date School Advisor	Title	Functional Area Research Method Topic pages
MILLER, JEFFREY REED	PHD 1985 THE LOUISIANA STATE UNIVERSITY AND AGRICULTURAL AND MECHANICAL COL.	AN EXPERIMENTAL RESEARCH STUDY ON THE EFFECTS OF THE TYPE OF ACCOUNTING SERVICE ON A BANK LENDING DECISION FOR NONPUBLIC BUSINESSES	Auditing Experimental Bank Loan Officers 201
MILLS, KATHLEEN DARBY	PHD 1992 THE UNIVERSITY OF ARIZONA WALLER, WILLIAM S.	AUDITORS' INHERENT RISK ASSESSMENTS: THE RELATIONSHIPS AMONG TASK EXPERIENCE, INFERABILITY OF CONDITIONING INFORMATION, SECOND-ORDER UNCERTAINTY AND EXTENT OF TESTING	Auditing Experimental Judgment & Decision Making - Cognitive Processes 101
MILLS, SHERRY KAY SNODGRASS	PHD 1989 TEXAS TECH UNIVERSITY CLANCY, DONALD K.	EFFECTS OF THE SERVICE ENCOUNTER ON CPA FIRM RETENTION	General Survey CPA Firm Issues 176
MILLS, TINA YOUNGBLOOD	PHD 1993 THE UNIVERSITY OF TENNESSEE SCHEINER, JAMES H.	THE EXTERNAL AUDITOR'S RELIANCE DECISION ON THE INTERNAL AUDIT FUNCTION: A TEST OF COGNITIVE STYLE AND ITS ROLE IN THE RELIANCE DECISION	Auditing Experimental Judgment & Decision Making - Cognitive Processes 197
MINYARD, DONALD HOYT	PHD 1988 UNIVERSITY OF ILLINOIS AT URBANA-CHAMPAIGN	AN EXAMINATION OF VARIABLES ASSOCIATED WITH DIVESTMENT DECISIONS	General Archival - Primary Other 128
MITCHELL, ELIZABETH ANN	PHD 1987 TEXAS A&M UNIVERSITY	AN INTEGRATIVE MODEL FOR THE STUDY OF PUBLIC ACCOUNTING FIRMS	General Survey CPA Firm Issues 350
MITCHELL, NAOMI CELIA	DBA 1994 CLEVELAND STATE UNIVERSITY KREISER, LAWRENCE A.	THE RELATIONSHIP OF CERTAIN ENVIRONMENTAL PERFORMANCE INDICATORS AND FINANCIAL STATEMENTS	Financial Accounting Archival - Primary Disclosures 191
MITCHEM, CHERYL EVELYN DRAKE	PHD 1990 VIRGINIA COMMONWEALTH UNIVERSITY SPERRY, JOHN B.; DICKINSON, HARRY D.	A CASH FLOW AND MACROECONOMIC MODEL OF FINANCIAL DISTRESS	Financial Accounting Archival - Primary Financial Distress or Bankruptcy 233
MITENKO, GRAHAM ROBERT	DBA 1987 MEMPHIS STATE UNIVERSITY BURNS, KENNETH J.	AN EMPIRICAL INVESTIGATION OF THE RELATIONSHIP AMONG AND PREDICTIVE ABILITY OF FOUR MEASURES OF CASH FLOW	Financial Accounting Archival - Primary Cash Flows 168

Listing by Author

Author	Degree & Date School Advisor	Title	Functional Area Research Method Topic pages
MITTELSTAEDT, H. FRED	PHD 1987 UNIVERSITY OF ILLINOIS AT URBANA-CHAMPAIGN	MANAGEMENT SURVIVAL STRATEGIES AND THE DECISION TO REDUCE PENSION PLAN FUNDING: AN EMPIRICAL TEST	General Archival - Primary Post Retirement Benefit Issues 121
MITTERMAIER, LINDA JEAN	PHD 1987 INDIANA UNIVERSITY	THE IMPACT OF INFLATION ON INDIVIDUAL FEDERAL INCOME TAX LIABILITIES: AN ANALYSIS OF REVENUE AND EQUITY EFFECTS	Taxation Archival - Primary Individual Taxation 385
MOECKEL, CINDY LEE	PHD 1987 THE UNIVERSITY OF NORTH CAROLINA AT CHAPEL HILL LANGENDERFER, HAROLD	THE EFFECTS OF EXPERIENCE ON AUDITORS' ABILITY TO INTEGRATE AUDIT EVIDENCE	Auditing Experimental Judgment & Decision Making 262
MOFFEIT, KATHERINE SOUTHERLAND	PHD 1985 UNIVERSITY OF NORTH TEXAS	THE EFFECT OF COGNITIVE STYLE ON AUDITOR INTERNAL CONTROL EVALUATION	Auditing Experimental Judgment & Decision Making - Cognitive Processes 154
MOHAMMED ABDULLA, MOHAMED ISMAIL	PHD 1991 UNIVERSITY OF EXETER (UNITED KINGDOM)	ADVANCED MEANS OF PREPARING THE PUBLIC BUDGET AND THEIR UTILISATION IN MODERNISING THE PUBLIC BUDGET IN THE UNITED ARAB EMIRATES. (VOLUMES I-III)	Not-for-Profit Analytical - Internal Budgeting 447
MOHRMAN, MARY BETH	PHD 1991 WASHINGTON UNIVERSITY DOPUCH, NICHOLAS	MANDATED ACCOUNTING CHANGES AND DEBT CONTRACTS	Financial Accounting Archival - Primary Accounting Change 82
MOHRWEIS, LAWRENCE CHARLES	PHD 1986 THE UNIVERSITY OF WISCONSIN - MADISON	AN EMPIRICAL INVESTIGATION OF FACTORS AFFECTING THE USE OF CONCURRENT EDP AUDIT TECHNIQUES	Auditing Survey EDP Controls 236
MONCADA, SUSAN MARY	PHD 1991 UNIVERSITY OF ILLINOIS AT URBANA-CHAMPAIGN NELSON, ROBERT	A HUMAN FACTORS ANALYSIS OF THE INTERPERSONAL COMMUNICATION EFFECTIVENESS OF PROGRAMMER ANALYSTS	Information Systems Survey Other 187
MONSERRAT JAUME, MAGDALENA	1993 Universitat Autonomade Barcelona (Spain)	CATALAN WORKER-SHAREHOLDER PUBLIC LIMITED COMPANIES: A COMPARATIVE ECONOMIC ANALYSIS (SPAIN) [LAS SOCIEDADES ANONIMAS LABORALES CATALANAS: UN ANALISIS ECONOMICO COMPARATIVO]	Financial Accounting Case International/Global Issues 400

Author	Degree & Date School Advisor	Title	Functional Area Research Method Topic pages
MONTONDON, LUCILLE MARIE	PHD 1990 UNIVERSITY OF HOUSTON	A STUDY OF MUNICIPAL RESOURCE ALLOCATION DECISIONS AND MUNICIPAL BOND RATINGS	Not-for-Profit Case Governmental 150
MOODY, SHARON MATHIS	PHD 1987 THE UNIVERSITY OF MISSISSIPPI	AN EMPIRICAL STUDY OF THE ASSOCIATION BETWEEN THE SALARY AND BONUS COMPONENTS OF EXECUTIVE COMPENSATION ANDPRINCIPAL-AGENT RISK SHARING AND PERFORMANCE MEASUREMENT	Cost/Managerial Archival - Primary Incentive Compensation 182
MOONEY, JULIAN LOWELL	PHD 1989 UNIVERSITY OF GEORGIA EDWARDS, JAMES DON	A COMPARISON OF EARNINGS AND CASH FLOW AS RISK MEASURES DURING DIFFERING ECONOMIC CONDITIONS	Financial Accounting Archival - Primary Risk 232
MOONEY, KATHLEEN KAYE BORN	PHD 1989 TEXAS A&M UNIVERSITY SHEARON, WINSTON T. JR.	AN INVESTIGATION OF THE ASSOCIATION OF CPAS WITH REAL ESTATE LIMITED PARTNERSHIPS	General Survey Industry - Real Estate 109
MOORE, ELMA LEE SCHMIDT	PHD 1993 THE UNION INSTITUTE	AN ANALYSIS OF LEARNING STYLES, INSTRUCTIONAL STYLES, AND CULTURE AMONG SELECTED ACCOUNTING STUDENTS AND INSTRUCTORS AT THE UNIVERSITY-LEVEL	Education Survey Instructional Methods 224
MOORE, JOHN WILLIAM	PHD 1992 VIRGINIA COMMONWEALTH UNIVERSITY SPERRY, JOHN B.; DICKINSON, HARRY D.	AN EMPIRICAL INVESTIGATION OF THE FINANCIAL EFFECTS OF UNION REPRESENTATION AND DECERTIFICATION ELECTIONS ONPUBLICLY TRADED FIRMS	Financial Accounting Archival - Primary Disclosures 205
MOORE, MICHAEL JOE	PHD 1992 THE UNIVERSITY OF ALABAMA INGRAM, ROBERT W.	AN EMPIRICAL INVESTIGATION OF THE DETERMINANTS OF LOAN LOSSES AT SMALL BANKS	Financial Accounting Archival - Primary Industry - Banking/Savings & Loan 182
MOORE, PERRY GLEN	PHD 1993 UNIVERSITY OF GEORGIA WARREN, CARL S.	EXTERNAL AUDITOR RELIANCE ON INTERNAL AUDITORS: AN EXAMINATION OF THE SIMILARITY OF AUDITOR JUDGMENTS	Auditing Survey Internal Auditing 151
MOORE, RONALD KENNETH	PHD 1987 UNIVERSITY OF NORTH TEXAS	PREDICTION OF BANKRUPTCY USING FINANCIAL RATIOS, INFORMATION MEASURES, NATIONAL ECONOMIC DATA AND TEXAS ECONOMIC DATA	Financial Accounting Archival - Primary Financial Distress or Bankruptcy 134

Author	Degree & Date School Advisor	Title	Functional Area Research Method Topic pages
MOORE, WALTER BURNIS	PHD 1989 THE UNIVERSITY OF NEBRASKA - LINCOLN BROWN, JAMES F. JR.	BUDGETARY SLACK BEHAVIOR IN MUNICIPAL GOVERNMENTS: AN EMPIRICAL BEHAVIORAL STUDY	Not-for-Profit Survey Budgeting 200
MORELAND, KEITH ARON	PHD 1992 UNIVERSITY OF CINCINNATI STEPHAN, JENS A.	AN EMPIRICAL STUDY OF THE EFFECT OF AUDITOR SANCTIONS ON THE ASSOCIATION BETWEEN EARNINGS AND SECURITY RETURNS	Financial Accounting Archival - Primary Audit Quality 115
MORGAN, JOHN DANIEL	PHD 1992 THE UNIVERSITY OF NEBRASKA - LINCOLN HUBBARD, THOMAS D.	PREDICTING 'VERY EARLY TURNOVER' IN PUBLIC ACCOUNTING WITH PERSONALITY AND DEMOGRAPHIC BACKGROUND VARIABLES	General Case Job Performance, Satisfaction &/or Turnover 165
MORRILL, CAMERON KEITH JOSEPH	PHD 1991 UNIVERSITY OF ALBERTA (CANADA)	CORPORATE LEADERS, FIRM PERFORMANCE AND ACCOUNTING EARNINGS	Financial Accounting Archival - Primary Accounting Choice 213
MORRIS, BARBARA SUE	PHD 1985 UNIVERSITY OF GEORGIA	AN EXPERIMENTAL STUDY OF AGENCY THEORY VARIABLES AS DETERMINANTS OF AUDIT INTENSIVENESS	Auditing Experimental Audit Planning 280
MORRIS, BONNIE WHITE	PHD 1992 UNIVERSITY OF PITTSBURGH	CASE-BASED REASONING IN INTERNAL AUDITOR EVALUATIONS OF EDP CONTROLS	Auditing Case Internal Control 184
MORRIS, JOSEPH LYNN	PHD 1986 THE UNIVERSITY OF MISSISSIPPI	A PROFILE OF WINNING AND LOSING CASES CONCERNING THE VALUATION OF CLOSELY HELD SHARES FOR ESTATE AND GIFT TAX PURPOSES	Taxation Archival - Secondary Tax Court 247
MORRIS, NORMA WILLIAMS	PHD 1989 TEXAS A&M UNIVERSITY WALLACE, WANDA A.	THE ASSOCIATION BETWEEN SELECTED CORPORATE ATTRIBUTES AND MANAGEMENT INCENTIVES FOR VOLUNTARY ACCOUNTING DISCLOSURE	Financial Accounting Archival - Primary Voluntary Management Disclosures 321
MORRIS, ROSELYN EVERTS	PHD 1993 UNIVERSITY OF HOUSTON STRAWSER, JERRY R.	THE PERFORMANCE OF AUDITORS IN MODIFYING OPINIONS OF FAILED BANKS	Auditing Archival - Primary Audit Opinion 181

Listing by Author

Author	Degree & Date School Advisor	Title	Functional Area Research Method Topic pages
MORRISON, THEODORE DAVIDSON, III	DBA 1993 MISSISSIPPI STATE UNIVERSITY HERRING, DORA R.	AN EMPIRICAL MODEL FOR THE DESCRIPTION AND FORECASTING OF QUARTERLY EARNINGS PER SHARE FOR SMALL AND NEGLECTED FIRMS	Financial Accounting Archival - Primary Earnings Per Share 218
MORROW, MITCHEL CRAWFORD	PHD 1992 UNIVERSITY OF GEORGIA BAREFIELD, R. M.	EFFECTS OF BUDGET PARTICIPATION, DIFFICULTY AND BUDGET CONTINGENT REWARD ON BUDGET PERFORMANCE	Cost/Managerial Experimental Budgeting 115
MORTON, JANE ELIZABETH	PHD 1993 THE UNIVERSITY OF ARIZONA FELIX, WILLIAM L. JR.	ORDER EFFECTS IN AUDITORS' INTERNAL CONTROL JUDGMENTS: BELIEF PERSEVERANCE VERSUS THE CONTRAST EFFECT	Auditing Experimental Judgment & Decision Making - Heuristics & Biases 195
MOSER, DONALD V.	PHD 1986 THE UNIVERSITY OF WISCONSIN - MADISON	THE EFFECTS OF INTERFERENCE, AVAILABILITY, AND ACCOUNTING INFORMATION ON INVESTORS' PREDICTIVE JUDGMENTS	Financial Accounting Experimental Judgment & Decision Making 237
MOSES, DUANE R.	PHD 1990 UNIVERSITY OF MISSOURI - COLUMBIA ECHTERNACHT, LONNIE	AUTOMATED VS. MANUAL SIMULATIONS IN HIGH SCHOOL ACCOUNTING: THE EFFECTS ON STUDENT ACHIEVEMENT, PERCEPTIONS AND TIME REQUIRED TO COMPLETE	Education Experimental Instructional Methods 64
MOUNT, CAROLE C.	PHD 1992 KENT STATE UNIVERSITY SEVERIENS, JACOBUS T.	THE MARGINAL IMPACT OF CASH FLOW INFORMATION ON BANK FAILURE PREDICTION: AN EMPIRICAL INVESTIGATION	Financial Accounting Archival - Primary Financial Distress or Bankruptcy 213
MOYER, SUSAN ELAINE	PHD 1989 THE UNIVERSITY OF ROCHESTER	ACCOUNTING CHOICES IN COMMERCIAL BANKS	Financial Accounting Archival - Primary Accounting Choice 93
MOYES, GLEN DAVID	DBA 1991 UNITED STATES INTERNATIONAL UNIVERSITY STOLAROW, JEROME	AN ANALYSIS OF THE EFFECTIVENESS OF SPECIFIC AUDITING TECHNIQUES FOR DETECTING FRAUD AS PERCEIVED BY THREE DIFFERENT AUDITOR GROUPS	Auditing Survey Fraud 331
MOYNIHAN, G.	DPHIL 1986 UNIVERSITY OF OXFORD (UNITED KINGDOM)	STOCK: THE LOWER OF COST OR MARKET VALUE IN THE COMPUTATION OF TRADING PROFIT FOR TAX PURPOSES	Taxation History 318

Listing by Author

Author	Degree & Date School Advisor	Title	Functional Area Research Method Topic pages
MOZES, CHAIM A.	PHD 1989 NEW YORK UNIVERSITY, GRADUATE SCHOOL OF BUSINESS ADMINISTRATION BILDERSEE, JOHN	PREANNOUNCEMENT ACCOUNTING INFORMATION: MEASUREMENT TECHNIQUES AND EMPIRICAL PROPERTIES	Financial Accounting Archival - Primary Earnings Announcements 140
MUKHERJI, ARIJIT	PHD 1991 UNIVERSITY OF PITTSBURGH	COSTLY MONITORING IN A PRINCIPAL-AGENT MODEL	Cost/Managerial Analytical - Internal Agency Theory 121
MULCAHY, LEIGH-ANN	LLM 1992 YORK UNIVERSITY (CANADA) CONDON, M.	ACCOUNTABLE TO WHOM? THE CHANGING ROLE OF THE CORPORATE AUDITOR	Auditing Analytical - Internal Legal Liability 191
MUNTORO, RONNY KUSUMA	PHD 1987 UNIVERSITY OF SOUTHERN CALIFORNIA	THE USE OF ORGANIZATION BEHAVIOR METHODS IN THE DEVELOPMENT OF COMPUTERIZED ACCOUNTING SYSTEMS IN INDONESIA: AN ATTITUDINAL SURVEY	Information Systems Survey International/Global Issues
MURDOCH, ALASTAIR	PHD 1992 UNIVERSITY OF WASHINGTON BOWEN, ROBERT M.	DIVIDENDS AND EARNINGS: THEIR EFFECT ON FIRM VALUE	Financial Accounting Archival - Primary Dividends 338
MURPHY, DANIEL PHILIP	PHD 1990 THE UNIVERSITY OF NORTH CAROLINA AT CHAPEL HILL COLLINS, JULIE H.	EXPERIMENTAL EVIDENCE REGARDING IMPLICIT TAXES AND TAX-INDUCED INVESTOR CLIENTELES	Taxation Experimental Capital Markets 118
MURPHY, DAVID SMITH	PHD 1989 WASHINGTON STATE UNIVERSITY FRAKES, ALBERT	AN EMPIRICAL INVESTIGATION OF THE EFFECT OF EXPERT SYSTEM USE ON THE DEVELOPMENT OF EXPERTISE IN AUDITING	Education Experimental Instructional Methods 186
MURPHY, JOHN ALOYSIUS DANIEL	PHD 1991 FLORIDA ATLANTIC UNIVERSITY HOFFMAN, MICHAEL J. R.	THE IMPACT OF A VALUE-ADDED TAX ON THE CASH FLOW OF CORPORATIONS	Taxation Public Policy 112
MURTHY, UDAY SIMHA	PHD 1989 INDIANA UNIVERSITY GROOMER, S. MICHAEL	THE RELATIONSHIP BETWEEN THE STABILITY OF COMPUTERIZED ACCOUNTING APPLICATIONS, COMPUTER AUDIT STRATEGY AND AUDIT RISK	Auditing Experimental Risk 192

Author	Degree & Date School Advisor	Title	Functional Area Research Method Topic pages
MYERS, JOAN JOETTE KLINGINSMITH	PHD 1993 SYRACUSE UNIVERSITY ISMAIL, BADR E.	THE EXPLORATION OF PRODUCT COSTING AND COST CONTROL METHODS IN THE CURRENT MANUFACTURING ENVIRONMENT: A FIELD STUDY	Cost/Managerial Case Management Control Systems 201
MYERS, MARLA ANN	PHD 1992 THE UNIVERSITY OF ARIZONA MUTCHLER, JANE F.	A TEST OF THE RELATION BETWEEN AUDIT TECHNOLOGY AND THE DEVELOPMENT OF EXPERTISE	Auditing Experimental Judgment & Decision Making - Cognitive Processes 150
MYERS, MARY DOVE	PHD 1988 UNIVERSITY OF MARYLAND COLLEGE PARK GORDON, LAWRENCE A.	AN EMPIRICAL INVESTIGATION OF POSTAUDIT PROCEDURES FOR CAPITAL EXPENDITURES AND THEIR ASSOCIATION WITH FIRM PERFORMANCE	Cost/Managerial Survey Capital Budgeting 206
MYNATT, PATRICIA GRAFF	PHD 1989 THE UNIVERSITY OF NORTH CAROLINA AT CHAPEL HILL BLOCHER, EDWARD; ALLEN, STEVEN A.	THE INFORMATION CONTENT OF FINANCIAL STATEMENT RELEASES	Financial Accounting Archival - Primary Information Content 110
NA, CHONGKIL	PHD 1993 WASHINGTON STATE UNIVERSITY ETTREDGE, MICHAEL	THE ASSOCIATION BETWEEN ACCOUNTING ACCRUALS AND MEAN REVERSION OF ANNUAL EARNINGS	Financial Accounting Archival - Primary Earnings Management 94
NA, IN-CHUL	PHD 1987 THE UNIVERSITY OF TEXAS AT AUSTIN	INVESTORS' REACTION TO THE EFFECT OF STATEMENT OF FINANCIAL ACCOUNTING STANDARDS NO. 52 ON 1981 EARNINGS FOR THE EARLY ADOPTERS: AN EMPIRICAL STUDY	Financial Accounting Archival - Primary Accounting Change 180
NA, YOUNG	PHD 1993 RUTGERS THE STATE UNIVERSITY OF NEW JERSEY - NEWARK SANNELLA, ALEXANDER	STOCK MARKET REACTION TO FASB NO. 106: THE DISCLOSURE OF POSTRETIREMENT BENEFIT COSTS	Financial Accounting Archival - Primary Post Retirement Benefit Issues 189
NABANGI, FABIAN KAFUKO	DPA 1992 THE UNIVERSITY OF ALABAMA CHAPPELL, WILLIAM	THE UTILITY OF ARIMA MODELS TO REVENUE FORECASTING FOR ALABAMA URBAN COUNTY GOVERNMENTS	Not-for-Profit Case Forecasting Financial Performance 148
NAGLE, BRIAN M.	PHD 1994 SAINT LOUIS UNIVERSITY PHILIPICH, KIRK	AUDIT REPORT MODIFICATIONS AND AUDITOR SWITCHES	Auditing Archival - Primary Auditor Changes 152

Author	Degree & Date School Advisor	Title	Functional Area Research Method Topic pages
NAM, YOUNG-HO	PHD 1990 MICHIGAN STATE UNIVERSITY	AN EMPIRICAL EXAMINATION OF THE ASSOCIATION BETWEEN FIRM CHARACTERISTICS AND THE ADOPTION OF LONG-TERM PERFORMANCE PLANS	Cost/Managerial Archival - Primary Performance Evaluation/Measurement 179
NANCE, WILLIAM DOUGLAS	PHD 1992 UNIVERSITY OF MINNESOTA DAVIS, GORDON B.	TASK/TECHNOLOGY FIT AND KNOWLEDGE WORKER USE OF INFORMATION TECHNOLOGY: A STUDY OF AUDITORS	Auditing Survey Audit Technology 216
NARASIMHAN, RAMESH	PHD 1987 VIRGINIA POLYTECHNIC INSTITUTE AND STATE UNIVERSITY LEININGER, WAYNE E.	PRELIMINARY CONTROL RISK ASSESSMENTS BY COMPUTER AUDIT SPECIALISTS AND NONSPECIALISTS	Auditing Experimental Judgment & Decision Making 266
NASSIRIPOUR, SIA	PHD 1993 WASHINGTON STATE UNIVERSITY GREENBERG, ROBERT R.	PREDICTING FUTURE CASH FLOW: CURRENT CASH FLOW VS. CURRENT EARNINGS	Financial Accounting Archival - Primary Cash Flows 92
NATARAJAN, RAMACHANDRAN	PHD 1992 UNIVERSITY OF PENNSYLVANIA LAMBERT, RICHARD A.	THE USE OF DISCRETIONARY ACCOUNTING REPORTS IN MANAGEMENT COMPENSATION CONTRACTS	Cost/Managerial Archival - Primary Incentive Compensation 123
NDUBIZU, GORDIAN ANUMUDU	PHD 1985 TEMPLE UNIVERSITY	AN EMPIRICAL INVESTIGATION OF THE SECURITY MARKET REACTION TO MULTINATIONAL ACCOUNTING CHANGES: STATEMENT OF FINANCIAL ACCOUNTING STANDARD NUMBER 52, FOREIGN CURRENCY TRANSLATION	Financial Accounting Archival - Primary Foreign Currency Translation 176
NDZINGE, SHABANI	PHD 1990 UNIVERSITY OF KENT AT CANTERBURY (UNITED KINGDOM)	REGIONAL HARMONISATION OF ACCOUNTING IN DEVELOPING COUNTRIES: THE CASE OF THE SADCC	General Case International/Global Issues 325
NECUNAZAR AZAD, ABBAS	PHD 1988 THE UNIVERSITY OF TEXAS AT AUSTIN CHARNES, A.	AN APPLICATION OF CHANCE-CONSTRAINED THEORY TO DYNAMIC BANK BALANCE SHEET MANAGEMENT	General Industry - Banking/Savings & Loan 164
NEEDY, KIM LA SCOLA	PHD 1993 WICHITA STATE UNIVERSITY MALZAHN, DON E.	PERFORMANCE COMPARISON OF ACTIVITY BASED COSTING VERSUS TRADITIONAL COST ACCOUNTING FOR STRATEGIC DECISION MAKING	Cost/Managerial Simulation Activity Based Costing 351

Author	Degree & Date School Advisor	Title	Functional Area Research Method Topic pages
NEHMER, ROBERT ALAN	PHD 1988 UNIVERSITY OF ILLINOIS AT URBANA-CHAMPAIGN CHANDLER, JOHN S.	ACCOUNTING INFORMATION SYSTEMS AS ALGEBRAS AND FIRST ORDER AXIOMATIC MODELS	Information Systems Analytical - Internal Systems Design &/or Development 169
NEILL, JOHN D., III	PHD 1990 UNIVERSITY OF FLORIDA AJINKYA, BIPIN B.	THE ROLE OF ACCOUNTING NUMBERS IN THE 'LONG-TERM' MISPRICING OF INITIAL PUBLIC SECURITY OFFERINGS	Financial Accounting Archival - Primary Initial Public Offerings 155
NEKRASZ, FRANK, JR.	PHD 1993 UNIVERSITY OF ILLINOIS AT URBANA-CHAMPAIGN NEUMANN, FREDERICK L.	A THEORETICAL INVESTIGATION OF MANADATORY AUDITOR REPORTS ON INTERNAL CONTROL STRUCTURES	Auditing Analytical - Internal Internal Control 233
NELSON, IRVIN TOM	PHD 1992 THE UNIVERSITY OF NEBRASKA - LINCOLN HUBBARD, THOMAS D.	IDENTIFYING AND RECRUITING FUTURE PROFESSIONALS: AN EMPIRICAL STUDY OF HIGHLY CAPABLE INDIVIDUALS' ATTITUDES TOWARD THE ACCOUNTING PROFESSION	General Experimental Accounting Career Issues 151
NELSON, JACOB JOHN	PHD 1992 WASHINGTON UNIVERSITY POWNALL, GRACE	CHANGES IN FIRMS' VOLUNTARY DISCLOSURES OF EARNINGS PROJECTIONS ASSOCIATED WITH OPTIONS LISTING	Financial Accounting Archival - Primary Voluntary Management Disclosures 86
NELSON, MARK WILLIAM	PHD 1990 THE OHIO STATE UNIVERSITY BAILEY, ANDREW D. JR.	AUDITOR LEARNING OF ERROR FREQUENCIES IN ANALYTICAL REVIEW	Auditing Experimental Analytical Review 212
NELSON, MARTHA KRUG	PHD 1990 UNIVERSITY OF PITTSBURGH BIRNBERG, JACOB G.	HEURISTIC AND NORMATIVE STRATEGIES: EVALUATION OF SAMPLE RESULTS BY AUDITORS	Auditing Experimental Judgment & Decision Making - Heuristics & Biases 193
NELSON, TONI LYNNE	PHD 1992 UNIVERSITY OF OREGON O'KEEFE, TERRENCE B.	THE EFFECT OF ACCOUNTING POLICY CHOICES ON THE RELATIONSHIP BETWEEN EARNINGS AND RETURNS	Financial Accounting Archival - Primary Accounting Choice 114
NEMEH, ALI G.	PHD 1986 UNIVERSITY OF STRATHCLYDE (UNITED KINGDOM)	OPERATIONAL AUDITING PRACTICES IN WESTERN DEVELOPED COUNTRIES: IMPLICATIONS FOR GOVERNMENT AUDIT IN THE STATE OF KUWAIT. (VOLUMES I AND II)	Auditing International/Global Issues 652

Author	Degree & Date School Advisor	Title	Functional Area Research Method Topic pages
NEWBERRY, KAYE JEANNE	PHD 1994 ARIZONA STATE UNIVERSITY CHRISTIAN, CHARLES W.	FOREIGN TAX CREDIT LIMITATIONS AND PUBLIC ISSUANCES BY UNITED STATES MULTINATIONALS: NEW EVIDENCE OF TAX CLIENTELES	Taxation Archival - Primary International/Global Issues 74
NEWMAN, SCOTT GARDINER	PHD 1986 THE UNIVERSITY OF TEXAS AT AUSTIN	A COMPREHENSIVE RANKING OF ESTATE FREEZING TRANSACTIONS	Taxation Analytical - Internal Estate & Gift Taxation 278
NG, A CHEW	PHD 1993 UNIVERSITY OF MELBOURNE (AUSTRALIA) HOUGHTON, KEITH	PREDICTION OF CORPORATE FAILURE: HUMAN JUDGMENTS AND FINANCIAL DECISION-MAKING	Financial Accounting Experimental Financial Distress or Bankruptcy 379
NIBBELIN, MICHAEL CHARLES	PHD 1988 THE FLORIDA STATE UNIVERSITY HILLISON, WILLIAM A.	THE EFFECTS OF MODE OF INFORMATION PRESENTATION AND PERCEPTUAL SKILL ON BOND RATING CHANGE DECISIONS: A LABORATORY STUDY	Financial Accounting Experimental Presentation Format 131
NICHOLS, DAVE LEROY	PHD 1992 OKLAHOMA STATE UNIVERSITY	SFAS 14'S GEOGRAPHIC SEGMENT DISCLOSURES AND THE ABILITY OF SECURITY ANALYSTS TO FORECAST EARNINGS	Financial Accounting Archival - Primary Segment Reporting 103
NICOLAOU, ANDREAS IACOVOU	DBA 1993 SOUTHERN ILLINOIS UNIVERSITY AT CARBONDALE MASONER, MICHAEL M.	AN EMPIRICAL EXAMINATION OF INFORMATION SYSTEMS SUCCESS IN RELATION WITH INFORMATION SYSTEMS DEVELOPMENT PHENOMENA	Information Systems Survey Systems Design &/or Development 158
NIGRINI, MARK JOHN	PHD 1993 UNIVERSITY OF CINCINNATI WOOD, WALLACE R.	THE DETECTION OF INCOME TAX EVASION THROUGH AN ANALYSIS OF DIGITAL DISTRIBUTIONS	Taxation Case Tax Compliance 326
NIKKHAH-AZAD, ALI	PHD 1988 UNIVERSITY OF NORTH TEXAS LUMSDEN, B.	PERCEPTIONS OF COLLEGE AND UNIVERSITY AUDITORS CONCERNING THE IMPORTANCE OF SELECTED FACTORS ASSOCIATED WITH OPERATIONAL AUDITING	Auditing Survey Internal Auditing 169
NISWANDER, FREDERICK DEAN	PHD 1993 TEXAS A&M UNIVERSITY SWANSON, EDWARD P.	ACCOUNTING AND FINANCING CHOICE AND CAPITAL ADEQUACY: AN EMPIRICAL STUDY OF PUBLIC AND PRIVATE COMMERCIAL BANKS	Financial Accounting Archival - Primary Industry - Banking/Savings & Loan 100

Author	Degree & Date School Advisor	Title	Functional Area Research Method Topic pages
NOGLER, GEORGE EDWARD	DBA 1987 BOSTON UNIVERSITY	AN EMPIRICAL STUDY OF BANKRUPTCY RESOLUTION AND COMMERCIAL BANK LOAN OFFICERS' PERCEPTIONS	Financial Accounting Bank Loan Officers 292
NOLAND, THOMAS RODNEY	PHD 1992 UNIVERSITY OF ILLINOIS AT URBANA-CHAMPAIGN ZIEBART, D.	THE SPEED OF THE MARKET RESPONSE TO EARNINGS ANNOUNCEMENTS AND THE BID-ASK SPREAD: AN EMPIRICAL STUDY	Financial Accounting Archival - Primary Earnings Announcements 119
NORWOOD, CYNTHIA JANE	PHD 1990 THE UNIVERSITY OF TENNESSEE SCHEINER, JAMES H.	MENTORING IN PUBLIC ACCOUNTING: AN EMPIRICAL INVESTIGATION	General Survey CPA Firm Issues 137
NOURI, HOSSEIN	PHD 1992 TEMPLE UNIVERSITY GREENBERG, PENELOPE SUE	THE EFFECT OF BUDGETARY PARTICIPATION ON JOB PERFORMANCE: A CONCEPTUAL MODEL AND ITS EMPIRICAL TEST	Cost/Managerial Survey Budgeting 293
NOVAK, EDWIN SHAWN	PHD 1991 UNIVERSITY OF HOUSTON THOMPSON, STEVEN C.	AN EMPIRICAL ANALYSIS OF FEDERAL INCOME TAX CAPITALIZATION IN THE PRICING OF INCOME PRODUCING REAL PROPERTY	Taxation Case Industry - Real Estate 181
NUGENT, DAVID ANTHONY	PHD 1992 UNIVERSITY OF PITTSBURGH BIRNBERG, JACOB G.	THE IMPACT OF WITHHOLDING POSITION AND PENALTY FACTORS ON TAXPAYER BEHAVIOR: A STUDY OF INTERACTION EFFECTS	Taxation Experimental Tax Compliance 176
NUGENT, JOHN HILLIARD	DBA 1989 BUSINESS SCHOOL LAUSANNE (SWITZERLAND)	CORPORATE DECLINE: CAUSES, SYMPTOMS, AND PRESCRIPTIONS FOR A TURNAROUND	Financial Accounting Financial Distress or Bankruptcy 177
NUTTER, SARAH EMMONS	PHD 1993 MICHIGAN STATE UNIVERSITY OUTSLAY, EDMUND	UNITED STATES FEDERAL TAXATION OF EXPATRIATES: AN EMPIRICAL INVESTIGATION OF THE EQUITY OF THE FOREIGN EARNED INCOME AND HOUSING EXCLUSIONS	Taxation Case International/Global Issues 144
NWAEZE, EMEKA T.	PHD 1992 THE UNIVERSITY OF CONNECTICUT HOSKIN, ROBERT E.	THE EFFECTS OF THE PARAMETERS OF EARNINGS EXPECTATION ON STOCK PRICES: A STRUCTURAL MODEL AND EMPIRICAL EVIDENCE	Financial Accounting Archival - Primary Earnings 168

Listing by Author

Author	Degree & Date School Advisor	Title	Functional Area Research Method Topic pages
NYCUM, VICKI L.	PHD 1985 THE UNIVERSITY OF NEBRASKA - LINCOLN	A STUDY OF THE APPLICATION OF THREE READABILITY INDICES AND THE CLOZE PROCEDURE TO EVALUATE THE UNDERSTANDABILITY OF NARRATIVE DISCLOSURES IN FINANCIAL REPORTS	Financial Accounting Disclosures 303
O'BRIEN, PATRICIA COLLEEN	PHD 1985 THE UNIVERSITY OF CHICAGO	AN EMPIRICAL ANALYSIS OF FORECASTS OF EARNINGS PER SHARE	Financial Accounting Archival - Primary Earnings Per Share
O'BRYAN, DAVID	PHD 1992 UNIVERSITY OF MISSOURI - COLUMBIA WILSON, EARL R.	THE ASSOCIATION OF EARNINGS AND CASH FLOW COMPONENTS WITH CORPORATE BOND RETURNS	Financial Accounting Archival - Primary Earnings Response Coefficients 230
O'CALLAGHAN, SUSANNE	PHD 1994 UNIVERSITY OF CINCINNATI SALE, J. TIMOTHY	AN ARTIFICIAL INTELLIGENCE APPLICATION OF BACKPROPAGATION NEURAL NETWORKS TO SIMULATE ACCOUNTANTS' ASSESSMENTS OF INTERNAL CONTROL SYSTEMS USING COSO GUIDELINES	Auditing Experimental Internal Control 170
O'CLOCK, PRISCILLA MARIE	PHD 1991 THE UNIVERSITY OF NEBRASKA - LINCOLN HUBBARD, THOMAS D.	THE EFFECT OF INFORMATION FRAMING ON THE AUDITOR'S GOING CONCERN EVALUATION	Auditing Experimental Judgment & Decision Making - Heuristics & Biases 201
O'LEARY, DANIEL EDMUND	PHD 1986 CASE WESTERN RESERVE UNIVERSITY	THE RELATIONSHIP OF NONACCOUNTING DISCLOSURES TO FIRM VALUATION AND PROFITABILITY: AN EMPIRICAL ANALYSIS OF TOBIN'S Q RATIO	Financial Accounting Archival - Primary Disclosures 186
O'SHAUGHNESSY, JOHN JOSEPH	PHD 1990 GOLDEN GATE UNIVERSITY CONATSER, R. GENE	AN EMPIRICAL STUDY OF THE EXTENT OF IMPLEMENTATION AND EFFECTIVENESS OF THE TREADWAY COMMISSION'S RECOMMENDATIONS AS PERCEIVED BY INTERNAL AUDIT MANAGERS OF CALIFORNIA'S 100 LARGEST PUBLICLY HELD COMPANIES	Auditing Survey Internal Auditing 269
OAKES, LESLIE SUSAN	PHD 1988 THE UNIVERSITY OF WISCONSIN - MADISON COVALESKI, MARK A.	ORGANIZATIONAL IMPLICATIONS OF ACCOUNTING-BASED INCENTIVE PLANS: AN HISTORICAL EXAMINATION OF ACCOUNTING IN THE LABOR PROCESS	General History 323
OCKREE, KANALIS A.	PHD 1993 UNIVERSITY OF KANSAS	A JUST-IN-TIME PRODUCTION PHILOSOPHY: EMPIRICAL ANALYSES AND FIELD STUDY	General Inventory 158

Listing by Author   153

Author	Degree & Date School Advisor	Title	Functional Area Research Method Topic pages
ODAIYAPPA, RAMASAMY	PHD 1985 UNIVERSITY OF FLORIDA	ECONOMIC CONSEQUENCES OF FINANCIAL ACCOUNTING STANDARDS BOARD STATEMENT NUMBER 33: AN INSIDER TRADING PERSPECTIVE	Financial Accounting Archival - Primary Insider Trading 137
ODOM, GARY LYNN	PHD 1986 UNIVERSITY OF SOUTH CAROLINA	THE EFFECT OF 1981 AND 1982 LEGISLATIVE ACTS ON SMALL CORPORATIONS' SELECTION OF A C OR S CORPORATE FORM	Taxation Simulation Business Form 148
ODOM, MARCUS DEAN	PHD 1993 OKLAHOMA STATE UNIVERSITY	AN EXAMINATION OF THE INTERACTION OF ELABORATION ALTERNATIVES AND ELABORATION PLACEMENT ON EXPERT SYSTEM-BASED INCIDENTAL LEARNING	Information Systems Experimental Decision Support Systems 159
OGILBY, SUZANNE MARIE	PHD 1991 THE UNIVERSITY OF WISCONSIN - MADISON COVALESKI, MARK	THE INSTITUTIONALIZATION OF BUDGETING PROCESSES: THE (RE)PRODUCTION OF POWER	Cost/Managerial Case Budgeting 375
OKCABOL, FAHRETTIN	PHD 1989 CITY UNIVERSITY OF NEW YORK TINKER, TONY	REGULATION AND ACCOUNTING PRACTICE: AN EVALUATION OF THE EFFICACY OF SEC MANDATORY REPORTING REQUIREMENTS	Financial Accounting Archival - Primary Standard Setting 165
OKLESHEN, MARILYN JEAN	PHD 1991 THE UNIVERSITY OF NEBRASKA - LINCOLN BROWN, JAMES F. JR.	THE SECURITY MARKET REACTION OF FINANCIAL INSTITUTIONS TO SFAS 95: THE STATEMENT OF CASH FLOWS	Financial Accounting Archival - Primary Cash Flows 159
OKOPNY, D. ROBERT	PHD 1985 TEXAS A&M UNIVERSITY	PLANNING AN INTERNATIONAL AUDIT: AN EMPIRICAL INVESTIGATION OF INTERNAL AUDITOR JUDGMENT	Auditing Experimental International/Global Issues 243
OLIVA, ROBERT ROGELIO	PHD 1993 FLORIDA INTERNATIONAL UNIVERSITY AVERCH, HARVEY	FEDERAL TAX DEDUCTIBILITY FOR LOCAL TAXES AND ITS EFFECT ON LOCAL REVENUE POLICIES	Taxation Public Policy 130
OLIVER, ELIZABETH GOAD	PHD 1992 TEXAS A&M UNIVERSITY GIROUX, GARY A.	MANAGERS' USE OF FASB'S MULTI-YEAR TRANSITION PERIODS: THE CASE OF PENSIONS	Financial Accounting Archival - Primary Standard Setting 148

Author	Degree & Date School Advisor	Title	Functional Area Research Method Topic pages
OLSON, CAROL ANN FELICIA	PHD 1989 UNIVERSITY OF FLORIDA KRAMER, JOHN L.	AN EXAMINATION OF THE FACTORS AFFECTING THE CHOICE OF EMPLOYEE FRINGE BENEFITS AND CAFETERIA PLANS	General Survey Other 185
OLSON, WILLIAM HALVER	PHD 1987 UNIVERSITY OF NORTH TEXAS	AN EMPIRICAL INVESTIGATION OF THE FACTORS CONSIDERED BY THE TAX COURT IN DETERMINING PRINCIPAL PURPOSE UNDER INTERNAL REVENUE CODE SECTION 269	Taxation Archival - Secondary Tax Court 76
OMER, KHURSHEED	DBA 1990 MEMPHIS STATE UNIVERSITY AGRAWAL, SURENDRA P.	AN INVESTIGATION OF PLOUGHBACK EARNINGS AS A FACTOR IN SECURITY PRICING	Financial Accounting Archival - Primary Earnings 172
OMER, THOMAS CLAYTON	PHD 1986 THE UNIVERSITY OF IOWA	ECONOMIC INCENTIVES AND ACCOUNTING POLICY CHOICES	Financial Accounting Archival - Primary Accounting Choice 140
ONIFADE, EMMANUEL ONAOLAPO	PHD 1993 UNIVERSITY OF SOUTH CAROLINA HARRISON, PAUL DAVID	AN EMPIRICAL EXAMINATION OF THE EFFECT OF CAUSAL ATTRIBUTIONS ON PROJECT CONTINUATION DECISION	Cost/Managerial Experimental Judgment & Decision Making 112
ONVURAL, NUR MEVLUDE	PHD 1990 NORTH CAROLINA STATE UNIVERSITY PEARCE, DOUGLAS K.	ECONOMIES OF SCALE AND ECONOMIES OF SCOPE IN NORTH CAROLINA SAVINGS AND LOAN INSTITUTIONS	General Archival - Primary Industry - Banking/Savings & Loan 125
ONYIRI, SUNNY O. G.	PHD 1994 THE UNION INSTITUTE SELLS, HALLOWAY C.	REPLACEMENT OF DEPRECIABLE TANGIBLE ASSETS: A MACRO APPROACH	Cost/Managerial Survey Capital Budgeting 141
OTT, RICHARD LAWRENCE	PHD 1986 TEXAS TECH UNIVERSITY	AN EMPIRICAL ANALYSIS OF THE INTERACTIVE EFFECTS BETWEEN THE INDIVIDUAL CHARACTERISTICS OF THE LEARNER AND THE METHOD OF INSTRUCTION--LECTURE OR COMPUTER-ASSISTED--ON STUDENT ACHIEVEMENT IN ELEMENTARY ACCOUNTING	Education Experimental Instructional Methods 134
OU, CHIN SHYH	PHD 1993 UNIVERSITY OF MINNESOTA BANKER, RAJIV D.; POTTER, GORDON	AN EMPIRICAL STUDY OF COST DRIVERS IN THE UNITED STATES BANKING INDUSTRY	Cost/Managerial Archival - Primary Industry - Banking/Savings & Loan 134

Author	Degree & Date School Advisor	Title	Functional Area Research Method Topic pages
PAGACH, DONALD PATRICK	PHD 1992 THE FLORIDA STATE UNIVERSITY BAGINSKI, STEPHEN P.	MANAGERIAL INCENTIVES AND THE INTRADAY TIMING OF EARNINGS ANNOUNCEMENTS	Financial Accounting Archival - Primary Earnings Announcements 98
PAIGE, KENNETH LEE	PHD 1985 UNIVERSITY OF PITTSBURGH	THE USE OF MANAGEMENT ACCOUNTING PRACTICES BY NONPROFIT ORGANIZATIONS: AN EXPLORATORY STUDY	Cost/Managerial Survey Not-for-Profit 162
PAIK, TAE-YOUNG	PHD 1989 UNIVERSITY OF CALIFORNIA, BERKELEY SEN, PRADYOT K.	THREE ESSAYS ON PARTICIPATIVE BUDGETING	Cost/Managerial Analytical - Internal Budgeting 164
PAK, HONG SEOK	PHD 1991 MEMPHIS STATE UNIVERSITY AUSTIN, KENNETH R.	THE EFFECTS OF INCOME SMOOTHING AND CONTRACTING COSTS ON MANAGERS' ATTITUDES TOWARDS THE SELECTION OF FOREIGN TRANSLATION ACCOUNTING PRINCIPLES: A STRUCTURAL EQUATION MODEL	Financial Accounting Archival - Primary Accounting Choice 122
PALMER, RICHARD JOSEPH	DBA 1990 SOUTHERN ILLINOIS UNIVERSITY AT CARBONDALE WELKER, ROBERT B.	THE EFFECT OF AN ANTICIPATED PERFORMANCE EVALUATION ON INDIVIDUAL PERFORMANCE AND CONTINUING MOTIVATION TOWARD THE TASK: THE INTERVENTION OF A SELF-PRESENTATION MOTIVE	Cost/Managerial Experimental Performance Evaluation/Measurement 149
PALOMINO BONILLA, LUIS MIGUEL	PHD 1992 UNIVERSITY OF PENNSYLVANIA SANTOMERO, ANTHONY	INFORMATIONAL ASYMMETRIES IN UNDERDEVELOPED SECURITIES MARKETS, OPTIMAL FINANCIAL CONTRACTS, AND REGULATION	Financial Accounting Analytical - Internal Capital Markets 123
PAN, ALEXANDER M.	PHD 1986 UNIVERSITY OF SOUTHERN CALIFORNIA	THE USE OF PANEL DATA IN ANALYTICAL REVIEW BY AUDITORS	Auditing Archival - Primary Analytical Review
PANDIT, GANESH MANGESH	DBA 1994 LOUISIANA TECH UNIVERSITY BYINGTON, J. RALPH	THE IMPACT OF CLIENTS' PERCEPTIONS ON AUDITOR SWITCHING	Auditing Survey Auditor Changes 166
PANG, YANG HOONG	PHD 1991 QUEEN'S UNIVERSITY AT KINGSTON (CANADA)	FINANCIAL DISCLOSURE AND ANALYSTS' FORECAST SUPERIORITY	Financial Accounting Archival - Primary Financial Analysts 216

Author	Degree & Date School Advisor	Title	Functional Area Research Method Topic pages
PANICH, RICHARD LOUIS	PHD 1985 ARIZONA STATE UNIVERSITY	AN EXAMINATION OF STRUCTURAL INCOME TAX REVISION FROM A PERSONAL WEALTH REDISTRIBUTION PERSPECTIVE	Taxation Individual Taxation 399
PANT, LAURIE W.	DBA 1986 BOSTON UNIVERSITY	THE DETERMINANTS OF CORPORATE TURNAROUND	Financial Accounting Archival - Primary Financial Distress or Bankruptcy 144
PAQUETTE, LAURENCE RICHARD	PHD 1985 UNIVERSITY OF MASSACHUSETTS	THE EFFECT OF DECISION STRATEGY AND TASK COMPLEXITY ON DECISION PERFORMANCE IN AN ACCOUNTING CONTEXT	General Experimental Judgment & Decision Making 139
PARK, CHANGHUN (PETER)	PHD 1993 PURDUE UNIVERSITY RO, BYUNG T.	THE RELEVANCE OF REPLACEMENT COST ASSET INFORMATION TO FIRM VALUATION	Financial Accounting Archival - Primary Inflation 98
PARK, GWANGHOON	PHD 1991 UNIVERSITY OF GEORGIA EDWARDS, JAMES DON	THE ASSOCIATION BETWEEN MANAGEMENT COMPENSATION AND ACCOUNTING POLICY DECISIONS: AN EXTENSION OF THE BONUS HYPOTHESIS	Financial Accounting Archival - Primary Accounting Choice 122
PARK, KYOUNG-HWAN	PHD 1993 GEORGIA STATE UNIVERSITY MEHTA, DILEEP R.	A SIMULATION MODEL OF TRANSFER PRICING FOR MULTINATIONAL CORPORATIONS BASED ON THE EQUIVALENT ANNUAL COST METHOD	Cost/Managerial Simulation Transfer Pricing 142
PARK, KYUNGJOO	PHD 1990 CITY UNIVERSITY OF NEW YORK HAW, IN-MU	QUALITY OF ACCOUNTING EARNINGS UNDER ALTERNATIVE PENSION ACCOUNTING METHODS	Financial Accounting Archival - Primary Post Retirement Benefit Issues 147
PARK, MANYONG	PHD 1988 THE UNIVERSITY OF TEXAS AT AUSTIN MAY, ROBERT G.	INCREMENTAL INFORMATION CONTAINED IN THE SFAS NO. 33 DISCLOSURES: A CLOSER EXAMINATION	Financial Accounting Archival - Primary Inflation 108
PARK, SECHOUL	PHD 1992 UNIVERSITY OF MARYLAND COLLEGE PARK LOEB, MARTIN P.	INSIDER TRADING ACTIVITY SURROUNDING CORPORATE EARNINGS ANNOUNCEMENT	Financial Accounting Archival - Primary Insider Trading 141

Listing by Author

Author	Degree & Date School Advisor	Title	Functional Area Research Method Topic pages
PARK, SEONG WHOE	PHD 1990 GEORGIA STATE UNIVERSITY - COLLEGE OF BUSINESS ADMINISTRATION DILLON, RAY D.	THE CHARACTERISTICS AND USAGE OF COMPUTERIZED INFORMATION SYSTEMS IN SMALL APPAREL AND TEXTILE COMPANIES	Information Systems Survey Small Business 173
PARKASH, MOHINDER	PHD 1987 THE UNIVERSITY OF ARIZONA	THE IMPACT OF A FIRM'S CONTRACTS AND SIZE ON THE ACCURACY, DISPERSION AND REVISIONS OF FINANCIAL ANALYSTS' FORECASTS: A THEORETICAL AND EMPIRICAL INVESTIGATION	Financial Accounting Archival - Primary Financial Analysts 118
PARKER, DOROTHY JANET	PHD 1992 UNIVERSITY OF ARKANSAS FRIES, CLARENCE E.	AN EXAMINATION OF A DIFFERENTIAL IN STANDARD COST DETERMINANTS AND ITS IMPACT ON VARIANCE INVESTIGATION PROCEDURES IN MANUFACTURING	Cost/Managerial Survey Standard Costs & Variance Analysis 119
PARKER, ROBERT JAMES	PHD 1993 TEMPLE UNIVERSITY GREENBERG, PENELOPE	BUDGETING EFFECTS AND EVALUATION BY SELF, PEERS, AND SUPERIORS WITH MODERATING EFFECTS OF PERSONAL AND SOCIAL IDENTITY	Cost/Managerial Experimental Budgeting 106
PARRISH, SHARON R.	DBA 1986 UNIVERSITY OF KENTUCKY	DEVELOPMENT OF A MODEL PEER REVIEW PROGRAM FOR STATE GOVERNMENT AUDIT AGENCIES	Not-for-Profit Governmental 327
PARRY, MICHAEL JOHN	PHD 1989 UNIVERSITY OF WALES COLLEGE OF CARDIFF (UNITED KINGDOM)	THE ROLE OF ACCOUNTING IN THE ECONOMIC DEVELOPMENT OF BANGLADESH	General International/Global Issues 563
PARSEGIAN, ELSA VARSENIG	PHD 1985 UNIVERSITY OF PITTSBURGH	A TEST OF SOME OF THE EFFECTS OF DIFFERENT PROPERTY RIGHTS STRUCTURES ON MANAGERIAL BEHAVIOR IN THE LIFE INSURANCE INDUSTRY	General Archival - Primary Industry - Insurance 168
PASEWARK, WILLIAM ROBERT	PHD 1986 TEXAS A&M UNIVERSITY	DETERMINING ECONOMIC INTEREST IN NATURAL RESOURCES	Taxation Archival - Secondary Tax Court 168
PASKIN, STEVEN	PHD 1991 UNIVERSITY OF COLORADO AT BOULDER BUCHMAN, THOMAS A.	SOME ECONOMIC DETERMINANTS OF DISCRETIONARY ACCOUNTING CHANGES	Financial Accounting Archival - Primary Accounting Change 143

Author	Degree & Date School Advisor	Title	Functional Area Research Method Topic pages
PASTORIA, GAIL	PHD 1993 KENT STATE UNIVERSITY ALAM, PERVAIZ	THE USE OF ACCOUNTING ACCRUALS AS A DEFENSIVE STRATEGY TO DETER TAKEOVERS	Financial Accounting Archival - Primary Earnings Management 253
PATE, GWENDOLYN RICHARDSON	PHD 1991 THE UNIVERSITY OF TENNESSEE STANGA, KEITH G.	A TEST OF THE THEORY OF MANAGEMENT'S PREFERENCES FOR ACCOUNTING STANDARDS: EVIDENCE FROM FASB STATEMENT NO. 94	Financial Accounting Archival - Primary Standard Setting 156
PATTEN, DENNIS MICHAEL	PHD 1987 THE UNIVERSITY OF NEBRASKA - LINCOLN	THE MARKET REACTION TO SOCIAL RESPONSIBILITY INFORMATION DISCLOSURES: THE CASE OF THE SULLIVAN PRINCIPLES SIGNINGS	Financial Accounting Archival - Primary Social/Environmental Responsibility 141
PATTERSON, EVELYN RUTH	PHD 1987 THE UNIVERSITY OF TEXAS AT AUSTIN	GAME THEORETIC APPLICATIONS TO AUDIT SAMPLING	Auditing Analytical - Internal Audit Sampling 217
PAULEY, PATRICIA ANN	PHD 1987 UNIVERSITY OF HOUSTON HORVITZ, JEROME	KNOWLEDGE OF THE TAX CONSEQUENCES OF PLAN DISTRIBUTIONS	Taxation Survey Post Retirement Benefit Issues 470
PAULSSON, GERT ARNE	EKONDR 1993 LUNDS UNIVERSITET (SWEDEN)	ACCOUNTING SYSTEMS IN TRANSITION: A CASE STUDY IN THE SWEDISH HEALTH CARE ORGANIZATION	Cost/Managerial Case Management Control Systems 221
PAVA, MOSES L.	PHD 1990 NEW YORK UNIVERSITY, GRADUATE SCHOOL OF BUSINESS ADMINISTRATION RONEN, JOSHUA	FINANCIAL ANALYSTS' FORECASTS AND FINANCIAL ANALYSTS' FORECASTING CUES	Financial Accounting Archival - Primary Financial Analysts 107
PAVELKA, DEBORAH DIANNE	PHD 1985 UNIVERSITY OF MISSOURI - COLUMBIA	PENSION LIABILITIES AND BANKERS' LOAN DECISIONS	Financial Accounting Experimental Post Retirement Benefit Issues 220
PAZ, ARMANDO J.	DBA 1993 UNITED STATES INTERNATIONAL UNIVERSITY KRISHNAMOORTHY, MEENAKSHI S.	FORECASTING SAVINGS AND LOAN FAILURES USING FINANCIAL ACCOUNTING INFORMATION	Financial Accounting Archival - Primary Financial Distress or Bankruptcy 119

Listing by Author

159

Author	Degree & Date School Advisor	Title	Functional Area Research Method Topic pages
PEARSON, TIMOTHY A.	PHD 1990 THE UNIVERSITY OF WISCONSIN - MADISON MATSUMURA, ELLA MAE	AN INVESTIGATION OF THE RELATIONSHIP BETWEEN AUDIT FEES AND AUDITOR REPUTATION: THE MARKET FOR INSURANCE AUDIT CLIENTS	Auditing Archival - Primary Audit Fees 109
PEECHER, MARK EVERETT	PHD 1994 UNIVERSITY OF ILLINOIS AT URBANA-CHAMPAIGN SOLOMON, IRA	CONSEQUENTIALITY, JUSTIFICATION AND AUDITORS' DECISION PROCESSES: A THEORETICAL FRAMEWORK AND TWO EXPERIMENTS	Auditing Experimental Auditor Behavior 205
PEEK, GEORGE SHERMAN	PHD 1990 UNIVERSITY OF GEORGIA EDWARDS, JAMES DON	AN EMPIRICAL STUDY OF RISK PREFERENCE ELICITATION WITH PRACTICING AUDITORS USING EXPERIMENTAL AND BUSINESS CONTEXTS	General Experimental Risk 207
PEEK, LUCIA ELIZABETH	PHD 1987 UNIVERSITY OF GEORGIA WARREN, CARL; NETER, JOHN	SAS NO. 39 GUIDELINES FOR NONSTATISTICAL SAMPLING: A SIMULATION STUDY	Auditing Simulation Audit Sampling 283
PEI, KER-WEI BUCK	PHD 1986 UNIVERSITY OF NORTH TEXAS	A COMPARATIVE STUDY OF INTERNAL AND EXTERNAL AUDITORS' JUDGMENT OF INTERNAL AUDITOR INDEPENDENCE	Auditing Experimental Internal Auditing 195
PEINO JANEIRO, VICTOR GABRIEL	PHD 1990 UNIVERSIDAD DE SANTIAGO DE COMPOSTELA (SPAIN)	ACCOUNTING AS A PROGRAM OF SCIENTIFIC INVESTIGATION: A TEST [LA CONTABILIDAD COMO PROGRAMA DE INVESTIGACION CIENTIFICA: UN ENSAYO]	General History
PENDLEBURY, MAURICE WILSON	PHD 1985 UNIVERSITY OF WALES (UNITED KINGDOM)	AN INVESTIGATION INTO THE ROLE AND NATURE OF MANAGEMENT ACCOUNTING IN LOCAL GOVERNMENT IN ENGLAND AND WALES	Cost/Managerial Survey Governmental 295
PEREIRA, EMILIO ANTHONY	PHD 1991 UNIVERSITY OF HOUSTON	ENVIRONMENTAL UNCERTAINTY AND MANAGERS' BUDGET-RELATED BEHAVIOR: A CROSS-CULTURAL FIELD STUDY	Cost/Managerial Survey Budgeting 252
PEREZ GARCIA, MARIA PILAR	DR 1989 UNIVERSIDAD DE VALLADOLID (SPAIN)	THE FAILURE OF A CENTRAL BANK: THE BANK OF VALLADOLID [LA BANCARROTA DE UN BANCO EMISOR: EL BANCO DE VALLADOLID]	General International/Global Issues 410

Author	Degree & Date School Advisor	Title	Functional Area Research Method Topic pages
PERKINS, WILLIAM DAVID	PHD 1991 TEXAS A&M UNIVERSITY STRAWSER, ROBERT H.	THE ASSOCIATION BETWEEN AUDIT STRUCTURE AND AUDITOR SATISFACTION: AN INTEGRATION OF BEHAVIORAL THEORIES	Auditing Survey Job Performance, Satisfaction &/or Turnover 104
PERRY, SUSAN ELIZABETH	PHD 1990 THE UNIVERSITY OF WISCONSIN - MADISON WILLIAMS, THOMAS H.	ACCOUNTING INFORMATION IN GOING-PRIVATE TRANSACTIONS	Financial Accounting Survey Merger, Acquisition, Reorganization 131
PERSELLIN, MARK BENNETT	PHD 1987 UNIVERSITY OF HOUSTON HOFFMAN, WILLIAM H. JR.	AN INVESTIGATION OF THE PLANNING AND POLICY IMPLICATIONS OF THE FOREIGN SALES CORPORATION LEGISLATION	Taxation Survey International/Global Issues 376
PERSONS, OBEUA SRICHANDRABHAN DHU	PHD 1991 THE UNIVERSITY OF TEXAS AT AUSTIN MAY, ROBERT G.	MARKET REACTIONS TO AUDITOR CHANGES BY FIRMS WITH DIFFERENT FINANCIAL CONDITIONS	Auditing Archival - Primary Auditor Changes 86
PETERS, JAMES MILTON	PHD 1989 UNIVERSITY OF PITTSBURGH	A KNOWLEDGE-BASED MODEL OF INHERENT AUDIT RISK ASSESSMENT	Auditing Survey Risk 317
PETRONI, KATHY RUBY	PHD 1990 THE UNIVERSITY OF MICHIGAN DEANGELO, LINDA E.	REGULATORY EFFICIENCY, FINANCIAL DISTRESS AND MANAGERIAL ACCOUNTING DISCRETION	General Archival - Primary Industry - Insurance 98
PFEFFER, MARY GRAVES	PHD 1987 UNIVERSITY OF NORTH TEXAS	VENTURE CAPITAL INVESTMENT AND PROTOCOL ANALYSIS	General Survey Investments 157
PHILHOURS, JOEL ELLIS	PHD 1991 UNIVERSITY OF KENTUCKY KNOBLETT, JAMES A.	NONLINEAR EFFECTS OF RESEARCH AND DEVELOPMENT EXPENDITURES ON MARKET VALUE	Financial Accounting Archival - Primary Research & Development 163
PHILLIPS, DAVID A.	PHD 1989 UNIVERSITY OF BRADFORD (UNITED KINGDOM)	ECONOMIC DEVELOPMENT, ACCOUNTING PRICES AND TECHNOLOGY: A CASE STUDY IN THE ESTIMATION OF ACCOUNTING PRICES AND THEIR APPLICATION TO ECONOMIC AND DISTRIBUTIONAL ANALYSIS OF THE CHOICE OF TECHNOLOGY IN THE NEPAL TEXTILE INDUSTRY	General Case International/Global Issues 484

Author	Degree & Date School Advisor	Title	Functional Area Research Method Topic pages
PHILLIPS, JEFFREY JOSEPH	PHD 1985 UNIVERSITY OF GEORGIA	BAYESIAN BOUNDS FOR MONETARY-UNIT SAMPLING USING ACTUAL ACCOUNTING POPULATIONS	Auditing Archival - Primary Audit Sampling 325
PHILLIPS, SAMUEL HORACE	PHD 1991 UNIVERSITY OF HOUSTON GAMBLE, GEORGE O.	AN EXPERIMENTAL INVESTIGATION OF THE ROLE OF COLLEGE AND UNIVERSITY FINANCIAL STATEMENTS IN ALUMNI SUPPORT DECISIONS	Not-for-Profit Experimental College & University 323
PICARD, ROBERT RAYMOND	PHD 1994 UNIVERSITY OF KENTUCKY COOPER, JEAN C.	MANAGERIAL ACCOUNTING PROBLEM-SOLVING SKILLS: AN EXPERIMENT INVESTIGATING GROUP-TO-INDIVIDUAL ACQUISITION AND TRANSFER	Education Experimental Instructional Methods 246
PICHLER, ANTON	DRSOCOEC 1990 UNIVERSITAET INNSBRUCK (AUSTRIA)	THE CONTROL OF PUBLIC BUILDINGS BY THE GENERAL ACCOUNTING OFFICE IN AUSTRIA [DIE KONTROLLE OEFFENTLICHER BAUTEN DURCH DEN RECHNUNGSHOF IN OESTERREICH]	Not-for-Profit Analytical - Internal Governmental 280
PIERCE, BARBARA GUGLIOTTA	PHD 1992 INDIANA UNIVERSITY SALAMON, GERALD L.	FIRM SIZE AND SEGMENTAL REPORTING: EVIDENCE ON DIFFERENTIAL MARKET REACTIONS	Financial Accounting Archival - Primary Standard Setting 106
PINAC-WARD, SUZANNE RESI	PHD 1986 THE LOUISIANA STATE UNIVERSITY AND AGRICULTURAL AND MECHANICAL COL.	AN EMPIRICAL INVESTIGATION OF THE COMPARABILITY OF REPORTED EARNINGS PER SHARE UNDER ACCOUNTING PRINCIPLES BOARD OPINION NO. 15	Financial Accounting Survey Earnings Per Share 173
PIROZZOLI, IRIS ANN	PHD 1990 THE UNIVERSITY OF WISCONSIN - MADISON FRANK, WERNER	PRICE-CUTTING AND TRANSACTION COSTS IN THE MARKET FOR AUDIT SERVICES	Auditing Archival - Primary Audit Fees 116
POCH Y TORRES, RAMON	DR 1988 UNIVERSITAT DE BARCELONA (SPAIN)	THE SYSTEM OF INTERNAL CONTROL OF BUSINESS FIRMS	Auditing Survey Internal Control 505
POE, CLYDE DOUGLAS	PHD 1985 TEXAS A&M UNIVERSITY	AN EXAMINATION OF THE STRENGTH OF THE CONTAGION EFFECT ON EVALUATIVE STYLE IN MANAGERIAL ACCOUNTING	Cost/Managerial Survey Performance Evaluation/Measuremen t 134

Author	Degree & Date School Advisor	Title	Functional Area Research Method Topic pages
POFF, J. KENT	PHD 1991 VIRGINIA POLYTECHNIC INSTITUTE AND STATE UNIVERSITY SEAGO, W. EUGENE	AN ECONOMIC ANALYSIS OF UNIFORM CAPITALIZATION OF INVENTORY COSTS UNDER SECTION 263A OF THE INTERNAL REVENUE CODE OF 1986	Taxation Analytical - Internal Inventory 164
POHLEN, TERRANCE LYNN	PHD 1993 THE OHIO STATE UNIVERSITY LALONDE, BERNARD J.	THE EFFECT OF ACTIVITY-BASED COSTING ON LOGISTICS MANAGEMENT	Cost/Managerial Case Activity Based Costing 397
POINTER, MARTHA MANNING	PHD 1992 UNIVERSITY OF SOUTH CAROLINA DOUPNIK, TIMOTHY S.	AN INVESTIGATION OF THE RELATIONSHIPS BETWEEN REQUIRED GEOGRAPHICAL SEGMENT DISCLOSURE AND SYSTEMATIC EQUITY RISK AND OPERATING RISK	Financial Accounting Archival - Primary Segment Reporting 104
PONEMON, LAWRENCE ANDREW	PHD 1988 UNION COLLEGE (NEW YORK) ARNOLD, DONALD F.	A COGNITIVE-DEVELOPMENTAL APPROACH TO THE ANALYSIS OF CERTIFIED PUBLIC ACCOUNTANTS' ETHICAL JUDGMENTS	General Survey Ethics 283
POONAKASEM, PORNSIRI PRINGSULAKA	PHD 1987 UNIVERSITY OF FLORIDA ABDEL-KHALIK, A. RASHAD	THE IMPACT OF MERGER ON THE FIRM'S EQUITY RISK: EX-ANTE VERSUS EX-POST ANALYSES	General Archival - Primary Risk 133
PORTER, SUSAN L.	PHD 1994 UNIVERSITY OF WASHINGTON BIDDLE, GARY	THE EFFECTS OF ALTERNATIVE STATE TAX REGIMES ON FIRMS' ACCOUNTING AND FINANCING DECISIONS	Taxation Archival - Primary State Taxation 136
PORTER, THOMAS LARSEN	PHD 1992 UNIVERSITY OF WASHINGTON BOWEN, ROBERT M.	THE EFFECT OF ECONOMIC REGULATION ON ACCOUNTING DECISIONS: EVIDENCE FROM THE UNITED STATES AIRLINE INDUSTRY	Financial Accounting Archival - Primary Industry - Airline 108
POTTER, GORDON SPOONER	PHD 1986 THE UNIVERSITY OF WISCONSIN - MADISON	ACCOUNTING EARNINGS ANNOUNCEMENTS, FUND CONCENTRATION AND COMMON STOCK RETURNS	Financial Accounting Archival - Primary Earnings Announcements 161
POULLAOS, CHRISTOPHER	PHD 1992 UNIVERSITY OF NEW SOUTH WALES (AUSTRALIA)	MAKING THE AUSTRALIAN CHARTERED ACCOUNTANT, 1886-1935	General Archival - Secondary History

Author	Degree & Date School Advisor	Title	Functional Area Research Method Topic pages
POURCIAU, SUSAN GRIBBLE	PHD 1988 ARIZONA STATE UNIVERSITY BOATSMAN, JIM	THE EFFECT OF ACCOUNTING DISCRETION ON EXECUTIVE COMPENSATION CONTRACTS	Cost/Managerial Archival - Primary Incentive Compensation 83
POURJALALI, HAMID	PHD 1992 OKLAHOMA STATE UNIVERSITY KIMBRELL, JANET	AN IMPROVED TEST OF POSITIVE ACCOUNTING THEORY: EXAMINATION OF THE CHANGES IN THE AMOUNT OF ACCRUALS IN RESPONSE TO THE CHANGES IN CONTRACTING VARIABLES	Financial Accounting Archival - Primary Accounting Choice 123
POWER, JACQUELINE LOU	PHD 1993 TEXAS A&M UNIVERSITY KRATCHMAN, STANLEY H.	ANNOUNCEMENTS OF STOCK REPURCHASES DURING 1988 AND 1989: AN EMPIRICAL ANALYSIS EXAMINING THE DISCLOSURE OF INTENDED OPEN MARKET REPURCHASES	Financial Accounting Archival - Primary Stock Transactions 169
POWER, JEFFREY WILLIAM	PHD 1991 PURDUE UNIVERSITY KROSS, WILLIAM	AN EMPIRICAL INVESTIGATION OF ANTITAKEOVER AMENDMENTS AND MANAGERIAL DISCRETION IN REPORTED EARNINGS	Financial Accounting Archival - Primary Earnings Management 140
POWNALL, JACQUELINE SUE	PHD 1985 THE UNIVERSITY OF CHICAGO	AN EMPIRICAL ANALYSIS OF THE REGULATION OF THE DEFENSE CONTRACTING INDUSTRY: THE COST ACCOUNTING STANDARDS BOARD	Cost/Managerial Archival - Primary Standard Setting
POZNANSKI, PETER JOHN	PHD 1991 TEXAS TECH UNIVERSITY FINN, DON W.	THE EFFECTS OF ORGANIZATIONAL COMMITMENT, PROFESSIONAL COMMITMENT, LIFE-SPAN CAREER DEVELOPMENT, AND SELF-MONITORING ON JOB SATISFACTION AND JOB PERFORMANCE AMONG STAFF ACCOUNTANTS	General Survey Job Performance, Satisfaction &/or Turnover 173
PRAWITT, DOUGLAS FRANK	PHD 1993 THE UNIVERSITY OF ARIZONA FELIX, WILLIAM L. JR.	A COMPARISON OF HUMAN RESOURCE ALLOCATION ACROSS AUDITING FIRMS: THE EFFECTS OF STRUCTURED AUDIT TECHNOLOGY AND ENVIRONMENT	Auditing Experimental Decision Aids 154
PRESS, ERIC GEOFFREY	PHD 1988 UNIVERSITY OF OREGON	THE ROLE OF ACCOUNTING BASED CONTRACTUAL PROVISIONS AND FINANCIAL STATEMENT EFFECTS IN EXPLAINING A DEBT EXTINGUISHMENT: THE CASE OF IN-SUBSTANCE DEFEASANCE	Financial Accounting Archival - Primary Long Term Debt 138
PRESSLY, THOMAS RICHARD	PHD 1989 KENT STATE UNIVERSITY FETYKO, DAVID F.	AN EMPIRICAL STUDY OF INVESTOR USE OF STATEMENT OF CASH FLOWS INFORMATION IN STOCK PRICE PREDICTION DECISIONS	Financial Accounting Experimental Cash Flows 207

Listing by Author 164

Author	Degree & Date School Advisor	Title	Functional Area Research Method Topic pages
PRESTON-THOMAS, AVERIL REI	PHD 1988 CORNELL UNIVERSITY	THE ASSOCIATION BETWEEN ACCOUNTING DISCLOSURES AND INSTITUTIONAL TRADING PATTERNS	Financial Accounting Archival - Primary Disclosures 172
PRESUTTI, ANTHONY HARRY, JR.	PHD 1988 UNIVERSITY OF CINCINNATI	AN EMPIRICAL INVESTIGATION OF THE IMPACT OF THE ANCHOR AND ADJUSTMENT HEURISTIC ON THE AUDIT JUDGMENT PROCESS	Auditing Experimental Judgment & Decision Making - Heuristics & Biases 95
PRICE, CAROL EILEEN	PHD 1992 TEXAS A&M UNIVERSITY SHEARON, WINSTON T. JR.	ACCOUNTING INFORMATION AND LOAN QUALITY ASSESSMENT: AN INVESTIGATION OF THE DECISION PROCESS	Financial Accounting Case Industry - Banking/Savings & Loan 119
PRICE, CHARLES EWELL	PHD 1987 UNIVERSITY OF GEORGIA	AN EMPIRICAL INQUIRY INTO THE PREDICTIVE POWER OF SELECTED ATTRIBUTES FROM DISPUTED FEDERAL TAX EXAMINATIONS	Taxation Archival - Primary Tax Court 134
PRICE, JEAN BOCKNIK	PHD 1992 INDIANA UNIVERSITY TILLER, MIKEL G.	OPERATIONALIZING INDUSTRY AFFILIATION AS A FACTOR IN THE BOND RATING DECISION: AN INVESTIGATION AND TEST OF A NEW APPROACH	Financial Accounting Archival - Primary Long Term Debt 116
PRICE, RENEE HALL	PHD 1993 TEXAS A&M UNIVERSITY CREADY, WILLIAM; WALLACE, WANDA	THE RELATIONS BETWEEN INSTITUTIONAL EQUITY OWNERSHIP, PRICE RESPONSIVENESS, AND ACCOUNTING DISCLOSURE QUALITY	Financial Accounting Archival - Primary Disclosures 120
PRIEBJRIVAT, ANGKARAT	PHD 1992 NEW YORK UNIVERSITY, GRADUATE SCHOOL OF BUSINESS ADMINISTRATION	CORPORATE DISCLOSURE: A CASE OF SECURITIES EXCHANGE OF THAILAND	Financial Accounting Archival - Primary International/Global Issues 187
PRINGLE, LYNN M.	DBA 1987 UNIVERSITY OF COLORADO AT BOULDER	A CATASTROPHE THEORY MODEL OF INVENTORY METHOD CHOICE	Financial Accounting Archival - Primary Inventory 182
PROBER, LARRY M.	PHD 1985 TEMPLE UNIVERSITY	A COMPARISON OF HISTORICAL COST AND GENERAL PRICE-LEVEL ADJUSTED MEASURES IN THE PREDICTION OF DIVIDEND CHANGES	Financial Accounting Archival - Primary Inflation 179

Author	Degree & Date School Advisor	Title	Functional Area Research Method Topic pages
PURCELL, THOMAS J., III	PHD 1988 THE UNIVERSITY OF NEBRASKA - LINCOLN RAYMOND, ROBERT H.	AN ANALYSIS OF THE FEDERAL INCOME TAX CONCEPT OF EARNINGS AND PROFITS AS COMPARED TO THE FINANCIAL ACCOUNTING CONCEPT OF RETAINED EARNINGS	Taxation Survey Earnings 214
PURVIS, S.E.C.	PHD 1985 COLUMBIA UNIVERSITY	THE AUDITOR'S PRELIMINARY EVALUATION OF INTERNAL ACCOUNTING CONTROL: A BEHAVIORAL ANALYSIS	Auditing Experimental Internal Control 408
PUTMAN, ROBERT LYNN	DBA 1988 MEMPHIS STATE UNIVERSITY RAYBURN, L. GAYLE	AN EMPIRICAL STUDY OF THE IMPACT OF PUBLIC LAW 98-21 ON THE FINANCIAL OPERATING ENVIRONMENT OF UNITED STATES HOSPITALS	General Archival - Primary Industry - Health Care 176
PYO, YOUNGIN	PHD 1987 PURDUE UNIVERSITY RO, BYUNG-TAK	INFORMATION TRANSFERS AND INFORMATION LEAKAGE ASSOCIATED WITH EARNINGS RELEASES	Financial Accounting Archival - Primary Information Transfer 114
QTAISHAT, MUNIF ABDELRAHMAN	EDD 1988 UNIVERSITY OF GEORGIA PERKINS, EDWARD A.	JORDANIAN ACCOUNTING PRACTITIONERS' PERCEPTIONS OF UNDERGRADUATE ACCOUNTING PROGRAM CONTENT	Education Survey Curriculum Issues 229
QUARLES, NOWLIN ROSS	PHD 1988 UNIVERSITY OF NORTH TEXAS	PROFESSIONAL COMMITMENT, ORGANIZATIONAL COMMITMENT, AND ORGANIZATIONAL - PROFESSIONAL CONFLICT IN THE INTERNAL AUDIT FUNCTION: MODEL DEVELOPMENT AND TEST	Auditing Survey Internal Auditing 259
QUE, ANTONIO L.	PHD 1985 NEW YORK UNIVERSITY, GRADUATE SCHOOL OF BUSINESS ADMINISTRATION	A CRITICAL EVALUATION OF FASB STATEMENT NO. 13	Financial Accounting Archival - Primary Leases 248
QUILLIAM, WILLIAM CLAYTON	PHD 1991 UNIVERSITY OF FLORIDA MESSIER, WILLIAM F. JR.	EXAMINING THE EFFECTS OF ACCOUNTABILITY ON AUDITORS' VALUATION DECISIONS	Auditing Experimental Auditor Behavior 107
QURESHI, ANIQUE AHMED	PHD 1993 RUTGERS THE STATE UNIVERSITY OF NEW JERSEY - NEWARK VASARHELYI, MIKLOS	AN INVESTIGATION OF AUDITOR JUDGMENT IN THE EVALUATION OF CONTINGENT LEGAL LIABILITIES	Auditing Experimental Judgment & Decision Making - Heuristics & Biases 166

Author	Degree & Date School Advisor	Title	Functional Area Research Method Topic pages
RABASEDA I TARRES, JOAQUIM	ECONOMD 1991 UNIVERSITAT DE BARCELONA (SPAIN)	THEORY AND TECHNIQUE OF CONSOLIDATION ACCOUNTING	Financial Accounting Analytical - Internal Merger, Acquisition, Reorganization 625
RADHAKRISHNAN, SURESH	PHD 1991 NEW YORK UNIVERSITY, GRADUATE SCHOOL OF BUSINESS ADMINISTRATION BALACHANDRAN, KASHI R.	THE RELEVANCE OF COST APPLICATION IN A COMMON FACILITY	Cost/Managerial Analytical - Internal Incentive Compensation 122
RADIG, WILLIAM J.	DBA 1988 MISSISSIPPI STATE UNIVERSITY DANIEL, TROY E.	THE EFFECTS OF INFORMATION REQUIRED BY STATEMENT OF FINANCIAL ACCOUNTING STANDARDS NO. 33 ON THE MANAGERIAL DECISIONS MADE IN SELECTED INDUSTRIAL CORPORATIONS	Financial Accounting Archival - Primary Inflation 138
RADTKE, ROBIN RAE	PHD 1992 UNIVERSITY OF FLORIDA AJINKYA, BIPIN B.	AN EXPERIMENTAL INVESTIGATION OF MANAGERS' ESCALATION ERRORS	Cost/Managerial Experimental Judgment & Decision Making 159
RAGHUNANDAN, KANNAN	PHD 1990 THE UNIVERSITY OF IOWA GRIMLUND, RICHARD	AN EMPIRICAL TEST OF THE PREDICTIVE ABILITY OF AUDITORS' LOSS CONTINGENCY DISCLOSURES	Auditing Archival - Primary Audit Opinion 98
RAGHUNATHAN, BHANU	PHD 1986 UNIVERSITY OF PITTSBURGH	ECONOMIC DETERMINANTS OF AUDITOR INDEPENDENCE	Auditing Independence 143
RAGLAND, BERNARD GRAFTON	PHD 1989 THE GEORGE WASHINGTON UNIVERSITY CORDES, JOSEPH E.	DEPRECIATION--CHOICE VARIABLE OR ONLY A MANAGEMENT CHOICE?	Financial Accounting Archival - Primary Accounting Choice 202
RAGOTHAMAN, SRINIVASAN	PHD 1991 UNIVERSITY OF KANSAS BUBLITZ, BRUCE O.	ECONOMIC IMPLICATIONS OF ASSET WRITEDOWN DISCLOSURE POLICY	Financial Accounting Archival - Primary Disclosures 169
RAHMAN, MONSURUR	PHD 1992 SOUTHERN ILLINOIS UNIVERSITY AT CARBONDALE WELKER, ROBERT B.	THE EFFECT OF A CONSTRAINED RESOURCE ON INDIVIDUAL PERFORMANCE, PERFORMANCE EFFORT, AND FEELINGS TOWARD THE TASK AND DECISION-MAKERS: THE INTERVENTION OF EQUITY	Cost/Managerial Experimental Agency Theory 208

Listing by Author

167

Author	Degree & Date School Advisor	Title	Functional Area Research Method Topic pages
RAJAN, MADHAV VASANTH	PHD 1990 CARNEGIE-MELLON UNIVERSITY BAIMAN, STANLEY	PERFORMANCE EVALUATION AND CONTROL IN MULTI-AGENT SETTINGS	Cost/Managerial Analytical - Internal Management Control Systems 146
RAMADAN, SAYEL S.	PHD 1985 UNIVERSITY OF GLASGOW (UNITED KINGDOM)	THE ALLOCATION OF CENTRAL OVERHEAD COSTS FOR THE PURPOSES OF PERFORMANCE EVALUATION: A STUDY OF UK DIVISIONALISED COMPANIES	Cost/Managerial Survey Cost Allocation 433
RAMAGLIA, JUDITH ANN	PHD 1988 UNIVERSITY OF WASHINGTON MUELLER, GERHARD G.	STRUCTURES IN THE ACCOUNTING LEXICON: AN INVESTIGATION OF SIMILARITIES STRUCTURES AND CONNOTATIVE DIMENSIONS IN FIVE NATIONS	General International/Global Issues 301
RAMANAN, RAMACHANDRAN	PHD 1986 NORTHWESTERN UNIVERSITY	MANAGERIAL INCENTIVES, ACCOUNTING FOR INTEREST COSTS AND CAPITAL INVESTMENT DECISIONS OF THE FIRM	Financial Accounting Archival - Primary Agency Theory 150
RAMASWAMY, KADANDOGE PADMANABHAN	PHD 1993 UNIVERSITY OF KANSAS WAEGELEIN, JAMES F.	LONG-TERM PERFORMANCE ISSUES OF MERGERS AND ACQUISITIONS	Financial Accounting Archival - Primary Merger, Acquisition, Reorganization 144
RAMBO, ROBERT GEORGE	PHD 1994 THE FLORIDA STATE UNIVERSITY BAGINSKI, STEPHEN P.	VARIATION IN THE STOCK MARKET RESPONSE TO EARNINGS ANNOUNCEMENTS ASSOCIATED WITH THE REPORTING FIRM'S POSITION IN ITS INDUSTRY'S EARNINGS RELEASE QUEUE	Financial Accounting Archival - Primary Earnings Announcements 106
RAMESH, KRISHNAMOORTHY	PHD 1991 MICHIGAN STATE UNIVERSITY	ESSAYS ON EARNINGS RESPONSE COEFFICIENT	Financial Accounting Archival - Primary Earnings Response Coefficients 121
RAMEZANI, AHMAD	PHD 1991 UNIVERSITY OF CALIFORNIA, BERKELEY	ASSET ATTRIBUTES AND PORTFOLIO CHOICE: IMPLICATIONS FOR CAPITAL ASSET PRICES	Financial Accounting Archival - Primary Capital Markets 134
RAMOS, VINCENT, JR.	PHD 1993 TEXAS A&M UNIVERSITY PALMER, DOUG; PARKER, RICHARD	EVALUATION OF THE IMPACT OF A 'SCHOOL WITHIN A SCHOOL'S ALTERNATIVE PROGRAM ON GRADES, ATTENDANCE, ACHIEVEMENT, AND SELF-CONCEPT BY ETHNIC GROUP	Education Case Academic Achievement 124

Author	Degree & Date School Advisor	Title	Functional Area Research Method Topic pages
RAMSAY, ROBERT JOE	PHD 1991 INDIANA UNIVERSITY TILLER, MIKEL G.	AN INVESTIGATION OF THE HIERARCHICAL, SEQUENTIAL NATURE OF AUDIT WORKING PAPER REVIEW	Auditing Experimental Judgment & Decision Making - Cognitive Processes 139
RAMZY, WAFAA ABDEL MAGID	PHD 1988 HERIOT-WATT UNIVERSITY (UNITED KINGDOM)	THE DETERMINANTS OF AUDIT FEES: AN ANALYTICAL STUDY	Auditing Survey Audit Fees 259
RAND, RICHARD SPAULDING, JR.	PHD 1989 UNIVERSITY OF SOUTH CAROLINA	THE EFFECT OF AUDITORS' KNOWLEDGE OF ERRORS ON PLANNING-STAGE ASSESSMENTS OF CLIENT-RELATED RISK COMPONENTS AND ON INITIAL AUDIT SCOPE DECISIONS	Auditing Experimental Risk 129
RANGANATHAN, KRISHNAN AYENGAR	PHD 1991 UNIVERSITY OF NORTH TEXAS MERINO, BARBARA D.	IMPACT OF THE GAIN/LOSS PROVISIONS OF FINANCIAL ACCOUNTING STANDARD NO. 88 ON BENEFIT SETTLEMENTS	Financial Accounting Archival - Primary Post Retirement Benefit Issues 210
RANKINE, GRAEME WILLIAM	PHD 1987 UNIVERSITY OF WASHINGTON	THE EFFECT OF TAXES AND AGENCY COSTS ON ORGANIZATIONAL CHOICE: THE CASE OF FRANCHISING	General Other 143
RAO, GITA RAMA	PHD 1990 THE UNIVERSITY OF ROCHESTER BALL, RAY	THE RELATION BETWEEN STOCK RETURNS AND EARNINGS: A STUDY OF NEWLY-PUBLIC FIRMS	Financial Accounting Archival - Primary Earnings Response Coefficients 131
RAO, HEMA	DBA 1990 MISSISSIPPI STATE UNIVERSITY HERRING, DORA	AN EMPIRICAL EVALUATION OF THE PRACTICE OF DISCOUNTING INITIAL AUDIT FEES AND THE EFFECT OF THE PRACTICE ON THE APPEARANCE OF AUDIT INDEPENDENCE (FEE DISCOUNTING)	Auditing Survey Audit Fees 177
RASTOGI, LOKESH CHANDRA	DBA 1985 NOVA UNIVERSITY	A COMPARISON OF JOB SATISFACTION OF CERTIFIED MANAGEMENT ACCOUNTANTS (CMAS) WORKING IN CPA FIRMS AND IN INDUSTRY	General Survey Job Performance, Satisfaction &/or Turnover 322
RAVENSCROFT, SUSAN PICKARD	PHD 1989 MICHIGAN STATE UNIVERSITY	INCENTIVE PLANS AND MULTI-AGENT INFORMATION SHARING	Cost/Managerial Experimental Incentive Compensation 167

Listing by Author

169

Author	Degree & Date School Advisor	Title	Functional Area Research Method Topic pages
RAVI, INDUMATHI	PHD 1990 STATE UNIVERSITY OF NEW YORK AT BUFFALO	THE EFFECT OF A MANDATORY ACCOUNTING CHANGE ON EXECUTIVE COMPENSATION: THE CASE OF SFAS NO. 2	General Archival - Primary Accounting Change 151
RAWASHDEH, MUFEED M.	PHD 1994 SAINT LOUIS UNIVERSITY JENNINGS, JAMES P.	DETERMINANTS OF GOING-PRIVATE: INFORMATION ASYMMETRY, HOSTILE TAKEOVER THREAT, AND/OR FREE CASH FLOW	Financial Accounting Archival - Primary Agency Theory 118
RAY, J. O., III	DBA 1985 MISSISSIPPI STATE UNIVERSITY	AN INTERACTIVE FINANCIAL FORECASTING MODEL FOR MISSISSIPPI DELTA FARMING	General Industry - Agricultural 307
RAY, MANASH RANJAN	PHD 1989 THE PENNSYLVANIA STATE UNIVERSITY CUSHING, BARRY E.	TOWARDS A POSITIVE AGENCY THEORY OF CONTROL: AN EMPIRICAL STUDY OF COMPENSATION CONTRACTS IN THE INSURANCE INDUSTRY	General Survey Industry - Insurance 219
RAYBURN, JUDY DAWSON	PHD 1985 THE UNIVERSITY OF IOWA	THE INCREMENTAL INFORMATION CONTENT OF ACCRUAL ACCOUNTING EARNINGS	Financial Accounting Archival - Primary Accruals 103
RAZAKI, KHALID AHMED	PHD 1986 UNIVERSITY OF ILLINOIS AT URBANA-CHAMPAIGN	THE INCREMENTAL PREDICTIVE ABILITY OF GENERAL PRICE LEVEL ADJUSTED ACCOUNTING NUMBERS FOR DOWNWARD BOND RATING CHANGES	Financial Accounting Archival - Primary Inflation 140
REBMANN-HUBER, ZELMA E.	PHD 1988 UNIVERSITY OF WASHINGTON MUELLER, GERHARD	THE INFLUENCE OF VARIOUS GROUPS ON ACCOUNTING STANDARD-SETTING IN SIXTEEN DEVELOPED COUNTRIES: MODEL AND EMPIRICAL INVESTIGATIONS	Financial Accounting Survey International/Global Issues 230
REBURN, JAMES PATRICK	DBA 1988 LOUISIANA TECH UNIVERSITY	AN EMPIRICAL EXAMINATION OF DISCLOSURES REQUIRED BY THE SECURITIES AND EXCHANGE COMMISSION: THE CASE OF STOCK OWNERSHIP REPORTING	Financial Accounting Archival - Primary Information Content 144
REDINBAUGH, DONNA FAYE HEERMANN	PHD 1986 THE UNIVERSITY OF NEBRASKA - LINCOLN	STRATEGIC PLANNING/MANAGEMENT IN SELECTED BIG EIGHT ACCOUNTING FIRMS	General Case CPA Firm Issues 341

Author	Degree & Date School Advisor	Title	Functional Area Research Method Topic pages
REDING, KURT F.	PHD 1988 THE UNIVERSITY OF TENNESSEE REEVE, JAMES M.	CONTROL CHARTS AS DECISION AIDS TO OPERATIONAL AUDITORS' ASSESSMENTS OF PRODUCTION PROCESS PERFORMANCE	Auditing Experimental Decision Aids 238
REDMER, TIMOTHY ALBERT ORAL	PHD 1988 VIRGINIA COMMONWEALTH UNIVERSITY SPERRY, JOHN	BUDGET ACTIVITIES AND THEIR IMPACT ON THE BUDGET PROCESS: AN EXPLORATORY STUDY	Cost/Managerial Survey Budgeting 162
REES, LYNN L.	PHD 1993 ARIZONA STATE UNIVERSITY	AN INVESTIGATION OF THE INFORMATION CONTAINED IN DISCLOSURES OF DIFFERENCES BETWEEN FOREIGN AND DOMESTIC EARNINGS	Financial Accounting Archival - Primary International/Global Issues 78
REGEL, ROY W.	DBA 1985 UNIVERSITY OF COLORADO AT BOULDER	STAFF PERFORMANCE EVALUATION BY AUDITORS: THE EFFECT OF TRAINING ON ACCURACY AND CONSENSUS	Auditing Survey Job Performance, Satisfaction &/or Turnover 165
REGIER, PHILIP ROGER	PHD 1987 UNIVERSITY OF ILLINOIS AT URBANA-CHAMPAIGN	THE DIFFERENTIAL EFFECTS OF UNEXPECTED PERMANENT AND TRANSITORY EARNINGS CHANGES ON EQUITY RETURNS	Financial Accounting Archival - Primary Earnings Announcements 102
REIDER, BARBARA POWELL	PHD 1991 KENT STATE UNIVERSITY PEARSON, MICHAEL A.	HYPOTHESIS CONFIRMATION AND DISCONFIRMATION BY INDEPENDENT AUDITORS: GENERAL AND AUDIT-SPECIFIC CONTEXTS	Auditing Experimental Judgment & Decision Making - Heuristics & Biases 278
REIS, PRISCILLA ROSE	PHD 1991 RENSSELAER POLYTECHNIC INSTITUTE PAULSON, ALBERT S.	ACCOUNTING FOR COMPLEXITY: AN EXPLORATORY STUDY	Cost/Managerial Case Management Control Systems 388
REITER, SARA ANN	PHD 1985 UNIVERSITY OF MISSOURI - COLUMBIA	THE EFFECT OF DEFINED BENEFIT PENSION PLAN DISCLOSURES ON BOND RISK PREMIUMS AND BOND RATINGS	Financial Accounting Archival - Primary Post Retirement Benefit Issues 181
REITHER, CHERI LYNN	PHD 1994 UNIVERSITY OF NORTH TEXAS KLAMMER, THOMAS	A PROCESS ANALYSIS OF LENDERS' USE OF FAS 95 CASH FLOW INFORMATION	Financial Accounting Experimental Cash Flows 220

Author	Degree & Date School Advisor	Title	Functional Area Research Method Topic pages
REMMELE, DAVID ALAN	PHD 1985 THE UNIVERSITY OF WISCONSIN - MADISON	COURT-DETERMINED MATERIALITY: AN EMPIRICAL ANALYSIS OF THE CRITERIA COURTS USE AND THE IMPLICATIONS FOR ACCOUNTANTS	Auditing Archival - Secondary Materiality 252
RESCHO, JOYCE ANNE	PHD 1987 THE UNIVERSITY OF MISSISSIPPI	PUBLIC ACCOUNTING FIRM STRATEGY AND INNOVATIVENESS: A STUDY OF THE ADOPTION OF PRODUCT, TECHNICAL, AND ADMINISTRATIVE INNOVATIONS USING A STRATEGIC TYPOLOGY	General Survey CPA Firm Issues 229
REYNOLDS, MARY ANN	PHD 1989 THE UNIVERSITY OF UTAH LOEBBECKE, JAMES K.	AN EXAMINATION OF THE AUDIT FUNCTION IN SOCIETY	Auditing Survey Accounting in Society 214
REZAEE, ZABIHOLLAH	PHD 1985 THE UNIVERSITY OF MISSISSIPPI	CAPITAL MARKET REACTIONS TO ACCOUNTING POLICY DELIBERATIONS: AN EMPIRICAL STUDY OF ACCOUNTING FOR THE TRANSLATION OF FOREIGN CURRENCY TRANSACTIONS AND FOREIGN CURRENCY FINANCIAL STATEMENTS, 1974-1982	Financial Accounting Archival - Primary Foreign Currency Translation 305
RICE, ERIC MARSHALL	PHD 1990 HARVARD UNIVERSITY SUMMERS, LAWRENCE H.	SKIRTING THE LAW: ESSAYS ON CORPORATE TAX EVASION AND AVOIDANCE	Taxation Archival - Primary Tax Compliance 173
RICH, JOHN CARR	PHD 1985 UNIVERSITY OF NORTH TEXAS	THE EQUITY METHOD OF ACCOUNTING AND UNCONSOLIDATED SUBSIDIARIES: AN EMPIRICAL STUDY	Financial Accounting Archival - Primary Merger, Acquisition, Reorganization 177
RICHARDSON, CLARA LUCILE	PHD 1985 TEXAS A&M UNIVERSITY	THE PREDICTIVE ABILITY OF ALTERNATIVE BASES FOR INTERPERIOD TAX ALLOCATION: AN EMPIRICAL STUDY	Financial Accounting Archival - Primary Taxes 179
RICKETTS, ROBERT CARLTON	PHD 1988 UNIVERSITY OF NORTH TEXAS BROCK, HORACE	ALTERNATIVE SOCIAL SECURITY TAXING SCHEMES: AN ANALYSIS OF VERTICAL AND HORIZONTAL EQUITY IN THE FEDERAL TAX SYSTEM	Taxation Archival - Primary Individual Taxation 232
RIFFE, SUSAN MICHELE	PHD 1992 UNIVERSITY OF SOUTHERN CALIFORNIA MANEGOLD, JAMES G.	AN EMPIRICAL ANALYSIS OF OFF-BALANCE-SHEET FINANCIAL INSTRUMENT DISCLOSURES IN THE BANKING INDUSTRY	Financial Accounting Archival - Primary Industry - Banking/Savings & Loan

Author	Degree & Date School Advisor	Title	Functional Area Research Method Topic pages
RIGSBY, JOHN THOMAS, JR.	DBA 1986 MEMPHIS STATE UNIVERSITY	AN ANALYSIS OF THE EFFECTS OF COMPLEXITY ON THE MATERIALITY DECISIONS OF AUDITORS	Auditing Experimental Judgment & Decision Making 168
RILEY, ANNE CURTIN	DBA 1987 THE GEORGE WASHINGTON UNIVERSITY	AN ANALYTICAL FRAMEWORK FOR THE EVALUATION OF INHERENT AUDIT RISK	Auditing Experimental Risk 277
RINKE, DOLORES FAY	EDD 1990 NORTHERN ILLINOIS UNIVERSITY	CREDENTIALING PROCESSES OF PROFESSIONAL PUBLIC ACCOUNTANTS IN FRANCE, ITALY, THE UNITED KINGDOM, AND WEST GERMANY	General Archival - Secondary International/Global Issues 339
RIORDAN, DIANE A.	PHD 1988 VIRGINIA POLYTECHNIC INSTITUTE AND STATE UNIVERSITY BROWN, ROBERT M.	THE NATURE AND EFFECTIVENESS OF MANAGEMENT CONTROL IN SMALL FAMILY BUSINESSES	Cost/Managerial Survey Small Business 173
RIORDAN, MICHAEL PATRICK	PHD 1989 VIRGINIA POLYTECHNIC INSTITUTE AND STATE UNIVERSITY BROWN, ROBERT M.	HOW COGNITIVE COMPLEXITY AFFECTS ACCOUNTING CAREER PATHS	General Survey Accounting Career Issues 173
RIPOLL FELIU, VICENTE MATEO	PHD 1987 UNIVERSITAT DE VALENCIA (SPAIN)	THE RESEARCH ABOUT THE VARIANCES IN THE STANDARD COST MODELS [LA INVESTIGACION DE LAS DESVIACIONES EN LOS MODELOS DE COSTE ESTANDAR]	Cost/Managerial Standard Costs & Variance Analysis 675
RIPPINGTON, FREDERICK ALFRED	PHD 1991 THE CITY UNIVERSITY (LONDON) (UNITED KINGDOM)	THE INCREMENTAL INFORMATION CONTENT OF THE ANNUAL REPORT AND ACCOUNTS	Financial Accounting Archival - Primary Information Content 262
ROARK, STEPHEN JOE	PHD 1986 ARIZONA STATE UNIVERSITY	AN EXAMINATION OF RISK ATTITUDES IN LEGAL TAX RESEARCH	Taxation Experimental Judgment & Decision Making - Heuristics & Biases 185
ROBERTS, CLYDE A.	DBA 1988 UNIVERSITY OF KENTUCKY FULKS, DANIEL	CPA CREDIBILITY AND THE CREDIT DECISION PROCESS OF COMMERCIAL LOAN OFFICERS	General Experimental Bank Loan Officers 134

Author	Degree & Date School Advisor	Title	Functional Area Research Method Topic pages
ROBERTS, MICHAEL L.	PHD 1988 GEORGIA STATE UNIVERSITY - COLLEGE OF BUSINESS ADMINISTRATION ENGLEBRECHT, TED D.	JUDGMENT AND THE VALUATION OF CLOSELY HELD CORPORATIONS FOR ESTATE TAXATION	Taxation Experimental Estate & Gift Taxation 181
ROBERTS, ROBIN WENDELL	PHD 1987 UNIVERSITY OF ARKANSAS	DETERMINANTS OF AUDITOR CHANGE IN THE PUBLIC SECTOR	Auditing Case Auditor Changes 135
ROBERTSON, DARROCH AITKENS	PHD 1987 THE UNIVERSITY OF WESTERN ONTARIO (CANADA)	AN INVESTIGATION OF DEFERRED INCOME TAXES DURING A RECESSIONARY PERIOD	Financial Accounting Archival - Primary Taxes
ROBERTSON, PAUL JEPSEN	DBA 1989 MISSISSIPPI STATE UNIVERSITY DAUGHTREY, ZOEL	DEBT OR EQUITY? AN EMPIRICAL ANALYSIS OF TAX COURT CLASSIFICATION DURING THE PERIOD 1955-1987	Taxation Archival - Secondary Tax Court 165
ROBINSON, CHRISTOPHER MICHAEL	PHD 1985 UNIVERSITY OF TORONTO (CANADA)	AN EMPIRICAL INVESTIGATION OF ERROR CORRECTION DECISIONS MADE BY AUDITORS IN PRACTICE	Auditing Analytical - Internal Errors
ROBINSON, IDA B.	PHD 1993 OKLAHOMA STATE UNIVERSITY HANSEN, DON R.	AN EXAMINATION OF BOND VALUATION IN THE PRESENCE OF LOSS CONTINGENCY DISCLOSURES: A CONTINUOUS-TIME FINANCE THEORY APPROACH	Financial Accounting Archival - Primary Disclosures 103
ROBINSON, THOMAS RICHARD	PHD 1993 CASE WESTERN RESERVE UNIVERSITY BRICKER, ROBERT	EXTERNAL DEMANDS FOR EARNINGS MANAGEMENT: THE ASSOCIATION BETWEEN EARNINGS VARIABILITY AND BOND RISK PREMIA	Financial Accounting Archival - Primary Earnings Management 266
ROBSON, GARY STEPHEN	PHD 1990 THE UNIVERSITY OF ARIZONA BAREFIELD, RUSSELL M.	CERTIFICATION EXPERIENCE REQUIREMENTS AND THE TIMING OF RESIGNATION IN PUBLIC ACCOUNTING	General Case CPA Firm Issues 159
ROBSON, KEITH	PHD 1988 UNIVERSITY OF MANCHESTER (UNITED KINGDOM)	ACCOUNTING, THE STATE AND THE REGULATORY PROCESS: THE CASE OF STANDARD SETTING, 1969-1975	General Archival - Secondary History 382

Author	Degree & Date School Advisor	Title	Functional Area Research Method Topic pages
ROCKWELL, STEPHEN RAYMOND	PHD 1993 MICHIGAN STATE UNIVERSITY MCCARTHY, WILLIAM E.	THE CONCEPTUAL MODELING AND AUTOMATED USE OF RECONSTRUCTIVE ACCOUNTING DOMAIN KNOWLEDGE	Information Systems Analytical - Internal Decision Support Systems 157
RODGERS, JACCI LOU SPEELMAN	PHD 1988 THE UNIVERSITY OF OKLAHOMA WARD, BART H.	USE OF THE INERTIA EFFECT TO EXPLAIN AND PREDICT AUDITOR MISADJUSTMENTS ARISING FROM THE ANCHORING AND ADJUSTMENT HEURISTIC	Auditing Experimental Judgment & Decision Making - Heuristics & Biases 139
ROGERS, LEON REED	PHD 1989 TEXAS A&M UNIVERSITY PUGH, DAVID	COMPARISON AND EVALUATION OF AN INTEGRATED COMPUTERIZED SPREADSHEET ESTIMATING SYSTEM VERSUS MANUAL ESTIMATING FOR RESIDENTIAL CONSTRUCTION PROJECTS	General Survey Microcomputer Applications 94
ROGERS, VIOLET CORLEY	PHD 1993 UNIVERSITY OF NORTH TEXAS KOCH, BRUCE	AN ANALYSIS OF CONFIDENCE LEVELS AND RETRIEVAL OF PROCEDURES ASSOCIATED WITH ACCOUNTS RECEIVABLE CONFIRMATIONS	Auditing Experimental Judgment & Decision Making - Cognitive Processes 197
ROLLINS, THERESA P.	PHD 1989 TEMPLE UNIVERSITY SAMI, HEIBATOLLAH	AN EMPIRICAL INVESTIGATION OF PENSION PLAN ACTUARIAL ASSUMPTION CHANGES AND FIRM CHARACTERISTICS: A POSITIVE THEORY APPROACH	Financial Accounting Archival - Primary Post Retirement Benefit Issues 210
ROMEO, GEORGE CHARLES	PHD 1991 DREXEL UNIVERSITY NDUBIZU, GORDIAN A.	THE EFFECTS OF SFAS NO. 90 AND 92 ON THE STOCK PRICES AND BETA OF NUCLEAR ELECTRIC UTILITIES	Financial Accounting Archival - primary Industry - Utilities 146
ROMINE, JEFFREY MORRIS	PHD 1992 MEMPHIS STATE UNIVERSITY AUSTIN, KENNETH	THE QUALITY REVIEW DECISION: AN ANALYSIS OF DECISION SEARCH PROCESSES, DECISION OUTCOMES, CONTEXTUAL BACKGROUND, AND EXPERIENCE EFFECTS	Auditing Experimental Audit Quality 219
RONNEN, URI	PHD 1989 STANFORD UNIVERSITY MELUMAD, NAHUM	ESSAYS IN AUDITING	Auditing Analytical - Internal Audit Quality 97
ROOF, BRADLEY MILLER	PHD 1985 UNIVERSITY OF VIRGINIA	A COMPARISON OF HISTORIC COST AND PRICE LEVEL FINANCIAL DISCLOSURES: THE ASSOCIATION OF FINANCIAL DISCLOSURES AND ASSESSMENTS OF FINANCIAL RISK	Financial Accounting Archival - Primary Inflation 350

Listing by Author

Author	Degree & Date School Advisor	Title	Functional Area Research Method Topic pages
ROOHANI, SAEED JAFARI	DBA 1991 MISSISSIPPI STATE UNIVERSITY HERRING, DORA ROSE	AN IMPROVED ACCOUNTING AND AUDITING INFORMATION REPORTING MODEL FOR SAVINGS AND LOAN INSTITUTIONS	Financial Accounting Archival - Primary Industry - Banking/Savings & Loan 158
ROSACKER, ROBERT EUGENE	PHD 1988 THE UNIVERSITY OF NEBRASKA - LINCOLN BALKE, THOMAS E.	A BOX-JENKINS TIME-SERIES INTERRUPTION ANALYSIS CONCERNING UNITED STATES FEDERAL TAX POLICY: AN EMPIRICAL EXAMINATION OF THE INVESTMENT TAX CREDIT	Taxation Archival - Primary Public Policy 148
ROSE-GREEN, ENA PATRICIA	PHD 1994 THE FLORIDA STATE UNIVERSITY SCHAEFER, THOMAS	THE EFFECTS OF MANAGEMENT CHANGE ON THE CAPITAL MARKET'S RESPONSE TO EARNINGS ANNOUNCEMENTS	Financial Accounting Archival - Primary Earnings Announcements 106
ROSMAN, ANDREW JOEL	PHD 1989 THE UNIVERSITY OF NORTH CAROLINA AT CHAPEL HILL PLUMLEE, DAVID	THE EFFECT OF LEARNING ENVIRONMENTS ON THE USE OF ACCOUNTING INFORMATION BY DIFFERENT TYPES OF LENDERS	General Experimental Judgment & Decision Making - Heuristics & Biases 139
ROUBI, RAAFAT RAMADAN	PHD 1985 UNIVERSITY OF NORTH TEXAS	THE ASSOCIATION BETWEEN THE ESTABLISHMENT OF AUDIT COMMITTEES COMPOSED OF OUTSIDE DIRECTORS AND A CHANGE IN THE OBJECTIVITY OF THE MANAGEMENT RESULTS-REPORTING FUNCTION: AN EMPIRICAL INVESTIGATION INTO INCOME SMOOTHING PATTERNS	Auditing Archival - Primary Audit Committees 216
ROUSH, PAMELA BARTON	PHD 1989 GEORGIA STATE UNIVERSITY - COLLEGE OF BUSINESS ADMINISTRATION STABLER, FRANK	AN INVESTIGATION OF THE EFFECTS OF NON-AUDIT SERVICES AND AUDITOR TENURE ON AUDITOR OBJECTIVITY	Auditing Archival - Primary CPA Firm Issues 109
ROVELSTAD, RICHARD GARY	PHD 1986 THE UNIVERSITY OF ALABAMA	DEFERRED TAXES AND TOBIN'S Q: AN EMPIRICAL INVESTIGATION OF SIGNIFICANCE AND ASSOCIATION	Financial Accounting Archival - Primary Taxes 175
ROWE, THOMAS MILTON	PHD 1985 TEXAS A&M UNIVERSITY	AN EMPIRICAL ANALYSIS OF THE QUALITY OF DIOCESAN FINANCIAL DISCLOSURE	Not-for-Profit Case Religious Organizations 241
ROXAS, MARIA LOURDES P.	PHD 1988 UNIVERSITY OF GEORGIA GODFREY, JAMES T.	EFFECT OF THE AMOUNT OF INFORMATION AND THE AMOUNT OF EXPERIENCE AND EDUCATION ON INVESTMENT DECISIONS	Financial Accounting Experimental Forecasting Financial Performance 163

Listing by Author

Author	Degree & Date School Advisor	Title	Functional Area Research Method Topic pages
ROY, DANIEL	PHD 1992 UNIVERSITY OF ILLINOIS AT URBANA-CHAMPAIGN MCKEOWN, J. C.	AN EVALUATION OF UNIVARIATE TIME-SERIES MODELS OF QUARTERLY EARNINGS PER SHARE AND THEIR GENERALIZATION TO MODELS WITH AUTOREGRESSIVE CONDITIONALLY HETEROSCEDASTIC DISTURBANCES	Financial Accounting Archival - Primary Earnings Per Share 112
ROZEN, ETZMUN S.	PHD 1986 NEW YORK UNIVERSITY, GRADUATE SCHOOL OF BUSINESS ADMINISTRATION	AN EMPIRICAL INVESTIGATION OF THE MOTIVATIONS UNDERLYING LIFO-FIRM INVENTORY LIQUIDATIONS	General Archival - Primary Inventory 127
RUBIN, MARC ALLEN	PHD 1985 THE UNIVERSITY OF TEXAS AT AUSTIN	AN EXAMINATION OF THE POLITICAL AND ECONOMIC DETERMINANTS OF MUNICIPAL AUDIT FEES: THEORY AND EVIDENCE	Auditing Governmental 211
RUBLE, AAFFIEN HENDERIKA	PHD 1990 ARIZONA STATE UNIVERSITY RENEAU, J. HAL	ADAPTIVE BEHAVIOR BY HOSPITALS IN RESPONSE TO MEDICARE'S PROSPECTIVE PAYMENT SYSTEM	General Archival - Primary Industry - Health Care 162
RUCHALA, LINDA VIRGINIA	PHD 1991 INDIANA UNIVERSITY HILL, JOHN W.	THE INFLUENCE OF BUDGET REPORTS AND INCENTIVE COMPENSATION ON ESCALATION	Cost/Managerial Experimental Judgment & Decision Making 176
RUDD, TORE FLEMMING	PHD 1988 THE UNIVERSITY OF UTAH STERLING, ROBERT R.	AUDITING AS VERIFICATION OF FINANCIAL INFORMATION	General Analytical - Internal Accounting in Society 289
RUDE, JOHN ARTHUR	PHD 1990 KENT STATE UNIVERSITY	AN EVALUATION OF THE USEFULNESS OF ALTERNATIVE ACCOUNTING TREATMENTS OF DEFERRED TAXES IN PREDICTING FINANCIAL FAILURE	Financial Accounting Archival - Primary Taxes 206
RUF, BERNADETTE MARY	PHD 1990 VIRGINIA POLYTECHNIC INSTITUTE AND STATE UNIVERSITY LEININGER, WAYNE E.	DECISION-MAKING IN A DECISION SUPPORT SYSTEMS ENVIRONMENT: AN EVALUATION OF SPATIAL ABILITY AND TASK STRUCTURE	Information Systems Experimental Decision Support Systems 201
RUHL, JACK MICHAEL	PHD 1991 CASE WESTERN RESERVE UNIVERSITY CAMPBELL, DAVID R.	AN EMPIRICAL STUDY OF THE EFFECTS OF INCONGRUENCE WITHIN A FIRM'S FINANCIAL PLANNING AND CONTROL SYSTEM ON MANAGERS' PROJECT SELECTIONS	Cost/Managerial Experimental Incentive Compensation 214

Listing by Author

Author	Degree & Date School Advisor	Title	Functional Area Research Method Topic pages
RUIZ, JANIS SHIPMAN	PHD 1986 UNIVERSITY OF CALIFORNIA, LOS ANGELES	LOBBYING, ECONOMIC CONSEQUENCES AND 'STATEMENT OF FINANCIAL ACCOUNTING STANDARD NUMBER 19'	Financial Accounting Standard Setting 502
RUJOUB, MOHAMMAD A.	PHD 1989 UNIVERSITY OF ARKANSAS COOK, DORIS M.	AN EMPIRICAL INVESTIGATION OF THE DISCRIMINANT AND PREDICTIVE ABILITY OF THE STATEMENT OF CASH FLOWS	Financial Accounting Archival - Primary Financial Distress or Bankruptcy 167
RUPERT, TIMOTHY J.	PHD 1994 THE PENNSYLVANIA STATE UNIVERSITY ENIS, CHARLES	PERFORMANCE FACILITATION ON TAX RULES: A PRAGMATIC REASONING SCHEMA APPROACH	Taxation Experimental Judgment & Decision Making - Cognitive Processes 323
RUSBARSKY, MARK KEVIN	PHD 1986 THE UNIVERSITY OF ARIZONA	THE CHANGES IN ECONOMIC INCENTIVES WHICH MOTIVATE DISCRETIONARY ACCOUNTING CHANGES: THE CASE OF THE SWITCH TO, AND THEN FROM, ACCELERATED DEPRECIATION	Financial Accounting Archival - Primary Accounting Change 134
RUSSO, JOSEPH A., JR.	PHD 1994 RUTGERS THE STATE UNIVERSITY OF NEW JERSEY - NEWARK VASARHELYI, MIKLOS	AN INVESTIGATION OF AUDITOR PROBLEM-SOLVING BEHAVIOR IN AN UNFAMILIAR TASK SITUATION	Auditing Experimental Judgment & Decision Making - Cognitive Processes 427
RUSTH, DOUGLAS BRUCE	PHD 1991 UNIVERSITY OF HOUSTON	MULTINATIONAL ENTITIES: PERCEIVED ENVIRONMENTAL UNCERTAINTY AND THE BUDGETARY PLANNING AND CONTROL SYSTEM	Cost/Managerial Survey Budgeting 126
RUTLEDGE, ROBERT WILLIAM	PHD 1989 UNIVERSITY OF SOUTH CAROLINA HARRELL, ADRIAN	THE EFFECTS OF FRAMING ACCOUNTING INFORMATION AND GROUP-SHIFT ON ESCALATION OF COMMITMENT	Cost/Managerial Experimental Judgment & Decision Making 114
RYAN, DAVID HARRISON	PHD 1989 UNIVERSITY OF SOUTH CAROLINA ROLFE, ROBERT J.	AN EMPIRICAL EXAMINATION OF THE INTERACTIVE EFFECTS OF FACTORS INFLUENCING TAX PRACTITIONERS' JUDGMENTS	Taxation Experimental Judgment & Decision Making 124
RYAN, STEPHEN G.	PHD 1988 STANFORD UNIVERSITY BEAVER, WILLIAM H.	STRUCTURAL MODELS OF THE ACCOUNTING PROCESS AND EARNINGS	Financial Accounting Archival - Primary Earnings 218

Author	Degree & Date School Advisor	Title	Functional Area Research Method Topic pages
RYU, TAE GHIL	PHD 1993 RUTGERS THE STATE UNIVERSITY OF NEW JERSEY - NEWARK MENSAH, YAW	A CROSS-SECTIONAL ANALYSIS OF THE ADOPTION OF STATEMENT OF FINANCIAL ACCOUNTING STANDARDS (SFAS) NO. 96, 'ACCOUNTING FOR INCOME TAXES'	Financial Accounting Archival - Primary Taxes 91
SAAYDAH, MANSOUR IBRAHIM	PHD 1991 SAINT LOUIS UNIVERSITY KISSINGER, JOHN N.	SFAS NO. 87, PENSION OBLIGATION DEFINITIONS AND THEIR RELATIONSHIP TO SYSTEMATIC RISK	Financial Accounting Archival - Primary Post Retirement Benefit Issues 173
SADLOWSKI, THEODORE STEPHEN	PHD 1993 UNIVERSITY OF ALBERTA (CANADA)	BUDGET ADMINISTRATION IN COLLEGES	Not-for-Profit Case College & University 287
SADOWSKI, SUSAN THERESA	PHD 1994 THE GEORGE WASHINGTON UNIVERSITY VAILL, PETER B.	CHANGES IN MANAGEMENT ACCOUNTING SYSTEMS WITH THE ADOPTION OF A TOTAL QUALITY MANAGEMENT PHILOSOPHY AND ITS OPERATIONALIZATION THROUGH CONTINUOUS PROCESS IMPROVEMENT AT THE LEVEL OF THE FIRM: A CASE STUDY OF THE YORK MANUFACTURING PLANT OF HARLEY-DAVIDSON, INC.	Cost/Managerial Case Management Control Systems 385
SAEMANN, GEORGIA PIERCE	PHD 1987 MICHIGAN STATE UNIVERSITY	A MODEL OF NYSE FIRM MANAGER POSITION AND PARTICIPATION CHOICE ON THE MARCH 1985 FASB EXPOSURE DRAFT: EMPLOYERS' ACCOUNTING FOR PENSIONS	Financial Accounting Survey Standard Setting 254
SAFA MIRHOSSEINY, ALI	EDD 1989 UNIVERSITY OF NORTHERN COLORADO STEWART, JOHN R.	CALIFORNIA ACCOUNTING MANAGERS' PERCEPTIONS OF THE EFFECTIVENESS AND RELEVANCY OF DIFFERENT MICROCOMPUTER TRAINING TECHNIQUES FOR GENERAL LEDGER ACCOUNTING PROGRAMS	Education Survey Continuing Education 70
SAGE, JUDITH ANN	PHD 1987 OKLAHOMA STATE UNIVERSITY	SELECTION OF QUALIFIED RETIREMENT PLAN DISTRIBUTION OPTIONS: A SIMULATION	Taxation Simulation Individual Taxation 301
SAILORS, JAMES FRANKLIN	PHD 1985 UNIVERSITY OF GEORGIA	AN INVESTIGATION OF THE STOCK MARKET REACTION TO A CHANGE IN ACCOUNTING METHODS	Financial Accounting Archival - Primary Accounting Change 152
SALAMONE, DIANE MARSAN	PHD 1991 SAINT LOUIS UNIVERSITY KISSINGER, JOHN N.	A PROBABILISTIC MODEL FOR PREDICTING MANAGEMENT BUYOUTS	Financial Accounting Archival - Primary Other 256

Listing by Author

Author	Degree & Date School Advisor	Title	Functional Area Research Method Topic pages
SALEM, AZIZA ABDEL-RAZIK AHMED	PHD 1986 THE UNIVERSITY OF MISSISSIPPI	A STUDY OF DETERMINANTS OF TRANSFER PRICING IN MULTINATIONAL CORPORATIONS: THE CASE BETWEEN U.S. PARENTS AND THE EGYPTIAN UNITS	Cost/Managerial Survey Transfer Pricing 226
SALLEE, LARRY	DBA 1991 UNITED STATES INTERNATIONAL UNIVERSITY MERRILL, GREGORY B.	AN EMPIRICAL ANALYSIS OF CONTINUING PROFESSIONAL EDUCATION FOR CERTIFIED PUBLIC ACCOUNTANTS EMPLOYED IN NON-PUBLIC OCCUPATIONS	Education Survey Continuing Education 166
SALTER, STEPHEN BRIAN	PHD 1991 UNIVERSITY OF SOUTH CAROLINA DOUPNIK, TIMOTHY	CLASSIFICATION OF FINANCIAL REPORTING SYSTEMS AND A TEST OF THEIR ENVIRONMENTAL DETERMINANTS	Financial Accounting Survey International/Global Issues 140
SALTERIO, STEVEN EARL	PHD 1993 THE UNIVERSITY OF MICHIGAN DANOS, PAUL	THE SEARCH FOR AND USE OF PRECEDENTS IN MAKING FINANCIAL ACCOUNTING DECISIONS	Auditing Other 135
SALY, P. JANE	PHD 1991 THE UNIVERSITY OF BRITISH COLUMBIA (CANADA)	THE EFFECT OF MAJOR STOCK DOWNTURNS ON EXECUTIVE STOCK OPTION CONTRACTS	Cost/Managerial Archival - Primary Incentive Compensation 177
SAMELSON, DONALD	PHD 1992 VIRGINIA POLYTECHNIC INSTITUTE AND STATE UNIVERSITY SEAGO, W. E.	AN EMPIRICAL INVESTIGATION OF ECONOMIC CONSEQUENCES OF THE TAX REFORM ACT OF 1986	Taxation Archival - Primary Public Policy 211
SAMIDI, JUHARI BIN	PHD 1989 UNIVERSITY OF ARKANSAS HAY, LEON E.	AN EMPIRICAL INVESTIGATION OF THE CAPITAL BUDGETING DECISION PROCESS OF GOVERNMENT-CONTROLLED ENTERPRISES AS COMPARED TO INVESTOR-OWNED ENTERPRISES: THE CASE OF MALAYSIA	Cost/Managerial Case Capital Budgeting 264
SAMPSELL, MARTHA EIBERFELD	EDD 1992 PEABODY COLLEGE FOR TEACHERS OF VANDERBILT UNIVERSITY MILLER, JACK W.	SURVEY RESPONSES OF DEPARTMENT CHAIRS OF THE ILLINOIS COLLEGIATE ACCOUNTING PROGRAM TO THE REVISED ILLINOIS PUBLIC ACCOUNTING ACT	Education Survey Curriculum Issues 191
SAMPSON, WESLEY CLAUDE	PHD 1985 UNIVERSITY OF MISSOURI - COLUMBIA	PERCEPTIONS OF AUDITOR INDEPENDENCE AND THE EFFECTS OF NONAUDIT SERVICES	Auditing Experimental Independence 165

Author	Degree & Date School Advisor	Title	Functional Area Research Method Topic pages
SANDER, JAMES FREDERICK	PHD 1987 UNIVERSITY OF ILLINOIS AT URBANA-CHAMPAIGN MCKEOWN, JAMES C.	AN EXAMINATION OF THE RELIABILITY OF VARIOUS INCOME MEASURES FOR ASSESSING THE MAINTENANCE OF OPERATING CAPABILITY	Financial Accounting Simulation Inflation 313
SANDERS, DEBRA LEE	PHD 1986 ARIZONA STATE UNIVERSITY	AN EMPIRICAL INVESTIGATION OF TAX PRACTITIONERS' DECISIONS UNDER UNCERTAINTY: A PROSPECT THEORY APPROACH	Taxation Experimental Judgment & Decision Making - Heuristics & Biases 148
SANDERS, GEORGE D.	PHD 1989 THE UNIVERSITY OF ALABAMA INGRAM, ROBERT W.	AN EMPIRICAL INVESTIGATION OF THE ASSOCIATION OF MUNICIPAL TAX STRUCTURE WITH MUNICIPAL ACCOUNTING CHOICE AND BIAS AND NOISE IN MUNICIPAL ACCOUNTING RATIOS	Not-for-Profit Governmental 114
SANDERS, JOSEPH CASH	PHD 1992 UNIVERSITY OF KENTUCKY FULKS, DANIEL L.; KNOBLETT, JAMES K.	A COMPREHENSIVE STUDY OF STRESS IN THE PUBLIC ACCOUNTING PROFESSION	General Survey Accounting Career Issues 159
SANDERSON, GEORGE NORMAN	PHD 1985 THE UNIVERSITY OF NEBRASKA - LINCOLN	CONTINUING PROFESSIONAL EDUCATION FOR CERTIFIED PUBLIC ACCOUNTANTS: STATE OF THE ART AND PREDICTIONS FOR CHANGE	Education Survey Continuing Education 188
SANDLIN, PETREA KAY	PHD 1987 THE UNIVERSITY OF TEXAS AT AUSTIN	THE EFFECT OF CAUSAL BACKGROUND ON AUDITORS' ANALYTICAL REVIEW JUDGMENTS	Auditing Experimental Analytical Review 202
SANKAR, MANDIRA ROY	PHD 1992 THE UNIVERSITY OF BRITISH COLUMBIA (CANADA) FELTHAM, GERALD A.	CORPORATE VOLUNTARY DISCLOSURES OF PREDECISION INFORMATION	Financial Accounting Archival - Primary Voluntary Management Disclosures 210
SANKARAN, VENKATESWAR	PHD 1989 UNIVERSITY OF GEORGIA WILKERSON, JACK E. JR.	IMPACT OF MANDATED DISCLOSURES ON MARKETMAKER BEHAVIOR: A CASE STUDY OF MANDATED REPLACEMENT COST DISCLOSURES	Financial Accounting Case Disclosures 114
SANSING, RICHARD CHALLES	PHD 1990 THE UNIVERSITY OF TEXAS AT AUSTIN NEWMAN, D. PAUL	STRATEGIC AUDITING AND STRATEGIC INFORMATION TRANSMISSION IN REPUTATION GAMES	General Analytical - Internal CPA Firm Issues 149

Author	Degree & Date School Advisor	Title	Functional Area Research Method Topic pages
SARATH, BHARAT	PHD 1988 STANFORD UNIVERSITY WOLFSON, MARK	AUDITING, LITIGATION, AND INSURANCE	Auditing Analytical - Internal Legal Liability 138
SARATHY, PRIYA	PHD 1993 RUTGERS THE STATE UNIVERSITY OF NEW JERSEY - NEW BRUNSWICK PERRY, MARTIN K.	THE INVESTMENT DECISION OF A CREDITOR UNDER REORGANIZATION: EMPIRICAL AND THEORETICAL ISSUES	Financial Accounting Archival - Primary Financial Distress or Bankruptcy 128
SARIKAS, ROBERT HENRY STEPHEN	PHD 1992 UNIVERSITY OF ILLINOIS AT URBANA-CHAMPAIGN BRIGHTON, GERALD D.	A MARKET TEST OF AN ACCOUNTING BASED MEASURE OF PUBLIC UTILITY COMMISSION REGULATORY CLIMATE	Financial Accounting Archival - Primary Industry - Utilities
SATIN, DIANE CAROL	PHD 1992 UNIVERSITY OF CALIFORNIA, BERKELEY	ACCOUNTING INFORMATION AND THE VALUATION OF LOSS FIRMS	Financial Accounting Archival - Primary Financial Ratios 170
SAUDAGARAN, SHAHROKH MOHAMED	PHD 1986 UNIVERSITY OF WASHINGTON	AN EMPIRICAL STUDY OF SELECTED FACTORS INFLUENCING THE DECISION TO LIST ON FOREIGN STOCK EXCHANGES	General Archival - Primary Capital Markets 201
SAUERLENDER, KARIN MARIE	PHD 1992 THE PENNSYLVANIA STATE UNIVERSITY JABLONSKY, STEPHEN	AMENDING THE FINANCIAL ACCOUNTING STANDARDS BOARD'S CONCEPTUAL FRAMEWORK: AN EMPIRICAL INVESTIGATION OF RESPONDENT COMMENTS	Financial Accounting Case Standard Setting 318
SAVAGE, HELEN MARY	PHD 1989 KENT STATE UNIVERSITY ALAM, PERVAIZ; FETYKO, DAVID F.	REGULATORY ACCOUNTING PRACTICES IN THE SAVINGS AND LOAN INDUSTRY: A STUDY OF THE EFFECTS OF ACCOUNTING CHOICE	General Archival - Primary Industry - Banking/Savings & Loan 169
SAVAGE, KATHRYN S.	PHD 1993 THE PENNSYLVANIA STATE UNIVERSITY JABLONSKY, STEPHEN F.	THE VALUE-AND-BELIEF STRUCTURES OF TOP FINANCIAL EXECUTIVES	General Survey CPA Firm Issues 313
SAWYERS, ROBY BLAKE	PHD 1990 ARIZONA STATE UNIVERSITY	THE IMPACT OF UNCERTAINTY AND AMBIGUITY ON INCOME TAX DECISION-MAKING	Taxation Experimental Tax Compliance 107

Author	Degree & Date School Advisor	Title	Functional Area Research Method Topic pages
SAYERS, DAVID L.	PHD 1985 THE UNIVERSITY OF NEBRASKA - LINCOLN	THE IMPACT OF SEGMENT REPORTING ON ANALYSTS' EARNINGS FORECASTS: THE CASE OF FASB STATEMENT NO. 14	Financial Accounting Archival - Primary Segment Reporting 83
SCARBROUGH, D. PAUL	PHD 1987 VIRGINIA POLYTECHNIC INSTITUTE AND STATE UNIVERSITY	THE EFFECTS OF ALTERNATIVE GROUPING METHODS ON EMPLOYEE TURNOVER RESEARCH IN CPA FIRMS	General Survey Job Performance, Satisfaction &/or Turnover 161
SCHADEWALD, MICHAEL STEVEN	PHD 1988 UNIVERSITY OF MINNESOTA JOYCE, ED	REFERENCE OUTCOME EFFECTS IN TAXPAYER DECISION-MAKING	Taxation Experimental Judgment & Decision Making- Heuristics & Biases 182
SCHAEFER, JAMES CLARK	DBA 1990 SOUTHERN ILLINOIS UNIVERSITY AT CARBONDALE WELKER, ROBERT B.	A STUDY OF THE PROPENSITY OF CERTIFIED PUBLIC ACCOUNTANTS TO ACT UNPROFESSIONALLY	General Survey Ethics 108
SCHAFERMEYER, KENNETH WILLIAM	PHD 1990 PURDUE UNIVERSITY SCHONDELMEYER, STEPHEN W.	AN ANALYSIS OF CHAIN PHARMACIES' COSTS OF DISPENSING A THIRD PARTY PRESCRIPTION	General Survey Industry - Health Care 268
SCHALOW, CHRISTINE MARIE	PHD 1992 UNIVERSITY OF ARKANSAS HAY, LEON E.	LOBBYING ACTIVITY IN THE STANDARDS SETTING PROCESS: FASB STATEMENT ON FINANCIAL ACCOUNTING STANDARDS NO. 106, 'EMPLOYERS' ACCOUNTING FOR POSTRETIREMENT BENEFITS OTHER THAN PENSIONS'	Financial Accounting Archival - Primary Standard Setting 133
SCHATZBERG, JEFFREY WAYNE	PHD 1987 THE UNIVERSITY OF IOWA	A THEORETICAL AND EMPIRICAL EXAMINATION OF INDEPENDENCE AND 'LOW BALLING'	Auditing Experimental Independence 191
SCHATZEL, JOHN A.	DBA 1988 BOSTON UNIVERSITY	AN EXPERIMENTAL STUDY OF FACTORS AFFECTING AUDITORS' RELIANCE ON ANALYTICAL PROCEDURES	Auditing Experimental Analytical Review 206
SCHEIDT, MARSHA ANN	DBA 1991 MISSISSIPPI STATE UNIVERSITY HERRING, DORA R.	AN EMPIRICAL ANALYSIS OF PARENT COMPANY BOND YIELD PREMIA SUBSEQUENT TO CONSOLIDATION OF NONHOMOGENEOUS FINANCIAL-ACTIVITIES SUBSIDIARIES	Financial Accounting Archival - Primary Merger, Acquisition, Reorganization 210

Author	Degree & Date School Advisor	Title	Functional Area Research Method Topic pages
SCHIFF, ANDREW DAVID	PHD 1993 RUTGERS THE STATE UNIVERSITY OF NEW JERSEY - NEWARK HOFFMAN, L. RICHARD	AN EXPLORATION OF THE USE OF FINANCIAL AND NONFINANCIAL MEASURES OF OPERATING PERFORMANCE BY EXECUTIVES IN A SERVICE ORGANIZATION	Cost/Managerial Experimental Performance Evaluation/Measurement 276
SCHILLER, STEFAN	EKONDR 1987 GOTEBORGS UNIVERSITET (SWEDEN)	MANAGEMENT ACCOUNTING SYSTEMS--USE AND DESIGN	Cost/Managerial Survey Management Control Systems 350
SCHISLER, DANIEL LAWRENCE	PHD 1992 MEMPHIS STATE UNIVERSITY MALLOY, JOHN M.	AN EXPERIMENTAL EXAMINATION OF TAXPAYERS' AND TAX PROFESSIONALS' AGGRESSIVE TAX PREFERENCES: A PROSPECT THEORY FOUNDATION	Taxation Experimental Tax Compliance 160
SCHLACHTER, PAUL JUSTIN	PHD 1986 THE UNIVERSITY OF NORTH CAROLINA AT CHAPEL HILL	A TWO-STAGE ANALYSIS OF INTERDIVISIONAL TRANSFER PRICING NEGOTIATIONS	Cost/Managerial Experimental Transfer Pricing 146
SCHLEIFER, LYDIA LANCASTER FOLGER	PHD 1988 UNIVERSITY OF GEORGIA SHOCKLEY, RANDOLPH A.	AN INVESTIGATION OF PERCEPTIONS AND ATTRIBUTES OF THE CONCEPT OF INDEPENDENCE	Auditing Survey Independence 313
SCHLICHTING, DAVID KENNETH	PHD 1988 THE UNIVERSITY OF WISCONSIN - MADISON STEVENSON, WILLIS C.	AN EMPIRICAL ANALYSIS OF THE IMPACT OF THE DEFICIT REDUCTION ACT OF 1984 ON CORPORATE DIVIDEND CAPTURE ACTIVITY	Taxation Archival - Primary Dividends 276
SCHLICTMAN, MARIBETH COLLER	PHD 1991 INDIANA UNIVERSITY SALAMON, GERALD L.	EXTERNAL REPORTING SYSTEMS AND ASSET PRICES: AN EXPERIMENTAL STUDY	Financial Accounting Experimental Earnings Response Coefficients 146
SCHLOEMER, PAUL G.	PHD 1991 VIRGINIA POLYTECHNIC INSTITUTE AND STATE UNIVERSITY	INTERNAL REVENUE CODE SECTION 263A: AN ASSESSMENT OF ITS IMPACT AND PROPOSALS FOR SIMPLIFICATION	Taxation Archival - Primary Public Policy 93
SCHMELZLE, GEORGE DANIEL	PHD 1992 THE UNIVERSITY OF MISSISSIPPI CASSIDY, JUDITH; FLESHER, DALE	A STUDY OF THE EFFECTS OF DOGMATISM AND THE EVENTS APPROACH TO ACCOUNTING ON DECISION-MAKING IN THE NEW MANUFACTURING ENVIRONMENT	Information Systems Experimental Systems Design &/or Development 184

Author	Degree & Date School Advisor	Title	Functional Area Research Method Topic pages
SCHMIDT, DENNIS R.	PHD 1985 THE UNIVERSITY OF NEBRASKA - LINCOLN	STATE TAXATION OF MULTIJURISDICTIONAL CORPORATE INCOME: AN EMPIRICAL ANALYSIS OF FORMULARY APPORTIONMENT	Taxation Archival - Primary State Taxation 219
SCHMIDT, TOM WILLIAMS	PHD 1993 UNIVERSITY OF MISSOURI COLUMBIA PARKER, JAMES E.	IMPACT OF CRITICAL THINKING ABILITY ON TAX PRACTITIONER JUDGMENT	Taxation Experimental Judgment & Decision Making - Cognitive Processes 143
SCHNEIDER, DOUGLAS KENNETH	PHD 1989 UNIVERSITY OF GEORGIA WINDAL, FLOYD W.	RESPONDENT PERCEPTION OF THE CREDIBILITY OF GAAP	Financial Accounting Survey Standard Setting 180
SCHNEIDER, GARY PAUL	PHD 1993 THE UNIVERSITY OF TENNESSEE BORTHICK, A. FAYE; SCHEINER, JAMES H.	ESCALATION BEHAVIOR IN INFORMATION SYSTEMS DEVELOPMENT: ALTERNATIVE MOTIVATIONS, EXPERIENCE, AND THE SUNK COST EFFECT	Cost/Managerial Experimental Judgment & Decision Making 123
SCHNEIDER, WM. BRUCE	PHD 1988 CLAREMONT GRADUATE SCHOOL MACIARIELLO, JOSEPH A.	CERTIFIED PUBLIC ACCOUNTANTS: A PROFESSION IN CRISIS	General Survey CPA Firm Issues 301
SCHODERBEK, MICHAEL PAUL	PHD 1992 INDIANA UNIVERSITY SALAMON, GERALD L.	THE EFFECT OF MARKET STRUCTURE ON THE BEHAVIOR OF INTRA-INDUSTRY INFORMATION TRANSFERS: EMPIRICAL TESTS USING FIRMS' QUARTERLY EARNINGS ANNOUNCEMENTS	Financial Accounting Archival - Primary Information Transfer 150
SCHRADER, RICHARD WILLIAM	PHD 1993 THE FLORIDA STATE UNIVERSITY HILLISON, WILLIAM A.	AN EMPIRICAL INVESTIGATION OF THE USEFULNESS OF SERVICE EFFORTS AND ACCOMPLISHMENTS MEASURES	General Experimental Job Performance, Satisfaction &/or Turnover 177
SCHRAMM, ELFRIEDE	DR 1991 JOHANNES KEPLER UNIVERSITAET LINZ (AUSTRIA)	EFFECTS OF THE ACCOUNTING REFORM ON VALUATION OF BALANCE SHEET UNDER SPECIAL CONSIDERATION OF HIDDEN RESERVES [AUSWIRKUNGEN DER RECHNUNGSLEGUNGSREFORM AUF DIE BILANZBEWERTUNG UNTER BESONDERER BERUECKSICHTIGUNG DER STILLEN RESERVEN]	Financial Accounting Analytical - Internal International/Global Issues
SCHROEDER, ANGELIKA THERESA HELKE	PHD 1988 UNIVERSITY OF COLORADO AT BOULDER SCHATTKE, RUDOLPH W.	CASH FLOW PREDICTIONS USING ALTERNATIVE INCOME MEASURES	Financial Accounting Archival - Primary Cash Flows 322

Author	Degree & Date School Advisor	Title	Functional Area Research Method Topic pages
SCHULTZ, SALLY M.	PHD 1986 THE PENNSYLVANIA STATE UNIVERSITY	AUDIT OPINION DECISIONS AND LITIGATION LOSS CONTINGENCIES	Auditing Archival - Primary Audit Opinion 123
SCHWARZ, FREDERICK H.	PHD 1986 SAINT LOUIS UNIVERSITY	AN ALTERNATIVE METHOD OF EVALUATING THE FINANCIAL PERFORMANCE OF FOREIGN SUBSIDIARIES	Financial Accounting Case Segment Reporting 155
SCHWINGHAMMER, PAUL HENRY	PHD 1986 UNIVERSITY OF ARKANSAS	AN EMPIRICAL INVESTIGATION OF METHODS OF COMPUTING THE CURRENT PORTION OF CAPITALIZED LEASE OBLIGATIONS AND THE EFFECTS ON SELECTED FINANCIAL MEASURES	Financial Accounting Archival - Primary Leases 220
SCOFIELD, BARBARA WILD	PHD 1989 THE UNIVERSITY OF TEXAS AT AUSTIN MAY, ROBERT G.	THE EFFECT OF THE INDUSTRY DISCLOSURE POLICY ON INTRA-INDUSTRY INFORMATION TRANSFER ASSOCIATED WITH QUARTERLY EARNINGS ANNOUNCEMENTS	Financial Accounting Archival - Primary Information Transfer 182
SCOTT, BERT G., JR.	DBA 1985 MISSISSIPPI STATE UNIVERSITY	AN INQUIRY INTO MITIGATING THE EFFECTS OF THE ANCHORING AND ADJUSTMENT HEURISTIC IN THE JUDGMENTAL EVALUATION OF UNDERRELIANCE RISK	Auditing Experimental Judgment & Decision Making - Heuristics & Biases 156
SCRIBNER, EDMUND ARTHUR	PHD 1985 OKLAHOMA STATE UNIVERSITY	TOWARD AN ECONOMIC MODEL OF TAXPAYER-IRS INTERACTION	Taxation Analytical - Internal Estate & Gift Taxation 107
SEAL, W. B.	PHD 1991 COUNCIL FOR NATIONAL ACADEMIC AWARDS (UNITED KINGDOM)	ACCOUNTING AND MANAGEMENT CONTROL IN THE THEORY OF THE FIRM	Cost/Managerial Analytical - Internal Management Control Systems 302
SEAMANS, DANA GERALD	DBA 1985 TEXAS TECH UNIVERSITY	AN ANALYSIS OF THE FEDERAL TAX RAMIFICATIONS OF GOODWILL	Taxation Archival - Secondary Corporate Taxation
SEATON, LLOYD, III	PHD 1991 THE UNIVERSITY OF NEBRASKA - LINCOLN RAYMOND, ROBERT H.	ECONOMIC CONSEQUENCES OF ACCOUNTING REGULATION: AN EMPIRICAL ANALYSIS OF CHANGES IN EMPLOYERS' ACCOUNTING FOR PENSIONS	Financial Accounting Archival - Primary Post Retirement Benefit Issues 105

Author	Degree & Date School Advisor	Title	Functional Area Research Method Topic pages
SEAY, ROBERT ALAN	DBA 1986 MISSISSIPPI STATE UNIVERSITY	AN EMPIRICAL INVESTIGATION INTO HOSPITAL UTILIZATION AND SUPPORT OF THE INTERNAL AUDIT FUNCTION	Auditing Survey Industry - Health Care 121
SEAY, SHARON SMITH	PHD 1993 UNIVERSITY OF GEORGIA EDWARDS, JAMES DON	AN EMPIRICAL ANALYSIS OF THE RATIO ADJUSTMENT PROCESS: THE CONTRIBUTION OF FIRM-SPECIFIC FACTORS	Financial Accounting Archival - Primary Capital Structure 108
SEDAGHAT, ALI M.	DBA 1987 THE GEORGE WASHINGTON UNIVERSITY	THE INTERACTIVE PROCESS OF ACCOUNTING: AN ANALYSIS OF THE DEVELOPMENT OF FINANCIAL ACCOUNTING AND REPORTING STANDARDS FOR OIL AND GAS PRODUCING ACTIVITIES	Financial Accounting Archival - Secondary Standard Setting 328
SEETHARAMAN, ANANTH	PHD 1991 GEORGIA STATE UNIVERSITY - COLLEGE OF BUSINESS ADMINISTRATION ENGLEBRECHT, TED D.	AN EMPIRICAL VALIDATION OF SOME EXTANT MEASURES OF VERTICAL AND HORIZONTAL EQUITY	Taxation Archival - Primary Public Policy 194
SEIPEL, CINDY L.	PHD 1990 OKLAHOMA STATE UNIVERSITY KIMBRELL, JANET	'SUBJECT TO' QUALIFIED OPINIONS AND THE SIGNALLING OF RISK SHIFTS	Auditing Archival - Primary Audit Opinion 132
SELLANI, ROBERT JOSEPH	DBA 1993 NOVA UNIVERSITY	ORGANIZATIONAL LAG AND ITS EFFECTS ON FINANCIAL PERFORMANCE IN THE ELECTRONICS INDUSTRY	Cost/Managerial Archival - Primary Performance Evaluation/Measurement 154
SELVY, PATRICIA MILLER	PHD 1991 GEORGIA STATE UNIVERSITY - COLLEGE OF BUSINESS ADMINISTRATION STABLER, H. F.	AN EMPIRICAL MODEL BUILDING ANALYSIS OF THE FIRM AND/OR REPORT VARIABLES ASSOCIATED WITH THE RATINGS RECEIVED ON STATE BOARD OF ACCOUNTANCY REVIEWED REPORTS ISSUED BY CPA FIRMS	General Archival - Primary CPA Firm Issues 138
SEN, KAUSTAV	PHD 1994 RUTGERS THE STATE UNIVERSITY OF NEW JERSEY - NEWARK SRINIDHI, B. N.	MECHANISM DESIGN IN AUDIT SETTINGS	Auditing Analytical - Internal Auditor Behavior 89
SEN, PRADYOT K.	PHD 1985 COLUMBIA UNIVERSITY	INCENTIVE SIGNALLING WITH IMPERFECT INFORMATION: ACCOUNTING DISCLOSURES AND CONTINGENT CONTRACTS	General Analytical - Internal Agency Theory 155

Listing by Author

Author	Degree & Date School Advisor	Title	Functional Area Research Method Topic pages
SENGE, STEPHEN V.	DBA 1985 KENT STATE UNIVERSITY	AN ANALYSIS OF THE MBA INTRODUCTORY FINANCIAL ACCOUNTING CURRICULUM	Education Survey Curriculum Issues 262
SENKOW, DAVID WILLIAM	PHD 1992 UNIVERSITY OF MINNESOTA DICKHAUT, JOHN W.	PRICING MECHANISMS FOR RESOURCE ALLOCATION IN DECENTRALIZED ORGANIZATIONS: EXPERIMENTAL EVIDENCE	Cost/Managerial Experimental Pricing 129
SENTENEY, DAVID L.	PHD 1987 UNIVERSITY OF ILLINOIS AT URBANA-CHAMPAIGN	AN INVESTIGATION INTO THE USEFULNESS OF PUBLICLY DISCLOSED ACCOUNTING EARNINGS DATA IN VALUING THE FOREIGN OPERATIONS OF U.S.-BASED MULTINATIONAL ENTERPRISES	Financial Accounting Archival - Primary International/Global Issues 158
SEOW, GIM-SEONG	PHD 1985 UNIVERSITY OF OREGON	THE VALUATION OF CORPORATE PENSION OBLIGATIONS: A CONTINGENT CLAIMS MODEL AND SOME EMPIRICAL TESTS	Financial Accounting Archival - Primary Post Retirement Benefit Issues 121
SERRETT, RANDALL KEITH	PHD 1986 UNIVERSITY OF HOUSTON	AN ANALYTICAL INVESTIGATION OF THE COOPERATIVE TAX ENTITY: PLANNING AND POLICY IMPLICATIONS	Taxation Analytical - Internal Corporate Taxation 242
SESHIE, GODWIN O.	PHD 1988 GEORGIA STATE UNIVERSITY - COLLEGE OF BUSINESS ADMINISTRATION HERMANSON, ROGER H.	THE ROLE OF PROSPECTIVE FINANCIAL INFORMATION ATTESTATION IN BANK LENDING DECISIONS	Auditing Experimental Bank Loan Officers 262
SHACKELFORD, DOUGLAS ALAN	PHD 1990 THE UNIVERSITY OF MICHIGAN BERNARD, VICTOR L.	THE MARKET FOR TAX BENEFITS: EVIDENCE FROM LEVERAGED ESOPS	Taxation Archival - Primary Public Policy 70
SHADBOLT, MICHAEL EARL	PHD 1990 THE UNIVERSITY OF NEBRASKA - LINCOLN HUBBARD, THOMAS D.	CALCULATING EARNINGS PER SHARE: AN EMPIRICAL ANALYSIS ESTIMATING THE DILUTIVE IMPACT OF CONVERTIBLE SECURITIES ON A CURRENT BASIS	Financial Accounting Archival - Primary Earnings Per Share 149
SHAFFER, RAYMOND JAMES	DBA 1990 UNIVERSITY OF KENTUCKY DANIKER, RELMOND P. VAN	FINANCIAL REPORTING OF DEFERRED MAINTENANCE FOR CAPITAL ASSETS IN GOVERNMENTAL ENTITIES: A SURVEY OF SELECTED USERS	Not-for-Profit Survey Governmental 300

Author	Degree & Date School Advisor	Title	Functional Area Research Method Topic pages
SHAHID, MD ABDUS	PHD 1992 TEMPLE UNIVERSITY SAMI, HEIBATOLLAH	DETERMINANTS OF EQUITY-FOR-DEBT SWAP: A POSITIVE THEORY APPROACH	Financial Accounting Archival - Primary Capital Structure 285
SHANHOLTZER, DENNIS DEAN	DBA 1989 MISSISSIPPI STATE UNIVERSITY	AN EXAMINATION OF THE RELATIONSHIP BETWEEN HISTORICAL COST AND CURRENT COST ACCOUNTING DATA AND REPORTED CASH PROVIDED BY OPERATIONS IN THE SUBSEQUENT PERIOD	Financial Accounting Archival-Primary Inflation 155
SHANKAR, S. GOWRI	PHD 1991 SYRACUSE UNIVERSITY KOVEOS, PETER	A REEXAMINATION OF THE CALLS OF CONVERTIBLE BONDS AND THEIR IMPACT ON SHAREHOLDER WEALTH	Financial Accounting Archival - Primary Long Term Debt 113
SHAPIRO, BRIAN PHILIP	PHD 1990 UNIVERSITY OF MINNESOTA	AUDITOR'S CAUSAL REASONING IN PRELIMINARY ANALYTICAL REVIEW: AN EMPIRICAL INVESTIGATION	Auditing Experimental Judgment & Decision Making - Cognitive Processes 262
SHARMA, SURESH RAJ	DBA 1993 SOUTHERN ILLINOIS UNIVERSITY AT CARBONDALE WELKER, ROBERT B.	THE EFFECTS OF THE SOCIAL ATTRACTIVENESS OF A GOAL SETTER ON GOAL ACCEPTANCE	General Experimental Judgment & Decision Making 218
SHARP, ANDREW DANIEL	PHD 1990 THE UNIVERSITY OF MISSISSIPPI TAYLOR, CHARLES W.	AN EMPIRICAL INVESTIGATION INTO THE EXTENT OF THE IMPACT OF FREE TRAVEL AWARDS ON REVENUE DISPLACEMENT IN THE AIRLINE INDUSTRY	General Archival - Primary Industry - Airline 107
SHASTRI, KAREN ANDREA	PHD 1990 UNIVERSITY OF PITTSBURGH BIRNBERG, JACOB G.	SELF TENDER OFFERS AS A TAKEOVER DEFENSE: AN ANALYSIS OF FIRM VALUE CHANGES, MANAGERIAL COMPENSATION AND OWNERSHIP CONTROL	General Archival - Primary Other 120
SHASTRI, TRIMBAK	PHD 1992 THE UNIVERSITY OF OKLAHOMA WARD, BART	A CONCEPTUAL FRAMEWORK FOR AUDIT COMMUNICATION RESEARCH AND SOME EMPIRICAL EVIDENCE	Auditing Experimental Audit Opinion 260
SHAUB, MICHAEL KENNETH	PHD 1989 TEXAS TECH UNIVERSITY FINN, DON W.	AN EMPIRICAL EXAMINATION OF THE DETERMINANTS OF AUDITORS' ETHICAL SENSITIVITY	General Survey Ethics 240

Listing by Author

189

Author	Degree & Date School Advisor	Title	Functional Area Research Method Topic pages
SHAVER, JAMES HOWARD	DBA 1985 LOUISIANA TECH UNIVERSITY	CERTIFICATION OF ACCOUNTING SPECIALISTS: VIEWPOINT OF THE SMALL FIRM PRACTITIONER	General Survey CPA Firm Issues 192
SHAW, WAYNE H.	PHD 1985 THE UNIVERSITY OF TEXAS AT AUSTIN	EMPIRICAL EVIDENCE ON THE MARKET IMPACT OF THE SAFE HARBOR LEASING LAW	Taxation Archival - Primary Leases 141
SHEHATA, MOHAMED MARGHANY	PHD 1988 UNIVERSITY OF FLORIDA ABDEL-KHALIK, A. RASHAD	THE IMPACT OF SFAS NO. 2 AND THE ECONOMIC RECOVERY TAX ACT OF 1981 ON FIRMS' R AND D SPENDING BEHAVIOR	Financial Accounting Archival - Primary Research & Development 116
SHEIKHOLESLAMI, MEHDI	PHD 1986 THE UNIVERSITY OF TEXAS AT DALLAS	THE IMPACT OF FOREIGN CURRENCY TRANSLATION METHOD CHANGE ON THE ACCURACY OF THE FINANCIAL ANALYSTS' EARNINGS FORECASTS	Financial Accounting Archival - Primary Foreign Currency Translation 99
SHELLEY, MARJORIE KAY	PHD 1989 THE UNIVERSITY OF TEXAS AT AUSTIN TOMASSINI, LAWRENCE A.; ANDERSON, URTON L.	AN EMPIRICAL INVESTIGATION OF DIFFERENTIAL SUBJECTIVE DISCOUNTING ACROSS THE POTENTIAL GAINS AND LOSSES FROM INVESTMENT OPTIONS	General Experimental Investments 179
SHELTON, JAMES BLAIR	PHD 1993 VIRGINIA COMMONWEALTH UNIVERSITY SCHWARTZ, BILL N.	MANAGEMENT'S CHOICE OF ADOPTION DATE OF STATEMENT OF FINANCIAL ACCOUNTING STANDARDS NO. 95: A POSITIVE THEORY APPROACH	Financial Accounting Archival - Primary Accounting Choice 126
SHELTON, MARGARET LOUISE	PHD 1986 UNIVERSITY OF HOUSTON	PREDICTION OF CORPORATE FAILURE WITH AN EXPANDED VARIABLE SET, USING MULTIPLE DISCRIMINANT ANALYSIS	Financial Accounting Archival - Primary Financial Distress or Bankruptcy 155
SHENG, WILLIAM W.	PHD 1994 PURDUE UNIVERSITY RO, BYUNG T.	ESSAYS ON BEHAVIORAL AUDITING: A GAME-THEORETIC APPROACH	Auditing Analytical - Internal CPA Firm Issues 87
SHERIF, HANAA ABDEL-GALIEL	PHD 1987 CITY UNIVERSITY OF NEW YORK	THE IMPACT OF LONG-TERM PERFORMANCE PLANS ON ACCOUNTING CHOICES	Cost/Managerial Archival - Primary Incentive Compensation 428

Author	Degree & Date School Advisor	Title	Functional Area Research Method Topic pages
SHEVLIN, TERRENCE J.	PHD 1986 STANFORD UNIVERSITY	RESEARCH AND DEVELOPMENT LIMITED PARTNERSHIPS: AN EMPIRICAL ANALYSIS OF TAXES AND INCENTIVES	Taxation Archival - Primary Partnership Taxation 242
SHIARAPPA, BARBARA JANUS	PHD 1988 TEMPLE UNIVERSITY LIPKA, ROLAND	THE ASSOCIATION BETWEEN MARKET RISK AND ACCOUNTING RISK ALTERNATIVELY MEASURED	Financial Accounting Archival - Primary Inflation 146
SHIBANO, TOSHIYUKI	PHD 1989 STANFORD UNIVERSITY	AN EQUILIBRIUM MODEL OF ATTESTATION BY PUBLIC ACCOUNTANTS	Auditing Analytical - Internal Legal Liability 161
SHIELDS, JEFFREY FRANKLIN	PHD 1991 UNIVERSITY OF PITTSBURGH	THE INFLUENCE OF INTERNAL AUDITING AND TRUST ON BUDGETARY SLACK	Cost/Managerial Experimental Budgeting 153
SHIH, MICHAEL SHENG-HUA	PHD 1989 UNIVERSITY OF MINNESOTA VIGELAND, ROBERT	FINANCIAL SYNERGY AND MERGER MOVEMENTS: PERSONAL AND CORPORATE INCOME TAXES AS AN EXPLANATION	Taxation Archival - Primary Merger, Acquisition, Reorganization 140
SHIM, EUN SUP	PHD 1993 RUTGERS THE STATE UNIVERSITY OF NEW JERSEY - NEWARK SUDIT, EPHRAIM F.	COST MANAGEMENT AND ACTIVITY-BASED COST ALLOCATION IN A NEW MANUFACTURING ENVIRONMENT	Cost/Managerial Survey Activity Based Costing 149
SHIM, KYU YOUNG	PHD 1990 KENT STATE UNIVERSITY FETYKO, DAVID F.; MCMATH, H. KENT	EMPIRICAL INVESTIGATION OF SHAREHOLDER REACTION TO THE INTRODUCTION OF MANAGEMENT INCENTIVE COMPENSATION PLANS	Cost/Managerial Archival - Primary Incentive Compensation 162
SHIN, DONG-IK	PHD 1992 THE UNIVERSITY OF NEBRASKA - LINCOLN LEE, SANG M.	DEVELOPMENT OF A COGNITIVE DIAGNOSIS SYSTEM FOR INTELLIGENT TUTORING: AN APPLICATION TO TRANSPORTATION PROBLEM-SOLVING	Information Systems Analytical - Internal Decision Support Systems 191
SHIN, DOUG YONG	PHD 1989 THE UNIVERSITY OF IOWA DEJONG, DOUGLAS V.	WHY MANAGERS VOLUNTARILY RELEASE EARNINGS FORECASTS?: THE ROLE OF THE MANAGERIAL LABOR MARKET	Financial Accounting Analytical - Internal Voluntary Management Disclosures 103

Author	Degree & Date School Advisor	Title	Functional Area Research Method Topic pages
SHIN, HONG CHUL	PHD 1985 THE UNIVERSITY OF TEXAS AT AUSTIN	OPTIMAL HIRING DECISIONS FOR ENTRY-LEVEL AUDITORS IN PUBLIC ACCOUNTING FIRMS	General CPA Firm Issues 186
SHIN, HUNG SIK	PHD 1991 THE PENNSYLVANIA STATE UNIVERSITY MILES, JAMES A.	TERMINATION OF OVERFUNDED PENSION PLANS AND SHAREHOLDER WEALTH	Financial Accounting Archival - Primary Post Retirement Benefit Issues 124
SHIUE, FU-JIING NORMAN	PHD 1990 THE GEORGE WASHINGTON UNIVERSITY	A POSITIVE THEORY OF ACCOUNTING STANDARDS DETERMINATION: THE CASE OF TAIWAN	Financial Accounting Archival - Primary International/Global Issues 158
SHOEMAKER, PAUL A.	PHD 1989 THE PENNSYLVANIA STATE UNIVERSITY MALCOM, ROBERT E.	THE SIGNIFICANCE OF THE INVESTMENT TAX CREDIT IN INVESTMENT DECISIONS: AN EMPIRICAL AND INTERNATIONAL ANALYSIS	Taxation Archival - Primary Investments 210
SHOENTHAL, EDWARD ROBERT	PHD 1985 NEW YORK UNIVERSITY	AN INVESTIGATION OF THE HARMONY OF COMPETENCIES FOUND IN CERTIFIED AND CHARTERED ACCOUNTANTS IN THE UNITED STATES AND GREAT BRITAIN	General Survey Accounting Career Issues 227
SHORES, DONNA J.	PHD 1986 STANFORD UNIVERSITY	DIFFERENTIAL INFORMATION AND SECURITY RETURNS SURROUNDING EARNINGS ANNOUNCEMENTS ON THE OVER-THE-COUNTER MARKET	Financial Accounting Archival - Primary Earnings Announcements 238
SHORNEY, MAYDA	PHD 1988 TEXAS A&M UNIVERSITY KRATCHMAN, STANLEY H.	AN EMPIRICAL INVESTIGATION OF THE EFFECT OF OWNERSHIP CONTROL ON THE CHOICE OF ACCOUNTING METHODS	Financial Accounting Archival - Primary Accounting Choice 109
SHREIM, OBEID SAAD	PHD 1989 UNIVERSITY OF WALES COLLEGE OF CARDIFF (UNITED KINGDOM)	VALUE FOR MONEY AUDITING: ITS DEVELOPMENT AND APPLICATION WITH SPECIAL REFERENCE TO THE U.K. PUBLIC SECTOR	General Survey International/Global Issues 357
SHROFF, PERVIN KEKI	PHD 1992 COLUMBIA UNIVERSITY OHLSON, JAMES A.	ESSAYS ON THE ASSOCIATION OF ACCOUNTING EARNINGS WITH SECURITY RETURNS	Financial Accounting Archival - Primary Earnings 138

Author	Degree & Date School Advisor	Title	Functional Area Research Method Topic pages
SIEGEL, PHILIP HARRIS	DBA 1985 MEMPHIS STATE UNIVERSITY	ALTERNATIVE EDUCATIONAL PROGRAMS FOR ENTRY INTO THE PUBLIC ACCOUNTING PROFESSION: AN ANALYSIS	General Survey Accounting Career Issues 173
SILVESTER, KATHERINE JOSEPHINE	PHD 1992 UNIVERSITY OF MARYLAND COLLEGE PARK GORDON, LAWRENCE A.	FIRM PERFORMANCE, ACCOUNTING SYSTEM CHOICE, AND NEWMANUFACTURING TECHNOLOGIES	Cost/Managerial Archival - Primary Activity Based Costing 362
SIMGA, CAN	PHD 1987 UNIVERSITY OF ILLINOIS AT URBANA-CHAMPAIGN SCHOENFELD, HANNS-MARTIN H.	NONFINANCIAL INDICATORS IN PERFORMANCE EVALUATION OF MNE'S; EXPLORING THE USE OF FUZZY OUTRANKING RELATIONS	Cost/Managerial Archival - Primary Performance Evaluation/Measurement 245
SIMNETT, ROGER	PHD 1992 UNIVERSITY OF NEW SOUTH WALES (AUSTRALIA)	INFORMATION SELECTION AND INFORMATION PROCESSING BY AUDITORS: EFFECT OF VARYING TASK COMPLEXITY	Auditing Experimental Judgment & Decision Making
SIMONS, KATHLEEN ANN	DBA 1991 BOSTON UNIVERSITY MEYER, PHILIP	AN INQUIRY INTO THE USEFULNESS OF A MEASURE OF CASH FLOW IN MODELING DIVIDEND CHANGES	Financial Accounting Archival - Primary Cash Flows 210
SINGER, RONALD MARTIN	PHD 1989 THE UNIVERSITY OF WISCONSIN - MADISON EICHENSEHER, JOHN W.	EXECUTIVE COMPENSATION AND RESEARCH AND DEVELOPMENT	Cost/Managerial Archival - Primary Incentive Compensation 148
SINGHAL, RAJ BAHADUR	PHD 1991 UNIVERSITY OF SOUTH CAROLINA	EFFECT OF FEEDBACK AND GOAL PRESENCE ON INFORMATION USAGE AND DECISION ACCURACY IN A HIGH INFORMATION LOAD ENVIRONMENT	General Experimental Judgment & Decision Making 112
SINGLETON, LARRY G.	PHD 1985 THE LOUISIANA STATE UNIVERSITY AND AGRICULTURAL AND MECHANICAL COL.	A FIELD TEST OF THE PERCEPTIONS OF THE QUALITATIVE CHARACTERISTICS OF STATEMENT OF FINANCIAL ACCOUNTING CONCEPTS NO. 2 BY PRACTICING CPAS	Financial Accounting Survey Accounting Choice 155
SINHA, PRAVEEN	PHD 1992 CARNEGIE-MELLON UNIVERSITY	VALUATION RELEVANCE OF CASH FLOWS AND ACCRUALS	Financial Accounting Archival - Primary Accruals 156

Author	Degree & Date School Advisor	Title	Functional Area Research Method Topic pages
SINHA, RANJAN	PHD 1993 UNIVERSITY OF CALIFORNIA, BERKELEY PENMAN, STEPHEN H.	AN ASSESSMENT OF MARKET REACTION TO EARNINGS AND BOOK VALUE INFORMATION	Financial Accounting Archival - Primary Earnings 317
SIPPLE, STANLEY ALFRED	PHD 1985 THE UNIVERSITY OF NEBRASKA - LINCOLN	AN EMPIRICAL INVESTIGATION TO DETERMINE IF A PARTNER MAY SERVE THE PARTNERSHIP AS AN EMPLOYEE	Taxation Survey Partnership Taxation 196
SISAYE, SELESHI	PHD 1988 UNIVERSITY OF PITTSBURGH	RESOURCE ALLOCATION PROCESSES IN DIVISIONALIZED BUSINESS ORGANIZATIONS: A POWER CONTROL MODEL OF ORGANIZATIONS	Cost/Managerial Experimental Management Control Systems 279
SIVAKUMAR, KUMAR N.	PHD 1989 RICE UNIVERSITY BELL, PHILIP W.	MANAGERIAL CHOICE OF DISCRETIONARY ACCOUNTING METHODS: AN EMPIRICAL EVALUATION OF SECURITY MARKET RESPONSE	Financial Accounting Archival - Primary Earnings Management 114
SIVARAMAKRISHNAN, KONDURU	PHD 1989 NORTHWESTERN UNIVERSITY	INFORMATION CONTENT OF EARNINGS COMPONENTS, REPORTING CHOICE AND LONG TERM CONTRACTS	Financial Accounting Analytical - Internal Agency Theory 218
SJOBLOM, LEIF MIKAEL	PHD 1993 STANFORD UNIVERSITY FOSTER, GEORGE	ESSAYS IN SHOP FLOOR QUALITY MANAGEMENT	Cost/Managerial Survey Quality Issues 253
SKARO, MATTHEW MARTIN	PHD 1987 THE UNIVERSITY OF NEBRASKA - LINCOLN	A THEORETICAL AND EMPIRICAL INVESTIGATION OF THE RELEVANCE AND RELIABILITY OF CERTAIN OPINIONS CONCERNING PENDING LITIGATION	Financial Accounting Archival - Primary Disclosures 130
SKINNER, DOUGLAS JOHN	PHD 1989 THE UNIVERSITY OF ROCHESTER WATTS, ROSS L.	OPTIONS MARKETS, STOCK RETURN VOLATILITY AND THE INFORMATION CONTENT OF ACCOUNTING EARNINGS RELEASES	Financial Accounting Archival - Primary Earnings Announcements 138
SKOGSVIK, KENTH HARRY GORAN	EKONDR 1988 HANDELSHOGSKOLAN I STOCKHOLM (SWEDEN)	ACCOUNTING MEASURES AS PREDICTORS OF BUSINESS FAILURE--A COMPARISON BETWEEN HISTORICAL COST ACCOUNTING AND CURRENT COST ACCOUNTING [PROGNOS AV FINANSIELL KRIS MED REDOVISNINGSMATT--EN JAMFORELSE MELLAN TRADITIONELL OCH INFLATIONSJUSTERAD REDOVISNING]	Financial Accounting Case Financial Ratios 366

Author	Degree & Date School Advisor	Title	Functional Area Research Method Topic pages
SLADE, PRISCILLA DEAN	PHD 1990 THE UNIVERSITY OF TEXAS AT AUSTIN DEAKIN, EDWARD; MAY, ROBERT	AN EMPIRICAL ANALYSIS OF DEFERRED TAX BALANCES FROM A STATEMENT OF FINANCIAL POSITION AND INCOME STATEMENT PERSPECTIVE	Financial Accounting Archival - Primary Taxes 104
SLAUBAUGH, MICHAEL DEAN	PHD 1992 INDIANA UNIVERSITY SALAMON, GERALD L.	INFORMATION SYSTEM NOISE AND THE SPEED OF STOCK PRICE ADJUSTMENTS	Financial Accounting Archival - Primary Earnings Announcements 159
SLOAN, RICHARD GEOFFREY	PHD 1992 THE UNIVERSITY OF ROCHESTER WATTS, ROSS L.	ACCOUNTING EARNINGS AND TOP EXECUTIVE COMPENSATION	Cost/Managerial Archival - Primary Incentive Compensation 128
SLOF, ERIC JOHN	PHD 1994 UNIVERSIDAD DE NAVARRA (SPAIN) ROSANAS, JOSEP MARIA	ECONOMIC MODELS OF TRANSFER PRICING IN DECENTRALIZED FIRMS	Cost/Managerial Analytical - Internal Transfer Pricing 132
SMITH, ANNE	EDD 1992 NORTHERN ILLINOIS UNIVERSITY	AN ASSESSMENT OF THE COGNITIVE LEVELS OF THE UNIFORM CERTIFIED PUBLIC ACCOUNTANT EXAMINATION AND THE CERTIFIED MANAGEMENT ACCOUNTANT EXAMINATION	General Survey CPA &/or CMA Examination 162
SMITH, BECKY LYNN	PHD 1994 UNITED STATES INTERNATIONAL UNIVERSITY KANTOR, JOHN	COMPETENCE, INFLUENCE, PROBLEM-SOLVING ABILITY, AND FEAR OF SUCCESS AMONG ACCOUNTANTS	General Survey Job Performance, Satisfaction &/or Turnover 117
SMITH, CARL STUART	PHD 1989 THE UNIVERSITY OF CONNECTICUT	AN ANALYSIS OF THE APPLICATION OF INDIRECT COST ALLOCATION METHODOLOGIES IN HIGHER EDUCATION	Not-for-Profit Survey College & University 147
SMITH, DARLENE A. PULLIAM	PHD 1987 UNIVERSITY OF NORTH TEXAS	AN ANALYSIS OF THE FACTORS USED BY THE TAX COURT IN APPLYING THE STEP TRANSACTION DOCTRINE	Taxation Archival - Secondary Tax Court 107
SMITH, EUGENE F.	PHD 1990 CITY UNIVERSITY OF NEW YORK KELLY, ROBERT	MONEY LAUNDERING: A STUDY IN THE CREATION OF LAW	General Analytical - Internal Industry - Banking/Savings & Loan 138

Author	Degree & Date School Advisor	Title	Functional Area Research Method Topic pages
SMITH, GEORGE MALCOLM	PHD 1989 THE CITY UNIVERSITY (LONDON) (UNITED KINGDOM)	IMPROVING THE DECISION USEFULNESS OF THE CORPORATE ANNUAL REPORT	Financial Accounting Experimental Presentation Format 342
SMITH, HENRY CLAY, III	PHD 1994 VIRGINIA COMMONWEALTH UNIVERSITY MCEWEN, RUTH ANN	AN EMPIRICAL INVESTIGATION OF THE INCREMENTAL VALUE OF FINANCIAL ANALYSTS' FORECASTS OF EARNINGS ERROR METRICS IN THE PREDICTION OF FINANCIAL DISTRESS	Financial Accounting Archival - Primary Financial Distress or Bankruptcy 179
SMITH, HOWARD GROMEL	DBA 1985 TEXAS TECH UNIVERSITY	THE STUDY OF THE IMPLICATIONS OF SFAS 33 TO THE SMALL BUSINESS ENTERPRISE: USEFULNESS IN LONG-TERM LOAN APPLICATIONS	Financial Accounting Experimental Small Business
SMITH, JOHN REED	PHD 1989 THE OHIO STATE UNIVERSITY BURNS, THOMAS J.	THE ECONOMIC VALUE OF AUDITING UNDER A NEGLIGENCE LIABILITY RULE	Auditing Analytical - Internal Legal Liability 124
SMITH, KEITH WRIGHT	PHD 1988 THE UNIVERSITY OF MISSISSIPPI (0131) BURKETT, HOMER A.	THE IMPLICATIONS OF ALLOWING COGNITIVE STYLE DECISION APPROACHES OF THE DECISION-MAKER TO DETERMINE THE INFORMATION FORMAT: AN EXPERIMENTAL EXAMINATION OF PERFORMANCE	Cost/Managerial Experimental Presentation Format 181
SMITH, KENNETH JONATHAN	DBA 1987 THE GEORGE WASHINGTON UNIVERSITY	AN INTERNAL AUDITING METHODOLOGY FOR THE EVALUATION OF CORPORATE WELLNESS INVESTMENTS	Auditing Case Internal Auditing 232
SMITH, M. AILEEN	PHD 1992 THE LOUISIANA STATE UNIVERSITY AND AGRICULTURAL AND MECHANICAL COL. APOSTOLOU, NICHOLAS	ATTITUDES TOWARD INTERNATIONAL HARMONIZATION EFFORTS: A CROSS-CULTURAL STUDY	Financial Accounting Survey International/Global Issues 140
SMITH, MARGARET C.	PHD 1986 DUKE UNIVERSITY	A MODEL OF THE OWNER/MANAGER/AUDITOR GAME: ON THE VALUE OF PEER REVIEW AND THE MATERIALITY STANDARD	Auditing Analytical - Internal Materiality 312
SMITH, MICHAEL ALLEN	PHD 1990 UNIVERSITY OF SOUTH CAROLINA	AN EMPIRICAL INVESTIGATION OF THE RELATIONSHIP BETWEEN HISTORIC REHABILITATION TAX CREDITS AND HISTORIC REHABILITATION EXPENDITURES IN THREE VIRGINIA CITIES	Taxation Case Public Policy 169

Listing by Author

Author	Degree & Date / School / Advisor	Title	Functional Area / Research Method / Topic / pages
SMITH, NANCY E.	PHD 1986 THE UNIVERSITY OF NEBRASKA - LINCOLN	THE IMPACT OF THE FASB'S CONCEPTUAL FRAMEWORK PROJECT ON INTERMEDIATE ACCOUNTING	Education Survey Curriculum Issues 140
SMITH, PAMELA ANN	PHD 1993 UNIVERSITY OF NORTH TEXAS BOYNTAN, CHARLES E. IV	THE EARLY ADOPTION OF ACCOUNTING STANDARDS AS AN EARNINGS MANAGEMENT TOOL	Financial Accounting Archival - Primary Earnings Management 102
SMITH, PAUL HESELTINE	PHD 1986 UNIVERSITY OF ARKANSAS	CORPORATE SOCIAL RESPONSE DISCLOSURE, STRUCTURE, AND REPUTATION RELATIONSHIPS FOR LARGE UNITED STATES CORPORATIONS IN THE NEW-FEDERALISM ERA	Financial Accounting Archival - Primary Social/Environmental Responsibility 206
SMITH, ROGER JOSEPH	DBA 1991 NOVA UNIVERSITY LEWIS, CHANTEE	THE EFFECTS OF THE TAX REFORM ACT OF 1986 ON CASH DIVIDEND VALUATION	Taxation Archival - Primary Dividends 162
SMITH, SHELDON RAY	PHD 1993 MICHIGAN STATE UNIVERSITY HAKA, SUSAN F.	ACCOUNTING INFORMATION IN GLOBAL MANUFACTURING NETWORKS: THE INFORMATION EFFECT ON COMPETITIVE POSITION	Cost/Managerial Survey International/Global Issues 167
SMITH, STERLING DUANE	PHD 1991 TEXAS A&M UNIVERSITY WALLACE, WANDA A.	AN EMPIRICAL INVESTIGATION OF THE PROPERTIES OF SEQUENTIAL DISCLOSURES TO THE EQUITY MARKETS	Financial Accounting Archival - Primary Disclosures 133
SMITH, W. ROBERT	PHD 1988 THE LOUISIANA STATE UNIVERSITY AND AGRICULTURAL AND MECHANICAL COL. CURATOLA, ANTHONY P.	A STUDY TO INVESTIGATE THE EFFECTS OF STATE TAXATION AND PLAN TYPE ON SMALL EMPLOYER RETIREMENT PLAN COST	General Simulation Small Business 165
SMOLINSKI, HAROLD CARL	DBA 1987 LOUISIANA TECH UNIVERSITY	AN EXAMINATION OF MEDIA INFORMATION PRECEDING POTENTIAL FIRM FINANCIAL DISTRESS: THE CASE OF DEBT RERATING TO CAA AND BELOW	Financial Accounting Archival - Primary Financial Distress or Bankruptcy 99
SNEAD, KENNETH CARTER, JR.	PHD 1988 UNIVERSITY OF SOUTH CAROLINA HARRELL, ADRIAN	AN APPLICATION OF VROOM'S EXPECTANCY THEORY AND MCCLELLAND'S TRICHOTOMY OF NEEDS THEORY TO EXAMINE MANAGERS' MOTIVATION TO IMPLEMENT A DECISION SUPPORT SYSTEM	Information Systems Experimental Decision Support Systems 166

Author	Degree & Date School Advisor	Title	Functional Area Research Method Topic pages
SNOW, CHARLES GRAN, JR.	PHD 1992 DREXEL UNIVERSITY SRINIVASAN, CADAMBI A.	AN EMPIRICAL INQUIRY INTO THE USE OF CERTAIN FINANCIAL AND NON-FINANCIAL MEASURES OF ENTITY PERFORMANCE	Financial Accounting Archival - Primary Performance Evaluation/Measurement 219
SNYDER, JOHN PAUL	PHD 1985 UNIVERSITY OF SOUTH CAROLINA	ANALYTICAL REVIEW: AN EMPIRICAL STUDY	Auditing Analytical Review 139
SODERSTROM, NAOMI SIEGEL	PHD 1990 NORTHWESTERN UNIVERSITY BALACHANDRAN, BALA; MAGEE, ROBERT P.	THE RESPONSE OF HOSPITALS TO INCENTIVES: THE CASE OF THE MEDICARE PROSPECTIVE PAYMENT SYSTEM	General Industry - Health Care 137
SOFFER, LEONARD CHARLES	PHD 1991 UNIVERSITY OF CALIFORNIA, BERKELEY PENMAN, STEPHEN	FINANCIAL STATEMENT INDICATORS OF TAKEOVER TARGETS: A MULTINOMIAL ANALYSIS	Financial Accounting Archival - Primary Merger, Acquisition, Reorganization 152
SOHN, PYUNG SIK	PHD 1993 THE UNIVERSITY OF TEXAS AT ARLINGTON HASSELL, JOHN M.	INTRADAY STOCK PRICE REACTION TO MANAGEMENT EARNINGS FORECASTS	Financial Accounting Archival - Primary Forecasting Financial Performance 197
SOHN, SUNGKYU	PHD 1992 NORTHWESTERN UNIVERSITY LYS, THOMAS	EX-POST REALIZATION AND VALUATION OF MANAGEMENT EARNINGS FORECASTS, MANAGER'S DISCRETION AND CHARACTERISTICS OF FORECASTING FIRMS	Financial Accounting Archival - Primary Forecasting Financial Performance 160
SOLIMAN, MAHMOUD EL-SAYED	PHD 1989 UNIVERSITY OF GEORGIA WILKERSON, JACK E.	THE DETERMINANTS OF ACCOUNTING CHOICES BY SMALL FIRMS: AN EMPIRICAL INVESTIGATION	Financial Accounting Archival - Primary Accounting Choice 187
SOMMERVILLE, PATRICIA MILLER	PHD 1991 SAINT LOUIS UNIVERSITY JENNINGS, JAMES P.	AN ANALYSIS OF THE ATTITUDES TOWARDS CASH FLOW PER SHARE AND A COMPARATIVE ANALYSIS OF ACCRUAL AND CASH BASIS ACCOUNTING IN EXPLAINING CASH FLOW PER SHARE	Financial Accounting Archival - Primary Cash Flows 200
SON, WON-IK	PHD 1993 THE UNIVERSITY OF WISCONSIN - MADISON DAVID, MARTIN H.	TAX TREATMENTS OF INVENTORY AND THEIR REAL EFFECTS: THEORY AND EVIDENCE	Taxation Archival - Primary Inventory 151

Author	Degree & Date School Advisor	Title	Functional Area Research Method Topic pages
SONG, IN-MAN	PHD 1986 THE UNIVERSITY OF WISCONSIN - MADISON	DIFFERENTIAL STOCK PRICE REACTION TO INFLATION-ADJUSTED INCOME DISCLOSURES UNDER SFAS 33: EFFECTS OF FIRM-SPECIFIC CHARACTERISTICS	Financial Accounting Archival - Primary Inflation 175
SOO, BILLY SY	PHD 1991 NORTHWESTERN UNIVERSITY MAGEE, ROBERT	MANAGERIAL RESPONSE TO MANDATORY ACCOUNTING PRINCIPLES: AN ACCRUALS PERSPECTIVE	Financial Accounting Archival - Primary Accounting Change 203
SOONGSWANG, ORANUJ	DBA 1991 MISSISSIPPI STATE UNIVERSITY PEARSON, RODNEY A.	THE PERCEIVED IMPORTANCE AND IMPLEMENTATION OF INTERNAL CONTROLS IN A DATABASE ENVIRONMENT	Information Systems Survey Internal Control 296
SOPARIWALA, PARVEZ R.	PHD 1985 MICHIGAN STATE UNIVERSITY	AN EMPIRICAL EXAMINATION OF THE ASSOCIATION BETWEEN THE ADOPTION OF LONG-TERM PERFORMANCE PLANS AND THE SUBSEQUENT GROWTH OF RESEARCH AND DEVELOPMENT EXPENDITURES	Cost/Managerial Archival - Primary Incentive Compensation 177
SOUGIANNIS, THEODORE	PHD 1990 UNIVERSITY OF CALIFORNIA, BERKELEY	THE VALUATION OF R AND D FIRMS AND THE ACCOUNTING RULES FOR R AND D COSTS	Financial Accounting Archival - Primary Research & Development 112
SOYBEL, VIRGINIA ELIZABETH EARLL	PHD 1989 COLUMBIA UNIVERSITY	MUNICIPAL FINANCIAL REPORTING AND THE NEW YORK CITY FISCAL CRISIS	Not-for-Profit Archival - Primary Governmental 162
SPEAR, NASSER ABDELMONEM	PHD 1992 UNIVERSITY OF NORTH TEXAS	THE INFORMATION CONTENT OF SUPPLEMENTAL RESERVE-BASED REPLACEMENT MEASURES RELATIVE TO THAT OF HISTORICAL COST INCOME AND ITS CASH AND ACCRUAL COMPONENTS OF OIL AND GAS PRODUCING COMPANIES	Financial Accounting Archival - Primary Industry - Oil & Gas 214
SPECHT, JAMES	PHD 1988 GEORGIA STATE UNIVERSITY - COLLEGE OF BUSINESS ADMINISTRATION ROBERTS, A. R.	AN EMPIRICAL EXAMINATION OF LITIGATION AGAINST AUDITORS OVER TIME	Auditing Archival - Primary Legal Liability 172
SPIKES, PAMELA ANN	PHD 1993 THE UNIVERSITY OF MISSISSIPPI FLESHER, TONYA K.	A STUDY OF THE APPLICATION OF THE UNRELATED BUSINESS INCOME TAX PROVISIONS TO COLLEGES AND UNIVERSITIES	Taxation Survey College & University 145

Listing by Author

Author	Degree & Date School Advisor	Title	Functional Area Research Method Topic pages
SPILKER, BRIAN CLARK	PHD 1993 THE UNIVERSITY OF TEXAS AT AUSTIN ANDERSON, URTON; LIMBERG, STEPHEN	THE EFFECTS OF TIME PRESSURE AND KNOWLEDGE ON KEY WORD SELECTION BEHAVIOR IN TAX RESEARCH	Taxation Experimental Judgment & Decision Making - Cognitive Processes 153
SPINDLE, ROXANNE MARIE	PHD 1991 UNIVERSITY OF COLORADO AT BOULDER JACKSON, BETTY R.	USING EX POST FORECASTING AND PANEL DATA TO EVALUATE LABOR SUPPLY ELASTICITIES	Taxation Archival - Primary Individual Taxation 209
SPIRES, ERIC EDWARD	PHD 1987 UNIVERSITY OF ILLINOIS AT URBANA-CHAMPAIGN	AN INVESTIGATION INTO AUDITORS' EVALUATIONS OF COMPLIANCE TESTS	Auditing Experimental Judgment & Decision Making 319
SPRADLING, DALE WARREN	PHD 1988 UNIVERSITY OF HOUSTON PRATT, JAMES W.	TOWARD PARITY BETWEEN S CORPORATIONS AND PARTNERSHIPS AND SIMPLIFICATION OF S CORPORATION TAXATION	Taxation Business Form 318
SPURRELL, A. C. LLOYD	PHD 1988 THE UNIVERSITY OF NEBRASKA - LINCOLN BALKE, THOMAS E.	AN EXAMINATION OF SELECTED FACTORS ASSOCIATED WITH AUDIT LITIGATION	Auditing Archival - Primary Legal Liability 158
SRIDHARAN, SWAMINATHAN	PHD 1990 UNIVERSITY OF PITTSBURGH EVANS, JOHN H. III	MANAGERIAL REPORTING INCENTIVES AND INVESTMENT DECISIONS	Cost/Managerial Analytical - Internal Agency Theory 175
SRIRAM, SRINIVASAN	PHD 1987 UNIVERSITY OF NORTH TEXAS	AN INVESTIGATION OF ASYMMETRICAL POWER RELATIONSHIPS EXISTING IN AUDITOR-CLIENT RELATIONSHIP DURING AUDITOR CHANGES	Auditing Archival - Primary Auditor Changes 177
ST. JOHN, WILLIAM CHARLES, JR.	PHD 1989 RENSSELAER POLYTECHNIC INSTITUTE ALDRICH, ALEXANDER	A STUDY OF THE VARIOUS CHANGES IN FEDERAL INCOME TAX LAWS AND THEIR EFFECTS ON THE RATE OF RETURN FOR REAL ESTATE INVESTORS	Taxation Industry - Real Estate 193
STAHEL, ANDREAS	DRSCTECH 1990 UNIVERSITAET ZURICH (SWITZERLAND)	CONCEPT OF THE DECISION-SUPPORTING MANAGEMENT ACCOUNTING SYSTEM [GESTALTUNG DES ENTSCHEIDUNGSORIENTIERTEN BETRIEBLICHEN RECHNUNGSWESENS]	Information Systems Analytical - Internal Decision Support Systems 199

Author	Degree & Date School Advisor	Title	Functional Area Research Method Topic pages
STANGL, ROBERT JOHN	PHD 1994 UNIVERSITY OF KANSAS WAEGELEIN, JAMES F.	CORPORATE AUDIT COMMITTEES: FACTORS ASSOCIATED WITH VOLUNTARY FORMATION AND MARKET REACTION TO MANDATORY FORMATION	Auditing Archival - Primary Audit Committees 146
STAPLES, CATHERINE LOVING	PHD 1990 THE UNIVERSITY OF NORTH CAROLINA AT CHAPEL HILL RUBIN, MARC A.	THE RELATION BETWEEN THE MEDIA, MONITORING DEVICES, AND THE SCHOOL DISTRICT BUDGETARY PROCESS	Not-for-Profit Case Budgeting 203
STEADMAN, MARK EDWARD	PHD 1990 THE UNIVERSITY OF TENNESSEE REEVE, JAMES	THE COMMON STOCK PRICE EFFECTS OF BOND RATING CHANGES: AN EXAMINATION OF ASYMMETRIC MARKET REACTIONS USING STAKEHOLDER THEORY	Financial Accounting Archival - Primary Long Term Debt 169
STEED, STEVE ALAN	PHD 1985 UNIVERSITY OF NORTH TEXAS	AN EMPIRICAL STUDY OF THE EFFECTIVENESS OF INDEPENDENCE DISCRIMINATION RESULTING FROM THE APPLICATION OF AICPA ETHICAL INTERPRETATION 101-3--ACCOUNTING SERVICES	General Experimental Ethics 177
STEIN, DOUGLAS MITCHELL	PHD 1992 THE UNIVERSITY OF WISCONSIN - MADISON RITTENBERG, LARRY E.	THE IMPACT OF PAPERLESS INFORMATION SYSTEMS ON SUBSTANTIVE AUDIT EVIDENCE	Auditing EDP Controls 271
STEINBART, PAUL JOHN	PHD 1985 MICHIGAN STATE UNIVERSITY	THE CONSTRUCTION OF AN EXPERT SYSTEM TO MAKE MATERIALITY JUDGMENTS	Information Systems Analytical - Internal Decision Support Systems 158
STEPHAN, JENS A.	PHD 1985 CORNELL UNIVERSITY	INFORMATION CONTENT OF SECURITY PRICES: EVIDENCE ON THE RATIONAL EXPECTATIONS HYPOTHESIS	General Archival - Primary Capital Markets 94
STEPHENSON, CRAIG ALLEN	PHD 1994 THE UNIVERSITY OF ARIZONA DYL, EDWARD A.	ESSAYS ON REPURCHASES AND TENDER OFFERS	Financial Accounting Archival - Primary Stock Transactions 134
STERNBURG, THOMAS JAMES	PHD 1993 ARIZONA STATE UNIVERSITY WYNDELTS, ROBERT	AN EMPIRICAL INVESTIGATION OF DETERRENCE THEORY AND INFLUENCE THEORY ON PROFESSIONAL TAX PREPARERS' RECOMMENDATIONS	Taxation Experimental Tax Professionals 132

Listing by Author

Author	Degree & Date School Advisor	Title	Functional Area Research Method Topic pages
STEVENS, KEVIN TIMOTHY	DBA 1989 UNIVERSITY OF KENTUCKY POPE, THOMAS R.	AN EMPIRICAL ANALYSIS OF THE NATURE OF SELECTED TAX EXPENDITURES IN A STATE INDIVIDUAL INCOME TAX SYSTEM	Taxation Archival - Primary State Taxation 285
STEWART, DANIEL VAN	PHD 1990 UNIVERSITY OF PITTSBURGH WEIDMAN, JOHN C.	A STUDY OF CHANGES IN ARTICLE PUBLICATION PRODUCTIVITY AMONG ACCOUNTING FACULTY PROMOTED DURING THE 1980'S	Education Archival - Primary Academic Issues 145
STEWART, JENICE PRATHER	PHD 1985 THE UNIVERSITY OF ALABAMA	AN EMPIRICAL INVESTIGATION OF THE USEFULNESS OF ALTERNATIVE EARNING CLASSIFICATIONS IN PREDICTING CASH FLOWS	Financial Accounting Archival - Primary Cash Flows 253
STICE, EARL KAY	PHD 1989 CORNELL UNIVERSITY	THE MARKET REACTION TO 10-K AND 10-Q FILINGS AND TO SUBSEQUENT 'WALL STREET JOURNAL' EARNINGS ANNOUNCEMENTS	Financial Accounting Archival - Primary Earnings Announcements 139
STICE, JAMES DAVID	PHD 1989 UNIVERSITY OF WASHINGTON PRATT, JAMES H.	PREDICTING LAWSUITS AGAINST AUDITORS USING FINANCIAL AND MARKET INFORMATION	Auditing Archival - Primary Legal Liability 158
STINSON, CHRISTOPHER HALL	PHD 1993 STANFORD UNIVERSITY BEAVER, WILLIAM H.	THE MANAGEMENT OF PROVISIONS AND ALLOWANCES IN THE SAVINGS AND LOAN INDUSTRY	Financial Accounting Archival - Primary Industry - Banking/Savings & Loan 219
STITTS, RANDAL HAYES	PHD 1991 TEXAS TECH UNIVERSITY BURNS, JANE O.	TAX PREFERENCES, FAIRNESS, AND THE ELDERLY: A COMPARATIVE ANALYSIS OF TAX LIABILITIES	Taxation Archival - Primary Public Policy 251
STOCKS, MORRIS H., JR.	PHD 1991 UNIVERSITY OF SOUTH CAROLINA HARRELL, ADRIAN	AN EMPIRICAL EXAMINATION OF THE IMPACT OF INFORMATION OVERLOAD ON GROUPS AND INDIVIDUALS IN A FINANCIAL DISTRESS DECISION TASK	General Experimental Judgment & Decision Making 106
STOLT, SUSAN MARIE JESZKA	PHD 1985 ARIZONA STATE UNIVERSITY	AN ATTRIBUTIONAL ANALYSIS OF PERFORMANCE EVALUATION IN PUBLIC ACCOUNTING	General Experimental Job Performance, Satisfaction &/or Turnover 252

Author	Degree & Date School Advisor	Title	Functional Area Research Method Topic pages
STONE, DAN NORMAN, JR.	PHD 1987 THE UNIVERSITY OF TEXAS AT AUSTIN	THE IMPACT OF INFORMATION FORM ON COGNITIVE PROCESSES AND CHOICE IN AN INFORMATION SYSTEM SELECTION TASK	Information Systems Experimental Presentation Format 275
STONEBACK, JANE YOUNG	PHD 1992 UNIVERSITY OF KANSAS	ESSAYS ON THE INFLUENCE OF THE STAGES OF ORGANIZATIONAL DEVELOPMENT UPON POLICY CHOICE	Cost/Managerial Management Control Systems 313
STRAWSER, JERRY ROBERT	PHD 1985 TEXAS A&M UNIVERSITY	AN EMPIRICAL INVESTIGATION OF AUDITOR JUDGMENT: FACTORS AFFECTING PERCEIVED AUDIT RISK	Auditing Experimental Judgment & Decision Making 217
STREET, DONNA LEE	PHD 1987 THE UNIVERSITY OF TENNESSEE	SEGMENT CASH FLOW STATEMENT: AN EMPIRICAL EXAMINATION OF ITS IMPACT ON THE LENDING DECISION	Financial Accounting Experimental Segment Reporting 155
STREULY, CAROLYN	PHD 1987 THE UNIVERSITY OF WISCONSIN - MADISON	TWO ESSAYS: AN EMPIRICAL INVESTIGATION INTO THE DETERMINANTS OF SECURITY RETURNS; AND, THE ASSOCIATION BETWEEN MARKET-DETERMINED AND ACCOUNTING-DETERMINED RISK MEASURES REVISITED	Financial Accounting Archival - Primary Risk 188
STROOPE, JOHN CLARENCE	PHD 1988 UNIVERSITY OF NORTH TEXAS ANDERSON, HERSHEL	INCOME TAX EVASION AND THE EFFECTIVENESS OF TAX COMPLIANCE LEGISLATION, 1979-1982	Taxation Archival - Primary Tax Compliance 85
STROUD, J. B., JR.	DBA 1985 MISSISSIPPI STATE UNIVERSITY	PERCEPTIONS OF CITY MANAGERS CONCERNING MUNICIPAL FINANCIAL STATEMENT USERS, USER IMPORTANCE, AND IMPORTANCE OF SELECTED ITEMS OF DISCLOSURE	Not-for-Profit Survey Governmental 140
STUART, IRIS C.	PHD 1993 THE UNIVERSITY OF IOWA GRIMLUND, RICHARD A.; CHRISTENSEN-SZALANSK I, JAY J.	ANALYTICAL PROCEDURES AND JUDGMENT ACCURACY: A COMPARISON OF STRUCTURED AND UNSTRUCTURED AUDIT METHODOLOGY	Auditing Experimental Job Performance, Satisfaction &/or Turnover 210
STYRON, WILLIAM JOEY	PHD 1993 TEXAS A&M UNIVERSITY STRAWSER, ROBERT H.	AN EMPIRICAL EXAMINATION OF THE GOING-CONCERN AUDIT OPINION: THE AUDITOR'S DECISION REGARDING CONTINUING GOING-CONCERN OPINIONS AND THE SUBSEQUENT FATE OF COMPANIES THAT HAVE RECEIVED GOING-CONCERN OPINIONS	Auditing Archival - Primary Audit Opinion 150

Author	Degree & Date / School / Advisor	Title	Functional Area / Research Method / Topic / pages
SU, ROBERT KUATERNG	PHD 1987 THE LOUISIANA STATE UNIVERSITY AND AGRICULTURAL AND MECHANICAL COL.	AN EMPIRICAL INVESTIGATION OF THE USEFULNESS OF CURRENT COST INFORMATION IN MERGER PREDICTION	Financial Accounting Archival - Primary Inflation 182
SUBRAMANIAM, CHANDRA	PHD 1993 UNIVERSITY OF MINNESOTA DALEY, LANE A.; JAGANNATHAN, RAVI K.	MEASURING INFORMATION CONTENT OF CORPORATE ANNOUNCEMENTS	Financial Accounting Simulation Capital Markets 103
SUBRAMANYAM, K. R.	PHD 1993 THE UNIVERSITY OF WISCONSIN - MADISON WILD, JOHN J.	STOCHASTIC PRECISION AND MARKET REACTIONS TO EARNINGS ANNOUNCEMENTS	Financial Accounting Archival - Primary Earnings Announcements 151
SUDIBYO, BAMBANG	DBA 1985 UNIVERSITY OF KENTUCKY	THE ADEQUACY OF CPAS' UNDERSTANDING OF THE RELATIVE SERIOUSNESS OF ALPHA AND BETA RISKS IN STATISTICAL AUDIT SAMPLING	Auditing Survey Audit Sampling 196
SUH, CHUNG WOO	PHD 1988 UNIVERSITY OF ILLINOIS AT URBANA-CHAMPAIGN KWON, YOUNG K.	DISCLOSURE TIMING OF ACCOUNTING INFORMATION AND STOCK MARKET REACTION UNDER ASYMMETRIC INFORMATION	Financial Accounting Analytical - Internal Earnings Announcements 142
SUH, YOON SUCK	PHD 1985 THE UNIVERSITY OF TEXAS AT AUSTIN	NONCONTROLLABLE COSTS AND OPTIMAL PERFORMANCE MEASUREMENT	Cost/Managerial Analytical - Internal Performance Evaluation/Measurement 124
SULLIVAN, M. CATHY	PHD 1994 THE UNIVERSITY OF TENNESSEE BORTHICK, A. FAYE	AN INVESTIGATION OF AGENCY THEORY'S ASSUMPTION OF STRICT EFFORT AVERSION: THE ROLE OF INTRINSIC MOTIVATION	General Experimental Agency Theory 135
SUMMERS, SUZANNE BURGER	PHD 1992 UNIVERSITY OF GEORGIA BAREFIELD, RUSSELL M.	THE IMPACT OF THE PROPOSED LICENSING REQUIREMENTS ON TURNOVER IN PUBLIC ACCOUNTING	General Archival - Primary Job Performance, Satisfaction &/or Turnover 120
SUMNER, JEANIE GRACE	PHD 1989 PORTLAND STATE UNIVERSITY RODICH, GROVER	AN ANALYSIS OF THE EFFECT OF STATE REGULATION OF COMMERCIAL INCOME TAX PREPARERS ON THE QUALITY OF INCOME TAX RETURNS	Taxation Archival - Primary State Taxation 166

Listing by Author

Author	Degree & Date School Advisor	Title	Functional Area Research Method Topic pages
SUN, HUEY-LIAN	PHD 1991 UNIVERSITY OF HOUSTON HOPWOOD, WILLIAM S.	INFORMATION CONTENT OF EXTERNAL FINANCING AND FIRM-SPECIFIC CHARACTERISTICS	Financial Accounting Archival - Primary Information Content 205
SUNG, HEEKYUNG	PHD 1993 THE UNIVERSITY OF OKLAHOMA AYRES, FRANCES L.	INFORMATION CONTENT OF THE TIMING OF EARNINGS ANNOUNCEMENTS	Financial Accounting Archival - Primary Earnings Announcements 111
SUNG, KYU YOUNG	PHD 1988 UNIVERSITY OF WASHINGTON SUNDEM, GARY L.	VALUE AND OPTIMAL TIMING OF MANAGERIAL ACCOUNTING INFORMATION IN A MULTIPERIOD SETTING WITH LEARNING	Cost/Managerial Analytical - Internal Agency Theory 101
SURDICK, JOHN JOSEPH, JR.	PHD 1988 THE UNIVERSITY OF WISCONSIN - MADISON FRANK, WERNER G.	AN INVESTIGATION OF THE BOND RATINGS ASSIGNED TO TAX-EXEMPT HOSPITAL REVENUE BONDS: AN EMPIRICAL MODEL FOR NOT-FOR-PROFIT HOSPITALS	Not-for-Profit Archival - Primary Industry - Health Care 215
SUSANTO, DJOKO	PHD 1992 UNIVERSITY OF ARKANSAS HAY, LEON E.	AN EMPIRICAL INVESTIGATION OF THE EXTENT OF CORPORATE DISCLOSURE IN ANNUAL REPORTS OF COMPANIES LISTED ON THE JAKARTA STOCK EXCHANGE	Financial Accounting Archival - Primary International/Global Issues 149
SUTLEY, KENNETH R.	PHD 1994 THE UNIVERSITY OF CHICAGO SCHIPPER, KATHERINE	AN EMPIRICAL INVESTIGATION INTO THE RELATION BETWEEN DIFFERENTIAL ANNUAL REPORT INFORMATIVENESS AND THE ASSOCIATION OF STOCK RETURNS WITH ACCOUNTING EARNINGS: THE CASE OF THE 'FINANCIAL POST' ANNUAL REPORT AWARDS	Financial Accounting Archival - Primary Information Content 123
SUTTER, MARK D.	PHD 1990 UNIVERSITY OF MISSOURI - COLUMBIA WILSON, EARL R.	A TEST OF FACTORS AFFECTING BUDGETING CHARACTERISTICS OF MUNICIPALITIES	Not-for-Profit Survey Budgeting 190
SUTTON, STEVEN GALE	PHD 1987 UNIVERSITY OF MISSOURI - COLUMBIA	FORMULATING QUALITY MEASURES FOR AUDIT ENGAGEMENTS	Auditing Survey Audit Quality 203
SUWANMALA, CHARAS	PHD 1991 NORTHERN ILLINOIS UNIVERSITY	CENTRAL CONTROL AND LOCAL PRODUCTIVITY: A CASE STUDY IN THAILAND	Not-for-Profit Case International/Global Issues 210

Author	Degree & Date School Advisor	Title	Functional Area Research Method Topic pages
SWAIN, MONTE RAY	PHD 1992 MICHIGAN STATE UNIVERSITY	EXPERIENCE AND INFORMATION EFFECTS ON SEARCH STRATEGIES IN A CAPITAL BUDGETING TASK	Cost/Managerial Experimental Capital Budgeting 202
SWAMINATHAN, SIVAKUMAR	PHD 1989 STATE UNIVERSITY OF NEW YORK AT BUFFALO	THE EFFECT OF INFORMATION PRECISION ON INVESTOR BELIEFS AND SECURITY PRICES: THE SEGMENT-REPORTING ISSUE	Financial Accounting Archival - Primary Segment Reporting 152
SWANSON, ZANE LEWIS	PHD 1991 THE UNIVERSITY OF OKLAHOMA AYRES, FRANCES	THE INFORMATION CONTENT OF EARNINGS COMPONENTS AND DIVIDENDS	Financial Accounting Archival - Primary Dividends 168
SWARTZ, LEE MICHAEL	PHD 1994 THE UNIVERSITY OF IOWA SA-AADU, JAY	THE IMPACT OF STATE ANTITAKEOVER LAWS ON SECURITY VALUE	General Archival - Primary Merger, Acquisition, Reorganization 108
SWAYZE, JAMES PRENTISS	PHD 1992 UNIVERSITY OF HOUSTON	THE EFFECT OF CORPORATE INCOME TAX INTEGRATION ON THE DEMAND FOR RISKY STOCK	Taxation Experimental Investments 199
SWEENEY, AMY PATRICIA	PHD 1992 THE UNIVERSITY OF ROCHESTER SMITH, CLIFFORD W.; WATTS, ROSS L.	DEBT-COVENANT VIOLATIONS AND MANAGERS' ACCOUNTING-CHOICE AND PRODUCTION-INVESTMENT DECISIONS	Financial Accounting Archival - Primary Accounting Choice 202
SWEENEY, JOHN THOMAS	PHD 1992 UNIVERSITY OF MISSOURI - COLUMBIA ROBERTS, ROBIN W.	COGNITIVE MORAL DEVELOPMENT AND AUDITOR INDEPENDENCE: AN EMPIRICAL INVESTIGATION	Auditing Survey Ethics 201
SWEENEY, MICHAEL PETER	PHD 1994 UNIVERSITY OF KENTUCKY VANDANIKER, RELMOND	MANAGEMENT ACCOUNTING IN MUNICIPAL GOVERNMENTS	Cost/Managerial Survey Governmental 166
SWENSON, DAN WILLIAM	PHD 1993 THE UNIVERSITY OF MISSISSIPPI FLESHER, DALE L.	AN EMPIRICAL INVESTIGATION OF HOW FIRM DIFFERENCES AFFECT MANAGEMENT SATISFACTION WITH ACTIVITY-BASED COSTING	Cost/Managerial Survey Activity Based Costing 237

Author	Degree & Date School Advisor	Title	Functional Area Research Method Topic pages
SWIFT, KENTON D.	PHD 1991 THE UNIVERSITY OF WISCONSIN - MADISON WEYGANDT, JERRY J.	AN EXPERIMENTAL INVESTIGATION INTO THE EFFECTS OF RISKS AND UNCERTAINTIES ON COMMERCIAL LENDING DECISIONS	Financial Accounting Experimental Industry - Banking/Savings & Loan 172
SWINNEY, LAURIE S.	PHD 1993 THE UNIVERSITY OF NEBRASKA - LINCOLN CHEN, KUNG H.	EXPERT SYSTEMS IN AUDITING: DECISION AID OR DECISION SUBJUGATION	Auditing Experimental Decision Aids 179
SYKES, VICEOLA DELORIS	PHD 1989 UNIVERSITY OF FLORIDA KRAMER, JOHN L.	AN ANALYSIS OF THE TAX EFFECTS OF FOREIGN INVESTMENTS IN U.S. AGRICULTURAL LAND	Taxation Analytical - Internal Public Policy 221
TAN, HUN-TONG	PHD 1992 THE UNIVERSITY OF MICHIGAN LIBBY, ROBERT	EFFECTS OF EXPECTATION AND PRIOR INVOLVEMENT ON MEMORY FOR AUDIT EVIDENCE AND JUDGMENT: THE MODERATING ROLE OF ACCOUNTABILITY	Auditing Experimental Judgment & Decision Making - Heuristics & Biases 98
TANDY, PAULETTE REDFERN	PHD 1987 TEXAS A&M UNIVERSITY	AN EMPIRICAL STUDY OF THE EXTENT, TIMING, AND NATURE OF ANALYTICAL REVIEW PROCEDURES IN ACTUAL AUDIT SETTINGS	Auditing Archival - Primary Analytical Review 180
TANNER, MARGARET MORGAN	PHD 1992 UNIVERSITY OF NORTH TEXAS DAVIS, FRED	AN ANALYSIS OF FACTORS ASSOCIATED WITH VOLUNTARY DISCLOSURE OF MANAGEMENT'S RESPONSIBILITIES FOR INTERNALCONTROL	Financial Accounting Archival - Primary Voluntary Management Disclosures 177
TATUM, KAY WARD	PHD 1986 TEXAS TECH UNIVERSITY	AN EMPIRICAL STUDY OF AUDIT SAMPLING PROBLEMS	Auditing Survey Audit Sampling 222
TEALL, HOWARD DOUGLAS	PHD 1987 THE UNIVERSITY OF WESTERN ONTARIO (CANADA)	AN EMPIRICAL STUDY OF THE ABILITY OF CANADIAN OIL AND GAS COMPANIES' RESERVES DISCLOSURES TO ACCOUNT FOR RELATIVE CHANGES IN COMMON STOCK PRICES	Financial Accounting Archival - Primary Industry - Oil & Gas
TEEUWEN, TERESA DIANE TRAPANI	PHD 1990 UNIVERSITY OF KANSAS JOY, O. MAURICE; LARCKER, DAVID F.	AN INVESTIGATION OF THE RELATIONSHIP BETWEEN CEO COMPENSATION AND CEO TRADING PROFITS	Cost/Managerial Archival - Primary Incentive Compensation 179

Author	Degree & Date School Advisor	Title	Functional Area Research Method Topic pages
TEO, SUSAN PIN PIN	PHD 1989 THE UNIVERSITY OF WISCONSIN - MADISON EICHENSEHER, JOHN W.	THE DEVELOPMENT OF AN INTERNATIONAL AUDITING HARMONIZATION MODEL AND THE EMPIRICAL TESTING OF ONE OF ITS COMPONENTS: AUDIT QUALITY	Auditing Survey International/Global Issues 130
TERANDO, WILLIAM DAVID	PHD 1993 UNIVERSITY OF ILLINOIS AT URBANA-CHAMPAIGN DIETRICH, J. RICHARD	THE INFLUENCE OF TAXES AND OTHER FACTORS ON DEBT RATIO DIFFERENCES BETWEEN MASTER LIMITED PARTNERSHIPS AND CORPORATIONS	Taxation Business Form 140
TESSONI, DANIEL DAVID	PHD 1986 SYRACUSE UNIVERSITY	AN EMPIRICAL EVALUATION OF THE POSITIVE THEORY OF ACCOUNTING IN THE CONTEXT OF ACCOUNTING FOR CHANGING PRICES	Financial Accounting Archival - Primary Inflation 278
THEVARANJAN, ALEX	PHD 1993 UNIVERSITY OF MINNESOTA BANKER, RAJIV D.	EFFORT ALLOCATION AND EXECUTIVE COMPENSATION	Cost/Managerial Incentive Compensation 104
THIAGARAJAN, SUNDARARAMAN	PHD 1989 UNIVERSITY OF FLORIDA FREEMAN, ROBERT N.	ECONOMIC DETERMINANTS OF EARNINGS PERSISTENCE	Financial Accounting Archival - Primary Earnings Response Coefficients 106
THOMAS, CHARLES WILLIS	DBA 1985 NOVA UNIVERSITY	EFFECTS OF COMPUTER TUTORIAL LESSONS ON ACCOUNTING I SKILLS AND ATTRITION	Education Experimental Instructional Methods 296
THOMAS, MICHAEL FRANCIS	PHD 1985 THE UNIVERSITY OF WISCONSIN - MADISON	AN APPLICATION OF SOCIO-TECHNICAL SYSTEMS ANALYSIS TO ACCOUNTING VARIANCE CONTROL THEORY	Cost/Managerial Standard Costs & Variance Analysis 546
THOMAS, PAULA BEVELS	DBA 1987 MISSISSIPPI STATE UNIVERSITY	PUSH DOWN ACCOUNTING: A CONCEPTUAL ANALYSIS OF ITS THEORETICAL IMPLICATIONS	Financial Accounting Analytical - Internal Segment Reporting 203
THOMAS, WILLIAM FRANCIS	PHD 1985 THE UNIVERSITY OF NORTH CAROLINA AT CHAPEL HILL	THE AUDITOR SELECTION DECISION: A MULTIATTRIBUTE APPROACH	Auditing Experimental CPA Firm Issues 173

Listing by Author

Author	Degree & Date School Advisor	Title	Functional Area Research Method Topic pages
THOMPSON, PETER MACLEOD	PHD 1991 UNIVERSITY OF CALGARY (CANADA) GELIJN, ANTON W.	A TEMPORAL DATA MODEL BASED ON ACCOUNTING PRINCIPLES	Information Systems Analytical - Internal Systems Design &/or Development 244
THORNE, DANIEL T.	DBA 1986 UNIVERSITY OF KENTUCKY	INFORMATION CONTENT OF HISTORIC COST-CURRENT COST TRENDS, DERIVED FROM SFAS NO. 33 DISCLOSURES	Financial Accounting Archival - Primary Inflation 149
THORNTON, PHILLIP WYNN	PHD 1993 UNIVERSITY OF NORTH TEXAS RAMON, KRIS	THE ROLE OF ACCOUNTING INFORMATION IN INVESTOR ASSESSMENTS OF CORPORATE TAKEOVERS	Financial Accounting Archival - Primary Merger, Acquisition, Reorganization 114
THRONEBERRY, MARY BETH	PHD 1993 THE UNIVERSITY OF MISSISSIPPI WALLACE, WILLIAM D.	DETERMINATION OF THE EFFECTS OF THE TAX REFORM ACT OF 1986 ON THE INCOME TAXES OF INDIVIDUAL PASSIVE ACTIVITY INVESTORS	Taxation Individual Taxation 193
TICHICH, MARY CAROL	PHD 1989 TEXAS A&M UNIVERSITY CRUMBLEY, D. LARRY	THE SEC INTERACTION IN THE ACCOUNTING STANDARDS SETTING PROCESS: AN ANALYSIS OF THE FASB STATEMENTS	Financial Accounting Survey Standard Setting 193
TIDD, RONALD ROBERT	PHD 1992 UNIVERSITY OF MINNESOTA DUKE, GORDON L.	GEOPOLITICAL CONSIDERATIONS IN THE ADMINISTRATION OF UNITED STATES INCOME TAX POLICY: AN ASSESSMENT OF INCOME TAX ENFORCEMENT EFFORTS, 1975-1988.	Taxation Archival - Primary Other 352
TIDRICK, DONALD EUGENE	PHD 1987 THE OHIO STATE UNIVERSITY BURNS, THOMAS J.	AUDITORS' PLANNING STAGE MATERIALITY JUDGMENTS AND THE MEDIATING EFFECTS OF LEVEL OF RESPONSIBILITY, FIRM AFFILIATION, AND AUDIT TECHNOLOGY: AN EXPERIMENT	Auditing Experimental Materiality 333
TOCCO, ANTHONY LEONARD	PHD 1986 SAINT LOUIS UNIVERSITY	AN EMPIRICAL INVESTIGATION OF THE OPINIONS OF SELECTED FINANCIAL STATEMENT USERS TOWARD THE ADOPTION OF ADDITIONAL SEGMENT INFORMATION TO 'FINANCIAL ACCOUNTING STANDARD NO. 14'	Financial Accounting Survey Segment Reporting 270
TODD, REBECCA	PHD 1986 THE UNIVERSITY OF NORTH CAROLINA AT CHAPEL HILL	AN INVESTIGATION OF THE CASH FLOW PROPERTIES OF ACCRUAL ACCOUNTING DATA: A STRUCTURAL EQUATION APPROACH	Financial Accounting Archival - Primary Accruals 81

Author	Degree & Date School Advisor	Title	Functional Area Research Method Topic pages
TOERNER, MICHAEL CHARLES	PHD 1990 THE LOUISIANA STATE UNIVERSITY AND AGRICULTURAL AND MECHANICAL COL. SUMNERS, GLENN	AN INVESTIGATION OF THE EFFECT OF A FAVORABLE EXTERNAL QUALITY ASSURANCE REVIEW ON THE SCOPE OF THE EXTERNAL AUDITOR'S EXAMINATION OF AN ORGANIZATION'S FINANCIAL STATEMENTS	Auditing Survey Internal Auditing 162
TOGO, DENNIS FUMIO	PHD 1986 ARIZONA STATE UNIVERSITY	THE MATCHING OF DECISION SUPPORT SYSTEMS TO TASKS AND ITS EFFECT ON DECISION-MAKING	Information Systems Decision Support Systems 121
TOLLIVER, ROBERT WAYNE	DBA 1987 UNIVERSITY OF KENTUCKY JOHNSON, KEITH H.	THE RELATIVE INFORMATION CONTENT OF EARNINGS AND FUNDS FLOW ACCOUNTING NUMBERS IMPOUNDED IN THE CAPITAL MARKET'S ASSESSMENT OF THE SYSTEMATIC RISK OF EQUITY SECURITIES	Financial Accounting Archival - Primary Risk 197
TONGE, STANLEY D.	DBA 1988 MEMPHIS STATE UNIVERSITY (0124) SPICELAND, J. DAVID	THE DIFFERENTIAL EFFECT OF FAS 33 DISCLOSURES ON SECURITY PRICES	Financial Accounting Archival - Primary Inflation 178
TONGTHARADOL, VAJANA	PHD 1986 ARIZONA STATE UNIVERSITY	FACTOR INFLUENCING SUPERVISOR'S RESPONSES TO SUBORDINATE'S BEHAVIOR: AN ATTRIBUTIONAL ANALYSIS	Cost/Managerial Experimental Performance Evaluation/Measurement 178
TOOLSON, RICHARD BURNS	PHD 1986 ARIZONA STATE UNIVERSITY	THE TAX INCENTIVE EFFECT OF THE CHARITABLE CONTRIBUTION DEDUCTION	Taxation Experimental Charitable Organizations 134
TOSH, DAVID EDWARD	PHD 1985 THE PENNSYLVANIA STATE UNIVERSITY	AN EMPIRICAL EVALUATION OF ALTERNATIVE ACCOUNTING MEASURES OF DEFINED BENEFIT PENSION PLAN LIABILITIES	Financial Accounting Post Retirement Benefit Issues 209
TOTTERDALE, GWENDOLYN	PHD 1985 UNIVERSITY OF OREGON	AN EXAMINATION OF THE DECISION-MAKING PROCESSES UNDERLYING THE DEVELOPMENT OF STANDARD COSTS FOR MANUFACTURED PRODUCTS	Cost/Managerial Experimental Standard Costs & Variance Analysis 257
TREWIN, JANET	PHD 1991 MICHIGAN STATE UNIVERSITY	THE IMPACT OF AN EXPERT SYSTEM ON A PROFESSIONAL ACCOUNTING ORGANIZATION	Information systems Case Decision Support Systems 183

Author	Degree & Date School Advisor	Title	Functional Area Research Method Topic pages
TREZEVANT, ROBERT HEATH	PHD 1989 THE UNIVERSITY OF ARIZONA DHALIWAL, DAN S.	THE EFFECT OF TAX LAW CHANGES ON CORPORATE INVESTMENT AND FINANCING BEHAVIOR: EMPIRICAL EVIDENCE FROM CHANGES BROUGHT ABOUT BY THE ECONOMIC RECOVERY TAX ACT OF 1981	Taxation Archival - Primary Investments 109
TRIMBLE, CHARLIE JOE	DBA 1991 LOUISIANA TECH UNIVERSITY	A MULTIPLE DISCRIMINANT ANALYSIS OF FIRM-SPECIFIC CHARACTERISTICS USEFUL IN PREDICTING MANAGEMENTS' USE OF DISCRETIONARY CASH FLOWS	Cost/Managerial Archival - Primary Agency Theory 145
TRIMBLE, DIXIE CLARK	DBA 1991 LOUISIANA TECH UNIVERSITY	AN ANALYSIS OF USER'S PERCEIVED INFORMATION NEEDS, FIRM'S CURRENT REPORTING PRACTICES, AND THE STOCK PRICE EFFECTS OF ANNOUNCEMENTS OF IMPAIRMENT IN VALUE OF LONG-LIVED OPERATING ASSETS	Financial Accounting Archival - Primary Information Content 167
TRIPPEER, DONALD RICHARD	PHD 1993 UNIVERSITY OF SOUTH CAROLINA WHITE, RICHARD	THE FUNDING OF GOVERNMENT PROGRAMS UNDER THE BUDGET ENFORCEMENT ACT: THE EFFECT OF THE EXCHANGE RELATIONSHIP ON TAXPAYER COMPLIANCE	Taxation Experimental Tax Compliance 83
TROMBLEY, MARK ALAN	PHD 1990 UNIVERSITY OF WASHINGTON KELLY, LAUREN	THE EFFECT OF CORPORATE MERGER TRANSACTIONS ON THE INFORMATION CONTENT OF EARNINGS ANNOUNCEMENTS	Financial Accounting Archival - Primary Merger, Acquisition, Reorganization 184
TROMPETER, GREGORY MICHAEL	PHD 1988 THE UNIVERSITY OF WISCONSIN - MADISON RITTENBERG, LARRY E.	AN INVESTIGATION INTO THE EFFECT OF COMPETITION, PARTNER COMPENSATION, LEGAL LIABILITY, AND AUTHORITATIVE PRONOUNCEMENTS ON AUDITOR JUDGMENT AND INDEPENDENCE	Auditing Experimental Judgment & Decision Making 209
TROUTMAN, COLEEN S.	PHD 1993 OKLAHOMA STATE UNIVERSITY	MORAL COMMITMENT TO TAX COMPLIANCE AS MEASURED BY THE DEVELOPMENT OF MORAL REASONING AND ATTITUDES TOWARDS THE FAIRNESS OF THE TAX LAWS	Taxation Survey Tax Compliance 97
TRUSSEL, JOHN M.	PHD 1993 THE GEORGE WASHINGTON UNIVERSITY PAIK, CHEI-MIN	ASSESSING THE PROBABILITY OF FINANCIAL DISTRESS: AN OPTION PRICING FRAMEWORK	Financial Accounting Archival - Primary Financial Distress or Bankruptcy 188
TSAI, YANN-CHING	PHD 1989 UNIVERSITY OF CALIFORNIA, LOS ANGELES MILLER, BRUCE L.	THE TIMING EFFECT OF EARNINGS REPORTS AND THE STOCK MARKET REACTION TO LATE-REPORTING FIRMS	Financial Accounting Archival - Primary Earnings Announcements 83

Listing by Author

Author	Degree & Date School Advisor	Title	Functional Area Research Method Topic pages
TSAY, BOR-YI	PHD 1986 UNIVERSITY OF HOUSTON	THE RELATIONSHIP BETWEEN PENSION DISCLOSURE AND BOND RISK PREMIUM	Financial Accounting Archival - Primary Post Retirement Benefit Issues 113
TSAY, YANG-TZONG	PHD 1988 UNIVERSITY OF MARYLAND COLLEGE PARK (0117) GORDON, LAWRENCE A.	THE INFORMATION CONTENT OF CORPORATE CAPITAL EXPENDITURE DECISIONS: INTERVENTION ANALYSIS	Financial Accounting Archival - Primary Investments 103
TUBBS, RICHARD MONROE	PHD 1988 UNIVERSITY OF FLORIDA MESSIER, WILLIAM F. JR.	THE EFFECT OF EXPERIENCE ON THE AUDITOR'S ORGANIZATION AND AMOUNT OF KNOWLEDGE	Auditing Experimental Judgment & Decision Making - Cognitive Processes 119
TUCKER, JAMES JOSEPH, III	PHD 1985 THE PENNSYLVANIA STATE UNIVERSITY	STOCK DIVIDENDS: HISTORICAL, CONCEPTUAL AND REPORTING PERSPECTIVES	Financial Accounting Archival - Primary Dividends 108
TUCKER, ROBERT RILEY	PHD 1987 THE FLORIDA STATE UNIVERSITY HILLISON, WILLIAM	AN INVESTIGATION OF THE RELATIONSHIP BETWEEN PUBLIC AND PRIVATE INFORMATION: AN EXPERIMENTAL MARKET STUDY	Financial Accounting Experimental Information Content 288
TUNG, SAMUEL S.	PHD 1987 THE UNIVERSITY OF WISCONSIN - MADISON	STOCK MARKET REACTIONS TO MANDATORY CHANGES IN ACCOUNTING FOR PENSIONS	Financial Accounting Archival - Primary Post Retirement Benefit Issues 125
TUNNELL, PERRY LAWRENCE	PHD 1990 OKLAHOMA STATE UNIVERSITY HAMMER, LAWRENCE H.	AN INVESTIGATION INTO THE EFFECTS OF FREQUENT TAX POLICY CHANGES ON FIRM RISK	Taxation Archival - Primary Public Policy 116
TUNTIWONGPIBOON, NARONK	PHD 1990 THE UNIVERSITY OF ALABAMA DUGAN, MICHAEL T.	AN INVESTIGATION OF CLIENT ATTRIBUTES AND AUDIT STRUCTURE	Auditing Archival - Primary Audit Structure 112
TURMEL, FRANCINE	PHD 1991 UNIVERSITE LAVAL (CANADA)	FACTEURS DETERMINANTS DE L'IMPACT DES CHANGEMENTS COMPTABLES OBLIGATOIRES SUR LE PRIX DES ACTIONS: LE CAS DE LA NORME AMERICAINE SUR LA COMPTABILISATION DES FRAIS D'INTERET	General International/Global Issues 160

Author	Degree & Date School Advisor	Title	Functional Area Research Method Topic pages
TURNER, DEBORAH HANSON	PHD 1985 GEORGIA STATE UNIVERSITY - COLLEGE OF BUSINESS ADMINISTRATION	THE EFFECT OF ALTERNATIVE METHODS OF ACCOUNTING FOR INCOME TAXES ON THE ASSOCIATION BETWEEN ACCOUNTING RISK MEASURES AND THE MARKET RISK MEASURE	Financial Accounting Archival - Primary Taxes 155
TURNER, LESLIE DANIEL	DBA 1988 UNIVERSITY OF KENTUCKY MADDEN, DONALD L.	IMPROVED MEASURES OF MANUFACTURING MAINTENANCE IN A CAPITAL BUDGETING CONTEXT: AN APPLICATION OF DATA ENVELOPMENT ANALYSIS EFFICIENCY MEASURES	Cost/Managerial Survey Performance Evaluation/Measurement 211
TURNER, MARK ALAN	DBA 1987 MEMPHIS STATE UNIVERSITY LAMBERT, KENNETH R.	JUDICIAL AND ADMINISTRATIVE DETERMINATION OF UNRELATED BUSINESS INCOME OF TAX EXEMPT ORGANIZATIONS	Taxation Archival - Secondary Not-for-Profit 253
TURNER, MARTHA J.	PHD 1991 CORNELL UNIVERSITY	THE USEFULNESS OF COST ALLOCATIONS: AN EXPERIMENTAL INVESTIGATION	Cost/Managerial Experimental Cost Allocation 199
TURNER, ROBERT M.	DBA 1992 BOSTON UNIVERSITY MENON, KRISHNAGOPAL	AN EXAMINATION OF EXTERNAL FINANCIAL REPORTING BY COLLEGES AND UNIVERSITIES	Not-for-Profit Survey College & University 236
TURPEN, RICHARD ALLEN	PHD 1987 THE UNIVERSITY OF ALABAMA	AUDIT PRICING AND AUDITOR CHOICE: AN EMPIRICAL INVESTIGATION OF THE MARKET FOR AUDITING SERVICES	Auditing Experimental Auditor Changes 136
TUTTLE, BRAD M.	PHD 1991 ARIZONA STATE UNIVERSITY	THE ROLE OF CONTEXT IN AUDITOR DIAGNOSIS	Auditing Experimental Judgment & Decision Making 97
TYPPO, ERIC WILHELM	PHD 1994 THE FLORIDA STATE UNIVERSITY BAGINSKI, STEPHEN P.	AN EMPIRICAL INVESTIGATION OF THE RELATIONSHIP BETWEEN INSIDER TRADING AND MANAGEMENT EARNINGS FORECAST CHARACTERISTICS	Financial Accounting Archival - Primary Insider Trading 121
TYSON, THOMAS N.	PHD 1987 GEORGIA STATE UNIVERSITY - COLLEGE OF BUSINESS ADMINISTRATION	FACTORS ASSOCIATED WITH CONTROLLER DEPARTMENT PARTICIPATION IN MEASURING QUALITY COSTS	Cost/Managerial Survey Quality Issues 258

Author	Degree & Date School Advisor	Title	Functional Area Research Method Topic pages
UDPA, SUNEEL CHANDRASHEKHAR	PHD 1990 WASHINGTON UNIVERSITY PINCUS, MORTON	THE EFFECT OF INSIDER TRADING ON THE STOCK PRICE RESPONSE TO EARNINGS	Financial Accounting Archival - Primary Insider Trading 150
UENO, SUSUMU	DBA 1991 SOUTHERN ILLINOIS UNIVERSITY AT CARBONDALE WU, FREDERICK; SEKARAN, UMA	THE INFLUENCE OF CULTURE ON BUDGET CONTROL PRACTICES IN THE U.S.A. AND JAPAN: AN EMPIRICAL STUDY	Cost/Managerial Survey Budgeting 143
UGRAS, YUSUF JOSEPH	PHD 1992 TEMPLE UNIVERSITY GREENBERG, RALPH H.	AN EMPIRICAL EXAMINATION OF THE FACTORS AFFECTING PERFORMANCE EVALUATION USE OF COST ALLOCATION	Cost/Managerial Survey Cost Allocation 127
UKAEGBU, EBEN O.	PHD 1987 UNIVERSITY OF STIRLING (UNITED KINGDOM)	MOTIVES FOR CORPORATE MERGERS AND TAKEOVERS: AN INVESTIGATION OF THE 'FAILING COMPANY' HYPOTHESIS AND OFPOST-MERGER PERFORMANCE	Financial Accounting Archival - Primary Financial Distress or Bankruptcy 423
ULINSKI, MICHAEL	PHD 1987 NEW YORK UNIVERSITY SAPRE, PADMAKAR M.	AN ANALYSIS OF THE RELATIONSHIP OF JOB NEED FULFILLMENT AND MICROCOMPUTER TRAINING TO MICROCOMPUTER USER SATISFACTION LEVELS OF PUBLIC ACCOUNTANTS	General Survey Microcomputer Applications 114
ULISS, BARBARA TURK	PHD 1991 CASE WESTERN RESERVE UNIVERSITY PREVITS, GARY JOHN	REPORTING INTEREST RATE SWAPS: THE ASSOCIATION OF DISCLOSURE QUALITY WITH CREDIT RISK AND OWNERSHIP STRUCTURE	Financial Accounting Archival - Primary Disclosures 193
USOFF, CATHERINE ANNE	PHD 1994 THE OHIO STATE UNIVERSITY SPIRES, ERIC E.	AN EXAMINATION OF FACTORS AFFECTING AUDIT PLANNING ACROSS ACCOUNTS	Auditing Experimental Errors 169
VACHARAJITTIPAN, SUCHITRA TUNLAYADECHANO	PHD 1991 THE GEORGE WASHINGTON UNIVERSITY HILMY, JOSEPH	THE INFORMATION CONTENT OF QUARTERLY EARNINGS: THE CASE OF THAILAND	Financial Accounting Archival - Primary International/Global Issues 157
VANSYCKLE, LARRY D.	DBA 1985 UNIVERSITY OF KENTUCKY	A CRITICAL EVALUATION OF THE CPA'S PERFORMANCE OF INTERNAL CONTROL REVIEWS OF EDP SYSTEMS IN COMPLIANCE WITH GENERALLY ACCEPTED AUDITING STANDARDS	Auditing Survey EDP Controls 196

Author	Degree & Date / School / Advisor	Title	Functional Area / Research Method / Topic / pages
VARNON, ANTHONY WAYNE	DBA 1990 MISSISSIPPI STATE UNIVERSITY DAUGHTREY, ZOEL	AN EMPIRICAL EXAMINATION OF FINANCIAL ACCOUNTING PRINCIPLES FOR AGRICULTURAL PRODUCERS: THE CASE OF PREPRODUCTIVE COSTS OF PERENNIAL FRUIT AND NUT CROPS	General Survey Industry - Agricultural 166
VAYSMAN, IGOR	PHD 1993 STANFORD UNIVERSITY	MODELS OF TRANSFER PRICING	Cost/Managerial Analytical - Internal Transfer Pricing 128
VELA PASTOR, JUAN	DR 1989 UNIVERSITAT DE BARCELONA (SPAIN)	THE ACCOUNTING SYSTEM RELATED TO DOCTRINE AND TECHNIQUE IN BUSINESS CONTROL	Cost/Managerial Analytical - Internal Management Control Systems 378
VENABLE, CAROL FRANCES	PHD 1988 THE UNIVERSITY OF ARIZONA FELIX, WILLIAM L. JR.	AN ANALYSIS OF AUDITOR INDEPENDENCE AND ITS DETERMINANTS	Auditing Survey Independence 151
VENDRZYK, VALARIA PAULINE	PHD 1993 TEXAS A&M UNIVERSITY GIROUX, GARY A.	AN EXAMINATION OF THE INFORMATION CONTENT OF ALLEGATIONS OF PROCUREMENT FRAUD IN THE DEFENSE CONTRACTING INDUSTRY	Financial Accounting Archival - Primary Fraud 129
VERGHESE, THOMAS	PHD 1988 COLUMBIA UNIVERSITY	A FORMALIZATION OF INTERNAL CONTROL EVALUATION	Auditing Analytical - Internal Internal Control 169
VERMA, KIRAN	PHD 1987 MICHIGAN STATE UNIVERSITY	EFFECTS OF ACCOUNTING TECHNIQUES ON THE STUDY OF MARKET POWER	Financial Accounting Accounting Choice 130
VESSEL, HERBERT	PHD 1986 UNIVERSITY OF MISSOURI - COLUMBIA	MANAGEMENT INCENTIVES FOR SOCIAL RESPONSIBILITY ACCOUNTING DISCLOSURE: AN EMPIRICAL ANALYSIS	Financial Accounting Archival - Primary Social/Environmental Responsibility 161
VIATOR, RALPH EDWARD	PHD 1986 TEXAS A&M UNIVERSITY	A COMPUTER-BASED APPROACH TO THE ASSESSMENT OF PRIOR PROBABILITY DISTRIBUTIONS: AN EMPIRICAL INVESTIGATION	Information Systems Experimental Decision Support Systems 162

Listing by Author

215

Author	Degree & Date School Advisor	Title	Functional Area Research Method Topic pages
VICKERY, KENNETH VERNON	DMIN 1988 DREW UNIVERSITY	ENABLING FOUR UNITED METHODIST CHURCHES' FINANCE COMMITTEES TO IMPLEMENT THE UNITED METHODIST INFORMATION SYSTEM PLUS' ACCOUNTING PROGRAM	Not-for-Profit Experimental Religious Organizations 268
VICKREY, DONN WILLIAM	PHD 1993 OKLAHOMA STATE UNIVERSITY	THE INCREMENTAL INFORMATION PROVIDED BY DISCLOSING CASH FLOW AND ACCRUAL COMPONENTS OF EARNINGS	Financial Accounting Archival - Primary Accruals 112
VIJAYAKUMAR, JAYARAMAN	PHD 1990 UNIVERSITY OF PITTSBURGH PATTON, JAMES	AN EMPIRICAL ANALYSIS OF THE FACTORS INFLUENCING CALL DECISIONS CONCERNING LOCAL GOVERNMENT BONDS	Not-for-Profit Governmental 165
VIJAYAN, ANIL KUMAR	PHD 1993 RUTGERS THE STATE UNIVERSITY OF NEW JERSEY - NEWARK MENSAH, YAW M.	CREDIT LOSS DISCLOSURE IN FAS #105 (EMPHASIS ON SWAPS) AND ITS TREATMENT IN RISK-BASED CAPITAL: AN EMPIRICAL ANALYSIS OF SIMILAR CREDIT LOSSES AND ITS DECISION USEFULNESS IN A BANK'S CREDIT RATING	Financial Accounting Archival - Primary Industry - Banking/Savings & Loan 203
VILLADSEN, BENTE	PHD 1994 YALE UNIVERSITY DEMSKI, JOEL S.	COLLUSION: EFFECTS ON INTERNAL CONTROL	Cost/Managerial Analytical - Internal Agency Theory 202
VILLAIRE, SONJA ANN SANDERS	EDD 1991 THE COLLEGE OF WILLIAM AND MARY RIES, ROGER R.	A CASE STUDY OF THE PREDICTIVE ABILITY OF PLACEMENT TESTS FOR PRINCIPLES OF ACCOUNTING	Education Case Academic Achievement 114
VIOLETTE, GEORGE R.	PHD 1987 ARIZONA STATE UNIVERSITY	THE DETERRENCE EFFECTS OF SANCTION COMMUNICATIONS ON TAXPAYER LEVEL OF INCOME TAX COMPLIANCE	Taxation Experimental Tax Compliance 108
VOGEL, THOMAS JOSEPH	PHD 1993 THE PENNSYLVANIA STATE UNIVERSITY CURLEY, ANTHONY J.	MONITORING NORMATIVE CORPORATE DECISIONS: A RECONCILIATION OF FINANCIAL AND ACCOUNTING CRITERIA	Financial Accounting Archival - Primary Financial Ratios 99
VOLK, GARY A.	PHD 1986 THE UNIVERSITY OF NEBRASKA - LINCOLN	A REEXAMINATION OF ACCOUNTING FOR STOCK DIVIDENDS: IS IT TIME FOR A CHANGE?	Financial Accounting Archival - Primary Dividends 133

Author	Degree & Date / School / Advisor	Title	Functional Area / Research Method / Topic / pages
VOLK, GERRIT JURGEN	DRERPOL 1989 FERNUNIVERSITAET-GES AMTHOCHSCHULE-HAGEN (GERMANY) SCHNEEL, DIETER	JAHRESABSCHLUSS UND INFORMATION: ZUR FORMALEN STRUKTUR DES JAHRESABSCHLUSSES EINER KAPITALGESELLSCHAFT	Financial Accounting Analytical - Internal International/Global Issues 287
VOLLMERS, GLORIA LUCEY	PHD 1994 UNIVERSITY OF NORTH TEXAS MERINO, BARBARA	AN ANALYSIS OF THE COST ACCOUNTING LITERATURE OF THE UNITED STATES FROM 1925 TO 1950	Cost/Managerial Archival - Secondary History 307
VREELAND, JANNET MARGARET	PHD 1993 TEXAS A&M UNIVERSITY STRAWSER, ROBERT H.	AN INVESTIGATION OF DISCLOSURE PRACTICES OF PRIVATE FIRMS	Financial Accounting Archival - Primary Disclosures 102
WACKER, RAYMOND FRANCIS	PHD 1989 UNIVERSITY OF HOUSTON HOFFMAN, WILLIAM H. JR.	THE EFFECTS OF INTERNATIONAL TAX TREATIES ON THE LOCATION OF U.S. MANUFACTURING DIRECT INVESTMENT ABROAD IN LESS-DEVELOPED NATIONS: A PANEL MODEL ANALYSIS	Taxation Archival - Primary International/Global Issues 226
WADHWA, DARSHAN L.	DBA 1988 LOUISIANA TECH UNIVERSITY	PERCEPTIONS OF CPAS REGARDING THE IMPACT OF THE ECONOMIC RECOVERY TAX ACT OF 1981 AND THE TAX REFORM ACT OF 1986 ON THE DOLLAR-VALUE LIFO INVENTORY METHOD FOR SMALL BUSINESSES	Taxation Survey Small Business 200
WAGGONER, JERI BROCKETT	PHD 1986 UNIVERSITY OF CINCINNATI	NONSAMPLING RISK: AUDITOR DETECTION OF COMPLIANCE DEVIATIONS	Auditing Experimental Risk 141
WAHLEN, JAMES MICHAEL	PHD 1991 THE UNIVERSITY OF MICHIGAN BERNARD, VICTOR L.	THE NATURE OF INFORMATION IN COMMERCIAL BANK LOAN LOSS DISCLOSURES	Financial Accounting Archival - Primary Industry - Banking/Savings & Loan 136
WALDEN, W. DARRELL	PHD 1993 VIRGINIA COMMONWEALTH UNIVERSITY SCHWARTZ, BILL N.	AN EMPIRICAL INVESTIGATION OF ENVIRONMENTAL DISCLOSURES ANALYZING REACTIONS TO PUBLIC POLICY AND REGULATOR EFFECTS	Financial Accounting Archival - Primary Social/Environmental Responsibility 206
WALDRON, MARILYN A.	DBA 1988 LOUISIANA TECH UNIVERSITY	A COMPARATIVE ANALYSIS OF ACCRUAL AND CASH BASIS ACCOUNTING IN PREDICTING CASH FLOWS FROM OPERATIONS IN THE OIL AND GAS INDUSTRY	Financial Accounting Archival - Primary Cash Flows 127

Listing by Author

Author	Degree & Date School Advisor	Title	Functional Area Research Method Topic pages
WALKER, KENTON BLAIR	PHD 1986 TEXAS A&M UNIVERSITY	AN EMPIRICAL FIELD STUDY OF STATISTICAL AND MANAGEMENT PREDICTION MODELS AND THE EFFECTS OF A BUDGET-BASED INCENTIVE PROGRAM	Cost/Managerial Case Incentive Compensation 136
WALKER, LOUELLA	PHD 1986 UNIVERSITY OF ARKANSAS	EMPIRICAL TESTS OF AN EXPLANATORY MODEL OF PERFORMANCE IN INTERMEDIATE ACCOUNTING I	Education Survey Academic Achievement 178
WALKER, ROBERT ATKINS	PHD 1991 THE UNIVERSITY OF TEXAS AT AUSTIN JONES, SALLY MORROW	DO TAXES MATTER? THE CASE OF THE PROPERTY-CASUALTY INSURANCE INDUSTRY	Taxation Archival - Primary Industry - Insurance 284
WALLACE, REGINALD SYLVANUS	PHD 1987 UNIVERSITY OF EXETER (UNITED KINGDOM)	DISCLOSURE OF ACCOUNTING INFORMATION IN DEVELOPING COUNTRIES: A CASE STUDY OF NIGERIA	General Case International/Global Issues 808
WALLIN, DAVID ERNEST	PHD 1990 THE UNIVERSITY OF ARIZONA WALLER, WILLIAM S.	ALTERNATIVE ECONOMIC INSTITUTIONS TO MOTIVATE MANAGERIAL DISCLOSURE OF PRIVATE INFORMATION: AN EXPERIMENTAL MARKETS EXAMINATION	General Experimental Accounting in Society 180
WALO, JUDITH CHRISTINA	PHD 1990 MICHIGAN STATE UNIVERSITY	LABORATORY STUDY OF THE EFFECTS OF AUDITOR'S BUSINESS RISK ON AUDIT SCOPE	Auditing Experimental Risk 248
WALTER, RICHARD M.	PHD 1988 THE UNIVERSITY OF TENNESSEE HERRING, HARTWELL C. III	A COMPARISON OF THE USEFULNESS OF CURRENT COST, CONSTANT DOLLAR, AND HISTORICAL COST INFORMATION FOR IDENTIFYING TAKEOVER TARGETS	Financial Accounting Case Inflation 169
WALTERS-YORK, L. MELISSA	PHD 1993 UNIVERSITY OF CENTRAL FLORIDA BAILEY, CHARLES D.	PATTERN PERCEPTIVENESS AND ACQUISITION OF ACCOUNTING SKILLS	General Experimental Judgment & Decision Making - Cognitive Processes 163
WALTON, KAREN SCHUELE	PHD 1991 KENT STATE UNIVERSITY ALAM, PERVAIZ; FETYKO, DAVID	THE DEBT/EQUITY CHOICE WITH ASYMMETRIC INFORMATION: AN EMPIRICAL STUDY	Financial Accounting Archival - Primary Capital Structure 180

Listing by Author

Author	Degree & Date School Advisor	Title	Functional Area Research Method Topic pages
WAMBSGANSS, JACOB R.	PHD 1985 THE UNIVERSITY OF NEBRASKA - LINCOLN	THE SIGNIFICANCE OF HUMAN RESOURCE ACCOUNTING	Cost/Managerial Other 151
WAMPLER, BRUCE M.	DBA 1994 LOUISIANA TECH UNIVERSITY	THE RELATIONSHIP BETWEEN EQUITY VALUES AND THE COMPONENTS OF UNRECORDED PENSION ASSETS AND LIABILITIES	Financial Accounting Archival - Primary Post Retirement Benefit Issues 126
WANG, SHIING-WU	PHD 1988 THE UNIVERSITY OF MICHIGAN (0127) KENNEY, WILLIAM JR.	FIRM SIZE AND TAX RATES RELATION: AN APPROPRIATE TEST OF FIRMS' POLITICAL SUCCESS?	Taxation Archival - Primary Corporate Taxation 129
WANG, YI-HSIN	PHD 1991 UNIVERSITY OF KENTUCKY MADDEN, DONALD L.; KELLER, STUART B.	AN EXPLORATORY EMPIRICAL INVESTIGATION OF RELATIONSHIPS BETWEEN CHANGES IN CATALYST FINANCIAL COMMITMENTS AND CHANGES IN PRODUCTIVITY AND PROFITABILITY IN SELECTED UNITED STATES MANUFACTURING INDUSTRIES AND COMPANIES	Cost/Managerial Archival - Primary Management Control Systems 169
WANG, ZHEMIN	PHD 1991 THE UNIVERSITY OF WISCONSIN - MADISON WILLIAMS, THOMAS H.	INFORMATIVENESS AND PREDICTABILITY OF EARNINGS AND CASH FLOWS	Financial Accounting Archival - Primary Cash Flows 113
WARD, TERRY JOE	PHD 1991 THE UNIVERSITY OF TENNESSEE WILLIAMS, JAN R.	FINANCIAL DISTRESS: AN EVALUATION OF THE PREDICTIVE POWER OF ACCRUAL AND CASH FLOW INFORMATION USING ORDINAL MULTI-STATE PREDICTION MODELS	Financial Accounting Archival - Primary Financial Distress or Bankruptcy 205
WARDLOW, PENELOPE S.	PHD 1985 UNIVERSITY OF GEORGIA	TOWARDS BUILDING A CONCEPTUAL FRAMEWORK OF FINANCIALREPORTING FOR STATE AND LOCAL GOVERNMENT DEFINED-BENEFIT PENSION PLANS	Not-for-Profit Post Retirement Benefit Issues 398
WARFIELD, TERRY DEE	PHD 1989 THE UNIVERSITY OF IOWA LINSMEIER, THOMAS J.	THE EFFECTS OF ACCOUNTING DISCLOSURES ON BANK INFORMATION ENVIRONMENTS	General Archival - Primary Industry - Banking/Savings & Loan 100
WARTICK, MARTHA LORRAINE	PHD 1991 THE PENNSYLVANIA STATE UNIVERSITY MILLIRON, VALERIE C.	THE EFFECT OF KNOWLEDGE OF LEGISLATIVE INTENT ON TAXPAYER PERCEPTIONS OF FAIRNESS	Taxation Experimental Tax Compliance 426

Author	Degree & Date School Advisor	Title	Functional Area Research Method Topic pages
WASLEY, CHARLES EDWARD	PHD 1987 THE UNIVERSITY OF IOWA	DIFFERENTIAL INFORMATION CONTENT OF EARNINGS ANNOUNCEMENTS: THEORETICAL AND EMPIRICAL ANALYSIS OF THE ROLE OF INFORMATION TRANSFERS	Financial Accounting Archival - Primary Information Transfer 117
WATANABE, JUDITH ELLEN	PHD 1985 THE UNIVERSITY OF NEBRASKA - LINCOLN	INDEXATION OF CAPITAL GAINS AND LOSSES: A COMPLEXITY STUDY	Taxation Experimental Individual Taxation 174
WATERS, BRENDA NELL	DBA 1993 LOUISIANA TECH UNIVERSITY	THE IMPACT OF INFORMATION AND PERSONALITY CHARACTERISTICS ON THE LENDING DECISION	Financial Accounting Experimental Bank Loan Officers 245
WATERS, JOHN MILBOURNE, II	PHD 1988 THE UNIVERSITY OF TENNESSEE HERRING, HARTWELL C. III	AN EMPIRICAL ASSESSMENT OF ATTITUDES TOWARD AUDIT OPINIONS AND ATTITUDES TOWARD AUDIT REPORTING	Auditing Survey Audit Opinion 245
WATTERS, MICHAEL PAUL	DBA 1989 MISSISSIPPI STATE UNIVERSITY DAUGHTREY, ZOEL W.	ACCOUNTING AND REPORTING PRACTICES OF MISSISSIPPI CATFISH PRODUCERS: AN EMPIRICAL STUDY	General Survey Industry - Agricultural 151
WATTS, SUSAN GAIL	PHD 1990 THE UNIVERSITY OF IOWA COLLINS, DANIEL W.	MARKET MICROSTRUCTURE AND THE TIMING OF EARNINGS RELEASES: AN EMPIRICAL ANALYSIS	Financial Accounting Archival - Primary Market Microstructure 107
WEBB, JUDITH L.	PHD 1989 UNIVERSITY OF WASHINGTON SUNDEM, GARY	TRANSACTION COSTS AND CONTROL SYSTEM CHOICE IN MULTINATIONAL ENTERPRISES: AN EMPIRICAL TEST	Cost/Managerial Survey Management Control Systems 155
WEBER, SANDRA LEE LIGON	PHD 1990 UNIVERSITY OF MISSOURI - COLUMBIA STEWART, JENICE P.	THE IMPACT OF THE FINANCIAL CONDITION OF THE FIRM ON THE ACCURACY OF ANNUAL EARNINGS FORECASTS	Financial Accounting Archival - Primary Forecasting Financial Performance 172
WEBSTER, ROBERT LEE	DBA 1993 LOUISIANA TECH UNIVERSITY	THE EFFECTS OF MANAGERIAL FINANCIAL FORECASTS ON USER PERCEPTIONS RELATING TO FINANCIAL STRENGTH OF PUBLIC UTILITY COMPANIES	Financial Accounting Experimental Forecasting Financial Performance 214

Author	Degree & Date School Advisor	Title	Functional Area Research Method Topic pages
WEIDA, NANCY COUGHLIN	PHD 1988 UNIVERSITY OF DELAWARE BROWN, PAMELA C.	GAME-THEORETIC MODELS OF THE TRANSFER PRICING PROBLEM	Cost/Managerial Analytical - Internal Transfer Pricing 215
WEINSTEIN, GERALD PAUL	PHD 1990 KENT STATE UNIVERSITY FETYKO, DAVID; ALAM, PERVAIZ	AN EMPIRICAL INVESTIGATION OF DIVESTITURE ANNOUNCEMENTS: THE SOUTH AFRICA EFFECT	Financial Accounting Archival - Primary Information Content 203
WEISEL, JAMES ALLEN	DBA 1991 UNIVERSITY OF KENTUCKY MADDEN, DONALD L.; KELLER, STUART B.	AN EMPIRICAL MODEL FOR CLASSIFYING AND PREDICTING THE FINANCIAL PERFORMANCE OF FEDERALLY INSURED SAVINGS ASSOCIATIONS	Financial Accounting Archival - Primary Industry - Banking/Savings & Loan 178
WEISENFELD, LESLIE WIGHT	PHD 1987 VIRGINIA POLYTECHNIC INSTITUTE AND STATE UNIVERSITY	EXAMINING THE EFFECT OF EVALUATING PERFORMANCE WITH PERFORMANCE REPORT VARIANCES ON REPORTED PERFORMANCE: A FIELD RESEARCH APPROACH	Cost/Managerial Case Standard Costs & Variance Analysis 292
WEISFELDER, CHRISTINE J.	PHD 1991 THE UNIVERSITY OF MICHIGAN DUFEY, GUNTER	LINKAGES BETWEEN TAX SYSTEMS: AN ANALYSIS OF THE CORPORATE TAX CONSEQUENCES OF TRANSFERRING ROYALTIES, INTEREST AND DIVIDENDS BETWEEN GERMANY, JAPAN AND THE UNITED STATES	Taxation Simulation International/Global Issues 295
WEISS, LAWRENCE ALAN	DBA 1989 HARVARD UNIVERSITY	BANKRUPTCY: THE EXPERIENCE OF NYSE AND ASE FIRMS--1980-1986	Financial Accounting Archival - Primary Financial Distress or Bankruptcy 190
WELCH, JUDITH KAYE	PHD 1985 THE FLORIDA STATE UNIVERSITY	AUDITOR INTERPRETATIONS OF AUDIT EVIDENCE: AN INFORMATIONAL ATTRIBUTE APPROACH	Auditing Experimental Judgment & Decision Making 96
WELCH, SANDRA THOMAS	PHD 1991 TEXAS A&M UNIVERSITY STRAWSER, ROBERT H.	AN INVESTIGATION OF THE DECISION REVISION PROCESS: DEFENSE CONTRACT AUDIT AGENCY AUDITORS DETERMINING THE EXISTENCE OF DEFECTIVE PRICING IN FIXED PRICE CONTRACTS	Auditing Experimental Judgment & Decision Making - Heuristics & Biases 228
WELD, LEONARD GREER	PHD 1989 TEXAS A&M UNIVERSITY CRUMBLEY, D. LARRY	AN EMPIRICAL STUDY OF THE EFFECT OF THE TAX REFORM ACT OF 1986 LOAN LOSS RESERVE REPEAL ON BANK LOAN CHARGE-OFFS	Taxation Archival - Primary Industry - Banking/Savings & Loan 154

Author	Degree & Date School Advisor	Title	Functional Area Research Method Topic pages
WELKER, DONNA-LYNN	PHD 1985 TEXAS A&M UNIVERSITY	BACKGROUND FACTORS AND THE ANCHORING AND ADJUSTMENT HEURISTIC: AN EMPIRICAL INVESTIGATION	Auditing Experimental Judgment & Decision Making - Heuristics & Biases 174
WELKER, MICHAEL ALAN	PHD 1993 THE UNIVERSITY OF IOWA COLLINS, DANIEL W.	DISCLOSURE POLICY, INFORMATION ASYMMETRY, LIQUIDITY AND THE COST OF EQUITY CAPITAL: A THEORETICAL AND EMPIRICAL INVESTIGATION	Financial Accounting Archival - Primary Disclosures 130
WELLS, DONALD WAYNE	PHD 1993 TEXAS A&M UNIVERSITY STRAWSER, ROBERT H.	THE MARKET EFFECTS OF AUDITOR RESIGNATIONS	Auditing Archival - Primary Auditor Changes 84
WELLS, STEVE CARROLL	PHD 1994 THE UNIVERSITY OF MISSISSIPPI WALLACE, WILLIAM D.	AN EMPIRICAL STUDY OF THE EFFECT OF VALUE-ADDED TAX FORM ON REVENUE VOLATILITY	Taxation Archival - Primary State Taxation 228
WELSH, MARY JEANNE	PHD 1987 THE LOUISIANA STATE UNIVERSITY AND AGRICULTURAL AND MECHANICAL COL.	AN EXPERIMENTAL RESEARCH STUDY ON THE EFFECT OF RECOGNITION AND DISCLOSURE OF CORPORATE PENSION PLAN ASSETS AND OBLIGATIONS ON INVESTMENT DECISIONS	Financial Accounting Experimental Post Retirement Benefit Issues 198
WENZEL, LOREN ALVIN	DBA 1990 MEMPHIS STATE UNIVERSITY AGRAWAL, SURENDRA P.	THE PREDICTIVE ABILITY OF QUARTERLY ACCRUAL AND CASH FLOW VARIABLES: A MULTIPLE TIME SERIES APPROACH	Financial Accounting Archival - Primary Forecasting Financial Performance 181
WERTHEIM, PAUL	PHD 1987 UNIVERSITY OF KANSAS	AN EMPIRICAL ANALYSIS OF CURRENT STATE TRENDING FORMULAS	Taxation State Taxation 218
WEST, TIMOTHY DAVID	PHD 1993 THE UNIVERSITY OF TENNESSEE ROTH, HAROLD P.	EXTERNAL AUDITORS' RISK ASSESSMENT DECISIONS: THE IMPACT OF IMPLEMENTING ACTIVITY-BASED COSTING	Auditing Experimental Activity Based Costing 190
WESTBROOK, LESTER CURTIS, JR.	PHD 1992 UNIVERSITY OF GEORGIA CLARK, RONALD L.	THE USE OF FINANCIAL AND NONFINANCIAL INFORMATION FOR PERFORMANCE EVALUATION OF SEGMENTS AND MANAGERS IN DECENTRALIZED MANUFACTURING COMPANIES: A CONTINGENCY APPROACH	Cost/Managerial Survey Performance Evaluation/Measurement 132

Author	Degree & Date School Advisor	Title	Functional Area Research Method Topic pages
WESTLAND, JAMES CHRISTOPHER	PHD 1987 THE UNIVERSITY OF MICHIGAN	SEMANTIC NETWORKS: A STOCHASTIC MODEL OF THEIR PERFORMANCE IN INFORMATION RETRIEVAL	Information Systems Decision Support Systems 259
WESTORT, PETER JOSEPH	PHD 1990 UNIVERSITY OF OREGON O'KEEFE, TERRENCE B.; KING, RAYMOND D.	INVESTMENTS IN HUMAN CAPITAL BY ACCOUNTANTS IN PUBLIC PRACTICE	Education Survey Continuing Education 177
WESTPHAL, CATHERINE MARGARET	PHD 1987 UNIVERSITY OF ILLINOIS AT URBANA-CHAMPAIGN	A PROJECT-BASED ANALYSIS OF THE EFFECTS OF FEDERAL TAX CREDITS ON HISTORIC REHABILITATION	Taxation Archival - Primary Other 190
WEYNS, GUY JOSEPH	PHD 1993 STANFORD UNIVERSITY MELUMAD, NAHUM	ANALYTICAL ESSAYS ON THE ECONOMIC CONSEQUENCES OF FINANCIAL ACCOUNTING STANDARDS	Financial Accounting Analytical - Internal Standard Setting 113
WHEELER, STEPHEN W.	PHD 1988 ARIZONA STATE UNIVERSITY	ASSESSING THE PERFORMANCE OF ANALYTICAL PROCEDURES: A BEST CASE SCENARIO	Auditing Case Analytical Review 122
WHELAN, ADELAIDE KATE	PHD 1990 CITY UNIVERSITY OF NEW YORK PASTENA, VICTOR	STOCK DIVIDENDS: MARKET REACTIONS AND MOTIVATIONS	Financial Accounting Archival - Primary Dividends 111
WHITE, GWENDOLEN BARNETT	PHD 1989 INDIANA UNIVERSITY HEINTZ, JAMES A.	AUDITORS' HYPOTHESIS GENERATION SKILLS: THE INFLUENCE OF EXPERIENCE AND AUDIT METHODOLOGY STRUCTURE	Auditing Experimental Audit Structure 143
WHITE, STEVEN DALE	PHD 1988 UNIVERSITY OF ARKANSAS	AN EMPIRICAL STUDY OF THE USER SATISFACTION OF ACCOUNTANTS WITH THE SOFTWARE MAINTENANCE FUNCTION	Information Systems Survey Systems Design &/or Development 174
WHITECOTTON, STACEY MARIE	PHD 1993 THE UNIVERSITY OF OKLAHOMA BUTLER, STEPHEN	DECISION AID RELIANCE AS A DETERMINANT OF ACCURACY IN EARNINGS FORECASTING JUDGMENTS: THE IMPACT OF CONTEXTUAL AND DECISION MAKER CHARACTERISTICS	General Experimental Decision Aids 144

Listing by Author

Author	Degree & Date School Advisor	Title	Functional Area Research Method Topic pages
WHITTEN, RUTH ANN	PHD 1993 UNIVERSITY OF WASHINGTON SUNDEM, GARY	CONTRACTS, RISK AND INFORMATION ASYMMETRY	General Analytical - Internal Agency Theory 53
WICK, MADALYN HELEN	PHD 1993 THE UNIVERSITY OF NEBRASKA - LINCOLN BALKE, THOMAS E.	AN EMPIRICAL STUDY OF DETERMINANTS OF CASH FLOW RESPONSE COEFFICIENTS	Financial Accounting Archival - Primary Cash Flows 155
WIEDMAN, CHRISTINE INGEBORG	PHD 1994 CORNELL UNIVERSITY ELLIOTT, JOHN A.	PROXIES FOR EARNINGS EXPECTATIONS: THE ROLE OF LOSS FUNCTIONS	Financial Accounting Archival - Primary Forecasting Financial Performance 159
WIER, BENSON	PHD 1993 TEXAS TECH UNIVERSITY FINN, DON W.	THE EFFECTS OF TASK RELEVANT KNOWLEDGE, GOAL LEVEL, GOAL COMMITMENT, AND MOTIVATION ON THE PARTICIPATION-PERFORMANCE LINKAGE: AN EMPIRICAL EXAMINATION	Cost/Managerial Experimental Budgeting 153
WIER, HEATHER ANN	PHD 1994 CORNELL UNIVERSITY SHAW, WAYNE	THE EFFECT OF SFAS 94 ON INVESTOR RISK ASSESSMENTS AND MANAGEMENT ACTIVITIES	Financial Accounting Archival - Primary Standard Setting 132
WIEST, DAVID NEVIN	PHD 1992 THE UNIVERSITY OF NORTH CAROLINA AT CHAPEL HILL BLOCHER, EDWARD J.	THE EFFECT OF SEC SANCTIONS ON AUDITOR SWITCHES	Auditing Archival - Primary Auditor Changes 163
WILBURN, NANCY LOU	PHD 1987 TEXAS A&M UNIVERSITY	AN EMPIRICAL ANALYSIS OF THE RELATIVE POWER OF CONSTITUENTS PARTICIPATING IN THE STANDARD-SETTING PROCESS OF THE FINANCIAL ACCOUNTING STANDARDS BOARD: EMPLOYERS' ACCOUNTING FOR PENSIONS	Financial Accounting Archival - Secondary Standard Setting 232
WILCZAK, MONIKA J.	PHD 1991 NEW YORK UNIVERSITY, GRADUATE SCHOOL OF BUSINESS ADMINISTRATION PADBERG, MANFRED	CONTRIBUTIONS TO THE CAPITAL BUDGETING PROBLEM	Cost/Managerial Analytical - Internal Capital Budgeting 168
WILDER, WALLACE MARK	PHD 1994 THE FLORIDA STATE UNIVERSITY LOREK, KENNETH S.	A MULTI-INDUSTRY ANALYSIS OF STRUCTURAL CHANGES AND EARNINGS FORECASTS	Financial Accounting Archival - Primary Forecasting Financial Performance 298

Author	Degree & Date School Advisor	Title	Functional Area Research Method Topic pages
WILLIAMS, JOANNE DEAHL	PHD 1987 TEXAS A&M UNIVERSITY	AN INVESTIGATION OF AUDITORS' DECISION PROCESSES IN A RISK ASSESSMENT DURING THE PLANNING STAGE OF AN AUDIT	Auditing Experimental Risk 225
WILLIAMS, JOHN RICHARD, SR.	PHD 1992 THE UNIVERSITY OF MISSISSIPPI GRAVES, O. FINLEY	THE IMPACT OF COMPANY-SPECIFIC VERSUS COUNTRY-SPECIFIC CHARACTERISTICS ON FINANCIAL ACCOUNTING DISCLOSURE: AN EMPIRICAL STUDY OF THIRTEEN COUNTRIES	Financial Accounting Case International/Global Issues 139
WILLIAMS, LOWELL KIM	DBA 1987 UNIVERSITY OF KENTUCKY	ACCOUNTING STANDARDS OVERLOAD: A DESCRIPTIVE MODEL FOR EVALUATING PERCEPTIONS OF ACCOUNTING STANDARDS	Financial Accounting Survey Standard Setting 136
WILLIAMS, PATRICIA ANN	DBA 1992 BOSTON UNIVERSITY BELL, PHILIP W.	THE EFFECT OF PRIOR FORECAST USEFULNESS ON USER REACTION TO A MANAGEMENT EARNINGS FORECAST	Financial Accounting Archival - Primary Voluntary Management Disclosures 213
WILLIAMS, RAY ELLIS	DBA 1987 MEMPHIS STATE UNIVERSITY AGRAWAL, SURENDRA P.	THE INFORMATIONAL CONTENT OF THE CURRENT MARKET VALUE OF LONG-TERM DEBT	Financial Accounting Archival - Primary Long Term Debt 96
WILLIS, DAVID MITCHELL	PHD 1992 UNIVERSITY OF CINCINNATI RICKETTS, DONALD E.	THE CHOICE OF COST SYSTEMS: A LABORATORY SIMULATION	Cost/Managerial Experimental Cost Systems 178
WILLITS, STEPHEN D.	PHD 1986 TEXAS TECH UNIVERSITY	PUBLIC EMPLOYEE RETIREMENT SYSTEM REPORTS: A STUDY OF USER INFORMATION PROCESSING ABILITY	General Experimental Judgment & Decision Making 197
WILSON, GORDON PETER	PHD 1985 CARNEGIE-MELLON UNIVERSITY	THE INCREMENTAL INFORMATION CONTENT OF ACCRUALS AND CASH FLOWS AFTER CONTROLLING FOR EARNINGS	Financial Accounting Archival - Primary Accruals 123
WILSON, PAULA ANNE	PHD 1989 UNIVERSITY OF WASHINGTON NOREEN, ERIC	CONTRACTING INCENTIVES OF MANAGERS' ADOPTION OF SFAS 87, 'EMPLOYERS' ACCOUNTING FOR PENSIONS'	Financial Accounting Accounting Choice 219

Author	Degree & Date School Advisor	Title	Functional Area Research Method Topic pages
WILSON, THOMAS E., JR.	PHD 1991 THE LOUISIANA STATE UNIVERSITY AND AGRICULTURAL AND MECHANICAL COL. APOSTOLOU, NICHOLAS G.	AN EXAMINATION OF AUDITOR CHANGES FOLLOWING EVENTS ADVERSELY AFFECTING EXTERNAL AUDITOR CREDIBILITY	Auditing Archival - Primary Auditor Changes 110
WINKLER, LESLIE ANN RICHESON	PHD 1989 TEXAS TECH UNIVERSITY ANDERSON, LANE K.	AN EMPIRICAL ANALYSIS OF THE EFFECTS OF STRUCTURE, BEHAVIOR, AND COMMUNICATION IN A JUST-IN-TIME RELATIONSHIP	Cost/Managerial Survey Inventory 161
WINTER, KENNETH	PHD 1988 THE UNIVERSITY OF WISCONSIN - MADISON WILLIAMS, THOMAS H.	THE EFFECT OF TASK DEMAND ON EXPERTS AND NONEXPERTS IN INTERNAL CONTROL EVALUATION	Auditing Experimental Judgment & Decision Making - Cognitive Processes 154
WITMER, PHILIP ROY	PHD 1993 THE GEORGE WASHINGTON UNIVERSITY	AUDITOR CHANGES AS OPPORTUNISTIC BEHAVIOR	Auditing Archival - Primary Auditor Changes 143
WOAN, RONALD JEN-JIN	PHD 1988 THE FLORIDA STATE UNIVERSITY LOREK, KENNETH STANLEY	THE IMPACT OF MEASUREMENT ERRORS AND MULTICOLLINEARITY ON THE STUDY OF THE RELATIONSHIP BETWEEN ACCOUNTING INFORMATION AND MARKET-DETERMINED RISKS	General Archival - Primary Risk 280
WOLCOTT, SUSAN KAY	PHD 1993 NORTHWESTERN UNIVERSITY MAGEE, ROBERT P.	THE EFFECTS OF PRIOR SHAREHOLDER ANTICIPATION AND RESTRUCTURING ACTIONS ON THE STOCK PRICE RESPONSE TO WRITEDOWN ANNOUNCEMENTS	Financial Accounting Archival - Primary Information Content 274
WOLK, CAREL MARIE	PHD 1992 UNIVERSITY OF MISSOURI - COLUMBIA NIKOLAI, LOREN A.	CAUSAL ATTRIBUTIONS FOR PERFORMANCE: IMPLICATIONS FOR AUDITOR TURNOVER	Auditing Survey Job Performance, Satisfaction &/or Turnover 232
WONG, JONATHAN WAITAK	PHD 1992 THE OHIO STATE UNIVERSITY BURNS, THOMAS J.	VALUATION RELEVANCE OF MARKET VALUE DISCLOSURES OF DEBT SECURITIES IN THE INSURANCE INDUSTRY	Financial Accounting Archival - Primary Industry - Insurance 105
WONG, TAK-JUN	PHD 1990 UNIVERSITY OF CALIFORNIA, LOS ANGELES MILLER, BRUCE L.; TEOH, SIEW HONG	ESSAYS ON THE DETERMINANTS OF THE RELATION BETWEEN STOCK PRICES AND ACCOUNTING EARNINGS	Financial Accounting Archival - Primary Earnings 132

Author	Degree & Date School Advisor	Title	Functional Area Research Method Topic pages
WONG, YUE KEE	PHD 1989 THE UNIVERSITY OF MICHIGAN SEVERANCE, DENNIS G.	COMPUTER-AIDED GROUP JUDGMENT: A STUDY OF GROUP DECISION SUPPORT SYSTEMS EFFECTIVENESS	Information systems Experimental Decision Support Systems 168
WONG-ON-WING, BERNARD	PHD 1986 ARIZONA STATE UNIVERSITY	AUDITOR'S PERCEPTION OF MANAGEMENT: ITS DETERMINANTS AND CONSEQUENCES	Auditing Experimental Judgment & Decision Making 107
WOOD, RAHNL ANTHONY	PHD 1993 SAINT LOUIS UNIVERSITY PHILIPICH, KIRK	AN EMPIRICAL STUDY OF THE ASSOCIATIONS AMONG CROSS-NATIONAL AUDIT CHARACTERISTICS AND ENVIRONMENTAL FACTORS	Auditing International/Global Issues 139
WOOD, ROYCE WILBURN, JR.	EDD 1989 THE UNIVERSITY OF ALABAMA BEACH, ROBERT H.	AN ANALYSIS OF SELECTED INTERNAL CONTROLS FOR FINANCIAL ACCOUNTING AT THE CENTRAL OFFICE LEVEL OF ALABAMA BOARDS OF EDUCATION	Not-for-Profit Survey Internal Control 211
WOODLOCK, PETER DAVID	PHD 1990 THE OHIO STATE UNIVERSITY BURNS, THOMAS J.	AUDITING AS THE OWNER'S RESPONSE TO THE NEED FOR RELIABLE MANAGER REPORTING: A PROBLEM OF SUPPLY AND DEMAND OF AUDIT SERVICES IN THE PRESENCE OF HIDDEN AUDITOR ACTIONS	Auditing Analytical - Internal Agency Theory 153
WRIGHT, DAVID WILLIAM	PHD 1986 MICHIGAN STATE UNIVERSITY	THE USE OF EMPIRICAL BAYES ESTIMATION IN AUDIT TESTING	Auditing Simulation Audit Sampling 224
WRIGHT, GAIL B.	DBA 1985 THE GEORGE WASHINGTON UNIVERSITY	ACCOUNTING ALTERNATIVES FOR COST RECOGNITION: AN EMPIRICAL ANALYSIS OF THE MATCHING PRINCIPLE EMPLOYED IN THE OIL-PRODUCING INDUSTRY	Financial Accounting Archival - Primary Accounting Choice 218
WRIGHT, SALLY	DBA 1993 BOSTON UNIVERSITY NANNI, ALFRED J. JR.	PARTICIPATIVE BUDGETING: AN EXAMINATION OF BUDGETARY SLACK AND MANAGERIAL PERFORMANCE OVER MULTIPLE PERIODS	Cost/Managerial Experimental Budgeting 180
WU, ANNE	PHD 1990 THE GEORGE WASHINGTON UNIVERSITY	THE DETERMINANTS OF VOLUNTARY RELEASE OF EARNINGS FORECASTS INFORMATION TO THE PUBLIC	Financial Accounting Archival - Primary Voluntary Management Disclosures 128

Author	Degree & Date School Advisor	Title	Functional Area Research Method Topic pages
WU, TSING TZAI	PHD 1988 CITY UNIVERSITY OF NEW YORK LILIEN, STEVEN B.	AN EXAMINATION OF THE MARKET REACTION TO THE ADOPTION OF SFAS NO.52: A NEW-INFORMATION-DE-FACTO APPROACH	Financial Accounting Archival - Primary Foreign Currency Translation 180
WU, YUWU	PHD 1992 NEW YORK UNIVERSITY, GRADUATE SCHOOL OF BUSINESS ADMINISTRATION LIVNAT, JOSHUA	MANAGEMENT BUYOUTS: A TEST OF THE MANAGEMENT MANIPULATION HYPOTHESIS	Financial Accounting Archival - Primary Earnings Management 75
WULSIN, FREDERICK ROELKER	DBA 1994 GOLDEN GATE UNIVERSITY TABARA, TATSUHIKO J.	AN INQUIRY INTO THE CAUSES OF AUDIT FAILURE	Auditing Survey Fraud 359
WURST, JOHN CHARLES	PHD 1987 UNIVERSITY OF GEORGIA NETER, JOHN; GODFREY, JAMES T.	AN INVESTIGATION OF THE SIEVE METHOD AND OF RECTIFICATION SAMPLING FOR AUDITING	Auditing Simulation Audit Sampling 380
WYATT, ROBERT LANE	PHD 1993 MEMPHIS STATE UNIVERSITY STEINBART, PAUL J.	THE EFFECT OF ELECTRONIC MEETING SYSTEMS ON GROUP PERFORMANCE: THE CASE OF THE BUDGETING DECISION	Cost/Managerial Experimental Budgeting 135
XIANG, BING	PHD 1991 UNIVERSITY OF ALBERTA (CANADA)	THE CHOICE OF RETURN-GENERATING MODELS IN EVENT STUDIES AND RATIONALITY OF VALUE LINE'S QUARTERLY EARNINGS FORECASTS	Financial Accounting Archival - Primary Forecasting Financial Performance 97
XIE, JIA-ZHENG (JAMES)	PHD 1991 THE UNIVERSITY OF BRITISH COLUMBIA (CANADA)	CONTRACT NEGOTIATION, INCOMPLETE CONTRACTING, AND ASYMMETRIC INFORMATION	Cost/Managerial Analytical - Internal Management Control Systems 274
YAHYAZADEH, MASOUD	PHD 1992 SYRACUSE UNIVERSITY ANDERSON, JOHN C.	THREE ESSAYS ON THE STRUCTURE OF AUDITING INDUSTRY, AUDITOR LIABILITY AND THE REGULATION OF AUDIT QUALITY	Auditing Analytical - Internal CPA Firm Issues 136
YAKHOU, MEHENNA	PHD 1985 UNIVERSITY OF CALIFORNIA, IRVINE	A COMPARATIVE STUDY OF THE ADOPTION PROCESS OF MANAGEMENT ACCOUNTING INNOVATIONS BY PUBLIC AND PRIVATE MANUFACTURING AND SERVICE ORGANIZATIONS IN FRANCE	Cost/Managerial Survey International/Global Issues 277

Author	Degree & Date School Advisor	Title	Functional Area Research Method Topic pages
YANCEY, WILLIAM FREDERICK	PHD 1993 THE UNIVERSITY OF TEXAS AT AUSTIN SMITH, J. REED	A MODEL OF ASSET RESTRUCTURING ANNOUNCEMENTS	Financial Accounting Analytical - Internal Agency Theory 184
YANG, BONG-JIN	PHD 1986 UNIVERSITY OF KANSAS	THE EFFECT OF THE FEDERAL RESERVE BOARD'S MARGIN CREDIT CONTROL ON THE DEALERS' BID-ASK SPREAD IN THE OTC STOCK MARKET	General Archival - Primary Capital Markets 127
YANG, DAVID CHIE-HWA	PHD 1985 COLUMBIA UNIVERSITY	THE ASSOCIATION BETWEEN SFAS 33 INFORMATION AND BOND RATINGS	Financial Accounting Archival - Primary Inflation 145
YARDLEY, JAMES A.	PHD 1986 UNIVERSITY OF ILLINOIS AT URBANA-CHAMPAIGN	LENDERS' AND ACCOUNTANTS' PERCEPTIONS OF THE INFORMATION RISK REDUCTION PROVIDED BY PRESCRIBED PROCEDURES	Financial Accounting Experimental Risk 183
YEATON, KATHRYN GIVENS	PHD 1994 UNIVERSITY OF SOUTH FLORIDA HOLSTRUM, GARY L.; GIFT, MICHAEL J.	AN INVESTIGATION OF THE IMPACT OF NON-ACCOUNTING INFORMATION (PLANT CLOSING ANNOUNCEMENTS) ON THE EXPECTATIONS OF FUTURE ACCOUNTING OUTCOMES	Financial Accounting Archival - Primary Information Content 193
YEH, SHU	PHD 1990 UNIVERSITY OF CALIFORNIA, LOS ANGELES LANDSMAN, WAYNE R.	LINE OF BUSINESS REPORTING, THE MARGINAL INFORMATION CONTENT OF EARNINGS ANNOUNCEMENTS, AND THE ACCURACY OF ANALYST EARNINGS FORECASTS	Financial Accounting Archival - Primary Segment Reporting 105
YEO, GILLIAN HIAN HENG	PHD 1990 UNIVERSITY OF ILLINOIS AT URBANA-CHAMPAIGN ZIEBART, DAVID A.	A FRAMEWORK TO ANALYZE MANAGEMENT'S VOLUNTARY FORECAST DISCLOSURE DECISIONS	Financial Accounting Archival - Primary Voluntary Management Disclosures 160
YEOM, SUNGSOO	PHD 1991 NEW YORK UNIVERSITY, GRADUATE SCHOOL OF BUSINESS ADMINISTRATION BALACHANDRAN, KASHI R.; RONEN, JOSHUA	THE ROLE OF TRANSFER PRICE FOR COORDINATION AND CONTROL WITHIN A FIRM	Cost/Managerial Analytical - Internal Transfer Pricing 104
YHIM, HARK-PPIN	DBA 1994 MISSISSIPPI STATE UNIVERSITY ADDY, NOEL D.	VOLUNTARY MANAGEMENT EARNINGS FORECASTS: AN ASSOCIATION BETWEEN DISCLOSURE LEVEL AND INFORMATION QUALITY	Financial Accounting Archival - Primary Forecasting Financial Performance 156

Listing by Author

Author	Degree & Date / School / Advisor	Title	Functional Area / Research Method / Topic / pages
YI, HWA DEUK	PHD 1994 / UNIVERSITY OF CALIFORNIA, LOS ANGELES / KIM, OLIVER; MILLER, BRUCE L.	MANAGEMENT EARNINGS FORECASTS: THE MARKET RESPONSE AND FIRMS' DISCLOSURE INCENTIVES	Financial Accounting / Archival - Primary / Voluntary Management Disclosures / 113
YI, JAEKYUNG	PHD 1992 / THE UNIVERSITY OF TEXAS AT AUSTIN / FREEMAN, ROBERT N.	THE EFFECT OF STOCK SPLITS ON THE REASSESSMENT OF EARNINGS PERSISTENCE	Financial Accounting / Archival - Primary / Forecasting Financial Performance / 115
YOHN, TERI LOMBARDI	PHD 1991 / INDIANA UNIVERSITY / SALAMON, GERALD L.	THE EFFECT OF THE EXISTENCE AND QUALITY OF EARNINGS DISCLOSURES ON BID-ASK SPREADS: THEORY AND EMPIRICAL EVIDENCE	Financial Accounting / Archival - Primary / Market Microstructure / 118
YOO, CHUNG EUL	PHD 1988 / PURDUE UNIVERSITY / ESKEW, ROBERT K.	THE INFORMATION CONTENT OF DISCONTINUED OPERATIONS ASSOCIATED WITH APB OPINION NO. 30	Financial Accounting / Archival - Primary / Information Content / 110
YOON, MYUNG-HO	PHD 1988 / UNIVERSITY OF HOUSTON / LIAO, WOODY M.	AN EXAMINATION OF THE EFFECT OF THE SAFE HARBOR RULE ON THE PREDICTION ERROR OF MANAGEMENT EARNINGS FORECASTS: SOME EMPIRICAL EVIDENCE	Financial Accounting / Archival - Primary / Voluntary Management Disclosures / 168
YOON, SOON SUK	PHD 1987 / THE UNIVERSITY OF WISCONSIN - MADISON	THE ECONOMIC CONSEQUENCES OF SFAS NO. 2: ITS IMPACT ON BUSINESS FIRMS AND INVESTORS	Financial Accounting / Archival - Primary / Research & Development / 119
YOON, SUNG SIG	PHD 1987 / UNIVERSITY OF CALIFORNIA, BERKELEY / SEN, PRADYOT K.	THE EFFECTS OF AUDITING ON MORAL HAZARD AND INFORMATION ASYMMETRIES	Auditing / Analytical - Internal / Agency Theory / 135
YOST, JEFFREY ALLAN	PHD 1989 / THE OHIO STATE UNIVERSITY / BURNS, THOMAS J.	INTRAFIRM RESOURCE ALLOCATION AND TRANSFER PRICING UNDER ASYMMETRIC INFORMATION: A PRINCIPAL-AGENT ANALYSIS OF DECENTRALIZED DECISION-MAKING IN A MULTIDIVISION FIRM	Cost/Managerial / Analytical - Internal / Transfer Pricing / 115
YOUNG, GAIL THIBAULT	DBA 1986 / THE GEORGE WASHINGTON UNIVERSITY	AN INVESTIGATION OF THE USEFULNESS OF THE FINANCIAL STATEMENTS AS SUPPLEMENTED BY OIL AND GAS PRODUCING ACTIVITIES DISCLOSURES	Financial Accounting / Survey / Industry - Oil & Gas / 534

Author	Degree & Date School Advisor	Title	Functional Area Research Method Topic pages
YOUNG, JAMES CHRISTIAN	PHD 1988 MICHIGAN STATE UNIVERSITY	FACTORS IN THE NONCOMPLIANCE DECISION: AN ANALYSIS OF MICHIGAN TAX AMNESTY PARTICIPANTS	Taxation Archival - Primary Tax Compliance 294
YOUNG, JONI J.	PHD 1991 UNIVERSITY OF ILLINOIS AT URBANA-CHAMPAIGN JOHNSON, O.	AGENDA FORMATION AND THE FINANCIAL ACCOUNTING STANDARDS BOARD	Financial Accounting Case Standard Setting 187
YOUNG, RONALD MAURICE	PHD 1992 TEXAS TECH UNIVERSITY SUTTON, STEVE G.	THE EFFECTS OF THE METHOD OF ALLOCATING SYSTEM COSTS ON THE INFORMATION SYSTEM	Cost/Managerial Survey Cost Allocation 167
YOUNG, SAUL DAVID	PHD 1985 UNIVERSITY OF VIRGINIA	AN ECONOMIC AND HISTORICAL ANALYSIS OF LICENSURE IN PUBLIC ACCOUNTANCY	General History 210
YU, PING KUEN	PHD 1992 THE UNIVERSITY OF TEXAS AT DALLAS GUISINGER, STEPHEN E.	TAX IMPACT ON U.S. FIRMS' CHOICE OF FOREIGN INCOME REMITTANCE METHODS: DIVIDENDS AND ROYALTIES	Taxation Archival - Primary International/Global Issues 129
YUEN, ALEXANDER E. C.	PHD 1989 GOLDEN GATE UNIVERSITY VINCENT, CHARLES F.	THE CALIFORNIA EXPERIENCE: AN EMPIRICAL STUDY OF THE USEFULNESS OF MUNICIPAL FINANCIAL REPORTS FOR NEWSPAPER REPORTERS	Not-for-Profit Survey Governmental 246
YUN, JOO-KWANG	PHD 1989 THE UNIVERSITY OF WISCONSIN - MADISON WILLIAMS, THOMAS H.	MEASURING RATES OF RETURN	Cost/Managerial Archival - Primary Capital Budgeting 240
YUNDT, CHARLES LEROY	PHD 1985 THE UNIVERSITY OF ALABAMA	FACTORS RELATING TO THE UNDERSTANDING OF COLLEGE AND UNIVERSITY FINANCIAL STATEMENTS FOR NONFINANCIAL UNIVERSITY PERSONNEL	Not-for-Profit College & University 158
YUTHAS, KRISTI JANE	PHD 1990 THE UNIVERSITY OF UTAH EINING, MARTHA M.	CONSTRUCT VALIDITY IN THE MEASUREMENT OF DECISION SUPPORT	Information Systems Experimental Decision Support Systems 207

Listing by Author

Author	Degree & Date School Advisor	Title	Functional Area Research Method Topic pages
ZAITEGI SARRIA, MIREN ITXASO	DR 1993 UNIVERSIDAD DEL PAIS VASCO/EUSKAL HERRIKO UNIBERTSITATEA (SPAIN)	ACCOUNTANT REFLECTIONS IN THE ASSUMPTION OF INSURED RISK [REFLEXIONES CONTABLES EN LA ASUNCION DEL RIESGO ASEGURADO]	General International/Global Issues 612
ZEBUN, ABDULWAHAB HAIDER	PHD 1988 UNIVERSITY OF HULL (UNITED KINGDOM)	LINKAGES BETWEEN MICROACCOUNTING AND MACROACCOUNTING: AN IRAQI CASE STUDY	General Analytical - Internal International/Global Issues 829
ZEKANY, KAY E.	PHD 1994 UNIVERSITY OF SOUTH CAROLINA LEITCH, ROBERT A.	THE INFORMATION CONTENT OF INVENTORY AND RECEIVABLES OF MERCHANDISERS	Financial Accounting Archival - Primary Accruals 145
ZELCER, MOISHE	PHD 1991 CITY UNIVERSITY OF NEW YORK PASTENA, VICTOR	MANAGEMENT BUYOUTS: THE MANAGEMENT/SHAREHOLDER CONFLICT	Financial Accounting Archival - Primary Other 113
ZELIN, ROBERT CLAYTON, II	PHD 1991 INDIANA UNIVERSITY TILLER, MIKEL G.	THE EFFECTS OF INDUSTRY DISTRIBUTIONAL INFORMATION ON AUDITORS' ANALYTICAL REVIEW INVESTIGATION PARAMETERS	Auditing Experimental Analytical Review 198
ZELLER, THOMAS LOUIS	PHD 1991 KENT STATE UNIVERSITY BROWN, RICHARD E.; FIGLEWICZ, RAYMOND E.	AN EMPIRICAL INVESTIGATION OF A NET OPERATING CASH FLOW RATE OF RETURN AS A PROXY MEASURE FOR FIRM ECONOMIC PERFORMANCE	Financial Accounting Archival - Primary Cash Flows 165
ZHANG, HUA	PHD 1993 MCGILL UNIVERSITY (CANADA) WHITMORE, G. A.	THE DYNAMIC BEHAVIOUR OF THE TERM STRUCTURE OF INTEREST RATES AND ITS IMPLICATION FOR INTEREST-RATE SENSITIVE ASSET PRICING	General Archival - Primary Other 164
ZIEGENFUSS, DOUGLAS EDWIN	PHD 1989 VIRGINIA COMMONWEALTH UNIVERSITY OLDS, PHILIP R.	AN EMPIRICAL INVESTIGATION OF THE EFFECTS OF QUALIFIED OPINIONS ON AUDIT FIRMS' GROWTH RATES AND LEGAL LIABILITY	Auditing Archival - Primary Audit Opinion 162
ZILL, SHARON	PHD 1991 THE UNIV. OF TEXAS H.S.C. AT HOUSTON SCH. OF PUBLIC HEALTH GRIMES, RICHARD E.	A STUDY IN NURSING HOME EFFECTIVENESS IN TEXAS	General Archival - Primary Industry - Health Care 83

Author	Degree & Date School Advisor	Title	Functional Area Research Method Topic pages
ZIMMERMANN, RAYMOND ARTHUR	PHD 1991 TEXAS TECH UNIVERSITY GATELY, MARY SUE	ALIMONY: AN EMPIRICAL ANALYSIS OF THE EFFECT ON TAX REVENUES AND EQUITY	Taxation Archival - Primary Public Policy 200
ZIV, AMIR	PHD 1990 STANFORD UNIVERSITY MELUMAD, NAHUM D.	INFORMATIONAL ISSUES IN ORGANIZATIONS	Cost/Managerial Analytical - Internal Agency Theory 103
ZUCCA, LINDA JEANNE	PHD 1989 CASE WESTERN RESERVE UNIVERSITY CAMPBELL, DAVID R.	AN EMPIRICAL STUDY OF FIRMS ENGAGING IN PARTIAL WRITEDOWNS OF LONG-LIVED ASSETS	Financial Accounting Archival - Primary Accounting Change 205

Dissertations
Listed
Alphabetically
by Topic

Academic Achievement

COKER, DIANNA ROSS	THE ROLE OF VISUAL-SPATIAL APTITUDE IN ACCOUNTING COURSEWORK
DENT D'ALMUANO, ROSELINE	TRANSFER STUDENTS' ACHIEVEMENT IN INTERMEDIATE ACCOUNTING: AN EMPIRICAL STUDY OF ARIZONA STATE UNIVERSITY STUDENTS
DICKEY, HAZEL VIRGINIA COLEMAN	RELATIONSHIP OF STUDENTS' PREPARATION AND PERCEPTIONS WITH FINAL GRADES IN PRINCIPLES OF ACCOUNTING I IN PUBLIC TWO-YEAR COLLEGES IN ARKANSAS
MANKO, KENNETH MICHAEL	THE RELATIONSHIP OF MEASURES OF SELF-CONCEPT AND ANXIETY TO ACADEMIC ACHIEVEMENT IN ACCOUNTING
RAMOS, VINCENT, JR.	EVALUATION OF THE IMPACT OF A 'SCHOOL WITHIN A SCHOOL'S ALTERNATIVE PROGRAM ON GRADES, ATTENDANCE, ACHIEVEMENT, AND SELF-CONCEPT BY ETHNIC GROUP
VILLAIRE, SONJA ANN SANDERS	A CASE STUDY OF THE PREDICTIVE ABILITY OF PLACEMENT TESTS FOR PRINCIPLES OF ACCOUNTING
WALKER, LOUELLA	EMPIRICAL TESTS OF AN EXPLANATORY MODEL OF PERFORMANCE IN INTERMEDIATE ACCOUNTING I

Academic Issues

BRICKER, ROBERT JAMES	AN EMPIRICAL INVESTIGATION OF THE INTELLECTUAL STRUCTURE OF THE ACCOUNTING DISCIPLINE: A CITATIONAL ANALYSIS OF SELECTED SCHOLARLY JOURNALS, 1983-1986
COOPER-FEDLER, PAMELA ANN	A CHARACTERIZATION AND ANALYSIS OF FACULTY ACTIVITY AND PRODUCTIVITY REPORTING SYSTEMS IN RESEARCH UNIVERSITIES
DANCER, WELDON TERRY	A STUDY OF THE ATTITUDES AND PERCEPTIONS OF MASTER'S LEVEL ACCOUNTING STUDENTS TOWARD A CAREER IN ACCOUNTING EDUCATION
ERIKSEN, SCOTT DOUGLAS	A CRITICAL INVESTIGATION OF POSITIVISM: ITS ADEQUACY AS AN APPROACH FOR ACCOUNTING RESEARCH
GEKAS, GEORGE ANDREW	ACCOUNTING EDUCATION AT DOCTORAL LEVEL: A CANADIAN PERSPECTIVE WITH SPECIAL REFERENCE TO THE DEMAND AND SUPPLY OF ACADEMIC ACCOUNTANTS
KENNEDY, DUANE BRIAN	CLASSIFICATION TECHNIQUES IN ACCOUNTING RESEARCH: EMPIRICAL EVIDENCE OF COMPARATIVE PERFORMANCE
STEWART, DANIEL VAN	A STUDY OF CHANGES IN ARTICLE PUBLICATION PRODUCTIVITY AMONG ACCOUNTING FACULTY PROMOTED DURING THE 1980'S

Accounting Career Issues

BEAN, LUANN G.	AN EXAMINATION OF STATUS-RISK AND PERSONALITY VARIABLES OF PRACTICING PUBLIC ACCOUNTANTS AND ACCOUNTING ACADEMICIANS AS EXPLANATIONS OF RECEPTIVITY/RESISTANCE TO INNOVATIONS
CHEW, ANDREW SWEE-CHUNG	A STRUCTURATIONAL ANALYSIS OF MANAGEMENT ACCOUNTING PRACTICE IN ITS ORGANISATIONAL CONTEXTS: A SOCIAL SCIENCE PERSPECTIVE
COLLINS, KAREN MARIE	A COMPREHENSIVE STUDY OF STRESS ON INDIVIDUALS IN MIDDLE-MANAGEMENT POSITIONS IN PUBLIC ACCOUNTING
DEUTSCH, ROBERT ALLEN	RECRUITING DECISIONS BY SELECTED BIG SIX CPA FIRMS: AN INVESTIGATION OF CHARACTERISTICS THAT INFLUENCE DECISIONS TO SELECT ACCOUNTING STUDENTS FOR OFFICE VISITS
DONABEDIAN, BAIRJ	STANDARD-SETTING IN CPA LICENSURE: A STUDY IN PROFESSIONAL SELF-REGULATION
FERN, RICHARD HULL	AN INQUIRY INTO THE ROLE OF THE CORPORATE CONTROLLER IN STRATEGIC PLANNING
FRENCH, GEORGE RICHARD	AN ANALYSIS OF THE INTERPERSONAL STYLE OF PERSONAL FINANCIAL PLANNERS (CPAS AND NONACCOUNTANTS) AND TRADITIONAL ACCOUNTANTS WITH IMPLICATIONS FOR THE ACCOUNTING PROFESSION

Listing by Topic 235

GABBIN, ALEXANDER L.	AN EMPIRICAL INVESTIGATION OF CANDIDATE ATTRIBUTES SIGNIFICANTLY AFFECTING RECRUITING OF ACCOUNTING GRADUATES BY A NATIONAL CPA FIRM
GERSICH, FRANK, III	AN INVESTIGATION OF THE IMPORTANCE OF SELECTED KNOWLEDGE AREAS AND SKILLS FOR A PUBLIC ACCOUNTING AUDITING CAREER AND THE EXTENT OF ACADEMIC PREPARATION AS PERCEIVED BY AUDIT SENIORS AND AUDIT MANAGERS
GONZALEZ, LUIS	LEVELS OF INFORMATION TECHNOLOGIES INTEGRATION AS FACTORS AFFECTING PERCEPTIONS OF JOB CHARACTERISTICS AND PROFESSIONALISM OF MANAGEMENT ACCOUNTANTS
HAMMOND, THERESA ANNE	THE MINORITY RECRUITMENT EFFORTS OF THE MAJOR PUBLIC ACCOUNTING FIRMS IN NEW YORK: A SOCIOLOGICAL ANALYSIS
HEIAN, JAMES BERNARD	A STUDY OF THE DETERMINANTS OF SENIOR CERTIFIED PUBLIC ACCOUNTANT LEADERSHIP EFFECTIVENESS
LILLIE, RICHARD EUGENE	AN ANALYSIS OF LEARNING STYLES OF PROFESSIONAL PERSONNEL BY LEVEL AND BY FUNCTION WITHIN A NATIONAL PUBLIC ACCOUNTING FIRM (ACCOUNTING EDUCATION)
MARTIN, LISA CLINE	AN EMPIRICAL INVESTIGATION OF THE JOB MOBILITY OF CERTIFIED PUBLIC ACCOUNTANTS WORKING IN INDUSTRY
NELSON, IRVIN TOM	IDENTIFYING AND RECRUITING FUTURE PROFESSIONALS: AN EMPIRICAL STUDY OF HIGHLY CAPABLE INDIVIDUALS' ATTITUDES TOWARD THE ACCOUNTING PROFESSION
RIORDAN, MICHAEL PATRICK	HOW COGNITIVE COMPLEXITY AFFECTS ACCOUNTING CAREER PATHS
SANDERS, JOSEPH CASH	A COMPREHENSIVE STUDY OF STRESS IN THE PUBLIC ACCOUNTING PROFESSION
SHOENTHAL, EDWARD ROBERT	AN INVESTIGATION OF THE HARMONY OF COMPETENCIES FOUND IN CERTIFIED AND CHARTERED ACCOUNTANTS IN THE UNITED STATES AND GREAT BRITAIN
SIEGEL, PHILIP HARRIS	ALTERNATIVE EDUCATIONAL PROGRAMS FOR ENTRY INTO THE PUBLIC ACCOUNTING PROFESSION: AN ANALYSIS

Accounting Change

ALCIATORE, MIMI LOUISE	THE INFORMATION CONTENT OF THE COMPONENTS OF THE CHANGE IN THE STANDARDIZED MEASURE
CHUNG, KUN YOUNG	FIRM SIZE, INDUSTRY ACCOUNTING NORMS, AND THE INFORMATION CONTENT OF ACCOUNTING CHANGE ANNOUNCEMENTS
DAVIS, KAREL ANN	AN EMPIRICAL INVESTIGATION OF THE STOCK MARKET'S RESPONSE TO CHANGES IN INVENTORY AND DEPRECIATION METHODS
EAKIN, CYNTHIA FIREY	ACCOUNTING CHANGES AND EARNINGS MANAGEMENT: EVIDENCE FROM THE EARLY ADOPTION OF SFAS NO. 96 'ACCOUNTING FOR INCOME
FINN, PHILIP MORTON	AN EXAMINATION OF THE MARKET REACTION TO A MANDATED ACCOUNTING CHANGE: THE CASE FOR THE COSTS OF COMPUTER SOFTWARE
FORT, CHARLES PATRICK	ANALYSTS' FORECAST ACCURACY AND THE PRESENTATION OF MANDATED ACCOUNTING CHANGES
FOSS, HELGA BERTA	THE EFFECT OF ACCOUNTING CHANGES AND TAX CONSEQUENCES ON INVESTOR BEHAVIOR
KHURANA, INDER KRISHAN	AN EMPIRICAL INVESTIGATION INTO THE SECURITY MARKET EFFECTS OF FASB STATEMENT NUMBER 94
KOPEL, ROANN RAE	VOLUNTARY CHANGES IN ACCOUNTING POLICIES: AN APPLICATION OF THE POSITIVE THEORY OF ACCOUNTING
LINDAHL, FREDERICK WILLIAM	QUANTAL CHOICE MODELS AND ACCOUNTING CHANGE

LINSMEIER, THOMAS J.	A DEBT COVENANT RATIONALE FOR A MARKET REACTION TO A MANDATED ACCOUNTING CHANGE: THE CASE OF THE INVESTMENT TAX CREDIT
MOHRMAN, MARY BETH	MANDATED ACCOUNTING CHANGES AND DEBT CONTRACTS
NA, IN-CHUL	INVESTORS' REACTION TO THE EFFECT OF STATEMENT OF FINANCIAL ACCOUNTING STANDARDS NO. 52 ON 1981 EARNINGS FOR THE EARLY ADOPTERS: AN EMPIRICAL STUDY
PASKIN, STEVEN	SOME ECONOMIC DETERMINANTS OF DISCRETIONARY ACCOUNTING CHANGES
RAVI, INDUMATHI	THE EFFECT OF A MANDATORY ACCOUNTING CHANGE ON EXECUTIVE COMPENSATION: THE CASE OF SFAS NO. 2
RUSBARSKY, MARK KEVIN	THE CHANGES IN ECONOMIC INCENTIVES WHICH MOTIVATE DISCRETIONARY ACCOUNTING CHANGES: THE CASE OF THE SWITCH TO, AND THEN FROM, ACCELERATED DEPRECIATION
SAILORS, JAMES FRANKLIN	AN INVESTIGATION OF THE STOCK MARKET REACTION TO A CHANGE IN ACCOUNTING METHODS
SOO, BILLY SY	MANAGERIAL RESPONSE TO MANDATORY ACCOUNTING PRINCIPLES: AN ACCRUALS PERSPECTIVE
ZUCCA, LINDA JEANNE	AN EMPIRICAL STUDY OF FIRMS ENGAGING IN PARTIAL WRITEDOWNS OF LONG-LIVED ASSETS

Accounting Choice

BERG, GARY GENE	EARLY VERSUS LATE COMPLIANCE TO SFAS 52: AN EMPIRICAL INVESTIGATION OF FIRM CHARACTERISTICS AND THE MARKET RESPONSE
BROWN, BETTY COFFEE	AN EMPIRICAL INVESTIGATION INTO DIFFERENCES BETWEEN COMPANIES THAT ELECTED AN EARLY COMPLIANCE WITH SFAS 52 AND COMPANIES NOT ELECTING AN EARLY COMPLIANCE
CAMPBELL, RONALD LOUIS	A CROSS-SECTIONAL AND TIME-SERIES INVESTIGATION OF MANAGERIAL DISCRETION REGARDING METHODS, RATES, PERIODS, AND DISCLOSURE: THE CASE OF EMPLOYERS' ACCOUNTING FOR PENSIONS
CASLAN, DAVID FREDERICK	AN EXAMINATION OF THE DETERMINANTS OF DISCRETIONARY ACCOUNTING CHOICE BY MANAGEMENT
CHESTER, MICHAEL CARTER, JR.	AN EMPIRICAL STUDY OF CORPORATE MANAGEMENT SUPPORT FOR PUSH DOWN ACCOUNTING
CHOI, YEONG CHAN	EARLY ADOPTION OF SFAS NO. 87 AND THE DEFENSIVE ACTION HYPOTHESIS: A POSITIVE THEORY ANALYSIS
CHUNG, TSAI-YEN	MANAGEMENT MOTIVATION FOR SELECTING ACCOUNTING PRINCIPLES: A MARKET-BASED EMPIRICAL INVESTIGATION
COWLING, JOHN FREDERICK	THE VARIATION OF ACCOUNTING INFORMATION FOR SEASONAL FIRMS ACROSS ALTERNATIVE FISCAL YEAR ENDS
CULLINAN, CHARLES P.	LABOR ORGANIZATION AND ACCOUNTING POLICY CHOICE: AN EMPIRICAL STUDY
DUKE, JOANNE CHRISTINE	DEBT COVENANT RESTRICTIONS AND ACCOUNTING TECHNIQUE CHOICE: AN EMPIRICAL STUDY
GODWIN, JOSEPH HUDSON	THE ECONOMIC DETERMINANTS OF ACCOUNTING CHOICE: THE CASE OF ACCOUNTING FOR PENSIONS
GUPTA, SANJAY	DETERMINANTS OF THE CHOICE BETWEEN COMPREHENSIVE AND PARTIAL INCOME TAX ALLOCATION: THE CASE OF THE DOMESTIC INTERNATIONAL SALES CORPORATION
HALL, STEVEN C.	ECONOMIC MOTIVATIONS FOR ACCOUNTING STRATEGY CHOICES

HARGADON, JOSEPH MICHAEL	ADOPTION CHOICE OF MANDATED ACCOUNTING CHANGES: A JOINT DECISION APPROACH
HARWOOD, ELAINE MARIE	ADOPTION OF REGULATORY ACCOUNTING PRINCIPLES BY STOCKHELD SAVINGS AND LOAN ASSOCIATIONS: AN EVENT STUDY OF DISCRETIONARY ACCOUNTING CHOICE
HOGAN, THOMAS JEFFERY	MANAGEMENT DECISIONS REGARDING CHOICES OF ACCOUNTING METHODS AND SUBMISSIONS TO THE FASB: AN EMPIRICAL STUDY OF FIRM CHARACTERISTICS
JONES, JENNIFER JEAN	THE EFFECT OF FOREIGN TRADE REGULATION ON ACCOUNTING CHOICES, AND PRODUCTION AND INVESTMENT DECISIONS
JUNG, WOON-OH	ACCOUNTING DECISIONS UNDER ASYMMETRIC INFORMATION
KANDIEL, EL-SAYED HUSSEIN AHMED	ACCOUNTING FOR INTERNALLY DEVELOPED SOFTWARE COSTS: A POSITIVE APPROACH
KIM, KYUNGHO	THE EFFECT OF ACCOUNTING BASED BONUS PLAN INCENTIVES ON MANAGERS' FINANCIAL REPORTING BEHAVIOR AND ANALYSTS' FORECAST ACCURACY
KOCH, PAULA LOUISE	THE EFFECTS OF FINANCIAL DISTRESS ON ACCOUNTING METHOD CHOICE
KOH, SEUNGHEE	RATIONAL ACCOUNTING CHOICE UNDER INFORMATION ASYMMETRY: THE CASE OF INVENTORY ACCOUNTING
KWON, SOON-YONG	INCOME STRATEGY AND EARNINGS RESPONSE COEFFICIENTS
MCINNES, WILLIAM MCKENZIE	ACCOUNTING CHOICES AND REPORTED FINANCIAL PERFORMANCE: THE UNITED KINGDOM GAS INDUSTRY, 1970-1980. (VOLUMES I AND II)
MORRILL, CAMERON KEITH JOSEPH	CORPORATE LEADERS, FIRM PERFORMANCE AND ACCOUNTING EARNINGS
MOYER, SUSAN ELAINE	ACCOUNTING CHOICES IN COMMERCIAL BANKS
NELSON, TONI LYNNE	THE EFFECT OF ACCOUNTING POLICY CHOICES ON THE RELATIONSHIP BETWEEN EARNINGS AND RETURNS
OMER, THOMAS CLAYTON	ECONOMIC INCENTIVES AND ACCOUNTING POLICY CHOICES
PAK, HONG SEOK	THE EFFECTS OF INCOME SMOOTHING AND CONTRACTING COSTS ON MANAGERS' ATTITUDES TOWARDS THE SELECTION OF FOREIGN TRANSLATION ACCOUNTING PRINCIPLES: A STRUCTURAL EQUATION MODEL
PARK, GWANGHOON	THE ASSOCIATION BETWEEN MANAGEMENT COMPENSATION AND ACCOUNTING POLICY DECISIONS: AN EXTENSION OF THE BONUS HYPOTHESIS
POURJALALI, HAMID	AN IMPROVED TEST OF POSITIVE ACCOUNTING THEORY: EXAMINATION OF THE CHANGES IN THE AMOUNT OF ACCRUALS IN RESPONSE TO THE CHANGES IN CONTRACTING VARIABLES
RAGLAND, BERNARD GRAFTON	DEPRECIATION--CHOICE VARIABLE OR ONLY A MANAGEMENT CHOICE?
SHELTON, JAMES BLAIR	MANAGEMENT'S CHOICE OF ADOPTION DATE OF STATEMENT OF FINANCIAL ACCOUNTING STANDARDS NO. 95: A POSITIVE THEORY APPROACH
SHORNEY, MAYDA	AN EMPIRICAL INVESTIGATION OF THE EFFECT OF OWNERSHIP CONTROL ON THE CHOICE OF ACCOUNTING METHODS
SINGLETON, LARRY G.	A FIELD TEST OF THE PERCEPTIONS OF THE QUALITATIVE CHARACTERISTICS OF STATEMENT OF FINANCIAL ACCOUNTING CONCEPTS NO. 2 BY PRACTICING CPAS

Listing by Topic

SOLIMAN, MAHMOUD EL-SAYED	THE DETERMINANTS OF ACCOUNTING CHOICES BY SMALL FIRMS: AN EMPIRICAL INVESTIGATION
SWEENEY, AMY PATRICIA	DEBT-COVENANT VIOLATIONS AND MANAGERS' ACCOUNTING-CHOICE AND PRODUCTION-INVESTMENT DECISIONS
VERMA, KIRAN	EFFECTS OF ACCOUNTING TECHNIQUES ON THE STUDY OF MARKET POWER
WILSON, PAULA ANNE	CONTRACTING INCENTIVES OF MANAGERS' ADOPTION OF SFAS 87, 'EMPLOYERS' ACCOUNTING FOR PENSIONS'
WRIGHT, GAIL B.	ACCOUNTING ALTERNATIVES FOR COST RECOGNITION: AN EMPIRICAL ANALYSIS OF THE MATCHING PRINCIPLE EMPLOYED IN THE OIL-PRODUCING INDUSTRY

Accounting in Society

HARPER, RICHARD ROBERT	AN ETHNOGRAPHIC EXAMINATION OF ACCOUNTANCY
REYNOLDS, MARY ANN	AN EXAMINATION OF THE AUDIT FUNCTION IN SOCIETY
RUDD, TORE FLEMMING	AUDITING AS VERIFICATION OF FINANCIAL INFORMATION
WALLIN, DAVID ERNEST	ALTERNATIVE ECONOMIC INSTITUTIONS TO MOTIVATE MANAGERIAL DISCLOSURE OF PRIVATE INFORMATION: AN EXPERIMENTAL MARKETS EXAMINATION

Accruals

BAE, GIL SOO	FURTHER INVESTIGATION OF POSTANNOUNCEMENT DRIFTS ASSOCIATED WITH EARNINGS, CASH FLOWS, AND ACCRUAL ADJUSTMENTS
CHARITOU, ANDREAS G.	THE INFORMATION CONTENT OF ACCRUAL AND CASH FLOW MEASURES: A CROSS-SECTIONAL VALUATION STUDY
CHOI, KWAN	DETERMINANTS OF TIME SERIES PROPERTIES OF ANNUAL EARNINGS AND CASH FLOWS
COSTIGAN, MICHAEL LAWRENCE	THE MARGINAL PREDICTIVE ABILITY OF ACCRUAL ACCOUNTING INFORMATION WITH RESPECT TO FUTURE CASH FLOWS FROM OPERATIONS
DECHOW, PATRICIA MARY	ACCOUNTING EARNINGS AND CASH FLOWS AS MEASURES OF FIRM PERFORMANCE: THE ROLE OF ACCOUNTING ACCRUALS
ETHERIDGE, HARLAN LYNN	AN EXAMINATION OF SEMIOTIC THEORIES OF ACCOUNTING ACCRUALS
KIM, BYOUNG HO	THE ASSOCIATION BETWEEN UNEXPECTED CHANGES IN INVENTORY AND RECEIVABLE BALANCES AND SECURITY PRICE CHANGES: CROSS-SECTIONAL ANALYSES
RAYBURN, JUDY DAWSON	THE INCREMENTAL INFORMATION CONTENT OF ACCRUAL ACCOUNTING EARNINGS
SINHA, PRAVEEN	VALUATION RELEVANCE OF CASH FLOWS AND ACCRUALS
TODD, REBECCA	AN INVESTIGATION OF THE CASH FLOW PROPERTIES OF ACCRUAL ACCOUNTING DATA: A STRUCTURAL EQUATION APPROACH
VICKREY, DONN WILLIAM	THE INCREMENTAL INFORMATION PROVIDED BY DISCLOSING CASH FLOW AND ACCRUAL COMPONENTS OF EARNINGS
WILSON, GORDON PETER	THE INCREMENTAL INFORMATION CONTENT OF ACCRUALS AND CASH FLOWS AFTER CONTROLLING FOR EARNINGS

ZEKANY, KAY E.   THE INFORMATION CONTENT OF INVENTORY AND RECEIVABLES OF MERCHANDISERS

Activity Based Costing

ALBRIGHT, THOMAS LYNN   THE IMPACT OF PROCESS VARIATION ON UNIT MANUFACTURING COST

BOST, PATRICIA JAMES   MOVEMENT TOWARD UNIFORMITY IN THE DESIGN OF ABC SYSTEMS

GREENWOOD, THOMAS G.   AN ACTIVITY-BASED CONCEPTUAL MODEL FOR EVALUATING PROCESS COST
                                  INFORMATION

HARSH, MARY FRANCES   THE IMPACT OF ACTIVITY-BASED COSTING ON MANAGERIAL DECISIONS: AN EMPIRICAL
                                  ANALYSIS

KIM, GYUTAI   AN ECONOMIC ANALYSIS OF AN ADVANCED MANUFACTURING SYSTEM WITH
                                  ACTIVITY-BASED COSTING SYSTEMS

MCGOWAN, ANNIE SMITH   AN INVESTIGATION OF THE BEHAVIORAL IMPLICATIONS OF ADOPTING ACTIVITY-BASED
                                  COST MANAGEMENT SYSTEMS: AN EXPLORATORY STUDY

NEEDY, KIM LA SCOLA   PERFORMANCE COMPARISON OF ACTIVITY BASED COSTING VERSUS TRADITIONAL COST
                                  ACCOUNTING FOR STRATEGIC DECISION MAKING

POHLEN, TERRANCE LYNN   THE EFFECT OF ACTIVITY-BASED COSTING ON LOGISTICS MANAGEMENT

SHIM, EUN SUP   COST MANAGEMENT AND ACTIVITY-BASED COST ALLOCATION IN A NEW
                                  MANUFACTURING ENVIRONMENT

SILVESTER, KATHERINE JOSEPHINE   FIRM PERFORMANCE, ACCOUNTING SYSTEM CHOICE, AND NEWMANUFACTURING
                                  TECHNOLOGIES

SWENSON, DAN WILLIAM   AN EMPIRICAL INVESTIGATION OF HOW FIRM DIFFERENCES AFFECT MANAGEMENT
                                  SATISFACTION WITH ACTIVITY-BASED COSTING

WEST, TIMOTHY DAVID   EXTERNAL AUDITORS' RISK ASSESSMENT DECISIONS: THE IMPACT OF IMPLEMENTING
                                  ACTIVITY-BASED COSTING

Agency Theory

ALBRECHT, WILLIAM DAVID   THE DETERMINANTS OF THE MARKET REACTION TO AN ANNOUNCEMENT OF A
                                  CHANGE IN AUDITOR

ASECHEMIE, DANIEL PELE SAMUEL   AN EXPERIMENTAL STUDY OF TOURNAMENTS AND CONTRACTS: A PRINCIPAL'S
                                  PERSPECTIVE

BALAKRISHNAN, RAMAMURTHY   APPLICATIONS OF MULTIPERIOD AGENCY MODELS: AN ACCOUNTING CONTEXT

BASAK, SULEYMAN   GENERAL EQUILIBRIUM CONTINUOUS-TIME ASSET PRICING IN THE PRESENCE OF: (1)
                                  PORTFOLIO INSURERS AND (2) NON-PRICE-TAKING INVESTORS

BERG, JOYCE ELLEN   INFORMATIVENESS AND VALUE OF PUBLIC INFORMATION: AN EXPERIMENTAL TEST

CHEH, JONGWOOK   INCENTIVE EFFECTS OF INTER-AGENT MONITORING: IMPLICATIONS FOR
                                  RESPONSIBILITY ACCOUNTING AND AUDITOR-CONSULTANT INTERACTION

CHIPALKATTI, NIRANJAN H.   ADVERSE SELECTION COSTS AND THE DEALERS' BID-ASK SPREAD AROUND EARNINGS
                                  ANNOUNCEMENTS: DIFFERENTIAL INFORMATION AND SIGNAL QUALITY

CHUNG, MOON-CHONG   AN INVESTMENT CENTER VS. A PROFIT CENTER: CAPITAL INVESTMENT UNDER
                                  INFORMATIONAL ASYMMETRY

Listing by Topic   240

Listing by Topic   241

SRIDHARAN, SWAMINATHAN	MANAGERIAL REPORTING INCENTIVES AND INVESTMENT DECISIONS
SULLIVAN, M. CATHY	AN INVESTIGATION OF AGENCY THEORY'S ASSUMPTION OF STRICT EFFORT AVERSION: THE ROLE OF INTRINSIC MOTIVATION
SUNG, KYU YOUNG	VALUE AND OPTIMAL TIMING OF MANAGERIAL ACCOUNTING INFORMATION IN A MULTIPERIOD SETTING WITH LEARNING
TRIMBLE, CHARLIE JOE	A MULTIPLE DISCRIMINANT ANALYSIS OF FIRM-SPECIFIC CHARACTERISTICS USEFUL IN PREDICTING MANAGEMENTS' USE OF DISCRETIONARY CASH FLOWS
VILLADSEN, BENTE	COLLUSION: EFFECTS ON INTERNAL CONTROL
WHITTEN, RUTH ANN	CONTRACTS, RISK AND INFORMATION ASYMMETRY
WOODLOCK, PETER DAVID	AUDITING AS THE OWNER'S RESPONSE TO THE NEED FOR RELIABLE MANAGER REPORTING: A PROBLEM OF SUPPLY AND DEMAND OF AUDIT SERVICES IN THE PRESENCE OF HIDDEN AUDITOR ACTIONS
YANCEY, WILLIAM FREDERICK	A MODEL OF ASSET RESTRUCTURING ANNOUNCEMENTS
YOON, SUNG SIG	THE EFFECTS OF AUDITING ON MORAL HAZARD AND INFORMATION ASYMMETRIES
ZIV, AMIR	INFORMATIONAL ISSUES IN ORGANIZATIONS

Analytical Review

ALLEN, ROBERT DREW	STATISTICAL ANALYTICAL PROCEDURES USING INDUSTRY SPECIFIC INFORMATION: AN EMPIRICAL STUDY
AMEEN, ELSIE COKER	THE EFFECTIVENESS AND EFFICIENCY OF STATISTICAL ANALYTICAL REVIEW IN AN AUDITING STRATEGY: A COMPARISON OF REGRESSION AND THE X-11 MODEL
BUSH, HOWARD FRANCIS	THE USE OF REGRESSION MODELS IN ANALYTICAL REVIEW JUDGMENT: A LABORATORY EXPERIMENT
CHAU, CHAK-TONG	COMPARING FORECASTING PERFORMANCE IN ANALYTICAL PROCEDURES: AN INTEGRATED STUDY USING STATE SPACE, EXPONENTIAL SMOOTHING AND REGRESSION MODELS
CHEN, YI-NING	THE ERROR DETECTION OF STRUCTURAL ANALYTICAL REVIEW PROCEDURES: A SIMULATION STUDY
COHEN, JEFFREY R.	THE IMPACT OF CONSERVATISM, INTERNAL CONTROL RELIABILITY, AND EXPERIENCE ON THE USE OF ANALYTICAL REVIEW
DZENG, SIMON C.	A COMPARISON OF VECTOR AUTOREGRESSION MODELS AND ORDINARY LEAST SQUARES MULTIPLE REGRESSION MODELS FOR ANALYTICAL PROCEDURES PERFORMED AS SUBSTANTIVE TEST
GREEN, BRIAN PATRICK	IDENTIFYING MANAGEMENT IRREGULARITIES THROUGH PRELIMINARY ANALYTICAL PROCEDURES
HO, JOANNA LEE-YUN	CONJUNCTION FALLACY IN AUDITORS' PROBABILITY JUDGMENT PROCESSES
JONES, SCOTT KENNETH	THE RISK PROPERTIES OF ANALYTICAL PROCEDURES THAT USE ORTHOGONAL POLYNOMIAL REGRESSIONS
NELSON, MARK WILLIAM	AUDITOR LEARNING OF ERROR FREQUENCIES IN ANALYTICAL REVIEW
PAN, ALEXANDER M.	THE USE OF PANEL DATA IN ANALYTICAL REVIEW BY AUDITORS

SANDLIN, PETREA KAY	THE EFFECT OF CAUSAL BACKGROUND ON AUDITORS' ANALYTICAL REVIEW JUDGMENTS
SCHATZEL, JOHN A.	AN EXPERIMENTAL STUDY OF FACTORS AFFECTING AUDITORS' RELIANCE ON ANALYTICAL PROCEDURES
SNYDER, JOHN PAUL	ANALYTICAL REVIEW: AN EMPIRICAL STUDY
TANDY, PAULETTE REDFERN	AN EMPIRICAL STUDY OF THE EXTENT, TIMING, AND NATURE OF ANALYTICAL REVIEW PROCEDURES IN ACTUAL AUDIT SETTINGS
WHEELER, STEPHEN W.	ASSESSING THE PERFORMANCE OF ANALYTICAL PROCEDURES: A BEST CASE SCENARIO
ZELIN, ROBERT CLAYTON, II	THE EFFECTS OF INDUSTRY DISTRIBUTIONAL INFORMATION ON AUDITORS' ANALYTICAL REVIEW INVESTIGATION PARAMETERS

Audit Committees

BROWN, SARAH	AN INVESTIGATION INTO THE ASSOCIATION BETWEEN AUDIT FAILURES AND THE PRESENCE OR ABSENCE OF A CORPORATE AUDIT COMMITTEE
CRAWFORD, JEAN GREENE	AN EMPIRICAL INVESTIGATION OF THE CHARACTERISTICS OF COMPANIES WITH AUDIT COMMITTEES
EDMONDS, CYNTHIA D.	AGENCY COST EXPLANATIONS FOR THE DEMAND FOR AUDIT QUALITY: AN EMPIRICAL INQUIRY INTO THE REASONS FOR THE PRESENCE OF AUDIT COMMITTEES OF THE BOARD OF DIRECTORS
JACKSON-HEARD, MARY FRANCES	THE EFFECT OF THE AUDIT COMMITTEE AND OTHER SELECTED FACTORS ON THE PERCEPTION OF AUDITORS' INDEPENDENCE
KALBERS, LAWRENCE PACKARD	THE AUDIT COMMITTEE: A POWER NEXUS FOR FINANCIAL REPORTING AND CORPORATE ACCOUNTABILITY
MCMULLEN, DOROTHY ANN	AUDIT COMMITTEE STRUCTURE AND PERFORMANCE: AN EMPIRICAL INVESTIGATION OF THE CONSEQUENCES AND ATTRIBUTES OF AUDIT COMMITTEES
ROUBI, RAAFAT RAMADAN	THE ASSOCIATION BETWEEN THE ESTABLISHMENT OF AUDIT COMMITTEES COMPOSED OF OUTSIDE DIRECTORS AND A CHANGE IN THE OBJECTIVITY OF THE MANAGEMENT RESULTS-REPORTING FUNCTION: AN EMPIRICAL INVESTIGATION INTO INCOME
STANGL, ROBERT JOHN	CORPORATE AUDIT COMMITTEES: FACTORS ASSOCIATED WITH VOLUNTARY FORMATION AND MARKET REACTION TO MANDATORY FORMATION

Audit Fees

BROZOVSKY, JOHN ALLWIN	THE EFFECT OF AUDITOR REPUTATION ON THE PRICING OF AUDIT SERVICES: AN EXPERIMENTAL STUDY
GIST, WILLIE EARL	AN EXPLORATORY STUDY OF THE EFFECTS OF PRODUCT DIFFERENTIATION AND ECONOMIES OF SCALE ON EXTERNAL AUDIT FEES
PEARSON, TIMOTHY A.	AN INVESTIGATION OF THE RELATIONSHIP BETWEEN AUDIT FEES AND AUDITOR REPUTATION: THE MARKET FOR INSURANCE AUDIT CLIENTS
PIROZZOLI, IRIS ANN	PRICE-CUTTING AND TRANSACTION COSTS IN THE MARKET FOR AUDIT SERVICES
RAMZY, WAFAA ABDEL MAGID	THE DETERMINANTS OF AUDIT FEES: AN ANALYTICAL STUDY
RAO, HEMA	AN EMPIRICAL EVALUATION OF THE PRACTICE OF DISCOUNTING INITIAL AUDIT FEES AND THE EFFECT OF THE PRACTICE ON THE APPEARANCE OF AUDIT INDEPENDENCE (FEE DISCOUNTING)

Audit Opinion

CARLSON, STEVEN JAMES	AN EXAMINATION OF THE EFFECT OF A GOING CONCERN AUDIT REPORT ON SECURITY RETURNS AND TRADING VOLUME WHILE CONTROLLING FOR THE CONCURRENT RELEASE OF FINANCIAL STATEMENT INFORMATION

CORBIN, DONNA PHILLIPS	AN INVESTIGATION OF THE PREDICTABILITY OF THE AUDITOR'S OPINION IN A MULTINOMIAL LOGISTIC REGRESSION FRAMEWORK
FLEAK, SANDRA KREISEL	THE GOING-CONCERN AUDIT OPINION AND SHARE PRICE BEHAVIOR
FRANZ, DIANA RUTH	AN ANALYSIS OF THE EFFECT OF THE EXPECTATION GAP STATEMENTS ON AUDITING STANDARDS ON THE REPORTING OF GOING CONCERN
GEIGER, MARSHALL ALLEN	SETTING THE STANDARD FOR A NEW AUDITOR'S REPORT: AN ANALYSIS OF ATTEMPTS TO INFLUENCE THE AUDITING STANDARDS BOARD
GEORGE, CAROLYN R.	THE EFFECT OF THE GOING-CONCERN AUDIT DECISION ON SURVIVAL
JONES, FREDERICK LAWSON	THE MARKET REACTION TO THE AUDITOR'S GOING CONCERN EVALUATION
KIM, JEONG-JAE	PRICE AND VOLUME REACTION TO THE ANNOUNCEMENT OF QUALIFIED AUDIT OPINIONS
LAWRENCE, JANICE ELIZABETH	AUDITS OF A FEDERAL LOAN PROGRAM: A CLASSIFICATION MODEL OF REPORTED IRREGULARITIES
LOUWERS, TIMOTHY JAMES	AN EMPIRICAL INVESTIGATION OF THE RELATIONSHIP BETWEEN FINANCIAL DISTRESS, EXTERNAL FACTORS, AND THE AUDITOR'S GOING CONCERN OPINION MODIFICATION
MORRIS, ROSELYN EVERTS	THE PERFORMANCE OF AUDITORS IN MODIFYING OPINIONS OF FAILED BANKS
RAGHUNANDAN, KANNAN	AN EMPIRICAL TEST OF THE PREDICTIVE ABILITY OF AUDITORS' LOSS CONTINGENCY DISCLOSURES
SCHULTZ, SALLY M.	AUDIT OPINION DECISIONS AND LITIGATION LOSS CONTINGENCIES
SEIPEL, CINDY L.	'SUBJECT TO' QUALIFIED OPINIONS AND THE SIGNALLING OF RISK SHIFTS
SHASTRI, TRIMBAK	A CONCEPTUAL FRAMEWORK FOR AUDIT COMMUNICATION RESEARCH AND SOME EMPIRICAL EVIDENCE
STYRON, WILLIAM JOEY	AN EMPIRICAL EXAMINATION OF THE GOING-CONCERN AUDIT OPINION: THE AUDITOR'S DECISION REGARDING CONTINUING GOING-CONCERN OPINIONS AND THE SUBSEQUENT FATE OF COMPANIES THAT HAVE RECEIVED GOING-CONCERN OPINIONS
WATERS, JOHN MILBOURNE, II	AN EMPIRICAL ASSESSMENT OF ATTITUDES TOWARD AUDIT OPINIONS AND ATTITUDES TOWARD AUDIT REPORTING
ZIEGENFUSS, DOUGLAS EDWIN	AN EMPIRICAL INVESTIGATION OF THE EFFECTS OF QUALIFIED OPINIONS ON AUDIT FIRMS' GROWTH RATES AND LEGAL LIABILITY

Audit Planning

BOHAC, DARLENE MARIE	THE EFFECT OF MANAGEMENT BUDGETARY CONTROLS ON AUDIT PLANNING
COOMER, SUSAN DARLENE	THE EFFECT OF PRIOR YEAR'S ERRORS AND IRREGULARITIES AND MANAGEMENT'S CHARACTERISTICS ON AUDIT PLANNING: AN EMPIRICAL INVESTIGATION
DUTTA, SAURAV KUMAR	EVIDENCE AGGREGATION FOR PLANNING AND EVALUATION OF AUDIT: A THEORETICAL STUDY
GUPTA, PARVEEN PARKASH	THE AUDIT PROCESS AS A FUNCTION OF DIFFERENTIATED ENVIRONMENT: AN EMPIRICAL STUDY
HILL, MARY CALLAHAN	THE AVAILABILITY AND USE OF FEEDBACK IN AUDIT PLANNING

HOPPE, PAUL PETER, III	ACCIDENTAL DATA IN A STATISTICAL AUDITING PLAN
KELTING, WILLIAM ROBERT	AUDIT PLANNING: AN EMPIRICAL INVESTIGATION INTO THE TIMING OF PRINCIPAL SUBSTANTIVE TESTS
KERR, DAVID SAMUEL	INFORMATION INTEGRATION IN AUDIT PLANNING
LEWIS, MERRILL TIM	EX ANTE EVALUATION OF AUDIT EVIDENCE
MARXEN, DALE EDWIN	GROUP POLARIZATION IN THE SETTING OF AUDIT TIME BUDGETS
MCNAIR, CAROL JEAN	THE EFFECTS OF BUDGET PRESSURE ON AUDIT FIRMS: AN EMPIRICAL EXAMINATION OF THE UNDERREPORTING OF CHARGEABLE TIME
MORRIS, BARBARA SUE	AN EXPERIMENTAL STUDY OF AGENCY THEORY VARIABLES AS DETERMINANTS OF AUDIT INTENSIVENESS

Audit Quality

BRYAN, BARRY JEROME	AN EMPIRICAL INVESTIGATION OF THE DETERMINANTS OF REPORTING QUALITY AND THE EFFECTIVENESS OF THE QUALITY REVIEW PROGRAM FOR SMALL ACCOUNTING FIRMS
CARCELLO, JOSEPH VINCENT	A COMPARATIVE STUDY OF AUDIT QUALITY AMONG THE BIG EIGHT ACCOUNTING FIRMS
CORY, SUZANNE NELLIE	AN INVESTIGATION OF AUDIT PRACTICE QUALITY
COTTRELL, DAVID MARK	MARKET-BASED AUDITING STANDARDS: EXPERIMENTAL TESTS OF MARKET DISCLOSURES AS SUBSTITUTES FOR EXTERNAL REGULATION
HAZERA, ALEJANDRO	A NORMATIVE MODEL FOR ASSESSING THE COMPETENCE OF EVIDENTIAL MATTER IN AUDITING
MALONE, CHARLES FRANCIS	AN EMPIRICAL INVESTIGATION OF THE RELATIONSHIPS BETWEEN INDIVIDUAL AND FIRM CHARACTERISTICS AND REDUCED AUDIT QUALITY
MCDANIEL, LINDA SUE	THE EFFECTS OF TIME PRESSURE AND AUDIT PROGRAM STRUCTURE ON AUDIT EFFECTIVENESS AND EFFICIENCY
MORELAND, KEITH ARON	AN EMPIRICAL STUDY OF THE EFFECT OF AUDITOR SANCTIONS ON THE ASSOCIATION BETWEEN EARNINGS AND SECURITY RETURNS
ROMINE, JEFFREY MORRIS	THE QUALITY REVIEW DECISION: AN ANALYSIS OF DECISION SEARCH PROCESSES, DECISION OUTCOMES, CONTEXTUAL BACKGROUND, AND EXPERIENCE EFFECTS
RONNEN, URI	ESSAYS IN AUDITING
SUTTON, STEVEN GALE	FORMULATING QUALITY MEASURES FOR AUDIT ENGAGEMENTS

Audit Sampling

ATKINSON, MARYANNE	A STUDY OF POPULATION CHARACTERISTICS AFFECTING THE PERFORMANCE OF AUDIT SAMPLING TECHNIQUES IN SUBSTANTIVE TESTS
CLAYTON, HOWARD ROBERTSON	CONFIDENCE BOUNDS BASED ON THE BOOTSTRAP AND HOEFFDING'S INEQUALITY FOR DOLLAR UNIT SAMPLING IN AUDITING
ETZIONI, RUTH	BAYESIAN GROUP SEQUENTIAL SAMPLING WITH APPLICATION TO TAX AUDITING

GAUNTT, JAMES EDWARD, JR.	A SIMULATION STUDY OF STATISTICAL ESTIMATORS USED IN VARIABLES SAMPLING
HERMANSON, HEATHER MARIE	THE IMPACT OF CONTROL RISK AND BUSINESS RISK ON SAMPLE EVIDENCE EVALUATION
HITZIG, NEAL B.	SUBSTANTIVE AUDIT TESTS OF DETAILS AND THE ESTIMATION OF RARE ERRORS BY DOUBLE SAMPLING WITH PROBABILITY PROPORTIONAL TO SIZE
ILDERTON, ROBERT BLAIR	EVALUATION OF SAMPLES WITH FEW NON-ZERO ITEMS
KO, CHEN-EN	MODEL-BASED SAMPLING IN AUDITING
LEE, IHNSHIK	A SIMULATION STUDY COMPARING VARIOUS CONFIDENCE INTERVALS FOR THE MEAN OF VOUCHER POPULATIONS IN ACCOUNTING
PATTERSON, EVELYN RUTH	GAME THEORETIC APPLICATIONS TO AUDIT SAMPLING
PEEK, LUCIA ELIZABETH	SAS NO. 39 GUIDELINES FOR NONSTATISTICAL SAMPLING: A SIMULATION STUDY
PHILLIPS, JEFFREY JOSEPH	BAYESIAN BOUNDS FOR MONETARY-UNIT SAMPLING USING ACTUAL ACCOUNTING POPULATIONS
SUDIBYO, BAMBANG	THE ADEQUACY OF CPAS' UNDERSTANDING OF THE RELATIVE SERIOUSNESS OF ALPHA AND BETA RISKS IN STATISTICAL AUDIT SAMPLING
TATUM, KAY WARD	AN EMPIRICAL STUDY OF AUDIT SAMPLING PROBLEMS
WRIGHT, DAVID WILLIAM	THE USE OF EMPIRICAL BAYES ESTIMATION IN AUDIT TESTING
WURST, JOHN CHARLES	AN INVESTIGATION OF THE SIEVE METHOD AND OF RECTIFICATION SAMPLING FOR AUDITING

Audit Structure

DRAKE, PHILIP D.	AN ANALYSIS OF THE AUDIT SERVICES MARKET: THE EFFECT OF AUDIT STRUCTURE ON AUDITOR EFFICIENCY, A DATA ENVELOPMENT ANALYSIS APPROACH
GLOVER, HUBERT DARNELL	MEASURING AUDIT STRUCTURE AND DETERMINING THE SOURCES OF VARIATION: AN APPLICATION OF ORGANIZATIONAL SCIENCE
TUNTIWONGPIBOON, NARONK	AN INVESTIGATION OF CLIENT ATTRIBUTES AND AUDIT STRUCTURE
WHITE, GWENDOLEN BARNETT	AUDITORS' HYPOTHESIS GENERATION SKILLS: THE INFLUENCE OF EXPERIENCE AND AUDIT METHODOLOGY STRUCTURE

Audit Technology

DESHMUKH, ASHUTOSH VASANT	THE ROLE OF AUDIT TECHNOLOGY AND EXTENSION OF AUDIT PROCEDURES IN STRATEGIC AUDITING
FISCHER, MICHAEL J.	'REAL-IZING' THE BENEFITS OF NEW TECHNOLOGIES AS A SOURCE OF AUDIT EVIDENCE: AN INTERPRETIVE FIELD STUDY
NANCE, WILLIAM DOUGLAS	TASK/TECHNOLOGY FIT AND KNOWLEDGE WORKER USE OF INFORMATION TECHNOLOGY: A STUDY OF AUDITORS

Auditor Behavior

IBRAHIM, MOHAMED EL HADY M.	AN EXAMINATION OF AN INTEGRATIVE EXPECTANCY MODEL FOR AUDITORS' PERFORMANCE BEHAVIORS UNDER TIME BUDGET PRESSURE

PEECHER, MARK EVERETT — CONSEQUENTIALITY, JUSTIFICATION AND AUDITORS' DECISION PROCESSES: A THEORETICAL FRAMEWORK AND TWO EXPERIMENTS

QUILLIAM, WILLIAM CLAYTON — EXAMINING THE EFFECTS OF ACCOUNTABILITY ON AUDITORS' VALUATION DECISIONS

SEN, KAUSTAV — MECHANISM DESIGN IN AUDIT SETTINGS

Auditor Changes

CHRISTENSEN, JO ANN — AUDITOR SWITCHING AND WHITE COLLAR CRIME

COATE, CHARLES JOSEPH — A TWO PERIOD BIDDING MODEL OF THE AUDIT MARKET

DEFOND, MARK LEROY — AN EMPIRICAL TEST OF THE ASSOCIATION BETWEEN CLIENT FIRM AGENCY COSTS AND AUDIT FIRM CHARACTERISTICS

DENNIS, PAMELA ERICKSON — THE EFFECTS OF BANNING DIRECT UNINVITED SOLICITATION ON PRICING, BIDDING, SEARCH AND SWITCHING DECISIONS IN THE MARKET FOR AUDIT SERVICES

EDWARDS, RANDAL KEITH — GROWTH COMPANIES AND CHANGES TO LARGER AUDIT FIRMS: AN EXAMINATION

FISHER, JOSEPH GERALD — THE ALLOCATION MECHANISM OF AUDITS: AN EXPERIMENTAL APPROACH

HA, GOOKLAK — THE INFORMATION CONTENT OF AUDITOR SWITCHES

JOHNSON, RICHARD ALAN — AN EMPIRICAL INVESTIGATION OF THE ASSOCIATION OF ACCOUNTING-BASED PERFORMANCE MEASURES WITH THE AUDITOR REPLACEMENT DECISION

KRISHNAN, JAGANNATHAN — AUDITOR SWITCHING, OPINION SHOPPING AND CLIENT SIZE

NAGLE, BRIAN M. — AUDIT REPORT MODIFICATIONS AND AUDITOR SWITCHES

PANDIT, GANESH MANGESH — THE IMPACT OF CLIENTS' PERCEPTIONS ON AUDITOR SWITCHING

PERSONS, OBEUA SRICHANDRABHANDHU — MARKET REACTIONS TO AUDITOR CHANGES BY FIRMS WITH DIFFERENT FINANCIAL CONDITIONS

ROBERTS, ROBIN WENDELL — DETERMINANTS OF AUDITOR CHANGE IN THE PUBLIC SECTOR

SRIRAM, SRINIVASAN — AN INVESTIGATION OF ASYMMETRICAL POWER RELATIONSHIPS EXISTING IN AUDITOR-CLIENT RELATIONSHIP DURING AUDITOR CHANGES

TURPEN, RICHARD ALLEN — AUDIT PRICING AND AUDITOR CHOICE: AN EMPIRICAL INVESTIGATION OF THE MARKET FOR AUDITING SERVICES

WELLS, DONALD WAYNE — THE MARKET EFFECTS OF AUDITOR RESIGNATIONS

WIEST, DAVID NEVIN — THE EFFECT OF SEC SANCTIONS ON AUDITOR SWITCHES

WILSON, THOMAS E., JR. — AN EXAMINATION OF AUDITOR CHANGES FOLLOWING EVENTS ADVERSELY AFFECTING EXTERNAL AUDITOR CREDIBILITY

WITMER, PHILIP ROY — AUDITOR CHANGES AS OPPORTUNISTIC BEHAVIOR

Bank Loan Officers

BAKER, WILLIAM MAURICE — THE EFFECTS OF ACCOUNTING REPORTS ON LOAN OFFICERS: AN EXPERIMENT

CALDERON, THOMAS GEORGE — BANKER NEEDS FOR ACCOUNTING INFORMATION

COKER, JOHN WILLIAM — AN EMPIRICAL ANALYSIS OF THE USE OF THE INCOME TAX BASIS OF ACCOUNTING ON THE LENDING DECISIONS OF BANKERS: AN EXPERIMENT

EPELLE, CHUKUEMERIE TAMUNOTONYE — THE IMPACT OF ORGANIZATIONAL GOALS UPON BANK LOAN OFFICERS' CREDIT WORTHINESS DECISIONS

GADDIS, MARCUS DAMON — INVESTIGATING THE INFLUENCE OF ASSERTIONS BY ACCOUNTING AND APPRAISAL PROFESSIONALS ON REAL ESTATE LENDING DECISIONS

HILTEBEITEL, KENNETH MERRILL — THE ACCOUNTING STANDARDS OVERLOAD ISSUE: AN EMPIRICAL TEST OF THE EFFECT OF FOUR SELECTED FINANCIAL ACCOUNTING STANDARDS ON THE LENDING DECISIONS OF BANKERS

LIN, PAO-CHUAN — INFORMATION ACQUISITION AND DECISION MAKING IN CREDITORS' DECISION ENVIRONMENT

MEREDITH, VICKI BANET — AN EMPIRICAL EXAMINATION OF BANKERS' PERCEPTIONS OF PROCEDURES PERFORMED BY CPAS IN LIMITED ASSURANCE ENGAGEMENTS

MILLER, JEFFREY REED — AN EXPERIMENTAL RESEARCH STUDY ON THE EFFECTS OF THE TYPE OF ACCOUNTING SERVICE ON A BANK LENDING DECISION FOR NONPUBLIC BUSINESSES

NOGLER, GEORGE EDWARD — AN EMPIRICAL STUDY OF BANKRUPTCY RESOLUTION AND COMMERCIAL BANK LOAN OFFICERS' PERCEPTIONS

ROBERTS, CLYDE A. — CPA CREDIBILITY AND THE CREDIT DECISION PROCESS OF COMMERCIAL LOAN OFFICERS

SESHIE, GODWIN O. — THE ROLE OF PROSPECTIVE FINANCIAL INFORMATION ATTESTATION IN BANK LENDING DECISIONS

WATERS, BRENDA NELL — THE IMPACT OF INFORMATION AND PERSONALITY CHARACTERISTICS ON THE LENDING DECISION

Budgeting

ANELL, ANDERS LARS — FROM CENTRAL PLANNING TO LOCAL RESPONSIBILITIES: THE ROLE OF BUDGETING IN SWEDISH COUNTY COUNCIL HEALTH CARE [FRAN CENTRAL PLANERING TILL LOKALT ANSVAR: BUDGETERINGENS ROLL I LANDSTINGSKOMMUNAL SJUKVARD]

AWASTHI, VIDYA NIDHI — BUDGETARY SLACK AND PERFORMANCE UNDER PARTICIPATIVE BUDGETING: AN EXPERIMENTAL STUDY OF THE EFFECTS OF MONITORING, THE AGENT'S RISK PREFERENCE, AND THE QUALITY OF THE AGENT'S PRE-DECISION INFORMATION

BARBEE, RONALD F. — PARTICIPATION IN THE BUDGETARY PROCESS: AN ATTRIBUTIONAL ANALYSIS

BETTNER, MARK STEVEN — THE EFFECTS OF PERCEIVED ACCOUNTING COMPETENCE, MACHIAVELLIANISM, PAST BUDGETING BEHAVIOR, AND BELIEFS ABOUT THE EFFECTIVENESS OF PAST BUDGETING BEHAVIOR ON BUDGETARY ATTITUDE: AN EMPIRICAL ANALYSIS

BILBEISI, KHAMIS MOHAMAD — CULTURAL EFFECTS ON THE RELATIONSHIPS BETWEEN BUDGETARY PARTICIPATION AND MANAGERIAL PERFORMANCE

CATHEY, JACK M. — CONTINGENT FACTORS AFFECTING BUDGET SYSTEM USEFULNESS: AN INFORMATION PROCESSING PERSPECTIVE

COLLINS, MARY KATHERINE — THE BUDGETARY PROCESS: A BEHAVIORAL PERSPECTIVE

COOK, HAROLD BARTLEY — THE RELATIONSHIP BETWEEN MANAGERIAL OWNERSHIP AND THE USE OF ACCOUNTING-BASED BUDGETING SYSTEMS TO MONITOR SUBORDINATES

CUMMINGS, CHARLES WILLIAM	BUDGET SLACK AND PREDICTION PERFORMANCE IN AN UNCERTAIN ENVIRONMENT: AN EXPERIMENTAL INVESTIGATION
CZYZEWSKI, ALAN BENJAMIN	THE PRODUCT LIFE CYCLE AND BUDGETING FUNCTIONS: PLANNING, CONTROL, AND MOTIVATION
DAVIS, DOROTHY A.	AN EMPIRICAL INVESTIGATION INTO EXISTING BUDGETING PRACTICES TO DETERMINE DIVERSITY IN INTERPRETATIONS OF THE LAW ON BUDGETING AT THE MUNICIPAL LEVEL IN MISSISSIPPI
FERRERI, LINDA BARLOW	UNIVERSITY BUDGET SYSTEMS: A TEST OF CONTINGENCY THEORY AT PRIVATE INSTITUTIONS
GORDON, TERESA PEALE	BOUNDED RATIONALITY AND BUDGETING: RESOURCE DEPENDENCE, AGENCY POWER, INDIVIDUAL MOTIVATION AND INCREMENTALISM IN BUDGETARY DECISION-MAKING
GRAFF, LOIS MARIE	COMPUTERIZED FINANCIAL PLANNING FOR SCHOOL DISTRICTS IN THE UNITED STATES
HAYES, ROBERT D.	THE CONSTANT - INPUT - PROPORTION ASSUMPTION IN THE BUDGETARY PROCESS
IMOISILI, OLUMHENSE ANTHONY	TASK COMPLEXITY, BUDGET STYLE OF EVALUATING PERFORMANCE AND MANAGERIAL STRESS: AN EMPIRICAL INVESTIGATION
INDRIANTORO, NUR	THE EFFECT OF PARTICIPATIVE BUDGETING ON JOB PERFORMANCE AND JOB SATISFACTION WITH LOCUS-OF-CONTROL AND CULTURAL DIMENSIONS AS MODERATING VARIABLES
KIM, DONG CHULL	RISK PREFERENCES IN PARTICIPATIVE BUDGETING
LEAVINS, JOHN R.	AN EXAMINATION OF BUDGET SLACK WITHIN AN EXPECTANCY THEORY FRAMEWORK
LENK, MARGARITA MARIA	PRIVATE INFORMATION AND A MANAGER'S MOTIVATION: AN EXPECTANCY THEORY TEST OF AGENCY THEORY'S EFFORT-AVERSION ASSUMPTION IN A PARTICIPATIVE BUDGETING SETTING
LEUNG, VICTOR KWAN LAP	BUDGETING IN RESPECT TO INFORMATION ASYMMETRY, PARTICIPATION AND EVALUATION FROM PERSPECTIVES OF AGENCY THEORY AND SOCIAL BEHAVIOR THEORY
MACKIE, JAMES JAY	AN EMPIRICAL INVESTIGATION OF THE IMPACT OF PERSONALITY TYPE ON SUPERVISOR-SUBORDINATE RELATIONSHIPS IN A BUDGETARY SETTING
MAGNER, NACE RICHARD	A FIELD STUDY OF PROCEDURAL JUSTICE AS AN INTERVENING VARIABLE BETWEEN PARTICIPATION IN BUDGETING AND ORGANIZATIONAL OUTCOMES
MCDERMOTT, EUGENE WILLIS	THE IMPACT OF TASK COMPLEXITY AND SELECTED COGNITIONS ON THE MOTIVATING ASPECTS OF BUDGETING
MOHAMMED ABDULLA, MOHAMED ISMAIL	ADVANCED MEANS OF PREPARING THE PUBLIC BUDGET AND THEIR UTILISATION IN MODERNISING THE PUBLIC BUDGET IN THE UNITED ARAB EMIRATES. (VOLUMES I-III)
MOORE, WALTER BURNIS	BUDGETARY SLACK BEHAVIOR IN MUNICIPAL GOVERNMENTS: AN EMPIRICAL BEHAVIORAL STUDY
MORROW, MITCHEL CRAWFORD	EFFECTS OF BUDGET PARTICIPATION, DIFFICULTY AND BUDGET CONTINGENT REWARD ON BUDGET PERFORMANCE
NOURI, HOSSEIN	THE EFFECT OF BUDGETARY PARTICIPATION ON JOB PERFORMANCE: A CONCEPTUAL MODEL AND ITS EMPIRICAL TEST
OGILBY, SUZANNE MARIE	THE INSTITUTIONALIZATION OF BUDGETING PROCESSES: THE (RE)PRODUCTION OF POWER
PAIK, TAE-YOUNG	THREE ESSAYS ON PARTICIPATIVE BUDGETING

Listing by Topic

PARKER, ROBERT JAMES	BUDGETING EFFECTS AND EVALUATION BY SELF, PEERS, AND SUPERIORS WITH MODERATING EFFECTS OF PERSONAL AND SOCIAL IDENTITY
PEREIRA, EMILIO ANTHONY	ENVIRONMENTAL UNCERTAINTY AND MANAGERS' BUDGET-RELATED BEHAVIOR: A CROSS-CULTURAL FIELD STUDY
REDMER, TIMOTHY ALBERT ORAL	BUDGET ACTIVITIES AND THEIR IMPACT ON THE BUDGET PROCESS: AN EXPLORATORY STUDY
RUSTH, DOUGLAS BRUCE	MULTINATIONAL ENTITIES: PERCEIVED ENVIRONMENTAL UNCERTAINTY AND THE BUDGETARY PLANNING AND CONTROL SYSTEM
SHIELDS, JEFFREY FRANKLIN	THE INFLUENCE OF INTERNAL AUDITING AND TRUST ON BUDGETARY SLACK
STAPLES, CATHERINE LOVING	THE RELATION BETWEEN THE MEDIA, MONITORING DEVICES, AND THE SCHOOL DISTRICT BUDGETARY PROCESS
SUTTER, MARK D.	A TEST OF FACTORS AFFECTING BUDGETING CHARACTERISTICS OF MUNICIPALITIES
UENO, SUSUMU	THE INFLUENCE OF CULTURE ON BUDGET CONTROL PRACTICES IN THE U.S.A. AND JAPAN: AN EMPIRICAL STUDY
WIER, BENSON	THE EFFECTS OF TASK RELEVANT KNOWLEDGE, GOAL LEVEL, GOAL COMMITMENT, AND MOTIVATION ON THE PARTICIPATION-PERFORMANCE LINKAGE: AN EMPIRICAL EXAMINATION
WRIGHT, SALLY	PARTICIPATIVE BUDGETING: AN EXAMINATION OF BUDGETARY SLACK AND MANAGERIAL PERFORMANCE OVER MULTIPLE PERIODS
WYATT, ROBERT LANE	THE EFFECT OF ELECTRONIC MEETING SYSTEMS ON GROUP PERFORMANCE: THE CASE OF THE BUDGETING DECISION

Business Form

FRESE, PHILLIP BRUCE	THE EFFECT OF CHANGES IN TAX STRUCTURE ON THE BEHAVIOR OF RATIONAL INVESTORS IN MARKETS FOR RISKY ASSETS: AN EMPIRICAL STUDY OF THE IMPACT OF THE OMNIBUS BUDGET RECONCILIATION ACT OF 1987 ON THE INVESTORS IN
GUENTHER, DAVID A.	THE EFFECT OF INCOME TAXES ON THE FORM OF BUSINESS ENTITY
LANGEMEIER, BRIAN LEON	A MODEL OF CHOICE OF BUSINESS ENTITY USING DISCRIMINANT ANALYSIS
ODOM, GARY LYNN	THE EFFECT OF 1981 AND 1982 LEGISLATIVE ACTS ON SMALL CORPORATIONS' SELECTION OF A C OR S CORPORATE FORM
SPRADLING, DALE WARREN	TOWARD PARITY BETWEEN S CORPORATIONS AND PARTNERSHIPS AND SIMPLIFICATION OF S CORPORATION TAXATION
TERANDO, WILLIAM DAVID	THE INFLUENCE OF TAXES AND OTHER FACTORS ON DEBT RATIO DIFFERENCES BETWEEN MASTER LIMITED PARTNERSHIPS AND CORPORATIONS

Capital Budgeting

ACCOLA, WILTON LEE	AN EMPIRICAL INVESTIGATION OF THE EFFECTS OF A CAPITAL BUDGETING COMPUTERIZED DECISION AID AND COGNITIVE STYLE DIFFERENCES ON INVESTMENT DECISIONS
ANCTIL, REGINA MARIE	CAPITAL BUDGETING USING RESIDUAL INCOME MAXIMIZATION
BROWN, MATTHEW J.	A MEAN-VARIANCE SERIAL REPLACEMENT DECISION MODEL
CHEN, SHIMIN	AN EMPIRICAL INVESTIGATION OF THE USE OF PAYBACK METHOD IN CAPITAL BUDGETING: EFFICIENT VIEW VS OPPORTUNISTIC VIEW

CHRISTENSEN, DAVID SCOTT	THE APPLICATION OF MATHEMATICAL PROGRAMMING TO THE PRODUCTIVITY INVESTMENT FUND PROGRAM: A CAPITAL RATIONING PROBLEM
CHURCH, PAMELA HARMON	ENVIRONMENTAL VOLATILITY AND CAPITAL BUDGETING PRACTICES
FRITSCHE, STEVEN RODNEY	ACCOUNTING RATE OF RETURN AND CONDITIONAL ESTIMATE OF INTERNAL RATE OF RETURN: AN INVESTIGATION OF TWO SURROGATES FOR INTERNAL RATE OF RETURN
ISSA, HUSSEIN MOHAMED AHMED	A PROPOSED MODEL FOR CAPITAL BUDGETARY CONTROL IN THE AMERICAN FOOD PRODUCT CORPORATION SECTOR
KEATING, PATRICK J.	'MANAGING BY THE NUMBERS': AN EMPIRICALLY INFORMED THEORETICAL STUDY OF CORPORATE FINANCIAL WORK
KITE, DEVAUN MARIE	THE IMPACT OF THE FREQUENCY OF ACCOUNTING-BASED PERFORMANCE REPORTS ON CAPITAL BUDGETING DECISIONS
MYERS, MARY DOVE	AN EMPIRICAL INVESTIGATION OF POSTAUDIT PROCEDURES FOR CAPITAL EXPENDITURES AND THEIR ASSOCIATION WITH FIRM PERFORMANCE
ONYIRI, SUNNY O. G.	REPLACEMENT OF DEPRECIABLE TANGIBLE ASSETS: A MACRO APPROACH
SAMIDI, JUHARI BIN	AN EMPIRICAL INVESTIGATION OF THE CAPITAL BUDGETING DECISION PROCESS OF GOVERNMENT-CONTROLLED ENTERPRISES AS COMPARED TO INVESTOR-OWNED ENTERPRISES: THE CASE OF MALAYSIA
SWAIN, MONTE RAY	EXPERIENCE AND INFORMATION EFFECTS ON SEARCH STRATEGIES IN A CAPITAL BUDGETING TASK
WILCZAK, MONIKA J.	CONTRIBUTIONS TO THE CAPITAL BUDGETING PROBLEM
YUN, JOO-KWANG	MEASURING RATES OF RETURN

Capital Markets

ABRAHAM, REBECCA JACOB	COMPARISON OF COMPUTATIONAL METHODS AND INVESTIGATION OF THE TERM STRUCTURE OF INTEREST RATES IMPLIED IN OPTION PRICES
BARRON, ORIE EDWIN	COSTLY TRADING: THE RELATION BETWEEN DISAGREEMENT (OR INFORMATION ASYMMETRIES) AND TRADING IN A WORLD WITH TRADING COSTS
CHANDRA, RAMESH	AN EXAMINATION OF EVENT STUDY METHODOLOGY
CHOI, WON WOOK	FINANCIAL STATEMENT ANALYSIS: THE STUDY OF RETURN ON COMMON EQUITY AND INTANGIBLE ASSETS
COLE, CHARLES STEVEN	THE IMPACT OF PRIVATE DEFAULT RISK INSURANCE ON THE YIELDS OF SEASONED TAX-EXEMPT BONDS
DALTON, THOMAS M.	AN EMPIRICAL INVESTIGATION OF THE RELATIONSHIP BETWEEN TAX-LOSS SELLING AND THE JANUARY EFFECT
DUH, RONG RUEY	ECONOMIC MAN AS AN INTUITIVE BAYESIAN: AN EXPERIMENTAL STUDY
GARLICK, JOHN RICHARD, SR.	CUMULATIVE ABNORMAL RETURNS; INTERVENTION ANALYSIS: A METHODOLOGICAL COMPARISON
GOVINDARAJ, SURESH	ESSAYS ON FINANCIAL MARKETS WITH APPLICATIONS TO ACCOUNTING
HUDSON, CARL DEERING	EXTERNAL MONITORING AND SECURITY OFFERING ANNOUNCEMENTS

Listing by Topic

HWANG, NEN-CHEN	FINANCIAL CHARACTERISTICS OF CORPORATIONS CHANGING COMMON STOCK LISTING FROM THE OVER-THE-COUNTER MARKET TO THE NEW YORK STOCK EXCHANGE
KEMERER, KEVIN L.	ACCOUNTING VARIABLES, STOCK SPLITS AND WHEN-ISSUED TRADING
KERCSMAR, JOHN	INDIVIDUAL INVESTORS' INFORMATION CHOICE, INFORMATION PROCESSING, AND JUDGMENT BEHAVIOR: A PROCESS-TRACING STUDY OF THE VERBAL PROTOCOLS ASSOCIATED WITH STOCK SELECTION
KRUEGER, THOMAS MICHAEL	AN EMPIRICAL ANALYSIS OF THE EFFICIENT MARKET HYPOTHESIS BASED ON WIDELY DISSEMINATED ANOMALY INFORMATION
MCGOWAN, JOHN R.	AN ANALYSIS OF THE EFFECT OF THE TAX REFORM ACT OF 1986 ON STOCK PRICES: A MARKET STUDY
MURPHY, DANIEL PHILIP	EXPERIMENTAL EVIDENCE REGARDING IMPLICIT TAXES AND TAX-INDUCED INVESTOR CLIENTELES
PALOMINO BONILLA, LUIS MIGUEL	INFORMATIONAL ASYMMETRIES IN UNDERDEVELOPED SECURITIES MARKETS, OPTIMAL FINANCIAL CONTRACTS, AND REGULATION
RAMEZANI, AHMAD	ASSET ATTRIBUTES AND PORTFOLIO CHOICE: IMPLICATIONS FOR CAPITAL ASSET PRICES
SAUDAGARAN, SHAHROKH MOHAMED	AN EMPIRICAL STUDY OF SELECTED FACTORS INFLUENCING THE DECISION TO LIST ON FOREIGN STOCK EXCHANGES
STEPHAN, JENS A.	INFORMATION CONTENT OF SECURITY PRICES: EVIDENCE ON THE RATIONAL EXPECTATIONS HYPOTHESIS
SUBRAMANIAM, CHANDRA	MEASURING INFORMATION CONTENT OF CORPORATE ANNOUNCEMENTS
YANG, BONG-JIN	THE EFFECT OF THE FEDERAL RESERVE BOARD'S MARGIN CREDIT CONTROL ON THE DEALERS' BID-ASK SPREAD IN THE OTC STOCK MARKET

Capital Structure

ELITZUR, RACHAMIM RAMY	FINANCIAL REPORTING AND MARKET DATA--A SIGNALLING EQUILIBRIUM PERSPECTIVE
FUGLISTER, JAYNE	CORPORATE CAPITAL STRUCTURE AND TAXES: SOME EVIDENCE
GNIZAK, CHARLES JAMES	INTEREST CAPITALIZATION TAX LAW: ITS EFFECT ON CAPITAL STRUCTURE AND MARKET VALUE
KIM, IL-WOON	AN EMPIRICAL STUDY ON THE INFORMATION CONTENT OF FINANCIAL LEVERAGE TO STOCKHOLDERS
KINNEY, MICHAEL RICHARD	CHANGES IN CORPORATE CAPITAL STRUCTURES AND INVESTMENT IN RESPONSE TO TAX INCENTIVES IN THE ECONOMIC RECOVERY TAX ACT OF 1981
LUKAWITZ, JAMES MARTIN	THE EFFECT OF PARTIAL EQUITY ISSUES ON THE MEASUREMENT OF FINANCIAL LEVERAGE
MAZHAR, NAHEED	FACTORS RELATED TO CORPORATE CAPITAL STRUCTURE
SEAY, SHARON SMITH	AN EMPIRICAL ANALYSIS OF THE RATIO ADJUSTMENT PROCESS: THE CONTRIBUTION OF FIRM-SPECIFIC FACTORS
SHAHID, MD ABDUS	DETERMINANTS OF EQUITY-FOR-DEBT SWAP: A POSITIVE THEORY APPROACH
WALTON, KAREN SCHUELE	THE DEBT/EQUITY CHOICE WITH ASYMMETRIC INFORMATION: AN EMPIRICAL STUDY

Listing by Topic

PRESSLY, THOMAS RICHARD	AN EMPIRICAL STUDY OF INVESTOR USE OF STATEMENT OF CASH FLOWS INFORMATION IN STOCK PRICE PREDICTION DECISIONS
REITHER, CHERI LYNN	A PROCESS ANALYSIS OF LENDERS' USE OF FAS 95 CASH FLOW INFORMATION
SCHROEDER, ANGELIKA THERESA HELKE	CASH FLOW PREDICTIONS USING ALTERNATIVE INCOME MEASURES
SIMONS, KATHLEEN ANN	AN INQUIRY INTO THE USEFULNESS OF A MEASURE OF CASH FLOW IN MODELING DIVIDEND CHANGES
SOMMERVILLE, PATRICIA MILLER	AN ANALYSIS OF THE ATTITUDES TOWARDS CASH FLOW PER SHARE AND A COMPARATIVE ANALYSIS OF ACCRUAL AND CASH BASIS ACCOUNTING IN EXPLAINING CASH FLOW PER SHARE
STEWART, JENICE PRATHER	AN EMPIRICAL INVESTIGATION OF THE USEFULNESS OF ALTERNATIVE EARNING CLASSIFICATIONS IN PREDICTING CASH FLOWS
WALDRON, MARILYN A.	A COMPARATIVE ANALYSIS OF ACCRUAL AND CASH BASIS ACCOUNTING IN PREDICTING CASH FLOWS FROM OPERATIONS IN THE OIL AND GAS INDUSTRY
WANG, ZHEMIN	INFORMATIVENESS AND PREDICTABILITY OF EARNINGS AND CASH FLOWS
WICK, MADALYN HELEN	AN EMPIRICAL STUDY OF DETERMINANTS OF CASH FLOW RESPONSE COEFFICIENTS
ZELLER, THOMAS LOUIS	AN EMPIRICAL INVESTIGATION OF A NET OPERATING CASH FLOW RATE OF RETURN AS A PROXY MEASURE FOR FIRM ECONOMIC PERFORMANCE

Charitable Organizations

BROMAN, AMY J.	THE IMPACT OF FEDERAL INCOME TAX POLICY ON THE CHARITABLE CONTRIBUTIONS BEHAVIOR OF HOUSEHOLDS
FULTS, GAIL JOHNSON	HOW PARTICIPATORY EVALUATION RESEARCH AFFECTS THE MANAGEMENT CONTROL PROCESS OF A MULTINATIONAL NON-PROFIT ORGANIZATION
GREENLEE, JANET STELLE	THE USE OF ACCOUNTING AND OTHER INFORMATION IN DETERMINING THE ALLOCATION OF RESOURCES TO VOLUNTARY HEALTH AND WELFARE ORGANIZATIONS: AN EMPIRICAL ANALYSIS
MCCLURE, RONNIE CLYDE	THE IMPACT ON CHARITABLE CLASSES IN DALLAS COUNTY, TEXAS, RESULTING FROM CHANGES IN THE TAX ECONOMICS OF PRIVATE PHILANTHROPY
TOOLSON, RICHARD BURNS	THE TAX INCENTIVE EFFECT OF THE CHARITABLE CONTRIBUTION DEDUCTION

College & University

AHN, TAE SIK	EFFICIENCY AND RELATED ISSUES IN HIGHER EDUCATION: A DATA ENVELOPMENT ANALYSIS APPROACH
ALRAWI, HIKMAT AHMAD ABDULGHAFOOR	ACCOUNTING, RESOURCE ALLOCATION, PLANNING AND EFFICIENCY: CASE STUDIES OF THE UNITED KINGDOM AND IRAQI UNIVERSITIES
AMMONS, JANICE LEE	THE IMPACT OF STATE CONTROL OF INDIRECT COST RECOVERIES ON AMERICAN RESEARCH UNIVERSITIES
BANAS, EDWARD JOSEPH, JR.	A DECONSTRUCTIONIST ANALYSIS OF ACCOUNTING METHODS FOR COMMUNITY COLLEGES IN THE STATE OF VIRGINIA
BROWN, KENNETH WAYNE	AN EXAMINATION OF DECISION-RELEVANT FINANCIAL AND NONFINANCIAL INDICATORS IN COLLEGES AND UNIVERSITIES
CASCINI, KAREN T.	A COMPARATIVE STUDY OF INVESTMENT STRATEGIES OF COLLEGES AND UNIVERSITIES AND COMMERCIAL CORPORATIONS

CHAMBERLAIN, DARNLEY HUGH, JR.	FINANCIAL REPORTING IN THE HIGHER EDUCATION ENVIRONMENT: ASSESSING THE VIEWS OF SELECTED USERS ON THE USEFULNESS AND ACCESSIBILITY OF SPECIFIED OUTCOMES INFORMATION
CHASE, BRUCE W.	AN EMPIRICAL INVESTIGATION OF A CHOICE OF ACCOUNTING METHOD FOR INVESTMENTS BY COLLEGES AND UNIVERSITIES: POSITIVE ACCOUNTING THEORY APPLIED IN A NOT-FOR-PROFIT ENVIRONMENT
GATIAN, AMY ELIZABETH WILLIAMS	USER INFORMATION SATISFACTION (UIS) AND USER PRODUCTIVITY: AN EMPIRICAL EXAMINATION
GIBSON, THOMAS HARRISON, JR.	THE 1985 NCAA FINANCIAL AUDIT LEGISLATION: IS IT WORKING, FROM COLLEGE AND UNIVERSITY PRESIDENTS' PERSPECTIVE?
HERRING, CLYDE EDSEL	AN EMPIRICAL ANALYSIS OF THE SELECTION OF FINANCIAL ACCOUNTING PRACTICES BY COLLEGES AND UNIVERSITIES
KEASLER, HUBERT LEVERT, JR.	A COMPOSITE PROFILE OF PROPOSED INDIRECT COST RATES APPLICABLE TO ORGANIZED RESEARCH AND DEVELOPMENT AT COLLEGES AND UNIVERSITIES THAT USE MODIFIED TOTAL DIRECT COSTS BASIS FOR FEDERAL IC RATE NEGOTIATIONS
PHILLIPS, SAMUEL HORACE	AN EXPERIMENTAL INVESTIGATION OF THE ROLE OF COLLEGE AND UNIVERSITY FINANCIAL STATEMENTS IN ALUMNI SUPPORT DECISIONS
SADLOWSKI, THEODORE STEPHEN	BUDGET ADMINISTRATION IN COLLEGES
SMITH, CARL STUART	AN ANALYSIS OF THE APPLICATION OF INDIRECT COST ALLOCATION METHODOLOGIES IN HIGHER EDUCATION
SPIKES, PAMELA ANN	A STUDY OF THE APPLICATION OF THE UNRELATED BUSINESS INCOME TAX PROVISIONS TO COLLEGES AND UNIVERSITIES
TURNER, ROBERT M.	AN EXAMINATION OF EXTERNAL FINANCIAL REPORTING BY COLLEGES AND UNIVERSITIES
YUNDT, CHARLES LEROY	FACTORS RELATING TO THE UNDERSTANDING OF COLLEGE AND UNIVERSITY FINANCIAL STATEMENTS FOR NONFINANCIAL UNIVERSITY PERSONNEL

Confirmations

ARMITAGE, JACK LONNIE	EFFECTIVENESS OF AUDIT CONFIRMATIONS FOR TRADE ACCOUNTS RECEIVABLE
CASTER, PAUL	THE EFFECTS OF MISSING DATA ON AUDIT INFERENCE AND AN INVESTIGATION INTO THE VALIDITY OF ACCOUNTS RECEIVABLE CONFIRMATIONS AS AUDIT EVIDENCE
CHOU, LING-TAI LYNETTE	A SURVEY EXAMINATION OF THE OBJECTIVE OF ACCOUNTS RECEIVABLE CONFIRMATION AND THE BEHAVIOR PATTERN OF CONFIRMATION RESPONDENTS

Continuing Education

ENGELBRET, WILLIAM G.	ASSESSING PARTICIPATION BY CERTIFIED PUBLIC ACCOUNTANTS IN CONTINUING PROFESSIONAL EDUCATION AND THE RELATIONSHIP BETWEEN EDUCATION AND CAREER PERFORMANCE
HOPE, NORMAN PHILLIP	MODES OF CONTINUING PROFESSIONAL EDUCATION: A FACTOR ANALYTIC TEST OF HOULE'S MODES OF LEARNING WITH CERTIFIED PUBLIC ACCOUNTANTS
HRNCIR, THERESA JUNE	ACCOUNTANTS IN BUSINESS AND INDUSTRY: DIFFUSION OF INNOVATION WITH REGULATED CHANGE
SAFA MIRHOSSEINY, ALI	CALIFORNIA ACCOUNTING MANAGERS' PERCEPTIONS OF THE EFFECTIVENESS AND RELEVANCY OF DIFFERENT MICROCOMPUTER TRAINING TECHNIQUES FOR GENERAL LEDGER ACCOUNTING PROGRAMS
SALLEE, LARRY	AN EMPIRICAL ANALYSIS OF CONTINUING PROFESSIONAL EDUCATION FOR CERTIFIED PUBLIC ACCOUNTANTS EMPLOYED IN NON-PUBLIC OCCUPATIONS
SANDERSON, GEORGE NORMAN	CONTINUING PROFESSIONAL EDUCATION FOR CERTIFIED PUBLIC ACCOUNTANTS: STATE OF THE ART AND PREDICTIONS FOR CHANGE

WESTORT, PETER JOSEPH   INVESTMENTS IN HUMAN CAPITAL BY ACCOUNTANTS IN PUBLIC PRACTICE

Corporate Taxation

CALLIHAN, DEBRA SALBADOR   AN ANALYSIS OF THE RELATION BETWEEN IMPLICIT TAXES AND MARKET
                               CONCENTRATION

CRAIG, CAROLINE KERN   THE SHIFTING OF CORPORATE CAPITAL ACQUISITION TAX SUBSIDIES: AN EMPIRICAL
                               ANALYSIS

CRAIN, TERRY LYNN   AN EMPIRICAL ANALYSIS OF THE EFFECT OF ALTERNATIVE CAPITAL GAIN TAX
                               PROVISIONS ON HORIZONTAL AND VERTICAL EQUITY

GRANGE, EDWARD VANCE, JR.   AN EXAMINATION OF THE IMPACT OF SELECTED FEDERAL INCOME TAX CHANGES ON
                               BIOTECHNOLOGY COMPANIES IN THE UNITED STATES

HIGGINS, MARK MATTHEW   AN EMPIRICAL ANALYSIS OF THE RELATIONSHIP BETWEEN CORPORATE EFFECTIVE
                               TAX RATES AND BOOK EFFECTIVE TAX RATES WITH AN ANALYSIS OF THE FINANCIAL
                               CHARACTERISTICS THAT INFLUENCE CORPORATE EFFECTIVE TAX RATES

LYNCH, HOWELL JACKSON, JR.   EFFECTIVE CORPORATE INCOME TAX RATES AND THEIR RELATIONSHIP TO
                               CORPORATE ATTRIBUTES: A MULTIDEFINITIONAL, MULTIPERIOD VIEW

SEAMANS, DANA GERALD   AN ANALYSIS OF THE FEDERAL TAX RAMIFICATIONS OF GOODWILL

SERRETT, RANDALL KEITH   AN ANALYTICAL INVESTIGATION OF THE COOPERATIVE TAX ENTITY: PLANNING AND
                               POLICY IMPLICATIONS

WANG, SHIING-WU   FIRM SIZE AND TAX RATES RELATION: AN APPROPRIATE TEST OF   FIRMS'
                               POLITICAL SUCCESS?

Cost Allocation

BARCLAY, RODERICK STUART   COMPUTER CHARGEBACK SYSTEMS: A CRITICAL ANALYSIS AND NEW METHODOLOGY

GUPTA, MAHENDRA R.   AGGREGATION ISSUES IN PRODUCT COSTING

HUFNAGEL, ELLEN M.   SOME DETERMINANTS OF PERCEIVED FAIRNESS IN CHARGEBACK SYSTEMS AND THE
                                EFFECTS OF PERCEIVED FAIRNESS ON USER DECISION MAKING

MAKRIGEORGIS, CHRISTOS N.   DEVELOPMENT OF AN OPTIMAL DURABILITY-BASED HIGHWAY COST ALLOCATION
                                MODEL

RAMADAN, SAYEL S.   THE ALLOCATION OF CENTRAL OVERHEAD COSTS FOR THE PURPOSES OF
                                PERFORMANCE EVALUATION: A STUDY OF UK DIVISIONALISED COMPANIES

TURNER, MARTHA J.   THE USEFULNESS OF COST ALLOCATIONS: AN EXPERIMENTAL INVESTIGATION

UGRAS, YUSUF JOSEPH   AN EMPIRICAL EXAMINATION OF THE FACTORS AFFECTING PERFORMANCE
                                EVALUATION USE OF COST ALLOCATION

YOUNG, RONALD MAURICE   THE EFFECTS OF THE METHOD OF ALLOCATING SYSTEM COSTS ON THE INFORMATION
                                SYSTEM

Cost Behaviors & Estimation

BANAFA, AHMED MOHAMMED   DESIGN RELIABILITY FOR ESTIMATING COSTS OF PILE FOUNDATIONS: FROM THEORY
                                TO APPLICATION OF A PROBABILISTIC-FUZZY APPROACH

CAVER, TROY VERNON   THE VALIDITY OF THE COST-IMPROVEMENT CURVE AS A COST PREDICTOR IN
                                CHANGING PRODUCTION ENVIRONMENTS

CHANG, HSI-HUI   LINEARITY AND SEPARABILITY ASSUMPTIONS IN COST ACCOUNTING

COULMAS, NANCY ELLEN — AN INTENSIVE CASE STUDY OF COST BEHAVIOR ANALYSIS IN AN INDUSTRIAL SETTING

FOWLER, CALVIN D. — AN EMPIRICAL STUDY OF LEARNING CURVES AMONG NON-REPETITIVE JOB SHOP OPERATIONS

Cost Systems

AKERS, MICHAEL DEWAYNE — AN EMPIRICAL INVESTIGATION OF PRODUCT COST METHODS

ALLES, MICHAEL GAMINI — INCENTIVE ASPECTS OF COSTING

GABRIEL, ELIZABETH ANN — MARKET COMPETITION AND THE INCENTIVE TO INVEST IN PRODUCT COST INFORMATION: AN EXPERIMENTAL INVESTIGATION

GOSSE, DARREL IRVIN — AN EMPIRICAL FIELD STUDY OF THE ROLE OF COST ACCOUNTING IN A COMPUTER-INTEGRATED MANUFACTURING ENVIRONMENT

HARRIS, JUDITH ANN BERMAN — A FIELD STUDY EXAMINING THE STRUCTURE AND SUBSTANCE OF COST ACCOUNTING SYSTEMS

LEE, HYUN-SOO — AUTOMATED INTERACTIVE COST ESTIMATING SYSTEM FOR REINFORCED CONCRETE BUILDING STRUCTURES

MCLANAHAN, JAMES CRAIG — COST AND ERROR CHARACTERISTICS OF THREE COST ACCOUNTING SYSTEM TYPES: FULL COSTING, MARGINAL COSTING, AND ACTIVITY BASED COSTING

WILLIS, DAVID MITCHELL — THE CHOICE OF COST SYSTEMS: A LABORATORY SIMULATION

CPA Firm Issues

ADEREMI, SYLVESTER OLUYEMISI — AN EMPIRICAL STUDY OF THE IMPORTANCE OF CERTAIN ATTRIBUTES TO ACCOUNTING FIRMS' SELECTION OF NEW PARTNERS

CENKER, WILLIAM JOHN — AN EMPIRICAL ANALYSIS OF THE RESOLUTION OF CONFLICT AND THE PERCEPTIONS OF AUTONOMY AND RESPONSIBILITY OF INDEPENDENT AUDITORS

DATAR, SRIKANT MADHAV — THE EFFECTS OF AUDITOR REPUTATION IN MORAL HAZARD AND ADVERSE SELECTION SETTINGS

DAVIDSON, RONALD ALLAN — SELECTION-SOCIALIZATION CONTROL IN AUDITING FIRMS: A TEST OF OUCHI'S MODEL OF CONTROL

DOUCET, THOMAS ARTHUR — THE DETERMINATION OF THE USEFUL LIFE OF A CLIENT BASE: AN EMPIRICAL STUDY

FRIEDLANDER, PHILIP HOWARD — INFORMATION TECHNOLOGY AND STRATEGIC ATTITUDES IN THE PUBLIC ACCOUNTING PROFESSION: A STRATEGIC GROUP ANALYSIS

GRUCA, STANLEY P. — ADVERTISING BY CPA FIRMS IN THE STATE OF ILLINOIS: AN ANALYSIS OF INCIDENCE, ATTITUDES, AND EFFICACY

HOLTER, NORMA C. — AUDITOR-FIRM CONFLICT IN THE DEFENSE CONTRACTING INDUSTRY: AN EMPIRICAL STUDY OF THE CONTRIBUTING FACTORS TO THE PERCEIVED IMBALANCE OF POWER

IYER, VENKATARAMAN MOHAN — FACTORS RELATED TO INCLINATION AND CAPACITY OF CPA FIRM ALUMNI TO BENEFIT THEIR FORMER FIRM: AN EMPIRICAL STUDY

LEINICKE, LINDA M. — AN ANALYSIS OF THE BUSINESS ADVISORY SERVICE ACCOUNTANT VERSUS THE TRADITIONAL ACCOUNTING SERVICE ACCOUNTANT, WITH IMPLICATIONS FOR THE ACCOUNTING PROFESSION

LOYLAND, MARY JENNIFER OLSON — AN EMPIRICAL INVESTIGATION OF CPA FIRM ATTRIBUTES AND PROFESSIONAL LIABILITY COVERAGE

MILLS, SHERRY KAY SNODGRASS	EFFECTS OF THE SERVICE ENCOUNTER ON CPA FIRM RETENTION
MITCHELL, ELIZABETH ANN	AN INTEGRATIVE MODEL FOR THE STUDY OF PUBLIC ACCOUNTING FIRMS
NORWOOD, CYNTHIA JANE	MENTORING IN PUBLIC ACCOUNTING: AN EMPIRICAL INVESTIGATION
REDINBAUGH, DONNA FAYE HEERMANN	STRATEGIC PLANNING/MANAGEMENT IN SELECTED BIG EIGHT ACCOUNTING FIRMS
RESCHO, JOYCE ANNE	PUBLIC ACCOUNTING FIRM STRATEGY AND INNOVATIVENESS: A STUDY OF THE ADOPTION OF PRODUCT, TECHNICAL, AND ADMINISTRATIVE INNOVATIONS USING A STRATEGIC TYPOLOGY
ROBSON, GARY STEPHEN	CERTIFICATION EXPERIENCE REQUIREMENTS AND THE TIMING OF RESIGNATION IN PUBLIC ACCOUNTING
ROUSH, PAMELA BARTON	AN INVESTIGATION OF THE EFFECTS OF NON-AUDIT SERVICES AND AUDITOR TENURE ON AUDITOR OBJECTIVITY
SANSING, RICHARD CHALLES	STRATEGIC AUDITING AND STRATEGIC INFORMATION TRANSMISSION IN REPUTATION GAMES
SAVAGE, KATHRYN S.	THE VALUE-AND-BELIEF STRUCTURES OF TOP FINANCIAL EXECUTIVES
SCHNEIDER, WM. BRUCE	CERTIFIED PUBLIC ACCOUNTANTS: A PROFESSION IN CRISIS
SELVY, PATRICIA MILLER	AN EMPIRICAL MODEL BUILDING ANALYSIS OF THE FIRM AND/OR REPORT VARIABLES ASSOCIATED WITH THE RATINGS RECEIVED ON STATE BOARD OF ACCOUNTANCY REVIEWED REPORTS ISSUED BY CPA FIRMS
SHAVER, JAMES HOWARD	CERTIFICATION OF ACCOUNTING SPECIALISTS: VIEWPOINT OF THE SMALL FIRM PRACTITIONER
SHENG, WILLIAM W.	ESSAYS ON BEHAVIORAL AUDITING: A GAME-THEORETIC APPROACH
SHIN, HONG CHUL	OPTIMAL HIRING DECISIONS FOR ENTRY-LEVEL AUDITORS IN PUBLIC ACCOUNTING FIRMS
THOMAS, WILLIAM FRANCIS	THE AUDITOR SELECTION DECISION: A MULTIATTRIBUTE APPROACH
YAHYAZADEH, MASOUD	THREE ESSAYS ON THE STRUCTURE OF AUDITING INDUSTRY, AUDITOR LIABILITY AND THE REGULATION OF AUDIT QUALITY

CPA &/or CMA Examination

DANIELS, ROGER B.	AN EMPIRICAL INVESTIGATION OF THE EFFECTS OF THE ADOPTION OF A SECURED PROCESS ON THE UNIFORM CERTIFIED PUBLIC ACCOUNTANT EXAMINATION
ELFRINK, JOHN ALBERT	AN EMPIRICAL INVESTIGATION INTO THE UTILITY OF THE UNIFORM CERTIFIED PUBLIC ACCOUNTANT EXAMINATION AS AN ENTRY REQUIREMENT FOR THE ACCOUNTING PROFESSION
FARRELL, BARBARA R.	ELEMENTS INFLUENCING SUCCESS ON THE CPA EXAMINATION
GRUBER, ROBERT ALLEN	AN EMPIRICAL INVESTIGATION INTO THE COGNITIVE LEVEL OF THE UNIFORM CPA EXAMINATION
SMITH, ANNE	AN ASSESSMENT OF THE COGNITIVE LEVELS OF THE UNIFORM CERTIFIED PUBLIC ACCOUNTANT EXAMINATION AND THE CERTIFIED MANAGEMENT ACCOUNTANT EXAMINATION

Curriculum Issues

ABRAMOVITCH, RAFAEL	A COST-BENEFIT ANALYSIS OF THE ALTERNATIVE FIVE-YEAR ACCOUNTING EDUCATION SYSTEM
BERRY, LUCILLE M.	THE CHANGES OF COMPUTER USAGE IN ACCOUNTING TEXTS FROM 1974-1984
CLARK, COROLYN ELIZABETH	AN EXPERIMENT TO DETERMINE THE EFFECTS OF A BEHAVIOR MODIFICATION INTERVENTION PROGRAM ON ANXIETY LEVELS AND ACHIEVEMENT OF STUDENTS IN PRINCIPLES OF ACCOUNTING CLASSES
CLEVENGER, THOMAS BENTON	THE DEVELOPMENT OF GUIDELINES FOR INTEGRATING MICROCOMPUTERS INTO THE ACCOUNTING CURRICULUM
DEFLORIA, JAMES DALE	THE PERCEPTIONS OF ACCOUNTING STUDENTS AS TO THE IMPORTANCE OF WRITTEN COMMUNICATION SKILLS FOR SUCCESS IN ACCOUNTING CAREERS
DESAI, SURYAKANT T.	DESIRABLE NON-CONTENT ATTRIBUTES IN PRINCIPLES OF ACCOUNTING MICROCOMPUTER TEST BANKS AMONG TWO-YEAR AND FOUR-YEAR COLLEGE ACCOUNTING INSTRUCTORS: A DELPHI STUDY
DIETZ, DONNA K.	INFORMATION SYSTEMS CONTENT IN UNDERGRADUATE ACCOUNTING PROGRAMS
DOBITZ, CAROL S.	FUND ACCOUNTING PRINCIPLES ADVOCATED BY ACCOUNTING EDUCATORS AND HOSPITAL/MUNICIPAL/COLLEGE CHIEF ACCOUNTANTS
HEAGY, CYNTHIA DONNELL	A NATIONAL STUDY AND EMPIRICAL INVESTIGATION OF THE ACCOUNTING SYSTEMS COURSE: ACADEMIC PRACTICE VERSUS PROFESSIONAL NEEDS
MATHEWS, MARTIN REGINALD	THE REACTIONS OF ACADEMIC ADMINISTRATORS TO THE ACCOUNTING EDUCATION CHANGE COMMISSION, 1989-1992
MCGEE, ROBERT WILLIAM	A MODEL PROGRAM FOR SCHOOLS OF PROFESSIONAL ACCOUNTANCY
MCKEAN, GERALD WILLIAM	CONGRUENCIES OF COMPUTER COMPETENCIES AS VIEWED BY ACCOUNTING PRACTITIONERS AND ACCOUNTING EDUCATORS
QTAISHAT, MUNIF ABDELRAHMAN	JORDANIAN ACCOUNTING PRACTITIONERS' PERCEPTIONS OF UNDERGRADUATE ACCOUNTING PROGRAM CONTENT
SAMPSELL, MARTHA EIBERFELD	SURVEY RESPONSES OF DEPARTMENT CHAIRS OF THE ILLINOIS COLLEGIATE ACCOUNTING PROGRAM TO THE REVISED ILLINOIS PUBLIC ACCOUNTING ACT
SENGE, STEPHEN V.	AN ANALYSIS OF THE MBA INTRODUCTORY FINANCIAL ACCOUNTING CURRICULUM
SMITH, NANCY E.	THE IMPACT OF THE FASB'S CONCEPTUAL FRAMEWORK PROJECT ON INTERMEDIATE ACCOUNTING

Decision Aids

BECKER, D'ARCY ANN	THE EFFECTS OF AUDIT DECISION AID DESIGN ON THE INTRINSIC MOTIVATION AND PERFORMANCE OF AUDITORS PREDICTING CORPORATE BANKRUPTCY
DAVIS, ELIZABETH BOOZER	AIDING GOING CONCERN JUDGMENTS: THE INFLUENCE OF DECISION AID TYPE AND ACCOUNTABILITY
EINING, MARTHA MCDONALD	THE IMPACT OF AN EXPERT SYSTEM AS A DECISION AID ON LEARNING DURING THE AUDIT PROCESS: AN EMPIRICAL TEST
JOSEPH, GILBERT WILLIAM	DESIGNING DECISION AIDS TO OVERCOME BELIEF REVISION BIASES: AN EMPIRICAL INVESTIGATION USING INTERNAL CONTROL RISK ASSESSMENTS IN A DATABASE ENVIRONMENT
KELLY, ANNE SULLIVAN	THE COMPARISON OF SEVERAL INTERNAL CONTROL EVALUATION METHODOLOGIES ON THE ASSESSMENT OF RISK AND OTHER AUDIT PLANNING DECISIONS: AN EMPIRICAL INVESTIGATION

KELLY, KIRK PATRICK	EXPERT PROBLEM SOLVING SYSTEM FOR THE AUDIT PLANNING PROCESS
LIGHTLE, SUSAN SANTALUCIA	AN EMPIRICAL INVESTIGATION OF THE EFFECT OF THE USE OF INTERNAL CONTROL CHECKLISTS ON AUDITORS' INTERNAL CONTROL EVALUATIONS
PRAWITT, DOUGLAS FRANK	A COMPARISON OF HUMAN RESOURCE ALLOCATION ACROSS AUDITING FIRMS: THE EFFECTS OF STRUCTURED AUDIT TECHNOLOGY AND ENVIRONMENT
REDING, KURT F.	CONTROL CHARTS AS DECISION AIDS TO OPERATIONAL AUDITORS' ASSESSMENTS OF PRODUCTION PROCESS PERFORMANCE
SWINNEY, LAURIE S.	EXPERT SYSTEMS IN AUDITING: DECISION AID OR DECISION SUBJUGATION
WHITECOTTON, STACEY MARIE	DECISION AID RELIANCE AS A DETERMINANT OF ACCURACY IN EARNINGS FORECASTING JUDGMENTS: THE IMPACT OF CONTEXTUAL AND DECISION MAKER CHARACTERISTICS

Decision Support Systems

ABBASI, NISHAT ULHASAN	IMPLEMENTATION OF DECISION SUPPORT SYSTEMS: A MODEL AND AN INVESTIGATION
BACK, BARBRO CHRISTINA	AN EXPERT SYSTEM FOR FINANCIAL STATEMENTS PLANNING
BALDWIN-MORGAN, AMELIA ANNETTE	THE IMPACT OF EXPERT SYSTEMS ON AUDITING FIRMS: AN INVESTIGATION USING THE DELPHI TECHNIQUE AND A CASE STUDY APPROACH
CAPOZZOLI, ERNEST ANTHONY	AN EXPERIMENTAL INVESTIGATION OF THE EFFECTS OF A DECISION SUPPORT SYSTEM UTILIZING HYPERTEXT-BASED ACCOUNTING DATA ON INDIVIDUAL DECISION-MAKING BEHAVIOR
CHIU, CHUI-YU	ARTIFICIAL INTELLIGENCE AND ITS APPLICATIONS TO CAPITAL BUDGETING DECISIONS UNDER UNCERTAINTY
CHOI, JONG UK	A CONSTRUCTIVE APPROACH TO BUILDING A KNOWLEDGE-BASED INTERNAL CONTROL EVALUATION REVIEW SYSTEM
COOK, GAIL LYNN	A SYSTEMIC STUDY OF COORDINATED DECISION-MAKING ACROSS FUNCTIONAL AREAS
DENNA, ERIC LEROY	TOWARD A REPRESENTATION OF AUDITOR KNOWLEDGE: EVIDENCE AGGREGATION AND EVALUATION
FEDHILA, HASSOUNA	THE CONSTRUCTION OF AN EXPERT SYSTEM TO MAKE COMMERCIAL LOAN CLASSIFICATIONS
HAN, MAN-HO	A KNOWLEDGE-BASED DECISION SUPPORT SYSTEM (KBDSS) FOR CORPORATE PORTFOLIO ANALYSIS: AN INTEGRATIVE MODEL APPROACH
HARRIS, CAROLYN REBECCA	AN EXPERT DECISION SUPPORT SYSTEM FOR AUDITOR GOING CONCERN EVALUATION
IRELAND, ALICE MARIE	AN INTELLIGENT DECISION SUPPORT SYSTEM FOR DEBT MANAGEMENT
KIANG, YIHWA	EXPLORATION OF QUALITATIVE REASONING AND ITS APPLICATIONS TO MANAGEMENT
KILLINGSWORTH, BRENDA LOU	THE DESIGN OF A KNOWLEDGE-BASED DECISION SUPPORT SYSTEM ENHANCING AUDIT PROGRAM PLANNING
MCDUFFIE, ROBERT STEPHEN	CONSTRUCTION AND VALIDATION OF AN EXPERT SYSTEM PROTOTYPE TO DETERMINE THE ACCOUNTING TREATMENT FOR BUSINESS COMBINATIONS
ODOM, MARCUS DEAN	AN EXAMINATION OF THE INTERACTION OF ELABORATION ALTERNATIVES AND ELABORATION PLACEMENT ON EXPERT SYSTEM-BASED INCIDENTAL LEARNING

Listing by Topic

ROCKWELL, STEPHEN RAYMOND	THE CONCEPTUAL MODELING AND AUTOMATED USE OF RECONSTRUCTIVE ACCOUNTING DOMAIN KNOWLEDGE
RUF, BERNADETTE MARY	DECISION-MAKING IN A DECISION SUPPORT SYSTEMS ENVIRONMENT: AN EVALUATION OF SPATIAL ABILITY AND TASK STRUCTURE
SHIN, DONG-IK	DEVELOPMENT OF A COGNITIVE DIAGNOSIS SYSTEM FOR INTELLIGENT TUTORING: AN APPLICATION TO TRANSPORTATION PROBLEM-SOLVING
SNEAD, KENNETH CARTER, JR.	AN APPLICATION OF VROOM'S EXPECTANCY THEORY AND MCCLELLAND'S TRICHOTOMY OF NEEDS THEORY TO EXAMINE MANAGERS' MOTIVATION TO IMPLEMENT A DECISION SUPPORT SYSTEM
STAHEL, ANDREAS	CONCEPT OF THE DECISION-SUPPORTING MANAGEMENT ACCOUNTING SYSTEM [GESTALTUNG DES ENTSCHEIDUNGSORIENTIERTEN BETRIEBLICHEN RECHNUNGSWESENS]
STEINBART, PAUL JOHN	THE CONSTRUCTION OF AN EXPERT SYSTEM TO MAKE MATERIALITY JUDGMENTS
TOGO, DENNIS FUMIO	THE MATCHING OF DECISION SUPPORT SYSTEMS TO TASKS AND ITS EFFECT ON DECISION-MAKING
TREWIN, JANET	THE IMPACT OF AN EXPERT SYSTEM ON A PROFESSIONAL ACCOUNTING ORGANIZATION
VIATOR, RALPH EDWARD	A COMPUTER-BASED APPROACH TO THE ASSESSMENT OF PRIOR PROBABILITY DISTRIBUTIONS: AN EMPIRICAL INVESTIGATION
WESTLAND, JAMES CHRISTOPHER	SEMANTIC NETWORKS: A STOCHASTIC MODEL OF THEIR PERFORMANCE IN INFORMATION RETRIEVAL
WONG, YUE KEE	COMPUTER-AIDED GROUP JUDGMENT: A STUDY OF GROUP DECISION SUPPORT SYSTEMS EFFECTIVENESS
YUTHAS, KRISTI JANE	CONSTRUCT VALIDITY IN THE MEASUREMENT OF DECISION SUPPORT

Disclosures

BRYAN, STEPHEN HART	MANAGEMENT DISCUSSION AND ANALYSIS: FIRM COMPLIANCE AND INFORMATION CONTENT
CAPRIOTTI, KIM BOYLAN	AN INVESTIGATION OF THE USE OF VERBAL AND NUMERICAL PROBABILITY EXPRESSIONS IN BANK LENDING DECISIONS
DEINES, DAN STUART	A TEST FOR THE SIMILARITY OF ANALYSTS' AND INVESTORS' EXPECTATIONS SUBJECT TO THE RELEASE OF MANDATED ACCOUNTING DISCLOSURES
GOTLOB, DAVID	INVESTOR AND CREDITOR PERCEPTIONS OF CORPORATE PERFORMANCE: A MULTIDIMENSIONAL SCALING APPROACH
INDJEJIKIAN, RAFFI J.	THE IMPACT OF INFORMATION ON THE EXTENT OF AGREEMENT AMONG INVESTORS: A NEW PERSPECTIVE ON FIRM DISCLOSURES
KILE, CHARLES OWEN, JR.	AN ANALYSIS OF THE IMPACT OF OMITTED EVALUATIVE INFORMATION ON FINANCIAL REPORTING: EVIDENCE FROM DISCLOSURES TO AMEND MANAGEMENT'S DISCUSSION AND ANALYSIS
KING, RONALD RAYMOND	EFFECTS OF CHANGES IN THE LEVEL OF PUBLIC DISCLOSURE ON THE ACQUISITION OF PRIVATE INFORMATION: AN EXPERIMENTAL MARKETS INVESTIGATION
MITCHELL, NAOMI CELIA	THE RELATIONSHIP OF CERTAIN ENVIRONMENTAL PERFORMANCE INDICATORS AND FINANCIAL STATEMENTS
MOORE, JOHN WILLIAM	AN EMPIRICAL INVESTIGATION OF THE FINANCIAL EFFECTS OF UNION REPRESENTATION AND DECERTIFICATION ELECTIONS ONPUBLICLY TRADED FIRMS
NYCUM, VICKI L.	A STUDY OF THE APPLICATION OF THREE READABILITY INDICES AND THE CLOZE PROCEDURE TO EVALUATE THE UNDERSTANDABILITY OF NARRATIVE DISCLOSURES IN FINANCIAL REPORTS

Listing by Topic

O'LEARY, DANIEL EDMUND	THE RELATIONSHIP OF NONACCOUNTING DISCLOSURES TO FIRM VALUATION AND PROFITABILITY: AN EMPIRICAL ANALYSIS OF TOBIN'S Q RATIO
PRESTON-THOMAS, AVERIL REI	THE ASSOCIATION BETWEEN ACCOUNTING DISCLOSURES AND INSTITUTIONAL TRADING PATTERNS
PRICE, RENEE HALL	THE RELATIONS BETWEEN INSTITUTIONAL EQUITY OWNERSHIP, PRICE RESPONSIVENESS, AND ACCOUNTING DISCLOSURE QUALITY
RAGOTHAMAN, SRINIVASAN	ECONOMIC IMPLICATIONS OF ASSET WRITEDOWN DISCLOSURE POLICY
ROBINSON, IDA B.	AN EXAMINATION OF BOND VALUATION IN THE PRESENCE OF LOSS CONTINGENCY DISCLOSURES: A CONTINUOUS-TIME FINANCE THEORY APPROACH
SANKARAN, VENKATESWAR	IMPACT OF MANDATED DISCLOSURES ON MARKETMAKER BEHAVIOR: A CASE STUDY OF MANDATED REPLACEMENT COST DISCLOSURES
SKARO, MATTHEW MARTIN	A THEORETICAL AND EMPIRICAL INVESTIGATION OF THE RELEVANCE AND RELIABILITY OF CERTAIN OPINIONS CONCERNING PENDING LITIGATION
SMITH, STERLING DUANE	AN EMPIRICAL INVESTIGATION OF THE PROPERTIES OF SEQUENTIAL DISCLOSURES TO THE EQUITY MARKETS
ULISS, BARBARA TURK	REPORTING INTEREST RATE SWAPS: THE ASSOCIATION OF DISCLOSURE QUALITY WITH CREDIT RISK AND OWNERSHIP STRUCTURE
VREELAND, JANNET MARGARET	AN INVESTIGATION OF DISCLOSURE PRACTICES OF PRIVATE FIRMS
WELKER, MICHAEL ALAN	DISCLOSURE POLICY, INFORMATION ASYMMETRY, LIQUIDITY AND THE COST OF EQUITY CAPITAL: A THEORETICAL AND EMPIRICAL INVESTIGATION

Dividends

ALLTIZER, RICHARD LEE	THE INTERACTION OF DIVIDEND POLICY AND TAXATION ON THE VALUE OF THE FIRM
BROOKS, RAYMOND MICHAEL	AN IMPLIED CASH DIVIDEND AND TRADING PATTERNS: VOLUME, SPREADS, SPREAD COMPONENTS AND ASYMMETRIC INFORMATION AROUND DIVIDEND AND EARNINGS ANNOUNCEMENTS
CARROLL, THOMAS JOSEPH	THE NATURE OF THE DIVIDEND SIGNAL OF FUTURE EARNINGS
DAS, SOMNATH	DIFFERENTIAL INFORMATION CONTENT OF STOCK DIVIDEND ANNOUNCEMENTS
FANG, CHIH-CHIANG	THREE EMPIRICAL INVESTIGATIONS INTO EARNINGS AND DIVIDENDS
FERREIRA, LOURDES DALTRO	LINKAGES BETWEEN EXECUTIVE COMPENSATION PROVISIONS AND THE DIVIDEND DECISION
GRUBE, NANCY WEATHERHOLT	EXAMINATION OF INITIATING DIVIDEND EFFECTS
KIM, JEONG YOUN	AN EMPIRICAL INVESTIGATION OF THE EFFECT OF LIFO ADOPTION ON DIVIDEND POLICIES
KLEIN, LINDA SCHMID	EARNINGS INFORMATION CONTENT OF STOCK DIVIDEND AND SPLIT ANNOUNCEMENTS
MANDE, VIVEK GOPAL	THE INFORMATION CONTENT OF EARNINGS AND DIVIDENDS: THE SUBSTITUTION HYPOTHESIS
MURDOCH, ALASTAIR	DIVIDENDS AND EARNINGS: THEIR EFFECT ON FIRM VALUE

SCHLICHTING, DAVID KENNETH	AN EMPIRICAL ANALYSIS OF THE IMPACT OF THE DEFICIT REDUCTION ACT OF 1984 ON CORPORATE DIVIDEND CAPTURE ACTIVITY
SMITH, ROGER JOSEPH	THE EFFECTS OF THE TAX REFORM ACT OF 1986 ON CASH DIVIDEND VALUATION
SWANSON, ZANE LEWIS	THE INFORMATION CONTENT OF EARNINGS COMPONENTS AND DIVIDENDS
TUCKER, JAMES JOSEPH, III	STOCK DIVIDENDS: HISTORICAL, CONCEPTUAL AND REPORTING PERSPECTIVES
VOLK, GARY A.	A REEXAMINATION OF ACCOUNTING FOR STOCK DIVIDENDS: IS IT TIME FOR A CHANGE?
WHELAN, ADELAIDE KATE	STOCK DIVIDENDS: MARKET REACTIONS AND MOTIVATIONS

Earnings

AHMED, ANWER SHEHAB	ACCOUNTING EARNINGS, ECONOMIC RENTS AND STOCK RETURNS: AN EMPIRICAL ANALYSIS
ANGIMA, JACOB M.	THE ASSOCIATION BETWEEN ALTERNATIVE EARNINGS AND PROFITABILITY MEASURES AND STOCK RETURN IN SELECTED INDUSTRIES
EASTERGARD, ALF MOODY	THE COMPATIBILITY OF MARKET RETURNS AND INCOME NUMBERS OBSERVED AFTER ADJUSTMENTS TO RETAINED EARNINGS
JENNINGS, ROSS GRANT	A STUDY OF THE CROSS-SECTIONAL HOMOGENEITY OF THE INFORMATION CONTENT OF ACCOUNTING INCOME AND ITS COMPONENTS
KIM, HWAN	THE SPEED OF SECURITY MARKET REACTION AND THE LEVEL OF UNCERTAINTY ASSOCIATED WITH ANNUAL EARNINGS INFORMATION: ANALYSIS AND EVIDENCE
KOTHARI, SRIPRAKASH	A COMPARISON OF ALTERNATIVE PROXIES FOR THE MARKET'S EXPECTATION OF QUARTERLY EARNINGS
KRIPPEL, GREGORY LEE	THE ECONOMIC DETERMINANTS OF THE TIME-SERIES PROPERTIES OF EARNINGS, SALES, AND CASH FLOWS FROM OPERATIONS
LIPE, ROBERT CALVIN	THE INFORMATION CONTAINED IN THE COMPONENTS OF EARNINGS
LO, MAY HWA	DIFFERENTIAL CAPITAL MARKET VALUATIONS OF FUNCTIONAL COMPONENTS OF EARNINGS: AN EMPIRICAL ANALYSIS
LYON, JOHN DOUGLAS	THE VALUATION INFORMATION ASSOCIATED WITH THE SEQUENCE OF ACCOUNTING EARNINGS
MASTRACCHIO, NICHOLAS JAMES, JR.	AN EXAMINATION OF THE THEORETICAL BASIS AND THE APPLICATION OF THE CAPITALIZATION OF EARNINGS METHOD AND THE EXCESS EARNINGS METHOD TO CLOSELY HELD BUSINESSES
NWAEZE, EMEKA T.	THE EFFECTS OF THE PARAMETERS OF EARNINGS EXPECTATION ON STOCK PRICES: A STRUCTURAL MODEL AND EMPIRICAL EVIDENCE
OMER, KHURSHEED	AN INVESTIGATION OF PLOUGHBACK EARNINGS AS A FACTOR IN SECURITY PRICING
PURCELL, THOMAS J., III	AN ANALYSIS OF THE FEDERAL INCOME TAX CONCEPT OF EARNINGS AND PROFITS AS COMPARED TO THE FINANCIAL ACCOUNTING CONCEPT OF RETAINED EARNINGS
RYAN, STEPHEN G.	STRUCTURAL MODELS OF THE ACCOUNTING PROCESS AND EARNINGS
SHROFF, PERVIN KEKI	ESSAYS ON THE ASSOCIATION OF ACCOUNTING EARNINGS WITH SECURITY RETURNS

Listing by Topic

263

SINHA, RANJAN	AN ASSESSMENT OF MARKET REACTION TO EARNINGS AND BOOK VALUE INFORMATION
WONG, TAK-JUN	ESSAYS ON THE DETERMINANTS OF THE RELATION BETWEEN STOCK PRICES AND ACCOUNTING EARNINGS

Earnings Announcements

AHN, BYUNGJUN	THE INFORMATION CONTENT OF EARNINGS ANNOUNCEMENTS WITH VARYING RETURN PARAMETERS
ANDERSON, MARILYN TERESA	ACCOUNTING EARNINGS ANNOUNCEMENTS AND DIFFERENTIAL PREDISCLOSURE INFORMATION
ARCHAMBAULT, JEFFREY JAY	FINANCING AND INVESTING ACTIVITIES AND THE PREEMPTION OF EARNINGS
ARCHAMBAULT, MARIE ELLEN EMMENDORFER	REACTION TO EARNINGS IN A TAKEOVER ENVIRONMENT
BRACKNEY, KENNARD SAMUEL, JR.	EARNINGS ANNOUNCEMENT TIMELINESS AND INVESTOR WEALTH
CHANDRA, UDAY	THE ASSOCIATION BETWEEN PREDISCLOSURE INDUSTRY INFORMATION AND THE INFORMATION CONTENT OF EARNINGS ANNOUNCEMENTS
CHEN, DAVID MING-DAU	THE INFORMATION CONTENT OF QUARTERLY EARNINGS DATA AND THE MARKET'S REVISION OF RISK PREDICTIONS IMPLIED IN OPTION PRICES
CHIEN, CHIN-CHEN	ALTERNATIVE METHODS FOR THE ESTIMATION OF EARNINGS AND DIVIDENDS ANNOUNCEMENT EFFECTS: REVIEW, INTEGRATION, AND EXTENSION
CHO, JANG YOUN	TIMELINESS OF EARNINGS REPORTS: A SIGNALLING APPROACH
CHOI, SUNG KYU	DIFFERENTIAL INFORMATION CONTENT OF PUBLICLY ANNOUNCED EARNINGS: THEORETICAL AND EMPIRICAL ANALYSIS
CHUNG, HAY YOUNG	EMPIRICAL INVESTIGATION INTO THE STOCK MARKET REACTIONS TO CORPORATE EARNINGS REPORTS
CONRAD, EDWARD JOHN	ENVIRONMENTAL AND FIRM CHARACTERISTICS AS DETERMINANTS OF TRADING VOLUME REACTION TO EARNINGS ANNOUNCEMENTS
CREADY, WILLIAM MONTGOMERY	AN EMPIRICAL INVESTIGATION INTO THE RELATIONSHIP BETWEEN THE VALUE OF ACCOUNTING EARNINGS ANNOUNCEMENTS AND EQUITY INVESTOR ENDOWMENT SIZES
DEMPSEY, STEPHEN JEFFREY	PARTITIONING MARKET EFFICIENCIES BY ANALYST ATTENTION: THE CASE OF ANNUAL EARNINGS ANNOUNCEMENTS
ETTER, EDWIN ROGER, JR.	THE INFORMATION CONTENT OF BRITISH AND JAPANESE EARNINGS ANNOUNCEMENTS: A PRICE AND TRADING VOLUME APPROACH
GRAHAM, ROGER CHARLTON, JR.	THE ASSOCIATION BETWEEN ORDER OF ANNOUNCEMENT AND SECURITY PRICE REACTIONS TO AN EARNINGS RELEASE
HAN, KI CHOONG	MARKET RESPONSE TO EARNINGS ANNOUNCEMENTS: THE EFFECTS OF FIRM CHARACTERISTICS
HO, LI-CHIN	THE EFFECTS OF OPTION TRADING ON THE INFORMATION CONTENT OF EARNINGS DISCLOSURES: AN EMPIRICAL ANALYSIS
IM, JONG-GEOL	DIFFERENTIAL INFORMATION ENVIRONMENT AND THE MAGNITUDE OF CAPITAL MARKET RESPONSES TO EARNINGS ANNOUNCEMENTS
JANG, HWEE-YONG	TRADING VOLUME AND ACCOUNTING RESEARCH: THEORY, IMPLICATION, AND EVIDENCE

Listing by Topic

TSAI, YANN-CHING   THE TIMING EFFECT OF EARNINGS REPORTS AND THE STOCK MARKET   REACTION TO LATE-REPORTING FIRMS

Earnings Management

BARKMAN, BERYL V.   INCOME SMOOTHING: A LABORATORY EXPERIMENT

CAHAN, STEVEN F.   LEGISLATIVE ACTION, POLITICAL COSTS, AND FIRM ACCOUNTING CHOICE

CARNES, GREGORY ALVIN   AN EMPIRICAL INVESTIGATION OF THE RELATIONSHIP BETWEEN TAX INCENTIVES AND FINANCIAL REPORTING POLICY

CARSTENS, ROBERT HUGO KONRAD   AN ANALYSIS OF THE EXPERT OPINIONS AND EXPERIENCES OF AUDITORS ON THE TOPIC OF INCOME SMOOTHING

COYLE, WILLIAM HENRY   THE DIFFERENTIAL EFFECTS OF INCENTIVES AND MONITORING ON EARNINGS MANAGEMENT AT THE TIME OF A CEO CHANGE

DUCHAC, JONATHAN EHRLICH   EARNINGS MANAGEMENT AND THE PRECISION OF EARNINGS SIGNALS IN THE BANKING INDUSTRY

EASTERWOOD, CINTIA MENDEZ   HOSTILE TAKEOVERS AND INCENTIVES FOR EARNINGS MANIPULATION: AN EMPIRICAL ANALYSIS

EL HOSSADE, SALEM ISMAIL   MANAGEMENT OF ANNUAL REPORTED INCOME IN THE U.K.: THE SEARCH FOR INDICATORS

EL-SABBAGH, AMAL   MARKET EVALUATION OF DISCOVERY OF DISTORTED EARNINGS SIGNALS: EMPIRICAL TESTS OF CHANGES IN CASH FLOW EXPECTATIONS, RISKINESS, AND EARNINGS QUALITY HYPOTHESES

GOSSELIN, DAVID J.   AN EMPIRICAL INVESTIGATION OF CORPORATE INCOME SMOOTHING: A FACTOR ANALYTIC AND DISCRIMINANT APPROACH TO FIRM IDENTIFICATION

GRAMLICH, JEFFREY DOUGLAS   AN EMPIRICAL ANALYSIS OF THE EFFECT OF THE ALTERNATIVE MINIMUM TAX BOOK INCOME ADJUSTMENT ON THE EXTENT OF DISCRETIONARY ACCOUNTING ACCRUALS

JOO, HYUNGHWAN   INCOME SMOOTHING: AN ASYMMETRIC INFORMATION APPROACH

LASALLE, RANDALL EUGENE   THE EFFECT OF CEO TENURE ON EARNINGS MANAGEMENT

LEGGETT, CARL LEE   AN EMPIRICAL INVESTIGATION OF THE MARKET REACTION TO SELECTED CATEGORIES OF DISCRETIONARY CHARGES

MAKAR, STEPHEN DOUGLAS   POLITICAL COSTS OVER THE BUSINESS CYCLE: THE INCENTIVES FOR THE MANAGEMENT OF ACCOUNTING ACCRUALS

MANZON, GIL B., JR.   AN INVESTIGATION OF FACTORS AFFECTING THE INCOME STRATEGIES OF FIRMS SUBJECT TO THE ALTERNATIVE MINIMUM TAX

MAYDEW, EDWARD LYLE   INCENTIVES TO MAGNIFY NET OPERATING LOSSES FOLLOWING THE TAX REFORM ACT OF 1986

NA, CHONGKIL   THE ASSOCIATION BETWEEN ACCOUNTING ACCRUALS AND MEAN REVERSION OF ANNUAL EARNINGS

PASTORIA, GAIL   THE USE OF ACCOUNTING ACCRUALS AS A DEFENSIVE STRATEGY TO DETER TAKEOVERS

POWER, JEFFREY WILLIAM   AN EMPIRICAL INVESTIGATION OF ANTITAKEOVER AMENDMENTS AND MANAGERIAL DISCRETION IN REPORTED EARNINGS

ROBINSON, THOMAS RICHARD   EXTERNAL DEMANDS FOR EARNINGS MANAGEMENT: THE ASSOCIATION BETWEEN EARNINGS VARIABILITY AND BOND RISK PREMIA

SIVAKUMAR, KUMAR N.	MANAGERIAL CHOICE OF DISCRETIONARY ACCOUNTING METHODS: AN EMPIRICAL EVALUATION OF SECURITY MARKET RESPONSE
SMITH, PAMELA ANN	THE EARLY ADOPTION OF ACCOUNTING STANDARDS AS AN EARNINGS MANAGEMENT TOOL
WU, YUWU	MANAGEMENT BUYOUTS: A TEST OF THE MANAGEMENT MANIPULATION HYPOTHESIS

Earnings Per Share

ABDELKARIM, NASER MOHAMMAD	AN EMPIRICAL EXAMINATION OF THE RELATIONSHIP BETWEEN ANNOUNCEMENT-PERIOD STOCK RETURNS AND THE POTENTIAL DILUTION EFFECT OF CONVERTIBLE BONDS ON EPS
DIMITRY, KENNETH ELIA	AN EMPIRICAL EXAMINATION OF THE TIME-SERIES PROPERTIES OF EARNINGS-PER-SHARE USING TRANSFER FUNCTION ANALYSIS AT THE INDUSTRY LEVEL
JANG, YEONG MIN	AN EMPIRICAL EVALUATION OF THE CURRENT ACCOUNTING COMMON STOCK EQUIVALENCY TEST AND AN ALTERNATIVE MARKET MODEL
JERRIS, SCOTT I.	THE ASSOCIATION BETWEEN STOCK RETURNS AND ALTERNATIVE EARNINGS PER SHARE NUMBERS
LAI, SYOUCHING	AN ANALYTICAL ANALYSIS OF EPS RULES FOR CONVERTIBLE SECURITIES, WARRANTS, AND OPTIONS
LUCAS, MARCIA J.	EARNINGS PER SHARE: A STUDY OF CURRENT REPORTING
MORRISON, THEODORE DAVIDSON, III	AN EMPIRICAL MODEL FOR THE DESCRIPTION AND FORECASTING OF QUARTERLY EARNINGS PER SHARE FOR SMALL AND NEGLECTED FIRMS
O'BRIEN, PATRICIA COLLEEN	AN EMPIRICAL ANALYSIS OF FORECASTS OF EARNINGS PER SHARE
PINAC-WARD, SUZANNE RESI	AN EMPIRICAL INVESTIGATION OF THE COMPARABILITY OF REPORTED EARNINGS PER SHARE UNDER ACCOUNTING PRINCIPLES BOARD OPINION NO. 15
ROY, DANIEL	AN EVALUATION OF UNIVARIATE TIME-SERIES MODELS OF QUARTERLY EARNINGS PER SHARE AND THEIR GENERALIZATION TO MODELS WITH AUTOREGRESSIVE CONDITIONALLY HETEROSCEDASTIC DISTURBANCES
SHADBOLT, MICHAEL EARL	CALCULATING EARNINGS PER SHARE: AN EMPIRICAL ANALYSIS ESTIMATING THE DILUTIVE IMPACT OF CONVERTIBLE SECURITIES ON A CURRENT BASIS

Earnings Response Coefficients

BANDYOPADHYAY, SATIPRASAD	THE RELATIVE INFORMATIVENESS OF SUCCESSFUL EFFORTS AND FULL COST EARNINGS IN THE OIL AND GAS INDUSTRY
CHANG, CHUNG-YUEH C.	AN EXAMINATION OF TIME-VARYING EARNINGS GROWTH AND EARNINGS LEVELS AND THEIR IMPACTS ON SECURITY RETURNS
COFFER, CURTIS ALAN	THE EFFECTS OF UNCERTAINTY AND THE INFORMATION ENVIRONMENT ON THE RELATION BETWEEN ACCOUNTING EARNINGS AND STOCK RETURNS FOR NEWLY PUBLIC FIRMS
FELDMANN, DOROTHY A.	THE MARKET REACTION TO UNEXPECTED EARNINGS: THE CASE OF INDIVIDUAL AND INSTITUTIONAL INVESTORS
FURZE, SALLY	SFAS 94 AND NOISY EARNINGS SIGNALS
GUO, MIIN HONG	DIFFERENTIAL EARNINGS RESPONSE COEFFICIENTS TO ACCOUNTING INFORMATION: THE CASE OF REVISIONS OF FINANCIAL ANALYSTS' FORECASTS
JOHNSON, MARILYN FRANCES	BUSINESS CYCLES AND THE RELATION BETWEEN SECURITY RETURNS AND EARNINGS

KALLAPUR, SANJAY GOKULDAS	DETERMINANTS OF THE STOCK PRICE RESPONSE TO EARNINGS
KWAK, WIKIL	EARNINGS RESPONSE COEFFICIENTS AND THE QUALITY OF EARNINGS: THE CASE OF AUDITOR CHANGE
O'BRYAN, DAVID	THE ASSOCIATION OF EARNINGS AND CASH FLOW COMPONENTS WITH CORPORATE BOND RETURNS
RAMESH, KRISHNAMOORTHY	ESSAYS ON EARNINGS RESPONSE COEFFICIENT
RAO, GITA RAMA	THE RELATION BETWEEN STOCK RETURNS AND EARNINGS: A STUDY OF NEWLY-PUBLIC FIRMS
SCHLICTMAN, MARIBETH COLLER	EXTERNAL REPORTING SYSTEMS AND ASSET PRICES: AN EXPERIMENTAL STUDY
THIAGARAJAN, SUNDARARAMAN	ECONOMIC DETERMINANTS OF EARNINGS PERSISTENCE

EDP Controls

BLOUCH, WILLIAM EDWARD	EDP CONTROLS TO MAINTAIN DATA INTEGRITY IN DISTRIBUTED PROCESSING SYSTEMS
LANDRY, RAYMOND MAURICE, JR.	AN EMPIRICAL INVESTIGATION OF EDP AUDIT JUDGMENTS AND CONSENSUS BETWEEN EXTERNAL AND INTERNAL AUDIT EXPERTS
MOHRWEIS, LAWRENCE CHARLES	AN EMPIRICAL INVESTIGATION OF FACTORS AFFECTING THE USE OF CONCURRENT EDP AUDIT TECHNIQUES
STEIN, DOUGLAS MITCHELL	THE IMPACT OF PAPERLESS INFORMATION SYSTEMS ON SUBSTANTIVE AUDIT EVIDENCE
VANSYCKLE, LARRY D.	A CRITICAL EVALUATION OF THE CPA'S PERFORMANCE OF INTERNAL CONTROL REVIEWS OF EDP SYSTEMS IN COMPLIANCE WITH GENERALLY ACCEPTED AUDITING STANDARDS

Errors

JAGANNATHAN, JAYASHRI V.	SEQUENTIAL STOPPING RULES FOR ESTIMATING THE TOTAL ERROR IN ACCOUNTING POPULATIONS USING MONETARY UNIT SAMPLING
KAZENSKI, PAUL M.	A NON-LINEAR APPROACH TO DETECTING ESTIMATION AND VALUATION ERRORS IN THE REPORTED RESERVES OF PROPERTY-LIABILITY INSURERS
MARCHANT, GARRY ALLEN	ANALOGICAL REASONING AND ERROR DETECTION
ROBINSON, CHRISTOPHER MICHAEL	AN EMPIRICAL INVESTIGATION OF ERROR CORRECTION DECISIONS MADE BY AUDITORS IN PRACTICE
USOFF, CATHERINE ANNE	AN EXAMINATION OF FACTORS AFFECTING AUDIT PLANNING ACROSS ACCOUNTS

Estate & Gift Taxation

ANDERSON, PHILIP NEIL	AN EMPIRICAL STUDY OF RECENT CHANGES IN FEDERAL ESTATE TAXATION AND THEIR RELATED IMPACT ON THE FAMILY FARM
GREENSTEIN, BRIAN RICHARD	AN EMPIRICAL ANALYSIS OF THE QUALIFIED TERMINABLE INTEREST PROPERTY ELECTION AND RELATED PROVISIONS
NEWMAN, SCOTT GARDINER	A COMPREHENSIVE RANKING OF ESTATE FREEZING TRANSACTIONS
ROBERTS, MICHAEL L.	JUDGMENT AND THE VALUATION OF CLOSELY HELD CORPORATIONS FOR ESTATE TAXATION

SCRIBNER, EDMUND ARTHUR   TOWARD AN ECONOMIC MODEL OF TAXPAYER-IRS INTERACTION

Ethics

ALLEN, PAUL WADE   EXPLAINING CPA PREFERENCES TOWARD ETHICAL ISSUES

BAKKE, MARILYN   A STUDY OF THE DISCIPLINE OF CPAS BY STATE BOARDS OF ACCOUNTANCY

BEETS, STEPHEN DOUGLAS   EFFECTIVENESS OF THE COMPLAINT-BASED ENFORCEMENT SYSTEM OF THE AICPA CODE OF PROFESSIONAL ETHICS

BUTTROSS, THOMAS EDWARD   THE EFFECT OF SELECTED PERSONALITY AND SITUATIONAL VARIABLES ON THE ETHICAL JUDGMENTS OF MANAGEMENT ACCOUNTANTS IN FEDERAL INCOME TAX COMPLIANCE

CARNES, KAY C.   THE EFFECTS OF CERTAIN PERSONAL AND ORGANIZATIONAL VARIABLES ON THE ATTITUDES OF INTERNAL AUDITORS TOWARD ETHICAL DILEMMAS

CHI, SUNG-KUON   ETHICS AND AGENCY THEORY

CHIASSON, MICHAEL ANTHONY   ORGANIZATIONAL-PROFESSIONAL CONFLICT AND THE WHISTLEBLOWING INTENTIONS OF PROFESSIONAL ACCOUNTANTS

CHILTON, ROBERT CARTER   THE AMERICAN ACCOUNTING PROFESSION AND ITS CODE OF ETHICS: 1887-1933

CLAYPOOL, GREGORY ALLEN   AN EXPLORATORY STUDY OF THE COGNITIVE FRAMEWORKS USED BY CPAS AND THEOLOGIANS WHEN CONFRONTED WITH ETHICAL DILEMMAS

COPPAGE, RICHARD EDWARD   AN EMPIRICAL DEFINITION OF ETHICS FOR MANAGEMENT ACCOUNTANTS

GIBSON, ANNETTA MAE   AN EMPIRICAL INVESTIGATION INTO ETHICAL DECISION-MAKING IN ACCOUNTING

HODGE, THOMAS GLEN   THE EMPIRICAL DEVELOPMENT OF ETHICS DECISION MODELS FOR MANAGEMENT ACCOUNTANTS

HWANG, HO-CHAN   PROFESSIONAL ACCOUNTANTS' ETHICAL BEHAVIOR: A POSITIVE APPROACH

ISAACS, PATRICIA COLE   IMA'S CODE OF ETHICS: AN EMPIRICAL EXAMINATION OF VIEWPOINTS OF CERTIFIED MANAGEMENT ACCOUNTANTS

KARCHER, JULIA NANCY   AUDITORS' ABILITY TO DISCERN THE PRESENCE OF ETHICAL PROBLEMS

KLEINMAN, GARY BRUCE   CONSTRUCTING THE AUDITOR AND ACCOUNTANT

MCCARTHY, IRENE N.   PROFESSIONAL ETHICS CODE CONFLICT SITUATIONS: ETHICAL AND VALUE ORIENTATION OF COLLEGIATE ACCOUNTING STUDENTS

MCCOY, TIMOTHY LYNN   AN ANALYSIS OF MORAL JUDGMENTS AND OTHER FACTORS AFFECTING BEHAVIORAL INTENTIONS OF CERTIFIED PUBLIC ACCOUNTANTS

MCKENNA, JOHN N.   ETHICAL DILEMMAS IN FINANCIAL REPORTING SITUATIONS AND THE PREFERRED MODE OF RESOLUTION OF ETHICAL CONFLICTS AS TAKEN BY CERTIFIED AND NONCERTIFIED MANAGEMENT ACCOUNTANTS IN ORGANIZATIONS WITH PERCEIVED

PONEMON, LAWRENCE ANDREW   A COGNITIVE-DEVELOPMENTAL APPROACH TO THE ANALYSIS OF CERTIFIED PUBLIC ACCOUNTANTS' ETHICAL JUDGMENTS

SCHAEFER, JAMES CLARK   A STUDY OF THE PROPENSITY OF CERTIFIED PUBLIC ACCOUNTANTS TO ACT UNPROFESSIONALLY

SHAUB, MICHAEL KENNETH   AN EMPIRICAL EXAMINATION OF THE DETERMINANTS OF AUDITORS' ETHICAL SENSITIVITY

STEED, STEVE ALAN   AN EMPIRICAL STUDY OF THE EFFECTIVENESS OF INDEPENDENCE DISCRIMINATION RESULTING FROM THE APPLICATION OF AICPA ETHICAL INTERPRETATION 101-3--ACCOUNTING SERVICES

SWEENEY, JOHN THOMAS   COGNITIVE MORAL DEVELOPMENT AND AUDITOR INDEPENDENCE: AN EMPIRICAL INVESTIGATION

Financial Analysts

ABARBANELL, JEFFERY STEVEN   INFORMATION ACQUISITION BY FINANCIAL ANALYSTS IN RESPONSE TO SECURITY PRICE CHANGES

ALKHALIALEH, MAHMOUD ABDUL-HALEEM   NON-EARNINGS INFORMATION AND ANALYSTS' REVISIONS OF FUTURE EARNINGS FORECASTS

BRANSON, BRUCE CLAYTON   AN EMPIRICAL EXAMINATION OF FIRM-SPECIFIC CHARACTERISTICS ASSOCIATED WITH DIFFERENTIAL INFORMATION ENVIRONMENTS

BROCE, PATRICIA ANN   THE USEFULNESS OF 'PRO FORMA' FINANCIAL STATEMENTS IN DECISION MAKING BY FINANCIAL ANALYSTS

BULLIS FRANSSON, DEBRA ALICE   THE EFFECT OF INVESTMENT DECISION GOAL ON FINANCIAL ANALYSTS' USE OF INFORMATION IN JUDGMENTS ABOUT FIRMS

CHEN, YUANG-SUNG AL   FINANCIAL ANALYST FORECAST DISPERSION: DETERMINANTS AND USEFULNESS AS AN EXANTE MEASURE OF RISK

CHOI, MUN SOO   THE EFFECT OF DISPERSION OF ANALYSTS' FORECASTS ON STOCK AND BOND PRICES

GAGNE, MARGARET LEE   THE IMPACT OF FIRM SIZE ON THE PRICE AND VOLUME REACTIONS TO ANALYSTS' EARNINGS FORECAST REVISIONS

GOSS, BETSY CATON   ACCOUNTING QUALITY AND DISPERSION OF FINANCIAL ANALYSTS' FORECASTS: AN EMPIRICAL INVESTIGATION

GRAHAM, LISE NEWMAN   THE MAGNITUDE AND TIMING OF ANALYST FORECAST RESPONSE TO QUARTERLY EARNINGS ANNOUNCEMENTS

GUNDERSON, ELIZABETH ANN WEISS   EXPERTISE IN SECURITY VALUATION: OPERATIONALIZING THE VALUATION PROCESS

GUNDERSON, KONRAD ERIK   DISPERSION OF FINANCIAL ANALYSTS' EARNINGS FORECASTS AS A RISK MEASURE: ARGUMENT AND EVIDENCE

HAN, BONG-HEUI   DISPERSION IN FINANCIAL ANALYSTS' EARNINGS FORECASTS: IMPLICATIONS ON RISK AND EARNINGS

JANG, JEE IN   FINANCIAL ANALYST EARNINGS FORECAST REVISIONS: FORMATION PROCESS AND INFORMATION VALUE

KIM, JUN   PRIOR AND POSTERIOR BELIEFS, DIVERGENCE OF ANALYSTS' FORECASTS, AND TRADING ACTIVITY

LEE, MYUNG GON   THE DIFFERENTIAL PREDICTIVE INFORMATION CONTENT OF EARNINGS ON ANALYSTS' FORECAST REVISIONS

LIN, HSIOU-WEI WILLIAM   SECURITY ANALYSTS' INVESTMENT RECOMMENDATIONS

MAHMOUD, AMAL ABDEL WAKIL   THE EFFECT OF DIFFERENTIAL AMOUNTS OF INTERIM INFORMATION ON STOCK PRICES VARIABILITY: THE CASE OF ANALYSTS' FORECASTS AND FIRM SIZE

MCEWEN, RUTH ANN   AN EMPIRICAL ASSESSMENT OF ERROR METRICS APPLIED TO ANALYSTS' FORECASTS OF EARNINGS

PANG, YANG HOONG	FINANCIAL DISCLOSURE AND ANALYSTS' FORECAST SUPERIORITY
PARKASH, MOHINDER	THE IMPACT OF A FIRM'S CONTRACTS AND SIZE ON THE ACCURACY, DISPERSION AND REVISIONS OF FINANCIAL ANALYSTS' FORECASTS: A THEORETICAL AND EMPIRICAL INVESTIGATION
PAVA, MOSES L.	FINANCIAL ANALYSTS' FORECASTS AND FINANCIAL ANALYSTS' FORECASTING CUES

Financial Distress or Bankruptcy

AKSU, MINE HATICE	MARKET RESPONSE TO TROUBLED DEBT RESTRUCTURING
AL-DARAYSEH, MUSA M.	CORPORATE FAILURE FOR MANUFACTURING INDUSTRIES USING FINANCIAL RATIOS AND MACROECONOMIC VARIABLES WITH LOGIT ANALYSIS
ALY, IBRAHIM M. MOHAMED	PREDICTION OF BUSINESS FAILURE AS A CRITERION FOR EVALUATING THE USEFULNESS OF ALTERNATIVE ACCOUNTING MEASURES
BAHNSON, PAUL RICHARD	AN ASSESSMENT OF THE CONTRIBUTION OF CASH FLOW AND THE OPERATING CASH FLOW COMPONENT IN CLASSIFYING FAILED COMPANIES
BALDWIN, JANE NORA	BANKRUPTCY PREDICTION USING QUARTERLY FINANCIAL STATEMENT DATA
BUKOWY, STEPHEN JOSEPH	AN EMPIRICAL ANALYSIS OF THE USEFULNESS OF ACCOUNTING INFORMATION IN PREDICTING CLOSURES OF SMALL AND MEDIUM-SIZED HOSPITALS
CAMPBELL, STEVEN VINCENT	THE SIGNIFICANCE OF DIRECT BANKRUPTCY COSTS IN DETERMINING THE OUTCOME OF BANKRUPTCY REORGANIZATION
CHEN, JIIN-FENG	AN EXPERT SYSTEM FOR THE IDENTIFICATION OF TROUBLED SAVINGS AND LOAN ASSOCIATIONS
CHEONG, INBUM	AN ANALYSIS OF SOLVENCY REGULATION AND FAILURE PREDICTION IN THE UNITED STATES LIFE INSURANCE INDUSTRY
DELEO, WANDA IRVIN	AN ANALYSIS OF FINANCIAL INFORMATION AS IT RELATES TO FAILED COMMERCIAL BANKS: A MULTIVARIATE APPROACH
DHANANI, KARIM A.	AN EMPIRICAL STUDY OF FINANCIALLY DISTRESSED COMMERCIAL BANKS: A DISCRIMINANT MODEL FOR PREDICTING FUTURE BANK FAILURES
DONADIO, PAUL JOSEPH	MANAGEMENT DEFECTS AS A CAUSE OF CORPORATE FAILURE: AN INVESTIGATION OF ARGENTI'S THEORY OF CORPORATE COLLAPSE
DWYER, MARGARET MARY DEVINE	A COMPARISON OF STATISTICAL TECHNIQUES AND ARTIFICIAL NEURAL NETWORK MODELS IN CORPORATE BANKRUPTCY PREDICTION
EL-ZAYATY, AHMED ISMAIL	BUSINESS FAILURE PREDICTION: AN ANALYSIS OF TYPE II PREDICTION ERRORS
ELDAHRAWY, KAMAL M.	AN EMPIRICAL INVESTIGATION OF THE DISCRIMINANT AND PREDICTIVE ABILITY OF THE SFAS NO. 69 SIGNALS FOR BUSINESS FAILURE IN THE OIL AND GAS INDUSTRY
FIGLEWICZ, RAYMOND E.	AN EXAMINATION INTO THE FEASIBILITY OF USING MEASURES OF SYSTEMATIC RISK VARIABILITY AS PREDICTORS OF CORPORATE FAILURE
FINNEY, SHARON GARY	AN EMPIRICAL INVESTIGATION INTO THE PREDICTABILITY OF FAILURE IN INSURED SAVINGS INSTITUTIONS
FLAGG, JAMES CALVIN	A DESCRIPTION AND ANALYSIS OF THE CORPORATE FAILURE PROCESS USING AN EVENTS-BASED LOGIT MODEL
FLETCHER, LESLIE B.	THE PREDICTION OF FINANCIAL TURNAROUND OF FINANCIALLY DISTRESSED FIRMS

FORSYTH, TIMOTHY BUSH	A STUDY OF THE ABILITY OF FINANCIAL RATIOS TO PREDICT CORPORATE FAILURE AND THE RELATIONSHIP BETWEEN BANKRUPTCY MODEL PROBABILITY ASSESSMENTS AND STOCK MARKET BEHAVIOR
GORDON, GUS ALLEN	A DISCRIMINANT MODEL TO PREDICT FINANCIAL DISTRESS IN OIL AND GAS COMPANIES
GRANT, CHARLES TERRELL	FINANCIAL DISTRESS PREDICTION WITH AN EXPANDED INFORMATION SET
GUFFEY, DARYL MAX	BANKRUPTCY COSTS: ADDITIONAL EVIDENCE FROM THE TRANSPORTATION INDUSTRY
GUIDRY, FLORA GAIL	A TEST OF THE DETERMINANTS OF AUDITOR TENDENCY TO ISSUE GOING-CONCERN AUDIT REPORTS TO NONFAILING COMPANIES
HERMANSON, DANA ROGER	THE ASSOCIATION BETWEEN AUDIT FIRM CHARACTERISTICS AND THE AUDITOR'S PROPENSITY TO QUALIFY BANKRUPTCY-RELATED OPINIONS
HOTCHKISS, EDITH HARRIET SHWALB	INVESTMENT DECISIONS UNDER CHAPTER 11 BANKRUPTCY
HSIEH, SU-JANE	THE ECONOMIC VALUE OF FINANCIAL DISTRESS INFORMATION: AN EMPIRICAL ASSESSMENT
JORDAN, LELAND GONCE	ARE THE INTERIM FINANCIAL STATEMENTS OF FAILING FIRMS BIASED?
KENNY, SARA YORK	PREDICTING FAILURE IN THE SAVINGS AND LOAN INDUSTRY: A COMPARISON OF RAP AND GAAP ACCOUNTING
KOH, HIAN CHYE	PREDICTION OF GOING-CONCERN STATUS: A PROBIT MODEL FOR THE AUDITORS
LAUX, JUDITH ANN	CONTENT ANALYSIS AND CORPORATE BANKRUPTCY
LITTLE, PHILIP LEE	AN EXAMINATION OF FACTORS RELEVANT TO THE PREDICTION OF GOING CONCERN SUBJECT-TO QUALIFICATIONS OR DISCLAIMERS OF OPINION IN THE OIL AND GAS INDUSTRY
MARSHALL, LEISA LYNN	AN EMPIRICAL INVESTIGATION OF FINANCIAL MEASURES' ABILITY TO PREDICT FINANCIAL DISTRESS LEVELS OF AGRICULTURAL PRODUCERS
MCLAUGHLIN, THOMAS DAVID	GOING CONCERN DETERMINATIONS UNDER SAS NO. 59 AND THE RESULTING IMPACT ON AUDIT OPINIONS: THE CASE OF THE SAVINGS AND LOAN INDUSTRY
MITCHEM, CHERYL EVELYN DRAKE	A CASH FLOW AND MACROECONOMIC MODEL OF FINANCIAL DISTRESS
MOORE, RONALD KENNETH	PREDICTION OF BANKRUPTCY USING FINANCIAL RATIOS, INFORMATION MEASURES, NATIONAL ECONOMIC DATA AND TEXAS ECONOMIC DATA
MOUNT, CAROLE C.	THE MARGINAL IMPACT OF CASH FLOW INFORMATION ON BANK FAILURE PREDICTION: AN EMPIRICAL INVESTIGATION
NG, A CHEW	PREDICTION OF CORPORATE FAILURE: HUMAN JUDGMENTS AND FINANCIAL DECISION-MAKING
NUGENT, JOHN HILLIARD	CORPORATE DECLINE: CAUSES, SYMPTOMS, AND PRESCRIPTIONS FOR A TURNAROUND
PANT, LAURIE W.	THE DETERMINANTS OF CORPORATE TURNAROUND
PAZ, ARMANDO J.	FORECASTING SAVINGS AND LOAN FAILURES USING FINANCIAL ACCOUNTING INFORMATION

RUJOUB, MOHAMMAD A.	AN EMPIRICAL INVESTIGATION OF THE DISCRIMINANT AND PREDICTIVE ABILITY OF THE STATEMENT OF CASH FLOWS
SARATHY, PRIYA	THE INVESTMENT DECISION OF A CREDITOR UNDER REORGANIZATION: EMPIRICAL AND THEORETICAL ISSUES
SHELTON, MARGARET LOUISE	PREDICTION OF CORPORATE FAILURE WITH AN EXPANDED VARIABLE SET, USING MULTIPLE DISCRIMINANT ANALYSIS
SMITH, HENRY CLAY, III	AN EMPIRICAL INVESTIGATION OF THE INCREMENTAL VALUE OF FINANCIAL ANALYSTS' FORECASTS OF EARNINGS ERROR METRICS IN THE PREDICTION OF FINANCIAL DISTRESS
SMOLINSKI, HAROLD CARL	AN EXAMINATION OF MEDIA INFORMATION PRECEDING POTENTIAL FIRM FINANCIAL DISTRESS: THE CASE OF DEBT RERATING TO CAA AND BELOW
TRUSSEL, JOHN M.	ASSESSING THE PROBABILITY OF FINANCIAL DISTRESS: AN OPTION PRICING FRAMEWORK
UKAEGBU, EBEN O.	MOTIVES FOR CORPORATE MERGERS AND TAKEOVERS: AN INVESTIGATION OF THE 'FAILING COMPANY' HYPOTHESIS AND OFPOST-MERGER PERFORMANCE
WARD, TERRY JOE	FINANCIAL DISTRESS: AN EVALUATION OF THE PREDICTIVE POWER OF ACCRUAL AND CASH FLOW INFORMATION USING ORDINAL MULTI-STATE PREDICTION MODELS
WEISS, LAWRENCE ALAN	BANKRUPTCY: THE EXPERIENCE OF NYSE AND ASE FIRMS--1980-1986

Financial Ratios

BARTON, THOMAS MICHAEL	ON THE PREDICTION OF MERGERS AND BANKRUPTCIES WITH RATIOS FROM THE STATEMENT OF CHANGES IN FINANCIAL POSITION AND DIFFERENT FUNDS FLOW MEASURES
BRAMBLE, HULDAH ALETHA	THE USE OF ACCOUNTING RATIOS AS MEASURES OF RISK IN THE DETERMINATION OF THE BID-ASK SPREAD
BUKOVINSKY, DAVID MARTIN	CASH FLOW AND CASH POSITION MEASURES IN THE PREDICTION OF BUSINESS FAILURE: AN EMPIRICAL STUDY
DEVANEY, SHARON ANN LOHR	AN EMPIRICAL ANALYSIS OF THE PREDICTIVE VALUE OF HOUSEHOLD FINANCIAL RATIOS
ECKSTEIN, CLAIRE	TIME-SERIES PROPERTIES AND FORECASTING OF FINANCIAL RATIOS
EL FEKEY, MAHMOUD ELSYED	AN EMPIRICAL INVESTIGATION OF THE ROLE OF ALTERNATIVE ACCOUNTING VARIABLES IN ASSESSING A FIRM'S ABILITY TO PAY INCREASED WAGES
EL SHAMY, MOSTAFA AHMED	THE PREDICTIVE ABILITY OF FINANCIAL RATIOS: A TEST OF ALTERNATIVE MODELS
FELTUS, OLIVER LEONARD	THE INFORMATION CONTENT OF FINANCIAL STATEMENTS: PREDICTING EARNINGS PER SHARE USING FINANCIAL RATIOS
GREIG, ANTHONY CHARLTON	FUNDAMENTAL ANALYSIS AND SUBSEQUENT STOCK RETURNS
KANE, GREGORY DALE	ACCOUNTING DATA AND STOCK RETURNS ACROSS BUSINESS-CYCLE ASSOCIATED VALUATION CHANGE PERIODS
MCCARRON, KAREN ELIZABETH BRADSHAW	AN EMPIRICAL INVESTIGATION OF THE USEFULNESS OF FINANCIAL ACCOUNTING RATIOS IN PREDICTING THE EFFECTS OF A TROUBLED DEBT RESTRUCTURING
SATIN, DIANE CAROL	ACCOUNTING INFORMATION AND THE VALUATION OF LOSS FIRMS
SKOGSVIK, KENTH HARRY GORAN	ACCOUNTING MEASURES AS PREDICTORS OF BUSINESS FAILURE--A COMPARISON BETWEEN HISTORICAL COST ACCOUNTING AND CURRENT COST ACCOUNTING [PROGNOS AV FINANSIELL KRIS MED REDOVISNINGSMATT--EN JAMFORELSE MELLAN

VOGEL, THOMAS JOSEPH	MONITORING NORMATIVE CORPORATE DECISIONS: A RECONCILIATION OF FINANCIAL AND ACCOUNTING CRITERIA

Forecasting Financial Performance

ALEXANDER, JOHN C., JR.	EARNINGS EXPECTATIONS AND THE MARKET REACTION TO EARNINGS SURPRISE
BYINGTON, JAMES RALPH	ANALYSIS OF TIME SERIES PROPERTIES OF EARNINGS: COMPARISONS OF INDUSTRY MODELS AND BIVARIATE ANALYSIS FOR MODEL IMPROVEMENT
CALDERON, DARRYL PATRICK	THE USE OF A FORMAL REVIEW PROCESS ON PROSPECTIVE FINANCIAL STATEMENTS BY NONPROFIT ORGANIZATIONS AS A PREDICTOR OF EFFECTIVENESS
CARABALLO-ESTEBAN, TEODORO ANTONIO	PROSPECTIVE FINANCIAL STATEMENTS: COMPARATIVE ANALYSIS AND DEVELOPMENT PROPOSAL [LOS DOCUMENTOS CONTABLES PREVISIONALES: ANALISIS COMPARADO Y PROPUESTA DE DESARROLLO]
ELHOSSEINY, MOHAMED AHMED	PROSPECTIVE INFORMATION IN SEC FILINGS: AN ANALYSIS OF MANAGEMENT CHOICE AND THE EFFECT OF AUDITOR INVOLVEMENT--A SIGNALING APPROACH
FORNEY, CHARLES T.	AN INVESTIGATION INTO THE TIME-SERIES NATURE OF FOREIGN SUBSIDIARY EARNINGS AND MANAGEMENT'S ABILITY TO FORECAST THEM
HARRINGTON, ROBERT PICKENS	FORECASTING CORPORATE PERFORMANCE
KEARNS, FRANCIS E., JR.	AN INVESTIGATION OF THE RELATIVE PREDICTIVE VALIDITY OF QUARTERLY REPORTS BEFORE AND AFTER AUDITOR INVOLVEMENT UNDER ASR #177
KIM, JEEHONG	THE E/P EFFECT AND THE EARNINGS FORECAST ERROR EFFECT: A COMPARISON OF TWO STOCK MARKET ANOMALIES
KIM, JONG HO	A BETTER SURROGATE FOR MARKET EXPECTATION OF QUARTERLY EARNINGS
KOPCZYNSKI, FRANK JOSEPH	THE SYSTEMS PARADIGM IN THE ANALYSIS OF PROSPECTIVE FINANCIAL INFORMATION: A PRAXIS BASED MODEL REFLECTING THE SYSTEMS VIEW OF THE FIRM
LAGRONE, R. MICHAEL	AN EVALUATION OF MULTIVARIATE EARNINGS FORECASTING
LEE, KYUNG JOO	THE EFFECT OF TIME-SERIES PROPERTIES ON THE PREDICTIVE VALUE OF QUARTERLY EARNINGS FOR FORECASTING ANNUAL EARNINGS
LEE, NAM JOO	AN EMPIRICAL EVALUATION OF OUTLIER ADJUSTED QUARTERLY EARNINGS
NABANGI, FABIAN KAFUKO	THE UTILITY OF ARIMA MODELS TO REVENUE FORECASTING FOR ALABAMA URBAN COUNTY GOVERNMENTS
ROXAS, MARIA LOURDES P.	EFFECT OF THE AMOUNT OF INFORMATION AND THE AMOUNT OF EXPERIENCE AND EDUCATION ON INVESTMENT DECISIONS
SOHN, PYUNG SIK	INTRADAY STOCK PRICE REACTION TO MANAGEMENT EARNINGS FORECASTS
SOHN, SUNGKYU	EX-POST REALIZATION AND VALUATION OF MANAGEMENT EARNINGS FORECASTS, MANAGER'S DISCRETION AND CHARACTERISTICS OF FORECASTING FIRMS
WEBER, SANDRA LEE LIGON	THE IMPACT OF THE FINANCIAL CONDITION OF THE FIRM ON THE ACCURACY OF ANNUAL EARNINGS FORECASTS
WEBSTER, ROBERT LEE	THE EFFECTS OF MANAGERIAL FINANCIAL FORECASTS ON USER PERCEPTIONS RELATING TO FINANCIAL STRENGTH OF PUBLIC UTILITY COMPANIES
WENZEL, LOREN ALVIN	THE PREDICTIVE ABILITY OF QUARTERLY ACCRUAL AND CASH FLOW VARIABLES: A MULTIPLE TIME SERIES APPROACH

Listing by Topic   274

WIEDMAN, CHRISTINE INGEBORG	PROXIES FOR EARNINGS EXPECTATIONS: THE ROLE OF LOSS FUNCTIONS
WILDER, WALLACE MARK	A MULTI-INDUSTRY ANALYSIS OF STRUCTURAL CHANGES AND EARNINGS FORECASTS
XIANG, BING	THE CHOICE OF RETURN-GENERATING MODELS IN EVENT STUDIES AND RATIONALITY OF VALUE LINE'S QUARTERLY EARNINGS FORECASTS
YHIM, HARK-PPIN	VOLUNTARY MANAGEMENT EARNINGS FORECASTS: AN ASSOCIATION BETWEEN DISCLOSURE LEVEL AND INFORMATION QUALITY
YI, JAEKYUNG	THE EFFECT OF STOCK SPLITS ON THE REASSESSMENT OF EARNINGS PERSISTENCE

Foreign Currency Translation

ABEKAH, JOSEPH YAW	USEFULNESS OF REQUIRED QUANTITATIVE DISCLOSURES UNDER FOREIGN CURRENCY TRANSLATION STANDARDS: AN EMPIRICAL EXAMINATION
BOULEY, JUDITH NOREEN	AN EMPIRICAL INVESTIGATION OF SFAS NO. 52 AND THE IMPLICATIONS FOR PERFORMANCE EVALUATION SYSTEMS
BOYER, BENOI T NOEL	THE IMPACT OF FINANCIAL ACCOUNTING STANDARDS BOARD STATEMENTS NUMBERS 8 AND 52 ON MULTINATIONAL CORPORATIONS
CHI, CHARLES CHI-WEI	THE INFORMATION CONTENT AND HEDGING PERFORMANCE OF FOREIGN CURRENCY TRANSLATIONS: AN EVALUATION OF SFAS NO. 8 VS NO 52
CONOVER, TERESA LYNN	AN EMPIRICAL INVESTIGATION OF THE EFFECTS OF THE ACCOUNTING TREATMENT OF FOREIGN CURRENCY TRANSLATION ON MANAGEMENT ACTIONS IN MULTINATIONAL FIRMS
DEVINE, WILFRED FRANCIS	THE INFLUENCE OF CONSTITUENCY INPUT IN SETTING ACCOUNTING STANDARDS
EL-REFADI, IDRIS ABDULSALAM	FOREIGN EXCHANGE RISK MANAGEMENT IN U.S. MULTINATIONALS UNDER SFAS NO. 52: CHANGE IN MANAGEMENT DECISION-MAKING IN RESPONSE TO ACCOUNTING POLICY CHANGE
ELSAYED-AHMED, SAMEH METWALLY	AN EMPIRICAL EXAMINATION OF THE EFFECTS OF FASB STATEMENT NO. 52 ON SECURITY RETURNS AND REPORTED EARNINGS OF U.S.-BASED MULTINATIONAL CORPORATIONS
FISHER, STEVEN ALLEN	AN EMPIRICAL INVESTIGATION OF EXPERT JUDGMENTS CONCERNING THE SELECTION STATEMENT OF FINANCIAL ACCOUNTING STANDARDS NUMBER 52'S FUNCTIONAL CURRENCY
GILBERT, LISA R.	ACCOUNTING STANDARDS, EARNINGS EXPECTATIONS, AND MARKET PRICES: THE CASE OF SFAS 52
HADDAD, AMIN MOHAMMED	THE MARKET REACTION TO FOREIGN CURRENCY TRANSLATION POLICY-SETTING PROCESS: A NEW APPROACH
HOFFMANS, SHARRON RAE DYE	THE CHANGE FROM FINANCIAL ACCOUNTING STANDARD NO. 8 TO FINANCIAL ACCOUNTING STANDARD NO. 52 AND MANAGEMENT FINANCING DECISIONS
HOLT, PAUL EDWIN	A COMPARATIVE EXAMINATION OF THE EARNINGS EFFECTS OF ALTERNATIVE TRANSLATION METHODS
HOUSTON, CAROL OLSON	U.S. MANAGEMENT HEDGING PRACTICES SUBSEQUENT TO THE ADOPTION OF SFAS NO. 52 'FOREIGN CURRENCY TRANSLATION'
JOHNSON, CAROL BAUMAN	THE IMPACT OF CURRENCY CHANGES ON THE PERSISTENCE AND PRICING OF MULTINATIONAL CORPORATION EARNINGS
KIM, HYUK	AN EMPIRICAL STUDY OF THE MARKET REACTION TO STATEMENT OF FINANCIAL ACCOUNTING STANDARDS NO. 52: 'FOREIGN CURRENCYTRANSLATION'
KIM, JEONGKUK	THE EFFECT OF SFAS NO. 52 ON THE SECURITY ANALYSTS' PERCEPTION OF THE PREDICTIVE USEFULNESS OF REPORTED EARNINGS

Listing by Topic

KING, JOHN WILLIAM	INFORMATION EFFECTS OF TRANSLATION ADJUSTMENTS UNDER SFAS 52 AND SFAS 70
KIRSCH, ROBERT JOHN	SFAS NO 52, AN ACCOUNTING POLICY INTERVENTION: U.S.-BASED MULTINATIONAL CORPORATE PRE-ENACTMENT LOBBYING BEHAVIOR AND POST-ENACTMENT REACTION
LI, JUNE FANG	AN EMPIRICAL STUDY OF THE PERCEPTIONS OF FINANCIAL EXECUTIVES AND FINANCIAL ANALYSTS REGARDING SELECTEDASPECTS OF FOREIGN CURRENCY TRANSLATION AS CURRENTLY PROMULGATED BY THE FINANCIAL ACCOUNTING
MANSFIELD, JON L.	THE EFFECTS OF SFAS NO. 8 AND NO. 52 ON MULTINATIONAL COMPANY STOCK RETURNS: 1973-1982
MCMATH, HERBERT KENT	THE IMPACT OF MANDATED ACCOUNTING CHANGES ON MANAGEMENT DECISIONS: THE STATEMENT NO. 8 EPISODE
NDUBIZU, GORDIAN ANUMUDU	AN EMPIRICAL INVESTIGATION OF THE SECURITY MARKET REACTION TO MULTINATIONAL ACCOUNTING CHANGES: STATEMENT OF FINANCIAL ACCOUNTING STANDARD NUMBER 52, FOREIGN CURRENCY TRANSLATION
REZAEE, ZABIHOLLAH	CAPITAL MARKET REACTIONS TO ACCOUNTING POLICY DELIBERATIONS: AN EMPIRICAL STUDY OF ACCOUNTING FOR THE TRANSLATION OF FOREIGN CURRENCY TRANSACTIONS AND FOREIGN CURRENCY FINANCIAL STATEMENTS, 1974-1982
SHEIKHOLESLAMI, MEHDI	THE IMPACT OF FOREIGN CURRENCY TRANSLATION METHOD CHANGE ON THE ACCURACY OF THE FINANCIAL ANALYSTS' EARNINGS FORECASTS
WU, TSING TZAI	AN EXAMINATION OF THE MARKET REACTION TO THE ADOPTION OF SFAS NO.52: A NEW-INFORMATION-DE-FACTO APPROACH

Fraud

APOSTOLOU, BARBARA ANN	AN INVESTIGATION OF INTERNAL AUDITOR JUDGMENT ON THE IMPORTANCE OF INDICATORS OF POTENTIAL FINANCIAL FRAUD: AN ANALYTIC HIERARCHY PROCESS APPROACH
BAKER, DONALD R.	RELATIONSHIPS OF INTERNAL ACCOUNTING CONTROLS AND OCCURRENCES OF COMPUTER FRAUD
BHATTACHARYA, SOMNATH	THE USE OF RECALL AND RECOGNITION TECHNIQUES IN ELICITING EXPRIENCED-INEXPERIENCED AUDITOR DIFFERENCES IN THE DETECTION OF MANAGEMENT FRAUD
COBB, LAUREL GORDON	AN INVESTIGATION INTO THE EFFECT OF SELECTED AUDIT COMMITTEE CHARACTERISTICS ON FRAUDULENT FINANCIAL REPORTING
GILL, JOHN WAITS	THE EFFECTS OF A RED FLAGS QUESTIONNAIRE AND SELECTED ELEMENTS OF COGNITIVE STYLE ON THE AUDIT PLANNING TASK OF ASSESSING THE PROBABILITY OF MATERIAL MANAGEMENT FRAUD
HACKENBRACK, KARL EDWARD	ASSESSING A COMPANY'S EXPOSURE TO FRAUDULENT FINANCIAL REPORTING: IMPLICATIONS OF SEEMINGLY IRRELEVANT EVIDENCE
MOYES, GLEN DAVID	AN ANALYSIS OF THE EFFECTIVENESS OF SPECIFIC AUDITING TECHNIQUES FOR DETECTING FRAUD AS PERCEIVED BY THREE DIFFERENT AUDITOR GROUPS
VENDRZYK, VALARIA PAULINE	AN EXAMINATION OF THE INFORMATION CONTENT OF ALLEGATIONS OF PROCUREMENT FRAUD IN THE DEFENSE CONTRACTING INDUSTRY
WULSIN, FREDERICK ROELKER	AN INQUIRY INTO THE CAUSES OF AUDIT FAILURE

Governmental

AL-KAZEMI, ALI ABDUL-RAZZAQ	THE UTILIZATION OF MANAGEMENT ACCOUNTING TECHNIQUES WITH EMPHASIS ON QUANTITATIVE ANALYSIS IN THE PUBLIC SECTOR: BUILDING AN EFFECTIVE FINANCIAL MANAGEMENT SYSTEM
ALLEN, ARTHUR CONRAD, JR.	EFFECTS OF LOCAL GOVERNMENT AUDIT QUALITY ON THE RELIABILITY OF ACCOUNTING NUMBERS AND INVESTOR DECISIONS
BASU, ONKER NATH	MANAGING THE ORGANIZATIONAL ENVIRONMENT: AN INTERPRETIVE FIELD STUDY OF THE UNITED STATES GENERAL ACCOUNTING OFFICE AND THE MAINTENANCE OF PROFESSIONAL INDEPENDENCE

BLESSING, LINDA JANE	REPORTING OF GOVERNMENTAL PERFORMANCE INDICATORS FOR ASSESSMENT OF PUBLIC ACCOUNTABILITY
BRANNAN, RODGER LLOYD	THE SINGLE AUDIT ACT OF 1984: AN EXAMINATION OF THE AUDIT PROCESS IN THE GOVERNMENT SECTOR
BROOKS, RICHARD C.	AN INVESTIGATION OF THE DETERMINANTS OF THE MUNICIPAL DECISION TO PRIVATIZE RESIDENTIAL SANITATION COLLECTION
CARPENTER, FRANCES HORVATH	THE IMPACT OF MUNICIPAL REPORTING REQUIREMENTS ON MUNICIPAL OFFICIALS' FIXED ASSET ACQUISITION DECISIONS: A LABORATORY EXPERIMENT
CARPENTER, VIVIAN LAVERNE	THE INCENTIVES FOR THE EVOLUTION OF PERFORMANCE-ORIENTED ACCOUNTING INFORMATION SYSTEMS IN THE GOVERNMENTAL SETTING
CHANG, STANLEY YI	A STUDY OF THE BASIC CRITERIA AND STANDARDS BY INTERNAL SERVICE FUNDS
CHENG, RITA HARTUNG	TOWARD A POSITIVE THEORY OF STATE GOVERNMENT ACCOUNTING DISCLOSURE
CHWASTIAK, MICHELE EILEEN	AN EMPIRICAL INVESTIGATION INTO THE DOD'S CHOICE OF CONTRACT TYPE
COCKRELL, SUSAN ROBERTA	TESTING THE DETERMINANTS OF DISCLOSURE COMPLIANCE BY MUNICIPALITIES USING CONFIRMATION FACTOR ANALYSIS
COPLEY, PAUL ANDREW	AN EMPIRICAL INVESTIGATION OF THE DETERMINANTS OF LOCAL GOVERNMENT AUDIT FEES
DANIELS, JANET DELUCA	AN INVESTIGATION OF MUNICIPAL FINANCIAL REPORT FORMAT, USER PREFERENCE, AND DECISION-MAKING
DREWS-BRYAN, ALISON LUEDTKE	THE PERCEIVED USEFULNESS OF SELECTED INFORMATION CHARACTERISTICS FOR MUNICIPAL BUDGETING
GEIGER, DALE RAIMONDE	FEDERAL MANAGEMENT ACCOUNTING: DETERMINANTS, MOTIVATING CONTINGENCIES, AND DECISION MAKING RELEVANCE
HEBERT, MARCEL G.	AN INVESTIGATION OF THE EFFECT OF ALTERNATIVE PRESENTATION FORMATS ON PREPARERS AND USERS OF CITY FINANCIAL REPORTS
HOLLEY, JOYCE MARIE HIGGINS	AN INVESTIGATION OF INTERNAL INTERIM REPORTING BY MUNICIPALITIES
JAKUBOWSKI, STEPHEN THOMAS	THE EFFECT OF THE SINGLE AUDIT ACT OF 1984 ON THE INTERNAL CONTROL SYSTEMS OF LOCAL GOVERNMENTAL UNITS
JOHNSON, GARY GENE	COMPLIANCE AUDITING IN THE PUBLIC SECTOR: AN EMPIRICAL INVESTIGATION INTO THE EXTENT OF NONCOMPLIANCE WITH STATE LAWS BY COUNTY GOVERNMENTS
JOHNSON, LAURENCE ERNEST	AN INVESTIGATION OF CITY FINANCIAL STATEMENT READERS' REACTION TO DUAL-BASIS REPORTING OF GENERAL FUND OPERATING RESULTS: INTEGRATION OR EMPHASIS?
KENYON, PETER B.	AN INVESTIGATION OF THE EFFECT OF ANNUAL ACCOUNTING REPORTS ON MUNICIPAL BOND INTEREST COST
KIDWELL, LINDA ACHEY	THE IMPACT OF BUDGET VARIANCE, FISCAL STRESS, POLITICAL TURNOVER, AND EMPLOYMENT SECTOR ON COMPLIANCE REPORTING DECISIONS
KURTENBACH, JAMES MATTHEW	ENTITY RELATIONSHIPS: MARKET IMPACT AND MANAGEMENT INCENTIVES
KWIATKOWSKI, VERNON EVERETT	INFRASTRUCTURE ASSETS: AN ASSESSMENT OF USER NEEDS AND RECOMMENDATIONS FOR FINANCIAL REPORTING

Listing by Topic

LANDRY, STEVEN PAUL	ACCOUNTING INFORMATION IN THE BUDGETING DECISION-MAKING PROCESS IN A UNITED STATES GOVERNMENT ASSET INFRASTRUCTURE ENVIRONMENT
LANGSAM, SHELDON ALLEN	THE EFFECT OF MANDATORY INCLUSION OF COMPONENT UNITS ON THE REPORTED FINANCIAL CONDITION OF SELECTED LOCAL GOVERNMENTAL UNITS
MARTIN, SUSAN WORK	MODELING THE LOCAL GOVERNMENT GENERAL FUND DEFICIT
MILLER, GERALD JOHN	AN EMPIRICAL STUDY OF THE IMPROVEMENT IN FINANCIAL MANAGEMENT PRACTICES OF STATE AND LOCAL GOVERNMENTS IN RESPONSE TO THE SINGLE AUDIT ACT
MONTONDON, LUCILLE MARIE	A STUDY OF MUNICIPAL RESOURCE ALLOCATION DECISIONS AND MUNICIPAL BOND RATINGS
PARRISH, SHARON R.	DEVELOPMENT OF A MODEL PEER REVIEW PROGRAM FOR STATE GOVERNMENT AUDIT AGENCIES
PENDLEBURY, MAURICE WILSON	AN INVESTIGATION INTO THE ROLE AND NATURE OF MANAGEMENT ACCOUNTING IN LOCAL GOVERNMENT IN ENGLAND AND WALES
PICHLER, ANTON	THE CONTROL OF PUBLIC BUILDINGS BY THE GENERAL ACCOUNTING OFFICE IN AUSTRIA [DIE KONTROLLE OEFFENTLICHER BAUTEN DURCH DEN RECHNUNGSHOF IN OESTERREICH]
RUBIN, MARC ALLEN	AN EXAMINATION OF THE POLITICAL AND ECONOMIC DETERMINANTS OF MUNICIPAL AUDIT FEES: THEORY AND EVIDENCE
SANDERS, GEORGE D.	AN EMPIRICAL INVESTIGATION OF THE ASSOCIATION OF MUNICIPAL TAX STRUCTURE WITH MUNICIPAL ACCOUNTING CHOICE AND BIAS AND NOISE IN MUNICIPAL ACCOUNTING RATIOS
SHAFFER, RAYMOND JAMES	FINANCIAL REPORTING OF DEFERRED MAINTENANCE FOR CAPITAL ASSETS IN GOVERNMENTAL ENTITIES: A SURVEY OF SELECTED USERS
SOYBEL, VIRGINIA ELIZABETH EARLL	MUNICIPAL FINANCIAL REPORTING AND THE NEW YORK CITY FISCAL CRISIS
STROUD, J. B., JR.	PERCEPTIONS OF CITY MANAGERS CONCERNING MUNICIPAL FINANCIAL STATEMENT USERS, USER IMPORTANCE, AND IMPORTANCE OF SELECTED ITEMS OF DISCLOSURE
SWEENEY, MICHAEL PETER	MANAGEMENT ACCOUNTING IN MUNICIPAL GOVERNMENTS
VIJAYAKUMAR, JAYARAMAN	AN EMPIRICAL ANALYSIS OF THE FACTORS INFLUENCING CALL DECISIONS CONCERNING LOCAL GOVERNMENT BONDS
YUEN, ALEXANDER E. C.	THE CALIFORNIA EXPERIENCE: AN EMPIRICAL STUDY OF THE USEFULNESS OF MUNICIPAL FINANCIAL REPORTS FOR NEWSPAPER REPORTERS

History

BRAND, JOHN DAVID	THE EXCHEQUER IN THE LATER TWELFTH CENTURY
CALVO SANCHEZ, JOSE ANTONIO	THE RADICAL THINKING IN ACCOUNTING: FOUNDATIONS FOR ITS DEVELOPMENT [EL PENSAMIENTO RADICAL EN LA CONTABILIDAD: FUNDAMENTOS PARA SU DESARROLLO]
CRIPPS, JEREMY	ON ACCOUNTING
FORTIN, ANNE	THE EVOLUTION OF FRENCH ACCOUNTING THOUGHT AS REFLECTED BY THE SUCCESSIVE UNIFORM SYSTEMS (PLANS COMPTABLES GENERAUX)
GARNER, ROBERT MICHAEL	S. PAUL GARNER: A STUDY OF SELECTED CONTRIBUTIONS TO THE ACCOUNTING PROFESSION
HARSTON, MARY ELIZABETH	A COMPARISON OF THE EVOLUTION OF ACCOUNTING INSTITUTIONS IN GERMANY AND THE UNITED STATES

HASLAM, JIM	ON THE PRESCRIBING OF ACCOUNTING AND ACCOUNTING PUBLICITY BY THE STATE IN EARLY TO MID-NINETEENTH CENTURY BRITAIN: ACCOUNTING HISTORY AS CRITIQUE
HEIER, JAN RICHARD	A QUANTITATIVE STUDY OF ACCOUNTING METHODS AND USAGE IN MID - NINETEENTH-CENTURY ALABAMA AND MISSISSIPPI
HOSKINS, MARGARET ANN	THE MURPHY MODELS FOR ACCOUNTING: A TEST OF RELEVANCE
JOHNSON, ROXANNE THERESE	AN ANALYSIS OF THE EARLY RECORD-KEEPING IN THE DUPONT COMPANY--1800-1818
JORDAN, ROBERT EARL	THE INSTITUTE OF MANAGEMENT ACCOUNTANTS' CONTRIBUTION TO ACCOUNTING THOUGHT: A DESCRIPTIVE AND EVALUATIVE STUDY
KEDSLIE, MOYRA JEAN MCINTYRE	AN ANALYSIS OF THE FACTORS INFLUENCING THE FORMATION AND POLICIES OF PROFESSIONAL ACCOUNTING BODIES IN SCOTLAND, 1850-1900
KING, TERESA ANN TYSON	AN ANALYTIC STUDY OF SELECTED CONTRIBUTIONS OF PAUL F. GRADY TO THE DEVELOPMENT OF ACCOUNTANCY
LEGGE, REBECCA SUE SCRUGGS	A HISTORY OF WOMEN CERTIFIED PUBLIC ACCOUNTANTS IN THE UNITED STATES
LEHMAN, CHERYL R.	DISCOURSE ANALYSIS AND ACCOUNTING LITERATURE: TRANSFORMATION OF STATE HEGEMONY, 1960 - 1973
MATIKA, LAWRENCE A.	THE CONTRIBUTIONS OF FREDERICK ALBERT CLEVELAND TO THE DEVELOPMENT OF A SYSTEM OF MUNICIPAL ACCOUNTING IN THE PROGRESSIVE ERA
MICHAEL, RODNEY RICHARD	AN ANALYSIS OF THE ACCOUNTING SYSTEM OF THE QUINCY MINING COMPANY: 1846-1900
MOYNIHAN, G.	STOCK: THE LOWER OF COST OR MARKET VALUE IN THE COMPUTATION OF TRADING PROFIT FOR TAX PURPOSES
OAKES, LESLIE SUSAN	ORGANIZATIONAL IMPLICATIONS OF ACCOUNTING-BASED INCENTIVE PLANS: AN HISTORICAL EXAMINATION OF ACCOUNTING IN THE LABOR PROCESS
PEINO JANEIRO, VICTOR GABRIEL	ACCOUNTING AS A PROGRAM OF SCIENTIFIC INVESTIGATION: A TEST [LA CONTABILIDAD COMO PROGRAMA DE INVESTIGACION CIENTIFICA: UN ENSAYO]
POULLAOS, CHRISTOPHER	MAKING THE AUSTRALIAN CHARTERED ACCOUNTANT, 1886-1935
ROBSON, KEITH	ACCOUNTING, THE STATE AND THE REGULATORY PROCESS: THE CASE OF STANDARD SETTING, 1969-1975
VOLLMERS, GLORIA LUCEY	AN ANALYSIS OF THE COST ACCOUNTING LITERATURE OF THE UNITED STATES FROM 1925 TO 1950
YOUNG, SAUL DAVID	AN ECONOMIC AND HISTORICAL ANALYSIS OF LICENSURE IN PUBLIC ACCOUNTANCY

Incentive Compensation

ADAMSON, STANLEY RAY	THE EFFECT OF ESOP IMPLEMENTATION ON THE VALUE OF LARGE PUBLICLY-HELD FIRMS
BALSAM, STEVEN	EXECUTIVE COMPENSATION PACKAGES: A TOOL FOR RESOLVING THE OWNER-MANAGER CONFLICT
BARIL, CHARLES PURDOM	LONG-TERM INCENTIVE COMPENSATION PLAN ADOPTION AND THE CAPITAL SPENDING DECISIONS OF MANAGERS
BATTISTEL, GEORGE PETER	AN EMPIRICAL ANALYSIS OF THE STOCK MARKET REACTION TO BONUS PLAN ADOPTIONS

BISHOP, RACHEL ANN	INCENTIVE SCHEMES, MORAL HAZARD, AND RISK AVERSION: INTRAFIRM RESOURCE ALLOCATION AND DETERMINANTS OF BUDGETARY SLACK
BOSCIA, MARIAN W. LARSON	THE RELATIONSHIP BETWEEN ESOP VOTING RIGHTS AND EMPLOYEES' JOB PERFORMANCE
BUTLER, JANET ANN BASEMAN	SELF-INTEREST IN ACCOUNTING: AN EXAMINATION OF DECISION-MAKING
CHEN, RING DING	BUDGET-BASED CONTRACTS AND TOP-LEVEL EXECUTIVE COMPENSATION: AN EMPIRICAL EVALUATION
CLINCH, GREGORY JOHN	INFORMATION AND MOTIVATION ISSUES IN COMPENSATION DESIGN: AN APPLICATION TO HIGH TECHNOLOGY COMPANIES
CULPEPPER, DAVID HUNT	EXECUTIVE COMPENSATION PLANS: EMPIRICAL ANALYSIS OF THE TAX EXPLANATION OF COMPENSATION PLAN CHOICE
DUNBAR, AMY ELINOR	AN EMPIRICAL INVESTIGATION OF THE ASSOCIATION OF PRODUCTIVITY WITH EMPLOYEE STOCK OWNERSHIP PLANS OF PUBLICLY HELD CORPORATIONS
EL-HASHASH, HADEYA A.	THE ASSOCIATION BETWEEN FIRM CHARACTERISTICS AND EXECUTIVE COMPENSATION SCHEMES AND THE EFFECT OF ADOPTION OF SUCH SCHEMES ON FIRM PERFORMANCE
GAVER, JENNIFER JANE	INCENTIVE EFFECTS AND MANAGERIAL COMPENSATION CONTRACTS: A STUDY OF PERFORMANCE PLAN ADOPTIONS
GRASSO, LAWRENCE PETER	THE ORGANIZATIONAL DETERMINANTS OF THE USE OF INCENTIVES IN COMPENSATING BUSINESS UNIT MANAGERS
GRINER, EMMETT HAMILTON	INSIDER OWNERSHIP AND THE LEVEL OF CAPITAL EXPENDITURES IN THE LARGE INDUSTRIAL FIRM: AN EMPIRICAL INVESTIGATION
HUH, SUNGKWAN	ON THE DETERMINANTS OF PERFORMANCE-DEPENDENT MANAGEMENT COMPENSATION: A THEORETICAL AND EMPIRICAL INVESTIGATION
HWANG, IN TAE	THE DETERMINANTS OF EXECUTIVE INCENTIVE CONTRACTS
JANAKIRAMAN, SURYA N.	STRATEGIC CHOICE OF CHIEF EXECUTIVE OFFICERS' COMPENSATION: AN EMPIRICAL ANALYSIS
JENKINS, ELIZABETH KLAFF	EXECUTIVE COMPENSATION SCHEMES AND SHORT-RUN DECISION-MAKING: AN EMPIRICAL EXAMINATION
JUNG, KOOYUL	THE RELATIONSHIP BETWEEN CHANGES IN CERTAIN FIRM CHARACTERISTICS AND THE CHANGES IN THE STRUCTURE OF TOP MANAGEMENT COMPENSATION PLANS
KIM, NEUNG JIP	THE ASSOCIATION OF PERFORMANCE ATTAINMENT PLANS WITH CORPORATE PERFORMANCE
KUMAR, KRISHNA RADHAKRISHNAN	THE DETERMINANTS OF PERFORMANCE PLAN ADOPTION: AN EMPIRICAL STUDY
LEE, MANWOO	IMPACT OF UTILIZING LONG-TERM EXECUTIVE COMPENSATION PLANS ON CAPITAL INVESTMENT DECISIONS
LEE, SEOK-YOUNG	ESSAYS ON MANAGEMENT ACCOUNTING AND INCENTIVE CONTRACTS FOR SOME NEW PRODUCTION AND SELLING STRATEGIES
LEONG, KENNETH KIN ON	THE EXISTENCE OF BONUS COMPENSATION PLANS AND THE RELATED EFFECT ON THE SIZE OF REPORTED ACCOUNTING EARNINGS
LINDQUIST, TIMOTHY MARK	DISTRIBUTIVE AND PROCEDURAL JUSTICE: IMPLICATIONS FOR MANAGEMENT CONTROLS AND INCENTIVE SYSTEMS

Listing by Topic

LUFT, JOAN LUISE	BONUS AND PENALTY INCENTIVES: CONTRACT CHOICE BY EMPLOYEES
MAGNAN, MICHEL LOUIS	THE RELATION BETWEEN INDUSTRY-SPECIFIC VARIABLES AND COMPENSATION: THE CASE OF COMMERCIAL BANKS
MATSUNAGA, STEVEN ROY	THE EFFECTS OF FINANCIAL REPORTING AND TAX COSTS ON THE RELATIVE USE OF EMPLOYEE STOCK OPTIONS
MIDDLEMIST, MELANIE R.	THE RELATIONSHIP BETWEEN OUTCOME MEASURABILITY AND PRINCIPAL'S PREFERENCE FOR CONTRACT TYPE: A LABORATORY EXPERIMENT
MOODY, SHARON MATHIS	AN EMPIRICAL STUDY OF THE ASSOCIATION BETWEEN THE SALARY AND BONUS COMPONENTS OF EXECUTIVE COMPENSATION ANDPRINCIPAL-AGENT RISK SHARING AND PERFORMANCE MEASUREMENT
NATARAJAN, RAMACHANDRAN	THE USE OF DISCRETIONARY ACCOUNTING REPORTS IN MANAGEMENT COMPENSATION CONTRACTS
POURCIAU, SUSAN GRIBBLE	THE EFFECT OF ACCOUNTING DISCRETION ON EXECUTIVE COMPENSATION CONTRACTS
RADHAKRISHNAN, SURESH	THE RELEVANCE OF COST APPLICATION IN A COMMON FACILITY
RAVENSCROFT, SUSAN PICKARD	INCENTIVE PLANS AND MULTI-AGENT INFORMATION SHARING
RUHL, JACK MICHAEL	AN EMPIRICAL STUDY OF THE EFFECTS OF INCONGRUENCE WITHIN A FIRM'S FINANCIAL PLANNING AND CONTROL SYSTEM ON MANAGERS' PROJECT SELECTIONS
SALY, P. JANE	THE EFFECT OF MAJOR STOCK DOWNTURNS ON EXECUTIVE STOCK OPTION CONTRACTS
SHERIF, HANAA ABDEL-GALIEL	THE IMPACT OF LONG-TERM PERFORMANCE PLANS ON ACCOUNTING CHOICES
SHIM, KYU YOUNG	EMPIRICAL INVESTIGATION OF SHAREHOLDER REACTION TO THE INTRODUCTION OF MANAGEMENT INCENTIVE COMPENSATION PLANS
SINGER, RONALD MARTIN	EXECUTIVE COMPENSATION AND RESEARCH AND DEVELOPMENT
SLOAN, RICHARD GEOFFREY	ACCOUNTING EARNINGS AND TOP EXECUTIVE COMPENSATION
SOPARIWALA, PARVEZ R.	AN EMPIRICAL EXAMINATION OF THE ASSOCIATION BETWEEN THE ADOPTION OF LONG-TERM PERFORMANCE PLANS AND THE SUBSEQUENT GROWTH OF RESEARCH AND DEVELOPMENT EXPENDITURES
TEEUWEN, TERESA DIANE TRAPANI	AN INVESTIGATION OF THE RELATIONSHIP BETWEEN CEO COMPENSATION AND CEO TRADING PROFITS
THEVARANJAN, ALEX	EFFORT ALLOCATION AND EXECUTIVE COMPENSATION
WALKER, KENTON BLAIR	AN EMPIRICAL FIELD STUDY OF STATISTICAL AND MANAGEMENT PREDICTION MODELS AND THE EFFECTS OF A BUDGET-BASED INCENTIVE PROGRAM

Independence

AGACER, GILDA MONTEAGUDO	PERCEPTIONS OF THE AUDITOR'S INDEPENDENCE: A CROSS-CULTURAL STUDY
BAILEY, JAMES ALMA	AUDIT FEE EFFECTS ON AUDITOR INDEPENDENCE
DAVIS, JON STUART	AUDITOR BIDDING AND INDEPENDENCE: A LABORATORY MARKETS INVESTIGATION

Listing by Topic

ENGLISH, THOMAS JAMES	AN EXAMINATION OF THE EFFECT OF SOCIAL INFLUENCE ON AUDITORS' MATERIALITY JUDGMENTS
RAGHUNATHAN, BHANU	ECONOMIC DETERMINANTS OF AUDITOR INDEPENDENCE
SAMPSON, WESLEY CLAUDE	PERCEPTIONS OF AUDITOR INDEPENDENCE AND THE EFFECTS OF NONAUDIT SERVICES
SCHATZBERG, JEFFREY WAYNE	A THEORETICAL AND EMPIRICAL EXAMINATION OF INDEPENDENCE AND 'LOW BALLING'
SCHLEIFER, LYDIA LANCASTER FOLGER	AN INVESTIGATION OF PERCEPTIONS AND ATTRIBUTES OF THE CONCEPT OF INDEPENDENCE
VENABLE, CAROL FRANCES	AN ANALYSIS OF AUDITOR INDEPENDENCE AND ITS DETERMINANTS

Individual Taxation

BRYANT, JEFFREY JACK	THE EFFECTS OF LOCAL TAXES ON ECONOMIC BEHAVIOR IN THE HOUSING MARKET
BUCKHOLD, J. W.	ANALYSIS OF INDIVIDUAL TAXPAYER USE OF SELECTED TAX PREFERENCES--EMPIRICAL EVIDENCE
CRAMER, LOWELL JAMES	AN AFTER TAX ECONOMIC ANALYSIS OF HOME EQUITY CONVERSION FOR THE ELDERLY
EASON, PATRICIA LEE	AN EMPIRICAL ANALYSIS OF CONSUMPTION SENSITIVITY TO TAX POLICY UNCERTAINTY
FORAN, NANCY JOYCE HOFFMAN	THE EFFECT OF THE ECONOMIC RECOVERY TAX ACT OF 1981 AND THE TAX EQUITY AND FISCAL RESPONSIBILITY ACT OF 1982 ON THE FORM OF DISPOSITION BY INDIVIDUALS OF NONRESIDENTIAL REAL PROPERTY
HALL, BETHANE JO PIERCE	AN ANALYSIS OF THE EQUITY AND REVENUE EFFECTS OF THE ELIMINATION OR REDUCTION OF HOMEOWNER PREFERENCES
HEBBLE, ANNETTE	THE EFFECT OF ALTERNATIVE SYSTEMS OF TAXATION ON INDIVIDUAL SAVINGS: AN EXPERIMENTAL APPROACH
HESLOP, GORDON B.	AN ANALYSIS OF THE TAXATION TREATMENT UNDER SECTION 280A OF THE INTERNAL REVENUE CODE OF 1954 OF EXPENSES INCURRED IN CONNECTION WITH THE BUSINESS USE OF A DWELLING UNIT
KAENZIG, REBECCA	THE INDIVIDUAL VERSUS THE FAMILY: AN EMPIRICAL ANALYSIS OF HORIZONTAL EQUITY AND TAX-PAYER FILING STATUS
LANESE, KAREN BENNETT	VISIBILITY OF INCOME: A MODEL TO PREDICT USE OF THE CHILD CARE CREDIT
LEE, EUNSANG	TAX TREATMENT UNCERTAINTY AND THE IRS INDIVIDUAL RULINGS PROGRAM--A COMPREHENSIVE ANALYSIS
MCGHEE, THOMAS MITCHELL	A COMPARISON OF THE STATUTORY AND ECONOMIC INCIDENCE AMONG THE TAX REFORM ACT OF 1986, PRIOR LAW AND THREE TAX PROPOSALS
MCNETT, STEPHEN ALLEN	AN EXAMINATION OF THE IMPACT OF SECTION 911 ON ENTRY-LEVEL JOB SELECTION DECISIONS IN SELECTED SITUATIONS
MEADE, JANET ALICE	THE LOCK-IN EFFECT OF CAPITAL GAINS TAXATION AND THE WILLINGNESS TO UNDERTAKE RISKY NEW INVESTMENT
MEYER, DAN WESLEY	SOME CHARACTERISTICS AND ENVIRONMENTAL SENSITIVITIES OF TAXPAYERS TAKING THE UNITED STATES POLITICAL CONTRIBUTION TAX CREDIT DURING 1979-1982
MITTERMAIER, LINDA JEAN	THE IMPACT OF INFLATION ON INDIVIDUAL FEDERAL INCOME TAX LIABILITIES: AN ANALYSIS OF REVENUE AND EQUITY EFFECTS

PANICH, RICHARD LOUIS	AN EXAMINATION OF STRUCTURAL INCOME TAX REVISION FROM A PERSONAL WEALTH REDISTRIBUTION PERSPECTIVE
RICKETTS, ROBERT CARLTON	ALTERNATIVE SOCIAL SECURITY TAXING SCHEMES: AN ANALYSIS OF VERTICAL AND HORIZONTAL EQUITY IN THE FEDERAL TAX SYSTEM
SAGE, JUDITH ANN	SELECTION OF QUALIFIED RETIREMENT PLAN DISTRIBUTION OPTIONS: A SIMULATION
SPINDLE, ROXANNE MARIE	USING EX POST FORECASTING AND PANEL DATA TO EVALUATE LABOR SUPPLY ELASTICITIES
THRONEBERRY, MARY BETH	DETERMINATION OF THE EFFECTS OF THE TAX REFORM ACT OF 1986 ON THE INCOME TAXES OF INDIVIDUAL PASSIVE ACTIVITY INVESTORS
WATANABE, JUDITH ELLEN	INDEXATION OF CAPITAL GAINS AND LOSSES: A COMPLEXITY STUDY

Industry - Agricultural

BARNEY, DOUGLAS KEVIN	MODELING FARM DEBT FAILURE: THE FARMERS HOME ADMINISTRATION
BURCKEL, DARYL VINCENT	AN EMPIRICAL INVESTIGATION INTO DEVELOPING A FAILURE PREDICTION MODEL FOR FARMING ENTERPRISES: THE FIFTH FARM CREDIT DISTRICT
FOSHEE, KENNETH HAROLD	ESTIMATING THE COSTS OF PRODUCING CONTAINER GROWN PLANTS WITH THE ASSISTANCE OF COMPUTER ACCOUNTING SOFTWARE
GONZALEZ CABAN, ARMANDO	FIRE MANAGEMENT COSTS AND SOURCES OF VARIABILITY IN PRESCRIBED BURNING COSTS IN THE FOREST SERVICE'S NORTHERN, INTERMOUNTAIN, AND PACIFIC NORTHWEST REGIONS
MESSINA, FRANK MICHAEL	PREDICTION MODELS FOR DEBT COVENANT VIOLATIONS OF AGRICULTURAL COOPERATIVES
RAY, J. O., III	AN INTERACTIVE FINANCIAL FORECASTING MODEL FOR MISSISSIPPI DELTA FARMING
VARNON, ANTHONY WAYNE	AN EMPIRICAL EXAMINATION OF FINANCIAL ACCOUNTING PRINCIPLES FOR AGRICULTURAL PRODUCERS: THE CASE OF PREPRODUCTIVE COSTS OF PERENNIAL FRUIT AND NUT CROPS
WATTERS, MICHAEL PAUL	ACCOUNTING AND REPORTING PRACTICES OF MISSISSIPPI CATFISH PRODUCERS: AN EMPIRICAL STUDY

Industry - Airline

FINDORFF, PAUL CURTIS	ACQUISITIONS AND ECONOMIC PERFORMANCE IN THE AIRLINE INDUSTRY SINCE THE AIRLINE DEREGULATION ACT OF 1978
JOHNSTON, HOLLY HANSON	EMPIRICAL STUDIES IN MANAGEMENT ACCOUNTING: THREE ESSAYS ON THE U.S. AIRLINE INDUSTRY, 1981-1985
PORTER, THOMAS LARSEN	THE EFFECT OF ECONOMIC REGULATION ON ACCOUNTING DECISIONS: EVIDENCE FROM THE UNITED STATES AIRLINE INDUSTRY
SHARP, ANDREW DANIEL	AN EMPIRICAL INVESTIGATION INTO THE EXTENT OF THE IMPACT OF FREE TRAVEL AWARDS ON REVENUE DISPLACEMENT IN THE AIRLINE INDUSTRY

Industry - Banking/Savings & Loan

AHMED, ELTEGANI ABDELGADER	ISLAMIC BANKING: DISTRIBUTION OF PROFIT
AL-SHIRAWI, BASHIR ISSA	PERFORMANCE OF COMMERCIAL BANKS OPERATING IN THE STATE OF QATAR: A MULTIVARIATE ANALYSIS OF FINANCIAL STATEMENTS
BEAULIEU, PHILIP RAYMOND	COMMERCIAL LENDERS' USE OF ACCOUNTING INFORMATION: THE EFFECTS OF CHARACTER INFORMATION AND EXPERIENCE

Listing by Topic 283

BLACCONIERE, WALTER GEORGE	ACCOUNTING REGULATIONS IN THE SAVINGS AND LOAN INDUSTRY: EVIDENCE OF MARKET REACTIONS AND IMPLICATIONS OF CONTRACTING THEORY
CATANACH, ANTHONY HENRY, JR.	A CAUSAL INVESTIGATION OF RISK, CASH FLOW, AND SOLVENCY IN THE SAVINGS AND LOAN INDUSTRY
CUNNINGHAM, REBA LOVE	AN EMPIRICAL INVESTIGATION OF COMMON CHARACTERISTICS OF COMMERCIAL BANKS USING STANDBY LETTERS OF CREDIT, LETTERS OF CREDIT, INTEREST RATE SWAPS, AND LOAN SALES
DAHER, AHMAD HASAN ABDEL-RAHIM	GAP MANAGEMENT, SIZE AND RISK OF COMMERCIAL BANKS
DUVALL, LINDA GRIFFITH	REGULATORY VALUE OF UNREALIZED SECURITY GAINS AND LOSSES IN THE BANKING INDUSTRY
GREENAWALT, MARY BRADY	AN EMPIRICAL INVESTIGATION OF THE ACCOUNTING ESTIMATES OF LOAN LOSSES IN THE BANKING INDUSTRY
HARRISON, PATRICIA MACKEL	INVESTMENT, ENTRY, AND PERFORMANCE OF SAVINGS AND LOAN ASSOCIATIONS IN THE 1980S
HILL, JOHN WARREN	THE ECONOMIC CONSEQUENCES OF ACCOUNTING CHOICE: DEFERRAL OF LOAN SALE LOSSES IN THE SAVINGS AND LOAN INDUSTRY
HINDI, NITHAM MOHD	AN EMPIRICAL INVESTIGATION INTO THE IMPACT OF OFF-BALANCE SHEET ACTIVITIES ON THE RISKINESS OF COMMERCIAL BANKS: A MARKET-BASED ANALYSIS
HOLLINGSWORTH, DANNY P.	AN EMPIRICAL INVESTIGATION INTO THE CHANGE IN TAX EQUITY WITHIN THE FINANCIAL SERVICES INDUSTRY AS A RESULT OF THE 1986 TAX REFORM ACT
HUBBARD, DANIEL JULIAN	AN ACCOUNTING STUDY OF AMERICAN DEPOSITARY RECEIPTS
JORDAN, CHARLES EDWARD	THE DEVELOPMENT OF A STATISTICAL ANALYTICAL REVIEW MODEL FOR USE BY EXTERNAL AUDITORS IN EVALUATING BANKS' LOAN-LOSS RESERVES
KIMMEL, PAUL DAVID	AN INVESTIGATION OF THE USE OF ACCOUNTING NUMBERS IN THE REGULATION OF BANK CAPITAL
KORTE, LEON	SYSTEMATIC BIAS EFFECTS AND REGULATOR INTERVENTION: THE SAVINGS AND LOAN INDUSTRY
LIU, SHUEN-ZEN	SIGNALING, CAPITAL ADEQUACY RATIO REGULATIONS, AND THE RECOGNITION OF LOAN IMPAIRMENT BY COMMERCIAL BANKS
MARGAVIO, GEANIE WADGE	PORTFOLIO RESPONSES OF SAVINGS AND LOANS TO THE TAX REFORM ACT OF 1986
MOORE, MICHAEL JOE	AN EMPIRICAL INVESTIGATION OF THE DETERMINANTS OF LOAN LOSSES AT SMALL BANKS
NECUNAZAR AZAD, ABBAS	AN APPLICATION OF CHANCE-CONSTRAINED THEORY TO DYNAMIC BANK BALANCE SHEET MANAGEMENT
NISWANDER, FREDERICK DEAN	ACCOUNTING AND FINANCING CHOICE AND CAPITAL ADEQUACY: AN EMPIRICAL STUDY OF PUBLIC AND PRIVATE COMMERCIAL BANKS
ONVURAL, NUR MEVLUDE	ECONOMIES OF SCALE AND ECONOMIES OF SCOPE IN NORTH CAROLINA SAVINGS AND LOAN INSTITUTIONS
OU, CHIN SHYH	AN EMPIRICAL STUDY OF COST DRIVERS IN THE UNITED STATES BANKING INDUSTRY
PRICE, CAROL EILEEN	ACCOUNTING INFORMATION AND LOAN QUALITY ASSESSMENT: AN INVESTIGATION OF THE DECISION PROCESS

Listing by Topic

RIFFE, SUSAN MICHELE	AN EMPIRICAL ANALYSIS OF OFF-BALANCE-SHEET FINANCIAL INSTRUMENT DISCLOSURES IN THE BANKING INDUSTRY
ROOHANI, SAEED JAFARI	AN IMPROVED ACCOUNTING AND AUDITING INFORMATION REPORTING MODEL FOR SAVINGS AND LOAN INSTITUTIONS
SAVAGE, HELEN MARY	REGULATORY ACCOUNTING PRACTICES IN THE SAVINGS AND LOAN INDUSTRY: A STUDY OF THE EFFECTS OF ACCOUNTING CHOICE
SMITH, EUGENE F.	MONEY LAUNDERING: A STUDY IN THE CREATION OF LAW
STINSON, CHRISTOPHER HALL	THE MANAGEMENT OF PROVISIONS AND ALLOWANCES IN THE SAVINGS AND LOAN INDUSTRY
SWIFT, KENTON D.	AN EXPERIMENTAL INVESTIGATION INTO THE EFFECTS OF RISKS AND UNCERTAINTIES ON COMMERCIAL LENDING DECISIONS
VIJAYAN, ANIL KUMAR	CREDIT LOSS DISCLOSURE IN FAS #105 (EMPHASIS ON SWAPS) AND ITS TREATMENT IN RISK-BASED CAPITAL: AN EMPIRICAL ANALYSIS OF SIMILAR CREDIT LOSSES AND ITS DECISION USEFULNESS IN A BANK'S CREDIT RATING
WAHLEN, JAMES MICHAEL	THE NATURE OF INFORMATION IN COMMERCIAL BANK LOAN LOSS DISCLOSURES
WARFIELD, TERRY DEE	THE EFFECTS OF ACCOUNTING DISCLOSURES ON BANK INFORMATION ENVIRONMENTS
WEISEL, JAMES ALLEN	AN EMPIRICAL MODEL FOR CLASSIFYING AND PREDICTING THE FINANCIAL PERFORMANCE OF FEDERALLY INSURED SAVINGS ASSOCIATIONS
WELD, LEONARD GREER	AN EMPIRICAL STUDY OF THE EFFECT OF THE TAX REFORM ACT OF 1986 LOAN LOSS RESERVE REPEAL ON BANK LOAN CHARGE-OFFS

Industry - Health Care

ABBOTT, HAROLD DON	A COMPARISON OF ECONOMIC PERFORMANCE OF INVESTOR-OWNED CHAIN HOSPITALS AND NOT-FOR-PROFIT CHAIN HOSPITALS
ANGRISANI, DAVID PETER	AN ACQUISITION MODEL FOR THE HOSPITAL INDUSTRY
ARNESON, DEAN LEON	IMPACT OF MEDICAID DISCOUNTED AVERAGE WHOLESALE PRICE REIMBURSEMENT ON PHARMACISTS' DRUG PRODUCT SELECTION
ARNOLD, PATRICIA JOSEPHINE	CAPITAL COSTS, ACCOUNTING CHOICE AND MULTIHOSPITAL SYSTEMS
BEDARD, JEAN CATHERINE	USE OF DATA ENVELOPMENT ANALYSIS IN ACCOUNTING APPLICATIONS: EVALUATION AND ILLUSTRATION BY PROSPECTIVE HOSPITAL REIMBURSEMENT
BORDEN, JAMES PATRICK	AN ASSESSMENT OF THE IMPACT OF DIAGNOSIS RELATED GROUP (DRG)-BASED REIMBURSEMENT ON THE TECHNICAL EFFICIENCY OF NEW JERSEY HOSPITALS
CASSIDY, JUDITH HELEN	A STUDY OF THE IMPACT OF MEDICARE PROSPECTIVE PAYMENT SYSTEM ON HOSPITAL COST CONTAINMENT ACTIVITIES
CRAYCRAFT, CATHERINE ANN	THE RELEVANCE OF SOCIOECONOMIC INFORMATION IN EXPLAINING BOND RATINGS OF QUASI-CORPORATIONS
ELDENBURG, LESLIE GAY	THE USE OF INFORMATION IN A COST CONTAINMENT ENVIRONMENT: AN ANALYSIS OF THE AGENCY RELATIONSHIP BETWEEN HOSPITALS AND PHYSICIANS
FORGIONE, DANA ANTHONY	INCENTIVES AND PERFORMANCE IN THE HEALTH CARE INDUSTRY: THE CASE OF FOR/NON PROFIT MULTIHOSPITAL SYSTEMS
FOSTER, BENJAMIN PATRICK	TESTING THE APPROPRIATENESS OF NONPROFIT HOSPITALS' TAX EXEMPTIONS WITH LOGISTIC REGRESSION ANALYSES OF HOSPITAL FINANCIAL DATA

GUPTA, RAMESHWAR DASS	AN INQUIRY INTO THE ACCOUNTING PRINCIPLES AND REPORTING PRACTICES FOLLOWED BY SELECTED STATE UNIVERSITY HOSPITALS
HILL, NANCY THORLEY	THE ADOPTION OF COSTING SYSTEMS IN THE HOSPITAL INDUSTRY
HOLMES, RICHARD LAWRENCE	ON THE DETERMINATION AND REIMBURSEMENT OF COSTS IN THE PROVISION OF MEDICAID SERVICES BY LOCAL HEALTH DEPARTMENTS
JURAS, PAUL EDWARD	ANALYSIS OF RELATIVE EFFICIENCY MEASURES OF MEDICAL NURSING UNITS FOR MANAGERIAL DIAGNOSIS AND CONTROL
KLEINSORGE, ILENE K.	INCORPORATION OF QUALITY CONSIDERATIONS IN MEASURING RELATIVE TECHNICAL EFFICIENCY OF NURSING HOMES
LANGSTON, CAROLYN ANN PATTI	AN EVALUATION OF THE COST ACCOUNTING PROCEDURES FOR OUTPATIENT CARE AT A VA MEDICAL CENTER
LAWRENCE, CAROL MARTIN	THE EFFECT OF ACCOUNTING SYSTEM TYPE AND OWNERSHIP STRUCTURE ON HOSPITAL COSTS
MACQUARRIE, ALLAN JAMES	HEALTH CARE COST CONTAINMENT IN THE NEW ENVIRONMENT OF PROSPECTIVE PRICING OF SERVICES: THE IMPLICATIONS FOR THE ACCOUNTING AND FINANCIAL FUNCTION
MATTISON, DOROTHY MCCALL	THE INFLUENCE OF SELECTED VARIABLES ON THE FINANCIAL PERFORMANCE OF NOT-FOR-PROFIT AND FOR-PROFIT HOSPITALS: A COMPARATIVE ANALYSIS
MICHELMAN, JEFFREY ELIOT	THE DEVELOPMENT AND USES OF ACCOUNTING INFORMATION FOR MANAGERIAL REPORTING AND CONTROL IN A HEALTHCARE SETTING
PUTMAN, ROBERT LYNN	AN EMPIRICAL STUDY OF THE IMPACT OF PUBLIC LAW 98-21 ON THE FINANCIAL OPERATING ENVIRONMENT OF UNITED STATES HOSPITALS
RUBLE, AAFFIEN HENDERIKA	ADAPTIVE BEHAVIOR BY HOSPITALS IN RESPONSE TO MEDICARE'S PROSPECTIVE PAYMENT SYSTEM
SCHAFERMEYER, KENNETH WILLIAM	AN ANALYSIS OF CHAIN PHARMACIES' COSTS OF DISPENSING A THIRD PARTY PRESCRIPTION
SEAY, ROBERT ALAN	AN EMPIRICAL INVESTIGATION INTO HOSPITAL UTILIZATION AND SUPPORT OF THE INTERNAL AUDIT FUNCTION
SODERSTROM, NAOMI SIEGEL	THE RESPONSE OF HOSPITALS TO INCENTIVES: THE CASE OF THE MEDICARE PROSPECTIVE PAYMENT SYSTEM
SURDICK, JOHN JOSEPH, JR.	AN INVESTIGATION OF THE BOND RATINGS ASSIGNED TO TAX-EXEMPT HOSPITAL REVENUE BONDS: AN EMPIRICAL MODEL FOR NOT-FOR-PROFIT HOSPITALS
ZILL, SHARON	A STUDY IN NURSING HOME EFFECTIVENESS IN TEXAS

Industry - Insurance

ADIEL, RON	REINSURANCE AND THE MANAGEMENT OF EARNINGS IN THE PROPERTY-CASUALTY INSURANCE INDUSTRY
BURILOVICH, LINDA JEAN SKANTZ	GAAP ELASTICITIES IN THE LIFE INSURANCE INDUSTRY: THE EFFECT OF TAX LAW CHANGES ON THE ACCOUNTING BEHAVIOR OF MUTUAL AND STOCK LIFE INSURANCE COMPANIES
DEGG, MARTIN ROBERT	EARTHQUAKE HAZARD IN THE MIDDLE EAST: AN EVALUATION FOR INSURANCE AND REINSURANCE PURPOSES
FOUCH, SCOTT RANDALL	EMPIRICAL RESEARCH INTO THE SHIFTING OF THE CORPORATE INCOME TAX OF LIFE INSURANCE COMPANIES
HORN, BETTY C.	AN EXPERT SYSTEM MODEL TO EVALUATE MANAGEMENT'S ASSERTION OF VALUATION FOR AN ACCOUNTING ESTIMATE: AN APPLICATION TO PROPERTY/CASUALTY INSURANCE LOSS RESERVES

KAYE, GERALDINE DELLA	EXPENSES OF UNITED KINGDOM LIFE INSURERS WITH SPECIAL REFERENCE TO 1980-1986 DATA PROVIDED BY THE ASSOCIATION OF BRITISH INSURERS
KIM, DONG HOON	TWO ESSAYS ON ECONOMIC AND FINANCIAL THEORIES OF INSURANCE
MARTINEZ-MORALES, MANUEL	ADAPTIVE PREMIUM CONTROL IN AN INSURANCE RISK PROCESS
PARSEGIAN, ELSA VARSENIG	A TEST OF SOME OF THE EFFECTS OF DIFFERENT PROPERTY RIGHTS STRUCTURES ON MANAGERIAL BEHAVIOR IN THE LIFE INSURANCE INDUSTRY
PETRONI, KATHY RUBY	REGULATORY EFFICIENCY, FINANCIAL DISTRESS AND MANAGERIAL ACCOUNTING DISCRETION
RAY, MANASH RANJAN	TOWARDS A POSITIVE AGENCY THEORY OF CONTROL: AN EMPIRICAL STUDY OF COMPENSATION CONTRACTS IN THE INSURANCE INDUSTRY
WALKER, ROBERT ATKINS	DO TAXES MATTER? THE CASE OF THE PROPERTY-CASUALTY INSURANCE INDUSTRY
WONG, JONATHAN WAITAK	VALUATION RELEVANCE OF MARKET VALUE DISCLOSURES OF DEBT SECURITIES IN THE INSURANCE INDUSTRY

Industry - Oil & Gas

ALDIAB, TAISIER FARES	THE IMPACT OF THE CEILING TEST WRITE-OFF ON THE SECURITY RETURNS OF FULL COST OIL AND GAS FIRMS
BERGEVIN, PETER MICHAEL	EQUITY VALUATION OF PETROLEUM EXPLORATION AND PRODUCTION FIRMS USING ALTERNATIVE ACCOUNTING METHODS
CAMPBELL, ALAN DALE	AN ANALYSIS OF SMOOTHING OF PROVED OIL AND GAS RESERVE QUANTITIES AND AN ANALYSIS OF BIAS AND VARIABILITY IN REVISIONS OF PREVIOUS ESTIMATES OF PROVED OIL AND GAS RESERVE QUANTITIES
CHRISTIAN, CHARLES WILLIAM	AN EMPIRICAL TEST OF THE EFFECTS OF INTERNAL REVENUE CODE SECTION 465 ON RISK-TAKING BY INVESTORS IN OIL AND GAS DRILLING PROGRAMS
CRAIN, JOHN L.	AN INVESTIGATION OF THE USEFULNESS OF RESERVE QUANTITY DISCLOSURES FOR PETROLEUM ENTITIES
FRISKE, KARYN ANNE BYBEE	AN EXAMINATION OF THE EFFECTS OF STANDARD SETTING AND EARNINGS MANAGEMENT IN THE OIL AND GAS INDUSTRY: THE LESSON OF SFAS NO. 96
KIM, JEONG BON	EMPIRICAL EVALUATION OF THE VALUES OF ACCOUNTING ALTERNATIVES IN THE OIL AND GAS INDUSTRY IN THE CONTEXT OF RISK ASSESSMENT
KUMAR, AKHIL	BUDGET-RELATED PREDICTION MODELS IN THE BUSINESS ENVIRONMENT WITH SPECIAL REFERENCE TO SPOT PRICEPREDICTIONS
MALONE, JOHN DAVID, JR.	AN EMPIRICAL INVESTIGATION OF THE EXTENT OF CORPORATE FINANCIAL DISCLOSURE IN THE OIL AND GAS INDUSTRY
SPEAR, NASSER ABDELMONEM	THE INFORMATION CONTENT OF SUPPLEMENTAL RESERVE-BASED REPLACEMENT MEASURES RELATIVE TO THAT OF HISTORICAL COST INCOME AND ITS CASH AND ACCRUAL COMPONENTS OF OIL AND GAS PRODUCING COMPANIES
TEALL, HOWARD DOUGLAS	AN EMPIRICAL STUDY OF THE ABILITY OF CANADIAN OIL AND GAS COMPANIES' RESERVES DISCLOSURES TO ACCOUNT FOR RELATIVE CHANGES IN COMMON STOCK PRICES
YOUNG, GAIL THIBAULT	AN INVESTIGATION OF THE USEFULNESS OF THE FINANCIAL STATEMENTS AS SUPPLEMENTED BY OIL AND GAS PRODUCING ACTIVITIES DISCLOSURES

Industry - Real Estate

BIRD, CYNTHIA ELIZABETH	AN EXAMINATION OF THE EFFECT OF THE TAX REFORM ACT OF 1986 ON INDIVIDUAL AND CORPORATE INVESTMENT IN RESIDENTIAL RENTAL REALTY

COLBURN, STEVEN CHARLES	AN EMPIRICAL ANALYSIS OF THE IMPACT OF THE TAX REFORM ACT OF 1986 ON INVESTMENTS IN REAL ESTATE LIMITED PARTNERSHIPS
HUME, EVELYN C.	THE EFFECTS OF THE TAX REFORM ACT OF 1986 ON THE REAL ESTATE CAPITAL MARKETS AND ITS DIFFERENTIAL EFFECTS ON ENTITY AND FUNCTIONAL FORMS: AN EMPIRICAL INVESTIGATION
KRUMWIEDE, TIMOTHY GERARD	THE EFFECT OF TAXATION ON RESIDENTIAL REAL ESTATE: AN EMPIRICAL ANALYSIS OF REAL ESTATE CONSTRUCTION
MOONEY, KATHLEEN KAYE BORN	AN INVESTIGATION OF THE ASSOCIATION OF CPAS WITH REAL ESTATE LIMITED PARTNERSHIPS
NOVAK, EDWIN SHAWN	AN EMPIRICAL ANALYSIS OF FEDERAL INCOME TAX CAPITALIZATION IN THE PRICING OF INCOME PRODUCING REAL PROPERTY
ST. JOHN, WILLIAM CHARLES, JR.	A STUDY OF THE VARIOUS CHANGES IN FEDERAL INCOME TAX LAWS AND THEIR EFFECTS ON THE RATE OF RETURN FOR REAL ESTATE INVESTORS

Industry - Utilities

FINNEGAN, THOMAS ROBERT	THE EFFECT OF THE 1986 TAX REFORM ACT AND FINANCIAL ACCOUNTING CHANGES ON UTILITY RETURNS AND RATE SETTING
LOUDDER, MARTHA LYNN	AN EMPIRICAL INVESTIGATION OF THE ECONOMIC EFFECTS OF SFAS 90 AND 92 IN THE ELECTRIC UTILITY INDUSTRY
MCGILSKY, DEBRA ERTEL	AN EMPIRICAL STUDY OF A RATEMAKING ISSUE: DETERMINING THE FEDERAL INCOME TAX ALLOWANCE OF AN AFFILIATED UTILITY
ROMEO, GEORGE CHARLES	THE EFFECTS OF SFAS NO. 90 AND 92 ON THE STOCK PRICES AND BETA OF NUCLEAR ELECTRIC UTILITIES
SARIKAS, ROBERT HENRY STEPHEN	A MARKET TEST OF AN ACCOUNTING BASED MEASURE OF PUBLIC UTILITY COMMISSION REGULATORY CLIMATE

Inflation

BARIDWAN, ZAKI	FUNCTIONAL CURRENCY AND INFLATION RATE: AN ANALYSIS OF THE IMPACT ON FINANCIAL STATEMENTS: AN INDONESIAN CASE STUDY
BITNER, LARRY NEWELL	ACCOUNTING FOR CHANGING PRICES PER FASB 33 AND THE IMPACT ON INCOME SMOOTHING
CARGILL, WILLIE NEWTON	AN EQUITY RETENTION APPROACH TO ACCOUNTING FOR CHANGING PRICES
CHEN, KEVIN CHIEN-WEN	THE DETERMINANTS OF TOBIN'S Q RATIO AND AN EVALUATION OF SFAS 33 DATA
CHRISMAN, HEIDI HADLICH	THE EFFECTS OF THE MATURITY STRUCTURE OF NOMINAL CONTRACTS ON EQUITY RETURNS IN AN INFLATIONARY ENVIRONMENT
CHUNG, KEE-YOUNG	AN INVESTIGATION OF THE EFFECTS OF INFLATION-ADJUSTED ACCOUNTING DATA ON EQUITY VALUE
COLLINS, ALLISON BENNETT	A COMPARISON OF HISTORICAL COST DATA AND FASB STATEMENT NO. 33 CURRENT COST DATA IN THE PREDICTION OF CORPORATE BOND RATING
DEAN, DONALD C.	DECAPITALIZATION AND THE THEORY OF REPLACEMENT: ECONOMETRIC ANALYSIS OF SFAS 33
DEBERG, CURTIS LYNN	STRUCTURAL CHANGES IN SYSTEMATIC RISK AND INFLATION ACCOUNTING: A THEORETICAL AND EMPIRICAL EXAMINATION OF ASR190 AND FAS33
DRUKER, MOSHE	ACCOUNTING (INCLUDING TAXATION AND COMPANY LAW) IN AN INFLATIONARY PERIOD--INVESTIGATED ON ISRAELI MODEL

FREEMAN, GARY ROSS	AN INVESTIGATION OF THE USEFULNESS OF CURRENT COST INCOME TO CAPITAL MARKET PARTICIPANTS
GOMA, AHMED TAWFIK	EMPIRICAL INVESTIGATION OF THE INFORMATION CONTENT OF SPECIFIC PRICE CHANGE DISCLOSURES
GRAVES, OLIVER FINLEY	ACCOUNTING FOR INFLATION: GERMAN THEORY OF THE 1920S
HOOKS, JON ALLAN	INFLATION, INFLATION ACCOUNTING, AND REAL STOCK RETURNS: AN ALTERNATIVE TEST OF THE PROXY HYPOTHESIS
HUSSAEN, NIDHAM MOHAMMED ALI	THE EVOLUTION OF ACCOUNTING FOR INFLATION IN GERMANY, 1920-1923
JACKSON, STEVEN ROY	AN EMPIRICAL ASSESSMENT OF MEASUREMENT ERROR IN HISTORICAL COST AND SELECTED CHANGING PRICES INCOME NUMBERS
KENNEDY, JEFFREY LEE	A COMPARISON OF GENERALLY ACCEPTED ACCOUNTING PRACTICE AND STATEMENT OF FINANCIAL ACCOUNTING STANDARDS NO. 33 INCOME MEASUREMENT
KWON, SUNG SOO	FINENESS OF INFLATION-ADJUSTED ACCOUNTING DISCLOSURES AND STOCK PRICE VARIABILITY
LIM, SUK SIG	ACCURACY OF PARTIAL VALUATION RULES AND OPTIMAL USE OF PRICE INDEXES
LIN, YOU-AN ROBERT	THE USE OF SUPPLEMENTARY ACCOUNTING DISCLOSURES FOR CORPORATE TAKEOVER TARGETS PREDICTION
MAUTZ, RICHARD DAVID, JR.	THE IMPACT OF SUPPLEMENTARY, INFLATION-ADJUSTED FINANCIAL STATEMENT INFORMATION ON LABOR'S ASSESSMENT OF CORPORATE ABILITY TO PAY
PARK, CHANGHUN (PETER)	THE RELEVANCE OF REPLACEMENT COST ASSET INFORMATION TO FIRM VALUATION
PARK, MANYONG	INCREMENTAL INFORMATION CONTAINED IN THE SFAS NO. 33 DISCLOSURES: A CLOSER EXAMINATION
PROBER, LARRY M.	A COMPARISON OF HISTORICAL COST AND GENERAL PRICE-LEVEL ADJUSTED MEASURES IN THE PREDICTION OF DIVIDEND CHANGES
RADIG, WILLIAM J.	THE EFFECTS OF INFORMATION REQUIRED BY STATEMENT OF FINANCIAL ACCOUNTING STANDARDS NO. 33 ON THE MANAGERIAL DECISIONS MADE IN SELECTED INDUSTRIAL CORPORATIONS
RAZAKI, KHALID AHMED	THE INCREMENTAL PREDICTIVE ABILITY OF GENERAL PRICE LEVEL ADJUSTED ACCOUNTING NUMBERS FOR DOWNWARD BOND RATING CHANGES
ROOF, BRADLEY MILLER	A COMPARISON OF HISTORIC COST AND PRICE LEVEL FINANCIAL DISCLOSURES: THE ASSOCIATION OF FINANCIAL DISCLOSURES AND ASSESSMENTS OF FINANCIAL RISK
SANDER, JAMES FREDERICK	AN EXAMINATION OF THE RELIABILITY OF VARIOUS INCOME MEASURES FOR ASSESSING THE MAINTENANCE OF OPERATING CAPABILITY
SHANHOLTZER, DENNIS DEAN	AN EXAMINATION OF THE RELATIONSHIP BETWEEN HISTORICAL COST AND CURRENT COST ACCOUNTING DATA AND REPORTED CASH PROVIDED BY OPERATIONS IN THE SUBSEQUENT PERIOD
SHIARAPPA, BARBARA JANUS	THE ASSOCIATION BETWEEN MARKET RISK AND ACCOUNTING RISK ALTERNATIVELY MEASURED
SONG, IN-MAN	DIFFERENTIAL STOCK PRICE REACTION TO INFLATION-ADJUSTED INCOME DISCLOSURES UNDER SFAS 33: EFFECTS OF FIRM-SPECIFIC CHARACTERISTICS
SU, ROBERT KUATERNG	AN EMPIRICAL INVESTIGATION OF THE USEFULNESS OF CURRENT COST INFORMATION IN MERGER PREDICTION

Listing by Topic

TESSONI, DANIEL DAVID	AN EMPIRICAL EVALUATION OF THE POSITIVE THEORY OF ACCOUNTING IN THE CONTEXT OF ACCOUNTING FOR CHANGING PRICES
THORNE, DANIEL T.	INFORMATION CONTENT OF HISTORIC COST-CURRENT COST TRENDS, DERIVED FROM SFAS NO. 33 DISCLOSURES
TONGE, STANLEY D.	THE DIFFERENTIAL EFFECT OF FAS 33 DISCLOSURES ON SECURITY PRICES
WALTER, RICHARD M.	A COMPARISON OF THE USEFULNESS OF CURRENT COST, CONSTANT DOLLAR, AND HISTORICAL COST INFORMATION FOR IDENTIFYING TAKEOVER TARGETS
YANG, DAVID CHIE-HWA	THE ASSOCIATION BETWEEN SFAS 33 INFORMATION AND BOND RATINGS

Information Content

BASU, SOMNATH	INFORMATION, EXPECTATIONS AND EQUILIBRIUM: TRADING VOLUME HYPOTHESES
BETTS, NORMAN MURRAY	AN EMPIRICAL EXAMINATION OF THE REPORTING PRACTICES AND DIFFERENTIAL INFORMATION CONTENT OF EARNINGS COMPONENTS
CHOI, SOONJAE	THE INFORMATION CONTENT OF ACCOUNTING NUMBERS: USING A BELIEF REVISION MEASURE OF STOCK PRICES
DUGAR, AMITABH	THE INFORMATION CONTENT OF THE STATEMENT OF CHANGES IN FINANCIAL POSITION
HUANG-TSAI, CHUNGHUEY	THE ASSOCIATION BETWEEN FINANCIAL STATEMENT INFORMATION AND STOCK PRICES
JOHNSON, GEORGE ALFRED	THE INFORMATION VALUE OF NEW DISAGGREGATED ACCOUNTING INFORMATION: THE CASE OF VOLUNTARY CORPORATE SPINOFFS
JOO, INKI	INFORMATION CONTENT OF STOCK SPLITS IN RELATION WITH PRIOR YEAR'S EARNINGS' GROWTH, FIRM SIZE, SPLIT SIZE, AND REPUTATION: AN EMPIRICAL ANALYSIS
KIM, OLIVER	PRICE AND VOLUME REACTIONS TO PUBLIC ANNOUNCEMENTS AND ENDOGENOUS PRE-ANNOUNCEMENT INFORMATION
MYNATT, PATRICIA GRAFF	THE INFORMATION CONTENT OF FINANCIAL STATEMENT RELEASES
REBURN, JAMES PATRICK	AN EMPIRICAL EXAMINATION OF DISCLOSURES REQUIRED BY THE SECURITIES AND EXCHANGE COMMISSION: THE CASE OF STOCK OWNERSHIP REPORTING
RIPPINGTON, FREDERICK ALFRED	THE INCREMENTAL INFORMATION CONTENT OF THE ANNUAL REPORT AND ACCOUNTS
SUN, HUEY-LIAN	INFORMATION CONTENT OF EXTERNAL FINANCING AND FIRM-SPECIFIC CHARACTERISTICS
SUTLEY, KENNETH R.	AN EMPIRICAL INVESTIGATION INTO THE RELATION BETWEEN DIFFERENTIAL ANNUAL REPORT INFORMATIVENESS AND THE ASSOCIATION OF STOCK RETURNS WITH ACCOUNTING EARNINGS: THE CASE OF THE 'FINANCIAL POST' ANNUAL REPORT
TRIMBLE, DIXIE CLARK	AN ANALYSIS OF USER'S PERCEIVED INFORMATION NEEDS, FIRM'S CURRENT REPORTING PRACTICES, AND THE STOCK PRICE EFFECTS OF ANNOUNCEMENTS OF IMPAIRMENT IN VALUE OF LONG-LIVED OPERATING ASSETS
TUCKER, ROBERT RILEY	AN INVESTIGATION OF THE RELATIONSHIP BETWEEN PUBLIC AND PRIVATE INFORMATION: AN EXPERIMENTAL MARKET STUDY
WEINSTEIN, GERALD PAUL	AN EMPIRICAL INVESTIGATION OF DIVESTITURE ANNOUNCEMENTS: THE SOUTH AFRICA EFFECT
WOLCOTT, SUSAN KAY	THE EFFECTS OF PRIOR SHAREHOLDER ANTICIPATION AND RESTRUCTURING ACTIONS ON THE STOCK PRICE RESPONSE TO WRITEDOWN ANNOUNCEMENTS

| YEATON, KATHRYN GIVENS | AN INVESTIGATION OF THE IMPACT OF NON-ACCOUNTING INFORMATION (PLANT CLOSING ANNOUNCEMENTS) ON THE EXPECTATIONS OF FUTURE ACCOUNTING OUTCOMES |
| YOO, CHUNG EUL | THE INFORMATION CONTENT OF DISCONTINUED OPERATIONS ASSOCIATED WITH APB OPINION NO. 30 |

Information Transfer

BAGINSKI, STEPHEN PAUL	INTRA-INDUSTRY INFORMATION TRANSFERS ASSOCIATED WITH MANAGEMENT EARNINGS FORECASTS
BANNISTER, JAMES W.	EARNINGS SIGNALS AND INTER-FIRM INFORMATION TRANSFERS
JOH, GUN-HO	INTERFIRM INFORMATION TRANSFER AND DISCLOSURE TIMING
LIN, MEI-HWA	AN EMPIRICAL STUDY OF INFORMATION TRANSFER FROM A LEADING FIRM TO LARGE FIRMS AND SMALL FIRMS IN THE SAME INDUSTRY
PYO, YOUNGIN	INFORMATION TRANSFERS AND INFORMATION LEAKAGE ASSOCIATED WITH EARNINGS RELEASES
SCHODERBEK, MICHAEL PAUL	THE EFFECT OF MARKET STRUCTURE ON THE BEHAVIOR OF INTRA-INDUSTRY INFORMATION TRANSFERS: EMPIRICAL TESTS USING FIRMS' QUARTERLY EARNINGS ANNOUNCEMENTS
SCOFIELD, BARBARA WILD	THE EFFECT OF THE INDUSTRY DISCLOSURE POLICY ON INTRA-INDUSTRY INFORMATION TRANSFER ASSOCIATED WITH QUARTERLY EARNINGS ANNOUNCEMENTS
WASLEY, CHARLES EDWARD	DIFFERENTIAL INFORMATION CONTENT OF EARNINGS ANNOUNCEMENTS: THEORETICAL AND EMPIRICAL ANALYSIS OF THE ROLE OF INFORMATION TRANSFERS

Initial Public Offerings

DUCHARME, LARRY L.	IPOS: PRIVATE INFORMATION AND EARNINGS MANAGEMENT
ELDER, RANDAL JEFFREY	AUDITOR INDUSTRY EXPERIENCE AND INITIAL PUBLIC OFFERINGS
FRIEDLAN, JOHN MICHAEL	ACCOUNTING INFORMATION AND THE PRICING OF INITIAL PUBLIC OFFERINGS
KIM, MOONCHUL	THE ROLE OF ACCOUNTING INFORMATION IN THE PRICING OF IPOS
LEE, MINWOO	THE ROLES OF AUDITORS AND INVESTMENT BANKERS IN SIGNALLING PRIVATE INFORMATION AND INSURING LITIGATION RISK IN THE NEW EQUITY ISSUES MARKET
NEILL, JOHN D., III	THE ROLE OF ACCOUNTING NUMBERS IN THE 'LONG-TERM' MISPRICING OF INITIAL PUBLIC SECURITY OFFERINGS

Insider Trading

BETTIS, J. C. CARR	REVISITING THE PROFITABILITY OF INSIDER AND OUTSIDER TRADING
COLLURA RAPACCIOLI, DONNA	WEALTH REDISTRIBUTIONS OR CHANGES IN FIRM VALUE: AN ANALYSIS OF THE RETURNS TO BONDHOLDERS AND STOCKHOLDERS AROUND INSIDE TRADE EVENTS
LETOURNEAU, CLAIRE ANGELA	FINANCIAL DISCLOSURE AND THE ACCOUNTANT'S RESPONSIBILITY TO SHAREHOLDERS: THE CASE OF INSIDER TRADING
ODAIYAPPA, RAMASAMY	ECONOMIC CONSEQUENCES OF FINANCIAL ACCOUNTING STANDARDS BOARD STATEMENT NUMBER 33: AN INSIDER TRADING PERSPECTIVE
PARK, SECHOUL	INSIDER TRADING ACTIVITY SURROUNDING CORPORATE EARNINGS ANNOUNCEMENT

TYPPO, ERIC WILHELM	AN EMPIRICAL INVESTIGATION OF THE RELATIONSHIP BETWEEN INSIDER TRADING AND MANAGEMENT EARNINGS FORECAST CHARACTERISTICS
UDPA, SUNEEL CHANDRASHEKHAR	THE EFFECT OF INSIDER TRADING ON THE STOCK PRICE RESPONSE TO EARNINGS

Instructional Methods

AUSTIN, WALTER WADE	A STUDY OF THE EFFECTS OF INTEGRATING MICROCOMPUTERS INTO THE INTRODUCTORY FINANCIAL ACCOUNTING COURSE
DAY, MARY MARLENE	CRITICAL ACCOUNTING PEDAGOGY IN PRACTICE: (RE)CONSTRUCTIONS OF 'A TRUE AND FAIR VIEW'
HURT, ROBERT LEE	THE EFFECTS OF COMPUTER-ASSISTED INSTRUCTION ON MOTIVATION AND ANXIETY IN FIRST-YEAR UNDERGRADUATE ACCOUNTING STUDENTS
KOEN, MARIUS	UTILISING THE COMPUTER AS AN AID FOR TEACHING ACCOUNTING
MOORE, ELMA LEE SCHMIDT	AN ANALYSIS OF LEARNING STYLES, INSTRUCTIONAL STYLES, AND CULTURE AMONG SELECTED ACCOUNTING STUDENTS AND INSTRUCTORS AT THE UNIVERSITY-LEVEL
MOSES, DUANE R.	AUTOMATED VS. MANUAL SIMULATIONS IN HIGH SCHOOL ACCOUNTING: THE EFFECTS ON STUDENT ACHIEVEMENT, PERCEPTIONS AND TIME REQUIRED TO COMPLETE
MURPHY, DAVID SMITH	AN EMPIRICAL INVESTIGATION OF THE EFFECT OF EXPERT SYSTEM USE ON THE DEVELOPMENT OF EXPERTISE IN AUDITING
OTT, RICHARD LAWRENCE	AN EMPIRICAL ANALYSIS OF THE INTERACTIVE EFFECTS BETWEEN THE INDIVIDUAL CHARACTERISTICS OF THE LEARNER AND THE METHOD OF INSTRUCTION--LECTURE OR COMPUTER-ASSISTED--ON STUDENT ACHIEVEMENT IN ELEMENTARY ACCOUNTING
PICARD, ROBERT RAYMOND	MANAGERIAL ACCOUNTING PROBLEM-SOLVING SKILLS: AN EXPERIMENT INVESTIGATING GROUP-TO-INDIVIDUAL ACQUISITION AND TRANSFER
THOMAS, CHARLES WILLIS	EFFECTS OF COMPUTER TUTORIAL LESSONS ON ACCOUNTING I SKILLS AND ATTRITION

Interim Reporting

AL-SUDAIRY, SALMAN ABDULRAHMAN	THE DETECTION AND DETECTABILITY OF MATERIAL MISSTATEMENTS IN INTERIM FINANCIAL REPORTS BY CAPITAL MARKET PARTICIPANTS
BURROWES, ASHLEY WAYNE	A SURVEY OF SOPHISTICATED NEW ZEALAND USERS OF FINANCIAL STATEMENTS AND THEIR INTERIM REPORTING REQUIREMENTS
BUTTARS, THOMAS ALAN	A DISAGGREGATE APPROACH TO ACCOUNTING BASED MEASURES OF SYSTEMATIC RISK
LOPEZ GRACIA, JOSE	ACCOUNTING INFORMATION AND STOCK EXCHANGE: EMPIRICAL ANALYSIS OF THE INTERIM REPORTS AND THEIR RELEVANCE IN DECISION-MAKING [LA INFORMACION CONTABLE Y EL MERCADO DE VALORES: ANALISIS EMPIRICO DE LOS INFORMES

Internal Auditing

BETHEA, PRESTON, JR.	A DESCRIPTIVE EXPLORATORY EXAMINATION OF THE ROLE AND RESPONSIBILITIES OF INTERNAL AUDITORS IN HIGHER EDUCATION
BOYLE, EDMUND JOSEPH	THE ROLE OF INTERNAL AUDITING IN THE DEFENSE INDUSTRY: AN EMPIRICAL STUDY
BROWN, WILLIAM P.	SHARED AND DIFFERING PERCEPTIONS OF COSTS AND BENEFITS ASSOCIATED WITH INTERNAL/EXTERNAL AUDITOR SERVICES AND COOPERATION
CAMPBELL, ANNHENRIE	AUDIT CONTINUITY, CLIENT'S POLICY, AND THE INTERNAL AUDIT RELIANCE JUDGMENT
DEBRUINE, MARINUS	AN AGENCY-THEORETIC ANALYSIS OF THE EXTERNAL AUDITOR'S USE OF THE INTERNAL AUDITOR IN CONDUCTING THE FINANCIAL AUDIT

HABEGGER, JERRELL WAYNE	AN INTERNAL AUDITING INNOVATION DECISION: STATISTICAL SAMPLING
KLEMSTINE, CHARLES FREDERICK	INTERNAL AND EXTERNAL AUDIT SUBSTITUTION
MOORE, PERRY GLEN	EXTERNAL AUDITOR RELIANCE ON INTERNAL AUDITORS: AN EXAMINATION OF THE SIMILARITY OF AUDITOR JUDGMENTS
NIKKHAH-AZAD, ALI	PERCEPTIONS OF COLLEGE AND UNIVERSITY AUDITORS CONCERNING THE IMPORTANCE OF SELECTED FACTORS ASSOCIATED WITH OPERATIONAL AUDITING
O'SHAUGHNESSY, JOHN JOSEPH	AN EMPIRICAL STUDY OF THE EXTENT OF IMPLEMENTATION AND EFFECTIVENESS OF THE TREADWAY COMMISSION'S RECOMMENDATIONS AS PERCEIVED BY INTERNAL AUDIT MANAGERS OF CALIFORNIA'S 100 LARGEST PUBLICLY HELD COMPANIES
PEI, KER-WEI BUCK	A COMPARATIVE STUDY OF INTERNAL AND EXTERNAL AUDITORS' JUDGMENT OF INTERNAL AUDITOR INDEPENDENCE
QUARLES, NOWLIN ROSS	PROFESSIONAL COMMITMENT, ORGANIZATIONAL COMMITMENT, AND ORGANIZATIONAL - PROFESSIONAL CONFLICT IN THE INTERNAL AUDIT FUNCTION: MODEL DEVELOPMENT AND TEST
SMITH, KENNETH JONATHAN	AN INTERNAL AUDITING METHODOLOGY FOR THE EVALUATION OF CORPORATE WELLNESS INVESTMENTS
TOERNER, MICHAEL CHARLES	AN INVESTIGATION OF THE EFFECT OF A FAVORABLE EXTERNAL QUALITY ASSURANCE REVIEW ON THE SCOPE OF THE EXTERNAL AUDITOR'S EXAMINATION OF AN ORGANIZATION'S FINANCIAL STATEMENTS

Internal Control

CHEN, KUO-TAY	SCHEMATIC EVALUATION OF INTERNAL ACCOUNTING CONTROL SYSTEMS
HIGHSMITH, GWENDOLYN JANNETT	AN EMPIRICAL INVESTIGATION OF THE PERFORMANCE OF THE EDP QUALITY ASSURANCE FUNCTION ON THE INDEPENDENT AUDITOR'S EVALUATION OF INTERNAL CONTROL
KANNAN, RAMU S.	A KNOWLEDGE-BASED APPROACH FOR CONTROL DESIGN: A CASE STUDY IN THE PURCHASING CYCLE
MACUR, KENNETH MICHAEL	THE EFFECTS OF CLUSTERING AND RESPONSE MODE CORRESPONDENCE ON THE EVALUATION OF INTERNAL ACCOUNTING CONTROLS
MESERVY, RAYMAN DAVID	AUDITING INTERNAL CONTROLS: A COMPUTATIONAL MODEL OF THE REVIEW PROCESS
MORRIS, BONNIE WHITE	CASE-BASED REASONING IN INTERNAL AUDITOR EVALUATIONS OF EDP CONTROLS
NEKRASZ, FRANK, JR.	A THEORETICAL INVESTIGATION OF MANADATORY AUDITOR REPORTS ON INTERNAL CONTROL STRUCTURES
O'CALLAGHAN, SUSANNE	AN ARTIFICIAL INTELLIGENCE APPLICATION OF BACKPROPAGATION NEURAL NETWORKS TO SIMULATE ACCOUNTANTS' ASSESSMENTS OF INTERNAL CONTROL SYSTEMS USING COSO GUIDELINES
POCH Y TORRES, RAMON	THE SYSTEM OF INTERNAL CONTROL OF BUSINESS FIRMS
PURVIS, S.E.C.	THE AUDITOR'S PRELIMINARY EVALUATION OF INTERNAL ACCOUNTING CONTROL: A BEHAVIORAL ANALYSIS
SOONGSWANG, ORANUJ	THE PERCEIVED IMPORTANCE AND IMPLEMENTATION OF INTERNAL CONTROLS IN A DATABASE ENVIRONMENT
VERGHESE, THOMAS	A FORMALIZATION OF INTERNAL CONTROL EVALUATION
WOOD, ROYCE WILBURN, JR.	AN ANALYSIS OF SELECTED INTERNAL CONTROLS FOR FINANCIAL ACCOUNTING AT THE CENTRAL OFFICE LEVEL OF ALABAMA BOARDS OF EDUCATION

Listing by Topic

ABDUL-RAHIM, HASSAN MAHMOOD	AN ANALYSIS OF CORPORATE ACCOUNTING AND REPORTING PRACTICES IN BAHRAIN
ABOUEL-ENIN, MOHAMED A.	AN EMPIRICAL STUDY OF FACTORS INFLUENCING THE SUCCESS OF EGYPT-UNITED STATES OF AMERICA JOINT VENTURES ENGAGING IN BUSINESSES IN EGYPT
ACTON, DANIEL DICKSON	THE IMPACT ON DOMESTIC FINANCIAL STATEMENTS USERS OF DISCLOSING FOREIGN BUSINESS AND FINANCIAL PRACTICES: AN INVESTIGATION OF JAPANESE CORPORATIONS
ADHIKARI, AJAY	AN EMPIRICAL CROSS-NATIONAL STUDY OF ENVIRONMENTAL FACTORS INFLUENCING ACCOUNTING DISCLOSURE AND REPORTING REQUIREMENTS OF STOCK EXCHANGES
AL-NASRULLAH, ABDULAZIZ A.	AN EVALUATION OF INTERNAL CONTROLS OF COMMERCIAL LOANS IN SAUDI ARABIAN BANKS
AL-RASHED, WAEL E. R.	KUWAIT'S TAX REFORMATION, ITS ALTERNATIVES AND IMPACT ON A DEVELOPING ACCOUNTING PROFESSION
AL-RWITA, SAAD SALEH	OWNERSHIP, CONTROL, AND PERFORMANCE IN AN UNDERDEVELOPED MARKET ENVIRONMENT: THE CASE OF THE SAUDI BANKING INDUSTRY
ARTSBERG, KRISTINA ULRIKA	POLICY MAKING AND ACCOUNTING CHANGE: INFLUENCES ON THE CHOICE OF MEASUREMENT PRINCIPLES IN SWEDISH ACCOUNTING [NORMBILDNING OCH REDOVISNINGSFOERAENDRING: VAERDERINGAR VID VAL AV MAETPRINCIPER INOM
BARDO, FREDERIC S.	A NORMATIVE THEORY OF ACCOUNTING FOR ZIMBABWE: A THIRD WORLD COUNTRY
BILODEAU, JULIEN	THE USE OF ACCOUNTING NUMBERS IN DEBT AND PREFERRED SHARE COVENANTS: SOME CANADIAN EVIDENCE
BOOYSEN, STEFANES FRANCOIS	A FRAMEWORK FOR FINANCIAL REPORTING TO EMPLOYEES IN THE REPUBLIC OF SOUTH AFRICA
CERDA APARICIO, JOSE	COMPARATIVE ANALYSIS OF THE IMPLEMENTATION OF THE 4TH COMPANY LAW DIRECTIVE IN THE 12 MEMBER COUNTRIES OF THE EUROPEAN COMMUNITY [LA ADAPTACION DEL DERECHO DE SOCIEDADES A LA IV DIRECTIVA DE LA COMUNIDAD
CHANG, CHUN SHYONG	THE INFORMATION CONTENT OF TAIWANESE FINANCIAL STATEMENTS: THE CASE OF LOAN DEFAULT
CHANG, JINNDER	TRANSFER PRICING AND TAX STRATEGIES FOR MULTINATIONAL COMPANIES IN TAIWAN
CHANG, YOUNG HANG	A COMPARATIVE STUDY OF THE ACCOUNTING SYSTEMS OF FIVE COUNTRIES IN EAST AND SOUTHEAST ASIA
CHAWLA, GURDEEP KUMAR	UNITED STATES GAAP VERSUS EUROPEAN COMMUNITY AND PACIFIC RIM COUNTRIES' ACCOUNTING STANDARDS: AN EMPIRICAL STUDY
CHRISTENSEN, LINDA FAY	SUBSIDIARY MANAGEMENT ACCOUNTING SYSTEMS OF U.S.-BASED MULTINATIONAL ENTERPRISES
CHU, LILUAN ERIC	MARKET-BASED ACCOUNTING RESEARCH: AN INTERNATIONAL COMPARISON AND NEW EVIDENCE
CHUNG, KI-YOUNG	AN ESSAY ON THE INTERTEMPORAL GENERAL EQUILIBRIUM MODEL OF EXCHANGE RATES IN A CONTINUOUS-TIME VERSION
COOKE, T. E.	AN EMPIRICAL STUDY OF FINANCIAL DISCLOSURE BY SWEDISH COMPANIES
CREDLE, SID HOWARD	THE MARKET REACTION TO THE FORGIVENESS OF DEFERRED TAXES OF THE DOMESTIC INTERNATIONAL SALES CORPORATION (DISC): EMPIRICAL EVIDENCE REGARDING THE 'INDEFINITE REVERSAL CRITERION'
DEMIRAG, ISTEMIHAN SEFIK	FOREIGN CURRENCY ACCOUNTING AND MANAGEMENT EVALUATION OF FOREIGN SUBSIDIARY PERFORMANCE

EL-ISSA, YASIN AHMAD MOUSA	THE USEFULNESS OF CORPORATE FINANCIAL DISCLOSURE TO INVESTORS IN THE AMMAN FINANCIAL MARKET
ELECHIGUERRA ARRIZABALAGA, CRISANTA	ACCOUNTING INFORMATION DURING PERIODS OF ECONOMIC INSTABILITY [LA INFORMACION CONTABLE EN LOS PERIODOS DE INESTABILIDAD ECONOMICA]
EWER, SID ROY	A STUDY OF THE EFFECT OF TRANSBORDER DATA FLOW RESTRICTIONS ON U.S. MULTINATIONAL CORPORATE ACCOUNTING CONTROL SYSTEMS
FEENEY, P. W.	EURONOTES: RISK AND PRICING
FULKERSON, CHERYL LINTHICUM	EARNINGS EXPECTATIONS, FIRM VALUATION AND RISK ASSESSMENT USING FOREIGN AND RESTATED ACCOUNTING DATA
GABALLA, MAHMOUD A.	PERFORMANCE AND CONTROL OF PUBLIC ENTERPRISE IN EGYPT
GLOECK, JUERGEN DIETER	THE EXPECTATION GAP WITH REGARD TO THE AUDITING PROFESSION IN THE REPUBLIC OF SOUTH AFRICA
GOBER, JERALD ROBERT	THE BLEND OF TAXES USED TO FUND NATIONAL, STATE, AND LOCAL GOVERNMENTAL BODIES: A FACTOR IN THE ECONOMIES OF THE WORLD?
GOLDBERG, STEPHEN RICHARD	THE IMPACT OF EXCHANGE RATE CHANGES ON SECURITY RETURNS AND FINANCIAL REPORTING: THEORY AND EMPIRICAL FINDINGS
GUPTA, MANOJ	THE CURRENCY RISK FACTOR IN INTERNATIONAL EQUITY PRICING
HAMMOND, JOSEPH ANDREW	RISK EXPOSURE AND MANAGEMENT PRACTICES IN RESPONSE TO FLOATING EXCHANGE RATE VOLATILITY IN GHANA
HAN, JIN-SOO	INTERNAL CONTROL EVALUATION AND AUDIT PROGRAM PLANNING JUDGMENTS BY INDIVIDUAL AUDITORS AND AUDIT TEAMS: A STUDY OF SOUTH KOREAN CPA'S
HARRIS, DAVID GARLAND	THE IMPACT OF UNITED STATES TAX LAW REVISION ON MULTINATIONAL CORPORATIONS' CAPITAL LOCATION AND INCOME SHIFTING DECISIONS
HE, XIAOHONG	INTERNATIONAL TAX TRENDS AND COMPETITION: TAX SENSITIVITY OF U.S. FOREIGN INVESTMENT ABROAD
HIGSON, ANDREW WILLIAM	AN EMPIRICAL INVESTIGATION OF THE EXTERNAL AUDIT PROCESS: A STUDY OF THE REACTION OF PROFESSIONAL AUDITORS TO RECENT CHANGES IN THE AUDIT ENVIRONMENT
HILLEBRAND, ANDREAS WILHELM	A CONCEPT FOR A PERSONAL-COMPUTER-AIDED FINANCIAL STATEMENT ANALYSIS WITH REGARD TO THE GERMAN ACCOUNTING DIRECTIVES LAW [ENTWICKLUNG EINES KONZEPTS ZUR PERSONAL-COMPUTER-GESTUETZTEN ANALYSE PUBLIZIERTER
HUDACK, LAWRENCE RALPH	AN EXPLORATORY INVESTIGATION OF SOCIO-ECONOMIC PHENOMENA THAT MAY INFLUENCE ACCOUNTING DIFFERENCES IN THREE DIVERSE COUNTRIES
HUMAN, WILLEM ADRIAAN FRANS	THE ABILITY OF THE SOUTH AFRICAN AUDIT PROFESSION TO AUDIT IN THE ELECTRONIC DATA INTERCHANGE ERA
HUTCHINSON, PATRICK JOHN	THE FINANCIAL PROFILE OF GROWTH SMALL FIRMS: AN ANALYSIS OF THE ACCOUNTING RATIOS OF AUSTRALIAN COMPANIES AT AND AFTER FLOTATION, 1964/5-1983/4
IVANCEVICH, DANIEL MICHAEL	AN EMPIRICAL INVESTIGATION OF THE ACCOUNTING DIFFERENCES FOR GOODWILL IN THE UNITED STATES AND UNITED KINGDOM
JONNERGARD, KARIN	FEDERATIVE PROCESSES AND ADMINISTRATIVE DEVELOPMENT--A STUDY OF FEDERATIVE COOPERATIVE ORGANIZATIONS (SWEDEN, CANADA) [FEDERATIVA PROCESSER OCH ADMINISTRATIV UTVECKLING--EN STUDIE AV
KILANI, KILANI ABDULKERIM	THE EVOLUTION AND STATUS OF ACCOUNTING IN LIBYA. (VOLUMES I AND II)

Listing by Topic   295

LADNER, ROBERT	BALANCE SHEET ANALYSIS: OLD LEGAL SITUATION [BILANZANALYSE NACH NEUEM RECHT]
LARSON, ROBERT KEITH	AN EMPIRICAL INVESTIGATION OF THE RELATIONSHIPS BETWEEN INTERNATIONAL ACCOUNTING STANDARDS, EQUITY MARKETS AND ECONOMIC GROWTH IN DEVELOPING COUNTRIES
LEE, SUK JUN	THE EFFECT OF GAAP DIFFERENCES ON PRICE VARIABILITY AND DISPERSION OF BELIEFS
LIN, LIANGQI	ECONOMIC DETERMINANTS OF VOLUNTARY ACCOUNTING CHOICES FOR R&D EXPENDITURES IN BELGIUM
LUNDBLAD, HEIDEMARIE	VOLUNTARY FINANCIAL DISCLOSURE: AN INTERNATIONAL COMPARISON OF MANAGERIAL POLICIES
MALLADO RODRIGUEZ, JOSE ANTONIO	THE MEASURE OF EFFECTIVENESS AND EFFICACY IN PUBLIC EXPENSES: AN EMPIRICAL APPLICATION [LE MEDIDA DE LA EFICACIA Y DE LA EFICIENCIA DEL GASTO PUBLICO: UNA APLICACION EMPIRICA]
MCQUEEN, PATRICIA DORAN	THE INFORMATION CONTENT OF FOREIGN GAAP EARNINGS AND SHAREOWNERS' EQUITY AND THE UNITED STATES GAAP RECONCILIATION DISCLOSURES IN SEC FORM 20-F
MEYERMANS, ERIC AUGUST	ECONOMETRIC ALLOCATION SYSTEMS FOR THE FOREIGN EXCHANGE MARKET: SPECIFICATION, ESTIMATION AND TESTING OF TRANSMISSION MECHANISMS UNDER CURRENCY SUBSTITUTION
MONSERRAT JAUME, MAGDALENA	CATALAN WORKER-SHAREHOLDER PUBLIC LIMITED COMPANIES: A COMPARATIVE ECONOMIC ANALYSIS (SPAIN) [LAS SOCIEDADES ANONIMAS LABORALES CATALANAS: UN ANALISIS ECONOMICO COMPARATIVO]
MUNTORO, RONNY KUSUMA	THE USE OF ORGANIZATION BEHAVIOR METHODS IN THE DEVELOPMENT OF COMPUTERIZED ACCOUNTING SYSTEMS IN INDONESIA: AN ATTITUDINAL SURVEY
NDZINGE, SHABANI	REGIONAL HARMONISATION OF ACCOUNTING IN DEVELOPING COUNTRIES: THE CASE OF THE SADCC
NEMEH, ALI G.	OPERATIONAL AUDITING PRACTICES IN WESTERN DEVELOPED COUNTRIES: IMPLICATIONS FOR GOVERNMENT AUDIT IN THE STATE OF KUWAIT. (VOLUMES I AND II)
NEWBERRY, KAYE JEANNE	FOREIGN TAX CREDIT LIMITATIONS AND PUBLIC ISSUANCES BY UNITED STATES MULTINATIONALS: NEW EVIDENCE OF TAX CLIENTELES
NUTTER, SARAH EMMONS	UNITED STATES FEDERAL TAXATION OF EXPATRIATES: AN EMPIRICAL INVESTIGATION OF THE EQUITY OF THE FOREIGN EARNED INCOME AND HOUSING EXCLUSIONS
OKOPNY, D. ROBERT	PLANNING AN INTERNATIONAL AUDIT: AN EMPIRICAL INVESTIGATION OF INTERNAL AUDITOR JUDGMENT
PARRY, MICHAEL JOHN	THE ROLE OF ACCOUNTING IN THE ECONOMIC DEVELOPMENT OF BANGLADESH
PEREZ GARCIA, MARIA PILAR	THE FAILURE OF A CENTRAL BANK: THE BANK OF VALLADOLID [LA BANCARROTA DE UN BANCO EMISOR: EL BANCO DE VALLADOLID]
PERSELLIN, MARK BENNETT	AN INVESTIGATION OF THE PLANNING AND POLICY IMPLICATIONS OF THE FOREIGN SALES CORPORATION LEGISLATION
PHILLIPS, DAVID A.	ECONOMIC DEVELOPMENT, ACCOUNTING PRICES AND TECHNOLOGY: A CASE STUDY IN THE ESTIMATION OF ACCOUNTING PRICES AND THEIR APPLICATION TO ECONOMIC AND DISTRIBUTIONAL ANALYSIS OF THE CHOICE OF TECHNOLOGY IN THE NEPAL TEXTILE
PRIEBJRIVAT, ANGKARAT	CORPORATE DISCLOSURE: A CASE OF SECURITIES EXCHANGE OF THAILAND
RAMAGLIA, JUDITH ANN	STRUCTURES IN THE ACCOUNTING LEXICON: AN INVESTIGATION OF SIMILARITIES STRUCTURES AND CONNOTATIVE DIMENSIONS IN FIVE NATIONS
REBMANN-HUBER, ZELMA E.	THE INFLUENCE OF VARIOUS GROUPS ON ACCOUNTING STANDARD-SETTING IN SIXTEEN DEVELOPED COUNTRIES: MODEL AND EMPIRICAL INVESTIGATIONS

Listing by Topic 296

Listing by Topic   297

ZAITEGI SARRIA, MIREN ITXASO	ACCOUNTANT REFLECTIONS IN THE ASSUMPTION OF INSURED RISK [REFLEXIONES CONTABLES EN LA ASUNCION DEL RIESGO ASEGURADO]
ZEBUN, ABDULWAHAB HAIDER	LINKAGES BETWEEN MICROACCOUNTING AND MACROACCOUNTING: AN IRAQI CASE STUDY

Internships

BEARD, VICTORIA KNAPP	REFLECTIONS OF PUBLIC ACCOUNTING INTERNS: A QUALITATIVE ANALYSIS OF EXPERIENTIAL LEARNING
MARABELLO, CARMINE F., JR.	A STUDY OF PUBLIC ACCOUNTING INTERNSHIPS IN NEW ENGLAND: AN EVALUATION FROM THE VIEWPOINT OF CPA FIRMS

Inventory

AKATHAPORN, PARPORN	INVENTORY METHODS AND THE PRICE EARNINGS ANOMALY: AN EMPIRICAL EXAMINATION
BATCHELDER, WALTER IRVING	A STUDY OF THE LINK-CHAIN LIFO CONTROVERSY
BOUILLON, MARVIN L.	ECONOMIC DETERMINANTS OF THE DECISION TO LIQUIDATE LIFO INVENTORY QUANTITIES
CHAN, KAM CHU	A REEXAMINATION OF THE STOCK MARKET AND BOND MARKET REACTION TO LIFO ADOPTION
FILTER, WILLIAM VIGGO	A STUDY OF THE MARKET BEHAVIOR IN RESPONSE TO THE LIQUIDATION OF LIFO LAYERS
FRANKEL, MICAH PAUL	THE DETERMINANTS OF LIFO LAYER LIQUIDATIONS: TAX MINIMIZATION AND AGENCY COST FACTORS
GRIFFIN, LYNN DRAGER	AN EXPECTANCY THEORY EXAMINATION OF MANAGERIAL MOTIVATION TO IMPLEMENT JUST-IN-TIME
HE, XIN XIN	STOCHASTIC INVENTORY SYSTEMS WITH ORDER CROSSOVER
JAN, CHING-LIH	THE MARKET'S EVALUATION OF FOOTNOTE DISCLOSURES FOR FIRMS USING LIFO INVENTORY ACCOUNTING
KIM, JINSUN	AN EMPIRICAL ANALYSIS OF CHANGES IN INVENTORY ACCOUNTING METHODS IN 1974
LINNEGAR, GARY JOHN	AN INVESTIGATION INTO THE MANAGEMENT OF CHANGE IN COST ACCOUNTING INFORMATION SYSTEM REQUIREMENTS DURING THE TRANSITION FROM TRADITIONAL MANUFACTURING TO JUST IN TIME CONCEPTS
OCKREE, KANALIS A.	A JUST-IN-TIME PRODUCTION PHILOSOPHY: EMPIRICAL ANALYSES AND FIELD STUDY
POFF, J. KENT	AN ECONOMIC ANALYSIS OF UNIFORM CAPITALIZATION OF INVENTORY COSTS UNDER SECTION 263A OF THE INTERNAL REVENUE CODE OF 1986
PRINGLE, LYNN M.	A CATASTROPHE THEORY MODEL OF INVENTORY METHOD CHOICE
ROZEN, ETZMUN S.	AN EMPIRICAL INVESTIGATION OF THE MOTIVATIONS UNDERLYING LIFO-FIRM INVENTORY LIQUIDATIONS
SON, WON-IK	TAX TREATMENTS OF INVENTORY AND THEIR REAL EFFECTS: THEORY AND EVIDENCE
WINKLER, LESLIE ANN RICHESON	AN EMPIRICAL ANALYSIS OF THE EFFECTS OF STRUCTURE, BEHAVIOR, AND COMMUNICATION IN A JUST-IN-TIME RELATIONSHIP

Investments

COLDWELL, SUSAN GAIL	ERTA AS AN INVESTMENT STIMULUS: A MICRO BASED ANALYSIS OF FIRM INVESTMENT BEHAVIOR
CONNELL, JAMES ALLEN, JR.	INFORMATION SYSTEMS INVESTMENT EVALUATION
FARGHER, NEIL LAWRENCE	THE ASSOCIATION BETWEEN UNEXPECTED EARNINGS AND CAPITAL EXPENDITURE
KERN, BETH BURCHFIELD	THE IMPACT OF THE ECONOMIC RECOVERY TAX ACT OF 1981 ON CORPORATE INVESTMENT IN PLANT AND EQUIPMENT
KIM, CHANGSOO	A STUDY OF INVESTMENT IN INFORMATION TECHNOLOGY: FINANCIAL PERFORMANCE EFFECT AND FUTURE ECONOMIC BENEFIT TO THE FIRM
KIM, JOOHO	TOBIN'S Q VERSUS MODIFIED Q: AN INVESTIGATION OF SHAREHOLDERS' WEALTH MAXIMIZATION VERSUS FIRM VALUE MAXIMIZATION
LEFANOWICZ, CRAIG EDWARD	IMPLICATIONS OF CHANGES IN EQUITY VALUES ASSOCIATED WITH SIGNIFICANT EQUITY INVESTMENTS FOR INVESTEE AND INVESTOR FIRMS
MICHELSON, STUART EDWARD	CORPORATE CAPITAL EXPENDITURES, TAX LAWS, ASSETS-IN-PLACE, AND THE MARKET VALUE OF THE FIRM
MILACEK, EMIL CRAIG, JR.	AN ASSESSMENT OF THE EFFECT OF THE INVESTMENT TAX CREDIT ON CAPITAL INVESTMENT IN FARM SUPPLY COOPERATIVES IN MICHIGAN, MINNESOTA, NORTH DAKOTA, AND WISCONSIN
PFEFFER, MARY GRAVES	VENTURE CAPITAL INVESTMENT AND PROTOCOL ANALYSIS
SHELLEY, MARJORIE KAY	AN EMPIRICAL INVESTIGATION OF DIFFERENTIAL SUBJECTIVE DISCOUNTING ACROSS THE POTENTIAL GAINS AND LOSSES FROM INVESTMENT OPTIONS
SHOEMAKER, PAUL A.	THE SIGNIFICANCE OF THE INVESTMENT TAX CREDIT IN INVESTMENT DECISIONS: AN EMPIRICAL AND INTERNATIONAL ANALYSIS
SWAYZE, JAMES PRENTISS	THE EFFECT OF CORPORATE INCOME TAX INTEGRATION ON THE DEMAND FOR RISKY STOCK
TREZEVANT, ROBERT HEATH	THE EFFECT OF TAX LAW CHANGES ON CORPORATE INVESTMENT AND FINANCING BEHAVIOR: EMPIRICAL EVIDENCE FROM CHANGES BROUGHT ABOUT BY THE ECONOMIC RECOVERY TAX ACT OF 1981
TSAY, YANG-TZONG	THE INFORMATION CONTENT OF CORPORATE CAPITAL EXPENDITURE DECISIONS: INTERVENTION ANALYSIS

Job Performance, Satisfaction &/or Turnover

COLBERT, PAUL JOSEPH	THE INFLUENCE OF WORK CONTEXT PERCEPTIONS AND EXPERIENCES ON THE ORGANIZATIONAL COMMITMENT OF FIRST-YEAR EMPLOYEES: A LONGITUDINAL STUDY
COOPER, JEAN CLAIRE	COMPENSATION CONTRACT SELF-SELECTION, PARTICIPATIVE STANDARD SETTING AND JOB PERFORMANCE
DOBY, VICTORIA JEAN	THE RELATIONSHIP OF JOB STRAIN TO STAFF TURNOVER IN PUBLIC ACCOUNTING FIRMS
EMIG, JAMES MATTHEW	THE RELATIONSHIP BETWEEN LEADER BEHAVIOR AND SUBORDINATE SATISFACTION IN AN AUDIT ENVIRONMENT: AN EMPIRICAL INVESTIGATION
FOGARTY, TIMOTHY JOSEPH	AUDIT PERFORMANCE: AN EMPIRICAL SYNTHESIS OF THREE THEORETICAL EXPLANATIONS
FRAZER, JOHN DOUGLAS	PERFORMANCE EVALUATION OF AUDITORS: THE IMPORTANCE OF TIME-BUDGET PRESSURE THROUGH A FOCUS ON THE EVALUATOR

GREGSON, TERRY	AN EMPIRICAL INVESTIGATION OF THE RELATIONSHIP BETWEEN COMMUNICATION SATISFACTION, JOB SATISFACTION, TURNOVER, AND PERFORMANCE FOR PUBLIC ACCOUNTANTS
HARTWELL, CAROLYN L.	THE EFFECT OF PRIOR YEAR'S AUDIT INFORMATION AND PERFORMANCE FEEDBACK ON STAFF AUDITORS' PERFORMANCE
HENRY, LAURIE JANE	A PERSISTENCE-PERFORMANCE MODEL: AN OPERATIONAL MODEL TO ASSIST IN PREDICTING AN INDIVIDUAL'S FUTURE SUCCESS IN ACCOUNTING
HUNT, STEVEN CRAIG	CERTAIN COGNITIVE FACTORS AFFECTING PERFORMANCE EVALUATION IN CPA FIRMS
IGWE, VICTOR IHEUKWU	THE IMPACT OF AUDITORS' PERCEPTION OF PERFORMANCE APPRAISAL ON THE EFFORTS EXERTED TOWARDS JOB PERFORMANCE: A STUDY OF AUDITORS THAT AUDIT GOVERNMENTAL ENTITIES, COLLEGES AND UNIVERSITIES IN THE STATE OF FLORIDA
KAUFFMAN, NORMAN LEROY	PERFORMANCE EVALUATION AND JOB-DIRECTED EFFORT IN THE CPA FIRM: AN INTEGRATION OF EXPECTANCY THEORY, ATTRIBUTION THEORY, AND NEED THEORY
LARKIN, JOSEPH MICHAEL	A PERFORMANCE MODEL FOR STAFF AUDITORS IN AN INTERNAL AUDIT ENVIRONMENT
LEWELLYN, PATSY ANN GRANGER	AN INVESTIGATION OF FACTORS RELATED TO TERMINATION IN THE PUBLIC ACCOUNTING PROFESSION AND THE QUALITY OF LIFE OF CERTIFIED PUBLIC ACCOUNTANTS
MCGREGOR, CALVERT, JR.	AN INVESTIGATION OF ORGANIZATIONAL - PROFESSIONAL CONFLICT IN MANAGEMENT ACCOUNTING
MORGAN, JOHN DANIEL	PREDICTING 'VERY EARLY TURNOVER' IN PUBLIC ACCOUNTING WITH PERSONALITY AND DEMOGRAPHIC BACKGROUND VARIABLES
PERKINS, WILLIAM DAVID	THE ASSOCIATION BETWEEN AUDIT STRUCTURE AND AUDITOR SATISFACTION: AN INTEGRATION OF BEHAVIORAL THEORIES
POZNANSKI, PETER JOHN	THE EFFECTS OF ORGANIZATIONAL COMMITMENT, PROFESSIONAL COMMITMENT, LIFE-SPAN CAREER DEVELOPMENT, AND SELF-MONITORING ON JOB SATISFACTION AND JOB PERFORMANCE AMONG STAFF ACCOUNTANTS
RASTOGI, LOKESH CHANDRA	A COMPARISON OF JOB SATISFACTION OF CERTIFIED MANAGEMENT ACCOUNTANTS (CMAS) WORKING IN CPA FIRMS AND IN INDUSTRY
REGEL, ROY W.	STAFF PERFORMANCE EVALUATION BY AUDITORS: THE EFFECT OF TRAINING ON ACCURACY AND CONSENSUS
SCARBROUGH, D. PAUL	THE EFFECTS OF ALTERNATIVE GROUPING METHODS ON EMPLOYEE TURNOVER RESEARCH IN CPA FIRMS
SCHRADER, RICHARD WILLIAM	AN EMPIRICAL INVESTIGATION OF THE USEFULNESS OF SERVICE EFFORTS AND ACCOMPLISHMENTS MEASURES
SMITH, BECKY LYNN	COMPETENCE, INFLUENCE, PROBLEM-SOLVING ABILITY, AND FEAR OF SUCCESS AMONG ACCOUNTANTS
STOLT, SUSAN MARIE JESZKA	AN ATTRIBUTIONAL ANALYSIS OF PERFORMANCE EVALUATION IN PUBLIC ACCOUNTING
STUART, IRIS C.	ANALYTICAL PROCEDURES AND JUDGMENT ACCURACY: A COMPARISON OF STRUCTURED AND UNSTRUCTURED AUDIT METHODOLOGY
SUMMERS, SUZANNE BURGER	THE IMPACT OF THE PROPOSED LICENSING REQUIREMENTS ON TURNOVER IN PUBLIC ACCOUNTING
WOLK, CAREL MARIE	CAUSAL ATTRIBUTIONS FOR PERFORMANCE: IMPLICATIONS FOR AUDITOR TURNOVER

Judgment & Decision Making

AMER, TAREK SAAD	AN EXPERIMENTAL INVESTIGATION OF THE EFFECTS OF MULTI-CUE FINANCIAL INFORMATION DISPLAY AND TASK COMPLEXITY ON DECISION-MAKING

Listing by Topic

MOSER, DONALD V.	THE EFFECTS OF INTERFERENCE, AVAILABILITY, AND ACCOUNTING INFORMATION ON INVESTORS' PREDICTIVE JUDGMENTS
NARASIMHAN, RAMESH	PRELIMINARY CONTROL RISK ASSESSMENTS BY COMPUTER AUDIT SPECIALISTS AND NONSPECIALISTS
ONIFADE, EMMANUEL ONAOLAPO	AN EMPIRICAL EXAMINATION OF THE EFFECT OF CAUSAL ATTRIBUTIONS ON PROJECT CONTINUATION DECISION
PAQUETTE, LAURENCE RICHARD	THE EFFECT OF DECISION STRATEGY AND TASK COMPLEXITY ON DECISION PERFORMANCE IN AN ACCOUNTING CONTEXT
RADTKE, ROBIN RAE	AN EXPERIMENTAL INVESTIGATION OF MANAGERS' ESCALATION ERRORS
RIGSBY, JOHN THOMAS, JR.	AN ANALYSIS OF THE EFFECTS OF COMPLEXITY ON THE MATERIALITY DECISIONS OF AUDITORS
RUCHALA, LINDA VIRGINIA	THE INFLUENCE OF BUDGET REPORTS AND INCENTIVE COMPENSATION ON ESCALATION
RUTLEDGE, ROBERT WILLIAM	THE EFFECTS OF FRAMING ACCOUNTING INFORMATION AND GROUP-SHIFT ON ESCALATION OF COMMITMENT
RYAN, DAVID HARRISON	AN EMPIRICAL EXAMINATION OF THE INTERACTIVE EFFECTS OF FACTORS INFLUENCING TAX PRACTITIONERS' JUDGMENTS
SCHNEIDER, GARY PAUL	ESCALATION BEHAVIOR IN INFORMATION SYSTEMS DEVELOPMENT: ALTERNATIVE MOTIVATIONS, EXPERIENCE, AND THE SUNK COST EFFECT
SHARMA, SURESH RAJ	THE EFFECTS OF THE SOCIAL ATTRACTIVENESS OF A GOAL SETTER ON GOAL ACCEPTANCE
SIMNETT, ROGER	INFORMATION SELECTION AND INFORMATION PROCESSING BY AUDITORS: EFFECT OF VARYING TASK COMPLEXITY
SINGHAL, RAJ BAHADUR	EFFECT OF FEEDBACK AND GOAL PRESENCE ON INFORMATION USAGE AND DECISION ACCURACY IN A HIGH INFORMATION LOAD ENVIRONMENT
SPIRES, ERIC EDWARD	AN INVESTIGATION INTO AUDITORS' EVALUATIONS OF COMPLIANCE TESTS
STOCKS, MORRIS H., JR.	AN EMPIRICAL EXAMINATION OF THE IMPACT OF INFORMATION OVERLOAD ON GROUPS AND INDIVIDUALS IN A FINANCIAL DISTRESS DECISION TASK
STRAWSER, JERRY ROBERT	AN EMPIRICAL INVESTIGATION OF AUDITOR JUDGMENT: FACTORS AFFECTING PERCEIVED AUDIT RISK
TROMPETER, GREGORY MICHAEL	AN INVESTIGATION INTO THE EFFECT OF COMPETITION, PARTNER COMPENSATION, LEGAL LIABILITY, AND AUTHORITATIVE PRONOUNCEMENTS ON AUDITOR JUDGMENT AND INDEPENDENCE
TUTTLE, BRAD M.	THE ROLE OF CONTEXT IN AUDITOR DIAGNOSIS
WELCH, JUDITH KAYE	AUDITOR INTERPRETATIONS OF AUDIT EVIDENCE: AN INFORMATIONAL ATTRIBUTE APPROACH
WILLITS, STEPHEN D.	PUBLIC EMPLOYEE RETIREMENT SYSTEM REPORTS: A STUDY OF USER INFORMATION PROCESSING ABILITY
WONG-ON-WING, BERNARD	AUDITOR'S PERCEPTION OF MANAGEMENT: ITS DETERMINANTS AND CONSEQUENCES

Judgment & Decision Making - Cognitive Processes

BEDARD, JEAN	INTERNAL CONTROL EVALUATION IN COMPUTERIZED SYSTEMS: EXPERTS VERSUS NOVICES

BONNER, SARAH ELIZABETH	EXPERIENCE EFFECTS IN THE COMPONENTS OF ANALYTICAL RISK ASSESSMENT
BRANSON, LEONARD L.	ACCOUNTING INFORMATION, COGNITIVE PROCESSES, AND PERFORMANCE APPRAISAL
CHRIST, LEROY FREDERICK	A COMPARISON OF INSTRUCTIONAL STRATEGIES IN THE DEVELOPMENT OF CATEGORICAL TAX KNOWLEDGE WITH AN EXAMINATION OF THE EFFECT OF INCONSISTENT PRE-EXISTING KNOWLEDGE
CHRIST, MARY YORK	ATTENTION AND ENCODING DURING AUDIT PLANNING: AN EXPERIMENTAL STUDY USING A SCHEMATIC FRAMEWORK
CLAYTON, PENNY RENEE	AUDITOR DECISION PROCESSING AND THE IMPLICATIONS OF BRAIN DOMINANCE: A PREDECISIONAL BEHAVIOR STUDY
CLOYD, C. BRYAN	THE EFFECTS OF KNOWLEDGE AND INCENTIVES ON INFORMATION SEARCH IN TAX RESEARCH TASKS
COMSTOCK, S. MARK	THE COGNITIVE PROCESS UNDERLYING THE ACQUISITION OF ACCOUNTING EXPERTISE
DAVIS, CHARLES ELLIOT	THE EFFECTS OF AUDITOR KNOWLEDGE STRUCTURES AND EXPERIENCE ON PROBLEM IDENTIFICATION AND HYPOTHESIS GENERATION IN ANALYTICAL REVIEW
DAVIS, JEFFERSON TORONTO	AUDITOR EXPERIENCE IN PRELIMINARY CONTROL RISK ASSESSMENTS: NEURAL NETWORK MODELS OF AUDITORS' KNOWLEDGE STRUCTURES
DEL VECCHIO, STEPHEN CARL	AN EMPIRICAL STUDY OF THE FORGETTING OF AUDIT TASK EXPERTISE
DO, SANGHO	THE EFFECT OF OUTCOME FEEDBACK AND EXPERIENCE ON THE PREDICTION OF CORPORATE FAILURE: PERFORMANCE OF HUMAN VS. MODEL
DONADIO, JANETTE MARIE	AN EMPIRICAL STUDY OF THE JOINT EFFECTS OF KNOWLEDGE, INTELLECTUAL SKILL, AND TASK STRUCTURE ON THE ACCURACY OF AUDITORS' PERFORMANCE OF DIAGNOSTIC AUDIT TASKS
FREDERICK, DAVID MICHAEL	AUDITORS' REPRESENTATION AND RETRIEVAL OF KNOWLEDGE IN INTERNAL CONTROL EVALUATION
HANSEN, JAMES DAVID	THE EFFECT OF INFORMATION LOAD AND COGNITIVE STYLE ON DECISION QUALITY IN A FINANCIAL DISTRESS DECISION TASK
HEIMAN, VICKY BETH	AUDITORS' ASSESSMENTS OF THE LIKELIHOOD OF ANALYTICAL REVIEW EXPLANATIONS
HERZ, PAUL JOSEPH	AN INVESTIGATION OF PROCEDURAL MEMORY AS AN INGREDIENT OF TASK PERFORMANCE IN ACCOUNTING
HSU, KO-CHENG	THE EFFECTS OF COGNITIVE STYLES AND INTERFACE DESIGNS ON EXPERT SYSTEMS USAGE: AN ASSESSMENT OF KNOWLEDGE TRANSFER
KELLIHER, CHARLES FRANCIS, JR.	AN EMPIRICAL INVESTIGATION OF THE EFFECTS OF PERSONALITY TYPE AND VARIATION IN INFORMATION LOAD ON THE INFORMATION SEARCH STRATEGIES EMPLOYED BY DECISION-MAKERS
KRAWCZYK, KATHERINE ANN	REASONING WITHIN TAX RESEARCH: THE EFFECT OF TAX LAW FORM AND ORDER OF FACT PRESENTATION ON PROBLEM REPRESENTATIONS
MARONEY, JAMES JOSEPH	THE IMPACT OF KNOWLEDGE CONTENT AND STRUCTURE ON AUDITORS' HYPOTHESIS TESTING BEHAVIOR IN ANALYTICAL PROCEDURES
MILLS, KATHLEEN DARBY	AUDITORS' INHERENT RISK ASSESSMENTS: THE RELATIONSHIPS AMONG TASK EXPERIENCE, INFERABILITY OF CONDITIONING INFORMATION, SECOND-ORDER UNCERTAINTY AND EXTENT OF TESTING
MILLS, TINA YOUNGBLOOD	THE EXTERNAL AUDITOR'S RELIANCE DECISION ON THE INTERNAL AUDIT FUNCTION: A TEST OF COGNITIVE STYLE AND ITS ROLE IN THE RELIANCE DECISION

Listing by Topic

MOFFEIT, KATHERINE SOUTHERLAND	THE EFFECT OF COGNITIVE STYLE ON AUDITOR INTERNAL CONTROL EVALUATION
MYERS, MARLA ANN	A TEST OF THE RELATION BETWEEN AUDIT TECHNOLOGY AND THE DEVELOPMENT OF EXPERTISE
RAMSAY, ROBERT JOE	AN INVESTIGATION OF THE HIERARCHICAL, SEQUENTIAL NATURE OF AUDIT WORKING PAPER REVIEW
ROGERS, VIOLET CORLEY	AN ANALYSIS OF CONFIDENCE LEVELS AND RETRIEVAL OF PROCEDURES ASSOCIATED WITH ACCOUNTS RECEIVABLE CONFIRMATIONS
RUPERT, TIMOTHY J.	PERFORMANCE FACILITATION ON TAX RULES: A PRAGMATIC REASONING SCHEMA APPROACH
RUSSO, JOSEPH A., JR.	AN INVESTIGATION OF AUDITOR PROBLEM-SOLVING BEHAVIOR IN AN UNFAMILIAR TASK SITUATION
SCHMIDT, TOM WILLIAMS	IMPACT OF CRITICAL THINKING ABILITY ON TAX PRACTITIONER JUDGMENT
SHAPIRO, BRIAN PHILIP	AUDITOR'S CAUSAL REASONING IN PRELIMINARY ANALYTICAL REVIEW: AN EMPIRICAL INVESTIGATION
SPILKER, BRIAN CLARK	THE EFFECTS OF TIME PRESSURE AND KNOWLEDGE ON KEY WORD SELECTION BEHAVIOR IN TAX RESEARCH
TUBBS, RICHARD MONROE	THE EFFECT OF EXPERIENCE ON THE AUDITOR'S ORGANIZATION AND AMOUNT OF KNOWLEDGE
WALTERS-YORK, L. MELISSA	PATTERN PERCEPTIVENESS AND ACQUISITION OF ACCOUNTING SKILLS
WINTER, KENNETH	THE EFFECT OF TASK DEMAND ON EXPERTS AND NONEXPERTS IN INTERNAL CONTROL EVALUATION

Judgment & Decision Making - Heuristics & Biases

AHLAWAT, SUNITA SINGH	EXPLANATION EFFECTS IN SEQUENTIAL BELIEF-REVISION BY AUDIT GROUPS AND INDIVIDUALS
ASARE, STEPHEN KWAKU	THE AUDITORS' GOING CONCERN OPINION DECISION: INTERACTION OF TASK VARIABLES AND THE SEQUENTIAL PROCESSING OF EVIDENCE
BALCOM, NORMA JEAN	AN INVESTIGATION OF PROSPECT THEORY'S EFFECTS ON DECISIONS OF MANAGEMENT ACCOUNTANTS
BEAN, DAVID FRANCIS	THE FRAMING OF DECISION CHOICES BY INFORMATION PROVIDERS: AN EXPLORATORY STUDY
BLOOMFIELD, ROBERT JAMES	EVOLUTIONARY MODELS IN LABORATORY AND AUDITING GAMES
CHEN, SEAN SHAW-ZON	A MODEL OF BELIEF REVISION IN AUDIT RISK ASSESSMENT
CHO, WHAJOON	THE RELATIONSHIP BETWEEN EVIDENCE SEQUENCE AND TIME PRESSURE ON AUDITORS' CONTROL RISK ASSESSMENTS
CHOO, TECKMIN	AUDITORS' INFORMATION SEARCH AND EVALUATION IN HYPOTHESIS-TESTING: POSITIVITY, EXTREMITY, PSEUDODIAGNOSTICITY AND CONFIRMATION EFFECTS
CHUNG, LAI HONG	THE JOINT EFFECTS OF PRIOR OUTCOME AND PRESENTATION FORMAT ON INDIVIDUAL AND GROUP RESOURCE ALLOCATION DECISIONS: THE ROLE OF MENTAL ACCOUNTS
CHURCH, BRYAN KEVIN	AN INVESTIGATION OF CONFIRMATORY BIAS IN AN AUDIT SETTING: A CONCEPTUALIZATION AND LABORATORY EXPERIMENT

Listing by Topic

CONWAY, ROBERT C.	THE EFFECT OF ALTERNATE DECISION FRAMES ON DECISIONS THAT USE ACCOUNTING INFORMATION
COULTER, JOHN MICHAEL	THE EFFECTS OF AUDIT EXPERIENCE AND PROBABILITY KNOWLEDGE ON AUDITORS' USE OF HEURISTICS IN JUDGMENTS UNDER UNCERTAINTY
DEVINE, KEVIN MARK	THE EFFECTS OF INFORMATION FRAMING ON DECISION-MAKING BEHAVIOR RELATED TO RESOURCE ALLOCATIONS
DIPIETRO, JANICE DIANE	AN EMPIRICAL INVESTIGATION OF THE IMPACT OF AUDIT EXPERIENCE AND TASK ON THE UTILIZATION OF DECISION HEURISTICS
GELARDI, ALEXANDER MARIA GEORGE	THE EFFECT OF QUANTITY AND ORDER OF CUES ON SEQUENTIAL BELIEF REVISION IN TAX JUDGMENTS
HALL, SHEILA HUNTLEY	AN EXPERIMENTAL INVESTIGATION OF FINANCIAL STATEMENT USERS' SELF-INSIGHT IN REPORTING DECISION-MAKING PROCESSES
HANNO, DENNIS MICHAEL	THE USE OF INFORMATION IN THE SEQUENTIAL EVALUATION OF AUDIT EVIDENCE
HAYNES, CHRISTINE MILLER	AN EXAMINATION INTO THE EFFECTS OF CONTEXT AND EXPERIENCE ON AUDITORS' BELIEF REVISIONS IN CASCADED-INFERENCE TASKS
HELLELOID, RICHARD TRYGVE	HINDSIGHT BIAS AND JUDGMENTS BY TAX PROFESSIONALS
HIRST, DAVID ERIC	AUDITORS' SENSITIVITY TO FACTORS AFFECTING THE RELIABILITY OF EVIDENCE SOURCES IN BELIEF REVISION
HULME, RICHARD DOUGLAS	AN EMPIRICAL INVESTIGATION OF THE EFFECTS OF ORDER AND SAMPLE EVIDENCE REPRESENTATIONS ON AUDITORS' USE OF BASE RATES
JAMAL, KARIM	DETECTING FRAMING EFFECTS IN AUDIT JUDGMENT
JOHNSON, ERIC NOEL	EFFECTS OF EXPERIENCE, TASK VARIABLES, AND PRIOR BELIEFS ON AUDITORS' SEQUENTIAL JUDGMENTS
JOHNSON, LINDA MARIE	AN EMPIRICAL INVESTIGATION OF THE EFFECTS OF ADVOCACY ON PREPARERS' EVALUATIONS OF EVIDENCE
KENNEDY, SUSAN JANE	DEBIASING AUDIT JUDGMENT WITH ACCOUNTABILITY: A FRAMEWORK AND EXPERIMENTAL RESULTS
KING, VICKY ARNOLD	AUDITOR DECISION-MAKING; AN ANALYSIS OF THE EFFECTS OF ORDERING AND TESTS OF THE PREDICTIVE VALIDITY OF THE CONTRAST/SURPRISE MODEL
KOONCE, LISA LYNN	BELIEF PERSEVERANCE IN AUDIT ANALYTICAL REVIEW
LOWE, DAVID JORDAN	AN EMPIRICAL EXAMINATION OF THE HINDSIGHT BIAS PHENOMENON IN EVALUATION OF AUDITOR DECISIONS
MADDOCKS, PAULINE MERLE	OUTCOME KNOWLEDGE AND AUDITOR JUDGMENT
MCMILLAN, JEFFREY JOSEPH	THE ROLE OF CONFIRMATION BIAS, EXPERIENCE, AND MODE OF INFORMATION PROCESSING IN AUDIT JUDGMENT
MORTON, JANE ELIZABETH	ORDER EFFECTS IN AUDITORS' INTERNAL CONTROL JUDGMENTS: BELIEF PERSEVERANCE VERSUS THE CONTRAST EFFECT
NELSON, MARTHA KRUG	HEURISTIC AND NORMATIVE STRATEGIES: EVALUATION OF SAMPLE RESULTS BY AUDITORS

Listing by Topic

O'CLOCK, PRISCILLA MARIE	THE EFFECT OF INFORMATION FRAMING ON THE AUDITOR'S GOING CONCERN EVALUATION
PRESUTTI, ANTHONY HARRY, JR.	AN EMPIRICAL INVESTIGATION OF THE IMPACT OF THE ANCHOR AND ADJUSTMENT HEURISTIC ON THE AUDIT JUDGMENT PROCESS
QURESHI, ANIQUE AHMED	AN INVESTIGATION OF AUDITOR JUDGMENT IN THE EVALUATION OF CONTINGENT LEGAL LIABILITIES
REIDER, BARBARA POWELL	HYPOTHESIS CONFIRMATION AND DISCONFIRMATION BY INDEPENDENT AUDITORS: GENERAL AND AUDIT-SPECIFIC CONTEXTS
ROARK, STEPHEN JOE	AN EXAMINATION OF RISK ATTITUDES IN LEGAL TAX RESEARCH
RODGERS, JACCI LOU SPEELMAN	USE OF THE INERTIA EFFECT TO EXPLAIN AND PREDICT AUDITOR MISADJUSTMENTS ARISING FROM THE ANCHORING AND ADJUSTMENT HEURISTIC
ROSMAN, ANDREW JOEL	THE EFFECT OF LEARNING ENVIRONMENTS ON THE USE OF ACCOUNTING INFORMATION BY DIFFERENT TYPES OF LENDERS
SANDERS, DEBRA LEE	AN EMPIRICAL INVESTIGATION OF TAX PRACTITIONERS' DECISIONS UNDER UNCERTAINTY: A PROSPECT THEORY APPROACH
SCHADEWALD, MICHAEL STEVEN	REFERENCE OUTCOME EFFECTS IN TAXPAYER DECISION-MAKING
SCOTT, BERT G., JR.	AN INQUIRY INTO MITIGATING THE EFFECTS OF THE ANCHORING AND ADJUSTMENT HEURISTIC IN THE JUDGMENTAL EVALUATION OF UNDERRELIANCE RISK
TAN, HUN-TONG	EFFECTS OF EXPECTATION AND PRIOR INVOLVEMENT ON MEMORY FOR AUDIT EVIDENCE AND JUDGMENT: THE MODERATING ROLE OF ACCOUNTABILITY
WELCH, SANDRA THOMAS	AN INVESTIGATION OF THE DECISION REVISION PROCESS: DEFENSE CONTRACT AUDIT AGENCY AUDITORS DETERMINING THE EXISTENCE OF DEFECTIVE PRICING IN FIXED PRICE CONTRACTS
WELKER, DONNA-LYNN	BACKGROUND FACTORS AND THE ANCHORING AND ADJUSTMENT HEURISTIC: AN EMPIRICAL INVESTIGATION

Leases

BEARD, DEBORAH F.	THE IMPACT OF STATEMENT OF FINANCIAL ACCOUNTING STANDARDS NO. 13 ON SYSTEMATIC RISK AND ACCOUNTING VARIABLES
LEE, CHANGWOO	MARKET REACTIONS TO LEASE LIABILITIES AND REPORTING ENVIRONMENT CHANGES
QUE, ANTONIO L.	A CRITICAL EVALUATION OF FASB STATEMENT NO. 13
SCHWINGHAMMER, PAUL HENRY	AN EMPIRICAL INVESTIGATION OF METHODS OF COMPUTING THE CURRENT PORTION OF CAPITALIZED LEASE OBLIGATIONS AND THE EFFECTS ON SELECTED FINANCIAL MEASURES
SHAW, WAYNE H.	EMPIRICAL EVIDENCE ON THE MARKET IMPACT OF THE SAFE HARBOR LEASING LAW

Legal Liability

DONNELLY, WILLIAM JAMES, JR.	THE CPA'S LIABILITY IN TAX PRACTICE: HISTORY, TRENDS, PROBLEMS, POSSIBLE SOLUTIONS
FESLER, ROBERT DANIEL	LITIGATION REPORTING UNDER SFAS NO. 5: AN EMPIRICAL INVESTIGATION OF COMPARABILITY
HAWKINS, KYLEEN WHITEHEAD	AN EMPIRICAL ANALYSIS OF FACTORS USED BY COURTS WHEN DECIDING MOTIONS TO DISMISS RULE 10B-5 LITIGATION AGAINST ACCOUNTANTS

HONG, CHANGMOK	AUDITORS' LEGAL LIABILITY AND REPUTATION: A GAME-THEORETIC ANALYSIS OF THE DEMAND FOR AUDITING IN AN ADVERSE SELECTION SETTING
KO, WANSUK MATTHEW	AUDITOR'S INCENTIVE, LEGAL LIABILITY AND REPUTATION UNDER INFORMATION ASYMMETRY
MULCAHY, LEIGH-ANN	ACCOUNTABLE TO WHOM? THE CHANGING ROLE OF THE CORPORATE AUDITOR
SARATH, BHARAT	AUDITING, LITIGATION, AND INSURANCE
SHIBANO, TOSHIYUKI	AN EQUILIBRIUM MODEL OF ATTESTATION BY PUBLIC ACCOUNTANTS
SMITH, JOHN REED	THE ECONOMIC VALUE OF AUDITING UNDER A NEGLIGENCE LIABILITY RULE
SPECHT, JAMES	AN EMPIRICAL EXAMINATION OF LITIGATION AGAINST AUDITORS OVER TIME
SPURRELL, A. C. LLOYD	AN EXAMINATION OF SELECTED FACTORS ASSOCIATED WITH AUDIT LITIGATION
STICE, JAMES DAVID	PREDICTING LAWSUITS AGAINST AUDITORS USING FINANCIAL AND MARKET INFORMATION

Long Term Debt

BEGLEY, JOY	THE USE OF DEBT CONVENANTS TO CONTROL AGENCY PROBLEMS
BOYAS, ELISE A.	IDENTIFICATION AND EXAMINATION OF FACTORS BEHIND CORPORATE IN-SUBSTANCE DEFEASANCE OF DEBT
CARAYANNOPOULOS, PETER	THE IMPACT OF STOCHASTIC INTEREST RATES ON THE PRICING OF CONVERTIBLE BONDS
DEPPE, LARRY ARTHUR	AN EMPIRICAL INVESTIGATION OF THE IN-SUBSTANCE DEFEASANCE OF DEBT
DUHALA, KAREN	A GENERAL MODEL FOR BOND REFINANCING
FRANCIS, JENNIFER	CORPORATE COMPLIANCE WITH DEBT COVENANTS
HEFZI, HASSAN	ECONOMIC INCENTIVES OF MANAGEMENT FOR INSUBSTANCE DEFEASANCE OF DEBT: AN EMPIRICAL INVESTIGATION
KIM, SUNGSOO	INTEREST RATE SWAPS: FIRM CHARACTERISTICS, MOTIVATIONS AND DIFFERENTIAL MARKET REACTIONS
KIM, TAE-YONG	EARLY DEBT-REDEMPTION: AN EMPIRICAL INVESTIGATION OF MOTIVATION AND IMPACT
KOCHER, CLAUDIA SUE	COSTLY CONTRACTING: THE CASE OF EVENT RISK COVENANTS
KROPP, KARL V.	ASYMPTOTICS OF A FREE BOUNDARY PROBLEM RESULTING FROM THE DETERMINATION OF AN AMORTIZING LOAN'S REFINANCE OPTION
LAWRENCE, ROBYN	IN-SUBSTANCE DEFEASANCE: AN EMPIRICAL EXAMINATION OF THE FACTORS AFFECTING THE MARKET REACTION AND THE DECISION
PRESS, ERIC GEOFFREY	THE ROLE OF ACCOUNTING BASED CONTRACTUAL PROVISIONS AND FINANCIAL STATEMENT EFFECTS IN EXPLAINING A DEBT EXTINGUISHMENT: THE CASE OF IN-SUBSTANCE DEFEASANCE

PRICE, JEAN BOCKNIK	OPERATIONALIZING INDUSTRY AFFILIATION AS A FACTOR IN THE BOND RATING DECISION: AN INVESTIGATION AND TEST OF A NEW APPROACH
SHANKAR, S. GOWRI	A REEXAMINATION OF THE CALLS OF CONVERTIBLE BONDS AND THEIR IMPACT ON SHAREHOLDER WEALTH
STEADMAN, MARK EDWARD	THE COMMON STOCK PRICE EFFECTS OF BOND RATING CHANGES: AN EXAMINATION OF ASYMMETRIC MARKET REACTIONS USING STAKEHOLDER THEORY
WILLIAMS, RAY ELLIS	THE INFORMATIONAL CONTENT OF THE CURRENT MARKET VALUE OF LONG-TERM DEBT

Management Control Systems

ABDEL-WAHAB, MOSTAFA AHMED	DIVISIONAL PERFORMANCE CONTROL: AN INTERDISCIPLINARY-BASED MANAGEMENT SCIENCE/OPERATIONS RESEARCH APPROACH
BARNETT, DONALD JOSEPH	ATTRIBUTION BIASES, COMPETITIVE/COOPERATIVE WORK ENVIRONMENTS, AND THE MANAGEMENT CONTROL PROCESS
CARROLL, JAMES J.	CONTROL METHODOLOGIES FOR ACHIEVEMENT OF STRATEGIC OBJECTIVES
DEXTER, LEE	USAGE OF PROCEDURES AND CONTROLS IN INNOVATIVE MANUFACTURING COMPANIES
ELETR, AMR	A COMPARISON BETWEEN CONTROLLERS AND PRODUCTION MANAGERS IN THE ELECTRONICS MANUFACTURING INDUSTRY OF THE PERCEIVED RELEVANCE AND USE OF MANAGEMENT ACCOUNTING SYSTEMS' CHARACTERISTICS AND PROFITABILITY AS
ELMORE, ROBERT CLINTON	A CONTINGENCY THEORY APPROACH TO AN EMPIRICAL CLASSIFICATION OF MANAGEMENT ACCOUNTING INFORMATION SYSTEMS
EWING, PER	MANAGEMENT CONTROL OF INTERDEPENDENT UNITS [EKONOMISK STYRNING AV ENHETER MED INBORDE VERKSAMHETSSAMBAND]
GROSS, NORMA JEAN	CASH FLOW CONCEPTS IN THE FINANCIAL PERFORMANCE EVALUATION OF FOREIGN SUBSIDIARY MANAGERS
JACKSON, PAMELA GAIL ZIEMER	AN INVESTIGATION OF THE EFFECT OF CONTINGENCY THEORY VARIABLES ON THE DESIGN OF COST ACCOUNTING SYSTEMS IN SERVICE FIRMS
KREN, LESLIE	EFFECTS OF INCENTIVE EMPLOYMENT CONTRACTS ON PERFORMANCE AND INFORMATION REVELATION: EMPIRICAL EVIDENCE
LA GRANGE, JOHANNES FREDERICK	RESPONSIBILITY ACCOUNTING WITH THE RESTRUCTURING OF CERTAIN INSTITUTIONS
LOWE, DANA R.	THE RELATIONSHIP BETWEEN STRATEGY CHANGE AND THE DESIGN OF MANAGEMENT ACCOUNTING SYSTEMS: A MULTIPLE CASE STUDY
MYERS, JOAN JOETTE KLINGINSMITH	THE EXPLORATION OF PRODUCT COSTING AND COST CONTROL METHODS IN THE CURRENT MANUFACTURING ENVIRONMENT: A FIELD STUDY
PAULSSON, GERT ARNE	ACCOUNTING SYSTEMS IN TRANSITION: A CASE STUDY IN THE SWEDISH HEALTH CARE ORGANIZATION
RAJAN, MADHAV VASANTH	PERFORMANCE EVALUATION AND CONTROL IN MULTI-AGENT SETTINGS
REIS, PRISCILLA ROSE	ACCOUNTING FOR COMPLEXITY: AN EXPLORATORY STUDY
SADOWSKI, SUSAN THERESA	CHANGES IN MANAGEMENT ACCOUNTING SYSTEMS WITH THE ADOPTION OF A TOTAL QUALITY MANAGEMENT PHILOSOPHY AND ITS OPERATIONALIZATION THROUGH CONTINUOUS PROCESS IMPROVEMENT AT THE LEVEL OF THE FIRM: A CASE STUDY OF
SCHILLER, STEFAN	MANAGEMENT ACCOUNTING SYSTEMS--USE AND DESIGN

SEAL, W. B.	ACCOUNTING AND MANAGEMENT CONTROL IN THE THEORY OF THE FIRM
SISAYE, SELESHI	RESOURCE ALLOCATION PROCESSES IN DIVISIONALIZED BUSINESS ORGANIZATIONS: A POWER CONTROL MODEL OF ORGANIZATIONS
STONEBACK, JANE YOUNG	ESSAYS ON THE INFLUENCE OF THE STAGES OF ORGANIZATIONAL DEVELOPMENT UPON POLICY CHOICE
VELA PASTOR, JUAN	THE ACCOUNTING SYSTEM RELATED TO DOCTRINE AND TECHNIQUE IN BUSINESS CONTROL
WANG, YI-HSIN	AN EXPLORATORY EMPIRICAL INVESTIGATION OF RELATIONSHIPS BETWEEN CHANGES IN CATALYST FINANCIAL COMMITMENTS AND CHANGES IN PRODUCTIVITY AND PROFITABILITY IN SELECTED UNITED STATES MANUFACTURING INDUSTRIES AND
WEBB, JUDITH L.	TRANSACTION COSTS AND CONTROL SYSTEM CHOICE IN MULTINATIONAL ENTERPRISES: AN EMPIRICAL TEST
XIE, JIA-ZHENG (JAMES)	CONTRACT NEGOTIATION, INCOMPLETE CONTRACTING, AND ASYMMETRIC INFORMATION

Market Microstructure

BRUMETT, CLIFFORD	INVENTORY ADJUSTMENT AND ADVERSE INFORMATION MOTIVES IN SECURITY DEALER PRICING DECISIONS
KIM, YONG HWAN	LIQUIDITY, INFORMED TRADING, AND PUBLIC INFORMATION: THEORY AND EVIDENCE--A MARKET MICROSTRUCTURE ANALYSIS
WATTS, SUSAN GAIL	MARKET MICROSTRUCTURE AND THE TIMING OF EARNINGS RELEASES: AN EMPIRICAL ANALYSIS
YOHN, TERI LOMBARDI	THE EFFECT OF THE EXISTENCE AND QUALITY OF EARNINGS DISCLOSURES ON BID-ASK SPREADS: THEORY AND EMPIRICAL EVIDENCE

Materiality

CARPENTER, BRIAN WELLS	THE EFFECT OF NATURE OF TRANSACTION, RANK, EXPERIENCE, AND FAMILIARITY ON THE MATERIALITY JUDGMENTS OF AUDITORS: AN EMPIRICAL EXAMINATION
CHOI, NAHNHEE J.	THE MANAGER-AUDITOR GAME REVISITED: ON THE EFFECT OF INCOMPLETE INFORMATION, THE DUE CARE LEVEL, AND THE MATERIALITY LEVEL IMPOSED BY THE STANDARD-SETTING BOARDS
DOW, KATHY J.	AN EXAMINATION OF MATERIALITY FROM THE USER-DECISION PERSPECTIVE
ENGLISH, DENISE MAY	THE INFLUENCE OF TIME PRESSURE, FIRM METHODOLOGY, AND CLIENT SIZE ON AUDITORS' MATERIALITY JUDGMENTS: AN INFORMATION ACQUISITION APPROACH
EYLER, KEL-ANN SHELDON	AN EXAMINATION OF THE EFFECTS OF AUDIT STRUCTURE AND GROUP TASK SETTINGS ON THE MATERIALITY JUDGMENTS OF AUDITORS
GARCIA DELGADO, SONIA M.	MATERIALITY IN AUDITING
KHALIFA, ZAKAA MOHAMED	THE IMPACT OF THE FINANCIAL CONDITION OF THE FIRM ON AUDITORS' MATERIALITY/DISCLOSURE JUDGMENTS: AN EXPERIMENTAL STUDY
KING, JAMES B., II	INDIVIDUAL AND TEAM PLANNING MATERIALITY JUDGMENTS IN STRUCTURED AND UNSTRUCTURED ACCOUNTING FIRMS
MCEACHARN, ELIZABETH MICHELLE	A FUZZY REASONING EXPERT SYSTEM FOR PLANNING-STAGE MATERIALITY JUDGEMENTS
REMMELE, DAVID ALAN	COURT-DETERMINED MATERIALITY: AN EMPIRICAL ANALYSIS OF THE CRITERIA COURTS USE AND THE IMPLICATIONS FOR ACCOUNTANTS

SMITH, MARGARET C.	A MODEL OF THE OWNER/MANAGER/AUDITOR GAME: ON THE VALUE OF PEER REVIEW AND THE MATERIALITY STANDARD
TIDRICK, DONALD EUGENE	AUDITORS' PLANNING STAGE MATERIALITY JUDGMENTS AND THE MEDIATING EFFECTS OF LEVEL OF RESPONSIBILITY, FIRM AFFILIATION, AND AUDIT TECHNOLOGY: AN EXPERIMENT

Merger, Acquisition, Reorganization

ANDERSON, ELLEN G.	AGENCY THEORY AND CORPORATE ACQUISITIONS: EMPIRICAL TEST FOR A CERTAIN CLASS OF CORPORATE TAKEOVERS
BANERJEE, AJEYO	MANAGERIAL COMPENSATION AND SHAREHOLDER WEALTH CONSEQUENCES OF 'WHITE KNIGHT' BEHAVIOR
BECKMAN, JUDY KAY	PREDICTING THE LEVEL OF MINORITY INTEREST FOLLOWING A TENDER OFFER
BILLINGS, BOYSIE ANTHONY	BUSINESS COMBINATIONS: LITIGATION AND TAXPAYER STRATEGY
BULL, IVAN OLE	MANAGEMENT PERFORMANCE IN LEVERAGED BUYOUTS: AN EMPIRICAL ANALYSIS
COFF, RUSSELL W.	CORPORATE ACQUISITIONS OF HUMAN-ASSET-INTENSIVE FIRMS: LET THE BUYER BEWARE
COWAN, ARNOLD RICHARD	TWO-TIER TENDER OFFERS: COERCION, HUBRIS OR IMPROVED MANAGEMENT?
CRAWFORD, DEAN	THE STRUCTURE OF CORPORATE MERGERS: ACCOUNTING, TAX, AND FORM-OF-PAYMENT CHOICES
DAVIS, MICHAEL LEE	AN EMPIRICAL ANALYSIS OF THE IMPACT OF MERGER ACCOUNTING METHOD ON STOCK PRICES
DESAI, ARUN RAMADHAR	AN EMPIRICAL STUDY OF POST MERGER PERFORMANCE OF ACQUIRING FIRMS
DEVIDAL, DOUGLAS PAUL	THE ROLE OF PRIVATE LETTER RULINGS IN TAX-FREE REORGANIZATIONS
DUNNE, KATHLEEN M.	DETERMINANTS OF THE CHOICE OF ACCOUNTING TREATMENT FOR BUSINESS COMBINATIONS: A POSITIVE THEORY APPROACH
FLINN, RONALD EARL	AN INVESTIGATION OF PROPOSED CHANGES IN THE FEDERAL INCOME TAXATION OF ACQUISITIVE REORGANIZATIONS
GHANI, WAQAR I.	THE ECONOMIC IMPACT OF ACCOUNTING INFORMATION AGGREGATION AND DISAGGREGATION ON INFORMEDNESS AND CONSENSUS: THE CASE OF CONSOLIDATED NONHOMOGENEOUS SUBSIDIARIES
GHOSH, ALOKE	VALUATION OF GAINS FROM MERGERS: SOURCES AND ESTIMATION OF THESE GAINS FROM DISCIPLINARY TAKEOVERS AND DIFFERENT TAX-RELATED ISSUES
GONZALEZ, PEDRO	FINANCIAL CHARACTERISTICS OF COMPANIES INVOLVED IN CROSS-BORDER MERGERS AND ACQUISITIONS
GREENSPAN, JAMES WILLIAM	DISTINGUISHING A PURCHASE FROM A POOLING THROUGH THE USE OF HOSTILE AND FRIENDLY TENDER OFFERS
HAYN, CARLA K.	THE ROLE OF TAX ATTRIBUTES IN CORPORATE ACQUISITIONS
HETHCOX, KATHLEEN BLACKBURN	BUSINESS COMBINATIONS ACCOUNTED FOR BY THE PURCHASE METHOD: AN EMPIRICAL ANALYSIS OF THE MAGNITUDE OF GOODWILL AND ACQUIRING FIRMS' STOCK RETURNS
HUFFMAN, STEPHEN PHILLIP	TESTS OF THE FREE CASH FLOW THEORY OF TAKEOVERS

JOHN, TERESA ANNE	CORPORATE MERGERS, INVESTMENT INCENTIVES AND FIRM VALUE: AN AGENCY THEORETIC ANALYSIS
KELLEY, CLAUDIA LU	A STUDY OF THE STOCK MARKET REACTION TO SECTION 382 OF THE TAX REFORM ACT OF 1986 AND THE CHARACTERISTICS OF TARGETS WITH LOSS CARRYOVERS
KIRK, FLORENCE REARDON	THE ROLE OF TAXES IN ACQUISITIONS
MANRY, DAVID LEE	TARGET FIRM EARNINGS, GREENMAIL, AND SHAREHOLDERS' INTERESTS
PERRY, SUSAN ELIZABETH	ACCOUNTING INFORMATION IN GOING-PRIVATE TRANSACTIONS
RABASEDA I TARRES, JOAQUIM	THEORY AND TECHNIQUE OF CONSOLIDATION ACCOUNTING
RAMASWAMY, KADANDOGE PADMANABHAN	LONG-TERM PERFORMANCE ISSUES OF MERGERS AND ACQUISITIONS
RICH, JOHN CARR	THE EQUITY METHOD OF ACCOUNTING AND UNCONSOLIDATED SUBSIDIARIES: AN EMPIRICAL STUDY
SCHEIDT, MARSHA ANN	AN EMPIRICAL ANALYSIS OF PARENT COMPANY BOND YIELD PREMIA SUBSEQUENT TO CONSOLIDATION OF NONHOMOGENEOUS FINANCIAL-ACTIVITIES SUBSIDIARIES
SHIH, MICHAEL SHENG-HUA	FINANCIAL SYNERGY AND MERGER MOVEMENTS: PERSONAL AND CORPORATE INCOME TAXES AS AN EXPLANATION
SOFFER, LEONARD CHARLES	FINANCIAL STATEMENT INDICATORS OF TAKEOVER TARGETS: A MULTINOMIAL ANALYSIS
SWARTZ, LEE MICHAEL	THE IMPACT OF STATE ANTITAKEOVER LAWS ON SECURITY VALUE
THORNTON, PHILLIP WYNN	THE ROLE OF ACCOUNTING INFORMATION IN INVESTOR ASSESSMENTS OF CORPORATE TAKEOVERS
TROMBLEY, MARK ALAN	THE EFFECT OF CORPORATE MERGER TRANSACTIONS ON THE INFORMATION CONTENT OF EARNINGS ANNOUNCEMENTS

Methodology

DANIELS, DEANNA KAY	EVALUATING THE QUALITATIVE CHARACTERISTICS OF ACCOUNTING INFORMATION: A DESCRIPTIVE STUDY OF IMPORTANCE WEIGHTS AND LOCATION MEASURES
HAN, INGOO	THE IMPACT OF MEASUREMENT SCALE ON CLASSIFICATION PERFORMANCE OF INDUCTIVE LEARNING AND STATISTICAL APPROACHES
LINDSAY, ROGER MURRAY	THE USE OF TESTS OF SIGNIFICANCE IN ACCOUNTING RESEARCH: A METHODOLOGICAL, PHILOSOPHICAL AND EMPIRICAL INQUIRY
MARAIS, MARTHINUS LAURENTIUS	SOME APPLICATIONS OF COMPUTER INTENSIVE STATISTICAL METHODS TO EMPIRICAL RESEARCH IN ACCOUNTING

Microcomputer Applications

AMES, GARY ADNA	EDP AUDITING OF MICROCOMPUTER SYSTEMS: AN EXPERIMENTAL ANALYSIS OF AUDITOR REACTION TO A CHANGED ENVIRONMENT
ANDERSON, JOHN CHARLES	THE SELECTION DECISION FOR MICROCOMPUTER GENERAL LEDGER SOFTWARE: AN INVESTIGATION USING A KNOWLEDGE-BASED SYSTEM
COLLEY, JAMES RONALD	AN INVESTIGATION OF PERCEPTIONAL DIFFERENCES REGARDING MICROCOMPUTER USE BY CPA FIRMS

LANDOE, GENE ARLAN	THE IMPACT OF MICROCOMPUTER TECHNOLOGY ON NORTHERN CALIFORNIA CERTIFIED PUBLIC ACCOUNTING FIRMS
MCDERMOTT, NANCY ANN	THE INTERNAL ACCOUNTING CONTROL SYSTEM IN A MICROCOMPUTER ENVIRONMENT: AN ANALYTIC HIERARCHY PROCESS APPROACH
ROGERS, LEON REED	COMPARISON AND EVALUATION OF AN INTEGRATED COMPUTERIZED SPREADSHEET ESTIMATING SYSTEM VERSUS MANUAL ESTIMATING FOR RESIDENTIAL CONSTRUCTION PROJECTS
ULINSKI, MICHAEL	AN ANALYSIS OF THE RELATIONSHIP OF JOB NEED FULFILLMENT AND MICROCOMPUTER TRAINING TO MICROCOMPUTER USER SATISFACTION LEVELS OF PUBLIC ACCOUNTANTS

Not-for-Profit

BERRY, DELANO HOWARD	AN EXTENSION OF MANAGERIAL ACCOUNTING AND OPERATIONAL AUDITING IN THE PUBLIC SECTOR: A CASE STUDY OF SCHOOL FOOD SERVICE PROGRAMS IN SELECTED LOCAL SCHOOL DISTRICTS IN THE COMMONWEALTH OF KENTUCKY
DEIS, DONALD RAY, JR.	TOWARDS A THEORY OF THE ROLE OF THE PUBLIC SECTOR AUDIT AS A MONITORING DEVICE: A TEST USING TEXAS INDEPENDENT SCHOOL DISTRICTS
GAUMNITZ, CAROL BOTHAMLEY	AN ANALYSIS OF THE INTERNAL REVENUE SERVICE'S DECISION PROCESS WITH RESPECT TO THE UNRELATED BUSINESS INCOME TAXPROVISIONS CONTAINED IN CODE SECTIONS 511-513
PAIGE, KENNETH LEE	THE USE OF MANAGEMENT ACCOUNTING PRACTICES BY NONPROFIT ORGANIZATIONS: AN EXPLORATORY STUDY
TURNER, MARK ALAN	JUDICIAL AND ADMINISTRATIVE DETERMINATION OF UNRELATED BUSINESS INCOME OF TAX EXEMPT ORGANIZATIONS

Other

CHANDRA, AKHILESH	FIRM SIZE, A SELF-ORGANIZED CRITICAL PHENOMENON: EVIDENCE FROM THE DYNAMICAL SYSTEMS THEORY
DODD, JAMES LEE	ACCOUNTING INFORMATION TIMELINESS: AN EXPLORATORY STUDY OF INTERNAL DELAY
FULTZ, M. ELAINE	DELEGATED REGULATION: A STUDY OF THE NATIONAL FUTURES ASSOCIATION
GIRARD, ALINE CHANTAL	THE EFFECTS OF CONTEXT, TERMINOLOGY, AND EXPERTISE ON THE UNDERSTANDABILITY OF ACCOUNTING CONCEPTS: A LABORATORY EXPERIMENT
HENNING, STEVEN LYLE	ACCOUNTING FOR GOODWILL: CURRENT PRACTICES, VARIATION IN SOURCE AND COMPONENTS, AND MARKET VALUATION
HOWARD, ARLEY ANN	COST ANALYSIS OF DISTRIBUTION CHANNELS: AN EMPIRICAL DETERMINATION OF THE OPTIMAL CHANNEL STRATEGY
HUGHES, SUSAN BOEDEKER	THE IMPACT OF PRIVATE ACCOUNTING INFORMATION DISCLOSURE WITHIN THE CONTEXT OF COLLECTIVE BARGAINING: AN EMPIRICAL STUDY
JOHNSON, BRAD ROY	THE EXISTENCE AND NATURE OF DISPARATE VOLUME CAP CONSTRAINING EFFECTS ACROSS RURAL AND NONRURAL COMMUNITIES: AN EMPIRICAL ANALYSIS
JOHNSON, STEVEN D.	AN EMPIRICAL STUDY OF THE FIDELITY OF ORGANIZATIONAL ACCOUNTING COMMUNICATION AND THE IMPACT OF ORGANIZATIONAL CULTURE
KOFMAN, ALFREDO MARCOS	COLLUSION, REPUTATION AND COMMUNICATION: THREE ESSAYS IN ECONOMIC THEORY
LEE, SANGSOO	DECENTRALIZATION, INFORMATIONAL ASYMMETRY, AND THE VALUE OF COMMUNICATION AND DELEGATION
MCGOVERN, THOMAS WILLIAM	ACCOUNTING AND TRADE UNIONS: THE INCOMPATIBLES? A CASE STUDY OF CLOSURES AT DUNLOP

MEADE, NANCY MARGARET LOWMAN	ANTITAKEOVER DEVICES AND FIRM PERFORMANCE: AN EMPIRICAL STUDY USING ACCOUNTING MEASURES
MINYARD, DONALD HOYT	AN EXAMINATION OF VARIABLES ASSOCIATED WITH DIVESTMENT DECISIONS
MONCADA, SUSAN MARY	A HUMAN FACTORS ANALYSIS OF THE INTERPERSONAL COMMUNICATION EFFECTIVENESS OF PROGRAMMER ANALYSTS
OLSON, CAROL ANN FELICIA	AN EXAMINATION OF THE FACTORS AFFECTING THE CHOICE OF EMPLOYEE FRINGE BENEFITS AND CAFETERIA PLANS
RANKINE, GRAEME WILLIAM	THE EFFECT OF TAXES AND AGENCY COSTS ON ORGANIZATIONAL CHOICE: THE CASE OF FRANCHISING
SALAMONE, DIANE MARSAN	A PROBABILISTIC MODEL FOR PREDICTING MANAGEMENT BUYOUTS
SALTERIO, STEVEN EARL	THE SEARCH FOR AND USE OF PRECEDENTS IN MAKING FINANCIAL ACCOUNTING DECISIONS
SHASTRI, KAREN ANDREA	SELF TENDER OFFERS AS A TAKEOVER DEFENSE: AN ANALYSIS OF FIRM VALUE CHANGES, MANAGERIAL COMPENSATION AND OWNERSHIP CONTROL
TIDD, RONALD ROBERT	GEOPOLITICAL CONSIDERATIONS IN THE ADMINISTRATION OF UNITED STATES INCOME TAX POLICY: AN ASSESSMENT OF INCOME TAX ENFORCEMENT EFFORTS, 1975-1988.
WAMBSGANSS, JACOB R.	THE SIGNIFICANCE OF HUMAN RESOURCE ACCOUNTING
WESTPHAL, CATHERINE MARGARET	A PROJECT-BASED ANALYSIS OF THE EFFECTS OF FEDERAL TAX CREDITS ON HISTORIC REHABILITATION
ZELCER, MOISHE	MANAGEMENT BUYOUTS: THE MANAGEMENT/SHAREHOLDER CONFLICT
ZHANG, HUA	THE DYNAMIC BEHAVIOUR OF THE TERM STRUCTURE OF INTEREST RATES AND ITS IMPLICATION FOR INTEREST-RATE SENSITIVE ASSET PRICING

Partnership Taxation

KARAYAN, JOHN EDWARD	THE ECONOMIC IMPACT OF A TAX LAW CHANGE: PUBLICLY TRADED PARTNERSHIPS UNDER THE REVENUE ACT OF 1987
SHEVLIN, TERRENCE J.	RESEARCH AND DEVELOPMENT LIMITED PARTNERSHIPS: AN EMPIRICAL ANALYSIS OF TAXES AND INCENTIVES
SIPPLE, STANLEY ALFRED	AN EMPIRICAL INVESTIGATION TO DETERMINE IF A PARTNER MAY SERVE THE PARTNERSHIP AS AN EMPLOYEE

Performance Evaluation/Measurement

ADLER, RALPH WILLIAM	ACCOUNTING AND PERFORMANCE INDICATORS AS DETERMINANTS OF ORGANIZATIONAL DECLINE: THEORY AND EMPIRICAL EVIDENCE
ANDERSON, SHANNON WEEMS	MEASURING MANUFACTURING FLEXIBILITY: THE IMPACT OF PRODUCT MIX COMPLEXITY ON OPERATING PERFORMANCE AND MANUFACTURING OVERHEAD COST
ATKINSON, SUE ANDREWS	THE CONTRAST-INERTIA MODEL AND THE UPDATING OF ATTRIBUTIONS IN PERFORMANCE EVALUATION
BLEDSOE, NANCY LLEWELLYN	AN EMPIRICAL EXAMINATION OF THE EFFECTS OF PERFORMANCE EVALUATION ON GOAL CONGRUENCE WITHIN THE AUTOMOTIVE INDUSTRY
BRADLEY, MICHAEL P.	ACCOUNTING INFORMATION, INDIVIDUAL DIFFERENCES, AND ATTRIBUTIONS IN THE PERFORMANCE EVALUATION PROCESS

Listing by Topic

ETHRIDGE, JACK R., JR.	OPERATIONAL AUDITING AND ORGANIZATIONAL PERFORMANCE: SOME PERCEPTIONS OF EXECUTIVES AND INTERNAL AUDITORS
FREDERICKSON, JAMES RAY	RELATIVE PERFORMANCE INFORMATION: THE EFFECTS OF COMMON UNCERTAINTY AND CONTRACT TYPE ON AGENTS' GOALS AND EFFORT
JACKSON, ANTHONY WAYNE	THE INFLUENCE OF BUDGET RELATED PERFORMANCE EVALUATION MEASURES ON DECISION MAKING BEHAVIOR UNDER UNCERTAINTY
JOHNSON, GENE HERBERT	THE RELATIVE USE OF FORMAL AND INFORMAL INFORMATION IN THE EVALUATION OF INDIVIDUAL PERFORMANCE
KANG, JUNGPAO	GENERALIZED PROFITABILITY MEASURES UNDER STEADY-STATE CONDITIONS
KEINATH, ANNEMARIE KATHARINA	IMPACT OF ACCOUNTING INFORMATION ON ATTRIBUTIONAL CONFLICTS AND EMPLOYEE EFFORT IN A PERFORMANCE APPRAISAL SETTING
MANZONI, JEAN-FRANCOIS	USE OF QUANTITATIVE FEEDBACK BY SUPERIORS: CAUSES AND CONSEQUENCES
MAZACHEK, JULIANN	THE IMPACT OF ACCOUNTING PERFORMANCE MEASURES ON MANAGERIAL BEHAVIOR: A MODEL AND SURVEY
MCNAMEE, ALAN HOWARD	THE CONTINGENT EFFECT OF PERFORMANCE EVALUATION CRITERIA ON BUSINESS UNIT PERFORMANCE
NAM, YOUNG-HO	AN EMPIRICAL EXAMINATION OF THE ASSOCIATION BETWEEN FIRM CHARACTERISTICS AND THE ADOPTION OF LONG-TERM PERFORMANCE PLANS
PALMER, RICHARD JOSEPH	THE EFFECT OF AN ANTICIPATED PERFORMANCE EVALUATION ON INDIVIDUAL PERFORMANCE AND CONTINUING MOTIVATION TOWARD THE TASK: THE INTERVENTION OF A SELF-PRESENTATION MOTIVE
POE, CLYDE DOUGLAS	AN EXAMINATION OF THE STRENGTH OF THE CONTAGION EFFECT ON EVALUATIVE STYLE IN MANAGERIAL ACCOUNTING
SCHIFF, ANDREW DAVID	AN EXPLORATION OF THE USE OF FINANCIAL AND NONFINANCIAL MEASURES OF OPERATING PERFORMANCE BY EXECUTIVES IN A SERVICE ORGANIZATION
SELLANI, ROBERT JOSEPH	ORGANIZATIONAL LAG AND ITS EFFECTS ON FINANCIAL PERFORMANCE IN THE ELECTRONICS INDUSTRY
SIMGA, CAN	NONFINANCIAL INDICATORS IN PERFORMANCE EVALUATION OF MNE'S; EXPLORING THE USE OF FUZZY OUTRANKING RELATIONS
SNOW, CHARLES GRAN, JR.	AN EMPIRICAL INQUIRY INTO THE USE OF CERTAIN FINANCIAL AND NON-FINANCIAL MEASURES OF ENTITY PERFORMANCE
SUH, YOON SUCK	NONCONTROLLABLE COSTS AND OPTIMAL PERFORMANCE MEASUREMENT
TONGTHARADOL, VAJANA	FACTOR INFLUENCING SUPERVISOR'S RESPONSES TO SUBORDINATE'S BEHAVIOR: AN ATTRIBUTIONAL ANALYSIS
TURNER, LESLIE DANIEL	IMPROVED MEASURES OF MANUFACTURING MAINTENANCE IN A CAPITAL BUDGETING CONTEXT: AN APPLICATION OF DATA ENVELOPMENT ANALYSIS EFFICIENCY MEASURES
WESTBROOK, LESTER CURTIS, JR.	THE USE OF FINANCIAL AND NONFINANCIAL INFORMATION FOR PERFORMANCE EVALUATION OF SEGMENTS AND MANAGERS IN DECENTRALIZED MANUFACTURING COMPANIES: A CONTINGENCY APPROACH

Post Retirement Benefit Issues

ADDY, NOEL DOUGLAS, JR.	INTEREST RATE EXPECTATIONS FOR PENSION PLANS: INCENTIVES FOR DIVERGENT ACTUARIAL ASSUMPTIONS BETWEEN DOL AND FASB DISCLOSURES
ALI, ASHIQ	PENSION ASSETS AND THE MARKET RISK OF EQUITY

AMIR, ELI	ASSESSING ALTERNATIVE ACCOUNTING METHODS FOR POST-RETIREMENT BENEFITS OTHER THAN PENSIONS
ASKREN, BARBARA J.	MARKET VALUATION OF POSTEMPLOYMENT BENEFITS OTHER THAN PENSIONS
BARTH, MARY E.	ASSESSING FINANCIAL ACCOUNTING MEASUREMENT ALTERNATIVES FOR ASSETS AND LIABILITIES
BLANKLEY, ALAN IRVING	INCENTIVES IN PENSION ACCOUNTING: AN EMPIRICAL INVESTIGATION OF REPORTED RATE ESTIMATES
BRADLEY, LINDA JACOBSEN	THE IMPACT OF THE 1986 AND 1987 QUALIFIED PLAN REGULATION ON FIRMS' DECISION TO SWITCH FROM DEFINED BENEFIT TO DEFINED CONTRIBUTION FOR PLANS LARGER THAN 100 PARTICIPANTS
BURKS, EDDY J.	STATEMENT OF FINANCIAL ACCOUNTING STANDARDS NO. 87 AND MARKET RISK ADJUSTMENT
CAVANAGH, WALTER FORBES	THE ECONOMIC EFFECTS OF DEFINED BENEFIT PENSION FUNDING POLICY ON THE VALUE OF THE FIRM
CERF, DOUGLAS CLIFFORD	A STUDY OF INTERTEMPORAL VARIATION IN EARNINGS RESPONSE COEFFICIENTS: THE CASE OF THE MANDATED CHANGE IN ACCOUNTING RULES TO SFAS #87 ON PENSIONS
CHOI, BYEONGHEE	MARKET VALUATION OF POSTRETIREMENT OBLIGATIONS: A TEST OF HOW DIFFERENCES IN RELIABILITY AFFECT THE VALUATION IMPLICATIONS
CLEMENT, ROBIN PAULA	ACCOUNTING CHANGES AND THE DETERMINANTS OF SYSTEMATIC RISK: THE CASE OF FAS NO. 36: DISCLOSURE OF PENSION INFORMATION
COZORT, LARRY ALVIN	THE EFFECT OF ACCRUED PENSION BENEFIT PRESERVATION ON WORKER MOBILITY IN MULTIEMPLOYER PLANS
CROSBY, WILLIAM MORRIS	AN EXAMINATION OF THE EFFECTS WHICH A CHANGE IN THE INTEREST RATE HAS ON PENSION COSTS AND LIABILITIES INCOMPANIES WITH DEFINED-BENEFIT PENSION PLANS
DAVID, JEANNE MARIE	THE EFFECT OF DEFINED BENEFIT PENSION PLANS ON CORPORATE VALUATION: AN EMPIRICAL INVESTIGATION
DONELAN, JOSEPH G.	THE RELATIONSHIP BETWEEN PENSION ACCOUNTING INTEREST RATE ASSUMPTIONS AND FIRM RISK
DORIGAN, MICHAEL P.	CORPORATE DEFINED BENEFIT PENSION POLICIES: AN EMPIRICAL ANALYSIS OF ALTERNATIVE STRATEGIES
DUFFY, WENDY ANN	FINANCIAL REPORTING STANDARDS FOR PENSIONS: THE RELATIONSHIP BETWEEN FINANCIAL REPORTING AND CASH FLOW VARIABLES AND CHANGES IN THE INTEREST RATE ASSUMPTION
DURKEE, DAVID ALLEN	THE EFFECT OF COSTLY VS. COSTLESS PENSION DISCLOSURE ON COMMON SHARE PRICES
ELNATHAN, DAN	ANALYSIS OF ISSUES CONCERNING OTHER POST EMPLOYMENT BENEFITS
GHICAS, DIMITRIOS CHRISTOS	AN ANALYSIS OF THE CHANGE OF ACTUARIAL COST METHODS FOR PENSION ACCOUNTING AND FUNDING
GRANT, JULIA ELIZABETH STUART	NON-PENSION RETIREMENT BENEFITS
GURGANUS, FRANKIE EDWARDS	A STUDY OF THE UTILITY OF REPORTING POSTRETIREMENT HEALTH CARE BENEFITS
HAMDALLAH, AHMED EL-SAYED	AN INVESTIGATION OF MOTIVATION FOR VOLUNTARILY TERMINATING OVERFUNDED PENSION PLANS

Listing by Topic

HEFLIN, FRANK LEE	SECURITIES MARKET RESPONSE TO LEGISLATED CHANGES IN THE PENSION PLAN REVERSION EXCISE TAX
KWON, SUNKOOK	ECONOMIC DETERMINANTS OF THE ASSUMED INTEREST RATE IN PENSION ACCOUNTING
LAZAR, LAURA KRISTEN	EFFECTS OF PENSION INFORMATION ON CREDIT QUALITY JUDGMENTS OF MUNICIPAL BOND ANALYSTS
LIN, WENSHAN	ACCOUNTING REGULATION AND INFORMATION ASYMMETRY IN THE CAPITAL MARKETS: AN EMPIRICAL STUDY OF ACCOUNTING STANDARD SFAS NO 87
LOVE, WILLIAM H.	SIMULATED PENSION SCENARIOS WITH STOCHASTIC DEMOGRAPHIC AND INVESTMENT EXPERIENCE UTILIZING ALTERNATIVE ACTUARIAL COST METHODS AND ACCOUNTING PRINCIPLES
MA, SHEREE SHIOW-RU	AN EMPIRICAL EXAMINATION OF THE STOCK MARKET'S REACTION TO THE PENSION ACCOUNTING DELIBERATIONS OF THE FINANCIAL ACCOUNTING STANDARDS BOARD
MAHER, JOHN JOSEPH	PENSION OBLIGATIONS AND THE BOND CREDIT MARKET: AN EMPIRICAL ANALYSIS OF ACCOUNTING NUMBERS
MAHONEY, DANIEL PAUL	PENNSYLVANIA'S MUNICIPAL LABOR MARKET BEFORE AND AFTER THE ENACTMENT OF THE MUNICIPAL PENSION PLAN FUNDING STANDARD AND RECOVERY ACT: AN EMPIRICAL STUDY
MIDDLETON, MARY MARTIN	THE INFORMATIONAL IMPACT OF PENSION LIABILITIES ON CORPORATE RISK
MITTELSTAEDT, H. FRED	MANAGEMENT SURVIVAL STRATEGIES AND THE DECISION TO REDUCE PENSION PLAN FUNDING: AN EMPIRICAL TEST
NA, YOUNG	STOCK MARKET REACTION TO FASB NO. 106: THE DISCLOSURE OF POSTRETIREMENT BENEFIT COSTS
PARK, KYUNGJOO	QUALITY OF ACCOUNTING EARNINGS UNDER ALTERNATIVE PENSION ACCOUNTING METHODS
PAULEY, PATRICIA ANN	KNOWLEDGE OF THE TAX CONSEQUENCES OF PLAN DISTRIBUTIONS
PAVELKA, DEBORAH DIANNE	PENSION LIABILITIES AND BANKERS' LOAN DECISIONS
RANGANATHAN, KRISHNAN AYENGAR	IMPACT OF THE GAIN/LOSS PROVISIONS OF FINANCIAL ACCOUNTING STANDARD NO. 88 ON BENEFIT SETTLEMENTS
REITER, SARA ANN	THE EFFECT OF DEFINED BENEFIT PENSION PLAN DISCLOSURES ON BOND RISK PREMIUMS AND BOND RATINGS
ROLLINS, THERESA P.	AN EMPIRICAL INVESTIGATION OF PENSION PLAN ACTUARIAL ASSUMPTION CHANGES AND FIRM CHARACTERISTICS: A POSITIVE THEORY APPROACH
SAAYDAH, MANSOUR IBRAHIM	SFAS NO. 87, PENSION OBLIGATION DEFINITIONS AND THEIR RELATIONSHIP TO SYSTEMATIC RISK
SEATON, LLOYD, III	ECONOMIC CONSEQUENCES OF ACCOUNTING REGULATION: AN EMPIRICAL ANALYSIS OF CHANGES IN EMPLOYERS' ACCOUNTING FOR PENSIONS
SEOW, GIM-SEONG	THE VALUATION OF CORPORATE PENSION OBLIGATIONS: A CONTINGENT CLAIMS MODEL AND SOME EMPIRICAL TESTS
SHIN, HUNG SIK	TERMINATION OF OVERFUNDED PENSION PLANS AND SHAREHOLDER WEALTH
TOSH, DAVID EDWARD	AN EMPIRICAL EVALUATION OF ALTERNATIVE ACCOUNTING MEASURES OF DEFINED BENEFIT PENSION PLAN LIABILITIES

Listing by Topic

316

TSAY, BOR-YI	THE RELATIONSHIP BETWEEN PENSION DISCLOSURE AND BOND RISK PREMIUM
TUNG, SAMUEL S.	STOCK MARKET REACTIONS TO MANDATORY CHANGES IN ACCOUNTING FOR PENSIONS
WAMPLER, BRUCE M.	THE RELATIONSHIP BETWEEN EQUITY VALUES AND THE COMPONENTS OF UNRECORDED PENSION ASSETS AND LIABILITIES
WARDLOW, PENELOPE S.	TOWARDS BUILDING A CONCEPTUAL FRAMEWORK OF FINANCIALREPORTING FOR STATE AND LOCAL GOVERNMENT DEFINED-BENEFIT PENSION PLANS
WELSH, MARY JEANNE	AN EXPERIMENTAL RESEARCH STUDY ON THE EFFECT OF RECOGNITION AND DISCLOSURE OF CORPORATE PENSION PLAN ASSETS AND OBLIGATIONS ON INVESTMENT DECISIONS

Presentation Format

BROWN, DARRELL L.	THE INFLUENCE OF DECISION STYLE AND INFORMATION PRESENTATION FORMAT ON THE PERCEIVED USEFULNESS OF MANAGERIAL ACCOUNTING INFORMATION: AN EMPIRICAL INVESTIGATION
BURGESS, DEANNA OXENDER	THE EFFECTS OF GRAPHICAL DISTORTION OF ACCOUNTING INFORMATION ON FINANCIAL JUDGMENTS
DAVIS, LARRY R.	THE EFFECTS OF QUESTION COMPLEXITY AND FORM OF PRESENTATION ON THE EXTRACTION OF QUESTION-ANSWERS FROM AN INFORMATION PRESENTATION
FROWNFELTER, CYNTHIA ANN	THE EFFECTS OF DIFFERING INFORMATION PRESENTATIONS OF GENERAL PURPOSE FINANCIAL STATEMENTS ON USERS' DECISIONS
GIBSON, DANA L.	THE EFFECTS OF ALTERNATIVE SCREEN LAYOUTS AND FEEDBACK TYPES ON OCCASIONAL USER PRODUCTIVITY AND SATISFACTION IN A GENERAL LEDGER ENVIRONMENT
GREEN, SHARON L.	A BEHAVIORAL INVESTIGATION OF THE EFFECTS OF ALTERNATIVE GOVERNMENTAL FINANCIAL REPORTING FORMATS ON ANALYSTS' PREDICTIONS OF BOND RATINGS
NIBBELIN, MICHAEL CHARLES	THE EFFECTS OF MODE OF INFORMATION PRESENTATION AND PERCEPTUAL SKILL ON BOND RATING CHANGE DECISIONS: A LABORATORY STUDY
SMITH, GEORGE MALCOLM	IMPROVING THE DECISION USEFULNESS OF THE CORPORATE ANNUAL REPORT
SMITH, KEITH WRIGHT	THE IMPLICATIONS OF ALLOWING COGNITIVE STYLE DECISION APPROACHES OF THE DECISION-MAKER TO DETERMINE THE INFORMATION FORMAT: AN EXPERIMENTAL EXAMINATION OF PERFORMANCE
STONE, DAN NORMAN, JR.	THE IMPACT OF INFORMATION FORM ON COGNITIVE PROCESSES AND CHOICE IN AN INFORMATION SYSTEM SELECTION TASK

Pricing

GULLEY, LAWRENCE	A DETERMINATION OF THE EFFECTS OF A CHANGE IN INFORMATION-PROCESSING CAUSED BY A CHANGE IN ACCOUNTING METHODS
SENKOW, DAVID WILLIAM	PRICING MECHANISMS FOR RESOURCE ALLOCATION IN DECENTRALIZED ORGANIZATIONS: EXPERIMENTAL EVIDENCE

Public Policy

ANDERSON, SUSAN ELAINE G.	AN ANALYSIS OF THE EFFECT OF TAX LAW INSTABILITY AND PREFERENTIAL CAPITAL GAIN TREATMENT ON INVESTMENT IN RISKY ASSETS
BARRETT, KEVIN STANTON	CHARITABLE GIVING AND FEDERAL INCOME TAX POLICY: ADDITIONAL EVIDENCE BASED ON PANEL-DATA ELASTICITY ESTIMATES
BOYNTON, CHARLES EDWARD	TAX ACCOUNTING METHOD AND OFFSHORE PETROLEUM DEVELOPMENT: A POLICY EVALUATION MODEL EMPLOYING ROYALTY EQUIVALENTS AND EXCISE TAXES
BRAZELTON, JULIA K.	TAX SIMPLIFICATION: THE IMPLICATIONS OF A CONSUMPTION TAX BASE ON THE INDIVIDUAL TAXPAYER

BUSTA, BRUCE A.	A SIMULATION, REGRESSION ANALYSIS AND DELPHI SURVEY TO SEARCH FOR MATERIAL INEQUITIES RESULTING FROM THE REPEAL OF INCOME AVERAGING UNDER THE TAX REFORM ACT OF 1986
CARDWELL, PAUL HERMAN, JR.	THE EFFECT OF TAX REFORM ON THE EX ANTE VARIANCE OF SECURITY PRICES
CARR, JANICE LYNN	THE ACCELERATED COST RECOVERY SYSTEM: AN EXAMINATION OF ITS EFFECTS ON INCOME-PRODUCING PROPERTY
CASSILL, ARTHUR D.	AN EMPIRICAL ANALYSIS OF THE INFLUENCE OF SELECTED POLITICAL PROCESS VARIABLES UPON INDUSTRY INCOME TAX BURDENS
CLEMENTS, ALAN BRUCE	AN EMPIRICAL ANALYSIS OF LOW-INCOME HOUSING TAX INCENTIVES
FIEDERLEIN, KATHLEEN J.	AN EQUITY ANALYSIS OF SOCIAL SECURITY TAXING AND FINANCING SCHEMES: SIMULATIONS OF ALTERNATIVE TAX PROVISIONS
FRAZIER, JESSICA JOHNSON	AN ANALYSIS OF THE EFFECT OF THE PROPOSED AD VALOREM PROPERTY TAXATION OF UNMINED COAL PROPERTY IN KENTUCKY
HAGAN, JOSEPH MARTIN	AN EMPIRICAL STUDY OF THE EFFECT OF THE TAX REFORM ACT OF 1986 ON ECONOMIC EFFICIENCY AS MEASURED BY AVERAGE EFFECTIVE TAX RATES
HARVEY, PATRICK JAMES	ENHANCING TAX BENEFITS VIA PURCHASE OF LEGISLATIVE AUTHORITY: AN EXPERIMENTAL APPROACH
HULSE, DAVID STEWART	THE TIMING OF THE STOCK MARKET REACTION TO RIFLE-SHOT TRANSITION RULES IN THE TAX REFORM ACT OF 1986
KATTELUS, SUSAN CONVERY	PRIVATE NONOPERATING FOUNDATIONS: AN EMPIRICAL INVESTIGATION OF PAYOUT RATES AND FOUNDATION CHARACTERISTICS BEFORE AND AFTER THE ECONOMIC RECOVERY TAX ACT OF 1981
LANDER, JOEL MARTIN	ESSAYS ON THE CORPORATE TAX POLICY EFFECTS ON INVESTMENT AND FINANCING CHOICES
LECLERE, MARC JOSEPH	THE MEASUREMENT AND INTERPRETATION OF A CASHFLOW AVERAGE EFFECTIVE TAX RATE
LUTTMAN, SUZANNE MARIE	THE DISTRIBUTIONAL AND LABOR SUPPLY EFFECTS OF ALTERNATIVE INDIVIDUAL INCOME TAX PROPOSALS
MCBETH, KEVIN H.	REDEFINING THE FEDERAL INCOME TAX BASE FOR INCREASED EQUITY, NEUTRALITY, AND SIMPLICITY
MURPHY, JOHN ALOYSIUS DANIEL	THE IMPACT OF A VALUE-ADDED TAX ON THE CASH FLOW OF CORPORATIONS
OLIVA, ROBERT ROGELIO	FEDERAL TAX DEDUCTIBILITY FOR LOCAL TAXES AND ITS EFFECT ON LOCAL REVENUE POLICIES
ROSACKER, ROBERT EUGENE	A BOX-JENKINS TIME-SERIES INTERRUPTION ANALYSIS CONCERNING UNITED STATES FEDERAL TAX POLICY: AN EMPIRICAL EXAMINATION OF THE INVESTMENT TAX CREDIT
SAMELSON, DONALD	AN EMPIRICAL INVESTIGATION OF ECONOMIC CONSEQUENCES OF THE TAX REFORM ACT OF 1986
SCHLOEMER, PAUL G.	INTERNAL REVENUE CODE SECTION 263A: AN ASSESSMENT OF ITS IMPACT AND PROPOSALS FOR SIMPLIFICATION
SEETHARAMAN, ANANTH	AN EMPIRICAL VALIDATION OF SOME EXTANT MEASURES OF VERTICAL AND HORIZONTAL EQUITY
SHACKELFORD, DOUGLAS ALAN	THE MARKET FOR TAX BENEFITS: EVIDENCE FROM LEVERAGED ESOPS

Listing by Topic

SMITH, MICHAEL ALLEN	AN EMPIRICAL INVESTIGATION OF THE RELATIONSHIP BETWEEN HISTORIC REHABILITATION TAX CREDITS AND HISTORIC REHABILITATION EXPENDITURES IN THREE VIRGINIA CITIES
STITTS, RANDAL HAYES	TAX PREFERENCES, FAIRNESS, AND THE ELDERLY: A COMPARATIVE ANALYSIS OF TAX LIABILITIES
SYKES, VICEOLA DELORIS	AN ANALYSIS OF THE TAX EFFECTS OF FOREIGN INVESTMENTS IN U.S. AGRICULTURAL LAND
TUNNELL, PERRY LAWRENCE	AN INVESTIGATION INTO THE EFFECTS OF FREQUENT TAX POLICY CHANGES ON FIRM RISK
ZIMMERMANN, RAYMOND ARTHUR	ALIMONY: AN EMPIRICAL ANALYSIS OF THE EFFECT ON TAX REVENUES AND EQUITY

Quality Issues

BOWEN, PAUL LARRY	MANAGING DATA QUALITY IN ACCOUNTING INFORMATION SYSTEMS: A STOCHASTIC CLEARING SYSTEM APPROACH
ITTNER, CHRISTOPHER DEAN	THE ECONOMICS AND MEASUREMENT OF QUALITY COSTS: AN EMPIRICAL INVESTIGATION
SJOBLOM, LEIF MIKAEL	ESSAYS IN SHOP FLOOR QUALITY MANAGEMENT
TYSON, THOMAS N.	FACTORS ASSOCIATED WITH CONTROLLER DEPARTMENT PARTICIPATION IN MEASURING QUALITY COSTS

Religious Organizations

| ROWE, THOMAS MILTON | AN EMPIRICAL ANALYSIS OF THE QUALITY OF DIOCESAN FINANCIAL DISCLOSURE |
| VICKERY, KENNETH VERNON | ENABLING FOUR UNITED METHODIST CHURCHES' FINANCE COMMITTEES TO IMPLEMENT THE UNITED METHODIST INFORMATION SYSTEM PLUS' ACCOUNTING PROGRAM |

Research & Development

BERGER, PHILIP GARY	EXPLICIT AND IMPLICIT TAX EFFECTS OF THE RESEARCH AND DEVELOPMENT TAX CREDIT
COBERLY, JANET WOOD	AN ANALYSIS OF THE EFFECTIVENESS OF THE RESEARCH AND EXPERIMENTATION TAX CREDIT WITHIN A Q MODEL OF VALUATION
CROWELL, STEVEN JUDSON	AN EMPIRICAL ANALYSIS OF THE DIFFERENTIAL IMPACT OF THE RESEARCH AND EXPERIMENTATION TAX CREDIT ON U.S. CORPORATE RESEARCH EXPENDITURES
GUPTA, SANTOSH PRABHA	R&D INTENSITY, SIZE, RELATEDNESS, TAKEOVER PROCESS AND POST-MERGER CHANGE IN R&D
KIM, GWON HEE	LAG STRUCTURE, AMORTIZATION, AND PRODUCTIVITY CONTRIBUTION OF RESEARCH AND DEVELOPMENT COSTS
LINDSAY, DAVID HENDERSON	A TEST OF CONTRACTING COST THEORY ON STATEMENT OF FINANCIAL ACCOUNTING STANDARDS NO. 2: ACCOUNTING FOR RESEARCH AND DEVELOPMENT COSTS
PHILHOURS, JOEL ELLIS	NONLINEAR EFFECTS OF RESEARCH AND DEVELOPMENT EXPENDITURES ON MARKET VALUE
SHEHATA, MOHAMED MARGHANY	THE IMPACT OF SFAS NO. 2 AND THE ECONOMIC RECOVERY TAX ACT OF 1981 ON FIRMS' R AND D SPENDING BEHAVIOR
SOUGIANNIS, THEODORE	THE VALUATION OF R AND D FIRMS AND THE ACCOUNTING RULES FOR R AND D COSTS
YOON, SOON SUK	THE ECONOMIC CONSEQUENCES OF SFAS NO. 2: ITS IMPACT ON BUSINESS FIRMS AND INVESTORS

Listing by Topic

Risk

BRISCOE, NAT REEVE	UNCERTAINTY, RISK, AND PROFESSIONAL LIABILITY: AN EMPIRICAL ANALYSIS USING THE IN-BASKET TEST
BURKETTE, GARY DALE	A STUDY OF TASK UNCERTAINTY ASSOCIATED WITH PUBLIC ACCOUNTING FIRM SERVICES
CALLAHAN, CAROLYN MARGARET	A THEORETICAL AND EMPIRICAL EXAMINATION OF THE DETERMINANTS OF SYSTEMATIC RISK
CARMENT, THOMAS MAXWELL	THE MARKET EFFECT OF IN-SUBSTANCE DEFEASANCE ON BONDHOLDER DEFAULT RISK
CLARKE, DOUGLAS A.	AN EXAMINATION OF THE IMPACT OF INDIVIDUAL RISK ATTITUDES AND PERCEPTIONS ON AUDIT RISK ASSESSMENT
ELKHATIB, SOBHY MAHMOUD	AN EMPIRICAL TEST OF THE BERG PROCEDURE FOR INDUCING RISK PREFERENCES
FAIRFIELD, PATRICIA MARIE	THE INFORMATION CONTENT OF LEVERAGE: A TIME-SERIES ANALYSIS
GOULD, JOHN FRANKLIN	ESSAYS ON THE RELATION BETWEEN THE ACCOUNTING SYSTEM AND THE CAPITAL MARKET
GUESS, AUNDREA KAY	THE IMPACT OF AMBIGUITY AND RISK ON THE AUDITOR'S ASSESSMENT OF INHERENT RISK AND CONTROL RISK
LIU, SUPING	SFAS 94: AN EXAMINATION OF THE ASSOCIATION BETWEEN MARKET AND ACCOUNTING RISK MEASUREMENTS
LUEHLFING, MICHAEL STEVEN	THE IMPACT OF CLIENT RISK CHARACTERISTICS AND AUDIT PARTNER EXPERIENCE ON THE EXTENT OF THE SECOND PARTNER REVIEW IN AUDIT ENGAGEMENTS
MILLER, CHARLES ROBERT, II	ASSESSING AUDITORS' BUSINESS RISK
MOONEY, JULIAN LOWELL	A COMPARISON OF EARNINGS AND CASH FLOW AS RISK MEASURES DURING DIFFERING ECONOMIC CONDITIONS
MURTHY, UDAY SIMHA	THE RELATIONSHIP BETWEEN THE STABILITY OF COMPUTERIZED ACCOUNTING APPLICATIONS, COMPUTER AUDIT STRATEGY AND AUDIT RISK
PEEK, GEORGE SHERMAN	AN EMPIRICAL STUDY OF RISK PREFERENCE ELICITATION WITH PRACTICING AUDITORS USING EXPERIMENTAL AND BUSINESS CONTEXTS
PETERS, JAMES MILTON	A KNOWLEDGE-BASED MODEL OF INHERENT AUDIT RISK ASSESSMENT
POONAKASEM, PORNSIRI PRINGSULAKA	THE IMPACT OF MERGER ON THE FIRM'S EQUITY RISK: EX-ANTE VERSUS EX-POST ANALYSES
RAND, RICHARD SPAULDING, JR.	THE EFFECT OF AUDITORS' KNOWLEDGE OF ERRORS ON PLANNING-STAGE ASSESSMENTS OF CLIENT-RELATED RISK COMPONENTS AND ON INITIAL AUDIT SCOPE DECISIONS
RILEY, ANNE CURTIN	AN ANALYTICAL FRAMEWORK FOR THE EVALUATION OF INHERENT AUDIT RISK
STREULY, CAROLYN	TWO ESSAYS: AN EMPIRICAL INVESTIGATION INTO THE DETERMINANTS OF SECURITY RETURNS; AND, THE ASSOCIATION BETWEEN MARKET-DETERMINED AND ACCOUNTING-DETERMINED RISK MEASURES REVISITED
TOLLIVER, ROBERT WAYNE	THE RELATIVE INFORMATION CONTENT OF EARNINGS AND FUNDS FLOW ACCOUNTING NUMBERS IMPOUNDED IN THE CAPITAL MARKET'S ASSESSMENT OF THE SYSTEMATIC RISK OF EQUITY SECURITIES
WAGGONER, JERI BROCKETT	NONSAMPLING RISK: AUDITOR DETECTION OF COMPLIANCE DEVIATIONS

WALO, JUDITH CHRISTINA	LABORATORY STUDY OF THE EFFECTS OF AUDITOR'S BUSINESS RISK ON AUDIT SCOPE
WILLIAMS, JOANNE DEAHL	AN INVESTIGATION OF AUDITORS' DECISION PROCESSES IN A RISK ASSESSMENT DURING THE PLANNING STAGE OF AN AUDIT
WOAN, RONALD JEN-JIN	THE IMPACT OF MEASUREMENT ERRORS AND MULTICOLLINEARITY ON THE STUDY OF THE RELATIONSHIP BETWEEN ACCOUNTING INFORMATION AND MARKET-DETERMINED RISKS
YARDLEY, JAMES A.	LENDERS' AND ACCOUNTANTS' PERCEPTIONS OF THE INFORMATION RISK REDUCTION PROVIDED BY PRESCRIBED PROCEDURES

Segment Reporting

BENARTZI, SHLOMO	WITHIN-SEGMENT DIVERSITY AND THE INFORMATION CONTENT OF LINE-OF-BUSINESS REPORTING: EVIDENCE THAT STOCK PRICES DO NOT FULLY REFLECT THE IMPLICATIONS OF DIVIDEND CHANGES FOR SUBSEQUENT EARNINGS
COLLINS, DAVID THOMAS	AN EMPIRICAL INVESTIGATION INTO GEOGRAPHIC SEGMENT DISCLOSURE AND ITS ASSOCIATION WITH SYSTEMATIC RISK
EPPS, RUTH WILLIAMS	AN EMPIRICAL INVESTIGATION OF THE EFFECTS OF THE QUALITY OF SEGMENTAL DISCLOSURE ON THE BEHAVIOR OF SYSTEMATIC RISK OF DIVERSIFIED FIRMS
GREENSTEIN, MARILYN E. MAGEE	AN EMPIRICAL INVESTIGATION OF THE EFFECTS OF SEGMENT REPORTING ON THE BID-ASK SPREAD AND VOLUME OF TRADE
GULLEDGE, DEXTER EUGENE	AN INVESTIGATION OF MARKET REACTION TO RELATIVE CHANGES IN REPORTED AMOUNTS FOR BUSINESS SEGMENTS UNDER FASB NO. 14: AN APPLICATION OF SHANNON'S ENTROPY MEASURE
HARRIS, MARY ALICE STANFORD	THE IMPACT OF COMPETITION ON MANAGER'S REPORTING POLICIES FOR BUSINESS SEGMENTS
KIM, JAE-OH	SEGMENTAL DISCLOSURES AND INFORMATION CONTENT OF EARNINGS ANNOUNCEMENTS: THEORETICAL AND EMPIRICAL ANALYSIS
KWAK, SU KEUN	AN EMPIRICAL EVALUATION OF THE PREDICTIVE ABILITY OF SEGMENT DATA DISCLOSED IN ACCORDANCE WITH FASB STATEMENT NO. 14
LEE, DAISUN	INFORMATION CONTENT AND ECONOMIC CONSEQUENCES OF INTERIM SEGMENT REPORTING: AN EMPIRICAL TEST
NICHOLS, DAVE LEROY	SFAS 14'S GEOGRAPHIC SEGMENT DISCLOSURES AND THE ABILITY OF SECURITY ANALYSTS TO FORECAST EARNINGS
POINTER, MARTHA MANNING	AN INVESTIGATION OF THE RELATIONSHIPS BETWEEN REQUIRED GEOGRAPHICAL SEGMENT DISCLOSURE AND SYSTEMATIC EQUITY RISK AND OPERATING RISK
SAYERS, DAVID L.	THE IMPACT OF SEGMENT REPORTING ON ANALYSTS' EARNINGS FORECASTS: THE CASE OF FASB STATEMENT NO. 14
SCHWARZ, FREDERICK H.	AN ALTERNATIVE METHOD OF EVALUATING THE FINANCIAL PERFORMANCE OF FOREIGN SUBSIDIARIES
STREET, DONNA LEE	SEGMENT CASH FLOW STATEMENT: AN EMPIRICAL EXAMINATION OF ITS IMPACT ON THE LENDING DECISION
SWAMINATHAN, SIVAKUMAR	THE EFFECT OF INFORMATION PRECISION ON INVESTOR BELIEFS AND SECURITY PRICES: THE SEGMENT-REPORTING ISSUE
THOMAS, PAULA BEVELS	PUSH DOWN ACCOUNTING: A CONCEPTUAL ANALYSIS OF ITS THEORETICAL IMPLICATIONS
TOCCO, ANTHONY LEONARD	AN EMPIRICAL INVESTIGATION OF THE OPINIONS OF SELECTED FINANCIAL STATEMENT USERS TOWARD THE ADOPTION OF ADDITIONAL SEGMENT INFORMATION TO 'FINANCIAL ACCOUNTING STANDARD NO. 14'
YEH, SHU	LINE OF BUSINESS REPORTING, THE MARGINAL INFORMATION CONTENT OF EARNINGS ANNOUNCEMENTS, AND THE ACCURACY OF ANALYST EARNINGS FORECASTS

Small Business

BELL, ANGELA H.	AN EMPIRICAL STUDY OF THE TYPES AND FREQUENCIES OF ACCOUNTING PROBLEMS ENCOUNTERED DURING THE STAGES OF DEVELOPMENT OF SMALL BUSINESSES
BENSON, VAUGHN LEON	A STUDY OF THE USEFULNESS OF SELECTED GAAP BASIS ACCOUNTING INFORMATION AND ITS ACTUAL USE IN THE SMALL PRIVATE COMPANY LOAN DECISION PROCESS
BROCK, GLENDA CONERLY	AN EMPIRICAL RESEARCH STUDY OF THE IMPACT UPON SMALL BUSINESS OF THE CHANGE IN THE INVESTMENT TAX CREDIT DICTATED BY THE TAX REFORM ACT OF 1986
HAMBY, WILLIAM LYLE, JR.	AN INVESTIGATION OF INTERNAL ACCOUNTING CONTROL IN MICROCOMPUTER-BASED SMALL BUSINESS ACCOUNTING SYSTEMS
HUDSON, DENNIS HERSCHEL	AN INQUIRY INTO THE ACCOUNTING PRACTICES AND ATTITUDES OF SELECTED SMALL BUSINESSES: THE IMPACT OF RELEVANCE
KHALSA, JODHA SINGH	CONTEXT EFFECTS IN CERTIFIED PUBLIC ACCOUNTING FIRM SELECTION DECISIONS: THE SMALL BUSINESS ENVIRONMENT
PARK, SEONG WHOE	THE CHARACTERISTICS AND USAGE OF COMPUTERIZED INFORMATION SYSTEMS IN SMALL APPAREL AND TEXTILE COMPANIES
RIORDAN, DIANE A.	THE NATURE AND EFFECTIVENESS OF MANAGEMENT CONTROL IN SMALL FAMILY BUSINESSES
SMITH, HOWARD GROMEL	THE STUDY OF THE IMPLICATIONS OF SFAS 33 TO THE SMALL BUSINESS ENTERPRISE: USEFULNESS IN LONG-TERM LOAN APPLICATIONS
SMITH, W. ROBERT	A STUDY TO INVESTIGATE THE EFFECTS OF STATE TAXATION AND PLAN TYPE ON SMALL EMPLOYER RETIREMENT PLAN COST
WADHWA, DARSHAN L.	PERCEPTIONS OF CPAS REGARDING THE IMPACT OF THE ECONOMIC RECOVERY TAX ACT OF 1981 AND THE TAX REFORM ACT OF 1986 ON THE DOLLAR-VALUE LIFO INVENTORY METHOD FOR SMALL BUSINESSES

Social/Environmental Responsibility

ALLEN, FRAN MARIE	ENVIRONMENTAL RESPONSIBILITY, STAKEHOLDER THEORY AND THE VALUE OF THE FIRM
BEJAN, MARY RIORDAN	THE DIFFERENTIAL IMPACT ON NOISY AND NOISELESS PUBLIC INFORMATION ON SOCIAL WELFARE
DUNN, SARAH ANNE	A DESCRIPTIVE ANALYSIS AND EMPIRICAL INVESTIGATION OF CORPORATE ENVIRONMENTAL DISCLOSURES
HERREMANS, IRENE M.	AN INVESTIGATION OF THE TRIADIC RELATIONSHIP OF SOCIAL PERFORMANCE, SOCIAL DISCLOSURE, AND ECONOMIC PERFORMANCE
KASURINEN, VEIKKO ANTERO	CORPORATE SOCIAL ACCOUNTING: A MEASURING EXPERIMENT APPLIED TO THE PRODUCTION, TRADE AND CONSUMPTION OF ALCOHOL IN FINLAND [YRITYKSEN YHTEISKUNNALLISEN LASKENTATOIMEN MITTAAMISKOKEILU: SOVELLUS
PATTEN, DENNIS MICHAEL	THE MARKET REACTION TO SOCIAL RESPONSIBILITY INFORMATION DISCLOSURES: THE CASE OF THE SULLIVAN PRINCIPLES SIGNINGS
SMITH, PAUL HESELTINE	CORPORATE SOCIAL RESPONSE DISCLOSURE, STRUCTURE, AND REPUTATION RELATIONSHIPS FOR LARGE UNITED STATES CORPORATIONS IN THE NEW-FEDERALISM ERA
VESSEL, HERBERT	MANAGEMENT INCENTIVES FOR SOCIAL RESPONSIBILITY ACCOUNTING DISCLOSURE: AN EMPIRICAL ANALYSIS
WALDEN, W. DARRELL	AN EMPIRICAL INVESTIGATION OF ENVIRONMENTAL DISCLOSURES ANALYZING REACTIONS TO PUBLIC POLICY AND REGULATOR EFFECTS

Standard Costs & Variance Analysis

COCCO, ANTHONY F.	THE EFFECTS OF STANDARD DIFFICULTY AND COMPENSATION METHOD ON THE PARAMETERS OF THE INDUSTRIAL LEARNING CURVE AND OVERALL PERFORMANCE OF MANUAL ASSEMBLY AND DISASSEMBLY TASKS

GRIBBIN, DONALD WAYNE	ANALYSIS OF THE DISTRIBUTION PROPERTIES OF COST VARIANCES AND THEIR EFFECTS ON THE COST VARIANCE INVESTIGATION DECISION
HOLLANDER, ANITA SAWYER	A RULE-BASED APPROACH TO VARIANCE ANALYSIS
HUH, SUNG-KYOO	THE IMPACT OF PERCEIVED ENVIRONMENTAL UNCERTAINTY, COMPENSATION PLANS, AND SIZE ON THE CHOICE OF COST VARIANCE INVESTIGATION SYSTEMS IN LARGE MANUFACTURING FIRMS: AN EMPIRICAL STUDY
PARKER, DOROTHY JANET	AN EXAMINATION OF A DIFFERENTIAL IN STANDARD COST DETERMINANTS AND ITS IMPACT ON VARIANCE INVESTIGATION PROCEDURES IN MANUFACTURING
RIPOLL FELIU, VICENTE MATEO	THE RESEARCH ABOUT THE VARIANCES IN THE STANDARD COST MODELS [LA INVESTIGACION DE LAS DESVIACIONES EN LOS MODELOS DE COSTE ESTANDAR]
THOMAS, MICHAEL FRANCIS	AN APPLICATION OF SOCIO-TECHNICAL SYSTEMS ANALYSIS TO ACCOUNTING VARIANCE CONTROL THEORY
TOTTERDALE, GWENDOLYN	AN EXAMINATION OF THE DECISION-MAKING PROCESSES UNDERLYING THE DEVELOPMENT OF STANDARD COSTS FOR MANUFACTURED PRODUCTS
WEISENFELD, LESLIE WIGHT	EXAMINING THE EFFECT OF EVALUATING PERFORMANCE WITH PERFORMANCE REPORT VARIANCES ON REPORTED PERFORMANCE: A FIELD RESEARCH APPROACH

Standard Setting

AMOBI, EMMANUEL NNABUIKE	THE DEVELOPMENT AND EMPIRICAL VERIFICATION OF A PREDICTIVE MODEL FOR ACCOUNTING STANDARD LOBBYING BEHAVIOR OF OIL AND GAS FIRMS
BEALING, WILLIAM EARL, JR.	INSTITUTIONAL ASPECTS OF AUDITING REGULATION: THE BUDGETING RELATIONSHIPS AMONG THE SEC, CONGRESS AND THE PRESIDENT
BECKMAN, RONALD JAMES	AN EMPIRICAL INVESTIGATION OF THE LOBBYING INFLUENCE OF LARGE CORPORATIONS ON SELECTED FASB STANDARDS
CARPENTER, JANICE LEE	AN AGENCY THEORY ANALYSIS OF CORPORATE LOBBYING IN RESPONSE TO THE DISCUSSION MEMORANDUM ON ACCOUNTING FOR INCOME TAXES
CHUNG, DENNIS Y.	THE INFORMATIONAL EFFECT OF MANAGEMENT'S DECISION TO LOBBY AGAINST PROPOSED ACCOUNTING STANDARDS
CHUNG, KWANG-HYUN	CORPORATE LOBBYING AND MARKET REACTION TO PROPOSED ACCOUNTING RULES: THE CASE OF POSTRETIREMENT BENEFITS OTHER THAN PENSIONS
DEPREE, CHAUNCEY MARCELLOUS, JR.	TESTING THE CONCEPTUAL FRAMEWORK OF ACCOUNTING THROUGH AN APPLICATION OF A FORMAL STRUCTURE
DERESHIWSKY, MARY IRENE	ALIGNMENT OF SPECIAL-INTEREST SUBJECTS IN THE ACCOUNTING STANDARD-SETTING PROCESS: AN INVESTIGATION
FELTON, SANDRA	THE IMPACT OF LEASE ACCOUNTING REGULATION ON THE SHARE PRICES OF FIRMS WHICH LOBBIED ON SFAS NO. 13
FUHRMANN, JOHN STANLEY	THE ASSOCIATION BETWEEN SECURITY RETURNS AND FIRMS' LOBBYING POSITIONS ON ACCOUNTING STANDARDS
GOPALAKRISHNAN, VENKATARAMAN	MARKET REACTIONS TO ACCOUNTING POLICY DELIBERATIONS: THE CASE OF PENSIONS
HANDLANG, ALICE MAY	A CRITICAL ANALYSIS OF RESPONSES TO SELECTED FINANCIAL ACCOUNTING STANDARDS BOARD EXPOSURE DRAFTS TO DETERMINE THE IMPORTANT FACTORS RELEVANT TO ITS CONSTITUENCY
KERBY, DEBRA K.	CORPORATE LOBBYING AGAINST PROPOSED ACCOUNTING STANDARDS: EVIDENCE FROM THE FASB'S PENSION ACCOUNTING PROJECT
KWON, SOOYOUNG	CHOICE OF CONSOLIDATION POLICY AND PARENT FIRMS' RESPONSES TO SFAS NO. 94: CONSOLIDATION OF ALL MAJORITY-OWNED SUBSIDIARIES

Listing by Topic

LEE, BYUNG-CHULL	ECONOMIC CONSEQUENCES OF THE ACCOUNTING RULE FOR SOFTWARE COSTS
MEIER, HEIDI HYLTON	AUDITOR INDEPENDENCE: AN EXAMINATION OF AUDITOR LOBBYING BEFORE THE FINANCIAL ACCOUNTING STANDARDS BOARD ON FINANCIAL ACCOUNTING STANDARDS PERTAINING TO THE BANKING AND THRIFT INDUSTRIES
OKCABOL, FAHRETTIN	REGULATION AND ACCOUNTING PRACTICE: AN EVALUATION OF THE EFFICACY OF SEC MANDATORY REPORTING REQUIREMENTS
OLIVER, ELIZABETH GOAD	MANAGERS' USE OF FASB'S MULTI-YEAR TRANSITION PERIODS: THE CASE OF PENSIONS
PATE, GWENDOLYN RICHARDSON	A TEST OF THE THEORY OF MANAGEMENT'S PREFERENCES FOR ACCOUNTING STANDARDS: EVIDENCE FROM FASB STATEMENT NO. 94
PIERCE, BARBARA GUGLIOTTA	FIRM SIZE AND SEGMENTAL REPORTING: EVIDENCE ON DIFFERENTIAL MARKET REACTIONS
POWNALL, JACQUELINE SUE	AN EMPIRICAL ANALYSIS OF THE REGULATION OF THE DEFENSE CONTRACTING INDUSTRY: THE COST ACCOUNTING STANDARDS BOARD
RUIZ, JANIS SHIPMAN	LOBBYING, ECONOMIC CONSEQUENCES AND 'STATEMENT OF FINANCIAL ACCOUNTING STANDARD NUMBER 19'
SAEMANN, GEORGIA PIERCE	A MODEL OF NYSE FIRM MANAGER POSITION AND PARTICIPATION CHOICE ON THE MARCH 1985 FASB EXPOSURE DRAFT: EMPLOYERS' ACCOUNTING FOR PENSIONS
SAUERLENDER, KARIN MARIE	AMENDING THE FINANCIAL ACCOUNTING STANDARDS BOARD'S CONCEPTUAL FRAMEWORK: AN EMPIRICAL INVESTIGATION OF RESPONDENT COMMENTS
SCHALOW, CHRISTINE MARIE	LOBBYING ACTIVITY IN THE STANDARDS SETTING PROCESS: FASB STATEMENT ON FINANCIAL ACCOUNTING STANDARDS NO. 106, 'EMPLOYERS' ACCOUNTING FOR POSTRETIREMENT BENEFITS OTHER THAN PENSIONS'
SCHNEIDER, DOUGLAS KENNETH	RESPONDENT PERCEPTION OF THE CREDIBILITY OF GAAP
SEDAGHAT, ALI M.	THE INTERACTIVE PROCESS OF ACCOUNTING: AN ANALYSIS OF THE DEVELOPMENT OF FINANCIAL ACCOUNTING AND REPORTING STANDARDS FOR OIL AND GAS PRODUCING ACTIVITIES
TICHICH, MARY CAROL	THE SEC INTERACTION IN THE ACCOUNTING STANDARDS SETTING PROCESS: AN ANALYSIS OF THE FASB STATEMENTS
WEYNS, GUY JOSEPH	ANALYTICAL ESSAYS ON THE ECONOMIC CONSEQUENCES OF FINANCIAL ACCOUNTING STANDARDS
WIER, HEATHER ANN	THE EFFECT OF SFAS 94 ON INVESTOR RISK ASSESSMENTS AND MANAGEMENT ACTIVITIES
WILBURN, NANCY LOU	AN EMPIRICAL ANALYSIS OF THE RELATIVE POWER OF CONSTITUENTS PARTICIPATING IN THE STANDARD-SETTING PROCESS OF THE FINANCIAL ACCOUNTING STANDARDS BOARD: EMPLOYERS' ACCOUNTING FOR PENSIONS
WILLIAMS, LOWELL KIM	ACCOUNTING STANDARDS OVERLOAD: A DESCRIPTIVE MODEL FOR EVALUATING PERCEPTIONS OF ACCOUNTING STANDARDS
YOUNG, JONI J.	AGENDA FORMATION AND THE FINANCIAL ACCOUNTING STANDARDS BOARD

State Taxation

HARRIS, JEANNIE E.	TAX EXPENDITURES: REPORT UTILIZATION BY STATE POLICY MAKERS
IKEOKWU, FRANCIS AHAMEFULE	FLORIDA SALES TAX REVENUE: A COMPARATIVE STUDY TO DETERMINE THE RELATIONSHIP BETWEEN SALES TAX RATE AND SALES TAX REVENUE IN FLORIDA
LINTON, FRANK BRUCE	FEDERAL INCOME TAXING SYSTEM AND ITS EFFECT ON STATE INCOME TAX STRUCTURES

PORTER, SUSAN L.	THE EFFECTS OF ALTERNATIVE STATE TAX REGIMES ON FIRMS' ACCOUNTING AND FINANCING DECISIONS
SCHMIDT, DENNIS R.	STATE TAXATION OF MULTIJURISDICTIONAL CORPORATE INCOME: AN EMPIRICAL ANALYSIS OF FORMULARY APPORTIONMENT
STEVENS, KEVIN TIMOTHY	AN EMPIRICAL ANALYSIS OF THE NATURE OF SELECTED TAX EXPENDITURES IN A STATE INDIVIDUAL INCOME TAX SYSTEM
SUMNER, JEANIE GRACE	AN ANALYSIS OF THE EFFECT OF STATE REGULATION OF COMMERCIAL INCOME TAX PREPARERS ON THE QUALITY OF INCOME TAX RETURNS
WELLS, STEVE CARROLL	AN EMPIRICAL STUDY OF THE EFFECT OF VALUE-ADDED TAX FORM ON REVENUE VOLATILITY
WERTHEIM, PAUL	AN EMPIRICAL ANALYSIS OF CURRENT STATE TRENDING FORMULAS

Stock Transactions

BARTOV, ELIAHU	CHANGES IN FIRM FINANCIAL POLICY AS SIGNALS FOR FUTURE EARNINGS: AN EMPIRICAL INVESTIGATION OF UNSYSTEMATIC STOCK REPURCHASES
DORAN, DAVID THOMAS	STOCK DIVIDENDS, STOCK SPLITS, AND FUTURE EARNINGS: ACCOUNTING RELEVANCE AND EQUITY MARKET RESPONSE
KIMMELL, SHARON LEE	AN EXAMINATION OF MANAGEMENT MOTIVATION AND STOCK DISTRIBUTION SIZE
POWER, JACQUELINE LOU	ANNOUNCEMENTS OF STOCK REPURCHASES DURING 1988 AND 1989: AN EMPIRICAL ANALYSIS EXAMINING THE DISCLOSURE OF INTENDED OPEN MARKET REPURCHASES
STEPHENSON, CRAIG ALLEN	ESSAYS ON REPURCHASES AND TENDER OFFERS

Systems Design &/or Development

ADAMSON, IAN L.	AN OBJECT-ORIENTED FINANCIAL ACCOUNTING INFORMATION SYSTEM
BABA, ISLAHUDIN	THE ROLE OF AUDITORS IN INFORMATION SYSTEMS DEVELOPMENT APPLIED TO THE MALAYSIAN PUBLIC SECTOR
BAKER, JOHN HOWARD	A CONCEPTUAL DESIGN FOR SIMPLIFYING AND STRUCTURING ELECTRONIC DOCUMENTS: AN APPLICATION IN PROFESSIONAL CONDUCT STANDARDS
BERGER, HELMUT MAXIMILIAN	IMPROVEMENT AND IMPLEMENTATION OF A MODEL OF INTEGRATED ACCOUNTING [VERBESSERUNG UND IMPLEMENTIERUNG EINES MODELLES DER INTEGRIERTEN PLANUNGSRECHNUNG]
CERULLO, MARGARET VIRGINIA	A STUDY OF INTERNAL AUDITOR PERCEPTIONS OF SELECTED AUDIT ACTIVITIES PERFORMED DURING THE DESIGN PHASE OF SYSTEMS DEVELOPMENT
ESSEX, PATRICIA ANN	SYSTEMS DEVELOPMENT FRICTION: A CAUSAL MODEL BASED ON EQUITY CONSIDERATIONS
HAN, KYEONG SEOK	A FORMAL ALGORITHMIC MODEL COMPATIBLE WITH ACCOUNTING INFORMATION SYSTEMS
HARRIS, ELLEN KAY	FACTORS THAT INFLUENCE PRODUCT COSTING INFORMATION SYSTEM CHANGES
JACKSON, CYNTHIA MAPP	THE INFLUENCE OF USER INVOLVEMENT AND OTHER VARIABLES ON BEHAVIORAL INTENTION TO USE AN INFORMATION SYSTEM
JENSON, RICHARD L.	PARAMETRIC ESTIMATION OF PROGRAMMING EFFORT IN A MANUFACTURING DATABASE ENVIRONMENT

LEVENSTEIN, MARGARET CATHERINE	INFORMATION SYSTEMS AND INTERNAL ORGANIZATION: A STUDY OF THE DOW CHEMICAL COMPANY, 1890-1914
MANN, GARY J.	EFFECTS OF HUMAN NEEDS, GROUP INFLUENCE, AND MANAGEMENT STYLE ON CHANGE-RELATED BEHAVIORAL INTENTIONS IN INFORMATION SYSTEMS
NEHMER, ROBERT ALAN	ACCOUNTING INFORMATION SYSTEMS AS ALGEBRAS AND FIRST ORDER AXIOMATIC MODELS
NICOLAOU, ANDREAS IACOVOU	AN EMPIRICAL EXAMINATION OF INFORMATION SYSTEMS SUCCESS IN RELATION WITH INFORMATION SYSTEMS DEVELOPMENT PHENOMENA
SCHMELZLE, GEORGE DANIEL	A STUDY OF THE EFFECTS OF DOGMATISM AND THE EVENTS APPROACH TO ACCOUNTING ON DECISION-MAKING IN THE NEW MANUFACTURING ENVIRONMENT
THOMPSON, PETER MACLEOD	A TEMPORAL DATA MODEL BASED ON ACCOUNTING PRINCIPLES
WHITE, STEVEN DALE	AN EMPIRICAL STUDY OF THE USER SATISFACTION OF ACCOUNTANTS WITH THE SOFTWARE MAINTENANCE FUNCTION

Tax Compliance

ABRAMOWICZ, KENNETH FRANK	AN EMPIRICAL INVESTIGATION OF TAX COMPLIANCE RELATED TO SCHOLARSHIP INCOME
ANGELINI, JAMES PETER	AN INVESTIGATIVE ANALYSIS FOR THE DEVELOPMENT OF A FEDERAL TAX AMNESTY PROGRAM
BJORNSON, CHRIS E.	THE EFFECT OF INCOME TAX PREPAYMENTS ON TAXPAYER REPORTING BEHAVIOR: A BUSINESS SIMULATION
BRADLEY, CASSIE FRANCES	AN EMPIRICAL INVESTIGATION OF FACTORS AFFECTING CORPORATE TAX COMPLIANCE BEHAVIOR
CHOE, YONG SUN	THE EFFECT OF A TAX DEDUCTION ON CHARITABLE CONTRIBUTIONS BY LOW- AND MIDDLE-INCOME TAXPAYERS
COPP, CYNTHIA ANN	THE EFFECT OF TAX STRUCTURE VARIABLES ON THE DECISION FRAME ADOPTED AND THE TAX REPORTING CHOICE: TAXABLE INCOME COMPONENTS AND TAX PAYMENT TIMING
CROSSER, RICK LYNN	THE RELATIVE EFFECT OF PENALTY MAGNITUDES ON COMPLIANCE: AN EXPERIMENTAL EXAMINATION OF DETERRENCE
DUSENBURY, RICHARD BENNETT	TAX COMPLIANCE: THE EFFECT OF THE TIMING OF PAYMENTS
FISCHER, CAROL M.	PERCEIVED DETECTION PROBABILITY AND TAXPAYER COMPLIANCE: A CONCEPTUAL AND EMPIRICAL EXAMINATION
FISHER, DANN G.	ASSESSING TAXPAYER MORAL REASONING: THE DEVELOPMENT OF AN OBJECTIVE MEASURE
FRISCHMANN, PETER JAMES	TAXPAYER RESPONSE TO KINKED BUDGET CONSTRAINTS: NEW EMPIRICAL EVIDENCE OF TAX PRICE AWARENESS
GERBING, MONICA DIANE	AN EMPIRICAL STUDY OF TAXPAYER PERCEPTIONS OF FAIRNESS
HAMMER, SETH	THE CPA'S ROLE AS RISK ADVISER
HARRIS, THOMAS DONALD	THE EFFECT OF TYPE OF TAX KNOWLEDGE ON INDIVIDUALS' PERCEPTIONS OF FAIRNESS AND COMPLIANCE WITH THE FEDERAL INCOME TAX SYSTEM: AN EMPIRICAL STUDY
HITE, PEGGY SULLIVAN	AN EXPERIMENTAL INVESTIGATION OF TWO POSSIBLE EXPLANATIONS FOR TAXPAYER NONCOMPLIANCE: TAX SHELTERS AND NONCOMPLIANT PEERS

Listing by Topic

JOHNSON, JOYCE MARIE	AN EVALUATION OF THE FEDERAL CIVIL TAX PENALTY FOR THE FAILURE TO TIMELY DEPOSIT PAYROLL TAXES: A SURVEY OF GEORGIA TAX PRACTITIONERS
KEMPTON, PETER A.	THE CONTROL OF TAX EVASION--QUESTIONS FOR PRACTISING ACCOUNTANTS
LEAUBY, BRUCE ALAN	DETERMINANTS OF CORPORATE TAX AVOIDANCE STRATEGY: AN EMPIRICAL ANALYSIS
LEMLER, BRADLEY K.	TAXPAYER EXPECTATIONS, TAX INVESTMENT INCENTIVES AND TAXPAYER ECONOMIC BEHAVIOR: AN ANALYSIS OF INVESTMENT BEHAVIOR IN MANUFACTURING FIRMS FROM 1954 TO 1985
LUBICH, BRUCE HOWARD	THE IMPACT OF TAX NONCOMPLIANCE ON HORIZONTAL AND VERTICAL DISTRIBUTIONS OF INCOME
MARTINDALE, BOBBIE COOK	IMPACT OF TAX COMPLEXITY ON TAXPAYER UNDERSTANDING
MCCLENNY, RUTH LORRAINE	CHANGING TAXPAYER ATTITUDES AND INCREASING TAXPAYER COMPLIANCE: THE ROLE OF INDIVIDUAL DIFFERENCES IN TAXPAYERS
MCGILL, GARY ANDERSON	THE CPA'S ROLE IN INCOME TAX COMPLIANCE: AN EMPIRICAL STUDY OF VARIABILITY IN RECOMMENDING AGGRESSIVE TAX POSITIONS
MCNAIR, FRANCES ELIZABETH	AN EMPIRICAL INVESTIGATION OF THE PERCEIVED EFFECTS OF TAX REFORM ON TAXPAYER COMPLIANCE
NIGRINI, MARK JOHN	THE DETECTION OF INCOME TAX EVASION THROUGH AN ANALYSIS OF DIGITAL DISTRIBUTIONS
NUGENT, DAVID ANTHONY	THE IMPACT OF WITHHOLDING POSITION AND PENALTY FACTORS ON TAXPAYER BEHAVIOR: A STUDY OF INTERACTION EFFECTS
RICE, ERIC MARSHALL	SKIRTING THE LAW: ESSAYS ON CORPORATE TAX EVASION AND AVOIDANCE
SAWYERS, ROBY BLAKE	THE IMPACT OF UNCERTAINTY AND AMBIGUITY ON INCOME TAX DECISION-MAKING
SCHISLER, DANIEL LAWRENCE	AN EXPERIMENTAL EXAMINATION OF TAXPAYERS' AND TAX PROFESSIONALS' AGGRESSIVE TAX PREFERENCES: A PROSPECT THEORY FOUNDATION
STROOPE, JOHN CLARENCE	INCOME TAX EVASION AND THE EFFECTIVENESS OF TAX COMPLIANCE LEGISLATION, 1979-1982
TRIPPEER, DONALD RICHARD	THE FUNDING OF GOVERNMENT PROGRAMS UNDER THE BUDGET ENFORCEMENT ACT: THE EFFECT OF THE EXCHANGE RELATIONSHIP ON TAXPAYER COMPLIANCE
TROUTMAN, COLEEN S.	MORAL COMMITMENT TO TAX COMPLIANCE AS MEASURED BY THE DEVELOPMENT OF MORAL REASONING AND ATTITUDES TOWARDS THE FAIRNESS OF THE TAX LAWS
VIOLETTE, GEORGE R.	THE DETERRENCE EFFECTS OF SANCTION COMMUNICATIONS ON TAXPAYER LEVEL OF INCOME TAX COMPLIANCE
WARTICK, MARTHA LORRAINE	THE EFFECT OF KNOWLEDGE OF LEGISLATIVE INTENT ON TAXPAYER PERCEPTIONS OF FAIRNESS
YOUNG, JAMES CHRISTIAN	FACTORS IN THE NONCOMPLIANCE DECISION: AN ANALYSIS OF MICHIGAN TAX AMNESTY PARTICIPANTS

Tax Court

CARTER, GARY WILLIAM	THE ACQUIESCENCE/NONACQUIESCENCE POLICY OF THE COMMISSIONER WITH RESPECT TO TAX COURT DECISIONS - AN EMPIRICAL ANALYSIS
FENTON, EDMUND DAVID, JR.	AN EMPIRICAL INVESTIGATION INTO THE TAX COURT ASSESSMENT OF THE ECONOMIC INTEREST CONCEPT IN NATURAL RESOURCE TAXATION

Listing by Topic

GARRISON, LARRY RICHARD	THE EXCLUSION FROM INCOME OF SCHOLARSHIPS AND FELLOWSHIP GRANTS: AN EMPIRICAL INVESTIGATION OF TAX COURT DETERMINATIONS
JUDD, ANDREW JACKSON	AN EXAMINATION OF SIGNIFICANT VARIABLES USED BY COURTS IN WORTHLESS STOCK CASES
MORRIS, JOSEPH LYNN	A PROFILE OF WINNING AND LOSING CASES CONCERNING THE VALUATION OF CLOSELY HELD SHARES FOR ESTATE AND GIFT TAX PURPOSES
OLSON, WILLIAM HALVER	AN EMPIRICAL INVESTIGATION OF THE FACTORS CONSIDERED BY THE TAX COURT IN DETERMINING PRINCIPAL PURPOSE UNDER INTERNAL REVENUE CODE SECTION 269
PASEWARK, WILLIAM ROBERT	DETERMINING ECONOMIC INTEREST IN NATURAL RESOURCES
PRICE, CHARLES EWELL	AN EMPIRICAL INQUIRY INTO THE PREDICTIVE POWER OF SELECTED ATTRIBUTES FROM DISPUTED FEDERAL TAX EXAMINATIONS
ROBERTSON, PAUL JEPSEN	DEBT OR EQUITY? AN EMPIRICAL ANALYSIS OF TAX COURT CLASSIFICATION DURING THE PERIOD 1955-1987
SMITH, DARLENE A. PULLIAM	AN ANALYSIS OF THE FACTORS USED BY THE TAX COURT IN APPLYING THE STEP TRANSACTION DOCTRINE

Tax Professionals

BAIN, CRAIG EDGAR	EXPERTS' PERCEPTIONS OF SUBSTANTIAL AUTHORITY
CHRISTENSEN, ANNE LESLIE KEENEY	TAX RETURN QUALITY: A CLIENT AND PREPARER PERSPECTIVE
CUCCIA, ANDREW DANIEL	AN EXAMINATION OF THE EFFORT AND AGGRESSIVENESS OF PROFESSIONAL TAX PREPARERS: THE EFFECTS OF ECONOMIC SANCTIONS AND ROLE PERCEPTIONS
GOEDDE, HAROLD	AN EMPIRICAL STUDY OF TAX PRACTITIONERS PERCEPTIONS OF THE EFFECT OF THE 1986 TAX REFORM ACT ON SIMPLIFICATION AND FAIRNESS OF THE FEDERAL INCOME TAX
GURKA, GEOFFREY J.	THE ROLE OF NEUTRALIZATION STRATEGIES IN THE TRADEOFF BETWEEN PRACTITIONER RESPONSIBILITIES
GUTIERREZ, THERESA KAY	THE EFFECTS OF INTERACTIONS WITH IRS EMPLOYEES ON TAX PRACTITIONERS' ATTITUDES TOWARD THE IRS
HUTTON, MARGUERITE ROACH	PERCEPTUAL DIFFERENTIATION WITH REGARD TO PENALTIES IN PROFESSIONAL TAX PRACTICE
LIN, SUMING	INCOME TAX RETURN PREPARATION FEES AND TAX SAVINGS OF USING TAX RETURN PREPARERS
MALLEK, JAMES RANDOLPH	PROBLEM RECOGNITION IN PROFESSIONAL TAX ACCOUNTING
MASON, J. DAVID	A BEHAVIORAL MODEL OF SIMILARITY JUDGMENTS BY TAX PROFESSIONALS
MCCRAW, JOSEPH HARRISON, JR.	A STUDY OF THE FEASIBILITY OF USING LINEAR REGRESSION IN THE MANAGEMENT OF THE INDIVIDUAL TAX RETURN PREPARATION PROCESS
STERNBURG, THOMAS JAMES	AN EMPIRICAL INVESTIGATION OF DETERRENCE THEORY AND INFLUENCE THEORY ON PROFESSIONAL TAX PREPARERS' RECOMMENDATIONS

Taxes

BEEHLER, JOHN MICHAEL	AN EMPIRICAL EXAMINATION OF THE EFFECT OF THE SECTION 465 AT-RISK RULES ON EQUIPMENT LEASING TAX SHELTERS

CALLAGHAN, JOSEPH HENRY	THE NATURE OF DEFERRED INCOME TAXES ARISING FROM DIFFERENCES IN DEPRECIATION METHODS
CARTER, BEN DOUGLAS	AN EMPIRICAL INVESTIGATION INTO THE PREDICTABILITY OF CHANGES IN CASH FLOW FROM OPERATIONS UNDER ALTERNATIVE METHODS OF ACCOUNTING FOR INCOME TAXES
CLARK, STANLEY J.	AN EMPIRICAL EXAMINATION OF FIRMS' MOTIVATIONS FOR EARLY ADOPTION OF SFAS 96 AND THE INFORMATION CONTENT OF FIRMS' DECISION TO EARLY ADOPT SFAS 96
COLEMAN, CLARENCE, JR.	DEFERRED INCOME TAX CREDITS: AN EMPIRICAL ANALYSIS OF PERCEIVED MARKET RISK
HAMILL, JAMES ROBERT	AN EXPERIMENTAL ANALYSIS OF THE IMPACT OF INCOME TAXES ON NOMINAL INTEREST RATES
JETER, DEBRA COLEMAN	ACCOUNTING EARNINGS AND SECURITY RETURNS: STUDIES ON EARNINGS RESPONSE COEFFICIENTS, AUDIT REPORTS, AND DEFERRED TAXES
KHAN, ZAFAR ULLAH	THE IMPACT OF COMPREHENSIVE ALLOCATION AND FLOW-THROUGH METHOD OF ACCOUNTING FOR THE INCOME TAXES ON THE INVESTMENT DECISION: A FIELD EXPERIMENT
MILLER, GARY ARTHUR	THE COSTS AND BENEFITS OF INTERPERIOD INCOME TAX ALLOCATION
RICHARDSON, CLARA LUCILE	THE PREDICTIVE ABILITY OF ALTERNATIVE BASES FOR INTERPERIOD TAX ALLOCATION: AN EMPIRICAL STUDY
ROBERTSON, DARROCH AITKENS	AN INVESTIGATION OF DEFERRED INCOME TAXES DURING A RECESSIONARY PERIOD
ROVELSTAD, RICHARD GARY	DEFERRED TAXES AND TOBIN'S Q: AN EMPIRICAL INVESTIGATION OF SIGNIFICANCE AND ASSOCIATION
RUDE, JOHN ARTHUR	AN EVALUATION OF THE USEFULNESS OF ALTERNATIVE ACCOUNTING TREATMENTS OF DEFERRED TAXES IN PREDICTING FINANCIAL FAILURE
RYU, TAE GHIL	A CROSS-SECTIONAL ANALYSIS OF THE ADOPTION OF STATEMENT OF FINANCIAL ACCOUNTING STANDARDS (SFAS) NO. 96, 'ACCOUNTING FOR INCOME TAXES'
SLADE, PRISCILLA DEAN	AN EMPIRICAL ANALYSIS OF DEFERRED TAX BALANCES FROM A STATEMENT OF FINANCIAL POSITION AND INCOME STATEMENT PERSPECTIVE
TURNER, DEBORAH HANSON	THE EFFECT OF ALTERNATIVE METHODS OF ACCOUNTING FOR INCOME TAXES ON THE ASSOCIATION BETWEEN ACCOUNTING RISK MEASURES AND THE MARKET RISK MEASURE

Transfer Pricing

AL-ERYANI, MOHAMED FADL	POLICIES OF U.S. MULTINATIONAL CORPORATIONS ON PRICING INTRACOMPANY TRANSFERS WITH FOREIGN AFFILIATES IN MORE-DEVELOPED AND LESS-DEVELOPED COUNTRIES
ARUNACHALAM, VAIRAVAN	DECISION AIDING IN MULTI-PARTY TRANSFER PRICING NEGOTIATION: THE EFFECTS OF COMPUTER-MEDIATED COMMUNICATION AND STRUCTURED INTERACTION
AVILA, MARCOS GONCALVES	TRANSFER PRICING MECHANISMS: AN EXPERIMENTAL INVESTIGATION
BORKOWSKI, SUSAN CAROL	AN INVESTIGATION INTO THE DIVERGENCE OF THEORY FROM PRACTICE REGARDING TRANSFER PRICING METHODS
CHAN, CHRIS WAI-HONG	EFFECTS OF NEGOTIATOR ACCOUNTABILITY, PERFORMANCE EVALUATION SYSTEM, AND PERCEPTION OF DIVISIONAL POWER ON TRANSFER PRICING NEGOTIATION OUTCOMES
COLBERT, GARY J.	AN EMPIRICAL INVESTIGATION OF THE TRANSFER PROCESS AND TRANSFER PRICING: A MULTI-CASE RESEARCH DESIGN
CRAVENS, KAREN SUE	A COMPARATIVE INVESTIGATION OF TRANSFER PRICING PRACTICES IN AN INTERNATIONAL ENVIRONMENT

GHOSH, DIPANKAR	AN EXPERIMENT COMPARING NEGOTIATED AND CENTRALLY ADMINISTERED TRANSFER PRICES
HONG, YONG-SIK	A GAME-THEORETIC ANALYSIS OF TRANSFER PRICE NEGOTIATION UNDER INCOMPLETE INFORMATION CONDITIONS
JOY, ARTHUR C., JR.	AN EMPIRICAL INVESTIGATION INTO TRANSFER PRICING PRACTICES
LEE, KYUNG TAE	OPTIMAL CONTROL SYSTEMS IN MANAGERIAL ACCOUNTING
LI, SHU-HSING	TRANSFER PRICING UNDER INFORMATION ASYMMETRY IN MULTIAGENT SETTINGS
MAHENTHIRAN, SAKTHIHARAN	NEGOTIATED TRANSFER PRICING: AN INTEGRATED EMPIRICAL EXAMINATION
MEHAFDI, MESSAOUD	BEHAVIOURAL ASPECTS OF TRANSFER PRICING IN UNITED KINGDOM DECENTRALISED COMPANIES
PARK, KYOUNG-HWAN	A SIMULATION MODEL OF TRANSFER PRICING FOR MULTINATIONAL CORPORATIONS BASED ON THE EQUIVALENT ANNUAL COST METHOD
SALEM, AZIZA ABDEL-RAZIK AHMED	A STUDY OF DETERMINANTS OF TRANSFER PRICING IN MULTINATIONAL CORPORATIONS: THE CASE BETWEEN U.S. PARENTS AND THE EGYPTIAN UNITS
SCHLACHTER, PAUL JUSTIN	A TWO-STAGE ANALYSIS OF INTERDIVISIONAL TRANSFER PRICING NEGOTIATIONS
SLOF, ERIC JOHN	ECONOMIC MODELS OF TRANSFER PRICING IN DECENTRALIZED FIRMS
VAYSMAN, IGOR	MODELS OF TRANSFER PRICING
WEIDA, NANCY COUGHLIN	GAME-THEORETIC MODELS OF THE TRANSFER PRICING PROBLEM
YEOM, SUNGSOO	THE ROLE OF TRANSFER PRICE FOR COORDINATION AND CONTROL WITHIN A FIRM
YOST, JEFFREY ALLAN	INTRAFIRM RESOURCE ALLOCATION AND TRANSFER PRICING UNDER ASYMMETRIC INFORMATION: A PRINCIPAL-AGENT ANALYSIS OF DECENTRALIZED DECISION-MAKING IN A MULTIDIVISION FIRM

Voluntary Management Disclosures

BUSHMAN, ROBERT MICHAEL	PUBLIC DISCLOSURE BY FIRMS IN THE PRESENCE OF A MONOPOLISTIC SELLER OF PRIVATE INFORMATION
CHOI, JUNG HO	MANAGEMENT EARNINGS EXPECTATIONS, EARNINGS UNCERTAINTY, AND VOLUNTARY DISCLOSURE OF EARNINGS FORECASTS BY MANAGEMENT: AN EMPIRICAL EVALUATION OF CURRENT DISCLOSURE PRACTICES UNDER THE VOLUNTARY RULES
EL-RAJABI, MD-TAYSIR A	THE INFORMATION CONTENT OF ANNOUNCING THE CAPITAL INVESTMENT DECISIONS AND THE ACTUAL INVESTMENT NUMBERS
GABER, MOHAMED KHAIRAT ABDEL-GELIL	MANAGEMENT INCENTIVES TO REPORT FORECASTS OF CORPORATE EARNINGS
GEORGE, NASHWA ELGALLAB	MANAGEMENT EARNINGS FORECAST DISCLOSURE: AN EMPIRICAL STUDY OF FACTORS INFLUENCING THE DECISION
GIGLER, FRANK BARRY	SELF-ENFORCING VOLUNTARY DISCLOSURES
GILL, SUSAN	MOTIVATIONS FOR AND REACTIONS TO VOLUNTARY MANAGEMENT DISCLOSURES

GUSTAFSON, LYAL VAL	AN EMPIRICAL INVESTIGATION OF THE USEFULNESS OF MANAGEMENT EARNINGS FORECASTS AS EVIDENCED BY THEIR EFFECT ON ANALYSTS' PREDICTIONS
HAN, CHI-YING	MANAGEMENT FORECASTS: INCENTIVES AND EFFECTS
LIU, CHAO-SHIN	MANAGEMENT EARNINGS FORECASTS, SECURITY PRICE VARIABILITY, AND THE MARGINAL INFORMATION CONTENT OF EARNINGS ANNOUNCEMENTS
MORRIS, NORMA WILLIAMS	THE ASSOCIATION BETWEEN SELECTED CORPORATE ATTRIBUTES AND MANAGEMENT INCENTIVES FOR VOLUNTARY ACCOUNTING DISCLOSURE
NELSON, JACOB JOHN	CHANGES IN FIRMS' VOLUNTARY DISCLOSURES OF EARNINGS PROJECTIONS ASSOCIATED WITH OPTIONS LISTING
SANKAR, MANDIRA ROY	CORPORATE VOLUNTARY DISCLOSURES OF PREDECISION INFORMATION
SHIN, DOUG YONG	WHY MANAGERS VOLUNTARILY RELEASE EARNINGS FORECASTS?: THE ROLE OF THE MANAGERIAL LABOR MARKET
TANNER, MARGARET MORGAN	AN ANALYSIS OF FACTORS ASSOCIATED WITH VOLUNTARY DISCLOSURE OF MANAGEMENT'S RESPONSIBILITIES FOR INTERNALCONTROL
WILLIAMS, PATRICIA ANN	THE EFFECT OF PRIOR FORECAST USEFULNESS ON USER REACTION TO A MANAGEMENT EARNINGS FORECAST
WU, ANNE	THE DETERMINANTS OF VOLUNTARY RELEASE OF EARNINGS FORECASTS INFORMATION TO THE PUBLIC
YEO, GILLIAN HIAN HENG	A FRAMEWORK TO ANALYZE MANAGEMENT'S VOLUNTARY FORECAST DISCLOSURE DECISIONS
YI, HWA DEUK	MANAGEMENT EARNINGS FORECASTS: THE MARKET RESPONSE AND FIRMS' DISCLOSURE INCENTIVES
YOON, MYUNG-HO	AN EXAMINATION OF THE EFFECT OF THE SAFE HARBOR RULE ON THE PREDICTION ERROR OF MANAGEMENT EARNINGS FORECASTS: SOME EMPIRICAL EVIDENCE

Listing by Topic

Dissertations Listed Alphabetically by Research Method

Analytical - Internal Logic

ADAMSON, IAN L.	AN OBJECT-ORIENTED FINANCIAL ACCOUNTING INFORMATION SYSTEM
ALLES, MICHAEL GAMINI	INCENTIVE ASPECTS OF COSTING
ANCTIL, REGINA MARIE	CAPITAL BUDGETING USING RESIDUAL INCOME MAXIMIZATION
ANELL, ANDERS LARS	FROM CENTRAL PLANNING TO LOCAL RESPONSIBILITIES: THE ROLE OF BUDGETING IN SWEDISH COUNTY COUNCIL HEALTH CARE [FRAN CENTRAL PLANERING TILL LOKALT ANSVAR: BUDGETERINGENS ROLL I LANDSTINGSKOMMUNAL SJUKVARD]
ANGELINI, JAMES PETER	AN INVESTIGATIVE ANALYSIS FOR THE DEVELOPMENT OF A FEDERAL TAX AMNESTY PROGRAM
ARTSBERG, KRISTINA ULRIKA	POLICY MAKING AND ACCOUNTING CHANGE: INFLUENCES ON THE CHOICE OF MEASUREMENT PRINCIPLES IN SWEDISH ACCOUNTING [NORMBILDNING OCH REDOVISNINGSFOERAENDRING: VAERDERINGAR VID VAL AV MAETPRINCIPER INOM
BACK, BARBRO CHRISTINA	AN EXPERT SYSTEM FOR FINANCIAL STATEMENTS PLANNING
BAKER, JOHN HOWARD	A CONCEPTUAL DESIGN FOR SIMPLIFYING AND STRUCTURING ELECTRONIC DOCUMENTS: AN APPLICATION IN PROFESSIONAL CONDUCT STANDARDS
BALAKRISHNAN, RAMAMURTHY	APPLICATIONS OF MULTIPERIOD AGENCY MODELS: AN ACCOUNTING CONTEXT
BARCLAY, RODERICK STUART	COMPUTER CHARGEBACK SYSTEMS: A CRITICAL ANALYSIS AND NEW METHODOLOGY
BARDO, FREDERIC S.	A NORMATIVE THEORY OF ACCOUNTING FOR ZIMBABWE: A THIRD WORLD COUNTRY
BASAK, SULEYMAN	GENERAL EQUILIBRIUM CONTINUOUS-TIME ASSET PRICING IN THE PRESENCE OF: (1) PORTFOLIO INSURERS AND (2) NON-PRICE-TAKING INVESTORS
BEJAN, MARY RIORDAN	THE DIFFERENTIAL IMPACT ON NOISY AND NOISELESS PUBLIC INFORMATION ON SOCIAL WELFARE
BERGER, HELMUT MAXIMILIAN	IMPROVEMENT AND IMPLEMENTATION OF A MODEL OF INTEGRATED ACCOUNTING [VERBESSERUNG UND IMPLEMENTIERUNG EINES MODELLES DER INTEGRIERTEN PLANUNGSRECHNUNG]
BITNER, LARRY NEWELL	ACCOUNTING FOR CHANGING PRICES PER FASB 33 AND THE IMPACT ON INCOME SMOOTHING
BOWEN, PAUL LARRY	MANAGING DATA QUALITY IN ACCOUNTING INFORMATION SYSTEMS: A STOCHASTIC CLEARING SYSTEM APPROACH
CERDA APARICIO, JOSE	COMPARATIVE ANALYSIS OF THE IMPLEMENTATION OF THE 4TH COMPANY LAW DIRECTIVE IN THE 12 MEMBER COUNTRIES OF THE EUROPEAN COMMUNITY [LA ADAPTACION DEL DERECHO DE SOCIEDADES A LA IV DIRECTIVA DE LA COMUNIDAD
CHEH, JONGWOOK	INCENTIVE EFFECTS OF INTER-AGENT MONITORING: IMPLICATIONS FOR RESPONSIBILITY ACCOUNTING AND AUDITOR-CONSULTANT INTERACTION
CHEN, KUO-TAY	SCHEMATIC EVALUATION OF INTERNAL ACCOUNTING CONTROL SYSTEMS
CHI, SUNG-KUON	ETHICS AND AGENCY THEORY

CHILTON, ROBERT CARTER	THE AMERICAN ACCOUNTING PROFESSION AND ITS CODE OF ETHICS: 1887-1933
CHIU, CHUI-YU	ARTIFICIAL INTELLIGENCE AND ITS APPLICATIONS TO CAPITAL BUDGETING DECISIONS UNDER UNCERTAINTY
CHOI, JONG UK	A CONSTRUCTIVE APPROACH TO BUILDING A KNOWLEDGE-BASED INTERNAL CONTROL EVALUATION REVIEW SYSTEM
CHOI, NAHNHEE J.	THE MANAGER-AUDITOR GAME REVISITED: ON THE EFFECT OF INCOMPLETE INFORMATION, THE DUE CARE LEVEL, AND THE MATERIALITY LEVEL IMPOSED BY THE STANDARD-SETTING BOARDS
CHUNG, KI-YOUNG	AN ESSAY ON THE INTERTEMPORAL GENERAL EQUILIBRIUM MODEL OF EXCHANGE RATES IN A CONTINUOUS-TIME VERSION
CHUNG, MOON-CHONG	AN INVESTMENT CENTER VS. A PROFIT CENTER: CAPITAL INVESTMENT UNDER INFORMATIONAL ASYMMETRY
COATE, CHARLES JOSEPH	A TWO PERIOD BIDDING MODEL OF THE AUDIT MARKET
DATAR, SRIKANT MADHAV	THE EFFECTS OF AUDITOR REPUTATION IN MORAL HAZARD AND ADVERSE SELECTION SETTINGS
DAY, MARY MARLENE	CRITICAL ACCOUNTING PEDAGOGY IN PRACTICE: (RE)CONSTRUCTIONS OF 'A TRUE AND FAIR VIEW'
DE MELLO-E-SOUZA, CARLOS ALBERTO	OPTIMAL CONTRACTING BETWEEN AGENTS WITH DIFFERENT PLANNING HORIZONS IN THE PRESENCE OF INFORMATION ASYMMETRIES
DEBRUINE, MARINUS	AN AGENCY-THEORETIC ANALYSIS OF THE EXTERNAL AUDITOR'S USE OF THE INTERNAL AUDITOR IN CONDUCTING THE FINANCIAL AUDIT
DENNA, ERIC LEROY	TOWARD A REPRESENTATION OF AUDITOR KNOWLEDGE: EVIDENCE AGGREGATION AND EVALUATION
DENNIS, PAMELA ERICKSON	THE EFFECTS OF BANNING DIRECT UNINVITED SOLICITATION ON PRICING, BIDDING, SEARCH AND SWITCHING DECISIONS IN THE MARKET FOR AUDIT SERVICES
DEPREE, CHAUNCEY MARCELLOUS, JR.	TESTING THE CONCEPTUAL FRAMEWORK OF ACCOUNTING THROUGH AN APPLICATION OF A FORMAL STRUCTURE
DESHMUKH, ASHUTOSH VASANT	THE ROLE OF AUDIT TECHNOLOGY AND EXTENSION OF AUDIT PROCEDURES IN STRATEGIC AUDITING
DOOGAR, RAJIB KUMAR	THREE ANALYTICAL ESSAYS IN ACCOUNTING: INDUSTRY EQUILIBRIUM IN THE AUDIT MARKET AND PROCESS LEARNING IN AGENCIES
DUTTA, SAURAV KUMAR	EVIDENCE AGGREGATION FOR PLANNING AND EVALUATION OF AUDIT: A THEORETICAL STUDY
ETZIONI, RUTH	BAYESIAN GROUP SEQUENTIAL SAMPLING WITH APPLICATION TO TAX AUDITING
FLINN, RONALD EARL	AN INVESTIGATION OF PROPOSED CHANGES IN THE FEDERAL INCOME TAXATION OF ACQUISITIVE REORGANIZATIONS
GALANTINE, CAROLYN ANN	PRINCIPAL-AGENT THEORY WITH APPLICATIONS TO THE THREE-PARTY PROBLEM BETWEEN TAXPAYERS, EXAMINERS AND THE GOVERNMENT

GIGLER, FRANK BARRY	SELF-ENFORCING VOLUNTARY DISCLOSURES
GLOVER, JONATHAN CHARLES	IMPLEMENTATION USING SIMPLE MECHANISMS: SOME THEORETICAL RESULTS AND APPLICATIONS TO ACCOUNTING
GOVINDARAJ, SURESH	ESSAYS ON FINANCIAL MARKETS WITH APPLICATIONS TO ACCOUNTING
GREENWOOD, THOMAS G.	AN ACTIVITY-BASED CONCEPTUAL MODEL FOR EVALUATING PROCESS COST INFORMATION
GURKA, GEOFFREY J.	THE ROLE OF NEUTRALIZATION STRATEGIES IN THE TRADEOFF BETWEEN PRACTITIONER RESPONSIBILITIES
HAM, CHANGYONG	ESSAYS ON VALUE OF INFORMATION, COMMUNICATION, AND DELEGATION IN PRINCIPAL AND AGENT RELATIONSHIPS
HAN, KYEONG SEOK	A FORMAL ALGORITHMIC MODEL COMPATIBLE WITH ACCOUNTING INFORMATION SYSTEMS
HAN, MAN-HO	A KNOWLEDGE-BASED DECISION SUPPORT SYSTEM (KBDSS) FOR CORPORATE PORTFOLIO ANALYSIS: AN INTEGRATIVE MODEL APPROACH
HARPER, RICHARD ROBERT	AN ETHNOGRAPHIC EXAMINATION OF ACCOUNTANCY
HARSTON, MARY ELIZABETH	A COMPARISON OF THE EVOLUTION OF ACCOUNTING INSTITUTIONS IN GERMANY AND THE UNITED STATES
HASLAM, JIM	ON THE PRESCRIBING OF ACCOUNTING AND ACCOUNTING PUBLICITY BY THE STATE IN EARLY TO MID-NINETEENTH CENTURY BRITAIN: ACCOUNTING HISTORY AS CRITIQUE
HEFZI, HASSAN	ECONOMIC INCENTIVES OF MANAGEMENT FOR INSUBSTANCE DEFEASANCE OF DEBT: AN EMPIRICAL INVESTIGATION
HILLEBRAND, ANDREAS WILHELM	A CONCEPT FOR A PERSONAL-COMPUTER-AIDED FINANCIAL STATEMENT ANALYSIS WITH REGARD TO THE GERMAN ACCOUNTING DIRECTIVES LAW [ENTWICKLUNG EINES KONZEPTS ZUR PERSONAL-COMPUTER-GESTUETZTEN ANALYSE PUBLIZIERTER
HONG, CHANGMOK	AUDITORS' LEGAL LIABILITY AND REPUTATION: A GAME-THEORETIC ANALYSIS OF THE DEMAND FOR AUDITING IN AN ADVERSE SELECTION SETTING
HONG, YONG-SIK	A GAME-THEORETIC ANALYSIS OF TRANSFER PRICE NEGOTIATION UNDER INCOMPLETE INFORMATION CONDITIONS
HOSKINS, MARGARET ANN	THE MURPHY MODELS FOR ACCOUNTING: A TEST OF RELEVANCE
INDJEJIKIAN, RAFFI J.	THE IMPACT OF INFORMATION ON THE EXTENT OF AGREEMENT AMONG INVESTORS: A NEW PERSPECTIVE ON FIRM DISCLOSURES
JOHN, TERESA ANNE	CORPORATE MERGERS, INVESTMENT INCENTIVES AND FIRM VALUE: AN AGENCY THEORETIC ANALYSIS
JOO, HYUNGHWAN	INCOME SMOOTHING: AN ASYMMETRIC INFORMATION APPROACH
JUNG, WOON-OH	ACCOUNTING DECISIONS UNDER ASYMMETRIC INFORMATION

Listing by Research Method   335

KAYE, GERALDINE DELLA	EXPENSES OF UNITED KINGDOM LIFE INSURERS WITH SPECIAL REFERENCE TO 1980-1986 DATA PROVIDED BY THE ASSOCIATION OF BRITISH INSURERS
KIANG, YIHWA	EXPLORATION OF QUALITATIVE REASONING AND ITS APPLICATIONS TO MANAGEMENT
KILANI, KILANI ABDULKERIM	THE EVOLUTION AND STATUS OF ACCOUNTING IN LIBYA. (VOLUMES I AND II)
KILLINGSWORTH, BRENDA LOU	THE DESIGN OF A KNOWLEDGE-BASED DECISION SUPPORT SYSTEM ENHANCING AUDIT PROGRAM PLANNING
KIM, GYUTAI	AN ECONOMIC ANALYSIS OF AN ADVANCED MANUFACTURING SYSTEM WITH ACTIVITY-BASED COSTING SYSTEMS
KIM, TONG HUN	THE VALUE OF COMMUNICATION IN A MULTIPLE AGENT FRAMEWORK
KO, WANSUK MATTHEW	AUDITOR'S INCENTIVE, LEGAL LIABILITY AND REPUTATION UNDER INFORMATION ASYMMETRY
KOFMAN, ALFREDO MARCOS	COLLUSION, REPUTATION AND COMMUNICATION: THREE ESSAYS IN ECONOMIC THEORY
KROPP, KARL V.	ASYMPTOTICS OF A FREE BOUNDARY PROBLEM RESULTING FROM THE DETERMINATION OF AN AMORTIZING LOAN'S REFINANCE OPTION
KURTENBACH, JAMES MATTHEW	ENTITY RELATIONSHIPS: MARKET IMPACT AND MANAGEMENT INCENTIVES
LA GRANGE, JOHANNES FREDERICK	RESPONSIBILITY ACCOUNTING WITH THE RESTRUCTURING OF CERTAIN INSTITUTIONS
LADNER, ROBERT	BALANCE SHEET ANALYSIS: OLD LEGAL SITUATION [BILANZANALYSE NACH NEUEM RECHT]
LEE, EUNSANG	TAX TREATMENT UNCERTAINTY AND THE IRS INDIVIDUAL RULINGS PROGRAM--A COMPREHENSIVE ANALYSIS
LEE, HYUN-SOO	AUTOMATED INTERACTIVE COST ESTIMATING SYSTEM FOR REINFORCED CONCRETE BUILDING STRUCTURES
LEE, JONG-CHEON	OPTIMAL CONTRACTING WITH PREDECISION INFORMATION: COMMUNICATION PROBLEMS UNDER PURE ASYMMETRY OF INFORMATION
LEE, KYUNG TAE	OPTIMAL CONTROL SYSTEMS IN MANAGERIAL ACCOUNTING
LEE, SANGSOO	DECENTRALIZATION, INFORMATIONAL ASYMMETRY, AND THE VALUE OF COMMUNICATION AND DELEGATION
LEWIS, MERRILL TIM	EX ANTE EVALUATION OF AUDIT EVIDENCE
LI, SHU-HSING	TRANSFER PRICING UNDER INFORMATION ASYMMETRY IN MULTIAGENT SETTINGS
LIU, CHI-CHUN	TRADERS' MULTIPLE INFORMATION ACQUISITION AND ITS IMPACT ON MARKET BEHAVIOR: A RATIONAL EXPECTATIONS ANALYSIS

Listing by Research Method

MAKRIGEORGIS, CHRISTOS N.	DEVELOPMENT OF AN OPTIMAL DURABILITY-BASED HIGHWAY COST ALLOCATION MODEL
MCBETH, KEVIN H.	REDEFINING THE FEDERAL INCOME TAX BASE FOR INCREASED EQUITY, NEUTRALITY, AND SIMPLICITY
MCEACHARN, ELIZABETH MICHELLE	A FUZZY REASONING EXPERT SYSTEM FOR PLANNING-STAGE MATERIALITY JUDGEMENTS
MCGEE, ROBERT WILLIAM	A MODEL PROGRAM FOR SCHOOLS OF PROFESSIONAL ACCOUNTANCY
METH, BRACHA NAOMI	REDUCTION OF INCOME VARIANCE--OPTIMALITY AND INCENTIVES
MOHAMMED ABDULLA, MOHAMED ISMAIL	ADVANCED MEANS OF PREPARING THE PUBLIC BUDGET AND THEIR UTILISATION IN MODERNISING THE PUBLIC BUDGET IN THE UNITED ARAB EMIRATES. (VOLUMES I-III)
MUKHERJI, ARIJIT	COSTLY MONITORING IN A PRINCIPAL-AGENT MODEL
MULCAHY, LEIGH-ANN	ACCOUNTABLE TO WHOM? THE CHANGING ROLE OF THE CORPORATE AUDITOR
NEHMER, ROBERT ALAN	ACCOUNTING INFORMATION SYSTEMS AS ALGEBRAS AND FIRST ORDER AXIOMATIC MODELS
NEKRASZ, FRANK, JR.	A THEORETICAL INVESTIGATION OF MANADATORY AUDITOR REPORTS ON INTERNAL CONTROL STRUCTURES
NEWMAN, SCOTT GARDINER	A COMPREHENSIVE RANKING OF ESTATE FREEZING TRANSACTIONS
PAIK, TAE-YOUNG	THREE ESSAYS ON PARTICIPATIVE BUDGETING
PALOMINO BONILLA, LUIS MIGUEL	INFORMATIONAL ASYMMETRIES IN UNDERDEVELOPED SECURITIES MARKETS, OPTIMAL FINANCIAL CONTRACTS, AND REGULATION
PATTERSON, EVELYN RUTH	GAME THEORETIC APPLICATIONS TO AUDIT SAMPLING
PICHLER, ANTON	THE CONTROL OF PUBLIC BUILDINGS BY THE GENERAL ACCOUNTING OFFICE IN AUSTRIA [DIE KONTROLLE OEFFENTLICHER BAUTEN DURCH DEN RECHNUNGSHOF IN OESTERREICH]
POFF, J. KENT	AN ECONOMIC ANALYSIS OF UNIFORM CAPITALIZATION OF INVENTORY COSTS UNDER SECTION 263A OF THE INTERNAL REVENUE CODE OF 1986
RABASEDA I TARRES, JOAQUIM	THEORY AND TECHNIQUE OF CONSOLIDATION ACCOUNTING
RADHAKRISHNAN, SURESH	THE RELEVANCE OF COST APPLICATION IN A COMMON FACILITY
RAJAN, MADHAV VASANTH	PERFORMANCE EVALUATION AND CONTROL IN MULTI-AGENT SETTINGS
ROBINSON, CHRISTOPHER MICHAEL	AN EMPIRICAL INVESTIGATION OF ERROR CORRECTION DECISIONS MADE BY AUDITORS IN PRACTICE

ROCKWELL, STEPHEN RAYMOND   THE CONCEPTUAL MODELING AND AUTOMATED USE OF RECONSTRUCTIVE ACCOUNTING DOMAIN KNOWLEDGE

RONNEN, URI   ESSAYS IN AUDITING

RUDD, TORE FLEMMING   AUDITING AS VERIFICATION OF FINANCIAL INFORMATION

SANSING, RICHARD CHALLES   STRATEGIC AUDITING AND STRATEGIC INFORMATION TRANSMISSION IN REPUTATION GAMES

SARATH, BHARAT   AUDITING, LITIGATION, AND INSURANCE

SCHRAMM, ELFRIEDE   EFFECTS OF THE ACCOUNTING REFORM ON VALUATION OF BALANCE SHEET UNDER SPECIAL CONSIDERATION OF HIDDEN RESERVES [AUSWIRKUNGEN DER RECHNUNGSLEGUNGSREFORM AUF DIE BILANZBEWERTUNG UNTER BESONDERER

SCRIBNER, EDMUND ARTHUR   TOWARD AN ECONOMIC MODEL OF TAXPAYER-IRS INTERACTION

SEAL, W. B.   ACCOUNTING AND MANAGEMENT CONTROL IN THE THEORY OF THE FIRM

SEN, KAUSTAV   MECHANISM DESIGN IN AUDIT SETTINGS

SEN, PRADYOT K.   INCENTIVE SIGNALLING WITH IMPERFECT INFORMATION: ACCOUNTING DISCLOSURES AND CONTINGENT CONTRACTS

SERRETT, RANDALL KEITH   AN ANALYTICAL INVESTIGATION OF THE COOPERATIVE TAX ENTITY: PLANNING AND POLICY IMPLICATIONS

SHENG, WILLIAM W.   ESSAYS ON BEHAVIORAL AUDITING: A GAME-THEORETIC APPROACH

SHIBANO, TOSHIYUKI   AN EQUILIBRIUM MODEL OF ATTESTATION BY PUBLIC ACCOUNTANTS

SHIN, DONG-IK   DEVELOPMENT OF A COGNITIVE DIAGNOSIS SYSTEM FOR INTELLIGENT TUTORING: AN APPLICATION TO TRANSPORTATION PROBLEM-SOLVING

SHIN, DOUG YONG   WHY MANAGERS VOLUNTARILY RELEASE EARNINGS FORECASTS?: THE ROLE OF THE MANAGERIAL LABOR MARKET

SIVARAMAKRISHNAN, KONDURU   INFORMATION CONTENT OF EARNINGS COMPONENTS, REPORTING CHOICE AND LONG TERM CONTRACTS

SLOF, ERIC JOHN   ECONOMIC MODELS OF TRANSFER PRICING IN DECENTRALIZED FIRMS

SMITH, EUGENE F.   MONEY LAUNDERING: A STUDY IN THE CREATION OF LAW

SMITH, JOHN REED   THE ECONOMIC VALUE OF AUDITING UNDER A NEGLIGENCE LIABILITY RULE

SMITH, MARGARET C.   A MODEL OF THE OWNER/MANAGER/AUDITOR GAME: ON THE VALUE OF PEER REVIEW AND THE MATERIALITY STANDARD

Listing by Research Method   338

SRIDHARAN, SWAMINATHAN	MANAGERIAL REPORTING INCENTIVES AND INVESTMENT DECISIONS
STAHEL, ANDREAS	CONCEPT OF THE DECISION-SUPPORTING MANAGEMENT ACCOUNTING SYSTEM [GESTALTUNG DES ENTSCHEIDUNGSORIENTIERTEN BETRIEBLICHEN RECHNUNGSWESENS]
STEINBART, PAUL JOHN	THE CONSTRUCTION OF AN EXPERT SYSTEM TO MAKE MATERIALITY JUDGMENTS
SUH, CHUNG WOO	DISCLOSURE TIMING OF ACCOUNTING INFORMATION AND STOCK MARKET REACTION UNDER ASYMMETRIC INFORMATION
SUH, YOON SUCK	NONCONTROLLABLE COSTS AND OPTIMAL PERFORMANCE MEASUREMENT
SUNG, KYU YOUNG	VALUE AND OPTIMAL TIMING OF MANAGERIAL ACCOUNTING INFORMATION IN A MULTIPERIOD SETTING WITH LEARNING
SYKES, VICEOLA DELORIS	AN ANALYSIS OF THE TAX EFFECTS OF FOREIGN INVESTMENTS IN U.S. AGRICULTURAL LAND
THOMAS, PAULA BEVELS	PUSH DOWN ACCOUNTING: A CONCEPTUAL ANALYSIS OF ITS THEORETICAL IMPLICATIONS
THOMPSON, PETER MACLEOD	A TEMPORAL DATA MODEL BASED ON ACCOUNTING PRINCIPLES
VAYSMAN, IGOR	MODELS OF TRANSFER PRICING
VELA PASTOR, JUAN	THE ACCOUNTING SYSTEM RELATED TO DOCTRINE AND TECHNIQUE IN BUSINESS CONTROL
VERGHESE, THOMAS	A FORMALIZATION OF INTERNAL CONTROL EVALUATION
VILLADSEN, BENTE	COLLUSION: EFFECTS ON INTERNAL CONTROL
VOLK, GERRIT JURGEN	JAHRESABSCHLUSS UND INFORMATION: ZUR FORMALEN STRUKTUR DES JAHRESABSCHLUSSES EINER KAPITALGESELLSCHAFT
WEIDA, NANCY COUGHLIN	GAME-THEORETIC MODELS OF THE TRANSFER PRICING PROBLEM
WEYNS, GUY JOSEPH	ANALYTICAL ESSAYS ON THE ECONOMIC CONSEQUENCES OF FINANCIAL ACCOUNTING STANDARDS
WHITTEN, RUTH ANN	CONTRACTS, RISK AND INFORMATION ASYMMETRY
WILCZAK, MONIKA J.	CONTRIBUTIONS TO THE CAPITAL BUDGETING PROBLEM
WOODLOCK, PETER DAVID	AUDITING AS THE OWNER'S RESPONSE TO THE NEED FOR RELIABLE MANAGER REPORTING: A PROBLEM OF SUPPLY AND DEMAND OF AUDIT SERVICES IN THE PRESENCE OF HIDDEN AUDITOR ACTIONS
XIE, JIA-ZHENG (JAMES)	CONTRACT NEGOTIATION, INCOMPLETE CONTRACTING, AND ASYMMETRIC INFORMATION

YAHYAZADEH, MASOUD	THREE ESSAYS ON THE STRUCTURE OF AUDITING INDUSTRY, AUDITOR LIABILITY AND THE REGULATION OF AUDIT QUALITY
YANCEY, WILLIAM FREDERICK	A MODEL OF ASSET RESTRUCTURING ANNOUNCEMENTS
YEOM, SUNGSOO	THE ROLE OF TRANSFER PRICE FOR COORDINATION AND CONTROL WITHIN A FIRM
YOON, SUNG SIG	THE EFFECTS OF AUDITING ON MORAL HAZARD AND INFORMATION ASYMMETRIES
YOST, JEFFREY ALLAN	INTRAFIRM RESOURCE ALLOCATION AND TRANSFER PRICING UNDER ASYMMETRIC INFORMATION: A PRINCIPAL-AGENT ANALYSIS OF DECENTRALIZED DECISION-MAKING IN A MULTIDIVISION FIRM
ZEBUN, ABDULWAHAB HAIDER	LINKAGES BETWEEN MICROACCOUNTING AND MACROACCOUNTING: AN IRAQI CASE STUDY
ZIV, AMIR	INFORMATIONAL ISSUES IN ORGANIZATIONS

Archival - Primary

ABARBANELL, JEFFERY STEVEN	INFORMATION ACQUISITION BY FINANCIAL ANALYSTS IN RESPONSE TO SECURITY PRICE CHANGES
ABBOTT, HAROLD DON	A COMPARISON OF ECONOMIC PERFORMANCE OF INVESTOR-OWNED CHAIN HOSPITALS AND NOT-FOR-PROFIT CHAIN HOSPITALS
ABDELKARIM, NASER MOHAMMAD	AN EMPIRICAL EXAMINATION OF THE RELATIONSHIP BETWEEN ANNOUNCEMENT-PERIOD STOCK RETURNS AND THE POTENTIAL DILUTION EFFECT OF CONVERTIBLE BONDS ON EPS
ABDUL-RAHIM, HASSAN MAHMOOD	AN ANALYSIS OF CORPORATE ACCOUNTING AND REPORTING PRACTICES IN BAHRAIN
ABEKAH, JOSEPH YAW	USEFULNESS OF REQUIRED QUANTITATIVE DISCLOSURES UNDER FOREIGN CURRENCY TRANSLATION STANDARDS: AN EMPIRICAL EXAMINATION
ABRAHAM, REBECCA JACOB	COMPARISON OF COMPUTATIONAL METHODS AND INVESTIGATION OF THE TERM STRUCTURE OF INTEREST RATES IMPLIED IN OPTION PRICES
ADAMSON, STANLEY RAY	THE EFFECT OF ESOP IMPLEMENTATION ON THE VALUE OF LARGE PUBLICLY-HELD FIRMS
ADDY, NOEL DOUGLAS, JR.	INTEREST RATE EXPECTATIONS FOR PENSION PLANS: INCENTIVES FOR DIVERGENT ACTUARIAL ASSUMPTIONS BETWEEN DOL AND FASB DISCLOSURES
ADHIKARI, AJAY	AN EMPIRICAL CROSS-NATIONAL STUDY OF ENVIRONMENTAL FACTORS INFLUENCING ACCOUNTING DISCLOSURE AND REPORTING REQUIREMENTS OF STOCK EXCHANGES
ADIEL, RON	REINSURANCE AND THE MANAGEMENT OF EARNINGS IN THE PROPERTY-CASUALTY INSURANCE INDUSTRY
AHMED, ANWER SHEHAB	ACCOUNTING EARNINGS, ECONOMIC RENTS AND STOCK RETURNS: AN EMPIRICAL ANALYSIS
AHN, BYUNGJUN	THE INFORMATION CONTENT OF EARNINGS ANNOUNCEMENTS WITH VARYING RETURN PARAMETERS
AHN, TAE SIK	EFFICIENCY AND RELATED ISSUES IN HIGHER EDUCATION: A DATA ENVELOPMENT ANALYSIS APPROACH

Listing by Research Method   340

AINSWORTH, PENNE LYN	THE INFORMATION CONTENT OF CASH FLOW DATA: AN EMPIRICAL INVESTIGATION
AKATHAPORN, PARPORN	INVENTORY METHODS AND THE PRICE EARNINGS ANOMALY: AN EMPIRICAL EXAMINATION
AKSU, CELAL	AN EMPIRICAL INVESTIGATION OF TIME SERIES PROPERTIES OF QUARTERLY CASH FLOWS AND USEFULNESS OF EARNINGS IN PREDICTING CASH FLOWS
AKSU, MINE HATICE	MARKET RESPONSE TO TROUBLED DEBT RESTRUCTURING
AL-DARAYSEH, MUSA M.	CORPORATE FAILURE FOR MANUFACTURING INDUSTRIES USING FINANCIAL RATIOS AND MACROECONOMIC VARIABLES WITH LOGIT ANALYSIS
AL-SUDAIRY, SALMAN ABDULRAHMAN	THE DETECTION AND DETECTABILITY OF MATERIAL MISSTATEMENTS IN INTERIM FINANCIAL REPORTS BY CAPITAL MARKET PARTICIPANTS
ALBRECHT, WILLIAM DAVID	THE DETERMINANTS OF THE MARKET REACTION TO AN ANNOUNCEMENT OF A CHANGE IN AUDITOR
ALCIATORE, MIMI LOUISE	THE INFORMATION CONTENT OF THE COMPONENTS OF THE CHANGE IN THE STANDARDIZED MEASURE
ALDIAB, TAISIER FARES	THE IMPACT OF THE CEILING TEST WRITE-OFF ON THE SECURITY RETURNS OF FULL COST OIL AND GAS FIRMS
ALEXANDER, JOHN C., JR.	EARNINGS EXPECTATIONS AND THE MARKET REACTION TO EARNINGS SURPRISE
ALI, ASHIQ	PENSION ASSETS AND THE MARKET RISK OF EQUITY
ALKHALIALEH, MAHMOUD ABDUL-HALEEM	NON-EARNINGS INFORMATION AND ANALYSTS' REVISIONS OF FUTURE EARNINGS FORECASTS
ALLEN, ARTHUR CONRAD, JR.	EFFECTS OF LOCAL GOVERNMENT AUDIT QUALITY ON THE RELIABILITY OF ACCOUNTING NUMBERS AND INVESTOR DECISIONS
ALLEN, FRAN MARIE	ENVIRONMENTAL RESPONSIBILITY, STAKEHOLDER THEORY AND THE VALUE OF THE FIRM
ALLEN, ROBERT DREW	STATISTICAL ANALYTICAL PROCEDURES USING INDUSTRY SPECIFIC INFORMATION: AN EMPIRICAL STUDY
ALLTIZER, RICHARD LEE	THE INTERACTION OF DIVIDEND POLICY AND TAXATION ON THE VALUE OF THE FIRM
ALY, IBRAHIM M. MOHAMED	PREDICTION OF BUSINESS FAILURE AS A CRITERION FOR EVALUATING THE USEFULNESS OF ALTERNATIVE ACCOUNTING MEASURES
AMIR, ELI	ASSESSING ALTERNATIVE ACCOUNTING METHODS FOR POST-RETIREMENT BENEFITS OTHER THAN PENSIONS
AMOBI, EMMANUEL NNABUIKE	THE DEVELOPMENT AND EMPIRICAL VERIFICATION OF A PREDICTIVE MODEL FOR ACCOUNTING STANDARD LOBBYING BEHAVIOR OF OIL AND GAS FIRMS
ANDERSON, ELLEN G.	AGENCY THEORY AND CORPORATE ACQUISTIONS: EMPIRICAL TEST FOR A CERTAIN CLASS OF CORPORATE TAKEOVERS

ANDERSON, MARILYN TERESA	ACCOUNTING EARNINGS ANNOUNCEMENTS AND DIFFERENTIAL PREDISCLOSURE INFORMATION
ANDERSON, PHILIP NEIL	AN EMPIRICAL STUDY OF RECENT CHANGES IN FEDERAL ESTATE TAXATION AND THEIR RELATED IMPACT ON THE FAMILY FARM
ANGIMA, JACOB M.	THE ASSOCIATION BETWEEN ALTERNATIVE EARNINGS AND PROFITABILITY MEASURES AND STOCK RETURN IN SELECTED INDUSTRIES
ANGRISANI, DAVID PETER	AN ACQUISITION MODEL FOR THE HOSPITAL INDUSTRY
ARCHAMBAULT, JEFFREY JAY	FINANCING AND INVESTING ACTIVITIES AND THE PREEMPTION OF EARNINGS
ARCHAMBAULT, MARIE ELLEN EMMENDORFER	REACTION TO EARNINGS IN A TAKEOVER ENVIRONMENT
ARNESON, DEAN LEON	IMPACT OF MEDICAID DISCOUNTED AVERAGE WHOLESALE PRICE REIMBURSEMENT ON PHARMACISTS' DRUG PRODUCT SELECTION
ASKREN, BARBARA J.	MARKET VALUATION OF POSTEMPLOYMENT BENEFITS OTHER THAN PENSIONS
BAE, GIL SOO	FURTHER INVESTIGATION OF POSTANNOUNCEMENT DRIFTS ASSOCIATED WITH EARNINGS, CASH FLOWS, AND ACCRUAL ADJUSTMENTS
BAGINSKI, STEPHEN PAUL	INTRA-INDUSTRY INFORMATION TRANSFERS ASSOCIATED WITH MANAGEMENT EARNINGS FORECASTS
BAHNSON, PAUL RICHARD	AN ASSESSMENT OF THE CONTRIBUTION OF CASH FLOW AND THE OPERATING CASH FLOW COMPONENT IN CLASSIFYING FAILED COMPANIES
BALDWIN, JANE NORA	BANKRUPTCY PREDICTION USING QUARTERLY FINANCIAL STATEMENT DATA
BALSAM, STEVEN	EXECUTIVE COMPENSATION PACKAGES: A TOOL FOR RESOLVING THE OWNER-MANAGER CONFLICT
BANDYOPADHYAY, SATIPRASAD	THE RELATIVE INFORMATIVENESS OF SUCCESSFUL EFFORTS AND FULL COST EARNINGS IN THE OIL AND GAS INDUSTRY
BANERJEE, AJEYO	MANAGERIAL COMPENSATION AND SHAREHOLDER WEALTH CONSEQUENCES OF 'WHITE KNIGHT' BEHAVIOR
BANNISTER, JAMES W.	EARNINGS SIGNALS AND INTER-FIRM INFORMATION TRANSFERS
BARIL, CHARLES PURDOM	LONG-TERM INCENTIVE COMPENSATION PLAN ADOPTION AND THE CAPITAL SPENDING DECISIONS OF MANAGERS
BARNEY, DOUGLAS KEVIN	MODELING FARM DEBT FAILURE: THE FARMERS HOME ADMINISTRATION
BARRETT, KEVIN STANTON	CHARITABLE GIVING AND FEDERAL INCOME TAX POLICY: ADDITIONAL EVIDENCE BASED ON PANEL-DATA ELASTICITY ESTIMATES
BARRON, ORIE EDWIN	COSTLY TRADING: THE RELATION BETWEEN DISAGREEMENT (OR INFORMATION ASYMMETRIES) AND TRADING IN A WORLD WITH TRADING COSTS

Listing by Research Method

BARTH, MARY E.	ASSESSING FINANCIAL ACCOUNTING MEASUREMENT ALTERNATIVES FOR ASSETS AND LIABILITIES
BARTON, THOMAS MICHAEL	ON THE PREDICTION OF MERGERS AND BANKRUPTCIES WITH RATIOS FROM THE STATEMENT OF CHANGES IN FINANCIAL POSITION AND DIFFERENT FUNDS FLOW MEASURES
BARTOV, ELIAHU	CHANGES IN FIRM FINANCIAL POLICY AS SIGNALS FOR FUTURE EARNINGS: AN EMPIRICAL INVESTIGATION OF UNSYSTEMATIC STOCK REPURCHASES
BASU, SOMNATH	INFORMATION, EXPECTATIONS AND EQUILIBRIUM: TRADING VOLUME HYPOTHESES
BATTISTEL, GEORGE PETER	AN EMPIRICAL ANALYSIS OF THE STOCK MARKET REACTION TO BONUS PLAN ADOPTIONS
BEARD, DEBORAH F.	THE IMPACT OF STATEMENT OF FINANCIAL ACCOUNTING STANDARDS NO. 13 ON SYSTEMATIC RISK AND ACCOUNTING VARIABLES
BECKMAN, JUDY KAY	PREDICTING THE LEVEL OF MINORITY INTEREST FOLLOWING A TENDER OFFER
BEEHLER, JOHN MICHAEL	AN EMPIRICAL EXAMINATION OF THE EFFECT OF THE SECTION 465 AT-RISK RULES ON EQUIPMENT LEASING TAX SHELTERS
BEGLEY, JOY	THE USE OF DEBT CONVENANTS TO CONTROL AGENCY PROBLEMS
BENARTZI, SHLOMO	WITHIN-SEGMENT DIVERSITY AND THE INFORMATION CONTENT OF LINE-OF-BUSINESS REPORTING: EVIDENCE THAT STOCK PRICES DO NOT FULLY REFLECT THE IMPLICATIONS OF DIVIDEND CHANGES FOR SUBSEQUENT EARNINGS
BERG, GARY GENE	EARLY VERSUS LATE COMPLIANCE TO SFAS 52: AN EMPIRICAL INVESTIGATION OF FIRM CHARACTERISTICS AND THE MARKET RESPONSE
BERGEVIN, PETER MICHAEL	EQUITY VALUATION OF PETROLEUM EXPLORATION AND PRODUCTION FIRMS USING ALTERNATIVE ACCOUNTING METHODS
BETTIS, J. C. CARR	REVISITING THE PROFITABILITY OF INSIDER AND OUTSIDER TRADING
BETTS, NORMAN MURRAY	AN EMPIRICAL EXAMINATION OF THE REPORTING PRACTICES AND DIFFERENTIAL INFORMATION CONTENT OF EARNINGS COMPONENTS
BILODEAU, JULIEN	THE USE OF ACCOUNTING NUMBERS IN DEBT AND PREFERRED SHARE COVENANTS: SOME CANADIAN EVIDENCE
BLACCONIERE, WALTER GEORGE	ACCOUNTING REGULATIONS IN THE SAVINGS AND LOAN INDUSTRY: EVIDENCE OF MARKET REACTIONS AND IMPLICATIONS OF CONTRACTING THEORY
BLANKLEY, ALAN IRVING	INCENTIVES IN PENSION ACCOUNTING: AN EMPIRICAL INVESTIGATION OF REPORTED RATE ESTIMATES
BORDEN, JAMES PATRICK	AN ASSESSMENT OF THE IMPACT OF DIAGNOSIS RELATED GROUP (DRG)-BASED REIMBURSEMENT ON THE TECHNICAL EFFICIENCY OF NEW JERSEY HOSPITALS
BOYAS, ELISE A.	IDENTIFICATION AND EXAMINATION OF FACTORS BEHIND CORPORATE IN-SUBSTANCE DEFEASANCE OF DEBT
BOYER, BENOI T NOEL	THE IMPACT OF FINANCIAL ACCOUNTING STANDARDS BOARD STATEMENTS NUMBERS 8 AND 52 ON MULTINATIONAL CORPORATIONS

Listing by Research Method 343

BRACKNEY, KENNARD SAMUEL, JR.	EARNINGS ANNOUNCEMENT TIMELINESS AND INVESTOR WEALTH
BRADLEY, LINDA JACOBSEN	THE IMPACT OF THE 1986 AND 1987 QUALIFIED PLAN REGULATION ON FIRMS' DECISION TO SWITCH FROM DEFINED BENEFIT TO DEFINED CONTRIBUTION FOR PLANS LARGER THAN 100 PARTICIPANTS
BRAMBLE, HULDAH ALETHA	THE USE OF ACCOUNTING RATIOS AS MEASURES OF RISK IN THE DETERMINATION OF THE BID-ASK SPREAD
BRANSON, BRUCE CLAYTON	AN EMPIRICAL EXAMINATION OF FIRM-SPECIFIC CHARACTERISTICS ASSOCIATED WITH DIFFERENTIAL INFORMATION ENVIRONMENTS
BRAZELTON, JULIA K.	TAX SIMPLIFICATION: THE IMPLICATIONS OF A CONSUMPTION TAX BASE ON THE INDIVIDUAL TAXPAYER
BROCK, GLENDA CONERLY	AN EMPIRICAL RESEARCH STUDY OF THE IMPACT UPON SMALL BUSINESS OF THE CHANGE IN THE INVESTMENT TAX CREDIT DICTATED BY THE TAX REFORM ACT OF 1986
BROMAN, AMY J.	THE IMPACT OF FEDERAL INCOME TAX POLICY ON THE CHARITABLE CONTRIBUTIONS BEHAVIOR OF HOUSEHOLDS
BROOKS, RAYMOND MICHAEL	AN IMPLIED CASH DIVIDEND AND TRADING PATTERNS: VOLUME, SPREADS, SPREAD COMPONENTS AND ASYMMETRIC INFORMATION AROUND DIVIDEND AND EARNINGS ANNOUNCEMENTS
BROOKS, RICHARD C.	AN INVESTIGATION OF THE DETERMINANTS OF THE MUNICIPAL DECISION TO PRIVATIZE RESIDENTIAL SANITATION COLLECTION
BROWN, BETTY COFFEE	AN EMPIRICAL INVESTIGATION INTO DIFFERENCES BETWEEN COMPANIES THAT ELECTED AN EARLY COMPLIANCE WITH SFAS 52 AND COMPANIES NOT ELECTING AN EARLY COMPLIANCE
BROWN, SARAH	AN INVESTIGATION INTO THE ASSOCIATION BETWEEN AUDIT FAILURES AND THE PRESENCE OR ABSENCE OF A CORPORATE AUDIT COMMITTEE
BRUMETT, CLIFFORD	INVENTORY ADJUSTMENT AND ADVERSE INFORMATION MOTIVES IN SECURITY DEALER PRICING DECISIONS
BRYAN, BARRY JEROME	AN EMPIRICAL INVESTIGATION OF THE DETERMINANTS OF REPORTING QUALITY AND THE EFFECTIVENESS OF THE QUALITY REVIEW PROGRAM FOR SMALL ACCOUNTING FIRMS
BRYAN, STEPHEN HART	MANAGEMENT DISCUSSION AND ANALYSIS: FIRM COMPLIANCE AND INFORMATION CONTENT
BRYANT, JEFFREY JACK	THE EFFECTS OF LOCAL TAXES ON ECONOMIC BEHAVIOR IN THE HOUSING MARKET
BUCKHOLD, J. W.	ANALYSIS OF INDIVIDUAL TAXPAYER USE OF SELECTED TAX PREFERENCES--EMPIRICAL EVIDENCE
BUKOVINSKY, DAVID MARTIN	CASH FLOW AND CASH POSITION MEASURES IN THE PREDICTION OF BUSINESS FAILURE: AN EMPIRICAL STUDY
BUKOWY, STEPHEN JOSEPH	AN EMPIRICAL ANALYSIS OF THE USEFULNESS OF ACCOUNTING INFORMATION IN PREDICTING CLOSURES OF SMALL AND MEDIUM-SIZED HOSPITALS
BURCKEL, DARYL VINCENT	AN EMPIRICAL INVESTIGATION INTO DEVELOPING A FAILURE PREDICTION MODEL FOR FARMING ENTERPRISES: THE FIFTH FARM CREDIT DISTRICT
BURILOVICH, LINDA JEAN SKANTZ	GAAP ELASTICITIES IN THE LIFE INSURANCE INDUSTRY: THE EFFECT OF TAX LAW CHANGES ON THE ACCOUNTING BEHAVIOR OF MUTUAL AND STOCK LIFE INSURANCE COMPANIES

Listing by Research Method

BURKS, EDDY J.	STATEMENT OF FINANCIAL ACCOUNTING STANDARDS NO. 87 AND MARKET RISK ADJUSTMENT
BUTTARS, THOMAS ALAN	A DISAGGREGATE APPROACH TO ACCOUNTING BASED MEASURES OF SYSTEMATIC RISK
BYINGTON, JAMES RALPH	ANALYSIS OF TIME SERIES PROPERTIES OF EARNINGS: COMPARISONS OF INDUSTRY MODELS AND BIVARIATE ANALYSIS FOR MODEL IMPROVEMENT
CAHAN, STEVEN F.	LEGISLATIVE ACTION, POLITICAL COSTS, AND FIRM ACCOUNTING CHOICE
CALLAGHAN, JOSEPH HENRY	THE NATURE OF DEFERRED INCOME TAXES ARISING FROM DIFFERENCES IN DEPRECIATION METHODS
CALLAHAN, CAROLYN MARGARET	A THEORETICAL AND EMPIRICAL EXAMINATION OF THE DETERMINANTS OF SYSTEMATIC RISK
CALLIHAN, DEBRA SALBADOR	AN ANALYSIS OF THE RELATION BETWEEN IMPLICIT TAXES AND MARKET CONCENTRATION
CAMPBELL, ALAN DALE	AN ANALYSIS OF SMOOTHING OF PROVED OIL AND GAS RESERVE QUANTITIES AND AN ANALYSIS OF BIAS AND VARIABILITY IN REVISIONS OF PREVIOUS ESTIMATES OF PROVED OIL AND GAS RESERVE QUANTITIES
CAMPBELL, RONALD LOUIS	A CROSS-SECTIONAL AND TIME-SERIES INVESTIGATION OF MANAGERIAL DISCRETION REGARDING METHODS, RATES, PERIODS, AND DISCLOSURE: THE CASE OF EMPLOYERS' ACCOUNTING FOR PENSIONS
CAMPBELL, STEVEN VINCENT	THE SIGNIFICANCE OF DIRECT BANKRUPTCY COSTS IN DETERMINING THE OUTCOME OF BANKRUPTCY REORGANIZATION
CARAYANNOPOULOS, PETER	THE IMPACT OF STOCHASTIC INTEREST RATES ON THE PRICING OF CONVERTIBLE BONDS
CARCELLO, JOSEPH VINCENT	A COMPARATIVE STUDY OF AUDIT QUALITY AMONG THE BIG EIGHT ACCOUNTING FIRMS
CARDWELL, PAUL HERMAN, JR.	THE EFFECT OF TAX REFORM ON THE EX ANTE VARIANCE OF SECURITY PRICES
CARGILL, WILLIE NEWTON	AN EQUITY RETENTION APPROACH TO ACCOUNTING FOR CHANGING PRICES
CARLSON, STEVEN JAMES	AN EXAMINATION OF THE EFFECT OF A GOING CONCERN AUDIT REPORT ON SECURITY RETURNS AND TRADING VOLUME WHILE CONTROLLING FOR THE CONCURRENT RELEASE OF FINANCIAL STATEMENT INFORMATION
CARMENT, THOMAS MAXWELL	THE MARKET EFFECT OF IN-SUBSTANCE DEFEASANCE ON BONDHOLDER DEFAULT RISK
CARNES, GREGORY ALVIN	AN EMPIRICAL INVESTIGATION OF THE RELATIONSHIP BETWEEN TAX INCENTIVES AND FINANCIAL REPORTING POLICY
CARROLL, THOMAS JOSEPH	THE NATURE OF THE DIVIDEND SIGNAL OF FUTURE EARNINGS
CARTER, BEN DOUGLAS	AN EMPIRICAL INVESTIGATION INTO THE PREDICTABILITY OF CHANGES IN CASH FLOW FROM OPERATIONS UNDER ALTERNATIVE METHODS OF ACCOUNTING FOR INCOME TAXES
CASLAN, DAVID FREDERICK	AN EXAMINATION OF THE DETERMINANTS OF DISCRETIONARY ACCOUNTING CHOICE BY MANAGEMENT

CASSILL, ARTHUR D.	AN EMPIRICAL ANALYSIS OF THE INFLUENCE OF SELECTED POLITICAL PROCESS VARIABLES UPON INDUSTRY INCOME TAX BURDENS
CASTER, ARTHUR BRUCE	AN EMPIRICAL INVESTIGATION OF THE USEFULNESS OF FINANCIAL REPORTING INFORMATION IN PREDICTING FUTURE CASH FLOWS
CATANACH, ANTHONY HENRY, JR.	A CAUSAL INVESTIGATION OF RISK, CASH FLOW, AND SOLVENCY IN THE SAVINGS AND LOAN INDUSTRY
CAVANAGH, WALTER FORBES	THE ECONOMIC EFFECTS OF DEFINED BENEFIT PENSION FUNDING POLICY ON THE VALUE OF THE FIRM
CERF, DOUGLAS CLIFFORD	A STUDY OF INTERTEMPORAL VARIATION IN EARNINGS RESPONSE COEFFICIENTS: THE CASE OF THE MANDATED CHANGE IN ACCOUNTING RULES TO SFAS #87 ON PENSIONS
CHAN, KAM CHU	A REEXAMINATION OF THE STOCK MARKET AND BOND MARKET REACTION TO LIFO ADOPTION
CHANDRA, UDAY	THE ASSOCIATION BETWEEN PREDISCLOSURE INDUSTRY INFORMATION AND THE INFORMATION CONTENT OF EARNINGS ANNOUNCEMENTS
CHANG, CHUN SHYONG	THE INFORMATION CONTENT OF TAIWANESE FINANCIAL STATEMENTS: THE CASE OF LOAN DEFAULT
CHANG, CHUNG-YUEH C.	AN EXAMINATION OF TIME-VARYING EARNINGS GROWTH AND EARNINGS LEVELS AND THEIR IMPACTS ON SECURITY RETURNS
CHANG, HSI-HUI	LINEARITY AND SEPARABILITY ASSUMPTIONS IN COST ACCOUNTING
CHARITOU, ANDREAS G.	THE INFORMATION CONTENT OF ACCRUAL AND CASH FLOW MEASURES: A CROSS-SECTIONAL VALUATION STUDY
CHAWLA, GURDEEP KUMAR	UNITED STATES GAAP VERSUS EUROPEAN COMMUNITY AND PACIFIC RIM COUNTRIES' ACCOUNTING STANDARDS: AN EMPIRICAL STUDY
CHEN, DAVID MING-DAU	THE INFORMATION CONTENT OF QUARTERLY EARNINGS DATA AND THE MARKET'S REVISION OF RISK PREDICTIONS IMPLIED IN OPTION PRICES
CHEN, KEVIN CHIEN-WEN	THE DETERMINANTS OF TOBIN'S Q RATIO AND AN EVALUATION OF SFAS 33 DATA
CHEN, RING DING	BUDGET-BASED CONTRACTS AND TOP-LEVEL EXECUTIVE COMPENSATION: AN EMPIRICAL EVALUATION
CHEN, SHIMIN	AN EMPIRICAL INVESTIGATION OF THE USE OF PAYBACK METHOD IN CAPITAL BUDGETING: EFFICIENT VIEW VS OPPORTUNISTIC VIEW
CHEN, YUANG-SUNG AL	FINANCIAL ANALYST FORECAST DISPERSION: DETERMINANTS AND USEFULNESS AS AN EXANTE MEASURE OF RISK
CHENG, PAYYU	THE INCREMENTAL INFORMATION CONTENT OF FUND FLOW STATEMENTS: A QUARTERLY APPROACH
CHEONG, INBUM	AN ANALYSIS OF SOLVENCY REGULATION AND FAILURE PREDICTION IN THE UNITED STATES LIFE INSURANCE INDUSTRY
CHI, CHARLES CHI-WEI	THE INFORMATION CONTENT AND HEDGING PERFORMANCE OF FOREIGN CURRENCY TRANSLATIONS: AN EVALUATION OF SFAS NO. 8 VS NO 52

CHIEN, CHIN-CHEN — ALTERNATIVE METHODS FOR THE ESTIMATION OF EARNINGS AND DIVIDENDS ANNOUNCEMENT EFFECTS: REVIEW, INTEGRATION, AND EXTENSION

CHIPALKATTI, NIRANJAN H. — ADVERSE SELECTION COSTS AND THE DEALERS' BID-ASK SPREAD AROUND EARNINGS ANNOUNCEMENTS: DIFFERENTIAL INFORMATION AND SIGNAL QUALITY

CHO, JANG YOUN — TIMELINESS OF EARNINGS REPORTS: A SIGNALLING APPROACH

CHOE, YONG SUN — THE EFFECT OF A TAX DEDUCTION ON CHARITABLE CONTRIBUTIONS BY LOW- AND MIDDLE-INCOME TAXPAYERS

CHOI, BYEONGHEE — MARKET VALUATION OF POSTRETIREMENT OBLIGATIONS: A TEST OF HOW DIFFERENCES IN RELIABILITY AFFECT THE VALUATION IMPLICATIONS

CHOI, JUNG HO — MANAGEMENT EARNINGS EXPECTATIONS, EARNINGS UNCERTAINTY, AND VOLUNTARY DISCLOSURE OF EARNINGS FORECASTS BY MANAGEMENT: AN EMPIRICAL EVALUATION OF CURRENT DISCLOSURE PRACTICES UNDER THE VOLUNTARY RULES

CHOI, KWAN — DETERMINANTS OF TIME SERIES PROPERTIES OF ANNUAL EARNINGS AND CASH FLOWS

CHOI, MUN SOO — THE EFFECT OF DISPERSION OF ANALYSTS' FORECASTS ON STOCK AND BOND PRICES

CHOI, SOONJAE — THE INFORMATION CONTENT OF ACCOUNTING NUMBERS: USING A BELIEF REVISION MEASURE OF STOCK PRICES

CHOI, SUNG KYU — DIFFERENTIAL INFORMATION CONTENT OF PUBLICLY ANNOUNCED EARNINGS: THEORETICAL AND EMPIRICAL ANALYSIS

CHOI, WON WOOK — FINANCIAL STATEMENT ANALYSIS: THE STUDY OF RETURN ON COMMON EQUITY AND INTANGIBLE ASSETS

CHOI, YEONG CHAN — EARLY ADOPTION OF SFAS NO. 87 AND THE DEFENSIVE ACTION HYPOTHESIS: A POSITIVE THEORY ANALYSIS

CHRISMAN, HEIDI HADLICH — THE EFFECTS OF THE MATURITY STRUCTURE OF NOMINAL CONTRACTS ON EQUITY RETURNS IN AN INFLATIONARY ENVIRONMENT

CHRISTENSEN, DAVID SCOTT — THE APPLICATION OF MATHEMATICAL PROGRAMMING TO THE PRODUCTIVITY INVESTMENT FUND PROGRAM: A CAPITAL RATIONING PROBLEM

CHRISTIAN, CHARLES WILLIAM — AN EMPIRICAL TEST OF THE EFFECTS OF INTERNAL REVENUE CODE SECTION 465 ON RISK-TAKING BY INVESTORS IN OIL AND GAS DRILLING PROGRAMS

CHU, LILUAN ERIC — MARKET-BASED ACCOUNTING RESEARCH: AN INTERNATIONAL COMPARISON AND NEW EVIDENCE

CHUNG, DENNIS Y. — THE INFORMATIONAL EFFECT OF MANAGEMENT'S DECISION TO LOBBY AGAINST PROPOSED ACCOUNTING STANDARDS

CHUNG, HAY YOUNG — EMPIRICAL INVESTIGATION INTO THE STOCK MARKET REACTIONS TO CORPORATE EARNINGS REPORTS

CHUNG, KEE-YOUNG — AN INVESTIGATION OF THE EFFECTS OF INFLATION-ADJUSTED ACCOUNTING DATA ON EQUITY VALUE

CHUNG, KUN YOUNG — FIRM SIZE, INDUSTRY ACCOUNTING NORMS, AND THE INFORMATION CONTENT OF ACCOUNTING CHANGE ANNOUNCEMENTS

CHUNG, KWANG-HYUN	CORPORATE LOBBYING AND MARKET REACTION TO PROPOSED ACCOUNTING RULES: THE CASE OF POSTRETIREMENT BENEFITS OTHER THAN PENSIONS
CHUNG, TSAI-YEN	MANAGEMENT MOTIVATION FOR SELECTING ACCOUNTING PRINCIPLES: A MARKET-BASED EMPIRICAL INVESTIGATION
CHWASTIAK, MICHELE EILEEN	AN EMPIRICAL INVESTIGATION INTO THE DOD'S CHOICE OF CONTRACT TYPE
CLARK, STANLEY J.	AN EMPIRICAL EXAMINATION OF FIRMS' MOTIVATIONS FOR EARLY ADOPTION OF SFAS 96 AND THE INFORMATION CONTENT OF FIRMS' DECISION TO EARLY ADOPT SFAS 96
CLEMENT, ROBIN PAULA	ACCOUNTING CHANGES AND THE DETERMINANTS OF SYSTEMATIC RISK: THE CASE OF FAS NO. 36: DISCLOSURE OF PENSION INFORMATION
CLEMENTS, ALAN BRUCE	AN EMPIRICAL ANALYSIS OF LOW-INCOME HOUSING TAX INCENTIVES
COBB, LAUREL GORDON	AN INVESTIGATION INTO THE EFFECT OF SELECTED AUDIT COMMITTEE CHARACTERISTICS ON FRAUDULENT FINANCIAL REPORTING
COBERLY, JANET WOOD	AN ANALYSIS OF THE EFFECTIVENESS OF THE RESEARCH AND EXPERIMENTATION TAX CREDIT WITHIN A Q MODEL OF VALUATION
COFF, RUSSELL W.	CORPORATE ACQUISITIONS OF HUMAN-ASSET-INTENSIVE FIRMS: LET THE BUYER BEWARE
COFFER, CURTIS ALAN	THE EFFECTS OF UNCERTAINTY AND THE INFORMATION ENVIRONMENT ON THE RELATION BETWEEN ACCOUNTING EARNINGS AND STOCK RETURNS FOR NEWLY PUBLIC FIRMS
COLBURN, STEVEN CHARLES	AN EMPIRICAL ANALYSIS OF THE IMPACT OF THE TAX REFORM ACT OF 1986 ON INVESTMENTS IN REAL ESTATE LIMITED PARTNERSHIPS
COLDWELL, SUSAN GAIL	ERTA AS AN INVESTMENT STIMULUS: A MICRO BASED ANALYSIS OF FIRM INVESTMENT BEHAVIOR
COLE, CHARLES STEVEN	THE IMPACT OF PRIVATE DEFAULT RISK INSURANCE ON THE YIELDS OF SEASONED TAX-EXEMPT BONDS
COLEMAN, CLARENCE, JR.	DEFERRED INCOME TAX CREDITS: AN EMPIRICAL ANALYSIS OF PERCEIVED MARKET RISK
COLLINS, ALLISON BENNETT	A COMPARISON OF HISTORICAL COST DATA AND FASB STATEMENT NO. 33 CURRENT COST DATA IN THE PREDICTION OF CORPORATE BOND RATING
COLLINS, DAVID THOMAS	AN EMPIRICAL INVESTIGATION INTO GEOGRAPHIC SEGMENT DISCLOSURE AND ITS ASSOCIATION WITH SYSTEMATIC RISK
COLLURA RAPACCIOLI, DONNA	WEALTH REDISTRIBUTIONS OR CHANGES IN FIRM VALUE: AN ANALYSIS OF THE RETURNS TO BONDHOLDERS AND STOCKHOLDERS AROUND INSIDE TRADE EVENTS
CONNELL, JAMES ALLEN, JR.	INFORMATION SYSTEMS INVESTMENT EVALUATION
CONOVER, TERESA LYNN	AN EMPIRICAL INVESTIGATION OF THE EFFECTS OF THE ACCOUNTING TREATMENT OF FOREIGN CURRENCY TRANSLATION ON MANAGEMENT ACTIONS IN MULTINATIONAL FIRMS
CONRAD, EDWARD JOHN	ENVIRONMENTAL AND FIRM CHARACTERISTICS AS DETERMINANTS OF TRADING VOLUME REACTION TO EARNINGS ANNOUNCEMENTS

Listing by Research Method

COPLEY, PAUL ANDREW — AN EMPIRICAL INVESTIGATION OF THE DETERMINANTS OF LOCAL GOVERNMENT AUDIT FEES

CORBIN, DONNA PHILLIPS — AN INVESTIGATION OF THE PREDICTABILITY OF THE AUDITOR'S OPINION IN A MULTINOMIAL LOGISTIC REGRESSION FRAMEWORK

COSTIGAN, MICHAEL LAWRENCE — THE MARGINAL PREDICTIVE ABILITY OF ACCRUAL ACCOUNTING INFORMATION WITH RESPECT TO FUTURE CASH FLOWS FROM OPERATIONS

COWAN, ARNOLD RICHARD — TWO-TIER TENDER OFFERS: COERCION, HUBRIS OR IMPROVED MANAGEMENT?

COWLING, JOHN FREDERICK — THE VARIATION OF ACCOUNTING INFORMATION FOR SEASONAL FIRMS ACROSS ALTERNATIVE FISCAL YEAR ENDS

COYLE, WILLIAM HENRY — THE DIFFERENTIAL EFFECTS OF INCENTIVES AND MONITORING ON EARNINGS MANAGEMENT AT THE TIME OF A CEO CHANGE

CRAIG, CAROLINE KERN — THE SHIFTING OF CORPORATE CAPITAL ACQUISITION TAX SUBSIDIES: AN EMPIRICAL ANALYSIS

CRAIN, JOHN L. — AN INVESTIGATION OF THE USEFULNESS OF RESERVE QUANTITY DISCLOSURES FOR PETROLEUM ENTITIES

CRAIN, TERRY LYNN — AN EMPIRICAL ANALYSIS OF THE EFFECT OF ALTERNATIVE CAPITAL GAIN TAX PROVISIONS ON HORIZONTAL AND VERTICAL EQUITY

CRAWFORD, DEAN — THE STRUCTURE OF CORPORATE MERGERS: ACCOUNTING, TAX, AND FORM-OF-PAYMENT CHOICES

CRAWFORD, JEAN GREENE — AN EMPIRICAL INVESTIGATION OF THE CHARACTERISTICS OF COMPANIES WITH AUDIT COMMITTEES

CRAYCRAFT, CATHERINE ANN — THE RELEVANCE OF SOCIOECONOMIC INFORMATION IN EXPLAINING BOND RATINGS OF QUASI-CORPORATIONS

CREADY, WILLIAM MONTGOMERY — AN EMPIRICAL INVESTIGATION INTO THE RELATIONSHIP BETWEEN THE VALUE OF ACCOUNTING EARNINGS ANNOUNCEMENTS AND EQUITY INVESTOR ENDOWMENT SIZES

CREDLE, SID HOWARD — THE MARKET REACTION TO THE FORGIVENESS OF DEFERRED TAXES OF THE DOMESTIC INTERNATIONAL SALES CORPORATION (DISC): EMPIRICAL EVIDENCE REGARDING THE 'INDEFINITE REVERSAL CRITERION'

CROWELL, STEVEN JUDSON — AN EMPIRICAL ANALYSIS OF THE DIFFERENTIAL IMPACT OF THE RESEARCH AND EXPERIMENTATION TAX CREDIT ON U.S. CORPORATE RESEARCH EXPENDITURES

CULLINAN, CHARLES P. — LABOR ORGANIZATION AND ACCOUNTING POLICY CHOICE: AN EMPIRICAL STUDY

CULPEPPER, DAVID HUNT — EXECUTIVE COMPENSATION PLANS: EMPIRICAL ANALYSIS OF THE TAX EXPLANATION OF COMPENSATION PLAN CHOICE

CUNNINGHAM, REBA LOVE — AN EMPIRICAL INVESTIGATION OF COMMON CHARACTERISTICS OF COMMERCIAL BANKS USING STANDBY LETTERS OF CREDIT, LETTERS OF CREDIT, INTEREST RATE SWAPS, AND LOAN SALES

DAHER, AHMAD HASAN ABDEL-RAHIM — GAP MANAGEMENT, SIZE AND RISK OF COMMERCIAL BANKS

DALTON, THOMAS M. — AN EMPIRICAL INVESTIGATION OF THE RELATIONSHIP BETWEEN TAX-LOSS SELLING AND THE JANUARY EFFECT

DAS, SOMNATH — DIFFERENTIAL INFORMATION CONTENT OF STOCK DIVIDEND ANNOUNCEMENTS

DAVID, JEANNE MARIE — THE EFFECT OF DEFINED BENEFIT PENSION PLANS ON CORPORATE VALUATION: AN EMPIRICAL INVESTIGATION

DAVIS, DOROTHY A. — AN EMPIRICAL INVESTIGATION INTO EXISTING BUDGETING PRACTICES TO DETERMINE DIVERSITY IN INTERPRETATIONS OF THE LAW ON BUDGETING AT THE MUNICIPAL LEVEL IN MISSISSIPPI

DAVIS, KAREL ANN — AN EMPIRICAL INVESTIGATION OF THE STOCK MARKET'S RESPONSE TO CHANGES IN INVENTORY AND DEPRECIATION METHODS

DAVIS, MICHAEL LEE — AN EMPIRICAL ANALYSIS OF THE IMPACT OF MERGER ACCOUNTING METHOD ON STOCK PRICES

DEAN, DONALD C. — DECAPITALIZATION AND THE THEORY OF REPLACEMENT: ECONOMETRIC ANALYSIS OF SFAS 33

DEBERG, CURTIS LYNN — STRUCTURAL CHANGES IN SYSTEMATIC RISK AND INFLATION ACCOUNTING: A THEORETICAL AND EMPIRICAL EXAMINATION OF ASR190 AND FAS33

DECHOW, PATRICIA MARY — ACCOUNTING EARNINGS AND CASH FLOWS AS MEASURES OF FIRM PERFORMANCE: THE ROLE OF ACCOUNTING ACCRUALS

DEFOND, MARK LEROY — AN EMPIRICAL TEST OF THE ASSOCIATION BETWEEN CLIENT FIRM AGENCY COSTS AND AUDIT FIRM CHARACTERISTICS

DEINES, DAN STUART — A TEST FOR THE SIMILARITY OF ANALYSTS' AND INVESTORS' EXPECTATIONS SUBJECT TO THE RELEASE OF MANDATED ACCOUNTING DISCLOSURES

DELEO, WANDA IRVIN — AN ANALYSIS OF FINANCIAL INFORMATION AS IT RELATES TO FAILED COMMERCIAL BANKS: A MULTIVARIATE APPROACH

DEMPSEY, STEPHEN JEFFREY — PARTITIONING MARKET EFFICIENCIES BY ANALYST ATTENTION: THE CASE OF ANNUAL EARNINGS ANNOUNCEMENTS

DEPPE, LARRY ARTHUR — AN EMPIRICAL INVESTIGATION OF THE IN-SUBSTANCE DEFEASANCE OF DEBT

DESAI, ARUN RAMADHAR — AN EMPIRICAL STUDY OF POST MERGER PERFORMANCE OF ACQUIRING FIRMS

DEVANEY, SHARON ANN LOHR — AN EMPIRICAL ANALYSIS OF THE PREDICTIVE VALUE OF HOUSEHOLD FINANCIAL RATIOS

DEVIDAL, DOUGLAS PAUL — THE ROLE OF PRIVATE LETTER RULINGS IN TAX-FREE REORGANIZATIONS

DHANANI, KARIM A. — AN EMPIRICAL STUDY OF FINANCIALLY DISTRESSED COMMERCIAL BANKS: A DISCRIMINANT MODEL FOR PREDICTING FUTURE BANK FAILURES

DIMITRY, KENNETH ELIA — AN EMPIRICAL EXAMINATION OF THE TIME-SERIES PROPERTIES OF EARNINGS-PER-SHARE USING TRANSFER FUNCTION ANALYSIS AT THE INDUSTRY LEVEL

DONADIO, PAUL JOSEPH — MANAGEMENT DEFECTS AS A CAUSE OF CORPORATE FAILURE: AN INVESTIGATION OF ARGENTI'S THEORY OF CORPORATE COLLAPSE

DONELAN, JOSEPH G. — THE RELATIONSHIP BETWEEN PENSION ACCOUNTING INTEREST RATE ASSUMPTIONS AND FIRM RISK

Listing by Research Method 350

DORAN, DAVID THOMAS	STOCK DIVIDENDS, STOCK SPLITS, AND FUTURE EARNINGS: ACCOUNTING RELEVANCE AND EQUITY MARKET RESPONSE
DORIGAN, MICHAEL P.	CORPORATE DEFINED BENEFIT PENSION POLICIES: AN EMPIRICAL ANALYSIS OF ALTERNATIVE STRATEGIES
DRAKE, PHILIP D.	AN ANALYSIS OF THE AUDIT SERVICES MARKET: THE EFFECT OF AUDIT STRUCTURE ON AUDITOR EFFICIENCY, A DATA ENVELOPMENT ANALYSIS APPROACH
DUCHAC, JONATHAN EHRLICH	EARNINGS MANAGEMENT AND THE PRECISION OF EARNINGS SIGNALS IN THE BANKING INDUSTRY
DUCHARME, LARRY L.	IPOS: PRIVATE INFORMATION AND EARNINGS MANAGEMENT
DUFFY, WENDY ANN	FINANCIAL REPORTING STANDARDS FOR PENSIONS: THE RELATIONSHIP BETWEEN FINANCIAL REPORTING AND CASH FLOW VARIABLES AND CHANGES IN THE INTEREST RATE ASSUMPTION
DUGAR, AMITABH	THE INFORMATION CONTENT OF THE STATEMENT OF CHANGES IN FINANCIAL POSITION
DUKE, JOANNE CHRISTINE	DEBT COVENANT RESTRICTIONS AND ACCOUNTING TECHNIQUE CHOICE: AN EMPIRICAL STUDY
DUNBAR, AMY ELINOR	AN EMPIRICAL INVESTIGATION OF THE ASSOCIATION OF PRODUCTIVITY WITH EMPLOYEE STOCK OWNERSHIP PLANS OF PUBLICLY HELD CORPORATIONS
DUNN, SARAH ANNE	A DESCRIPTIVE ANALYSIS AND EMPIRICAL INVESTIGATION OF CORPORATE ENVIRONMENTAL DISCLOSURES
DURKEE, DAVID ALLEN	THE EFFECT OF COSTLY VS. COSTLESS PENSION DISCLOSURE ON COMMON SHARE PRICES
DUVALL, LINDA GRIFFITH	REGULATORY VALUE OF UNREALIZED SECURITY GAINS AND LOSSES IN THE BANKING INDUSTRY
DWYER, MARGARET MARY DEVINE	A COMPARISON OF STATISTICAL TECHNIQUES AND ARTIFICIAL NEURAL NETWORK MODELS IN CORPORATE BANKRUPTCY PREDICTION
EAKIN, CYNTHIA FIREY	ACCOUNTING CHANGES AND EARNINGS MANAGEMENT: EVIDENCE FROM THE EARLY ADOPTION OF SFAS NO. 96 'ACCOUNTING FOR INCOME
EASTERGARD, ALF MOODY	THE COMPATIBILITY OF MARKET RETURNS AND INCOME NUMBERS OBSERVED AFTER ADJUSTMENTS TO RETAINED EARNINGS
EASTERWOOD, CINTIA MENDEZ	HOSTILE TAKEOVERS AND INCENTIVES FOR EARNINGS MANIPULATION: AN EMPIRICAL ANALYSIS
ECKSTEIN, CLAIRE	TIME-SERIES PROPERTIES AND FORECASTING OF FINANCIAL RATIOS
EDMONDS, CYNTHIA D.	AGENCY COST EXPLANATIONS FOR THE DEMAND FOR AUDIT QUALITY: AN EMPIRICAL INQUIRY INTO THE REASONS FOR THE PRESENCE OF AUDIT COMMITTEES OF THE BOARD OF DIRECTORS
EL FEKEY, MAHMOUD ELSYED	AN EMPIRICAL INVESTIGATION OF THE ROLE OF ALTERNATIVE ACCOUNTING VARIABLES IN ASSESSING A FIRM'S ABILITY TO PAY INCREASED WAGES
EL HOSSADE, SALEM ISMAIL	MANAGEMENT OF ANNUAL REPORTED INCOME IN THE U.K.: THE SEARCH FOR INDICATORS

Listing by Research Method   351

EL SHAMY, MOSTAFA AHMED	THE PREDICTIVE ABILITY OF FINANCIAL RATIOS: A TEST OF ALTERNATIVE MODELS
EL-ISSA, YASIN AHMAD MOUSA	THE USEFULNESS OF CORPORATE FINANCIAL DISCLOSURE TO INVESTORS IN THE AMMAN FINANCIAL MARKET
EL-RAJABI, MD-TAYSIR A	THE INFORMATION CONTENT OF ANNOUNCING THE CAPITAL INVESTMENT DECISIONS AND THE ACTUAL INVESTMENT NUMBERS
EL-SABBAGH, AMAL	MARKET EVALUATION OF DISCOVERY OF DISTORTED EARNINGS SIGNALS: EMPIRICAL TESTS OF CHANGES IN CASH FLOW EXPECTATIONS, RISKINESS, AND EARNINGS QUALITY HYPOTHESES
EL-ZAYATY, AHMED ISMAIL	BUSINESS FAILURE PREDICTION: AN ANALYSIS OF TYPE II PREDICTION ERRORS
ELDAHRAWY, KAMAL M.	AN EMPIRICAL INVESTIGATION OF THE DISCRIMINANT AND PREDICTIVE ABILITY OF THE SFAS NO. 69 SIGNALS FOR BUSINESS FAILURE IN THE OIL AND GAS INDUSTRY
ELDENBURG, LESLIE GAY	THE USE OF INFORMATION IN A COST CONTAINMENT ENVIRONMENT: AN ANALYSIS OF THE AGENCY RELATIONSHIP BETWEEN HOSPITALS AND PHYSICIANS
ELDER, RANDAL JEFFREY	AUDITOR INDUSTRY EXPERIENCE AND INITIAL PUBLIC OFFERINGS
ELHOSSEINY, MOHAMED AHMED	PROSPECTIVE INFORMATION IN SEC FILINGS: AN ANALYSIS OF MANAGEMENT CHOICE AND THE EFFECT OF AUDITOR INVOLVEMENT--A SIGNALING APPROACH
ELITZUR, RACHAMIM RAMY	FINANCIAL REPORTING AND MARKET DATA--A SIGNALLING EQUILIBRIUM PERSPECTIVE
ELNATHAN, DAN	ANALYSIS OF ISSUES CONCERNING OTHER POST EMPLOYMENT BENEFITS
ELSAYED-AHMED, SAMEH METWALLY	AN EMPIRICAL EXAMINATION OF THE EFFECTS OF FASB STATEMENT NO. 52 ON SECURITY RETURNS AND REPORTED EARNINGS OF U.S.-BASED MULTINATIONAL CORPORATIONS
EPPS, RUTH WILLIAMS	AN EMPIRICAL INVESTIGATION OF THE EFFECTS OF THE QUALITY OF SEGMENTAL DISCLOSURE ON THE BEHAVIOR OF SYSTEMATIC RISK OF DIVERSIFIED FIRMS
ETHERIDGE, HARLAN LYNN	AN EXAMINATION OF SEMIOTIC THEORIES OF ACCOUNTING ACCRUALS
ETTER, EDWIN ROGER, JR.	THE INFORMATION CONTENT OF BRITISH AND JAPANESE EARNINGS ANNOUNCEMENTS: A PRICE AND TRADING VOLUME APPROACH
FAIRFIELD, PATRICIA MARIE	THE INFORMATION CONTENT OF LEVERAGE: A TIME-SERIES ANALYSIS
FANG, CHIH-CHIANG	THREE EMPIRICAL INVESTIGATIONS INTO EARNINGS AND DIVIDENDS
FARGHER, NEIL LAWRENCE	THE ASSOCIATION BETWEEN UNEXPECTED EARNINGS AND CAPITAL EXPENDITURE
FELDMANN, DOROTHY A.	THE MARKET REACTION TO UNEXPECTED EARNINGS: THE CASE OF INDIVIDUAL AND INSTITUTIONAL INVESTORS
FELTON, SANDRA	THE IMPACT OF LEASE ACCOUNTING REGULATION ON THE SHARE PRICES OF FIRMS WHICH LOBBIED ON SFAS NO. 13

Listing by Research Method

FELTUS, OLIVER LEONARD	THE INFORMATION CONTENT OF FINANCIAL STATEMENTS: PREDICTING EARNINGS PER SHARE USING FINANCIAL RATIOS
FERREIRA, LOURDES DALTRO	LINKAGES BETWEEN EXECUTIVE COMPENSATION PROVISIONS AND THE DIVIDEND DECISION
FESLER, ROBERT DANIEL	LITIGATION REPORTING UNDER SFAS NO. 5: AN EMPIRICAL INVESTIGATION OF COMPARABILITY
FIEDERLEIN, KATHLEEN J.	AN EQUITY ANALYSIS OF SOCIAL SECURITY TAXING AND FINANCING SCHEMES: SIMULATIONS OF ALTERNATIVE TAX PROVISIONS
FIGLEWICZ, RAYMOND E.	AN EXAMINATION INTO THE FEASIBILITY OF USING MEASURES OF SYSTEMATIC RISK VARIABILITY AS PREDICTORS OF CORPORATE FAILURE
FILTER, WILLIAM VIGGO	A STUDY OF THE MARKET BEHAVIOR IN RESPONSE TO THE LIQUIDATION OF LIFO LAYERS
FINDORFF, PAUL CURTIS	ACQUISITIONS AND ECONOMIC PERFORMANCE IN THE AIRLINE INDUSTRY SINCE THE AIRLINE DEREGULATION ACT OF 1978
FINGER, CATHERINE ANNE	THE RELATION BETWEEN FINANCIAL INFORMATION AND FUTURE CASH FLOWS
FINN, PHILIP MORTON	AN EXAMINATION OF THE MARKET REACTION TO A MANDATED ACCOUNTING CHANGE: THE CASE FOR THE COSTS OF COMPUTER SOFTWARE
FINNEGAN, THOMAS ROBERT	THE EFFECT OF THE 1986 TAX REFORM ACT AND FINANCIAL ACCOUNTING CHANGES ON UTILITY RETURNS AND RATE SETTING
FINNEY, SHARON GARY	AN EMPIRICAL INVESTIGATION INTO THE PREDICTABILITY OF FAILURE IN INSURED SAVINGS INSTITUTIONS
FLAGG, JAMES CALVIN	A DESCRIPTION AND ANALYSIS OF THE CORPORATE FAILURE PROCESS USING AN EVENTS-BASED LOGIT MODEL
FLEAK, SANDRA KREISEL	THE GOING-CONCERN AUDIT OPINION AND SHARE PRICE BEHAVIOR
FLETCHER, LESLIE B.	THE PREDICTION OF FINANCIAL TURNAROUND OF FINANCIALLY DISTRESSED FIRMS
FORGIONE, DANA ANTHONY	INCENTIVES AND PERFORMANCE IN THE HEALTH CARE INDUSTRY: THE CASE OF FOR/NON PROFIT MULTIHOSPITAL SYSTEMS
FORNEY, CHARLES T.	AN INVESTIGATION INTO THE TIME-SERIES NATURE OF FOREIGN SUBSIDIARY EARNINGS AND MANAGEMENT'S ABILITY TO FORECAST THEM
FORSYTH, TIMOTHY BUSH	A STUDY OF THE ABILITY OF FINANCIAL RATIOS TO PREDICT CORPORATE FAILURE AND THE RELATIONSHIP BETWEEN BANKRUPTCY MODEL PROBABILITY ASSESSMENTS AND STOCK MARKET BEHAVIOR
FORT, CHARLES PATRICK	ANALYSTS' FORECAST ACCURACY AND THE PRESENTATION OF MANDATED ACCOUNTING CHANGES
FOSTER, BENJAMIN PATRICK	TESTING THE APPROPRIATENESS OF NONPROFIT HOSPITALS' TAX EXEMPTIONS WITH LOGISTIC REGRESSION ANALYSES OF HOSPITAL FINANCIAL DATA
FOUCH, SCOTT RANDALL	EMPIRICAL RESEARCH INTO THE SHIFTING OF THE CORPORATE INCOME TAX OF LIFE INSURANCE COMPANIES

Listing by Research Method 353

FRANCIS, JENNIFER	CORPORATE COMPLIANCE WITH DEBT COVENANTS
FRANKEL, MICAH PAUL	THE DETERMINANTS OF LIFO LAYER LIQUIDATIONS: TAX MINIMIZATION AND AGENCY COST FACTORS
FRANKEL, RICHARD MOSES	ACCOUNTING INFORMATION AND FIRMS WITH LOW-GRADE BONDS
FRANZ, DAVID PAUL	THE INFORMATION CONTENT OF CASH FLOW MEASURES: AN EMPIRICAL ANALYSIS
FRANZ, DIANA RUTH	AN ANALYSIS OF THE EFFECT OF THE EXPECTATION GAP STATEMENTS ON AUDITING STANDARDS ON THE REPORTING OF GOING CONCERN
FRAZIER, JESSICA JOHNSON	AN ANALYSIS OF THE EFFECT OF THE PROPOSED AD VALOREM PROPERTY TAXATION OF UNMINED COAL PROPERTY IN KENTUCKY
FREEMAN, GARY ROSS	AN INVESTIGATION OF THE USEFULNESS OF CURRENT COST INCOME TO CAPITAL MARKET PARTICIPANTS
FRESE, PHILLIP BRUCE	THE EFFECT OF CHANGES IN TAX STRUCTURE ON THE BEHAVIOR OF RATIONAL INVESTORS IN MARKETS FOR RISKY ASSETS: AN EMPIRICAL STUDY OF THE IMPACT OF THE OMNIBUS BUDGET RECONCILIATION ACT OF 1987 ON THE INVESTORS IN PUBLICLY
FRIEDLAN, JOHN MICHAEL	ACCOUNTING INFORMATION AND THE PRICING OF INITIAL PUBLIC OFFERINGS
FRISCHMANN, PETER JAMES	TAXPAYER RESPONSE TO KINKED BUDGET CONSTRAINTS: NEW EMPIRICAL EVIDENCE OF TAX PRICE AWARENESS
FRISKE, KARYN ANNE BYBEE	AN EXAMINATION OF THE EFFECTS OF STANDARD SETTING AND EARNINGS MANAGEMENT IN THE OIL AND GAS INDUSTRY: THE LESSON OF SFAS NO. 96
FUHRMANN, JOHN STANLEY	THE ASSOCIATION BETWEEN SECURITY RETURNS AND FIRMS' LOBBYING POSITIONS ON ACCOUNTING STANDARDS
FULKERSON, CHERYL LINTHICUM	EARNINGS EXPECTATIONS, FIRM VALUATION AND RISK ASSESSMENT USING FOREIGN AND RESTATED ACCOUNTING DATA
FURZE, SALLY	SFAS 94 AND NOISY EARNINGS SIGNALS
GABER, MOHAMED KHAIRAT ABDEL-GELIL	MANAGEMENT INCENTIVES TO REPORT FORECASTS OF CORPORATE EARNINGS
GAGNE, MARGARET LEE	THE IMPACT OF FIRM SIZE ON THE PRICE AND VOLUME REACTIONS TO ANALYSTS' EARNINGS FORECAST REVISIONS
GAHARAN, CATHERINE INNES GREEN	A COMPARISON OF THE EFFECTIVENESS OF THE OPERATING FUNDS FLOW MEASURES OF CASH, NET QUICK ASSETS, AND WORKING CAPITAL IN PREDICTING FUTURE CASH FLOW
GARLICK, JOHN RICHARD, SR.	CUMULATIVE ABNORMAL RETURNS; INTERVENTION ANALYSIS: A METHODOLOGICAL COMPARISON
GAUMNITZ, CAROL BOTHAMLEY	AN ANALYSIS OF THE INTERNAL REVENUE SERVICE'S DECISION PROCESS WITH RESPECT TO THE UNRELATED BUSINESS INCOME TAXPROVISIONS CONTAINED IN CODE SECTIONS 511-513
GEORGE, CAROLYN R.	THE EFFECT OF THE GOING-CONCERN AUDIT DECISION ON SURVIVAL

Listing by Research Method

GEORGE, NASHWA ELGALLAB	MANAGEMENT EARNINGS FORECAST DISCLOSURE: AN EMPIRICAL STUDY OF FACTORS INFLUENCING THE DECISION
GHANI, WAQAR I.	THE ECONOMIC IMPACT OF ACCOUNTING INFORMATION AGGREGATION AND DISAGGREGATION ON INFORMEDNESS AND CONSENSUS: THE CASE OF CONSOLIDATED NONHOMOGENEOUS SUBSIDIARIES
GHICAS, DIMITRIOS CHRISTOS	AN ANALYSIS OF THE CHANGE OF ACTUARIAL COST METHODS FOR PENSION ACCOUNTING AND FUNDING
GHOSH, ALOKE	VALUATION OF GAINS FROM MERGERS: SOURCES AND ESTIMATION OF THESE GAINS FROM DISCIPLINARY TAKEOVERS AND DIFFERENT TAX-RELATED ISSUES
GILBERT, LISA R.	ACCOUNTING STANDARDS, EARNINGS EXPECTATIONS, AND MARKET PRICES: THE CASE OF SFAS 52
GILL, SUSAN	MOTIVATIONS FOR AND REACTIONS TO VOLUNTARY MANAGEMENT DISCLOSURES
GIST, WILLIE EARL	AN EXPLORATORY STUDY OF THE EFFECTS OF PRODUCT DIFFERENTIATION AND ECONOMIES OF SCALE ON EXTERNAL AUDIT FEES
GNIZAK, CHARLES JAMES	INTEREST CAPITALIZATION TAX LAW: ITS EFFECT ON CAPITAL STRUCTURE AND MARKET VALUE
GOBER, JERALD ROBERT	THE BLEND OF TAXES USED TO FUND NATIONAL, STATE, AND LOCAL GOVERNMENTAL BODIES: A FACTOR IN THE ECONOMIES OF THE WORLD?
GODWIN, JOSEPH HUDSON	THE ECONOMIC DETERMINANTS OF ACCOUNTING CHOICE: THE CASE OF ACCOUNTING FOR PENSIONS
GOLDBERG, STEPHEN RICHARD	THE IMPACT OF EXCHANGE RATE CHANGES ON SECURITY RETURNS AND FINANCIAL REPORTING: THEORY AND EMPIRICAL FINDINGS
GOMA, AHMED TAWFIK	EMPIRICAL INVESTIGATION OF THE INFORMATION CONTENT OF SPECIFIC PRICE CHANGE DISCLOSURES
GONZALEZ, PEDRO	FINANCIAL CHARACTERISTICS OF COMPANIES INVOLVED IN CROSS-BORDER MERGERS AND ACQUISITIONS
GOPALAKRISHNAN, VENKATARAMAN	MARKET REACTIONS TO ACCOUNTING POLICY DELIBERATIONS: THE CASE OF PENSIONS
GOSS, BETSY CATON	ACCOUNTING QUALITY AND DISPERSION OF FINANCIAL ANALYSTS' FORECASTS: AN EMPIRICAL INVESTIGATION
GOSSELIN, DAVID J.	AN EMPIRICAL INVESTIGATION OF CORPORATE INCOME SMOOTHING: A FACTOR ANALYTIC AND DISCRIMINANT APPROACH TO FIRM IDENTIFICATION
GOULD, JOHN FRANKLIN	ESSAYS ON THE RELATION BETWEEN THE ACCOUNTING SYSTEM AND THE CAPITAL MARKET
GRAHAM, LISE NEWMAN	THE MAGNITUDE AND TIMING OF ANALYST FORECAST RESPONSE TO QUARTERLY EARNINGS ANNOUNCEMENTS
GRAHAM, ROGER CHARLTON, JR.	THE ASSOCIATION BETWEEN ORDER OF ANNOUNCEMENT AND SECURITY PRICE REACTIONS TO AN EARNINGS RELEASE
GRAMLICH, JEFFREY DOUGLAS	AN EMPIRICAL ANALYSIS OF THE EFFECT OF THE ALTERNATIVE MINIMUM TAX BOOK INCOME ADJUSTMENT ON THE EXTENT OF DISCRETIONARY ACCOUNTING ACCRUALS

GRANT, CHARLES TERRELL	FINANCIAL DISTRESS PREDICTION WITH AN EXPANDED INFORMATION SET
GRANT, JULIA ELIZABETH STUART	NON-PENSION RETIREMENT BENEFITS
GREEN, BRIAN PATRICK	IDENTIFYING MANAGEMENT IRREGULARITIES THROUGH PRELIMINARY ANALYTICAL PROCEDURES
GREENAWALT, MARY BRADY	AN EMPIRICAL INVESTIGATION OF THE ACCOUNTING ESTIMATES OF LOAN LOSSES IN THE BANKING INDUSTRY
GREENSPAN, JAMES WILLIAM	DISTINGUISHING A PURCHASE FROM A POOLING THROUGH THE USE OF HOSTILE AND FRIENDLY TENDER OFFERS
GREENSTEIN, MARILYN E. MAGEE	AN EMPIRICAL INVESTIGATION OF THE EFFECTS OF SEGMENT REPORTING ON THE BID-ASK SPREAD AND VOLUME OF TRADE
GREIG, ANTHONY CHARLTON	FUNDAMENTAL ANALYSIS AND SUBSEQUENT STOCK RETURNS
GRINER, EMMETT HAMILTON	INSIDER OWNERSHIP AND THE LEVEL OF CAPITAL EXPENDITURES IN THE LARGE INDUSTRIAL FIRM: AN EMPIRICAL INVESTIGATION
GRUBE, NANCY WEATHERHOLT	EXAMINATION OF INITIATING DIVIDEND EFFECTS
GUENTHER, DAVID A.	THE EFFECT OF INCOME TAXES ON THE FORM OF BUSINESS ENTITY
GUIDRY, FLORA GAIL	A TEST OF THE DETERMINANTS OF AUDITOR TENDENCY TO ISSUE GOING-CONCERN AUDIT REPORTS TO NONFAILING COMPANIES
GULLEDGE, DEXTER EUGENE	AN INVESTIGATION OF MARKET REACTION TO RELATIVE CHANGES IN REPORTED AMOUNTS FOR BUSINESS SEGMENTS UNDER FASB NO. 14: AN APPLICATION OF SHANNON'S ENTROPY MEASURE
GUMENIK, ARTHUR JEFFREY	THE ASSOCIATION OF DISCRETIONARY CASH FLOW WITH SECURITY RETURNS
GUNDERSON, KONRAD ERIK	DISPERSION OF FINANCIAL ANALYSTS' EARNINGS FORECASTS AS A RISK MEASURE: ARGUMENT AND EVIDENCE
GUO, MIIN HONG	DIFFERENTIAL EARNINGS RESPONSE COEFFICIENTS TO ACCOUNTING INFORMATION: THE CASE OF REVISIONS OF FINANCIAL ANALYSTS' FORECASTS
GUPTA, MANOJ	THE CURRENCY RISK FACTOR IN INTERNATIONAL EQUITY PRICING
GUPTA, SANJAY	DETERMINANTS OF THE CHOICE BETWEEN COMPREHENSIVE AND PARTIAL INCOME TAX ALLOCATION: THE CASE OF THE DOMESTIC INTERNATIONAL SALES CORPORATION
GUPTA, SANTOSH PRABHA	R&D INTENSITY, SIZE, RELATEDNESS, TAKEOVER PROCESS AND POST-MERGER CHANGE IN R&D
GUSTAFSON, LYAL VAL	AN EMPIRICAL INVESTIGATION OF THE USEFULNESS OF MANAGEMENT EARNINGS FORECASTS AS EVIDENCED BY THEIR EFFECT ON ANALYSTS' PREDICTIONS
HADDAD, AMIN MOHAMMED	THE MARKET REACTION TO FOREIGN CURRENCY TRANSLATION POLICY-SETTING PROCESS: A NEW APPROACH

HAGAN, JOSEPH MARTIN	AN EMPIRICAL STUDY OF THE EFFECT OF THE TAX REFORM ACT OF 1986 ON ECONOMIC EFFICIENCY AS MEASURED BY AVERAGE EFFECTIVE TAX RATES
HALL, BETHANE JO PIERCE	AN ANALYSIS OF THE EQUITY AND REVENUE EFFECTS OF THE ELIMINATION OR REDUCTION OF HOMEOWNER PREFERENCES
HALL, STEVEN C.	ECONOMIC MOTIVATIONS FOR ACCOUNTING STRATEGY CHOICES
HAMDALLAH, AHMED EL-SAYED	AN INVESTIGATION OF MOTIVATION FOR VOLUNTARILY TERMINATING OVERFUNDED PENSION PLANS
HAN, BONG-HEUI	DISPERSION IN FINANCIAL ANALYSTS' EARNINGS FORECASTS: IMPLICATIONS ON RISK AND EARNINGS
HAN, CHI-YING	MANAGEMENT FORECASTS: INCENTIVES AND EFFECTS
HAN, KI CHOONG	MARKET RESPONSE TO EARNINGS ANNOUNCEMENTS: THE EFFECTS OF FIRM CHARACTERISTICS
HANNA, JOHN DOUGLAS	A FURTHER EXAMINATION OF THE INCREMENTAL INFORMATION CONTENT OF CASH-FLOW ANNOUNCEMENTS
HARGADON, JOSEPH MICHAEL	ADOPTION CHOICE OF MANDATED ACCOUNTING CHANGES: A JOINT DECISION APPROACH
HARRIS, DAVID GARLAND	THE IMPACT OF UNITED STATES TAX LAW REVISION ON MULTINATIONAL CORPORATIONS' CAPITAL LOCATION AND INCOME SHIFTING DECISIONS
HARRIS, MARY ALICE STANFORD	THE IMPACT OF COMPETITION ON MANAGER'S REPORTING POLICIES FOR BUSINESS SEGMENTS
HARRISON, PATRICIA MACKEL	INVESTMENT, ENTRY, AND PERFORMANCE OF SAVINGS AND LOAN ASSOCIATIONS IN THE 1980S
HARTER, CHARLES IVES	AN ANALYSIS OF THE EFFECT OF DISCRETIONARY CASH ON THE EARNINGS RESPONSE COEFFICIENT
HARWOOD, ELAINE MARIE	ADOPTION OF REGULATORY ACCOUNTING PRINCIPLES BY STOCKHELD SAVINGS AND LOAN ASSOCIATIONS: AN EVENT STUDY OF DISCRETIONARY ACCOUNTING CHOICE
HAYN, CARLA K.	THE ROLE OF TAX ATTRIBUTES IN CORPORATE ACQUISITIONS
HAZERA, ALEJANDRO	A NORMATIVE MODEL FOR ASSESSING THE COMPETENCE OF EVIDENTIAL MATTER IN AUDITING
HE, XIAOHONG	INTERNATIONAL TAX TRENDS AND COMPETITION: TAX SENSITIVITY OF U.S. FOREIGN INVESTMENT ABROAD
HEFLIN, FRANK LEE	SECURITIES MARKET RESPONSE TO LEGISLATED CHANGES IN THE PENSION PLAN REVERSION EXCISE TAX
HENNING, STEVEN LYLE	ACCOUNTING FOR GOODWILL: CURRENT PRACTICES, VARIATION IN SOURCE AND COMPONENTS, AND MARKET VALUATION
HERMANSON, DANA ROGER	THE ASSOCIATION BETWEEN AUDIT FIRM CHARACTERISTICS AND THE AUDITOR'S PROPENSITY TO QUALIFY BANKRUPTCY-RELATED OPINIONS

Listing by Research Method   357

HERREMANS, IRENE M.	AN INVESTIGATION OF THE TRIADIC RELATIONSHIP OF SOCIAL PERFORMANCE, SOCIAL DISCLOSURE, AND ECONOMIC PERFORMANCE
HETHCOX, KATHLEEN BLACKBURN	BUSINESS COMBINATIONS ACCOUNTED FOR BY THE PURCHASE METHOD: AN EMPIRICAL ANALYSIS OF THE MAGNITUDE OF GOODWILL AND ACQUIRING FIRMS' STOCK RETURNS
HIGGINS, MARK MATTHEW	AN EMPIRICAL ANALYSIS OF THE RELATIONSHIP BETWEEN CORPORATE EFFECTIVE TAX RATES AND BOOK EFFECTIVE TAX RATES WITH AN ANALYSIS OF THE FINANCIAL CHARACTERISTICS THAT INFLUENCE CORPORATE EFFECTIVE TAX RATES
HILL, JOHN WARREN	THE ECONOMIC CONSEQUENCES OF ACCOUNTING CHOICE: DEFERRAL OF LOAN SALE LOSSES IN THE SAVINGS AND LOAN INDUSTRY
HINDI, NITHAM MOHD	AN EMPIRICAL INVESTIGATION INTO THE IMPACT OF OFF-BALANCE SHEET ACTIVITIES ON THE RISKINESS OF COMMERCIAL BANKS: A MARKET-BASED ANALYSIS
HO, LI-CHIN	THE EFFECTS OF OPTION TRADING ON THE INFORMATION CONTENT OF EARNINGS DISCLOSURES: AN EMPIRICAL ANALYSIS
HO, SHIH-JEN KATHY	THE USEFULNESS OF CASH FLOWS RELATIVE TO ACCRUAL EARNINGS: A SECURITY VALUATION STUDY
HOFFMANS, SHARRON RAE DYE	THE CHANGE FROM FINANCIAL ACCOUNTING STANDARD NO. 8 TO FINANCIAL ACCOUNTING STANDARD NO. 52 AND MANAGEMENT FINANCING DECISIONS
HOGAN, THOMAS JEFFERY	MANAGEMENT DECISIONS REGARDING CHOICES OF ACCOUNTING METHODS AND SUBMISSIONS TO THE FASB: AN EMPIRICAL STUDY OF FIRM CHARACTERISTICS
HOLLEY, JOYCE MARIE HIGGINS	AN INVESTIGATION OF INTERNAL INTERIM REPORTING BY MUNICIPALITIES
HOLLINGSWORTH, DANNY P.	AN EMPIRICAL INVESTIGATION INTO THE CHANGE IN TAX EQUITY WITHIN THE FINANCIAL SERVICES INDUSTRY AS A RESULT OF THE 1986 TAX REFORM ACT
HOLT, PAUL EDWIN	A COMPARATIVE EXAMINATION OF THE EARNINGS EFFECTS OF ALTERNATIVE TRANSLATION METHODS
HOOKS, JON ALLAN	INFLATION, INFLATION ACCOUNTING, AND REAL STOCK RETURNS: AN ALTERNATIVE TEST OF THE PROXY HYPOTHESIS
HOTCHKISS, EDITH HARRIET SHWALB	INVESTMENT DECISIONS UNDER CHAPTER 11 BANKRUPTCY
HSIEH, SU-JANE	THE ECONOMIC VALUE OF FINANCIAL DISTRESS INFORMATION: AN EMPIRICAL ASSESSMENT
HUANG-TSAI, CHUNGHUEY	THE ASSOCIATION BETWEEN FINANCIAL STATEMENT INFORMATION AND STOCK PRICES
HUBBARD, DANIEL JULIAN	AN ACCOUNTING STUDY OF AMERICAN DEPOSITARY RECEIPTS
HUDSON, CARL DEERING	EXTERNAL MONITORING AND SECURITY OFFERING ANNOUNCEMENTS
HUFFMAN, STEPHEN PHILLIP	TESTS OF THE FREE CASH FLOW THEORY OF TAKEOVERS
HULSE, DAVID STEWART	THE TIMING OF THE STOCK MARKET REACTION TO RIFLE-SHOT TRANSITION RULES IN THE TAX REFORM ACT OF 1986

HUME, EVELYN C.	THE EFFECTS OF THE TAX REFORM ACT OF 1986 ON THE REAL ESTATE CAPITAL MARKETS AND ITS DIFFERENTIAL EFFECTS ON ENTITY AND FUNCTIONAL FORMS: AN EMPIRICAL INVESTIGATION
HUTCHINSON, PATRICK JOHN	THE FINANCIAL PROFILE OF GROWTH SMALL FIRMS: AN ANALYSIS OF THE ACCOUNTING RATIOS OF AUSTRALIAN COMPANIES AT AND AFTER FLOTATION, 1964/5-1983/4
HWANG, IN TAE	THE DETERMINANTS OF EXECUTIVE INCENTIVE CONTRACTS
HWANG, NEN-CHEN	FINANCIAL CHARACTERISTICS OF CORPORATIONS CHANGING COMMON STOCK LISTING FROM THE OVER-THE-COUNTER MARKET TO THE NEW YORK STOCK EXCHANGE
IKEOKWU, FRANCIS AHAMEFULE	FLORIDA SALES TAX REVENUE: A COMPARATIVE STUDY TO DETERMINE THE RELATIONSHIP BETWEEN SALES TAX RATE AND SALES TAX REVENUE IN FLORIDA
IM, JONG-GEOL	DIFFERENTIAL INFORMATION ENVIRONMENT AND THE MAGNITUDE OF CAPITAL MARKET RESPONSES TO EARNINGS ANNOUNCEMENTS
IVANCEVICH, DANIEL MICHAEL	AN EMPIRICAL INVESTIGATION OF THE ACCOUNTING DIFFERENCES FOR GOODWILL IN THE UNITED STATES AND UNITED KINGDOM
JACKSON, STEVEN ROY	AN EMPIRICAL ASSESSMENT OF MEASUREMENT ERROR IN HISTORICAL COST AND SELECTED CHANGING PRICES INCOME NUMBERS
JACOB, RUDOLPH AUBREY	THE TIME-SERIES BEHAVIOR AND INFORMATIONAL CONTENT OF SELECTED CASH FLOW VARIABLES
JAKUBOWSKI, STEPHEN THOMAS	THE EFFECT OF THE SINGLE AUDIT ACT OF 1984 ON THE INTERNAL CONTROL SYSTEMS OF LOCAL GOVERNMENTAL UNITS
JAN, CHING-LIH	THE MARKET'S EVALUATION OF FOOTNOTE DISCLOSURES FOR FIRMS USING LIFO INVENTORY ACCOUNTING
JANAKIRAMAN, SURYA N.	STRATEGIC CHOICE OF CHIEF EXECUTIVE OFFICERS' COMPENSATION: AN EMPIRICAL ANALYSIS
JANG, HWEE-YONG	TRADING VOLUME AND ACCOUNTING RESEARCH: THEORY, IMPLICATION, AND EVIDENCE
JANG, JEE IN	FINANCIAL ANALYST EARNINGS FORECAST REVISIONS: FORMATION PROCESS AND INFORMATION VALUE
JANG, YEONG MIN	AN EMPIRICAL EVALUATION OF THE CURRENT ACCOUNTING COMMON STOCK EQUIVALENCY TEST AND AN ALTERNATIVE MARKET MODEL
JENKINS, ELIZABETH KLAFF	EXECUTIVE COMPENSATION SCHEMES AND SHORT-RUN DECISION-MAKING: AN EMPIRICAL EXAMINATION
JENNINGS, ROSS GRANT	A STUDY OF THE CROSS-SECTIONAL HOMOGENEITY OF THE INFORMATION CONTENT OF ACCOUNTING INCOME AND ITS COMPONENTS
JENSEN, DAVID EDWARD	THE INFORMATION CONTENT OF CASH FLOW MEASURES IN REGARD TO ENTERPRISE DIVIDEND POLICY
JERRIS, SCOTT I.	THE ASSOCIATION BETWEEN STOCK RETURNS AND ALTERNATIVE EARNINGS PER SHARE NUMBERS
JETER, DEBRA COLEMAN	ACCOUNTING EARNINGS AND SECURITY RETURNS: STUDIES ON EARNINGS RESPONSE COEFFICIENTS, AUDIT REPORTS, AND DEFERRED TAXES

Listing by Research Method

359

JIN, JONG-DAE	THE IMPACT OF EARNINGS ANNOUNCEMENT ON BOND PRICE
JOH, GUN-HO	INTERFIRM INFORMATION TRANSFER AND DISCLOSURE TIMING
JOHNSON, CAROL BAUMAN	THE IMPACT OF CURRENCY CHANGES ON THE PERSISTENCE AND PRICING OF MULTINATIONAL CORPORATION EARNINGS
JOHNSON, DAVID MARK	INSIDER OWNERSHIP AND SIGNALS: A STUDY OF STOCK AND BOND ISSUE ANNOUNCEMENT EFFECTS
JOHNSON, GEORGE ALFRED	THE INFORMATION VALUE OF NEW DISAGGREGATED ACCOUNTING INFORMATION: THE CASE OF VOLUNTARY CORPORATE SPINOFFS
JOHNSON, KENNETH HAROLD	OWNERSHIP STRUCTURE AND THE INFORMATION CONTENT OF EARNINGS ANNOUNCEMENTS: AN EMPIRICAL INVESTIGATION
JOHNSON, MARILYN FRANCES	BUSINESS CYCLES AND THE RELATION BETWEEN SECURITY RETURNS AND EARNINGS
JOHNSON, RICHARD ALAN	AN EMPIRICAL INVESTIGATION OF THE ASSOCIATION OF ACCOUNTING-BASED PERFORMANCE MEASURES WITH THE AUDITOR REPLACEMENT DECISION
JOHNSTON, HOLLY HANSON	EMPIRICAL STUDIES IN MANAGEMENT ACCOUNTING: THREE ESSAYS ON THE U.S. AIRLINE INDUSTRY, 1981-1985
JONES, JENNIFER JEAN	THE EFFECT OF FOREIGN TRADE REGULATION ON ACCOUNTING CHOICES, AND PRODUCTION AND INVESTMENT DECISIONS
JOO, INKI	INFORMATION CONTENT OF STOCK SPLITS IN RELATION WITH PRIOR YEAR'S EARNINGS' GROWTH, FIRM SIZE, SPLIT SIZE, AND REPUTATION: AN EMPIRICAL ANALYSIS
JOO, JIN-KYU	EARNINGS SURPRISE AND EX-ANTE PRICE EFFECTS IN OPTIONS MARKETS
JORDAN, CHARLES EDWARD	THE DEVELOPMENT OF A STATISTICAL ANALYTICAL REVIEW MODEL FOR USE BY EXTERNAL AUDITORS IN EVALUATING BANKS' LOAN-LOSS RESERVES
JORDAN, LELAND GONCE	ARE THE INTERIM FINANCIAL STATEMENTS OF FAILING FIRMS BIASED?
KAENZIG, REBECCA	THE INDIVIDUAL VERSUS THE FAMILY: AN EMPIRICAL ANALYSIS OF HORIZONTAL EQUITY AND TAX-PAYER FILING STATUS
KALLAPUR, SANJAY GOKULDAS	DETERMINANTS OF THE STOCK PRICE RESPONSE TO EARNINGS
KANDIEL, EL-SAYED HUSSEIN AHMED	ACCOUNTING FOR INTERNALLY DEVELOPED SOFTWARE COSTS: A POSITIVE APPROACH
KANE, GREGORY DALE	ACCOUNTING DATA AND STOCK RETURNS ACROSS BUSINESS-CYCLE ASSOCIATED VALUATION CHANGE PERIODS
KARAYAN, JOHN EDWARD	THE ECONOMIC IMPACT OF A TAX LAW CHANGE: PUBLICLY TRADED PARTNERSHIPS UNDER THE REVENUE ACT OF 1987
KATTELUS, SUSAN CONVERY	PRIVATE NONOPERATING FOUNDATIONS: AN EMPIRICAL INVESTIGATION OF PAYOUT RATES AND FOUNDATION CHARACTERISTICS BEFORE AND AFTER THE ECONOMIC RECOVERY TAX ACT OF 1981

KAZENSKI, PAUL M.	A NON-LINEAR APPROACH TO DETECTING ESTIMATION AND VALUATION ERRORS IN THE REPORTED RESERVES OF PROPERTY-LIABILITY INSURERS
KEARNS, FRANCIS E., JR.	AN INVESTIGATION OF THE RELATIVE PREDICTIVE VALIDITY OF QUARTERLY REPORTS BEFORE AND AFTER AUDITOR INVOLVEMENT UNDER ASR #177
KEDSLIE, MOYRA JEAN MCINTYRE	AN ANALYSIS OF THE FACTORS INFLUENCING THE FORMATION AND POLICIES OF PROFESSIONAL ACCOUNTING BODIES IN SCOTLAND, 1850-1900
KELLEY, CLAUDIA LU	A STUDY OF THE STOCK MARKET REACTION TO SECTION 382 OF THE TAX REFORM ACT OF 1986 AND THE CHARACTERISTICS OF TARGETS WITH LOSS CARRYOVERS
KEMERER, KEVIN L.	ACCOUNTING VARIABLES, STOCK SPLITS AND WHEN-ISSUED TRADING
KENNEDY, JEFFREY LEE	A COMPARISON OF GENERALLY ACCEPTED ACCOUNTING PRACTICE AND STATEMENT OF FINANCIAL ACCOUNTING STANDARDS NO. 33 INCOME MEASUREMENT
KENNY, SARA YORK	PREDICTING FAILURE IN THE SAVINGS AND LOAN INDUSTRY: A COMPARISON OF RAP AND GAAP ACCOUNTING
KENYON, PETER B.	AN INVESTIGATION OF THE EFFECT OF ANNUAL ACCOUNTING REPORTS ON MUNICIPAL BOND INTEREST COST
KERBY, DEBRA K.	CORPORATE LOBBYING AGAINST PROPOSED ACCOUNTING STANDARDS: EVIDENCE FROM THE FASB'S PENSION ACCOUNTING PROJECT
KERN, BETH BURCHFIELD	THE IMPACT OF THE ECONOMIC RECOVERY TAX ACT OF 1981 ON CORPORATE INVESTMENT IN PLANT AND EQUIPMENT
KHURANA, INDER KRISHAN	AN EMPIRICAL INVESTIGATION INTO THE SECURITY MARKET EFFECTS OF FASB STATEMENT NUMBER 94
KILE, CHARLES OWEN, JR.	AN ANALYSIS OF THE IMPACT OF OMITTED EVALUATIVE INFORMATION ON FINANCIAL REPORTING: EVIDENCE FROM DISCLOSURES TO AMEND MANAGEMENT'S DISCUSSION AND ANALYSIS
KIM, BYOUNG HO	THE ASSOCIATION BETWEEN UNEXPECTED CHANGES IN INVENTORY AND RECEIVABLE BALANCES AND SECURITY PRICE CHANGES: CROSS-SECTIONAL ANALYSES
KIM, CHANGSOO	A STUDY OF INVESTMENT IN INFORMATION TECHNOLOGY: FINANCIAL PERFORMANCE EFFECT AND FUTURE ECONOMIC BENEFIT TO THE FIRM
KIM, GWON HEE	LAG STRUCTURE, AMORTIZATION, AND PRODUCTIVITY CONTRIBUTION OF RESEARCH AND DEVELOPMENT COSTS
KIM, HOJOONG	AN INVESTIGATION INTO FACTORS DETERMINING THE CASH FLOWS/STOCK RETURNS RELATIONSHIP
KIM, HWAN	THE SPEED OF SECURITY MARKET REACTION AND THE LEVEL OF UNCERTAINTY ASSOCIATED WITH ANNUAL EARNINGS INFORMATION: ANALYSIS AND EVIDENCE
KIM, HYUK	AN EMPIRICAL STUDY OF THE MARKET REACTION TO STATEMENT OF FINANCIAL ACCOUNTING STANDARDS NO. 52: 'FOREIGN CURRENCYTRANSLATION'
KIM, IL-WOON	AN EMPIRICAL STUDY ON THE INFORMATION CONTENT OF FINANCIAL LEVERAGE TO STOCKHOLDERS
KIM, JAE-OH	SEGMENTAL DISCLOSURES AND INFORMATION CONTENT OF EARNINGS ANNOUNCEMENTS: THEORETICAL AND EMPIRICAL ANALYSIS

KIM, JEEHONG	THE E/P EFFECT AND THE EARNINGS FORECAST ERROR EFFECT: A COMPARISON OF TWO STOCK MARKET ANOMALIES
KIM, JEONG BON	EMPIRICAL EVALUATION OF THE VALUES OF ACCOUNTING ALTERNATIVES IN THE OIL AND GAS INDUSTRY IN THE CONTEXT OF RISK ASSESSMENT
KIM, JEONG YOUN	AN EMPIRICAL INVESTIGATION OF THE EFFECT OF LIFO ADOPTION ON DIVIDEND POLICIES
KIM, JEONG-JAE	PRICE AND VOLUME REACTION TO THE ANNOUNCEMENT OF QUALIFIED AUDIT OPINIONS
KIM, JEONGKUK	THE EFFECT OF SFAS NO. 52 ON THE SECURITY ANALYSTS' PERCEPTION OF THE PREDICTIVE USEFULNESS OF REPORTED EARNINGS
KIM, JINSUN	AN EMPIRICAL ANALYSIS OF CHANGES IN INVENTORY ACCOUNTING METHODS IN 1974
KIM, JONG HO	A BETTER SURROGATE FOR MARKET EXPECTATION OF QUARTERLY EARNINGS
KIM, JOOHO	TOBIN'S Q VERSUS MODIFIED Q: AN INVESTIGATION OF SHAREHOLDERS' WEALTH MAXIMIZATION VERSUS FIRM VALUE MAXIMIZATION
KIM, JUN	PRIOR AND POSTERIOR BELIEFS, DIVERGENCE OF ANALYSTS' FORECASTS, AND TRADING ACTIVITY
KIM, KWON-JUNG	INFORMATION RELEASES, STOCK RETURNS, AND FIRM SIZE
KIM, KYUNGHO	THE EFFECT OF ACCOUNTING BASED BONUS PLAN INCENTIVES ON MANAGERS' FINANCIAL REPORTING BEHAVIOR AND ANALYSTS' FORECAST ACCURACY
KIM, MOON KYUM	INCREMENTAL INFORMATION CONTENT OF CASH FLOW VARIABLES: A SPANNING APPROACH
KIM, MOONCHUL	THE ROLE OF ACCOUNTING INFORMATION IN THE PRICING OF IPOS
KIM, OLIVER	PRICE AND VOLUME REACTIONS TO PUBLIC ANNOUNCEMENTS AND ENDOGENOUS PRE-ANNOUNCEMENT INFORMATION
KIM, SUNGSOO	INTEREST RATE SWAPS: FIRM CHARACTERISTICS, MOTIVATIONS AND DIFFERENTIAL MARKET REACTIONS
KIM, TAE-YONG	EARLY DEBT-REDEMPTION: AN EMPIRICAL INVESTIGATION OF MOTIVATION AND IMPACT
KIM, YONG HWAN	LIQUIDITY, INFORMED TRADING, AND PUBLIC INFORMATION: THEORY AND EVIDENCE--A MARKET MICROSTRUCTURE ANALYSIS
KIMMEL, PAUL DAVID	AN INVESTIGATION OF THE USE OF ACCOUNTING NUMBERS IN THE REGULATION OF BANK CAPITAL
KING, JOHN WILLIAM	INFORMATION EFFECTS OF TRANSLATION ADJUSTMENTS UNDER SFAS 52 AND SFAS 70
KINNEY, MICHAEL RICHARD	CHANGES IN CORPORATE CAPITAL STRUCTURES AND INVESTMENT IN RESPONSE TO TAX INCENTIVES IN THE ECONOMIC RECOVERY TAX ACT OF 1981

Listing by Research Method

KIRK, FLORENCE REARDON	THE ROLE OF TAXES IN ACQUISITIONS
KIRSCH, ROBERT JOHN	SFAS NO 52, AN ACCOUNTING POLICY INTERVENTION: U.S.-BASED MULTINATIONAL CORPORATE PRE-ENACTMENT LOBBYING BEHAVIOR AND POST-ENACTMENT REACTION
KLEIN, LINDA SCHMID	EARNINGS INFORMATION CONTENT OF STOCK DIVIDEND AND SPLIT ANNOUNCEMENTS
KLEINSORGE, ILENE K.	INCORPORATION OF QUALITY CONSIDERATIONS IN MEASURING RELATIVE TECHNICAL EFFICIENCY OF NURSING HOMES
KOCH, PAULA LOUISE	THE EFFECTS OF FINANCIAL DISTRESS ON ACCOUNTING METHOD CHOICE
KOCHER, CLAUDIA SUE	COSTLY CONTRACTING: THE CASE OF EVENT RISK COVENANTS
KOH, HIAN CHYE	PREDICTION OF GOING-CONCERN STATUS: A PROBIT MODEL FOR THE AUDITORS
KOH, SEUNGHEE	RATIONAL ACCOUNTING CHOICE UNDER INFORMATION ASYMMETRY: THE CASE OF INVENTORY ACCOUNTING
KOPEL, ROANN RAE	VOLUNTARY CHANGES IN ACCOUNTING POLICIES: AN APPLICATION OF THE POSITIVE THEORY OF ACCOUNTING
KORTE, LEON	SYSTEMATIC BIAS EFFECTS AND REGULATOR INTERVENTION: THE SAVINGS AND LOAN INDUSTRY
KOTHARI, SRIPRAKASH	A COMPARISON OF ALTERNATIVE PROXIES FOR THE MARKET'S EXPECTATION OF QUARTERLY EARNINGS
KRIPPEL, GREGORY LEE	THE ECONOMIC DETERMINANTS OF THE TIME-SERIES PROPERTIES OF EARNINGS, SALES, AND CASH FLOWS FROM OPERATIONS
KRISHNAN, JAGANNATHAN	AUDITOR SWITCHING, OPINION SHOPPING AND CLIENT SIZE
KRUEGER, THOMAS MICHAEL	AN EMPIRICAL ANALYSIS OF THE EFFICIENT MARKET HYPOTHESIS BASED ON WIDELY DISSEMINATED ANOMALY INFORMATION
KRUMWIEDE, TIMOTHY GERARD	THE EFFECT OF TAXATION ON RESIDENTIAL REAL ESTATE: AN EMPIRICAL ANALYSIS OF REAL ESTATE CONSTRUCTION
KUMAR, KRISHNA RADHAKRISHNAN	THE DETERMINANTS OF PERFORMANCE PLAN ADOPTION: AN EMPIRICAL STUDY
KWAK, SU KEUN	AN EMPIRICAL EVALUATION OF THE PREDICTIVE ABILITY OF SEGMENT DATA DISCLOSED IN ACCORDANCE WITH FASB STATEMENT NO. 14
KWAK, WIKIL	EARNINGS RESPONSE COEFFICIENTS AND THE QUALITY OF EARNINGS: THE CASE OF AUDITOR CHANGE
KWON, SOON-YONG	INCOME STRATEGY AND EARNINGS RESPONSE COEFFICIENTS
KWON, SOOYOUNG	CHOICE OF CONSOLIDATION POLICY AND PARENT FIRMS' RESPONSES TO SFAS NO. 94: CONSOLIDATION OF ALL MAJORITY-OWNED SUBSIDIARIES

Listing by Research Method   363

KWON, SUNG SOO — FINENESS OF INFLATION-ADJUSTED ACCOUNTING DISCLOSURES AND STOCK PRICE VARIABILITY

KWON, SUNKOOK — ECONOMIC DETERMINANTS OF THE ASSUMED INTEREST RATE IN PENSION ACCOUNTING

LAGRONE, R. MICHAEL — AN EVALUATION OF MULTIVARIATE EARNINGS FORECASTING

LAI, SYOUCHING — AN ANALYTICAL ANALYSIS OF EPS RULES FOR CONVERTIBLE SECURITIES, WARRANTS, AND OPTIONS

LANDER, JOEL MARTIN — ESSAYS ON THE CORPORATE TAX POLICY EFFECTS ON INVESTMENT AND FINANCING CHOICES

LANESE, KAREN BENNETT — VISIBILITY OF INCOME: A MODEL TO PREDICT USE OF THE CHILD CARE CREDIT

LANGSAM, SHELDON ALLEN — THE EFFECT OF MANDATORY INCLUSION OF COMPONENT UNITS ON THE REPORTED FINANCIAL CONDITION OF SELECTED LOCAL GOVERNMENTAL UNITS

LARSON, ROBERT KEITH — AN EMPIRICAL INVESTIGATION OF THE RELATIONSHIPS BETWEEN INTERNATIONAL ACCOUNTING STANDARDS, EQUITY MARKETS AND ECONOMIC GROWTH IN DEVELOPING COUNTRIES

LASALLE, RANDALL EUGENE — THE EFFECT OF CEO TENURE ON EARNINGS MANAGEMENT

LAUX, JUDITH ANN — CONTENT ANALYSIS AND CORPORATE BANKRUPTCY

LAWRENCE, CAROL MARTIN — THE EFFECT OF ACCOUNTING SYSTEM TYPE AND OWNERSHIP STRUCTURE ON HOSPITAL COSTS

LAWRENCE, ROBYN — IN-SUBSTANCE DEFEASANCE: AN EMPIRICAL EXAMINATION OF THE FACTORS AFFECTING THE MARKET REACTION AND THE DECISION

LEAUBY, BRUCE ALAN — DETERMINANTS OF CORPORATE TAX AVOIDANCE STRATEGY: AN EMPIRICAL ANALYSIS

LEE, ANDREW TONG KIN — ON DELAYED RESPONSES TO EARNINGS ANNOUNCEMENTS

LEE, BYUNG-CHULL — ECONOMIC CONSEQUENCES OF THE ACCOUNTING RULE FOR SOFTWARE COSTS

LEE, CHANGWOO — MARKET REACTIONS TO LEASE LIABILITIES AND REPORTING ENVIRONMENT CHANGES

LEE, CHARLES M. C. — INFORMATION DISSEMINATION AND THE SMALL TRADER: AN INTRADAY ANALYSIS OF THE SMALL TRADER RESPONSE TO ANNOUNCEMENTS OF CORPORATE EARNINGS AND CHANGES IN DIVIDEND POLICY

LEE, DAISUN — INFORMATION CONTENT AND ECONOMIC CONSEQUENCES OF INTERIM SEGMENT REPORTING: AN EMPIRICAL TEST

LEE, KYUNG JOO — THE EFFECT OF TIME-SERIES PROPERTIES ON THE PREDICTIVE VALUE OF QUARTERLY EARNINGS FOR FORECASTING ANNUAL EARNINGS

LEE, MANWOO — IMPACT OF UTILIZING LONG-TERM EXECUTIVE COMPENSATION PLANS ON CAPITAL INVESTMENT DECISIONS

LEE, MINWOO	THE ROLES OF AUDITORS AND INVESTMENT BANKERS IN SIGNALLING PRIVATE INFORMATION AND INSURING LITIGATION RISK IN THE NEW EQUITY ISSUES MARKET
LEE, MYUNG GON	THE DIFFERENTIAL PREDICTIVE INFORMATION CONTENT OF EARNINGS ON ANALYSTS' FORECAST REVISIONS
LEE, NAM JOO	AN EMPIRICAL EVALUATION OF OUTLIER ADJUSTED QUARTERLY EARNINGS
LEE, SUK JUN	THE EFFECT OF GAAP DIFFERENCES ON PRICE VARIABILITY AND DISPERSION OF BELIEFS
LEFANOWICZ, CRAIG EDWARD	IMPLICATIONS OF CHANGES IN EQUITY VALUES ASSOCIATED WITH SIGNIFICANT EQUITY INVESTMENTS FOR INVESTEE AND INVESTOR FIRMS
LEGGETT, CARL LEE	AN EMPIRICAL INVESTIGATION OF THE MARKET REACTION TO SELECTED CATEGORIES OF DISCRETIONARY CHARGES
LEMLER, BRADLEY K.	TAXPAYER EXPECTATIONS, TAX INVESTMENT INCENTIVES AND TAXPAYER ECONOMIC BEHAVIOR: AN ANALYSIS OF INVESTMENT BEHAVIOR IN MANUFACTURING FIRMS FROM 1954 TO 1985
LEONG, KENNETH KIN ON	THE EXISTENCE OF BONUS COMPENSATION PLANS AND THE RELATED EFFECT ON THE SIZE OF REPORTED ACCOUNTING EARNINGS
LETOURNEAU, CLAIRE ANGELA	FINANCIAL DISCLOSURE AND THE ACCOUNTANT'S RESPONSIBILITY TO SHAREHOLDERS: THE CASE OF INSIDER TRADING
LIM, SUK SIG	ACCURACY OF PARTIAL VALUATION RULES AND OPTIMAL USE OF PRICE INDEXES
LIM, TAYSEOP	THE EFFECT OF INFORMATION ASYMMETRY AROUND EARNINGS ANNOUNCEMENTS
LIN, HSIOU-WEI WILLIAM	SECURITY ANALYSTS' INVESTMENT RECOMMENDATIONS
LIN, LIANGQI	ECONOMIC DETERMINANTS OF VOLUNTARY ACCOUNTING CHOICES FOR R&D EXPENDITURES IN BELGIUM
LIN, MEI-HWA	AN EMPIRICAL STUDY OF INFORMATION TRANSFER FROM A LEADING FIRM TO LARGE FIRMS AND SMALL FIRMS IN THE SAME INDUSTRY
LIN, SUMING	INCOME TAX RETURN PREPARATION FEES AND TAX SAVINGS OF USING TAX RETURN PREPARERS
LIN, WENSHAN	ACCOUNTING REGULATION AND INFORMATION ASYMMETRY IN THE CAPITAL MARKETS: AN EMPIRICAL STUDY OF ACCOUNTING STANDARD SFAS NO 87
LIN, YOU-AN ROBERT	THE USE OF SUPPLEMENTARY ACCOUNTING DISCLOSURES FOR CORPORATE TAKEOVER TARGETS PREDICTION
LINDAHL, FREDERICK WILLIAM	QUANTAL CHOICE MODELS AND ACCOUNTING CHANGE
LINDSAY, DAVID HENDERSON	A TEST OF CONTRACTING COST THEORY ON STATEMENT OF FINANCIAL ACCOUNTING STANDARDS NO. 2: ACCOUNTING FOR RESEARCH AND DEVELOPMENT COSTS
LINSMEIER, THOMAS J.	A DEBT COVENANT RATIONALE FOR A MARKET REACTION TO A MANDATED ACCOUNTING CHANGE: THE CASE OF THE INVESTMENT TAX CREDIT

LINTON, FRANK BRUCE	FEDERAL INCOME TAXING SYSTEM AND ITS EFFECT ON STATE INCOME TAX STRUCTURES
LIPE, ROBERT CALVIN	THE INFORMATION CONTAINED IN THE COMPONENTS OF EARNINGS
LITTLE, PHILIP LEE	AN EXAMINATION OF FACTORS RELEVANT TO THE PREDICTION OF GOING CONCERN SUBJECT-TO QUALIFICATIONS OR DISCLAIMERS OF OPINION IN THE OIL AND GAS INDUSTRY
LIU, CHAO-SHIN	MANAGEMENT EARNINGS FORECASTS, SECURITY PRICE VARIABILITY, AND THE MARGINAL INFORMATION CONTENT OF EARNINGS ANNOUNCEMENTS
LIU, SHUEN-ZEN	SIGNALING, CAPITAL ADEQUACY RATIO REGULATIONS, AND THE RECOGNITION OF LOAN IMPAIRMENT BY COMMERCIAL BANKS
LIU, SUPING	SFAS 94: AN EXAMINATION OF THE ASSOCIATION BETWEEN MARKET AND ACCOUNTING RISK MEASUREMENTS
LO, MAY HWA	DIFFERENTIAL CAPITAL MARKET VALUATIONS OF FUNCTIONAL COMPONENTS OF EARNINGS: AN EMPIRICAL ANALYSIS
LOPEZ GRACIA, JOSE	ACCOUNTING INFORMATION AND STOCK EXCHANGE: EMPIRICAL ANALYSIS OF THE INTERIM REPORTS AND THEIR RELEVANCE IN DECISION-MAKING [LA INFORMACION CONTABLE Y EL MERCADO DE VALORES: ANALISIS EMPIRICO DE LOS INFORMES
LOUDDER, MARTHA LYNN	AN EMPIRICAL INVESTIGATION OF THE ECONOMIC EFFECTS OF SFAS 90 AND 92 IN THE ELECTRIC UTILITY INDUSTRY
LUBICH, BRUCE HOWARD	THE IMPACT OF TAX NONCOMPLIANCE ON HORIZONTAL AND VERTICAL DISTRIBUTIONS OF INCOME
LUCAS, MARCIA J.	EARNINGS PER SHARE: A STUDY OF CURRENT REPORTING
LUKAWITZ, JAMES MARTIN	THE EFFECT OF PARTIAL EQUITY ISSUES ON THE MEASUREMENT OF FINANCIAL LEVERAGE
LUTTMAN, SUZANNE MARIE	THE DISTRIBUTIONAL AND LABOR SUPPLY EFFECTS OF ALTERNATIVE INDIVIDUAL INCOME TAX PROPOSALS
LYNCH, HOWELL JACKSON, JR.	EFFECTIVE CORPORATE INCOME TAX RATES AND THEIR RELATIONSHIP TO CORPORATE ATTRIBUTES: A MULTIDEFINITIONAL, MULTIPERIOD VIEW
LYON, JOHN DOUGLAS	THE VALUATION INFORMATION ASSOCIATED WITH THE SEQUENCE OF ACCOUNTING EARNINGS
MA, SHEREE SHIOW-RU	AN EMPIRICAL EXAMINATION OF THE STOCK MARKET'S REACTION TO THE PENSION ACCOUNTING DELIBERATIONS OF THE FINANCIAL ACCOUNTING STANDARDS BOARD
MAGNAN, MICHEL LOUIS	THE RELATION BETWEEN INDUSTRY-SPECIFIC VARIABLES AND COMPENSATION: THE CASE OF COMMERCIAL BANKS
MAHER, JOHN JOSEPH	PENSION OBLIGATIONS AND THE BOND CREDIT MARKET: AN EMPIRICAL ANALYSIS OF ACCOUNTING NUMBERS
MAHMOUD, AMAL ABDEL WAKIL	THE EFFECT OF DIFFERENTIAL AMOUNTS OF INTERIM INFORMATION ON STOCK PRICES VARIABILITY: THE CASE OF ANALYSTS' FORECASTS AND FIRM SIZE
MAKAR, STEPHEN DOUGLAS	POLITICAL COSTS OVER THE BUSINESS CYCLE: THE INCENTIVES FOR THE MANAGEMENT OF ACCOUNTING ACCRUALS

MANDE, VIVEK GOPAL	THE INFORMATION CONTENT OF EARNINGS AND DIVIDENDS: THE SUBSTITUTION HYPOTHESIS
MANRY, DAVID LEE	TARGET FIRM EARNINGS, GREENMAIL, AND SHAREHOLDERS' INTERESTS
MANSFIELD, JON L.	THE EFFECTS OF SFAS NO. 8 AND NO. 52 ON MULTINATIONAL COMPANY STOCK RETURNS: 1973-1982
MANZON, GIL B., JR.	AN INVESTIGATION OF FACTORS AFFECTING THE INCOME STRATEGIES OF FIRMS SUBJECT TO THE ALTERNATIVE MINIMUM TAX
MARGAVIO, GEANIE WADGE	PORTFOLIO RESPONSES OF SAVINGS AND LOANS TO THE TAX REFORM ACT OF 1986
MARSHALL, LEISA LYNN	AN EMPIRICAL INVESTIGATION OF FINANCIAL MEASURES' ABILITY TO PREDICT FINANCIAL DISTRESS LEVELS OF AGRICULTURAL PRODUCERS
MARTIN, LOUISA ANN	PRIVATE INFORMATION AND BLOCK TRADING
MARTIN, SUSAN WORK	MODELING THE LOCAL GOVERNMENT GENERAL FUND DEFICIT
MASTRACCHIO, NICHOLAS JAMES, JR.	AN EXAMINATION OF THE THEORETICAL BASIS AND THE APPLICATION OF THE CAPITALIZATION OF EARNINGS METHOD AND THE EXCESS EARNINGS METHOD TO CLOSELY HELD BUSINESSES
MATSUNAGA, STEVEN ROY	THE EFFECTS OF FINANCIAL REPORTING AND TAX COSTS ON THE RELATIVE USE OF EMPLOYEE STOCK OPTIONS
MATTISON, DOROTHY MCCALL	THE INFLUENCE OF SELECTED VARIABLES ON THE FINANCIAL PERFORMANCE OF NOT-FOR-PROFIT AND FOR-PROFIT HOSPITALS: A COMPARATIVE ANALYSIS
MAZHAR, NAHEED	FACTORS RELATED TO CORPORATE CAPITAL STRUCTURE
MCCARRON, KAREN ELIZABETH BRADSHAW	AN EMPIRICAL INVESTIGATION OF THE USEFULNESS OF FINANCIAL ACCOUNTING RATIOS IN PREDICTING THE EFFECTS OF A TROUBLED DEBT RESTRUCTURING
MCCARTHY, MARK GOODWIN	THE INFORMATION CONTENT OF THE FORM 10-K AND ANNUAL REPORT TO SHAREHOLDERS: A TRADING VOLUME AND PRICE APPROACH
MCCLURE, RONNIE CLYDE	THE IMPACT ON CHARITABLE CLASSES IN DALLAS COUNTY, TEXAS, RESULTING FROM CHANGES IN THE TAX ECONOMICS OF PRIVATE PHILANTHROPY
MCEWEN, RUTH ANN	AN EMPIRICAL ASSESSMENT OF ERROR METRICS APPLIED TO ANALYSTS' FORECASTS OF EARNINGS
MCGHEE, THOMAS MITCHELL	A COMPARISON OF THE STATUTORY AND ECONOMIC INCIDENCE AMONG THE TAX REFORM ACT OF 1986, PRIOR LAW AND THREE TAX PROPOSALS
MCGOWAN, JOHN R.	AN ANALYSIS OF THE EFFECT OF THE TAX REFORM ACT OF 1986 ON STOCK PRICES: A MARKET STUDY
MCLAUGHLIN, THOMAS DAVID	GOING CONCERN DETERMINATIONS UNDER SAS NO. 59 AND THE RESULTING IMPACT ON AUDIT OPINIONS: THE CASE OF THE SAVINGS AND LOAN INDUSTRY
MCQUEEN, PATRICIA DORAN	THE INFORMATION CONTENT OF FOREIGN GAAP EARNINGS AND SHAREOWNERS' EQUITY AND THE UNITED STATES GAAP RECONCILIATION DISCLOSURES IN SEC FORM 20-F

Listing by Research Method   367

MEADE, NANCY MARGARET LOWMAN   ANTITAKEOVER DEVICES AND FIRM PERFORMANCE: AN EMPIRICAL STUDY USING
ACCOUNTING MEASURES

MENSAH, MICHAEL OFOSU   THE INCREMENTAL INFORMATION CONTENT OF CASH FLOW FROM OPERATIONS--AN
EXPLORATORY STUDY OF INTERTEMPORAL AND FIRM-SPECIFIC EFFECTS

MESSINA, FRANK MICHAEL   PREDICTION MODELS FOR DEBT COVENANT VIOLATIONS OF AGRICULTURAL
COOPERATIVES

MEYER, DAN WESLEY   SOME CHARACTERISTICS AND ENVIRONMENTAL SENSITIVITIES OF TAXPAYERS TAKING
THE UNITED STATES POLITICAL CONTRIBUTION TAX CREDIT DURING 1979-1982

MEYERMANS, ERIC AUGUST   ECONOMETRIC ALLOCATION SYSTEMS FOR THE FOREIGN EXCHANGE MARKET:
SPECIFICATION, ESTIMATION AND TESTING OF TRANSMISSION MECHANISMS UNDER
CURRENCY SUBSTITUTION

MICHELSON, STUART EDWARD   CORPORATE CAPITAL EXPENDITURES, TAX LAWS, ASSETS-IN-PLACE, AND THE MARKET
VALUE OF THE FIRM

MIDDLETON, MARY MARTIN   THE INFORMATIONAL IMPACT OF PENSION LIABILITIES ON CORPORATE RISK

MILACEK, EMIL CRAIG, JR.   AN ASSESSMENT OF THE EFFECT OF THE INVESTMENT TAX CREDIT ON CAPITAL
INVESTMENT IN FARM SUPPLY COOPERATIVES IN MICHIGAN, MINNESOTA, NORTH
DAKOTA, AND WISCONSIN

MINYARD, DONALD HOYT   AN EXAMINATION OF VARIABLES ASSOCIATED WITH DIVESTMENT DECISIONS

MITCHELL, NAOMI CELIA   THE RELATIONSHIP OF CERTAIN ENVIRONMENTAL PERFORMANCE INDICATORS AND
FINANCIAL STATEMENTS

MITCHEM, CHERYL EVELYN DRAKE   A CASH FLOW AND MACROECONOMIC MODEL OF FINANCIAL DISTRESS

MITENKO, GRAHAM ROBERT   AN EMPIRICAL INVESTIGATION OF THE RELATIONSHIP AMONG AND PREDICTIVE
ABILITY OF FOUR MEASURES OF CASH FLOW

MITTELSTAEDT, H. FRED   MANAGEMENT SURVIVAL STRATEGIES AND THE DECISION TO REDUCE PENSION PLAN
FUNDING: AN EMPIRICAL TEST

MITTERMAIER, LINDA JEAN   THE IMPACT OF INFLATION ON INDIVIDUAL FEDERAL INCOME TAX LIABILITIES: AN
ANALYSIS OF REVENUE AND EQUITY EFFECTS

MOHRMAN, MARY BETH   MANDATED ACCOUNTING CHANGES AND DEBT CONTRACTS

MOODY, SHARON MATHIS   AN EMPIRICAL STUDY OF THE ASSOCIATION BETWEEN THE SALARY AND BONUS
COMPONENTS OF EXECUTIVE COMPENSATION ANDPRINCIPAL-AGENT RISK SHARING AND
PERFORMANCE MEASUREMENT

MOONEY, JULIAN LOWELL   A COMPARISON OF EARNINGS AND CASH FLOW AS RISK MEASURES DURING DIFFERING
ECONOMIC CONDITIONS

MOORE, JOHN WILLIAM   AN EMPIRICAL INVESTIGATION OF THE FINANCIAL EFFECTS OF UNION REPRESENTATION
AND DECERTIFICATION ELECTIONS ONPUBLICLY TRADED FIRMS

MOORE, MICHAEL JOE   AN EMPIRICAL INVESTIGATION OF THE DETERMINANTS OF LOAN LOSSES AT SMALL
BANKS

MOORE, RONALD KENNETH   PREDICTION OF BANKRUPTCY USING FINANCIAL RATIOS, INFORMATION MEASURES,
NATIONAL ECONOMIC DATA AND TEXAS ECONOMIC DATA

Listing by Research Method

MORELAND, KEITH ARON	AN EMPIRICAL STUDY OF THE EFFECT OF AUDITOR SANCTIONS ON THE ASSOCIATION BETWEEN EARNINGS AND SECURITY RETURNS
MORRILL, CAMERON KEITH JOSEPH	CORPORATE LEADERS, FIRM PERFORMANCE AND ACCOUNTING EARNINGS
MORRIS, NORMA WILLIAMS	THE ASSOCIATION BETWEEN SELECTED CORPORATE ATTRIBUTES AND MANAGEMENT INCENTIVES FOR VOLUNTARY ACCOUNTING DISCLOSURE
MORRIS, ROSELYN EVERTS	THE PERFORMANCE OF AUDITORS IN MODIFYING OPINIONS OF FAILED BANKS
MORRISON, THEODORE DAVIDSON, III	AN EMPIRICAL MODEL FOR THE DESCRIPTION AND FORECASTING OF QUARTERLY EARNINGS PER SHARE FOR SMALL AND NEGLECTED FIRMS
MOUNT, CAROLE C.	THE MARGINAL IMPACT OF CASH FLOW INFORMATION ON BANK FAILURE PREDICTION: AN EMPIRICAL INVESTIGATION
MOYER, SUSAN ELAINE	ACCOUNTING CHOICES IN COMMERCIAL BANKS
MOZES, CHAIM A.	PREANNOUNCEMENT ACCOUNTING INFORMATION: MEASUREMENT TECHNIQUES AND EMPIRICAL PROPERTIES
MURDOCH, ALASTAIR	DIVIDENDS AND EARNINGS: THEIR EFFECT ON FIRM VALUE
MYNATT, PATRICIA GRAFF	THE INFORMATION CONTENT OF FINANCIAL STATEMENT RELEASES
NA, CHONGKIL	THE ASSOCIATION BETWEEN ACCOUNTING ACCRUALS AND MEAN REVERSION OF ANNUAL EARNINGS
NA, IN-CHUL	INVESTORS' REACTION TO THE EFFECT OF STATEMENT OF FINANCIAL ACCOUNTING STANDARDS NO. 52 ON 1981 EARNINGS FOR THE EARLY ADOPTERS: AN EMPIRICAL STUDY
NA, YOUNG	STOCK MARKET REACTION TO FASB NO. 106: THE DISCLOSURE OF POSTRETIREMENT BENEFIT COSTS
NAGLE, BRIAN M.	AUDIT REPORT MODIFICATIONS AND AUDITOR SWITCHES
NAM, YOUNG-HO	AN EMPIRICAL EXAMINATION OF THE ASSOCIATION BETWEEN FIRM CHARACTERISTICS AND THE ADOPTION OF LONG-TERM PERFORMANCE PLANS
NASSIRIPOUR, SIA	PREDICTING FUTURE CASH FLOW: CURRENT CASH FLOW VS. CURRENT EARNINGS
NATARAJAN, RAMACHANDRAN	THE USE OF DISCRETIONARY ACCOUNTING REPORTS IN MANAGEMENT COMPENSATION CONTRACTS
NDUBIZU, GORDIAN ANUMUDU	AN EMPIRICAL INVESTIGATION OF THE SECURITY MARKET REACTION TO MULTINATIONAL ACCOUNTING CHANGES: STATEMENT OF FINANCIAL ACCOUNTING STANDARD NUMBER 52, FOREIGN CURRENCY TRANSLATION
NEILL, JOHN D., III	THE ROLE OF ACCOUNTING NUMBERS IN THE 'LONG-TERM' MISPRICING OF INITIAL PUBLIC SECURITY OFFERINGS
NELSON, JACOB JOHN	CHANGES IN FIRMS' VOLUNTARY DISCLOSURES OF EARNINGS PROJECTIONS ASSOCIATED WITH OPTIONS LISTING

Listing by Research Method   369

NELSON, TONI LYNNE	THE EFFECT OF ACCOUNTING POLICY CHOICES ON THE RELATIONSHIP BETWEEN EARNINGS AND RETURNS
NEWBERRY, KAYE JEANNE	FOREIGN TAX CREDIT LIMITATIONS AND PUBLIC ISSUANCES BY UNITED STATES MULTINATIONALS: NEW EVIDENCE OF TAX CLIENTELES
NICHOLS, DAVE LEROY	SFAS 14'S GEOGRAPHIC SEGMENT DISCLOSURES AND THE ABILITY OF SECURITY ANALYSTS TO FORECAST EARNINGS
NISWANDER, FREDERICK DEAN	ACCOUNTING AND FINANCING CHOICE AND CAPITAL ADEQUACY: AN EMPIRICAL STUDY OF PUBLIC AND PRIVATE COMMERCIAL BANKS
NOLAND, THOMAS RODNEY	THE SPEED OF THE MARKET RESPONSE TO EARNINGS ANNOUNCEMENTS AND THE BID-ASK SPREAD: AN EMPIRICAL STUDY
NWAEZE, EMEKA T.	THE EFFECTS OF THE PARAMETERS OF EARNINGS EXPECTATION ON STOCK PRICES: A STRUCTURAL MODEL AND EMPIRICAL EVIDENCE
O'BRIEN, PATRICIA COLLEEN	AN EMPIRICAL ANALYSIS OF FORECASTS OF EARNINGS PER SHARE
O'BRYAN, DAVID	THE ASSOCIATION OF EARNINGS AND CASH FLOW COMPONENTS WITH CORPORATE BOND RETURNS
O'LEARY, DANIEL EDMUND	THE RELATIONSHIP OF NONACCOUNTING DISCLOSURES TO FIRM VALUATION AND PROFITABILITY: AN EMPIRICAL ANALYSIS OF TOBIN'S Q RATIO
ODAIYAPPA, RAMASAMY	ECONOMIC CONSEQUENCES OF FINANCIAL ACCOUNTING STANDARDS BOARD STATEMENT NUMBER 33: AN INSIDER TRADING PERSPECTIVE
OKCABOL, FAHRETTIN	REGULATION AND ACCOUNTING PRACTICE: AN EVALUATION OF THE EFFICACY OF SEC MANDATORY REPORTING REQUIREMENTS
OKLESHEN, MARILYN JEAN	THE SECURITY MARKET REACTION OF FINANCIAL INSTITUTIONS TO SFAS 95: THE STATEMENT OF CASH FLOWS
OLIVER, ELIZABETH GOAD	MANAGERS' USE OF FASB'S MULTI-YEAR TRANSITION PERIODS: THE CASE OF PENSIONS
OMER, KHURSHEED	AN INVESTIGATION OF PLOUGHBACK EARNINGS AS A FACTOR IN SECURITY PRICING
OMER, THOMAS CLAYTON	ECONOMIC INCENTIVES AND ACCOUNTING POLICY CHOICES
ONVURAL, NUR MEVLUDE	ECONOMIES OF SCALE AND ECONOMIES OF SCOPE IN NORTH CAROLINA SAVINGS AND LOAN INSTITUTIONS
OU, CHIN SHYH	AN EMPIRICAL STUDY OF COST DRIVERS IN THE UNITED STATES BANKING INDUSTRY
PAGACH, DONALD PATRICK	MANAGERIAL INCENTIVES AND THE INTRADAY TIMING OF EARNINGS ANNOUNCEMENTS
PAK, HONG SEOK	THE EFFECTS OF INCOME SMOOTHING AND CONTRACTING COSTS ON MANAGERS' ATTITUDES TOWARDS THE SELECTION OF FOREIGN TRANSLATION ACCOUNTING PRINCIPLES: A STRUCTURAL EQUATION MODEL
PAN, ALEXANDER M.	THE USE OF PANEL DATA IN ANALYTICAL REVIEW BY AUDITORS

Listing by Research Method 370

PANG, YANG HOONG   FINANCIAL DISCLOSURE AND ANALYSTS' FORECAST SUPERIORITY

PANT, LAURIE W.   THE DETERMINANTS OF CORPORATE TURNAROUND

PARK, CHANGHUN (PETER)   THE RELEVANCE OF REPLACEMENT COST ASSET INFORMATION TO FIRM VALUATION

PARK, GWANGHOON   THE ASSOCIATION BETWEEN MANAGEMENT COMPENSATION AND ACCOUNTING POLICY DECISIONS: AN EXTENSION OF THE BONUS HYPOTHESIS

PARK, KYUNGJOO   QUALITY OF ACCOUNTING EARNINGS UNDER ALTERNATIVE PENSION ACCOUNTING METHODS

PARK, MANYONG   INCREMENTAL INFORMATION CONTAINED IN THE SFAS NO. 33 DISCLOSURES: A CLOSER EXAMINATION

PARK, SECHOUL   INSIDER TRADING ACTIVITY SURROUNDING CORPORATE EARNINGS ANNOUNCEMENT

PARKASH, MOHINDER   THE IMPACT OF A FIRM'S CONTRACTS AND SIZE ON THE ACCURACY, DISPERSION AND REVISIONS OF FINANCIAL ANALYSTS' FORECASTS: A THEORETICAL AND EMPIRICAL INVESTIGATION

PARSEGIAN, ELSA VARSENIG   A TEST OF SOME OF THE EFFECTS OF DIFFERENT PROPERTY RIGHTS STRUCTURES ON MANAGERIAL BEHAVIOR IN THE LIFE INSURANCE INDUSTRY

PASKIN, STEVEN   SOME ECONOMIC DETERMINANTS OF DISCRETIONARY ACCOUNTING CHANGES

PASTORIA, GAIL   THE USE OF ACCOUNTING ACCRUALS AS A DEFENSIVE STRATEGY TO DETER TAKEOVERS

PATE, GWENDOLYN RICHARDSON   A TEST OF THE THEORY OF MANAGEMENT'S PREFERENCES FOR ACCOUNTING STANDARDS: EVIDENCE FROM FASB STATEMENT NO. 94

PATTEN, DENNIS MICHAEL   THE MARKET REACTION TO SOCIAL RESPONSIBILITY INFORMATION DISCLOSURES: THE CASE OF THE SULLIVAN PRINCIPLES SIGNINGS

PAVA, MOSES L.   FINANCIAL ANALYSTS' FORECASTS AND FINANCIAL ANALYSTS' FORECASTING CUES

PAZ, ARMANDO J.   FORECASTING SAVINGS AND LOAN FAILURES USING FINANCIAL ACCOUNTING INFORMATION

PEARSON, TIMOTHY A.   AN INVESTIGATION OF THE RELATIONSHIP BETWEEN AUDIT FEES AND AUDITOR REPUTATION: THE MARKET FOR INSURANCE AUDIT CLIENTS

PERSONS, OBEUA SRICHANDRABHANDHU   MARKET REACTIONS TO AUDITOR CHANGES BY FIRMS WITH DIFFERENT FINANCIAL CONDITIONS

PETRONI, KATHY RUBY   REGULATORY EFFICIENCY, FINANCIAL DISTRESS AND MANAGERIAL ACCOUNTING DISCRETION

PHILHOURS, JOEL ELLIS   NONLINEAR EFFECTS OF RESEARCH AND DEVELOPMENT EXPENDITURES ON MARKET VALUE

PHILLIPS, JEFFREY JOSEPH   BAYESIAN BOUNDS FOR MONETARY-UNIT SAMPLING USING ACTUAL ACCOUNTING POPULATIONS

PIERCE, BARBARA GUGLIOTTA	FIRM SIZE AND SEGMENTAL REPORTING: EVIDENCE ON DIFFERENTIAL MARKET REACTIONS
PIROZZOLI, IRIS ANN	PRICE-CUTTING AND TRANSACTION COSTS IN THE MARKET FOR AUDIT SERVICES
POINTER, MARTHA MANNING	AN INVESTIGATION OF THE RELATIONSHIPS BETWEEN REQUIRED GEOGRAPHICAL SEGMENT DISCLOSURE AND SYSTEMATIC EQUITY RISK AND OPERATING RISK
POONAKASEM, PORNSIRI PRINGSULAKA	THE IMPACT OF MERGER ON THE FIRM'S EQUITY RISK: EX-ANTE VERSUS EX-POST ANALYSES
PORTER, SUSAN L.	THE EFFECTS OF ALTERNATIVE STATE TAX REGIMES ON FIRMS' ACCOUNTING AND FINANCING DECISIONS
PORTER, THOMAS LARSEN	THE EFFECT OF ECONOMIC REGULATION ON ACCOUNTING DECISIONS: EVIDENCE FROM THE UNITED STATES AIRLINE INDUSTRY
POTTER, GORDON SPOONER	ACCOUNTING EARNINGS ANNOUNCEMENTS, FUND CONCENTRATION AND COMMON STOCK RETURNS
POURCIAU, SUSAN GRIBBLE	THE EFFECT OF ACCOUNTING DISCRETION ON EXECUTIVE COMPENSATION CONTRACTS
POURJALALI, HAMID	AN IMPROVED TEST OF POSITIVE ACCOUNTING THEORY: EXAMINATION OF THE CHANGES IN THE AMOUNT OF ACCRUALS IN RESPONSE TO THE CHANGES IN CONTRACTING VARIABLES
POWER, JACQUELINE LOU	ANNOUNCEMENTS OF STOCK REPURCHASES DURING 1988 AND 1989: AN EMPIRICAL ANALYSIS EXAMINING THE DISCLOSURE OF INTENDED OPEN MARKET REPURCHASES
POWER, JEFFREY WILLIAM	AN EMPIRICAL INVESTIGATION OF ANTITAKEOVER AMENDMENTS AND MANAGERIAL DISCRETION IN REPORTED EARNINGS
POWNALL, JACQUELINE SUE	AN EMPIRICAL ANALYSIS OF THE REGULATION OF THE DEFENSE CONTRACTING INDUSTRY: THE COST ACCOUNTING STANDARDS BOARD
PRESS, ERIC GEOFFREY	THE ROLE OF ACCOUNTING BASED CONTRACTUAL PROVISIONS AND FINANCIAL STATEMENT EFFECTS IN EXPLAINING A DEBT EXTINGUISHMENT: THE CASE OF IN-SUBSTANCE DEFEASANCE
PRESTON-THOMAS, AVERIL REI	THE ASSOCIATION BETWEEN ACCOUNTING DISCLOSURES AND INSTITUTIONAL TRADING PATTERNS
PRICE, CHARLES EWELL	AN EMPIRICAL INQUIRY INTO THE PREDICTIVE POWER OF SELECTED ATTRIBUTES FROM DISPUTED FEDERAL TAX EXAMINATIONS
PRICE, JEAN BOCKNIK	OPERATIONALIZING INDUSTRY AFFILIATION AS A FACTOR IN THE BOND RATING DECISION: AN INVESTIGATION AND TEST OF A NEW APPROACH
PRICE, RENEE HALL	THE RELATIONS BETWEEN INSTITUTIONAL EQUITY OWNERSHIP, PRICE RESPONSIVENESS, AND ACCOUNTING DISCLOSURE QUALITY
PRIEBJRIVAT, ANGKARAT	CORPORATE DISCLOSURE: A CASE OF SECURITIES EXCHANGE OF THAILAND
PRINGLE, LYNN M.	A CATASTROPHE THEORY MODEL OF INVENTORY METHOD CHOICE
PROBER, LARRY M.	A COMPARISON OF HISTORICAL COST AND GENERAL PRICE-LEVEL ADJUSTED MEASURES IN THE PREDICTION OF DIVIDEND CHANGES

Listing by Research Method

PUTMAN, ROBERT LYNN	AN EMPIRICAL STUDY OF THE IMPACT OF PUBLIC LAW 98-21 ON THE FINANCIAL OPERATING ENVIRONMENT OF UNITED STATES HOSPITALS
PYO, YOUNGIN	INFORMATION TRANSFERS AND INFORMATION LEAKAGE ASSOCIATED WITH EARNINGS RELEASES
QUE, ANTONIO L.	A CRITICAL EVALUATION OF FASB STATEMENT NO. 13
RADIG, WILLIAM J.	THE EFFECTS OF INFORMATION REQUIRED BY STATEMENT OF FINANCIAL ACCOUNTING STANDARDS NO. 33 ON THE MANAGERIAL DECISIONS MADE IN SELECTED INDUSTRIAL CORPORATIONS
RAGHUNANDAN, KANNAN	AN EMPIRICAL TEST OF THE PREDICTIVE ABILITY OF AUDITORS' LOSS CONTINGENCY DISCLOSURES
RAGLAND, BERNARD GRAFTON	DEPRECIATION--CHOICE VARIABLE OR ONLY A MANAGEMENT CHOICE?
RAGOTHAMAN, SRINIVASAN	ECONOMIC IMPLICATIONS OF ASSET WRITEDOWN DISCLOSURE POLICY
RAMANAN, RAMACHANDRAN	MANAGERIAL INCENTIVES, ACCOUNTING FOR INTEREST COSTS AND CAPITAL INVESTMENT DECISIONS OF THE FIRM
RAMASWAMY, KADANDOGE PADMANABHAN	LONG-TERM PERFORMANCE ISSUES OF MERGERS AND ACQUISITIONS
RAMBO, ROBERT GEORGE	VARIATION IN THE STOCK MARKET RESPONSE TO EARNINGS ANNOUNCEMENTS ASSOCIATED WITH THE REPORTING FIRM'S POSITION IN ITS INDUSTRY'S EARNINGS RELEASE QUEUE
RAMESH, KRISHNAMOORTHY	ESSAYS ON EARNINGS RESPONSE COEFFICIENT
RAMEZANI, AHMAD	ASSET ATTRIBUTES AND PORTFOLIO CHOICE: IMPLICATIONS FOR CAPITAL ASSET PRICES
RANGANATHAN, KRISHNAN AYENGAR	IMPACT OF THE GAIN/LOSS PROVISIONS OF FINANCIAL ACCOUNTING STANDARD NO. 88 ON BENEFIT SETTLEMENTS
RAO, GITA RAMA	THE RELATION BETWEEN STOCK RETURNS AND EARNINGS: A STUDY OF NEWLY-PUBLIC FIRMS
RAVI, INDUMATHI	THE EFFECT OF A MANDATORY ACCOUNTING CHANGE ON EXECUTIVE COMPENSATION: THE CASE OF SFAS NO. 2
RAWASHDEH, MUFEED M.	DETERMINANTS OF GOING-PRIVATE: INFORMATION ASYMMETRY, HOSTILE TAKEOVER THREAT, AND/OR FREE CASH FLOW
RAYBURN, JUDY DAWSON	THE INCREMENTAL INFORMATION CONTENT OF ACCRUAL ACCOUNTING EARNINGS
RAZAKI, KHALID AHMED	THE INCREMENTAL PREDICTIVE ABILITY OF GENERAL PRICE LEVEL ADJUSTED ACCOUNTING NUMBERS FOR DOWNWARD BOND RATING CHANGES
REBURN, JAMES PATRICK	AN EMPIRICAL EXAMINATION OF DISCLOSURES REQUIRED BY THE SECURITIES AND EXCHANGE COMMISSION: THE CASE OF STOCK OWNERSHIP REPORTING
REES, LYNN L.	AN INVESTIGATION OF THE INFORMATION CONTAINED IN DISCLOSURES OF DIFFERENCES BETWEEN FOREIGN AND DOMESTIC EARNINGS

REGIER, PHILIP ROGER	THE DIFFERENTIAL EFFECTS OF UNEXPECTED PERMANENT AND TRANSITORY EARNINGS CHANGES ON EQUITY RETURNS
REITER, SARA ANN	THE EFFECT OF DEFINED BENEFIT PENSION PLAN DISCLOSURES ON BOND RISK PREMIUMS AND BOND RATINGS
REZAEE, ZABIHOLLAH	CAPITAL MARKET REACTIONS TO ACCOUNTING POLICY DELIBERATIONS: AN EMPIRICAL STUDY OF ACCOUNTING FOR THE TRANSLATION OF FOREIGN CURRENCY TRANSACTIONS AND FOREIGN CURRENCY FINANCIAL STATEMENTS, 1974-1982
RICE, ERIC MARSHALL	SKIRTING THE LAW: ESSAYS ON CORPORATE TAX EVASION AND AVOIDANCE
RICH, JOHN CARR	THE EQUITY METHOD OF ACCOUNTING AND UNCONSOLIDATED SUBSIDIARIES: AN EMPIRICAL STUDY
RICHARDSON, CLARA LUCILE	THE PREDICTIVE ABILITY OF ALTERNATIVE BASES FOR INTERPERIOD TAX ALLOCATION: AN EMPIRICAL STUDY
RICKETTS, ROBERT CARLTON	ALTERNATIVE SOCIAL SECURITY TAXING SCHEMES: AN ANALYSIS OF VERTICAL AND HORIZONTAL EQUITY IN THE FEDERAL TAX SYSTEM
RIFFE, SUSAN MICHELE	AN EMPIRICAL ANALYSIS OF OFF-BALANCE-SHEET FINANCIAL INSTRUMENT DISCLOSURES IN THE BANKING INDUSTRY
RIPPINGTON, FREDERICK ALFRED	THE INCREMENTAL INFORMATION CONTENT OF THE ANNUAL REPORT AND ACCOUNTS
ROBERTSON, DARROCH AITKENS	AN INVESTIGATION OF DEFERRED INCOME TAXES DURING A RECESSIONARY PERIOD
ROBINSON, IDA B.	AN EXAMINATION OF BOND VALUATION IN THE PRESENCE OF LOSS CONTINGENCY DISCLOSURES: A CONTINUOUS-TIME FINANCE THEORY APPROACH
ROBINSON, THOMAS RICHARD	EXTERNAL DEMANDS FOR EARNINGS MANAGEMENT: THE ASSOCIATION BETWEEN EARNINGS VARIABILITY AND BOND RISK PREMIA
ROLLINS, THERESA P.	AN EMPIRICAL INVESTIGATION OF PENSION PLAN ACTUARIAL ASSUMPTION CHANGES AND FIRM CHARACTERISTICS: A POSITIVE THEORY APPROACH
ROMEO, GEORGE CHARLES	THE EFFECTS OF SFAS NO. 90 AND 92 ON THE STOCK PRICES AND BETA OF NUCLEAR ELECTRIC UTILITIES
ROOF, BRADLEY MILLER	A COMPARISON OF HISTORIC COST AND PRICE LEVEL FINANCIAL DISCLOSURES: THE ASSOCIATION OF FINANCIAL DISCLOSURES AND ASSESSMENTS OF FINANCIAL RISK
ROOHANI, SAEED JAFARI	AN IMPROVED ACCOUNTING AND AUDITING INFORMATION REPORTING MODEL FOR SAVINGS AND LOAN INSTITUTIONS
ROSACKER, ROBERT EUGENE	A BOX-JENKINS TIME-SERIES INTERRUPTION ANALYSIS CONCERNING UNITED STATES FEDERAL TAX POLICY: AN EMPIRICAL EXAMINATION OF THE INVESTMENT TAX CREDIT
ROSE-GREEN, ENA PATRICIA	THE EFFECTS OF MANAGEMENT CHANGE ON THE CAPITAL MARKET'S RESPONSE TO EARNINGS ANNOUNCEMENTS
ROUBI, RAAFAT RAMADAN	THE ASSOCIATION BETWEEN THE ESTABLISHMENT OF AUDIT COMMITTEES COMPOSED OF OUTSIDE DIRECTORS AND A CHANGE IN THE OBJECTIVITY OF THE MANAGEMENT RESULTS-REPORTING FUNCTION: AN EMPIRICAL INVESTIGATION INTO INCOME
ROUSH, PAMELA BARTON	AN INVESTIGATION OF THE EFFECTS OF NON-AUDIT SERVICES AND AUDITOR TENURE ON AUDITOR OBJECTIVITY

Listing by Research Method

ROVELSTAD, RICHARD GARY	DEFERRED TAXES AND TOBIN'S Q: AN EMPIRICAL INVESTIGATION OF SIGNIFICANCE AND ASSOCIATION
ROY, DANIEL	AN EVALUATION OF UNIVARIATE TIME-SERIES MODELS OF QUARTERLY EARNINGS PER SHARE AND THEIR GENERALIZATION TO MODELS WITH AUTOREGRESSIVE CONDITIONALLY HETEROSCEDASTIC DISTURBANCES
ROZEN, ETZMUN S.	AN EMPIRICAL INVESTIGATION OF THE MOTIVATIONS UNDERLYING LIFO-FIRM INVENTORY LIQUIDATIONS
RUBLE, AAFFIEN HENDERIKA	ADAPTIVE BEHAVIOR BY HOSPITALS IN RESPONSE TO MEDICARE'S PROSPECTIVE PAYMENT SYSTEM
RUDE, JOHN ARTHUR	AN EVALUATION OF THE USEFULNESS OF ALTERNATIVE ACCOUNTING TREATMENTS OF DEFERRED TAXES IN PREDICTING FINANCIAL FAILURE
RUJOUB, MOHAMMAD A.	AN EMPIRICAL INVESTIGATION OF THE DISCRIMINANT AND PREDICTIVE ABILITY OF THE STATEMENT OF CASH FLOWS
RUSBARSKY, MARK KEVIN	THE CHANGES IN ECONOMIC INCENTIVES WHICH MOTIVATE DISCRETIONARY ACCOUNTING CHANGES: THE CASE OF THE SWITCH TO, AND THEN FROM, ACCELERATED DEPRECIATION
RYAN, STEPHEN G.	STRUCTURAL MODELS OF THE ACCOUNTING PROCESS AND EARNINGS
RYU, TAE GHIL	A CROSS-SECTIONAL ANALYSIS OF THE ADOPTION OF STATEMENT OF FINANCIAL ACCOUNTING STANDARDS (SFAS) NO. 96, 'ACCOUNTING FOR INCOME TAXES'
SAAYDAH, MANSOUR IBRAHIM	SFAS NO. 87, PENSION OBLIGATION DEFINITIONS AND THEIR RELATIONSHIP TO SYSTEMATIC RISK
SAILORS, JAMES FRANKLIN	AN INVESTIGATION OF THE STOCK MARKET REACTION TO A CHANGE IN ACCOUNTING METHODS
SALAMONE, DIANE MARSAN	A PROBABILISTIC MODEL FOR PREDICTING MANAGEMENT BUYOUTS
SALY, P. JANE	THE EFFECT OF MAJOR STOCK DOWNTURNS ON EXECUTIVE STOCK OPTION CONTRACTS
SAMELSON, DONALD	AN EMPIRICAL INVESTIGATION OF ECONOMIC CONSEQUENCES OF THE TAX REFORM ACT OF 1986
SANKAR, MANDIRA ROY	CORPORATE VOLUNTARY DISCLOSURES OF PREDECISION INFORMATION
SARATHY, PRIYA	THE INVESTMENT DECISION OF A CREDITOR UNDER REORGANIZATION: EMPIRICAL AND THEORETICAL ISSUES
SARIKAS, ROBERT HENRY STEPHEN	A MARKET TEST OF AN ACCOUNTING BASED MEASURE OF PUBLIC UTILITY COMMISSION REGULATORY CLIMATE
SATIN, DIANE CAROL	ACCOUNTING INFORMATION AND THE VALUATION OF LOSS FIRMS
SAUDAGARAN, SHAHROKH MOHAMED	AN EMPIRICAL STUDY OF SELECTED FACTORS INFLUENCING THE DECISION TO LIST ON FOREIGN STOCK EXCHANGES
SAVAGE, HELEN MARY	REGULATORY ACCOUNTING PRACTICES IN THE SAVINGS AND LOAN INDUSTRY: A STUDY OF THE EFFECTS OF ACCOUNTING CHOICE

Listing by Research Method

SAYERS, DAVID L.	THE IMPACT OF SEGMENT REPORTING ON ANALYSTS' EARNINGS FORECASTS: THE CASE OF FASB STATEMENT NO. 14
SCHALOW, CHRISTINE MARIE	LOBBYING ACTIVITY IN THE STANDARDS SETTING PROCESS: FASB STATEMENT ON FINANCIAL ACCOUNTING STANDARDS NO. 106, 'EMPLOYERS' ACCOUNTING FOR POSTRETIREMENT BENEFITS OTHER THAN PENSIONS'
SCHEIDT, MARSHA ANN	AN EMPIRICAL ANALYSIS OF PARENT COMPANY BOND YIELD PREMIA SUBSEQUENT TO CONSOLIDATION OF NONHOMOGENEOUS FINANCIAL-ACTIVITIES SUBSIDIARIES
SCHLICHTING, DAVID KENNETH	AN EMPIRICAL ANALYSIS OF THE IMPACT OF THE DEFICIT REDUCTION ACT OF 1984 ON CORPORATE DIVIDEND CAPTURE ACTIVITY
SCHLOEMER, PAUL G.	INTERNAL REVENUE CODE SECTION 263A: AN ASSESSMENT OF ITS IMPACT AND PROPOSALS FOR SIMPLIFICATION
SCHMIDT, DENNIS R.	STATE TAXATION OF MULTIJURISDICTIONAL CORPORATE INCOME: AN EMPIRICAL ANALYSIS OF FORMULARY APPORTIONMENT
SCHODERBEK, MICHAEL PAUL	THE EFFECT OF MARKET STRUCTURE ON THE BEHAVIOR OF INTRA-INDUSTRY INFORMATION TRANSFERS: EMPIRICAL TESTS USING FIRMS' QUARTERLY EARNINGS ANNOUNCEMENTS
SCHROEDER, ANGELIKA THERESA HELKE	CASH FLOW PREDICTIONS USING ALTERNATIVE INCOME MEASURES
SCHULTZ, SALLY M.	AUDIT OPINION DECISIONS AND LITIGATION LOSS CONTINGENCIES
SCHWINGHAMMER, PAUL HENRY	AN EMPIRICAL INVESTIGATION OF METHODS OF COMPUTING THE CURRENT PORTION OF CAPITALIZED LEASE OBLIGATIONS AND THE EFFECTS ON SELECTED FINANCIAL MEASURES
SCOFIELD, BARBARA WILD	THE EFFECT OF THE INDUSTRY DISCLOSURE POLICY ON INTRA-INDUSTRY INFORMATION TRANSFER ASSOCIATED WITH QUARTERLY EARNINGS ANNOUNCEMENTS
SEATON, LLOYD, III	ECONOMIC CONSEQUENCES OF ACCOUNTING REGULATION: AN EMPIRICAL ANALYSIS OF CHANGES IN EMPLOYERS' ACCOUNTING FOR PENSIONS
SEAY, SHARON SMITH	AN EMPIRICAL ANALYSIS OF THE RATIO ADJUSTMENT PROCESS: THE CONTRIBUTION OF FIRM-SPECIFIC FACTORS
SEETHARAMAN, ANANTH	AN EMPIRICAL VALIDATION OF SOME EXTANT MEASURES OF VERTICAL AND HORIZONTAL EQUITY
SEIPEL, CINDY L.	'SUBJECT TO' QUALIFIED OPINIONS AND THE SIGNALLING OF RISK SHIFTS
SELLANI, ROBERT JOSEPH	ORGANIZATIONAL LAG AND ITS EFFECTS ON FINANCIAL PERFORMANCE IN THE ELECTRONICS INDUSTRY
SELVY, PATRICIA MILLER	AN EMPIRICAL MODEL BUILDING ANALYSIS OF THE FIRM AND/OR REPORT VARIABLES ASSOCIATED WITH THE RATINGS RECEIVED ON STATE BOARD OF ACCOUNTANCY REVIEWED REPORTS ISSUED BY CPA FIRMS
SENTENEY, DAVID L.	AN INVESTIGATION INTO THE USEFULNESS OF PUBLICLY DISCLOSED ACCOUNTING EARNINGS DATA IN VALUING THE FOREIGN OPERATIONS OF U.S.-BASED MULTINATIONAL ENTERPRISES
SEOW, GIM-SEONG	THE VALUATION OF CORPORATE PENSION OBLIGATIONS: A CONTINGENT CLAIMS MODEL AND SOME EMPIRICAL TESTS
SHACKELFORD, DOUGLAS ALAN	THE MARKET FOR TAX BENEFITS: EVIDENCE FROM LEVERAGED ESOPS

SHADBOLT, MICHAEL EARL	CALCULATING EARNINGS PER SHARE: AN EMPIRICAL ANALYSIS ESTIMATING THE DILUTIVE IMPACT OF CONVERTIBLE SECURITIES ON A CURRENT BASIS
SHAHID, MD ABDUS	DETERMINANTS OF EQUITY-FOR-DEBT SWAP: A POSITIVE THEORY APPROACH
SHANHOLTZER, DENNIS DEAN	AN EXAMINATION OF THE RELATIONSHIP BETWEEN HISTORICAL COST AND CURRENT COST ACCOUNTING DATA AND REPORTED CASH PROVIDED BY OPERATIONS IN THE SUBSEQUENT PERIOD
SHANKAR, S. GOWRI	A REEXAMINATION OF THE CALLS OF CONVERTIBLE BONDS AND THEIR IMPACT ON SHAREHOLDER WEALTH
SHARP, ANDREW DANIEL	AN EMPIRICAL INVESTIGATION INTO THE EXTENT OF THE IMPACT OF FREE TRAVEL AWARDS ON REVENUE DISPLACEMENT IN THE AIRLINE INDUSTRY
SHASTRI, KAREN ANDREA	SELF TENDER OFFERS AS A TAKEOVER DEFENSE: AN ANALYSIS OF FIRM VALUE CHANGES, MANAGERIAL COMPENSATION AND OWNERSHIP CONTROL
SHAW, WAYNE H.	EMPIRICAL EVIDENCE ON THE MARKET IMPACT OF THE SAFE HARBOR LEASING LAW
SHEHATA, MOHAMED MARGHANY	THE IMPACT OF SFAS NO. 2 AND THE ECONOMIC RECOVERY TAX ACT OF 1981 ON FIRMS' R AND D SPENDING BEHAVIOR
SHEIKHOLESLAMI, MEHDI	THE IMPACT OF FOREIGN CURRENCY TRANSLATION METHOD CHANGE ON THE ACCURACY OF THE FINANCIAL ANALYSTS' EARNINGS FORECASTS
SHELTON, JAMES BLAIR	MANAGEMENT'S CHOICE OF ADOPTION DATE OF STATEMENT OF FINANCIAL ACCOUNTING STANDARDS NO. 95: A POSITIVE THEORY APPROACH
SHELTON, MARGARET LOUISE	PREDICTION OF CORPORATE FAILURE WITH AN EXPANDED VARIABLE SET, USING MULTIPLE DISCRIMINANT ANALYSIS
SHERIF, HANAA ABDEL-GALIEL	THE IMPACT OF LONG-TERM PERFORMANCE PLANS ON ACCOUNTING CHOICES
SHEVLIN, TERRENCE J.	RESEARCH AND DEVELOPMENT LIMITED PARTNERSHIPS: AN EMPIRICAL ANALYSIS OF TAXES AND INCENTIVES
SHIARAPPA, BARBARA JANUS	THE ASSOCIATION BETWEEN MARKET RISK AND ACCOUNTING RISK ALTERNATIVELY MEASURED
SHIH, MICHAEL SHENG-HUA	FINANCIAL SYNERGY AND MERGER MOVEMENTS: PERSONAL AND CORPORATE INCOME TAXES AS AN EXPLANATION
SHIM, KYU YOUNG	EMPIRICAL INVESTIGATION OF SHAREHOLDER REACTION TO THE INTRODUCTION OF MANAGEMENT INCENTIVE COMPENSATION PLANS
SHIN, HUNG SIK	TERMINATION OF OVERFUNDED PENSION PLANS AND SHAREHOLDER WEALTH
SHIUE, FU-JIING NORMAN	A POSITIVE THEORY OF ACCOUNTING STANDARDS DETERMINATION: THE CASE OF TAIWAN
SHOEMAKER, PAUL A.	THE SIGNIFICANCE OF THE INVESTMENT TAX CREDIT IN INVESTMENT DECISIONS: AN EMPIRICAL AND INTERNATIONAL ANALYSIS
SHORES, DONNA J.	DIFFERENTIAL INFORMATION AND SECURITY RETURNS SURROUNDING EARNINGS ANNOUNCEMENTS ON THE OVER-THE-COUNTER MARKET

Listing by Research Method 377

SHORNEY, MAYDA	AN EMPIRICAL INVESTIGATION OF THE EFFECT OF OWNERSHIP CONTROL ON THE CHOICE OF ACCOUNTING METHODS
SHROFF, PERVIN KEKI	ESSAYS ON THE ASSOCIATION OF ACCOUNTING EARNINGS WITH SECURITY RETURNS
SILVESTER, KATHERINE JOSEPHINE	FIRM PERFORMANCE, ACCOUNTING SYSTEM CHOICE, AND NEW MANUFACTURING TECHNOLOGIES
SIMGA, CAN	NONFINANCIAL INDICATORS IN PERFORMANCE EVALUATION OF MNE'S; EXPLORING THE USE OF FUZZY OUTRANKING RELATIONS
SIMONS, KATHLEEN ANN	AN INQUIRY INTO THE USEFULNESS OF A MEASURE OF CASH FLOW IN MODELING DIVIDEND CHANGES
SINGER, RONALD MARTIN	EXECUTIVE COMPENSATION AND RESEARCH AND DEVELOPMENT
SINHA, PRAVEEN	VALUATION RELEVANCE OF CASH FLOWS AND ACCRUALS
SINHA, RANJAN	AN ASSESSMENT OF MARKET REACTION TO EARNINGS AND BOOK VALUE INFORMATION
SIVAKUMAR, KUMAR N.	MANAGERIAL CHOICE OF DISCRETIONARY ACCOUNTING METHODS: AN EMPIRICAL EVALUATION OF SECURITY MARKET RESPONSE
SKARO, MATTHEW MARTIN	A THEORETICAL AND EMPIRICAL INVESTIGATION OF THE RELEVANCE AND RELIABILITY OF CERTAIN OPINIONS CONCERNING PENDING LITIGATION
SKINNER, DOUGLAS JOHN	OPTIONS MARKETS, STOCK RETURN VOLATILITY AND THE INFORMATION CONTENT OF ACCOUNTING EARNINGS RELEASES
SLADE, PRISCILLA DEAN	AN EMPIRICAL ANALYSIS OF DEFERRED TAX BALANCES FROM A STATEMENT OF FINANCIAL POSITION AND INCOME STATEMENT PERSPECTIVE
SLAUBAUGH, MICHAEL DEAN	INFORMATION SYSTEM NOISE AND THE SPEED OF STOCK PRICE ADJUSTMENTS
SLOAN, RICHARD GEOFFREY	ACCOUNTING EARNINGS AND TOP EXECUTIVE COMPENSATION
SMITH, HENRY CLAY, III	AN EMPIRICAL INVESTIGATION OF THE INCREMENTAL VALUE OF FINANCIAL ANALYSTS' FORECASTS OF EARNINGS ERROR METRICS IN THE PREDICTION OF FINANCIAL DISTRESS
SMITH, PAMELA ANN	THE EARLY ADOPTION OF ACCOUNTING STANDARDS AS AN EARNINGS MANAGEMENT TOOL
SMITH, PAUL HESELTINE	CORPORATE SOCIAL RESPONSE DISCLOSURE, STRUCTURE, AND REPUTATION RELATIONSHIPS FOR LARGE UNITED STATES CORPORATIONS IN THE NEW-FEDERALISM ERA
SMITH, ROGER JOSEPH	THE EFFECTS OF THE TAX REFORM ACT OF 1986 ON CASH DIVIDEND VALUATION
SMITH, STERLING DUANE	AN EMPIRICAL INVESTIGATION OF THE PROPERTIES OF SEQUENTIAL DISCLOSURES TO THE EQUITY MARKETS
SMOLINSKI, HAROLD CARL	AN EXAMINATION OF MEDIA INFORMATION PRECEDING POTENTIAL FIRM FINANCIAL DISTRESS: THE CASE OF DEBT RERATING TO CAA AND BELOW

Listing by Research Method   378

SNOW, CHARLES GRAN, JR.	AN EMPIRICAL INQUIRY INTO THE USE OF CERTAIN FINANCIAL AND NON-FINANCIAL MEASURES OF ENTITY PERFORMANCE
SOFFER, LEONARD CHARLES	FINANCIAL STATEMENT INDICATORS OF TAKEOVER TARGETS: A MULTINOMIAL ANALYSIS
SOHN, PYUNG SIK	INTRADAY STOCK PRICE REACTION TO MANAGEMENT EARNINGS FORECASTS
SOHN, SUNGKYU	EX-POST REALIZATION AND VALUATION OF MANAGEMENT EARNINGS FORECASTS, MANAGER'S DISCRETION AND CHARACTERISTICS OF FORECASTING FIRMS
SOLIMAN, MAHMOUD EL-SAYED	THE DETERMINANTS OF ACCOUNTING CHOICES BY SMALL FIRMS: AN EMPIRICAL INVESTIGATION
SOMMERVILLE, PATRICIA MILLER	AN ANALYSIS OF THE ATTITUDES TOWARDS CASH FLOW PER SHARE AND A COMPARATIVE ANALYSIS OF ACCRUAL AND CASH BASIS ACCOUNTING IN EXPLAINING CASH FLOW PER SHARE
SON, WON-IK	TAX TREATMENTS OF INVENTORY AND THEIR REAL EFFECTS: THEORY AND EVIDENCE
SONG, IN-MAN	DIFFERENTIAL STOCK PRICE REACTION TO INFLATION-ADJUSTED INCOME DISCLOSURES UNDER SFAS 33: EFFECTS OF FIRM-SPECIFIC CHARACTERISTICS
SOO, BILLY SY	MANAGERIAL RESPONSE TO MANDATORY ACCOUNTING PRINCIPLES: AN ACCRUALS PERSPECTIVE
SOPARIWALA, PARVEZ R.	AN EMPIRICAL EXAMINATION OF THE ASSOCIATION BETWEEN THE ADOPTION OF LONG-TERM PERFORMANCE PLANS AND THE SUBSEQUENT GROWTH OF RESEARCH AND DEVELOPMENT EXPENDITURES
SOUGIANNIS, THEODORE	THE VALUATION OF R AND D FIRMS AND THE ACCOUNTING RULES FOR R AND D COSTS
SOYBEL, VIRGINIA ELIZABETH EARLL	MUNICIPAL FINANCIAL REPORTING AND THE NEW YORK CITY FISCAL CRISIS
SPEAR, NASSER ABDELMONEM	THE INFORMATION CONTENT OF SUPPLEMENTAL RESERVE-BASED REPLACEMENT MEASURES RELATIVE TO THAT OF HISTORICAL COST INCOME AND ITS CASH AND ACCRUAL COMPONENTS OF OIL AND GAS PRODUCING COMPANIES
SPECHT, JAMES	AN EMPIRICAL EXAMINATION OF LITIGATION AGAINST AUDITORS OVER TIME
SPINDLE, ROXANNE MARIE	USING EX POST FORECASTING AND PANEL DATA TO EVALUATE LABOR SUPPLY ELASTICITIES
SPURRELL, A. C. LLOYD	AN EXAMINATION OF SELECTED FACTORS ASSOCIATED WITH AUDIT LITIGATION
SRIRAM, SRINIVASAN	AN INVESTIGATION OF ASYMMETRICAL POWER RELATIONSHIPS EXISTING IN AUDITOR-CLIENT RELATIONSHIP DURING AUDITOR CHANGES
STANGL, ROBERT JOHN	CORPORATE AUDIT COMMITTEES: FACTORS ASSOCIATED WITH VOLUNTARY FORMATION AND MARKET REACTION TO MANDATORY FORMATION
STEADMAN, MARK EDWARD	THE COMMON STOCK PRICE EFFECTS OF BOND RATING CHANGES: AN EXAMINATION OF ASYMMETRIC MARKET REACTIONS USING STAKEHOLDER THEORY
STEPHAN, JENS A.	INFORMATION CONTENT OF SECURITY PRICES: EVIDENCE ON THE RATIONAL EXPECTATIONS HYPOTHESIS

STEPHENSON, CRAIG ALLEN	ESSAYS ON REPURCHASES AND TENDER OFFERS
STEVENS, KEVIN TIMOTHY	AN EMPIRICAL ANALYSIS OF THE NATURE OF SELECTED TAX EXPENDITURES IN A STATE INDIVIDUAL INCOME TAX SYSTEM
STEWART, DANIEL VAN	A STUDY OF CHANGES IN ARTICLE PUBLICATION PRODUCTIVITY AMONG ACCOUNTING FACULTY PROMOTED DURING THE 1980'S
STEWART, JENICE PRATHER	AN EMPIRICAL INVESTIGATION OF THE USEFULNESS OF ALTERNATIVE EARNING CLASSIFICATIONS IN PREDICTING CASH FLOWS
STICE, EARL KAY	THE MARKET REACTION TO 10-K AND 10-Q FILINGS AND TO SUBSEQUENT 'WALL STREET JOURNAL' EARNINGS ANNOUNCEMENTS
STICE, JAMES DAVID	PREDICTING LAWSUITS AGAINST AUDITORS USING FINANCIAL AND MARKET INFORMATION
STINSON, CHRISTOPHER HALL	THE MANAGEMENT OF PROVISIONS AND ALLOWANCES IN THE SAVINGS AND LOAN INDUSTRY
STITTS, RANDAL HAYES	TAX PREFERENCES, FAIRNESS, AND THE ELDERLY: A COMPARATIVE ANALYSIS OF TAX LIABILITIES
STREULY, CAROLYN	TWO ESSAYS: AN EMPIRICAL INVESTIGATION INTO THE DETERMINANTS OF SECURITY RETURNS; AND, THE ASSOCIATION BETWEEN MARKET-DETERMINED AND ACCOUNTING-DETERMINED RISK MEASURES REVISITED
STROOPE, JOHN CLARENCE	INCOME TAX EVASION AND THE EFFECTIVENESS OF TAX COMPLIANCE LEGISLATION, 1979-1982
STYRON, WILLIAM JOEY	AN EMPIRICAL EXAMINATION OF THE GOING-CONCERN AUDIT OPINION: THE AUDITOR'S DECISION REGARDING CONTINUING GOING-CONCERN OPINIONS AND THE SUBSEQUENT FATE OF COMPANIES THAT HAVE RECEIVED GOING-CONCERN OPINIONS
SU, ROBERT KUATERNG	AN EMPIRICAL INVESTIGATION OF THE USEFULNESS OF CURRENT COST INFORMATION IN MERGER PREDICTION
SUBRAMANYAM, K. R.	STOCHASTIC PRECISION AND MARKET REACTIONS TO EARNINGS ANNOUNCEMENTS
SUMMERS, SUZANNE BURGER	THE IMPACT OF THE PROPOSED LICENSING REQUIREMENTS ON TURNOVER IN PUBLIC ACCOUNTING
SUMNER, JEANIE GRACE	AN ANALYSIS OF THE EFFECT OF STATE REGULATION OF COMMERCIAL INCOME TAX PREPARERS ON THE QUALITY OF INCOME TAX RETURNS
SUN, HUEY-LIAN	INFORMATION CONTENT OF EXTERNAL FINANCING AND FIRM-SPECIFIC CHARACTERISTICS
SUNG, HEEKYUNG	INFORMATION CONTENT OF THE TIMING OF EARNINGS ANNOUNCEMENTS
SURDICK, JOHN JOSEPH, JR.	AN INVESTIGATION OF THE BOND RATINGS ASSIGNED TO TAX-EXEMPT HOSPITAL REVENUE BONDS: AN EMPIRICAL MODEL FOR NOT-FOR-PROFIT HOSPITALS
SUSANTO, DJOKO	AN EMPIRICAL INVESTIGATION OF THE EXTENT OF CORPORATE DISCLOSURE IN ANNUAL REPORTS OF COMPANIES LISTED ON THE JAKARTA STOCK EXCHANGE
SUTLEY, KENNETH R.	AN EMPIRICAL INVESTIGATION INTO THE RELATION BETWEEN DIFFERENTIAL ANNUAL REPORT INFORMATIVENESS AND THE ASSOCIATION OF STOCK RETURNS WITH ACCOUNTING EARNINGS: THE CASE OF THE 'FINANCIAL POST' ANNUAL REPORT AWARDS

Listing by Research Method

SWAMINATHAN, SIVAKUMAR	THE EFFECT OF INFORMATION PRECISION ON INVESTOR BELIEFS AND SECURITY PRICES: THE SEGMENT-REPORTING ISSUE
SWANSON, ZANE LEWIS	THE INFORMATION CONTENT OF EARNINGS COMPONENTS AND DIVIDENDS
SWARTZ, LEE MICHAEL	THE IMPACT OF STATE ANTITAKEOVER LAWS ON SECURITY VALUE
SWEENEY, AMY PATRICIA	DEBT-COVENANT VIOLATIONS AND MANAGERS' ACCOUNTING-CHOICE AND PRODUCTION-INVESTMENT DECISIONS
TANDY, PAULETTE REDFERN	AN EMPIRICAL STUDY OF THE EXTENT, TIMING, AND NATURE OF ANALYTICAL REVIEW PROCEDURES IN ACTUAL AUDIT SETTINGS
TANNER, MARGARET MORGAN	AN ANALYSIS OF FACTORS ASSOCIATED WITH VOLUNTARY DISCLOSURE OF MANAGEMENT'S RESPONSIBILITIES FOR INTERNALCONTROL
TEALL, HOWARD DOUGLAS	AN EMPIRICAL STUDY OF THE ABILITY OF CANADIAN OIL AND GAS COMPANIES' RESERVES DISCLOSURES TO ACCOUNT FOR RELATIVE CHANGES IN COMMON STOCK PRICES
TEEUWEN, TERESA DIANE TRAPANI	AN INVESTIGATION OF THE RELATIONSHIP BETWEEN CEO COMPENSATION AND CEO TRADING PROFITS
TESSONI, DANIEL DAVID	AN EMPIRICAL EVALUATION OF THE POSITIVE THEORY OF ACCOUNTING IN THE CONTEXT OF ACCOUNTING FOR CHANGING PRICES
THIAGARAJAN, SUNDARARAMAN	ECONOMIC DETERMINANTS OF EARNINGS PERSISTENCE
THORNE, DANIEL T.	INFORMATION CONTENT OF HISTORIC COST-CURRENT COST TRENDS, DERIVED FROM SFAS NO. 33 DISCLOSURES
THORNTON, PHILLIP WYNN	THE ROLE OF ACCOUNTING INFORMATION IN INVESTOR ASSESSMENTS OF CORPORATE TAKEOVERS
TIDD, RONALD ROBERT	GEOPOLITICAL CONSIDERATIONS IN THE ADMINISTRATION OF UNITED STATES INCOME TAX POLICY: AN ASSESSMENT OF INCOME TAX ENFORCEMENT EFFORTS, 1975-1988.
TODD, REBECCA	AN INVESTIGATION OF THE CASH FLOW PROPERTIES OF ACCRUAL ACCOUNTING DATA: A STRUCTURAL EQUATION APPROACH
TOLLIVER, ROBERT WAYNE	THE RELATIVE INFORMATION CONTENT OF EARNINGS AND FUNDS FLOW ACCOUNTING NUMBERS IMPOUNDED IN THE CAPITAL MARKET'S ASSESSMENT OF THE SYSTEMATIC RISK OF EQUITY SECURITIES
TONGE, STANLEY D.	THE DIFFERENTIAL EFFECT OF FAS 33 DISCLOSURES ON SECURITY PRICES
TREZEVANT, ROBERT HEATH	THE EFFECT OF TAX LAW CHANGES ON CORPORATE INVESTMENT AND FINANCING BEHAVIOR: EMPIRICAL EVIDENCE FROM CHANGES BROUGHT ABOUT BY THE ECONOMIC RECOVERY TAX ACT OF 1981
TRIMBLE, CHARLIE JOE	A MULTIPLE DISCRIMINANT ANALYSIS OF FIRM-SPECIFIC CHARACTERISTICS USEFUL IN PREDICTING MANAGEMENTS' USE OF DISCRETIONARY CASH FLOWS
TRIMBLE, DIXIE CLARK	AN ANALYSIS OF USER'S PERCEIVED INFORMATION NEEDS, FIRM'S CURRENT REPORTING PRACTICES, AND THE STOCK PRICE EFFECTS OF ANNOUNCEMENTS OF IMPAIRMENT IN VALUE OF LONG-LIVED OPERATING ASSETS
TROMBLEY, MARK ALAN	THE EFFECT OF CORPORATE MERGER TRANSACTIONS ON THE INFORMATION CONTENT OF EARNINGS ANNOUNCEMENTS

TRUSSEL, JOHN M.	ASSESSING THE PROBABILITY OF FINANCIAL DISTRESS: AN OPTION PRICING FRAMEWORK
TSAI, YANN-CHING	THE TIMING EFFECT OF EARNINGS REPORTS AND THE STOCK MARKET REACTION TO LATE-REPORTING FIRMS
TSAY, BOR-YI	THE RELATIONSHIP BETWEEN PENSION DISCLOSURE AND BOND RISK PREMIUM
TSAY, YANG-TZONG	THE INFORMATION CONTENT OF CORPORATE CAPITAL EXPENDITURE DECISIONS: INTERVENTION ANALYSIS
TUCKER, JAMES JOSEPH, III	STOCK DIVIDENDS: HISTORICAL, CONCEPTUAL AND REPORTING PERSPECTIVES
TUNG, SAMUEL S.	STOCK MARKET REACTIONS TO MANDATORY CHANGES IN ACCOUNTING FOR PENSIONS
TUNNELL, PERRY LAWRENCE	AN INVESTIGATION INTO THE EFFECTS OF FREQUENT TAX POLICY CHANGES ON FIRM RISK
TUNTIWONGPIBOON, NARONK	AN INVESTIGATION OF CLIENT ATTRIBUTES AND AUDIT STRUCTURE
TURNER, DEBORAH HANSON	THE EFFECT OF ALTERNATIVE METHODS OF ACCOUNTING FOR INCOME TAXES ON THE ASSOCIATION BETWEEN ACCOUNTING RISK MEASURES AND THE MARKET RISK MEASURE
TYPPO, ERIC WILHELM	AN EMPIRICAL INVESTIGATION OF THE RELATIONSHIP BETWEEN INSIDER TRADING AND MANAGEMENT EARNINGS FORECAST CHARACTERISTICS
UDPA, SUNEEL CHANDRASHEKHAR	THE EFFECT OF INSIDER TRADING ON THE STOCK PRICE RESPONSE TO EARNINGS
UKAEGBU, EBEN O.	MOTIVES FOR CORPORATE MERGERS AND TAKEOVERS: AN INVESTIGATION OF THE 'FAILING COMPANY' HYPOTHESIS AND OFPOST-MERGER PERFORMANCE
ULISS, BARBARA TURK	REPORTING INTEREST RATE SWAPS: THE ASSOCIATION OF DISCLOSURE QUALITY WITH CREDIT RISK AND OWNERSHIP STRUCTURE
VACHARAJITTIPAN, SUCHITRA TUNLAYADECHANONT	THE INFORMATION CONTENT OF QUARTERLY EARNINGS: THE CASE OF THAILAND
VENDRZYK, VALARIA PAULINE	AN EXAMINATION OF THE INFORMATION CONTENT OF ALLEGATIONS OF PROCUREMENT FRAUD IN THE DEFENSE CONTRACTING INDUSTRY
VESSEL, HERBERT	MANAGEMENT INCENTIVES FOR SOCIAL RESPONSIBILITY ACCOUNTING DISCLOSURE: AN EMPIRICAL ANALYSIS
VICKREY, DONN WILLIAM	THE INCREMENTAL INFORMATION PROVIDED BY DISCLOSING CASH FLOW AND ACCRUAL COMPONENTS OF EARNINGS
VIJAYAN, ANIL KUMAR	CREDIT LOSS DISCLOSURE IN FAS #105 (EMPHASIS ON SWAPS) AND ITS TREATMENT IN RISK-BASED CAPITAL: AN EMPIRICAL ANALYSIS OF SIMILAR CREDIT LOSSES AND ITS DECISION USEFULNESS IN A BANK'S CREDIT RATING
VOGEL, THOMAS JOSEPH	MONITORING NORMATIVE CORPORATE DECISIONS: A RECONCILIATION OF FINANCIAL AND ACCOUNTING CRITERIA
VOLK, GARY A.	A REEXAMINATION OF ACCOUNTING FOR STOCK DIVIDENDS: IS IT TIME FOR A CHANGE?

Listing by Research Method

VREELAND, JANNET MARGARET	AN INVESTIGATION OF DISCLOSURE PRACTICES OF PRIVATE FIRMS
WACKER, RAYMOND FRANCIS	THE EFFECTS OF INTERNATIONAL TAX TREATIES ON THE LOCATION OF U.S. MANUFACTURING DIRECT INVESTMENT ABROAD IN LESS-DEVELOPED NATIONS: A PANEL MODEL ANALYSIS
WAHLEN, JAMES MICHAEL	THE NATURE OF INFORMATION IN COMMERCIAL BANK LOAN LOSS DISCLOSURES
WALDEN, W. DARRELL	AN EMPIRICAL INVESTIGATION OF ENVIRONMENTAL DISCLOSURES ANALYZING REACTIONS TO PUBLIC POLICY AND REGULATOR EFFECTS
WALDRON, MARILYN A.	A COMPARATIVE ANALYSIS OF ACCRUAL AND CASH BASIS ACCOUNTING IN PREDICTING CASH FLOWS FROM OPERATIONS IN THE OIL AND GAS INDUSTRY
WALKER, ROBERT ATKINS	DO TAXES MATTER? THE CASE OF THE PROPERTY-CASUALTY INSURANCE INDUSTRY
WALTON, KAREN SCHUELE	THE DEBT/EQUITY CHOICE WITH ASYMMETRIC INFORMATION: AN EMPIRICAL STUDY
WAMPLER, BRUCE M.	THE RELATIONSHIP BETWEEN EQUITY VALUES AND THE COMPONENTS OF UNRECORDED PENSION ASSETS AND LIABILITIES
WANG, SHIING-WU	FIRM SIZE AND TAX RATES RELATION: AN APPROPRIATE TEST OF FIRMS' POLITICAL SUCCESS?
WANG, YI-HSIN	AN EXPLORATORY EMPIRICAL INVESTIGATION OF RELATIONSHIPS BETWEEN CHANGES IN CATALYST FINANCIAL COMMITMENTS AND CHANGES IN PRODUCTIVITY AND PROFITABILITY IN SELECTED UNITED STATES MANUFACTURING INDUSTRIES AND
WANG, ZHEMIN	INFORMATIVENESS AND PREDICTABILITY OF EARNINGS AND CASH FLOWS
WARD, TERRY JOE	FINANCIAL DISTRESS: AN EVALUATION OF THE PREDICTIVE POWER OF ACCRUAL AND CASH FLOW INFORMATION USING ORDINAL MULTI-STATE PREDICTION MODELS
WARFIELD, TERRY DEE	THE EFFECTS OF ACCOUNTING DISCLOSURES ON BANK INFORMATION ENVIRONMENTS
WASLEY, CHARLES EDWARD	DIFFERENTIAL INFORMATION CONTENT OF EARNINGS ANNOUNCEMENTS: THEORETICAL AND EMPIRICAL ANALYSIS OF THE ROLE OF INFORMATION TRANSFERS
WATTS, SUSAN GAIL	MARKET MICROSTRUCTURE AND THE TIMING OF EARNINGS RELEASES: AN EMPIRICAL ANALYSIS
WEBER, SANDRA LEE LIGON	THE IMPACT OF THE FINANCIAL CONDITION OF THE FIRM ON THE ACCURACY OF ANNUAL EARNINGS FORECASTS
WEINSTEIN, GERALD PAUL	AN EMPIRICAL INVESTIGATION OF DIVESTITURE ANNOUNCEMENTS: THE SOUTH AFRICA EFFECT
WEISEL, JAMES ALLEN	AN EMPIRICAL MODEL FOR CLASSIFYING AND PREDICTING THE FINANCIAL PERFORMANCE OF FEDERALLY INSURED SAVINGS ASSOCIATIONS
WEISS, LAWRENCE ALAN	BANKRUPTCY: THE EXPERIENCE OF NYSE AND ASE FIRMS--1980-1986
WELD, LEONARD GREER	AN EMPIRICAL STUDY OF THE EFFECT OF THE TAX REFORM ACT OF 1986 LOAN LOSS RESERVE REPEAL ON BANK LOAN CHARGE-OFFS

Listing by Research Method   383

WELKER, MICHAEL ALAN	DISCLOSURE POLICY, INFORMATION ASYMMETRY, LIQUIDITY AND THE COST OF EQUITY CAPITAL: A THEORETICAL AND EMPIRICAL INVESTIGATION
WELLS, DONALD WAYNE	THE MARKET EFFECTS OF AUDITOR RESIGNATIONS
WELLS, STEVE CARROLL	AN EMPIRICAL STUDY OF THE EFFECT OF VALUE-ADDED TAX FORM ON REVENUE VOLATILITY
WENZEL, LOREN ALVIN	THE PREDICTIVE ABILITY OF QUARTERLY ACCRUAL AND CASH FLOW VARIABLES: A MULTIPLE TIME SERIES APPROACH
WESTPHAL, CATHERINE MARGARET	A PROJECT-BASED ANALYSIS OF THE EFFECTS OF FEDERAL TAX CREDITS ON HISTORIC REHABILITATION
WHELAN, ADELAIDE KATE	STOCK DIVIDENDS: MARKET REACTIONS AND MOTIVATIONS
WICK, MADALYN HELEN	AN EMPIRICAL STUDY OF DETERMINANTS OF CASH FLOW RESPONSE COEFFICIENTS
WIEDMAN, CHRISTINE INGEBORG	PROXIES FOR EARNINGS EXPECTATIONS: THE ROLE OF LOSS FUNCTIONS
WIER, HEATHER ANN	THE EFFECT OF SFAS 94 ON INVESTOR RISK ASSESSMENTS AND MANAGEMENT ACTIVITIES
WIEST, DAVID NEVIN	THE EFFECT OF SEC SANCTIONS ON AUDITOR SWITCHES
WILDER, WALLACE MARK	A MULTI-INDUSTRY ANALYSIS OF STRUCTURAL CHANGES AND EARNINGS FORECASTS
WILLIAMS, PATRICIA ANN	THE EFFECT OF PRIOR FORECAST USEFULNESS ON USER REACTION TO A MANAGEMENT EARNINGS FORECAST
WILLIAMS, RAY ELLIS	THE INFORMATIONAL CONTENT OF THE CURRENT MARKET VALUE OF LONG-TERM DEBT
WILSON, GORDON PETER	THE INCREMENTAL INFORMATION CONTENT OF ACCRUALS AND CASH FLOWS AFTER CONTROLLING FOR EARNINGS
WILSON, THOMAS E., JR.	AN EXAMINATION OF AUDITOR CHANGES FOLLOWING EVENTS ADVERSELY AFFECTING EXTERNAL AUDITOR CREDIBILITY
WITMER, PHILIP ROY	AUDITOR CHANGES AS OPPORTUNISTIC BEHAVIOR
WOAN, RONALD JEN-JIN	THE IMPACT OF MEASUREMENT ERRORS AND MULTICOLLINEARITY ON THE STUDY OF THE RELATIONSHIP BETWEEN ACCOUNTING INFORMATION AND MARKET-DETERMINED RISKS
WOLCOTT, SUSAN KAY	THE EFFECTS OF PRIOR SHAREHOLDER ANTICIPATION AND RESTRUCTURING ACTIONS ON THE STOCK PRICE RESPONSE TO WRITEDOWN ANNOUNCEMENTS
WONG, JONATHAN WAITAK	VALUATION RELEVANCE OF MARKET VALUE DISCLOSURES OF DEBT SECURITIES IN THE INSURANCE INDUSTRY
WONG, TAK-JUN	ESSAYS ON THE DETERMINANTS OF THE RELATION BETWEEN STOCK PRICES AND ACCOUNTING EARNINGS

Listing by Research Method

WRIGHT, GAIL B.	ACCOUNTING ALTERNATIVES FOR COST RECOGNITION: AN EMPIRICAL ANALYSIS OF THE MATCHING PRINCIPLE EMPLOYED IN THE OIL-PRODUCING INDUSTRY
WU, ANNE	THE DETERMINANTS OF VOLUNTARY RELEASE OF EARNINGS FORECASTS INFORMATION TO THE PUBLIC
WU, TSING TZAI	AN EXAMINATION OF THE MARKET REACTION TO THE ADOPTION OF SFAS NO.52: A NEW-INFORMATION-DE-FACTO APPROACH
WU, YUWU	MANAGEMENT BUYOUTS: A TEST OF THE MANAGEMENT MANIPULATION HYPOTHESIS
XIANG, BING	THE CHOICE OF RETURN-GENERATING MODELS IN EVENT STUDIES AND RATIONALITY OF VALUE LINE'S QUARTERLY EARNINGS FORECASTS
YANG, BONG-JIN	THE EFFECT OF THE FEDERAL RESERVE BOARD'S MARGIN CREDIT CONTROL ON THE DEALERS' BID-ASK SPREAD IN THE OTC STOCK MARKET
YANG, DAVID CHIE-HWA	THE ASSOCIATION BETWEEN SFAS 33 INFORMATION AND BOND RATINGS
YEATON, KATHRYN GIVENS	AN INVESTIGATION OF THE IMPACT OF NON-ACCOUNTING INFORMATION (PLANT CLOSING ANNOUNCEMENTS) ON THE EXPECTATIONS OF FUTURE ACCOUNTING OUTCOMES
YEH, SHU	LINE OF BUSINESS REPORTING, THE MARGINAL INFORMATION CONTENT OF EARNINGS ANNOUNCEMENTS, AND THE ACCURACY OF ANALYST EARNINGS FORECASTS
YEO, GILLIAN HIAN HENG	A FRAMEWORK TO ANALYZE MANAGEMENT'S VOLUNTARY FORECAST DISCLOSURE DECISIONS
YHIM, HARK-PPIN	VOLUNTARY MANAGEMENT EARNINGS FORECASTS: AN ASSOCIATION BETWEEN DISCLOSURE LEVEL AND INFORMATION QUALITY
YI, HWA DEUK	MANAGEMENT EARNINGS FORECASTS: THE MARKET RESPONSE AND FIRMS' DISCLOSURE INCENTIVES
YI, JAEKYUNG	THE EFFECT OF STOCK SPLITS ON THE REASSESSMENT OF EARNINGS PERSISTENCE
YOHN, TERI LOMBARDI	THE EFFECT OF THE EXISTENCE AND QUALITY OF EARNINGS DISCLOSURES ON BID-ASK SPREADS: THEORY AND EMPIRICAL EVIDENCE
YOO, CHUNG EUL	THE INFORMATION CONTENT OF DISCONTINUED OPERATIONS ASSOCIATED WITH APB OPINION NO. 30
YOON, MYUNG-HO	AN EXAMINATION OF THE EFFECT OF THE SAFE HARBOR RULE ON THE PREDICTION ERROR OF MANAGEMENT EARNINGS FORECASTS: SOME EMPIRICAL EVIDENCE
YOON, SOON SUK	THE ECONOMIC CONSEQUENCES OF SFAS NO. 2: ITS IMPACT ON BUSINESS FIRMS AND INVESTORS
YOUNG, JAMES CHRISTIAN	FACTORS IN THE NONCOMPLIANCE DECISION: AN ANALYSIS OF MICHIGAN TAX AMNESTY PARTICIPANTS
YU, PING KUEN	TAX IMPACT ON U.S. FIRMS' CHOICE OF FOREIGN INCOME REMITTANCE METHODS: DIVIDENDS AND ROYALTIES
YUN, JOO-KWANG	MEASURING RATES OF RETURN

ZEKANY, KAY E.	THE INFORMATION CONTENT OF INVENTORY AND RECEIVABLES OF MERCHANDISERS
ZELCER, MOISHE	MANAGEMENT BUYOUTS: THE MANAGEMENT/SHAREHOLDER CONFLICT
ZELLER, THOMAS LOUIS	AN EMPIRICAL INVESTIGATION OF A NET OPERATING CASH FLOW RATE OF RETURN AS A PROXY MEASURE FOR FIRM ECONOMIC PERFORMANCE
ZHANG, HUA	THE DYNAMIC BEHAVIOUR OF THE TERM STRUCTURE OF INTEREST RATES AND ITS IMPLICATION FOR INTEREST-RATE SENSITIVE ASSET PRICING
ZIEGENFUSS, DOUGLAS EDWIN	AN EMPIRICAL INVESTIGATION OF THE EFFECTS OF QUALIFIED OPINIONS ON AUDIT FIRMS' GROWTH RATES AND LEGAL LIABILITY
ZILL, SHARON	A STUDY IN NURSING HOME EFFECTIVENESS IN TEXAS
ZIMMERMANN, RAYMOND ARTHUR	ALIMONY: AN EMPIRICAL ANALYSIS OF THE EFFECT ON TAX REVENUES AND EQUITY
ZUCCA, LINDA JEANNE	AN EMPIRICAL STUDY OF FIRMS ENGAGING IN PARTIAL WRITEDOWNS OF LONG-LIVED ASSETS

Archival - Secondary

BELL, ANGELA H.	AN EMPIRICAL STUDY OF THE TYPES AND FREQUENCIES OF ACCOUNTING PROBLEMS ENCOUNTERED DURING THE STAGES OF DEVELOPMENT OF SMALL BUSINESSES
BERRY, LUCILLE M.	THE CHANGES OF COMPUTER USAGE IN ACCOUNTING TEXTS FROM 1974-1984
BRAND, JOHN DAVID	THE EXCHEQUER IN THE LATER TWELFTH CENTURY
BRICKER, ROBERT JAMES	AN EMPIRICAL INVESTIGATION OF THE INTELLECTUAL STRUCTURE OF THE ACCOUNTING DISCIPLINE: A CITATIONAL ANALYSIS OF SELECTED SCHOLARLY JOURNALS, 1983-1986
CARPENTER, JANICE LEE	AN AGENCY THEORY ANALYSIS OF CORPORATE LOBBYING IN RESPONSE TO THE DISCUSSION MEMORANDUM ON ACCOUNTING FOR INCOME TAXES
CARTER, GARY WILLIAM	THE ACQUIESCENCE/NONACQUIESCENCE POLICY OF THE COMMISSIONER WITH RESPECT TO TAX COURT DECISIONS - AN EMPIRICAL ANALYSIS
CHESTER, MICHAEL CARTER, JR.	AN EMPIRICAL STUDY OF CORPORATE MANAGEMENT SUPPORT FOR PUSH DOWN ACCOUNTING
CRIPPS, JEREMY	ON ACCOUNTING
DONNELLY, WILLIAM JAMES, JR.	THE CPA'S LIABILITY IN TAX PRACTICE: HISTORY, TRENDS, PROBLEMS, POSSIBLE SOLUTIONS
ERIKSEN, SCOTT DOUGLAS	A CRITICAL INVESTIGATION OF POSITIVISM: ITS ADEQUACY AS AN APPROACH FOR ACCOUNTING RESEARCH
FENTON, EDMUND DAVID, JR.	AN EMPIRICAL INVESTIGATION INTO THE TAX COURT ASSESSMENT OF THE ECONOMIC INTEREST CONCEPT IN NATURAL RESOURCE TAXATION
FORTIN, ANNE	THE EVOLUTION OF FRENCH ACCOUNTING THOUGHT AS REFLECTED BY THE SUCCESSIVE UNIFORM SYSTEMS (PLANS COMPTABLES GENERAUX)

GARNER, ROBERT MICHAEL	S. PAUL GARNER: A STUDY OF SELECTED CONTRIBUTIONS TO THE ACCOUNTING PROFESSION
GARRISON, LARRY RICHARD	THE EXCLUSION FROM INCOME OF SCHOLARSHIPS AND FELLOWSHIP GRANTS: AN EMPIRICAL INVESTIGATION OF TAX COURT DETERMINATIONS
GEIGER, MARSHALL ALLEN	SETTING THE STANDARD FOR A NEW AUDITOR'S REPORT: AN ANALYSIS OF ATTEMPTS TO INFLUENCE THE AUDITING STANDARDS BOARD
GRAVES, OLIVER FINLEY	ACCOUNTING FOR INFLATION: GERMAN THEORY OF THE 1920S
GREENSTEIN, BRIAN RICHARD	AN EMPIRICAL ANALYSIS OF THE QUALIFIED TERMINABLE INTEREST PROPERTY ELECTION AND RELATED PROVISIONS
HEIER, JAN RICHARD	A QUANTITATIVE STUDY OF ACCOUNTING METHODS AND USAGE IN MID - NINETEENTH-CENTURY ALABAMA AND MISSISSIPPI
HESLOP, GORDON B.	AN ANALYSIS OF THE TAXATION TREATMENT UNDER SECTION 280A OF THE INTERNAL REVENUE CODE OF 1954 OF EXPENSES INCURRED IN CONNECTION WITH THE BUSINESS USE OF A DWELLING UNIT
HUSSAEN, NIDHAM MOHAMMED ALI	THE EVOLUTION OF ACCOUNTING FOR INFLATION IN GERMANY, 1920-1923
JUDD, ANDREW JACKSON	AN EXAMINATION OF SIGNIFICANT VARIABLES USED BY COURTS IN WORTHLESS STOCK CASES
KING, TERESA ANN TYSON	AN ANALYTIC STUDY OF SELECTED CONTRIBUTIONS OF PAUL F. GRADY TO THE DEVELOPMENT OF ACCOUNTANCY
LEGGE, REBECCA SUE SCRUGGS	A HISTORY OF WOMEN CERTIFIED PUBLIC ACCOUNTANTS IN THE UNITED STATES
LEHMAN, CHERYL R.	DISCOURSE ANALYSIS AND ACCOUNTING LITERATURE: TRANSFORMATION OF STATE HEGEMONY, 1960 - 1973
LINDSAY, ROGER MURRAY	THE USE OF TESTS OF SIGNIFICANCE IN ACCOUNTING RESEARCH: A METHODOLOGICAL, PHILOSOPHICAL AND EMPIRICAL INQUIRY
MARAIS, MARTHINUS LAURENTIUS	SOME APPLICATIONS OF COMPUTER INTENSIVE STATISTICAL METHODS TO EMPIRICAL RESEARCH IN ACCOUNTING
MATIKA, LAWRENCE A.	THE CONTRIBUTIONS OF FREDERICK ALBERT CLEVELAND TO THE DEVELOPMENT OF A SYSTEM OF MUNICIPAL ACCOUNTING IN THE PROGRESSIVE ERA
MORRIS, JOSEPH LYNN	A PROFILE OF WINNING AND LOSING CASES CONCERNING THE VALUATION OF CLOSELY HELD SHARES FOR ESTATE AND GIFT TAX PURPOSES
OLSON, WILLIAM HALVER	AN EMPIRICAL INVESTIGATION OF THE FACTORS CONSIDERED BY THE TAX COURT IN DETERMINING PRINCIPAL PURPOSE UNDER INTERNAL REVENUE CODE SECTION 269
PASEWARK, WILLIAM ROBERT	DETERMINING ECONOMIC INTEREST IN NATURAL RESOURCES
POULLAOS, CHRISTOPHER	MAKING THE AUSTRALIAN CHARTERED ACCOUNTANT, 1886-1935
REMMELE, DAVID ALAN	COURT-DETERMINED MATERIALITY: AN EMPIRICAL ANALYSIS OF THE CRITERIA COURTS USE AND THE IMPLICATIONS FOR ACCOUNTANTS

Listing by Research Method

RINKE, DOLORES FAY	CREDENTIALING PROCESSES OF PROFESSIONAL PUBLIC ACCOUNTANTS IN FRANCE, ITALY, THE UNITED KINGDOM, AND WEST GERMANY
ROBERTSON, PAUL JEPSEN	DEBT OR EQUITY? AN EMPIRICAL ANALYSIS OF TAX COURT CLASSIFICATION DURING THE PERIOD 1955-1987
ROBSON, KEITH	ACCOUNTING, THE STATE AND THE REGULATORY PROCESS: THE CASE OF STANDARD SETTING, 1969-1975
SEAMANS, DANA GERALD	AN ANALYSIS OF THE FEDERAL TAX RAMIFICATIONS OF GOODWILL
SEDAGHAT, ALI M.	THE INTERACTIVE PROCESS OF ACCOUNTING: AN ANALYSIS OF THE DEVELOPMENT OF FINANCIAL ACCOUNTING AND REPORTING STANDARDS FOR OIL AND GAS PRODUCING ACTIVITIES
SMITH, DARLENE A. PULLIAM	AN ANALYSIS OF THE FACTORS USED BY THE TAX COURT IN APPLYING THE STEP TRANSACTION DOCTRINE
TURNER, MARK ALAN	JUDICIAL AND ADMINISTRATIVE DETERMINATION OF UNRELATED BUSINESS INCOME OF TAX EXEMPT ORGANIZATIONS
VOLLMERS, GLORIA LUCEY	AN ANALYSIS OF THE COST ACCOUNTING LITERATURE OF THE UNITED STATES FROM 1925 TO 1950
WILBURN, NANCY LOU	AN EMPIRICAL ANALYSIS OF THE RELATIVE POWER OF CONSTITUENTS PARTICIPATING IN THE STANDARD-SETTING PROCESS OF THE FINANCIAL ACCOUNTING STANDARDS BOARD: EMPLOYERS' ACCOUNTING FOR PENSIONS

Case

AHMED, ELTEGANI ABDELGADER	ISLAMIC BANKING: DISTRIBUTION OF PROFIT
AL-RWITA, SAAD SALEH	OWNERSHIP, CONTROL, AND PERFORMANCE IN AN UNDERDEVELOPED MARKET ENVIRONMENT: THE CASE OF THE SAUDI BANKING INDUSTRY
AL-SHIRAWI, BASHIR ISSA	PERFORMANCE OF COMMERCIAL BANKS OPERATING IN THE STATE OF QATAR: A MULTIVARIATE ANALYSIS OF FINANCIAL STATEMENTS
ALBRIGHT, THOMAS LYNN	THE IMPACT OF PROCESS VARIATION ON UNIT MANUFACTURING COST
ALRAWI, HIKMAT AHMAD ABDULGHAFOOR	ACCOUNTING, RESOURCE ALLOCATION, PLANNING AND EFFICIENCY: CASE STUDIES OF THE UNITED KINGDOM AND IRAQI UNIVERSITIES
ANDERSON, SHANNON WEEMS	MEASURING MANUFACTURING FLEXIBILITY: THE IMPACT OF PRODUCT MIX COMPLEXITY ON OPERATING PERFORMANCE AND MANUFACTURING OVERHEAD COST
BAKKE, MARILYN	A STUDY OF THE DISCIPLINE OF CPAS BY STATE BOARDS OF ACCOUNTANCY
BALDWIN-MORGAN, AMELIA ANNETTE	THE IMPACT OF EXPERT SYSTEMS ON AUDITING FIRMS: AN INVESTIGATION USING THE DELPHI TECHNIQUE AND A CASE STUDY APPROACH
BANAFA, AHMED MOHAMMED	DESIGN RELIABILITY FOR ESTIMATING COSTS OF PILE FOUNDATIONS: FROM THEORY TO APPLICATION OF A PROBABILISTIC-FUZZY APPROACH
BANAS, EDWARD JOSEPH, JR.	A DECONSTRUCTIONIST ANALYSIS OF ACCOUNTING METHODS FOR COMMUNITY COLLEGES IN THE STATE OF VIRGINIA
BARIDWAN, ZAKI	FUNCTIONAL CURRENCY AND INFLATION RATE: AN ANALYSIS OF THE IMPACT ON FINANCIAL STATEMENTS: AN INDONESIAN CASE STUDY

BEALING, WILLIAM EARL, JR.	INSTITUTIONAL ASPECTS OF AUDITING REGULATION: THE BUDGETING RELATIONSHIPS AMONG THE SEC, CONGRESS AND THE PRESIDENT
BEARD, VICTORIA KNAPP	REFLECTIONS OF PUBLIC ACCOUNTING INTERNS: A QUALITATIVE ANALYSIS OF EXPERIENTIAL LEARNING
BERRY, DELANO HOWARD	AN EXTENSION OF MANAGERIAL ACCOUNTING AND OPERATIONAL AUDITING IN THE PUBLIC SECTOR: A CASE STUDY OF SCHOOL FOOD SERVICE PROGRAMS IN SELECTED LOCAL SCHOOL DISTRICTS IN THE COMMONWEALTH OF KENTUCKY
BORKOWSKI, SUSAN CAROL	AN INVESTIGATION INTO THE DIVERGENCE OF THEORY FROM PRACTICE REGARDING TRANSFER PRICING METHODS
BOST, PATRICIA JAMES	MOVEMENT TOWARD UNIFORMITY IN THE DESIGN OF ABC SYSTEMS
BOYLE, EDMUND JOSEPH	THE ROLE OF INTERNAL AUDITING IN THE DEFENSE INDUSTRY: AN EMPIRICAL STUDY
BULL, IVAN OLE	MANAGEMENT PERFORMANCE IN LEVERAGED BUYOUTS: AN EMPIRICAL ANALYSIS
BURKETTE, GARY DALE	A STUDY OF TASK UNCERTAINTY ASSOCIATED WITH PUBLIC ACCOUNTING FIRM SERVICES
CAVER, TROY VERNON	THE VALIDITY OF THE COST-IMPROVEMENT CURVE AS A COST PREDICTOR IN CHANGING PRODUCTION ENVIRONMENTS
CHANDRA, AKHILESH	FIRM SIZE, A SELF-ORGANIZED CRITICAL PHENOMENON: EVIDENCE FROM THE DYNAMICAL SYSTEMS THEORY
CHEN, JIIN-FENG	AN EXPERT SYSTEM FOR THE IDENTIFICATION OF TROUBLED SAVINGS AND LOAN ASSOCIATIONS
CHRISTENSEN, JO ANN	AUDITOR SWITCHING AND WHITE COLLAR CRIME
CLINCH, GREGORY JOHN	INFORMATION AND MOTIVATION ISSUES IN COMPENSATION DESIGN: AN APPLICATION TO HIGH TECHNOLOGY COMPANIES
COCKRELL, SUSAN ROBERTA	TESTING THE DETERMINANTS OF DISCLOSURE COMPLIANCE BY MUNICIPALITIES USING CONFIRMATION FACTOR ANALYSIS
COKER, DIANNA ROSS	THE ROLE OF VISUAL-SPATIAL APTITUDE IN ACCOUNTING COURSEWORK
COULMAS, NANCY ELLEN	AN INTENSIVE CASE STUDY OF COST BEHAVIOR ANALYSIS IN AN INDUSTRIAL SETTING
CROSBY, WILLIAM MORRIS	AN EXAMINATION OF THE EFFECTS WHICH A CHANGE IN THE INTEREST RATE HAS ON PENSION COSTS AND LIABILITIES INCOMPANIES WITH DEFINED-BENEFIT PENSION PLANS
DENT D'ALMUANO, ROSELINE	TRANSFER STUDENTS' ACHIEVEMENT IN INTERMEDIATE ACCOUNTING: AN EMPIRICAL STUDY OF ARIZONA STATE UNIVERSITY STUDENTS
DERESHIWSKY, MARY IRENE	ALIGNMENT OF SPECIAL-INTEREST SUBJECTS IN THE ACCOUNTING STANDARD-SETTING PROCESS: AN INVESTIGATION
DEVINE, WILFRED FRANCIS	THE INFLUENCE OF CONSTITUENCY INPUT IN SETTING ACCOUNTING STANDARDS

DICKEY, HAZEL VIRGINIA COLEMAN	RELATIONSHIP OF STUDENTS' PREPARATION AND PERCEPTIONS WITH FINAL GRADES IN PRINCIPLES OF ACCOUNTING I IN PUBLIC TWO-YEAR COLLEGES IN ARKANSAS
DRUKER, MOSHE	ACCOUNTING (INCLUDING TAXATION AND COMPANY LAW) IN AN INFLATIONARY PERIOD--INVESTIGATED ON ISRAELI MODEL
DUNNE, KATHLEEN M.	DETERMINANTS OF THE CHOICE OF ACCOUNTING TREATMENT FOR BUSINESS COMBINATIONS: A POSITIVE THEORY APPROACH
EDWARDS, RANDAL KEITH	GROWTH COMPANIES AND CHANGES TO LARGER AUDIT FIRMS: AN EXAMINATION
EWING, PER	MANAGEMENT CONTROL OF INTERDEPENDENT UNITS [EKONOMISK STYRNING AV ENHETER MED INBORDE VERKSAMHETSSAMBAND]
FARRELL, BARBARA R.	ELEMENTS INFLUENCING SUCCESS ON THE CPA EXAMINATION
FEDHILA, HASSOUNA	THE CONSTRUCTION OF AN EXPERT SYSTEM TO MAKE COMMERCIAL LOAN CLASSIFICATIONS
FOSHEE, KENNETH HAROLD	ESTIMATING THE COSTS OF PRODUCING CONTAINER GROWN PLANTS WITH THE ASSISTANCE OF COMPUTER ACCOUNTING SOFTWARE
FOUST, KAREN MCLAFFERTY	INTERNAL STRUCTURE AND THE TRANSITION FROM A TWO-TIER TO A THREE-TIER HIERARCHY
FOWLER, CALVIN D.	AN EMPIRICAL STUDY OF LEARNING CURVES AMONG NON-REPETITIVE JOB SHOP OPERATIONS
FULTZ, M. ELAINE	DELEGATED REGULATION: A STUDY OF THE NATIONAL FUTURES ASSOCIATION
GABBIN, ALEXANDER L.	AN EMPIRICAL INVESTIGATION OF CANDIDATE ATTRIBUTES SIGNIFICANTLY AFFECTING RECRUITING OF ACCOUNTING GRADUATES BY A NATIONAL CPA FIRM
GRUBER, ROBERT ALLEN	AN EMPIRICAL INVESTIGATION INTO THE COGNITIVE LEVEL OF THE UNIFORM CPA EXAMINATION
GUPTA, MAHENDRA R.	AGGREGATION ISSUES IN PRODUCT COSTING
GUPTA, RAMESHWAR DASS	AN INQUIRY INTO THE ACCOUNTING PRINCIPLES AND REPORTING PRACTICES FOLLOWED BY SELECTED STATE UNIVERSITY HOSPITALS
HANDLANG, ALICE MAY	A CRITICAL ANALYSIS OF RESPONSES TO SELECTED FINANCIAL ACCOUNTING STANDARDS BOARD EXPOSURE DRAFTS TO DETERMINE THE IMPORTANT FACTORS RELEVANT TO ITS CONSTITUENCY
HARRIS, ELLEN KAY	FACTORS THAT INFLUENCE PRODUCT COSTING INFORMATION SYSTEM CHANGES
HARRIS, JEANNIE E.	TAX EXPENDITURES: REPORT UTILIZATION BY STATE POLICY MAKERS
HAWKINS, KYLEEN WHITEHEAD	AN EMPIRICAL ANALYSIS OF FACTORS USED BY COURTS WHEN DECIDING MOTIONS TO DISMISS RULE 10B-5 LITIGATION AGAINST ACCOUNTANTS
HAYES, ROBERT D.	THE CONSTANT - INPUT - PROPORTION ASSUMPTION IN THE BUDGETARY PROCESS

HEIAN, JAMES BERNARD   A STUDY OF THE DETERMINANTS OF SENIOR CERTIFIED PUBLIC ACCOUNTANT LEADERSHIP EFFECTIVENESS

HOLMES, RICHARD LAWRENCE   ON THE DETERMINATION AND REIMBURSEMENT OF COSTS IN THE PROVISION OF MEDICAID SERVICES BY LOCAL HEALTH DEPARTMENTS

HOWARD, ARLEY ANN   COST ANALYSIS OF DISTRIBUTION CHANNELS: AN EMPIRICAL DETERMINATION OF THE OPTIMAL CHANNEL STRATEGY

HUDACK, LAWRENCE RALPH   AN EXPLORATORY INVESTIGATION OF SOCIO-ECONOMIC PHENOMENA THAT MAY INFLUENCE ACCOUNTING DIFFERENCES IN THREE DIVERSE COUNTRIES

JENSON, RICHARD L.   PARAMETRIC ESTIMATION OF PROGRAMMING EFFORT IN A MANUFACTURING DATABASE ENVIRONMENT

JOHNSON, ROXANNE THERESE   AN ANALYSIS OF THE EARLY RECORD-KEEPING IN THE DUPONT COMPANY--1800-1818

JONNERGARD, KARIN   FEDERATIVE PROCESSES AND ADMINISTRATIVE DEVELOPMENT--A   STUDY OF FEDERATIVE COOPERATIVE ORGANIZATIONS (SWEDEN,   CANADA) [FEDERATIVA PROCESSER OCH ADMINISTRATIV UTVECKLING--EN   STUDIE AV

JURAS, PAUL EDWARD   ANALYSIS OF RELATIVE EFFICIENCY MEASURES OF MEDICAL NURSING UNITS FOR MANAGERIAL DIAGNOSIS AND CONTROL

KANNAN, RAMU S.   A KNOWLEDGE-BASED APPROACH FOR CONTROL DESIGN: A CASE STUDY IN THE PURCHASING CYCLE

KEATING, PATRICK J.   'MANAGING BY THE NUMBERS': AN EMPIRICALLY INFORMED THEORETICAL STUDY OF CORPORATE FINANCIAL WORK

KELLY, KIRK PATRICK   EXPERT PROBLEM SOLVING SYSTEM FOR THE AUDIT PLANNING PROCESS

KIDWELL, LINDA ACHEY   THE IMPACT OF BUDGET VARIANCE, FISCAL STRESS, POLITICAL TURNOVER, AND EMPLOYMENT SECTOR ON COMPLIANCE REPORTING DECISIONS

KIM, NEUNG JIP   THE ASSOCIATION OF PERFORMANCE ATTAINMENT PLANS WITH CORPORATE PERFORMANCE

KOPCZYNSKI, FRANK JOSEPH   THE SYSTEMS PARADIGM IN THE ANALYSIS OF PROSPECTIVE FINANCIAL INFORMATION: A PRAXIS BASED MODEL REFLECTING THE SYSTEMS VIEW OF THE FIRM

LANDRY, STEVEN PAUL   ACCOUNTING INFORMATION IN THE BUDGETING DECISION-MAKING PROCESS IN A UNITED STATES GOVERNMENT ASSET INFRASTRUCTURE ENVIRONMENT

LANGSTON, CAROLYN ANN PATTI   AN EVALUATION OF THE COST ACCOUNTING PROCEDURES FOR OUTPATIENT CARE AT A VA MEDICAL CENTER

LARKIN, JOSEPH MICHAEL   A PERFORMANCE MODEL FOR STAFF AUDITORS IN AN INTERNAL AUDIT ENVIRONMENT

LAWRENCE, JANICE ELIZABETH   AUDITS OF A FEDERAL LOAN PROGRAM: A CLASSIFICATION MODEL OF REPORTED IRREGULARITIES

LEE, SEOK-YOUNG   ESSAYS ON MANAGEMENT ACCOUNTING AND INCENTIVE CONTRACTS FOR SOME NEW PRODUCTION AND SELLING STRATEGIES

LEVENSTEIN, MARGARET CATHERINE   INFORMATION SYSTEMS AND INTERNAL ORGANIZATION: A STUDY OF THE DOW CHEMICAL COMPANY, 1890-1914

LINNEGAR, GARY JOHN	AN INVESTIGATION INTO THE MANAGEMENT OF CHANGE IN COST ACCOUNTING INFORMATION SYSTEM REQUIREMENTS DURING THE TRANSITION FROM TRADITIONAL MANUFACTURING TO JUST IN TIME CONCEPTS
LOWE, DANA R.	THE RELATIONSHIP BETWEEN STRATEGY CHANGE AND THE DESIGN OF MANAGEMENT ACCOUNTING SYSTEMS: A MULTIPLE CASE STUDY
LUEHLFING, MICHAEL STEVEN	THE IMPACT OF CLIENT RISK CHARACTERISTICS AND AUDIT PARTNER EXPERIENCE ON THE EXTENT OF THE SECOND PARTNER REVIEW IN AUDIT ENGAGEMENTS
MACKIE, JAMES JAY	AN EMPIRICAL INVESTIGATION OF THE IMPACT OF PERSONALITY TYPE ON SUPERVISOR-SUBORDINATE RELATIONSHIPS IN A BUDGETARY SETTING
MAHONEY, DANIEL PAUL	PENNSYLVANIA'S MUNICIPAL LABOR MARKET BEFORE AND AFTER THE ENACTMENT OF THE MUNICIPAL PENSION PLAN FUNDING STANDARD AND RECOVERY ACT: AN EMPIRICAL STUDY
MALLADO RODRIGUEZ, JOSE ANTONIC	THE MEASURE OF EFFECTIVENESS AND EFFICACY IN PUBLIC EXPENSES: AN EMPIRICAL APPLICATION [LE MEDIDA DE LA EFICACIA Y DE LA EFICIENCIA DEL GASTO PUBLICO: UNA APLICACION EMPIRICA]
MANZONI, JEAN-FRANCOIS	USE OF QUANTITATIVE FEEDBACK BY SUPERIORS: CAUSES AND CONSEQUENCES
MASIMBA, RODERICK DAVID	THE AGENCY PROBLEM: AN EMPIRICAL INVESTIGATION OF MANAGERIAL BEHAVIOR UNDER EXOGENOUSLY IMPOSED PRINCIPAL-AGENT RELATIONSHIPS IN TANZANIA
MASON, J. DAVID	A BEHAVIORAL MODEL OF SIMILARITY JUDGMENTS BY TAX PROFESSIONALS
MCCRAW, JOSEPH HARRISON, JR.	A STUDY OF THE FEASIBILITY OF USING LINEAR REGRESSION IN THE MANAGEMENT OF THE INDIVIDUAL TAX RETURN PREPARATION PROCESS
MCGOVERN, THOMAS WILLIAM	ACCOUNTING AND TRADE UNIONS: THE INCOMPATIBLES? A CASE STUDY OF CLOSURES AT DUNLOP
MCINNES, WILLIAM MCKENZIE	ACCOUNTING CHOICES AND REPORTED FINANCIAL PERFORMANCE: THE UNITED KINGDOM GAS INDUSTRY, 1970-1980. (VOLUMES I AND II)
MCMATH, HERBERT KENT	THE IMPACT OF MANDATED ACCOUNTING CHANGES ON MANAGEMENT DECISIONS: THE STATEMENT NO. 8 EPISODE
MICHAEL, RODNEY RICHARD	AN ANALYSIS OF THE ACCOUNTING SYSTEM OF THE QUINCY MINING COMPANY: 1846-1900
MONSERRAT JAUME, MAGDALENA	CATALAN WORKER-SHAREHOLDER PUBLIC LIMITED COMPANIES: A COMPARATIVE ECONOMIC ANALYSIS (SPAIN) [LAS SOCIEDADES ANONIMAS LABORALES CATALANAS: UN ANALISIS ECONOMICO COMPARATIVO]
MONTONDON, LUCILLE MARIE	A STUDY OF MUNICIPAL RESOURCE ALLOCATION DECISIONS AND MUNICIPAL BOND RATINGS
MORGAN, JOHN DANIEL	PREDICTING 'VERY EARLY TURNOVER' IN PUBLIC ACCOUNTING WITH PERSONALITY AND DEMOGRAPHIC BACKGROUND VARIABLES
MORRIS, BONNIE WHITE	CASE-BASED REASONING IN INTERNAL AUDITOR EVALUATIONS OF EDP CONTROLS
MYERS, JOAN JOETTE KLINGINSMITH	THE EXPLORATION OF PRODUCT COSTING AND COST CONTROL METHODS IN THE CURRENT MANUFACTURING ENVIRONMENT: A FIELD STUDY
NABANGI, FABIAN KAFUKO	THE UTILITY OF ARIMA MODELS TO REVENUE FORECASTING FOR ALABAMA URBAN COUNTY GOVERNMENTS

Listing by Research Method

NDZINGE, SHABANI	REGIONAL HARMONISATION OF ACCOUNTING IN DEVELOPING COUNTRIES: THE CASE OF THE SADCC
NIGRINI, MARK JOHN	THE DETECTION OF INCOME TAX EVASION THROUGH AN ANALYSIS OF DIGITAL DISTRIBUTIONS
NOVAK, EDWIN SHAWN	AN EMPIRICAL ANALYSIS OF FEDERAL INCOME TAX CAPITALIZATION IN THE PRICING OF INCOME PRODUCING REAL PROPERTY
NUTTER, SARAH EMMONS	UNITED STATES FEDERAL TAXATION OF EXPATRIATES: AN EMPIRICAL INVESTIGATION OF THE EQUITY OF THE FOREIGN EARNED INCOME AND HOUSING EXCLUSIONS
OGILBY, SUZANNE MARIE	THE INSTITUTIONALIZATION OF BUDGETING PROCESSES: THE (RE)PRODUCTION OF POWER
PAULSSON, GERT ARNE	ACCOUNTING SYSTEMS IN TRANSITION: A CASE STUDY IN THE SWEDISH HEALTH CARE ORGANIZATION
PHILLIPS, DAVID A.	ECONOMIC DEVELOPMENT, ACCOUNTING PRICES AND TECHNOLOGY: A CASE STUDY IN THE ESTIMATION OF ACCOUNTING PRICES AND THEIR APPLICATION TO ECONOMIC AND DISTRIBUTIONAL ANALYSIS OF THE CHOICE OF TECHNOLOGY IN THE NEPAL TEXTILE
POHLEN, TERRANCE LYNN	THE EFFECT OF ACTIVITY-BASED COSTING ON LOGISTICS MANAGEMENT
PRICE, CAROL EILEEN	ACCOUNTING INFORMATION AND LOAN QUALITY ASSESSMENT: AN INVESTIGATION OF THE DECISION PROCESS
RAMOS, VINCENT, JR.	EVALUATION OF THE IMPACT OF A 'SCHOOL WITHIN A SCHOOL'S ALTERNATIVE PROGRAM ON GRADES, ATTENDANCE, ACHIEVEMENT, AND SELF-CONCEPT BY ETHNIC GROUP
REDINBAUGH, DONNA FAYE HEERMANN	STRATEGIC PLANNING/MANAGEMENT IN SELECTED BIG EIGHT ACCOUNTING FIRMS
REIS, PRISCILLA ROSE	ACCOUNTING FOR COMPLEXITY: AN EXPLORATORY STUDY
ROBERTS, ROBIN WENDELL	DETERMINANTS OF AUDITOR CHANGE IN THE PUBLIC SECTOR
ROBSON, GARY STEPHEN	CERTIFICATION EXPERIENCE REQUIREMENTS AND THE TIMING OF RESIGNATION IN PUBLIC ACCOUNTING
ROWE, THOMAS MILTON	AN EMPIRICAL ANALYSIS OF THE QUALITY OF DIOCESAN FINANCIAL DISCLOSURE
SADLOWSKI, THEODORE STEPHEN	BUDGET ADMINISTRATION IN COLLEGES
SADOWSKI, SUSAN THERESA	CHANGES IN MANAGEMENT ACCOUNTING SYSTEMS WITH THE ADOPTION OF A TOTAL QUALITY MANAGEMENT PHILOSOPHY AND ITS OPERATIONALIZATION THROUGH CONTINUOUS PROCESS IMPROVEMENT AT THE LEVEL OF THE FIRM: A CASE STUDY OF
SAMIDI, JUHARI BIN	AN EMPIRICAL INVESTIGATION OF THE CAPITAL BUDGETING DECISION PROCESS OF GOVERNMENT-CONTROLLED ENTERPRISES AS COMPARED TO INVESTOR-OWNED ENTERPRISES: THE CASE OF MALAYSIA
SANKARAN, VENKATESWAR	IMPACT OF MANDATED DISCLOSURES ON MARKETMAKER BEHAVIOR: A CASE STUDY OF MANDATED REPLACEMENT COST DISCLOSURES
SAUERLENDER, KARIN MARIE	AMENDING THE FINANCIAL ACCOUNTING STANDARDS BOARD'S CONCEPTUAL FRAMEWORK: AN EMPIRICAL INVESTIGATION OF RESPONDENT COMMENTS

SCHWARZ, FREDERICK H.	AN ALTERNATIVE METHOD OF EVALUATING THE FINANCIAL PERFORMANCE OF FOREIGN SUBSIDIARIES
SKOGSVIK, KENTH HARRY GORAN	ACCOUNTING MEASURES AS PREDICTORS OF BUSINESS FAILURE--A COMPARISON BETWEEN HISTORICAL COST ACCOUNTING AND CURRENT COST ACCOUNTING [PROGNOS AV FINANSIELL KRIS MED REDOVISNINGSMATT--EN JAMFORELSE MELLAN
SMITH, KENNETH JONATHAN	AN INTERNAL AUDITING METHODOLOGY FOR THE EVALUATION OF CORPORATE WELLNESS INVESTMENTS
SMITH, MICHAEL ALLEN	AN EMPIRICAL INVESTIGATION OF THE RELATIONSHIP BETWEEN HISTORIC REHABILITATION TAX CREDITS AND HISTORIC REHABILITATION EXPENDITURES IN THREE VIRGINIA CITIES
STAPLES, CATHERINE LOVING	THE RELATION BETWEEN THE MEDIA, MONITORING DEVICES, AND THE SCHOOL DISTRICT BUDGETARY PROCESS
SUWANMALA, CHARAS	CENTRAL CONTROL AND LOCAL PRODUCTIVITY: A CASE STUDY IN THAILAND
TREWIN, JANET	THE IMPACT OF AN EXPERT SYSTEM ON A PROFESSIONAL ACCOUNTING ORGANIZATION
VILLAIRE, SONJA ANN SANDERS	A CASE STUDY OF THE PREDICTIVE ABILITY OF PLACEMENT TESTS FOR PRINCIPLES OF ACCOUNTING
WALKER, KENTON BLAIR	AN EMPIRICAL FIELD STUDY OF STATISTICAL AND MANAGEMENT PREDICTION MODELS AND THE EFFECTS OF A BUDGET-BASED INCENTIVE PROGRAM
WALLACE, REGINALD SYLVANUS OLUSEGUN	DISCLOSURE OF ACCOUNTING INFORMATION IN DEVELOPING COUNTRIES: A CASE STUDY OF NIGERIA
WALTER, RICHARD M.	A COMPARISON OF THE USEFULNESS OF CURRENT COST, CONSTANT DOLLAR, AND HISTORICAL COST INFORMATION FOR IDENTIFYING TAKEOVER TARGETS
WEISENFELD, LESLIE WIGHT	EXAMINING THE EFFECT OF EVALUATING PERFORMANCE WITH PERFORMANCE REPORT VARIANCES ON REPORTED PERFORMANCE: A FIELD RESEARCH APPROACH
WHEELER, STEPHEN W.	ASSESSING THE PERFORMANCE OF ANALYTICAL PROCEDURES: A BEST CASE SCENARIO
WILLIAMS, JOHN RICHARD, SR.	THE IMPACT OF COMPANY-SPECIFIC VERSUS COUNTRY-SPECIFIC CHARACTERISTICS ON FINANCIAL ACCOUNTING DISCLOSURE: AN EMPIRICAL STUDY OF THIRTEEN COUNTRIES
YOUNG, JONI J.	AGENDA FORMATION AND THE FINANCIAL ACCOUNTING STANDARDS BOARD

Experimental

ACCOLA, WILTON LEE	AN EMPIRICAL INVESTIGATION OF THE EFFECTS OF A CAPITAL BUDGETING COMPUTERIZED DECISION AID AND COGNITIVE STYLE DIFFERENCES ON INVESTMENT DECISIONS
ACTON, DANIEL DICKSON	THE IMPACT ON DOMESTIC FINANCIAL STATEMENTS USERS OF DISCLOSING FOREIGN BUSINESS AND FINANCIAL PRACTICES: AN INVESTIGATION OF JAPANESE CORPORATIONS
ADLER, RALPH WILLIAM	ACCOUNTING AND PERFORMANCE INDICATORS AS DETERMINANTS OF ORGANIZATIONAL DECLINE: THEORY AND EMPIRICAL EVIDENCE
AHLAWAT, SUNITA SINGH	EXPLANATION EFFECTS IN SEQUENTIAL BELIEF-REVISION BY AUDIT GROUPS AND INDIVIDUALS
ALLEN, GEORGE LOUIS	AN EMPIRICAL INVESTIGATION OF THE COMPLEMENTARY VALUE OF A STATEMENT OF CASH FLOWS IN A SET OF PUBLISHED FINANCIAL STATEMENTS

AMER, TAREK SAAD | AN EXPERIMENTAL INVESTIGATION OF THE EFFECTS OF MULTI-CUE FINANCIAL INFORMATION DISPLAY AND TASK COMPLEXITY ON DECISION-MAKING

ANDERSON, SUSAN ELAINE G. | AN ANALYSIS OF THE EFFECT OF TAX LAW INSTABILITY AND PREFERENTIAL CAPITAL GAIN TREATMENT ON INVESTMENT IN RISKY ASSETS

ANDERSON, URTON LIGGETT | THE AUDITOR'S ASSESSMENT OF CONTROL RISK: THE EXPLANATION PHENOMENON IN JUDGMENTS OF EVENT UNCERTAINTY

APOSTOLOU, BARBARA ANN | AN INVESTIGATION OF INTERNAL AUDITOR JUDGMENT ON THE IMPORTANCE OF INDICATORS OF POTENTIAL FINANCIAL FRAUD: AN ANALYTIC HIERARCHY PROCESS APPROACH

ARUNACHALAM, VAIRAVAN | DECISION AIDING IN MULTI-PARTY TRANSFER PRICING NEGOTIATION: THE EFFECTS OF COMPUTER-MEDIATED COMMUNICATION AND STRUCTURED INTERACTION

ASARE, STEPHEN KWAKU | THE AUDITORS' GOING CONCERN OPINION DECISION: INTERACTION OF TASK VARIABLES AND THE SEQUENTIAL PROCESSING OF EVIDENCE

ASECHEMIE, DANIEL PELE SAMUEL | AN EXPERIMENTAL STUDY OF TOURNAMENTS AND CONTRACTS: A PRINCIPAL'S PERSPECTIVE

ATKINSON, SUE ANDREWS | THE CONTRAST-INERTIA MODEL AND THE UPDATING OF ATTRIBUTIONS IN PERFORMANCE EVALUATION

AUSTIN, WALTER WADE | A STUDY OF THE EFFECTS OF INTEGRATING MICROCOMPUTERS INTO THE INTRODUCTORY FINANCIAL ACCOUNTING COURSE

AVILA, MARCOS GONCALVES | TRANSFER PRICING MECHANISMS: AN EXPERIMENTAL INVESTIGATION

AWASTHI, VIDYA NIDHI | BUDGETARY SLACK AND PERFORMANCE UNDER PARTICIPATIVE BUDGETING: AN EXPERIMENTAL STUDY OF THE EFFECTS OF MONITORING, THE AGENT'S RISK PREFERENCE, AND THE QUALITY OF THE AGENT'S PRE-DECISION INFORMATION

BAILEY, JAMES ALMA | AUDIT FEE EFFECTS ON AUDITOR INDEPENDENCE

BAKER, WILLIAM MAURICE | THE EFFECTS OF ACCOUNTING REPORTS ON LOAN OFFICERS: AN EXPERIMENT

BALCOM, NORMA JEAN | AN INVESTIGATION OF PROSPECT THEORY'S EFFECTS ON DECISIONS OF MANAGEMENT ACCOUNTANTS

BARKMAN, BERYL V. | INCOME SMOOTHING: A LABORATORY EXPERIMENT

BASU, PROGYAN | THE INFLUENCE OF CLIENT CONTROL ENVIRONMENT ATTRIBUTES ON EVALUATION OF INTERNAL CONTROL: AN EMPIRICAL INVESTIGATION OF AUDITOR JUDGMENT

BATCHELDER, WALTER IRVING | A STUDY OF THE LINK-CHAIN LIFO CONTROVERSY

BEAN, DAVID FRANCIS | THE FRAMING OF DECISION CHOICES BY INFORMATION PROVIDERS: AN EXPLORATORY STUDY

BEAULIEU, PHILIP RAYMOND | COMMERCIAL LENDERS' USE OF ACCOUNTING INFORMATION: THE EFFECTS OF CHARACTER INFORMATION AND EXPERIENCE

BECKER, D'ARCY ANN | THE EFFECTS OF AUDIT DECISION AID DESIGN ON THE INTRINSIC MOTIVATION AND PERFORMANCE OF AUDITORS PREDICTING CORPORATE BANKRUPTCY

Listing by Research Method

BEDARD, JEAN	INTERNAL CONTROL EVALUATION IN COMPUTERIZED SYSTEMS: EXPERTS VERSUS NOVICES
BERG, JOYCE ELLEN	INFORMATIVENESS AND VALUE OF PUBLIC INFORMATION: AN EXPERIMENTAL TEST
BHATTACHARYA, SOMNATH	THE USE OF RECALL AND RECOGNITION TECHNIQUES IN ELICITING EXPRIENCED-INEXPERIENCED AUDITOR DIFFERENCES IN THE DETECTION OF MANAGEMENT FRAUD
BILBEISI, KHAMIS MOHAMAD	CULTURAL EFFECTS ON THE RELATIONSHIPS BETWEEN BUDGETARY PARTICIPATION AND MANAGERIAL PERFORMANCE
BISHOP, RACHEL ANN	INCENTIVE SCHEMES, MORAL HAZARD, AND RISK AVERSION: INTRAFIRM RESOURCE ALLOCATION AND DETERMINANTS OF BUDGETARY SLACK
BJORNSON, CHRIS E.	THE EFFECT OF INCOME TAX PREPAYMENTS ON TAXPAYER REPORTING BEHAVIOR: A BUSINESS SIMULATION
BLAZEK, MICHELE MCGLINCHY	AN EMPIRICAL STUDY OF BAYESIAN DECISION THEORY AND AUDITOR JUDGMENT UNDER UNCERTAINTY
BLOOMFIELD, ROBERT JAMES	EVOLUTIONARY MODELS IN LABORATORY AND AUDITING GAMES
BOHAC, DARLENE MARIE	THE EFFECT OF MANAGEMENT BUDGETARY CONTROLS ON AUDIT PLANNING
BONNER, SARAH ELIZABETH	EXPERIENCE EFFECTS IN THE COMPONENTS OF ANALYTICAL RISK ASSESSMENT
BOSCIA, MARIAN W. LARSON	THE RELATIONSHIP BETWEEN ESOP VOTING RIGHTS AND EMPLOYEES' JOB PERFORMANCE
BRADLEY, MICHAEL P.	ACCOUNTING INFORMATION, INDIVIDUAL DIFFERENCES, AND ATTRIBUTIONS IN THE PERFORMANCE EVALUATION PROCESS
BRANSON, LEONARD L.	ACCOUNTING INFORMATION, COGNITIVE PROCESSES, AND PERFORMANCE APPRAISAL
BRISCOE, NAT REEVE	UNCERTAINTY, RISK, AND PROFESSIONAL LIABILITY: AN EMPIRICAL ANALYSIS USING THE IN-BASKET TEST
BRODY, RICHARD GLEN	ESCALATION OF COMMITMENT AS A THREAT TO INTERNAL AUDITOR OBJECTIVITY
BROWN, DARRELL L.	THE INFLUENCE OF DECISION STYLE AND INFORMATION PRESENTATION FORMAT ON THE PERCEIVED USEFULNESS OF MANAGERIAL ACCOUNTING INFORMATION: AN EMPIRICAL INVESTIGATION
BROZOVSKY, JOHN ALLWIN	THE EFFECT OF AUDITOR REPUTATION ON THE PRICING OF AUDIT SERVICES: AN EXPERIMENTAL STUDY
BULLIS FRANSSON, DEBRA ALICE	THE EFFECT OF INVESTMENT DECISION GOAL ON FINANCIAL ANALYSTS' USE OF INFORMATION IN JUDGMENTS ABOUT FIRMS
BURGESS, DEANNA OXENDER	THE EFFECTS OF GRAPHICAL DISTORTION OF ACCOUNTING INFORMATION ON FINANCIAL JUDGMENTS
BUSH, HOWARD FRANCIS	THE USE OF REGRESSION MODELS IN ANALYTICAL REVIEW JUDGMENT: A LABORATORY EXPERIMENT

Listing by Research Method

BUSHMAN, ROBERT MICHAEL

PUBLIC DISCLOSURE BY FIRMS IN THE PRESENCE OF A MONOPOLISTIC SELLER OF PRIVATE INFORMATION

BUTLER, JANET ANN BASEMAN

SELF-INTEREST IN ACCOUNTING: AN EXAMINATION OF DECISION-MAKING

BUTT, JANE LOUISE

FREQUENCY JUDGMENTS IN AUDITING

BUTTROSS, THOMAS EDWARD

THE EFFECT OF SELECTED PERSONALITY AND SITUATIONAL VARIABLES ON THE ETHICAL JUDGMENTS OF MANAGEMENT ACCOUNTANTS IN FEDERAL INCOME TAX COMPLIANCE

CALDERON, THOMAS GEORGE

BANKER NEEDS FOR ACCOUNTING INFORMATION

CAMPBELL, ANNHENRIE

AUDIT CONTINUITY, CLIENT'S POLICY, AND THE INTERNAL AUDIT RELIANCE JUDGMENT

CAPOZZOLI, ERNEST ANTHONY

AN EXPERIMENTAL INVESTIGATION OF THE EFFECTS OF A DECISION SUPPORT SYSTEM UTILIZING HYPERTEXT-BASED ACCOUNTING DATA ON INDIVIDUAL DECISION-MAKING BEHAVIOR

CAPRIOTTI, KIM BOYLAN

AN INVESTIGATION OF THE USE OF VERBAL AND NUMERICAL PROBABILITY EXPRESSIONS IN BANK LENDING DECISIONS

CARNES, KAY C.

THE EFFECTS OF CERTAIN PERSONAL AND ORGANIZATIONAL VARIABLES ON THE ATTITUDES OF INTERNAL AUDITORS TOWARD ETHICAL DILEMMAS

CARPENTER, BRIAN WELLS

THE EFFECT OF NATURE OF TRANSACTION, RANK, EXPERIENCE, AND FAMILIARITY ON THE MATERIALITY JUDGMENTS OF AUDITORS: AN EMPIRICAL EXAMINATION

CARPENTER, FRANCES HORVATH

THE IMPACT OF MUNICIPAL REPORTING REQUIREMENTS ON MUNICIPAL OFFICIALS' FIXED ASSET ACQUISITION DECISIONS: A LABORATORY EXPERIMENT

CASTER, PAUL

THE EFFECTS OF MISSING DATA ON AUDIT INFERENCE AND AN INVESTIGATION INTO THE VALIDITY OF ACCOUNTS RECEIVABLE CONFIRMATIONS AS AUDIT EVIDENCE

CHAN, CHRIS WAI-HONG

EFFECTS OF NEGOTIATOR ACCOUNTABILITY, PERFORMANCE EVALUATION SYSTEM, AND PERCEPTION OF DIVISIONAL POWER ON TRANSFER PRICING NEGOTIATION OUTCOMES

CHEN, SEAN SHAW-ZON

A MODEL OF BELIEF REVISION IN AUDIT RISK ASSESSMENT

CHO, WHAJOON

THE RELATIONSHIP BETWEEN EVIDENCE SEQUENCE AND TIME PRESSURE ON AUDITORS' CONTROL RISK ASSESSMENTS

CHOO, TECKMIN

AUDITORS' INFORMATION SEARCH AND EVALUATION IN HYPOTHESIS-TESTING: POSITIVITY, EXTREMITY, PSEUDODIAGNOSTICITY AND CONFIRMATION EFFECTS

CHRIST, LEROY FREDERICK

A COMPARISON OF INSTRUCTIONAL STRATEGIES IN THE DEVELOPMENT OF CATEGORICAL TAX KNOWLEDGE WITH AN EXAMINATION OF THE EFFECT OF INCONSISTENT PRE-EXISTING KNOWLEDGE

CHRIST, MARY YORK

ATTENTION AND ENCODING DURING AUDIT PLANNING: AN EXPERIMENTAL STUDY USING A SCHEMATIC FRAMEWORK

CHUNG, LAI HONG

THE JOINT EFFECTS OF PRIOR OUTCOME AND PRESENTATION FORMAT ON INDIVIDUAL AND GROUP RESOURCE ALLOCATION DECISIONS: THE ROLE OF MENTAL ACCOUNTS

CHURCH, BRYAN KEVIN

AN INVESTIGATION OF CONFIRMATORY BIAS IN AN AUDIT SETTING: A CONCEPTUALIZATION AND LABORATORY EXPERIMENT

CLARK, COROLYN ELIZABETH	AN EXPERIMENT TO DETERMINE THE EFFECTS OF A BEHAVIOR MODIFICATION INTERVENTION PROGRAM ON ANXIETY LEVELS AND ACHIEVEMENT OF STUDENTS IN PRINCIPLES OF ACCOUNTING CLASSES
CLAYTON, PENNY RENEE	AUDITOR DECISION PROCESSING AND THE IMPLICATIONS OF BRAIN DOMINANCE: A PREDECISIONAL BEHAVIOR STUDY
CLOYD, C. BRYAN	THE EFFECTS OF KNOWLEDGE AND INCENTIVES ON INFORMATION SEARCH IN TAX RESEARCH TASKS
COCCO, ANTHONY F.	THE EFFECTS OF STANDARD DIFFICULTY AND COMPENSATION METHOD ON THE PARAMETERS OF THE INDUSTRIAL LEARNING CURVE AND OVERALL PERFORMANCE OF MANUAL ASSEMBLY AND DISASSEMBLY TASKS
COHEN, JEFFREY R.	THE IMPACT OF CONSERVATISM, INTERNAL CONTROL RELIABILITY, AND EXPERIENCE ON THE USE OF ANALYTICAL REVIEW
COKER, JOHN WILLIAM	AN EMPIRICAL ANALYSIS OF THE USE OF THE INCOME TAX BASIS OF ACCOUNTING ON THE LENDING DECISIONS OF BANKERS: AN EXPERIMENT
COMSTOCK, S. MARK	THE COGNITIVE PROCESS UNDERLYING THE ACQUISITION OF ACCOUNTING EXPERTISE
CONWAY, ROBERT C.	THE EFFECT OF ALTERNATE DECISION FRAMES ON DECISIONS THAT USE ACCOUNTING INFORMATION
COOK, GAIL LYNN	A SYSTEMIC STUDY OF COORDINATED DECISION-MAKING ACROSS FUNCTIONAL AREAS
COOPER, JEAN CLAIRE	COMPENSATION CONTRACT SELF-SELECTION, PARTICIPATIVE STANDARD SETTING AND JOB PERFORMANCE
COPP, CYNTHIA ANN	THE EFFECT OF TAX STRUCTURE VARIABLES ON THE DECISION FRAME ADOPTED AND THE TAX REPORTING CHOICE: TAXABLE INCOME COMPONENTS AND TAX PAYMENT TIMING
COTTRELL, DAVID MARK	MARKET-BASED AUDITING STANDARDS: EXPERIMENTAL TESTS OF MARKET DISCLOSURES AS SUBSTITUTES FOR EXTERNAL REGULATION
COULTER, JOHN MICHAEL	THE EFFECTS OF AUDIT EXPERIENCE AND PROBABILITY KNOWLEDGE ON AUDITORS' USE OF HEURISTICS IN JUDGMENTS UNDER UNCERTAINTY
CROSSER, RICK LYNN	THE RELATIVE EFFECT OF PENALTY MAGNITUDES ON COMPLIANCE: AN EXPERIMENTAL EXAMINATION OF DETERRENCE
CUCCIA, ANDREW DANIEL	AN EXAMINATION OF THE EFFORT AND AGGRESSIVENESS OF PROFESSIONAL TAX PREPARERS: THE EFFECTS OF ECONOMIC SANCTIONS AND ROLE PERCEPTIONS
CUMMINGS, CHARLES WILLIAM	BUDGET SLACK AND PREDICTION PERFORMANCE IN AN UNCERTAIN ENVIRONMENT: AN EXPERIMENTAL INVESTIGATION
DANIEL, SHIRLEY JUNE	AUDITOR JUDGMENTS: A DESCRIPTIVE STUDY OF THE ASSESSMENT OF AUDIT RISK
DAVIS, CHARLES ELLIOT	THE EFFECTS OF AUDITOR KNOWLEDGE STRUCTURES AND EXPERIENCE ON PROBLEM IDENTIFICATION AND HYPOTHESIS GENERATION IN ANALYTICAL REVIEW
DAVIS, ELIZABETH BOOZER	AIDING GOING CONCERN JUDGMENTS: THE INFLUENCE OF DECISION AID TYPE AND ACCOUNTABILITY
DAVIS, JEFFERSON TORONTO	AUDITOR EXPERIENCE IN PRELIMINARY CONTROL RISK ASSESSMENTS: NEURAL NETWORK MODELS OF AUDITORS' KNOWLEDGE STRUCTURES

DAVIS, JON STUART   AUDITOR BIDDING AND INDEPENDENCE: A LABORATORY MARKETS INVESTIGATION

DAVIS, LARRY R.   THE EFFECTS OF QUESTION COMPLEXITY AND FORM OF PRESENTATION ON THE EXTRACTION OF QUESTION-ANSWERS FROM AN INFORMATION PRESENTATION

DECKER, LARITA MARIE   INFORMATION AND INCENTIVE MECHANISMS FOR ALIGNING PRINCIPAL AND AGENT INTERESTS IN ESCALATION SITUATIONS

DEL VECCHIO, STEPHEN CARL   AN EMPIRICAL STUDY OF THE FORGETTING OF AUDIT TASK EXPERTISE

DELANEY, JOHN EDWARD   A DELPHI STUDY OF REVENUE CYCLE AUDITS

DEVINE, KEVIN MARK   THE EFFECTS OF INFORMATION FRAMING ON DECISION-MAKING BEHAVIOR RELATED TO RESOURCE ALLOCATIONS

DILLA, WILLIAM NOEL   TESTS OF INFORMATION EVALUATION BEHAVIOR IN A COMPETITIVE ENVIRONMENT

DIPIETRO, JANICE DIANE   AN EMPIRICAL INVESTIGATION OF THE IMPACT OF AUDIT EXPERIENCE AND TASK ON THE UTILIZATION OF DECISION HEURISTICS

DO, SANGHO   THE EFFECT OF OUTCOME FEEDBACK AND EXPERIENCE ON THE PREDICTION OF CORPORATE FAILURE: PERFORMANCE OF HUMAN VS. MODEL

DONADIO, JANETTE MARIE   AN EMPIRICAL STUDY OF THE JOINT EFFECTS OF KNOWLEDGE, INTELLECTUAL SKILL, AND TASK STRUCTURE ON THE ACCURACY OF AUDITORS' PERFORMANCE OF DIAGNOSTIC AUDIT TASKS

DOW, KATHY J.   AN EXAMINATION OF MATERIALITY FROM THE USER-DECISION PERSPECTIVE

DUH, RONG RUEY   ECONOMIC MAN AS AN INTUITIVE BAYESIAN: AN EXPERIMENTAL STUDY

DUNN, CHERYL LYNN   AN INVESTIGATION OF ABSTRACTION IN EVENTS-BASED ACCOUNTING SYSTEMS

DUSENBURY, RICHARD BENNETT   TAX COMPLIANCE: THE EFFECT OF THE TIMING OF PAYMENTS

DWYER, PEGGY DIANE   AN EMPIRICAL INVESTIGATION OF THE EFFECTS OF CERTAIN CLIENT CHARACTERISTICS ON AUDITORS' EVALUATIONS OF ACCOUNTING ESTIMATES

EINING, MARTHA MCDONALD   THE IMPACT OF AN EXPERT SYSTEM AS A DECISION AID ON LEARNING DURING THE AUDIT PROCESS: AN EMPIRICAL TEST

ELKHATIB, SOBHY MAHMOUD   AN EMPIRICAL TEST OF THE BERG PROCEDURE FOR INDUCING RISK PREFERENCES

ENGLISH, DENISE MAY   THE INFLUENCE OF TIME PRESSURE, FIRM METHODOLOGY, AND CLIENT SIZE ON AUDITORS' MATERIALITY JUDGMENTS: AN INFORMATION ACQUISITION APPROACH

ENGLISH, THOMAS JAMES   AN EXAMINATION OF THE EFFECT OF SOCIAL INFLUENCE ON AUDITORS' MATERIALITY JUDGMENTS

EPELLE, CHUKUEMERIE TAMUNOTONYE   THE IMPACT OF ORGANIZATIONAL GOALS UPON BANK LOAN OFFICERS' CREDIT WORTHINESS DECISIONS

ESSEX, PATRICIA ANN	SYSTEMS DEVELOPMENT FRICTION: A CAUSAL MODEL BASED ON EQUITY CONSIDERATIONS
EYLER, KEL-ANN SHELDON	AN EXAMINATION OF THE EFFECTS OF AUDIT STRUCTURE AND GROUP TASK SETTINGS ON THE MATERIALITY JUDGMENTS OF AUDITORS
FENNEMA, MARTIN GENE	ANTICIPATIONS OF EFFORT AND ACCURACY IN MULTIATTRIBUTE CHOICE
FISHER, JOSEPH GERALD	THE ALLOCATION MECHANISM OF AUDITS: AN EXPERIMENTAL APPROACH
FISHER, STEVEN ALLEN	AN EMPIRICAL INVESTIGATION OF EXPERT JUDGMENTS CONCERNING THE SELECTION STATEMENT OF FINANCIAL ACCOUNTING STANDARDS NUMBER 52'S FUNCTIONAL CURRENCY
FLYNN, RICHARD STEVEN	AN EMPIRICAL INVESTIGATION OF THE EFFECTS OF ALTERNATIVE PERFORMANCE MEASUREMENT SCHEMES ON THE AGENT'S DISCLOSURE OF PRIVATE INFORMATION
FORDHAM, DAVID RONALD	A COMMUNICATIONS-BASED TYPOLOGY OF COLLABORATION IN DECISION-MAKING
FOSS, HELGA BERTA	THE EFFECT OF ACCOUNTING CHANGES AND TAX CONSEQUENCES ON INVESTOR BEHAVIOR
FRAZER, JOHN DOUGLAS	PERFORMANCE EVALUATION OF AUDITORS: THE IMPORTANCE OF TIME-BUDGET PRESSURE THROUGH A FOCUS ON THE EVALUATOR
FREDERICK, DAVID MICHAEL	AUDITORS' REPRESENTATION AND RETRIEVAL OF KNOWLEDGE IN INTERNAL CONTROL EVALUATION
FREDERICKSON, JAMES RAY	RELATIVE PERFORMANCE INFORMATION: THE EFFECTS OF COMMON UNCERTAINTY AND CONTRACT TYPE ON AGENTS' GOALS AND EFFORT
FRENCH, GEORGE RICHARD	AN ANALYSIS OF THE INTERPERSONAL STYLE OF PERSONAL FINANCIAL PLANNERS (CPAS AND NONACCOUNTANTS) AND TRADITIONAL ACCOUNTANTS WITH IMPLICATIONS FOR THE ACCOUNTING PROFESSION
FRIAR, SHIRLEY ANNE	DECISION MAKING UNDER RISK: AN EXPERIMENTAL STUDY WITHIN A BUSINESS CONTEXT
FROWNFELTER, CYNTHIA ANN	THE EFFECTS OF DIFFERING INFORMATION PRESENTATIONS OF GENERAL PURPOSE FINANCIAL STATEMENTS ON USERS' DECISIONS
GABRIEL, ELIZABETH ANN	MARKET COMPETITION AND THE INCENTIVE TO INVEST IN PRODUCT COST INFORMATION: AN EXPERIMENTAL INVESTIGATION
GADDIS, MARCUS DAMON	INVESTIGATING THE INFLUENCE OF ASSERTIONS BY ACCOUNTING AND APPRAISAL PROFESSIONALS ON REAL ESTATE LENDING DECISIONS
GELARDI, ALEXANDER MARIA GEORGE	THE EFFECT OF QUANTITY AND ORDER OF CUES ON SEQUENTIAL BELIEF REVISION IN TAX JUDGMENTS
GHOSH, DIPANKAR	AN EXPERIMENT COMPARING NEGOTIATED AND CENTRALLY ADMINISTERED TRANSFER PRICES
GIBSON, DANA L.	THE EFFECTS OF ALTERNATIVE SCREEN LAYOUTS AND FEEDBACK TYPES ON OCCASIONAL USER PRODUCTIVITY AND SATISFACTION IN A GENERAL LEDGER ENVIRONMENT
GILL, JOHN WAITS	THE EFFECTS OF A RED FLAGS QUESTIONNAIRE AND SELECTED ELEMENTS OF COGNITIVE STYLE ON THE AUDIT PLANNING TASK OF ASSESSING THE PROBABILITY OF MATERIAL MANAGEMENT FRAUD

Listing by Research Method

GIRARD, ALINE CHANTAL	THE EFFECTS OF CONTEXT, TERMINOLOGY, AND EXPERTISE ON THE UNDERSTANDABILITY OF ACCOUNTING CONCEPTS: A LABORATORY EXPERIMENT
GREEN, SHARON L.	A BEHAVIORAL INVESTIGATION OF THE EFFECTS OF ALTERNATIVE GOVERNMENTAL FINANCIAL REPORTING FORMATS ON ANALYSTS' PREDICTIONS OF BOND RATINGS
GRIFFIN, LYNN DRAGER	AN EXPECTANCY THEORY EXAMINATION OF MANAGERIAL MOTIVATION TO IMPLEMENT JUST-IN-TIME
GUESS, AUNDREA KAY	THE IMPACT OF AMBIGUITY AND RISK ON THE AUDITOR'S ASSESSMENT OF INHERENT RISK AND CONTROL RISK
GULLEY, LAWRENCE	A DETERMINATION OF THE EFFECTS OF A CHANGE IN INFORMATION-PROCESSING CAUSED BY A CHANGE IN ACCOUNTING METHODS
GUNDERSON, ELIZABETH ANN WEISS	EXPERTISE IN SECURITY VALUATION: OPERATIONALIZING THE VALUATION PROCESS
GURGANUS, FRANKIE EDWARDS	A STUDY OF THE UTILITY OF REPORTING POSTRETIREMENT HEALTH CARE BENEFITS
HACKENBRACK, KARL EDWARD	ASSESSING A COMPANY'S EXPOSURE TO FRAUDULENT FINANCIAL REPORTING: IMPLICATIONS OF SEEMINGLY IRRELEVANT EVIDENCE
HALL, SHEILA HUNTLEY	AN EXPERIMENTAL INVESTIGATION OF FINANCIAL STATEMENT USERS' SELF-INSIGHT IN REPORTING DECISION-MAKING PROCESSES
HAMILL, JAMES ROBERT	AN EXPERIMENTAL ANALYSIS OF THE IMPACT OF INCOME TAXES ON NOMINAL INTEREST RATES
HAMILTON, CHARLES THOMAS	INDIVIDUAL JUDGMENT IN ANALYTICAL REVIEW PERFORMANCE
HAN, JIN-SOO	INTERNAL CONTROL EVALUATION AND AUDIT PROGRAM PLANNING JUDGMENTS BY INDIVIDUAL AUDITORS AND AUDIT TEAMS: A STUDY OF SOUTH KOREAN CPA'S
HANNO, DENNIS MICHAEL	THE USE OF INFORMATION IN THE SEQUENTIAL EVALUATION OF AUDIT EVIDENCE
HANSEN, JAMES DAVID	THE EFFECT OF INFORMATION LOAD AND COGNITIVE STYLE ON DECISION QUALITY IN A FINANCIAL DISTRESS DECISION TASK
HARRINGTON, ROBERT PICKENS	FORECASTING CORPORATE PERFORMANCE
HARSH, MARY FRANCES	THE IMPACT OF ACTIVITY-BASED COSTING ON MANAGERIAL DECISIONS: AN EMPIRICAL ANALYSIS
HARTWELL, CAROLYN L.	THE EFFECT OF PRIOR YEAR'S AUDIT INFORMATION AND PERFORMANCE FEEDBACK ON STAFF AUDITORS' PERFORMANCE
HARVEY, PATRICK JAMES	ENHANCING TAX BENEFITS VIA PURCHASE OF LEGISLATIVE AUTHORITY: AN EXPERIMENTAL APPROACH
HAYNES, CHRISTINE MILLER	AN EXAMINATION INTO THE EFFECTS OF CONTEXT AND EXPERIENCE ON AUDITORS' BELIEF REVISIONS IN CASCADED-INFERENCE TASKS
HEBBLE, ANNETTE	THE EFFECT OF ALTERNATIVE SYSTEMS OF TAXATION ON INDIVIDUAL SAVINGS: AN EXPERIMENTAL APPROACH

Listing by Research Method 401

HEIMAN, VICKY BETH	AUDITORS' ASSESSMENTS OF THE LIKELIHOOD OF ANALYTICAL REVIEW EXPLANATIONS
HELLELOID, RICHARD TRYGVE	HINDSIGHT BIAS AND JUDGMENTS BY TAX PROFESSIONALS
HERMANSON, HEATHER MARIE	THE IMPACT OF CONTROL RISK AND BUSINESS RISK ON SAMPLE EVIDENCE EVALUATION
HERZ, PAUL JOSEPH	AN INVESTIGATION OF PROCEDURAL MEMORY AS AN INGREDIENT OF TASK PERFORMANCE IN ACCOUNTING
HIGHSMITH, GWENDOLYN JANNETT	AN EMPIRICAL INVESTIGATION OF THE PERFORMANCE OF THE EDP QUALITY ASSURANCE FUNCTION ON THE INDEPENDENT AUDITOR'S EVALUATION OF INTERNAL CONTROL
HILL, MARY CALLAHAN	THE AVAILABILITY AND USE OF FEEDBACK IN AUDIT PLANNING
HILTEBEITEL, KENNETH MERRILL	THE ACCOUNTING STANDARDS OVERLOAD ISSUE: AN EMPIRICAL TEST OF THE EFFECT OF FOUR SELECTED FINANCIAL ACCOUNTING STANDARDS ON THE LENDING DECISIONS OF BANKERS
HIRST, DAVID ERIC	AUDITORS' SENSITIVITY TO FACTORS AFFECTING THE RELIABILITY OF EVIDENCE SOURCES IN BELIEF REVISION
HITE, PEGGY SULLIVAN	AN EXPERIMENTAL INVESTIGATION OF TWO POSSIBLE EXPLANATIONS FOR TAXPAYER NONCOMPLIANCE: TAX SHELTERS AND NONCOMPLIANT PEERS
HITZIG, NEAL B.	SUBSTANTIVE AUDIT TESTS OF DETAILS AND THE ESTIMATION OF RARE ERRORS BY DOUBLE SAMPLING WITH PROBABILITY PROPORTIONAL TO SIZE
HO, JOANNA LEE-YUN	CONJUNCTION FALLACY IN AUDITORS' PROBABILITY JUDGMENT PROCESSES
HSU, KO-CHENG	THE EFFECTS OF COGNITIVE STYLES AND INTERFACE DESIGNS ON EXPERT SYSTEMS USAGE: AN ASSESSMENT OF KNOWLEDGE TRANSFER
HUFNAGEL, ELLEN M.	SOME DETERMINANTS OF PERCEIVED FAIRNESS IN CHARGEBACK SYSTEMS AND THE EFFECTS OF PERCEIVED FAIRNESS ON USER DECISION MAKING
HUGHES, SUSAN BOEDEKER	THE IMPACT OF PRIVATE ACCOUNTING INFORMATION DISCLOSURE WITHIN THE CONTEXT OF COLLECTIVE BARGAINING: AN EMPIRICAL STUDY
HULME, RICHARD DOUGLAS	AN EMPIRICAL INVESTIGATION OF THE EFFECTS OF ORDER AND SAMPLE EVIDENCE REPRESENTATIONS ON AUDITORS' USE OF BASE RATES
HUNT, STEVEN CRAIG	CERTAIN COGNITIVE FACTORS AFFECTING PERFORMANCE EVALUATION IN CPA FIRMS
HURT, ROBERT LEE	THE EFFECTS OF COMPUTER-ASSISTED INSTRUCTION ON MOTIVATION AND ANXIETY IN FIRST-YEAR UNDERGRADUATE ACCOUNTING STUDENTS
ISMAIL, ZUBAIDAH BINTE	THE IMPACT OF THE REVIEW PROCESS IN HYPOTHESIS GENERATION TASKS
JACKSON, ANTHONY WAYNE	THE INFLUENCE OF BUDGET RELATED PERFORMANCE EVALUATION MEASURES ON DECISION MAKING BEHAVIOR UNDER UNCERTAINTY
JAMAL, KARIM	DETECTING FRAMING EFFECTS IN AUDIT JUDGMENT

JEFFREY, CYNTHIA GEISLER	THE IMPACT OF ESCALATION OF COMMITMENT ON LOAN EVALUATION JUDGMENTS OF INDEPENDENT AUDITORS AND BANK LOAN OFFICERS
JOHNSON, ERIC NOEL	EFFECTS OF EXPERIENCE, TASK VARIABLES, AND PRIOR BELIEFS ON AUDITORS' SEQUENTIAL JUDGMENTS
JOHNSON, LAURENCE ERNEST	AN INVESTIGATION OF CITY FINANCIAL STATEMENT READERS' REACTION TO DUAL-BASIS REPORTING OF GENERAL FUND OPERATING RESULTS: INTEGRATION OR EMPHASIS?
JOHNSON, LINDA MARIE	AN EMPIRICAL INVESTIGATION OF THE EFFECTS OF ADVOCACY ON PREPARERS' EVALUATIONS OF EVIDENCE
JOHNSON, VAN EDWARD	AN EXAMINATION OF THE EFFECTS OF ACCOUNTABILITY ON AUDITOR JUDGMENTS
JOSEPH, GILBERT WILLIAM	DESIGNING DECISION AIDS TO OVERCOME BELIEF REVISION BIASES: AN EMPIRICAL INVESTIGATION USING INTERNAL CONTROL RISK ASSESSMENTS IN A DATABASE ENVIRONMENT
KACHELMEIER, STEVEN JOHN	A LABORATORY MARKET INVESTIGATION OF THE DEMAND FOR AUDITING IN AN ENVIRONMENT OF MORAL HAZARD
KARCHER, JULIA NANCY	AUDITORS' ABILITY TO DISCERN THE PRESENCE OF ETHICAL PROBLEMS
KASURINEN, VEIKKO ANTERO	CORPORATE SOCIAL ACCOUNTING: A MEASURING EXPERIMENT APPLIED TO THE PRODUCTION, TRADE AND CONSUMPTION OF ALCOHOL IN FINLAND [YRITYKSEN YHTEISKUNNALLISEN LASKENTATOIMEN MITTAAMISKOKEILU: SOVELLUS
KEINATH, ANNEMARIE KATHARINA	IMPACT OF ACCOUNTING INFORMATION ON ATTRIBUTIONAL CONFLICTS AND EMPLOYEE EFFORT IN A PERFORMANCE APPRAISAL SETTING
KELLIHER, CHARLES FRANCIS, JR.	AN EMPIRICAL INVESTIGATION OF THE EFFECTS OF PERSONALITY TYPE AND VARIATION IN INFORMATION LOAD ON THE INFORMATION SEARCH STRATEGIES EMPLOYED BY DECISION-MAKERS
KELLY, ANNE SULLIVAN	THE COMPARISON OF SEVERAL INTERNAL CONTROL EVALUATION METHODOLOGIES ON THE ASSESSMENT OF RISK AND OTHER AUDIT PLANNING DECISIONS: AN EMPIRICAL INVESTIGATION
KELTING, WILLIAM ROBERT	AUDIT PLANNING: AN EMPIRICAL INVESTIGATION INTO THE TIMING OF PRINCIPAL SUBSTANTIVE TESTS
KENNEDY, SUSAN JANE	DEBIASING AUDIT JUDGMENT WITH ACCOUNTABILITY: A FRAMEWORK AND EXPERIMENTAL RESULTS
KERR, DAVID SAMUEL	INFORMATION INTEGRATION IN AUDIT PLANNING
KHALIFA, ZAKAA MOHAMED	THE IMPACT OF THE FINANCIAL CONDITION OF THE FIRM ON AUDITORS' MATERIALITY/DISCLOSURE JUDGMENTS: AN EXPERIMENTAL STUDY
KHAN, ZAFAR ULLAH	THE IMPACT OF COMPREHENSIVE ALLOCATION AND FLOW-THROUGH METHOD OF ACCOUNTING FOR THE INCOME TAXES ON THE INVESTMENT DECISION: A FIELD EXPERIMENT
KIM, DONG CHULL	RISK PREFERENCES IN PARTICIPATIVE BUDGETING
KING, JAMES B., II	INDIVIDUAL AND TEAM PLANNING MATERIALITY JUDGMENTS IN STRUCTURED AND UNSTRUCTURED ACCOUNTING FIRMS
KING, RONALD RAYMOND	EFFECTS OF CHANGES IN THE LEVEL OF PUBLIC DISCLOSURE ON THE ACQUISITION OF PRIVATE INFORMATION: AN EXPERIMENTAL MARKETS INVESTIGATION

KING, VICKY ARNOLD	AUDITOR DECISION-MAKING; AN ANALYSIS OF THE EFFECTS OF ORDERING AND TESTS OF THE PREDICTIVE VALIDITY OF THE CONTRAST/SURPRISE MODEL
KITE, DEVAUN MARIE	THE IMPACT OF THE FREQUENCY OF ACCOUNTING-BASED PERFORMANCE REPORTS ON CAPITAL BUDGETING DECISIONS
KOONCE, LISA LYNN	BELIEF PERSEVERANCE IN AUDIT ANALYTICAL REVIEW
KRAWCZYK, KATHERINE ANN	REASONING WITHIN TAX RESEARCH: THE EFFECT OF TAX LAW FORM AND ORDER OF FACT PRESENTATION ON PROBLEM REPRESENTATIONS
KREN, LESLIE	EFFECTS OF INCENTIVE EMPLOYMENT CONTRACTS ON PERFORMANCE AND INFORMATION REVELATION: EMPIRICAL EVIDENCE
KUMAR, AKHIL	BUDGET-RELATED PREDICTION MODELS IN THE BUSINESS ENVIRONMENT WITH SPECIAL REFERENCE TO SPOT PRICEPREDICTIONS
LAZAR, LAURA KRISTEN	EFFECTS OF PENSION INFORMATION ON CREDIT QUALITY JUDGMENTS OF MUNICIPAL BOND ANALYSTS
LENK, MARGARITA MARIA	PRIVATE INFORMATION AND A MANAGER'S MOTIVATION: AN EXPECTANCY THEORY TEST OF AGENCY THEORY'S EFFORT-AVERSION ASSUMPTION IN A PARTICIPATIVE BUDGETING SETTING
LIGHTLE, SUSAN SANTALUCIA	AN EMPIRICAL INVESTIGATION OF THE EFFECT OF THE USE OF INTERNAL CONTROL CHECKLISTS ON AUDITORS' INTERNAL CONTROL EVALUATIONS
LIN, PAO-CHUAN	INFORMATION ACQUISITION AND DECISION MAKING IN CREDITORS' DECISION ENVIRONMENT
LINDQUIST, TIMOTHY MARK	DISTRIBUTIVE AND PROCEDURAL JUSTICE: IMPLICATIONS FOR MANAGEMENT CONTROLS AND INCENTIVE SYSTEMS
LIPPMAN, ELLEN J.	AN INVESTIGATION OF THE EFFECTS OF LOAD, FORMAT, AND EXPERTISE ON DECISION QUALITY AND DECISION PROCESSING STRATEGIES
LORD, ALAN TUNIS	THE EFFECTS OF CONTEXTUAL FACTORS ON AUDITORS' DECISION BEHAVIOR UNDER PRESSURE
LOWE, DAVID JORDAN	AN EMPIRICAL EXAMINATION OF THE HINDSIGHT BIAS PHENOMENON IN EVALUATION OF AUDITOR DECISIONS
LUFT, JOAN LUISE	BONUS AND PENALTY INCENTIVES: CONTRACT CHOICE BY EMPLOYEES
MACUR, KENNETH MICHAEL	THE EFFECTS OF CLUSTERING AND RESPONSE MODE CORRESPONDENCE ON THE EVALUATION OF INTERNAL ACCOUNTING CONTROLS
MADDOCKS, PAULINE MERLE	OUTCOME KNOWLEDGE AND AUDITOR JUDGMENT
MAHENTHIRAN, SAKTHIHARAN	NEGOTIATED TRANSFER PRICING: AN INTEGRATED EMPIRICAL EXAMINATION
MAIN, DAPHNE	AUDITOR DECISION-MAKING UNDER AMBIGUITY: A TEST OF THE EINHORN AND HOGARTH AMBIGUITY MODEL
MALLEK, JAMES RANDOLPH	PROBLEM RECOGNITION IN PROFESSIONAL TAX ACCOUNTING

Listing by Research Method   404

MARCHANT, GARRY ALLEN	ANALOGICAL REASONING AND ERROR DETECTION
MARONEY, JAMES JOSEPH	THE IMPACT OF KNOWLEDGE CONTENT AND STRUCTURE ON AUDITORS' HYPOTHESIS TESTING BEHAVIOR IN ANALYTICAL PROCEDURES
MARTINDALE, BOBBIE COOK	IMPACT OF TAX COMPLEXITY ON TAXPAYER UNDERSTANDING
MARXEN, DALE EDWIN	GROUP POLARIZATION IN THE SETTING OF AUDIT TIME BUDGETS
MAUTZ, RICHARD DAVID, JR.	THE IMPACT OF SUPPLEMENTARY, INFLATION-ADJUSTED FINANCIAL STATEMENT INFORMATION ON LABOR'S ASSESSMENT OF CORPORATE ABILITY TO PAY
MAYDEW, EDWARD LYLE	INCENTIVES TO MAGNIFY NET OPERATING LOSSES FOLLOWING THE TAX REFORM ACT OF 1986
MCCLENNY, RUTH LORRAINE	CHANGING TAXPAYER ATTITUDES AND INCREASING TAXPAYER COMPLIANCE: THE ROLE OF INDIVIDUAL DIFFERENCES IN TAXPAYERS
MCCOY, TIMOTHY LYNN	AN ANALYSIS OF MORAL JUDGMENTS AND OTHER FACTORS AFFECTING BEHAVIORAL INTENTIONS OF CERTIFIED PUBLIC ACCOUNTANTS
MCDANIEL, LINDA SUE	THE EFFECTS OF TIME PRESSURE AND AUDIT PROGRAM STRUCTURE ON AUDIT EFFECTIVENESS AND EFFICIENCY
MCDERMOTT, EUGENE WILLIS	THE IMPACT OF TASK COMPLEXITY AND SELECTED COGNITIONS ON THE MOTIVATING ASPECTS OF BUDGETING
MCGILL, GARY ANDERSON	THE CPA'S ROLE IN INCOME TAX COMPLIANCE: AN EMPIRICAL STUDY OF VARIABILITY IN RECOMMENDING AGGRESSIVE TAX POSITIONS
MCLANAHAN, JAMES CRAIG	COST AND ERROR CHARACTERISTICS OF THREE COST ACCOUNTING SYSTEM TYPES: FULL COSTING, MARGINAL COSTING, AND ACTIVITY BASED COSTING
MCMILLAN, JEFFREY JOSEPH	THE ROLE OF CONFIRMATION BIAS, EXPERIENCE, AND MODE OF INFORMATION PROCESSING IN AUDIT JUDGMENT
MCMULLEN, DOROTHY ANN	AUDIT COMMITTEE STRUCTURE AND PERFORMANCE: AN EMPIRICAL INVESTIGATION OF THE CONSEQUENCES AND ATTRIBUTES OF AUDIT COMMITTEES
MCNAIR, FRANCES ELIZABETH	AN EMPIRICAL INVESTIGATION OF THE PERCEIVED EFFECTS OF TAX REFORM ON TAXPAYER COMPLIANCE
MCNETT, STEPHEN ALLEN	AN EXAMINATION OF THE IMPACT OF SECTION 911 ON ENTRY-LEVEL JOB SELECTION DECISIONS IN SELECTED SITUATIONS
MEADE, JANET ALICE	THE LOCK-IN EFFECT OF CAPITAL GAINS TAXATION AND THE WILLINGNESS TO UNDERTAKE RISKY NEW INVESTMENT
MEIXNER, WILDA FURR	THE EFFECT OF THE ORGANIZATIONAL ENVIRONMENT ON JUDGMENT CONSENSUS: THE CASE FOR PROFESSIONAL GOVERNMENT AUDITORS IN THE STATE OF TEXAS
MIDDLEMIST, MELANIE R.	THE RELATIONSHIP BETWEEN OUTCOME MEASURABILITY AND PRINCIPAL'S PREFERENCE FOR CONTRACT TYPE: A LABORATORY EXPERIMENT
MILLER, JEFFREY REED	AN EXPERIMENTAL RESEARCH STUDY ON THE EFFECTS OF THE TYPE OF ACCOUNTING SERVICE ON A BANK LENDING DECISION FOR NONPUBLIC BUSINESSES

Listing by Research Method

MILLS, KATHLEEN DARBY	AUDITORS' INHERENT RISK ASSESSMENTS: THE RELATIONSHIPS AMONG TASK EXPERIENCE, INFERABILITY OF CONDITIONING INFORMATION, SECOND-ORDER UNCERTAINTY AND EXTENT OF TESTING
MILLS, TINA YOUNGBLOOD	THE EXTERNAL AUDITOR'S RELIANCE DECISION ON THE INTERNAL AUDIT FUNCTION: A TEST OF COGNITIVE STYLE AND ITS ROLE IN THE RELIANCE DECISION
MOECKEL, CINDY LEE	THE EFFECTS OF EXPERIENCE ON AUDITORS' ABILITY TO INTEGRATE AUDIT EVIDENCE
MOFFEIT, KATHERINE SOUTHERLAND	THE EFFECT OF COGNITIVE STYLE ON AUDITOR INTERNAL CONTROL EVALUATION
MORRIS, BARBARA SUE	AN EXPERIMENTAL STUDY OF AGENCY THEORY VARIABLES AS DETERMINANTS OF AUDIT INTENSIVENESS
MORROW, MITCHEL CRAWFORD	EFFECTS OF BUDGET PARTICIPATION, DIFFICULTY AND BUDGET CONTINGENT REWARD ON BUDGET PERFORMANCE
MORTON, JANE ELIZABETH	ORDER EFFECTS IN AUDITORS' INTERNAL CONTROL JUDGMENTS: BELIEF PERSEVERANCE VERSUS THE CONTRAST EFFECT
MOSER, DONALD V.	THE EFFECTS OF INTERFERENCE, AVAILABILITY, AND ACCOUNTING INFORMATION ON INVESTORS' PREDICTIVE JUDGMENTS
MOSES, DUANE R.	AUTOMATED VS. MANUAL SIMULATIONS IN HIGH SCHOOL ACCOUNTING: THE EFFECTS ON STUDENT ACHIEVEMENT, PERCEPTIONS AND TIME REQUIRED TO COMPLETE
MURPHY, DANIEL PHILIP	EXPERIMENTAL EVIDENCE REGARDING IMPLICIT TAXES AND TAX-INDUCED INVESTOR CLIENTELES
MURPHY, DAVID SMITH	AN EMPIRICAL INVESTIGATION OF THE EFFECT OF EXPERT SYSTEM USE ON THE DEVELOPMENT OF EXPERTISE IN AUDITING
MURTHY, UDAY SIMHA	THE RELATIONSHIP BETWEEN THE STABILITY OF COMPUTERIZED ACCOUNTING APPLICATIONS, COMPUTER AUDIT STRATEGY AND AUDIT RISK
MYERS, MARLA ANN	A TEST OF THE RELATION BETWEEN AUDIT TECHNOLOGY AND THE DEVELOPMENT OF EXPERTISE
NARASIMHAN, RAMESH	PRELIMINARY CONTROL RISK ASSESSMENTS BY COMPUTER AUDIT SPECIALISTS AND NONSPECIALISTS
NELSON, IRVIN TOM	IDENTIFYING AND RECRUITING FUTURE PROFESSIONALS: AN EMPIRICAL STUDY OF HIGHLY CAPABLE INDIVIDUALS' ATTITUDES TOWARD THE ACCOUNTING PROFESSION
NELSON, MARK WILLIAM	AUDITOR LEARNING OF ERROR FREQUENCIES IN ANALYTICAL REVIEW
NELSON, MARTHA KRUG	HEURISTIC AND NORMATIVE STRATEGIES: EVALUATION OF SAMPLE RESULTS BY AUDITORS
NG, A CHEW	PREDICTION OF CORPORATE FAILURE: HUMAN JUDGMENTS AND FINANCIAL DECISION-MAKING
NIBBELIN, MICHAEL CHARLES	THE EFFECTS OF MODE OF INFORMATION PRESENTATION AND PERCEPTUAL SKILL ON BOND RATING CHANGE DECISIONS: A LABORATORY STUDY
NUGENT, DAVID ANTHONY	THE IMPACT OF WITHHOLDING POSITION AND PENALTY FACTORS ON TAXPAYER BEHAVIOR: A STUDY OF INTERACTION EFFECTS

Listing by Research Method

O'CALLAGHAN, SUSANNE	AN ARTIFICIAL INTELLIGENCE APPLICATION OF BACKPROPAGATION NEURAL NETWORKS TO SIMULATE ACCOUNTANTS' ASSESSMENTS OF INTERNAL CONTROL SYSTEMS USING COSO GUIDELINES
O'CLOCK, PRISCILLA MARIE	THE EFFECT OF INFORMATION FRAMING ON THE AUDITOR'S GOING CONCERN EVALUATION
ODOM, MARCUS DEAN	AN EXAMINATION OF THE INTERACTION OF ELABORATION ALTERNATIVES AND ELABORATION PLACEMENT ON EXPERT SYSTEM-BASED INCIDENTAL LEARNING
OKOPNY, D. ROBERT	PLANNING AN INTERNATIONAL AUDIT: AN EMPIRICAL INVESTIGATION OF INTERNAL AUDITOR JUDGMENT
ONIFADE, EMMANUEL ONAOLAPO	AN EMPIRICAL EXAMINATION OF THE EFFECT OF CAUSAL ATTRIBUTIONS ON PROJECT CONTINUATION DECISION
OTT, RICHARD LAWRENCE	AN EMPIRICAL ANALYSIS OF THE INTERACTIVE EFFECTS BETWEEN THE INDIVIDUAL CHARACTERISTICS OF THE LEARNER AND THE METHOD OF INSTRUCTION--LECTURE OR COMPUTER-ASSISTED--ON STUDENT ACHIEVEMENT IN ELEMENTARY ACCOUNTING
PALMER, RICHARD JOSEPH	THE EFFECT OF AN ANTICIPATED PERFORMANCE EVALUATION ON INDIVIDUAL PERFORMANCE AND CONTINUING MOTIVATION TOWARD THE TASK: THE INTERVENTION OF A SELF-PRESENTATION MOTIVE
PAQUETTE, LAURENCE RICHARD	THE EFFECT OF DECISION STRATEGY AND TASK COMPLEXITY ON DECISION PERFORMANCE IN AN ACCOUNTING CONTEXT
PARKER, ROBERT JAMES	BUDGETING EFFECTS AND EVALUATION BY SELF, PEERS, AND SUPERIORS WITH MODERATING EFFECTS OF PERSONAL AND SOCIAL IDENTITY
PAVELKA, DEBORAH DIANNE	PENSION LIABILITIES AND BANKERS' LOAN DECISIONS
PEECHER, MARK EVERETT	CONSEQUENTIALITY, JUSTIFICATION AND AUDITORS' DECISION PROCESSES: A THEORETICAL FRAMEWORK AND TWO EXPERIMENTS
PEEK, GEORGE SHERMAN	AN EMPIRICAL STUDY OF RISK PREFERENCE ELICITATION WITH PRACTICING AUDITORS USING EXPERIMENTAL AND BUSINESS CONTEXTS
PEI, KER-WEI BUCK	A COMPARATIVE STUDY OF INTERNAL AND EXTERNAL AUDITORS' JUDGMENT OF INTERNAL AUDITOR INDEPENDENCE
PHILLIPS, SAMUEL HORACE	AN EXPERIMENTAL INVESTIGATION OF THE ROLE OF COLLEGE AND UNIVERSITY FINANCIAL STATEMENTS IN ALUMNI SUPPORT DECISIONS
PICARD, ROBERT RAYMOND	MANAGERIAL ACCOUNTING PROBLEM-SOLVING SKILLS: AN EXPERIMENT INVESTIGATING GROUP-TO-INDIVIDUAL ACQUISITION AND TRANSFER
PRAWITT, DOUGLAS FRANK	A COMPARISON OF HUMAN RESOURCE ALLOCATION ACROSS AUDITING FIRMS: THE EFFECTS OF STRUCTURED AUDIT TECHNOLOGY AND ENVIRONMENT
PRESSLY, THOMAS RICHARD	AN EMPIRICAL STUDY OF INVESTOR USE OF STATEMENT OF CASH FLOWS INFORMATION IN STOCK PRICE PREDICTION DECISIONS
PRESUTTI, ANTHONY HARRY, JR.	AN EMPIRICAL INVESTIGATION OF THE IMPACT OF THE ANCHOR AND ADJUSTMENT HEURISTIC ON THE AUDIT JUDGMENT PROCESS
PURVIS, S.E.C.	THE AUDITOR'S PRELIMINARY EVALUATION OF INTERNAL ACCOUNTING CONTROL: A BEHAVIORAL ANALYSIS
QUILLIAM, WILLIAM CLAYTON	EXAMINING THE EFFECTS OF ACCOUNTABILITY ON AUDITORS' VALUATION DECISIONS

QURESHI, ANIQUE AHMED	AN INVESTIGATION OF AUDITOR JUDGMENT IN THE EVALUATION OF CONTINGENT LEGAL LIABILITIES
RADTKE, ROBIN RAE	AN EXPERIMENTAL INVESTIGATION OF MANAGERS' ESCALATION ERRORS
RAHMAN, MONSURUR	THE EFFECT OF A CONSTRAINED RESOURCE ON INDIVIDUAL PERFORMANCE, PERFORMANCE EFFORT, AND FEELINGS TOWARD THE TASK AND DECISION-MAKERS: THE INTERVENTION OF EQUITY
RAMSAY, ROBERT JOE	AN INVESTIGATION OF THE HIERARCHICAL, SEQUENTIAL NATURE OF AUDIT WORKING PAPER REVIEW
RAND, RICHARD SPAULDING, JR.	THE EFFECT OF AUDITORS' KNOWLEDGE OF ERRORS ON PLANNING-STAGE ASSESSMENTS OF CLIENT-RELATED RISK COMPONENTS AND ON INITIAL AUDIT SCOPE DECISIONS
RAVENSCROFT, SUSAN PICKARD	INCENTIVE PLANS AND MULTI-AGENT INFORMATION SHARING
REDING, KURT F.	CONTROL CHARTS AS DECISION AIDS TO OPERATIONAL AUDITORS' ASSESSMENTS OF PRODUCTION PROCESS PERFORMANCE
REIDER, BARBARA POWELL	HYPOTHESIS CONFIRMATION AND DISCONFIRMATION BY INDEPENDENT AUDITORS: GENERAL AND AUDIT-SPECIFIC CONTEXTS
REITHER, CHERI LYNN	A PROCESS ANALYSIS OF LENDERS' USE OF FAS 95 CASH FLOW INFORMATION
RIGSBY, JOHN THOMAS, JR.	AN ANALYSIS OF THE EFFECTS OF COMPLEXITY ON THE MATERIALITY DECISIONS OF AUDITORS
RILEY, ANNE CURTIN	AN ANALYTICAL FRAMEWORK FOR THE EVALUATION OF INHERENT AUDIT RISK
ROARK, STEPHEN JOE	AN EXAMINATION OF RISK ATTITUDES IN LEGAL TAX RESEARCH
ROBERTS, CLYDE A.	CPA CREDIBILITY AND THE CREDIT DECISION PROCESS OF COMMERCIAL LOAN OFFICERS
ROBERTS, MICHAEL L.	JUDGMENT AND THE VALUATION OF CLOSELY HELD CORPORATIONS FOR ESTATE TAXATION
RODGERS, JACCI LOU SPEELMAN	USE OF THE INERTIA EFFECT TO EXPLAIN AND PREDICT AUDITOR MISADJUSTMENTS ARISING FROM THE ANCHORING AND ADJUSTMENT HEURISTIC
ROGERS, VIOLET CORLEY	AN ANALYSIS OF CONFIDENCE LEVELS AND RETRIEVAL OF PROCEDURES ASSOCIATED WITH ACCOUNTS RECEIVABLE CONFIRMATIONS
ROMINE, JEFFREY MORRIS	THE QUALITY REVIEW DECISION: AN ANALYSIS OF DECISION SEARCH PROCESSES, DECISION OUTCOMES, CONTEXTUAL BACKGROUND, AND EXPERIENCE EFFECTS
ROSMAN, ANDREW JOEL	THE EFFECT OF LEARNING ENVIRONMENTS ON THE USE OF ACCOUNTING INFORMATION BY DIFFERENT TYPES OF LENDERS
ROXAS, MARIA LOURDES P.	EFFECT OF THE AMOUNT OF INFORMATION AND THE AMOUNT OF EXPERIENCE AND EDUCATION ON INVESTMENT DECISIONS
RUCHALA, LINDA VIRGINIA	THE INFLUENCE OF BUDGET REPORTS AND INCENTIVE COMPENSATION ON ESCALATION

RUF, BERNADETTE MARY	DECISION-MAKING IN A DECISION SUPPORT SYSTEMS ENVIRONMENT: AN EVALUATION OF SPATIAL ABILITY AND TASK STRUCTURE
RUHL, JACK MICHAEL	AN EMPIRICAL STUDY OF THE EFFECTS OF INCONGRUENCE WITHIN A FIRM'S FINANCIAL PLANNING AND CONTROL SYSTEM ON MANAGERS' PROJECT SELECTIONS
RUPERT, TIMOTHY J.	PERFORMANCE FACILITATION ON TAX RULES: A PRAGMATIC REASONING SCHEMA APPROACH
RUSSO, JOSEPH A., JR.	AN INVESTIGATION OF AUDITOR PROBLEM-SOLVING BEHAVIOR IN AN UNFAMILIAR TASK SITUATION
RUTLEDGE, ROBERT WILLIAM	THE EFFECTS OF FRAMING ACCOUNTING INFORMATION AND GROUP-SHIFT ON ESCALATION OF COMMITMENT
RYAN, DAVID HARRISON	AN EMPIRICAL EXAMINATION OF THE INTERACTIVE EFFECTS OF FACTORS INFLUENCING TAX PRACTITIONERS' JUDGMENTS
SAMPSON, WESLEY CLAUDE	PERCEPTIONS OF AUDITOR INDEPENDENCE AND THE EFFECTS OF NONAUDIT SERVICES
SANDERS, DEBRA LEE	AN EMPIRICAL INVESTIGATION OF TAX PRACTITIONERS' DECISIONS UNDER UNCERTAINTY: A PROSPECT THEORY APPROACH
SANDLIN, PETREA KAY	THE EFFECT OF CAUSAL BACKGROUND ON AUDITORS' ANALYTICAL REVIEW JUDGMENTS
SAWYERS, ROBY BLAKE	THE IMPACT OF UNCERTAINTY AND AMBIGUITY ON INCOME TAX DECISION-MAKING
SCHADEWALD, MICHAEL STEVEN	REFERENCE OUTCOME EFFECTS IN TAXPAYER DECISION-MAKING
SCHATZBERG, JEFFREY WAYNE	A THEORETICAL AND EMPIRICAL EXAMINATION OF INDEPENDENCE AND 'LOW BALLING'
SCHATZEL, JOHN A.	AN EXPERIMENTAL STUDY OF FACTORS AFFECTING AUDITORS' RELIANCE ON ANALYTICAL PROCEDURES
SCHIFF, ANDREW DAVID	AN EXPLORATION OF THE USE OF FINANCIAL AND NONFINANCIAL MEASURES OF OPERATING PERFORMANCE BY EXECUTIVES IN A SERVICE ORGANIZATION
SCHISLER, DANIEL LAWRENCE	AN EXPERIMENTAL EXAMINATION OF TAXPAYERS' AND TAX PROFESSIONALS' AGGRESSIVE TAX PREFERENCES: A PROSPECT THEORY FOUNDATION
SCHLACHTER, PAUL JUSTIN	A TWO-STAGE ANALYSIS OF INTERDIVISIONAL TRANSFER PRICING NEGOTIATIONS
SCHLICTMAN, MARIBETH COLLER	EXTERNAL REPORTING SYSTEMS AND ASSET PRICES: AN EXPERIMENTAL STUDY
SCHMELZLE, GEORGE DANIEL	A STUDY OF THE EFFECTS OF DOGMATISM AND THE EVENTS APPROACH TO ACCOUNTING ON DECISION-MAKING IN THE NEW MANUFACTURING ENVIRONMENT
SCHMIDT, TOM WILLIAMS	IMPACT OF CRITICAL THINKING ABILITY ON TAX PRACTITIONER JUDGMENT
SCHNEIDER, GARY PAUL	ESCALATION BEHAVIOR IN INFORMATION SYSTEMS DEVELOPMENT: ALTERNATIVE MOTIVATIONS, EXPERIENCE, AND THE SUNK COST EFFECT

SCHRADER, RICHARD WILLIAM	AN EMPIRICAL INVESTIGATION OF THE USEFULNESS OF SERVICE EFFORTS AND ACCOMPLISHMENTS MEASURES
SCOTT, BERT G., JR.	AN INQUIRY INTO MITIGATING THE EFFECTS OF THE ANCHORING AND ADJUSTMENT HEURISTIC IN THE JUDGMENTAL EVALUATION OF UNDERRELIANCE RISK
SENKOW, DAVID WILLIAM	PRICING MECHANISMS FOR RESOURCE ALLOCATION IN DECENTRALIZED ORGANIZATIONS: EXPERIMENTAL EVIDENCE
SESHIE, GODWIN O.	THE ROLE OF PROSPECTIVE FINANCIAL INFORMATION ATTESTATION IN BANK LENDING DECISIONS
SHAPIRO, BRIAN PHILIP	AUDITOR'S CAUSAL REASONING IN PRELIMINARY ANALYTICAL REVIEW: AN EMPIRICAL INVESTIGATION
SHARMA, SURESH RAJ	THE EFFECTS OF THE SOCIAL ATTRACTIVENESS OF A GOAL SETTER ON GOAL ACCEPTANCE
SHASTRI, TRIMBAK	A CONCEPTUAL FRAMEWORK FOR AUDIT COMMUNICATION RESEARCH AND SOME EMPIRICAL EVIDENCE
SHELLEY, MARJORIE KAY	AN EMPIRICAL INVESTIGATION OF DIFFERENTIAL SUBJECTIVE DISCOUNTING ACROSS THE POTENTIAL GAINS AND LOSSES FROM INVESTMENT OPTIONS
SHIELDS, JEFFREY FRANKLIN	THE INFLUENCE OF INTERNAL AUDITING AND TRUST ON BUDGETARY SLACK
SIMNETT, ROGER	INFORMATION SELECTION AND INFORMATION PROCESSING BY AUDITORS: EFFECT OF VARYING TASK COMPLEXITY
SINGHAL, RAJ BAHADUR	EFFECT OF FEEDBACK AND GOAL PRESENCE ON INFORMATION USAGE AND DECISION ACCURACY IN A HIGH INFORMATION LOAD ENVIRONMENT
SISAYE, SELESHI	RESOURCE ALLOCATION PROCESSES IN DIVISIONALIZED BUSINESS ORGANIZATIONS: A POWER CONTROL MODEL OF ORGANIZATIONS
SMITH, GEORGE MALCOLM	IMPROVING THE DECISION USEFULNESS OF THE CORPORATE ANNUAL REPORT
SMITH, HOWARD GROMEL	THE STUDY OF THE IMPLICATIONS OF SFAS 33 TO THE SMALL BUSINESS ENTERPRISE: USEFULNESS IN LONG-TERM LOAN APPLICATIONS
SMITH, KEITH WRIGHT	THE IMPLICATIONS OF ALLOWING COGNITIVE STYLE DECISION APPROACHES OF THE DECISION-MAKER TO DETERMINE THE INFORMATION FORMAT: AN EXPERIMENTAL EXAMINATION OF PERFORMANCE
SNEAD, KENNETH CARTER, JR.	AN APPLICATION OF VROOM'S EXPECTANCY THEORY AND MCCLELLAND'S TRICHOTOMY OF NEEDS THEORY TO EXAMINE MANAGERS' MOTIVATION TO IMPLEMENT A DECISION SUPPORT SYSTEM
SPILKER, BRIAN CLARK	THE EFFECTS OF TIME PRESSURE AND KNOWLEDGE ON KEY WORD SELECTION BEHAVIOR IN TAX RESEARCH
SPIRES, ERIC EDWARD	AN INVESTIGATION INTO AUDITORS' EVALUATIONS OF COMPLIANCE TESTS
STEED, STEVE ALAN	AN EMPIRICAL STUDY OF THE EFFECTIVENESS OF INDEPENDENCE DISCRIMINATION RESULTING FROM THE APPLICATION OF AICPA ETHICAL INTERPRETATION 101-3--ACCOUNTING SERVICES
STERNBURG, THOMAS JAMES	AN EMPIRICAL INVESTIGATION OF DETERRENCE THEORY AND INFLUENCE THEORY ON PROFESSIONAL TAX PREPARERS' RECOMMENDATIONS

STOCKS, MORRIS H., JR.	AN EMPIRICAL EXAMINATION OF THE IMPACT OF INFORMATION OVERLOAD ON GROUPS AND INDIVIDUALS IN A FINANCIAL DISTRESS DECISION TASK
STOLT, SUSAN MARIE JESZKA	AN ATTRIBUTIONAL ANALYSIS OF PERFORMANCE EVALUATION IN PUBLIC ACCOUNTING
STONE, DAN NORMAN, JR.	THE IMPACT OF INFORMATION FORM ON COGNITIVE PROCESSES AND CHOICE IN AN INFORMATION SYSTEM SELECTION TASK
STRAWSER, JERRY ROBERT	AN EMPIRICAL INVESTIGATION OF AUDITOR JUDGMENT: FACTORS AFFECTING PERCEIVED AUDIT RISK
STREET, DONNA LEE	SEGMENT CASH FLOW STATEMENT: AN EMPIRICAL EXAMINATION OF ITS IMPACT ON THE LENDING DECISION
STUART, IRIS C.	ANALYTICAL PROCEDURES AND JUDGMENT ACCURACY: A COMPARISON OF STRUCTURED AND UNSTRUCTURED AUDIT METHODOLOGY
SULLIVAN, M. CATHY	AN INVESTIGATION OF AGENCY THEORY'S ASSUMPTION OF STRICT EFFORT AVERSION: THE ROLE OF INTRINSIC MOTIVATION
SWAIN, MONTE RAY	EXPERIENCE AND INFORMATION EFFECTS ON SEARCH STRATEGIES IN A CAPITAL BUDGETING TASK
SWAYZE, JAMES PRENTISS	THE EFFECT OF CORPORATE INCOME TAX INTEGRATION ON THE DEMAND FOR RISKY STOCK
SWIFT, KENTON D.	AN EXPERIMENTAL INVESTIGATION INTO THE EFFECTS OF RISKS AND UNCERTAINTIES ON COMMERCIAL LENDING DECISIONS
SWINNEY, LAURIE S.	EXPERT SYSTEMS IN AUDITING: DECISION AID OR DECISION SUBJUGATION
TAN, HUN-TONG	EFFECTS OF EXPECTATION AND PRIOR INVOLVEMENT ON MEMORY FOR AUDIT EVIDENCE AND JUDGMENT: THE MODERATING ROLE OF ACCOUNTABILITY
THOMAS, CHARLES WILLIS	EFFECTS OF COMPUTER TUTORIAL LESSONS ON ACCOUNTING I SKILLS AND ATTRITION
THOMAS, WILLIAM FRANCIS	THE AUDITOR SELECTION DECISION: A MULTIATTRIBUTE APPROACH
TIDRICK, DONALD EUGENE	AUDITORS' PLANNING STAGE MATERIALITY JUDGMENTS AND THE MEDIATING EFFECTS OF LEVEL OF RESPONSIBILITY, FIRM AFFILIATION, AND AUDIT TECHNOLOGY: AN EXPERIMENT
TONGTHARADOL, VAJANA	FACTOR INFLUENCING SUPERVISOR'S RESPONSES TO SUBORDINATE'S BEHAVIOR: AN ATTRIBUTIONAL ANALYSIS
TOOLSON, RICHARD BURNS	THE TAX INCENTIVE EFFECT OF THE CHARITABLE CONTRIBUTION DEDUCTION
TOTTERDALE, GWENDOLYN	AN EXAMINATION OF THE DECISION-MAKING PROCESSES UNDERLYING THE DEVELOPMENT OF STANDARD COSTS FOR MANUFACTURED PRODUCTS
TRIPPEER, DONALD RICHARD	THE FUNDING OF GOVERNMENT PROGRAMS UNDER THE BUDGET ENFORCEMENT ACT: THE EFFECT OF THE EXCHANGE RELATIONSHIP ON TAXPAYER COMPLIANCE
TROMPETER, GREGORY MICHAEL	AN INVESTIGATION INTO THE EFFECT OF COMPETITION, PARTNER COMPENSATION, LEGAL LIABILITY, AND AUTHORITATIVE PRONOUNCEMENTS ON AUDITOR JUDGMENT AND INDEPENDENCE

Listing by Research Method   411

TUBBS, RICHARD MONROE	THE EFFECT OF EXPERIENCE ON THE AUDITOR'S ORGANIZATION AND AMOUNT OF KNOWLEDGE
TUCKER, ROBERT RILEY	AN INVESTIGATION OF THE RELATIONSHIP BETWEEN PUBLIC AND PRIVATE INFORMATION: AN EXPERIMENTAL MARKET STUDY
TURNER, MARTHA J.	THE USEFULNESS OF COST ALLOCATIONS: AN EXPERIMENTAL INVESTIGATION
TURPEN, RICHARD ALLEN	AUDIT PRICING AND AUDITOR CHOICE: AN EMPIRICAL INVESTIGATION OF THE MARKET FOR AUDITING SERVICES
TUTTLE, BRAD M.	THE ROLE OF CONTEXT IN AUDITOR DIAGNOSIS
USOFF, CATHERINE ANNE	AN EXAMINATION OF FACTORS AFFECTING AUDIT PLANNING ACROSS ACCOUNTS
VIATOR, RALPH EDWARD	A COMPUTER-BASED APPROACH TO THE ASSESSMENT OF PRIOR PROBABILITY DISTRIBUTIONS: AN EMPIRICAL INVESTIGATION
VICKERY, KENNETH VERNON	ENABLING FOUR UNITED METHODIST CHURCHES' FINANCE COMMITTEES TO IMPLEMENT THE UNITED METHODIST INFORMATION SYSTEM PLUS' ACCOUNTING PROGRAM
VIOLETTE, GEORGE R.	THE DETERRENCE EFFECTS OF SANCTION COMMUNICATIONS ON TAXPAYER LEVEL OF INCOME TAX COMPLIANCE
WAGGONER, JERI BROCKETT	NONSAMPLING RISK: AUDITOR DETECTION OF COMPLIANCE DEVIATIONS
WALLIN, DAVID ERNEST	ALTERNATIVE ECONOMIC INSTITUTIONS TO MOTIVATE MANAGERIAL DISCLOSURE OF PRIVATE INFORMATION: AN EXPERIMENTAL MARKETS EXAMINATION
WALO, JUDITH CHRISTINA	LABORATORY STUDY OF THE EFFECTS OF AUDITOR'S BUSINESS RISK ON AUDIT SCOPE
WALTERS-YORK, L. MELISSA	PATTERN PERCEPTIVENESS AND ACQUISITION OF ACCOUNTING SKILLS
WARTICK, MARTHA LORRAINE	THE EFFECT OF KNOWLEDGE OF LEGISLATIVE INTENT ON TAXPAYER PERCEPTIONS OF FAIRNESS
WATANABE, JUDITH ELLEN	INDEXATION OF CAPITAL GAINS AND LOSSES: A COMPLEXITY STUDY
WATERS, BRENDA NELL	THE IMPACT OF INFORMATION AND PERSONALITY CHARACTERISTICS ON THE LENDING DECISION
WEBSTER, ROBERT LEE	THE EFFECTS OF MANAGERIAL FINANCIAL FORECASTS ON USER PERCEPTIONS RELATING TO FINANCIAL STRENGTH OF PUBLIC UTILITY COMPANIES
WELCH, JUDITH KAYE	AUDITOR INTERPRETATIONS OF AUDIT EVIDENCE: AN INFORMATIONAL ATTRIBUTE APPROACH
WELCH, SANDRA THOMAS	AN INVESTIGATION OF THE DECISION REVISION PROCESS: DEFENSE CONTRACT AUDIT AGENCY AUDITORS DETERMINING THE EXISTENCE OF DEFECTIVE PRICING IN FIXED PRICE CONTRACTS
WELKER, DONNA-LYNN	BACKGROUND FACTORS AND THE ANCHORING AND ADJUSTMENT HEURISTIC: AN EMPIRICAL INVESTIGATION

WELSH, MARY JEANNE	AN EXPERIMENTAL RESEARCH STUDY ON THE EFFECT OF RECOGNITION AND DISCLOSURE OF CORPORATE PENSION PLAN ASSETS AND OBLIGATIONS ON INVESTMENT DECISIONS
WEST, TIMOTHY DAVID	EXTERNAL AUDITORS' RISK ASSESSMENT DECISIONS: THE IMPACT OF IMPLEMENTING ACTIVITY-BASED COSTING
WHITE, GWENDOLEN BARNETT	AUDITORS' HYPOTHESIS GENERATION SKILLS: THE INFLUENCE OF EXPERIENCE AND AUDIT METHODOLOGY STRUCTURE
WHITECOTTON, STACEY MARIE	DECISION AID RELIANCE AS A DETERMINANT OF ACCURACY IN EARNINGS FORECASTING JUDGMENTS: THE IMPACT OF CONTEXTUAL AND DECISION MAKER CHARACTERISTICS
WIER, BENSON	THE EFFECTS OF TASK RELEVANT KNOWLEDGE, GOAL LEVEL, GOAL COMMITMENT, AND MOTIVATION ON THE PARTICIPATION-PERFORMANCE LINKAGE: AN EMPIRICAL EXAMINATION
WILLIAMS, JOANNE DEAHL	AN INVESTIGATION OF AUDITORS' DECISION PROCESSES IN A RISK ASSESSMENT DURING THE PLANNING STAGE OF AN AUDIT
WILLIS, DAVID MITCHELL	THE CHOICE OF COST SYSTEMS: A LABORATORY SIMULATION
WILLITS, STEPHEN D.	PUBLIC EMPLOYEE RETIREMENT SYSTEM REPORTS: A STUDY OF USER INFORMATION PROCESSING ABILITY
WINTER, KENNETH	THE EFFECT OF TASK DEMAND ON EXPERTS AND NONEXPERTS IN INTERNAL CONTROL EVALUATION
WONG, YUE KEE	COMPUTER-AIDED GROUP JUDGMENT: A STUDY OF GROUP DECISION SUPPORT SYSTEMS EFFECTIVENESS
WONG-ON-WING, BERNARD	AUDITOR'S PERCEPTION OF MANAGEMENT: ITS DETERMINANTS AND CONSEQUENCES
WRIGHT, SALLY	PARTICIPATIVE BUDGETING: AN EXAMINATION OF BUDGETARY SLACK AND MANAGERIAL PERFORMANCE OVER MULTIPLE PERIODS
WYATT, ROBERT LANE	THE EFFECT OF ELECTRONIC MEETING SYSTEMS ON GROUP PERFORMANCE: THE CASE OF THE BUDGETING DECISION
YARDLEY, JAMES A.	LENDERS' AND ACCOUNTANTS' PERCEPTIONS OF THE INFORMATION RISK REDUCTION PROVIDED BY PRESCRIBED PROCEDURES
YUTHAS, KRISTI JANE	CONSTRUCT VALIDITY IN THE MEASUREMENT OF DECISION SUPPORT
ZELIN, ROBERT CLAYTON, II	THE EFFECTS OF INDUSTRY DISTRIBUTIONAL INFORMATION ON AUDITORS' ANALYTICAL REVIEW INVESTIGATION PARAMETERS

Simulation

ATKINSON, MARYANNE	A STUDY OF POPULATION CHARACTERISTICS AFFECTING THE PERFORMANCE OF AUDIT SAMPLING TECHNIQUES IN SUBSTANTIVE TESTS
BIRD, CYNTHIA ELIZABETH	AN EXAMINATION OF THE EFFECT OF THE TAX REFORM ACT OF 1986 ON INDIVIDUAL AND CORPORATE INVESTMENT IN RESIDENTIAL RENTAL REALTY
BOYNTON, CHARLES EDWARD	TAX ACCOUNTING METHOD AND OFFSHORE PETROLEUM DEVELOPMENT: A POLICY EVALUATION MODEL EMPLOYING ROYALTY EQUIVALENTS AND EXCISE TAXES
CARR, JANICE LYNN	THE ACCELERATED COST RECOVERY SYSTEM: AN EXAMINATION OF ITS EFFECTS ON INCOME-PRODUCING PROPERTY

CHANDRA, RAMESH	AN EXAMINATION OF EVENT STUDY METHODOLOGY
CHAU, CHAK-TONG	COMPARING FORECASTING PERFORMANCE IN ANALYTICAL PROCEDURES: AN INTEGRATED STUDY USING STATE SPACE, EXPONENTIAL SMOOTHING AND REGRESSION MODELS
CHEN, YI-NING	THE ERROR DETECTION OF STRUCTURAL ANALYTICAL REVIEW PROCEDURES: A SIMULATION STUDY
CLAYTON, HOWARD ROBERTSON	CONFIDENCE BOUNDS BASED ON THE BOOTSTRAP AND HOEFFDING'S INEQUALITY FOR DOLLAR UNIT SAMPLING IN AUDITING
CRAMER, LOWELL JAMES	AN AFTER TAX ECONOMIC ANALYSIS OF HOME EQUITY CONVERSION FOR THE ELDERLY
DUHALA, KAREN	A GENERAL MODEL FOR BOND REFINANCING
DZENG, SIMON C.	A COMPARISON OF VECTOR AUTOREGRESSION MODELS AND ORDINARY LEAST SQUARES MULTIPLE REGRESSION MODELS FOR ANALYTICAL PROCEDURES PERFORMED AS SUBSTANTIVE TEST
FORAN, NANCY JOYCE HOFFMAN	THE EFFECT OF THE ECONOMIC RECOVERY TAX ACT OF 1981 AND THE TAX EQUITY AND FISCAL RESPONSIBILITY ACT OF 1982 ON THE FORM OF DISPOSITION BY INDIVIDUALS OF NONRESIDENTIAL REAL PROPERTY
FRITSCHE, STEVEN RODNEY	ACCOUNTING RATE OF RETURN AND CONDITIONAL ESTIMATE OF INTERNAL RATE OF RETURN: AN INVESTIGATION OF TWO SURROGATES FOR INTERNAL RATE OF RETURN
GAUNTT, JAMES EDWARD, JR.	A SIMULATION STUDY OF STATISTICAL ESTIMATORS USED IN VARIABLES SAMPLING
GRIBBIN, DONALD WAYNE	ANALYSIS OF THE DISTRIBUTION PROPERTIES OF COST VARIANCES AND THEIR EFFECTS ON THE COST VARIANCE INVESTIGATION DECISION
HAN, INGOO	THE IMPACT OF MEASUREMENT SCALE ON CLASSIFICATION PERFORMANCE OF INDUCTIVE LEARNING AND STATISTICAL APPROACHES
HE, XIN XIN	STOCHASTIC INVENTORY SYSTEMS WITH ORDER CROSSOVER
HOPPE, PAUL PETER, III	ACCIDENTAL DATA IN A STATISTICAL AUDITING PLAN
ILDERTON, ROBERT BLAIR	EVALUATION OF SAMPLES WITH FEW NON-ZERO ITEMS
ISSA, HUSSEIN MOHAMED AHMED	A PROPOSED MODEL FOR CAPITAL BUDGETARY CONTROL IN THE AMERICAN FOOD PRODUCT CORPORATION SECTOR
JAGANNATHAN, JAYASHRI V.	SEQUENTIAL STOPPING RULES FOR ESTIMATING THE TOTAL ERROR IN ACCOUNTING POPULATIONS USING MONETARY UNIT SAMPLING
JONES, SCOTT KENNETH	THE RISK PROPERTIES OF ANALYTICAL PROCEDURES THAT USE ORTHOGONAL POLYNOMIAL REGRESSIONS
KANG, JUNGPAO	GENERALIZED PROFITABILITY MEASURES UNDER STEADY-STATE CONDITIONS
KENNEDY, DUANE BRIAN	CLASSIFICATION TECHNIQUES IN ACCOUNTING RESEARCH: EMPIRICAL EVIDENCE OF COMPARATIVE PERFORMANCE

KO, CHEN-EN	MODEL-BASED SAMPLING IN AUDITING
LEE, IHNSHIK	A SIMULATION STUDY COMPARING VARIOUS CONFIDENCE INTERVALS FOR THE MEAN OF VOUCHER POPULATIONS IN ACCOUNTING
LOVE, WILLIAM H.	SIMULATED PENSION SCENARIOS WITH STOCHASTIC DEMOGRAPHIC AND INVESTMENT EXPERIENCE UTILIZING ALTERNATIVE ACTUARIAL COST METHODS AND ACCOUNTING PRINCIPLES
MARTINEZ-MORALES, MANUEL	ADAPTIVE PREMIUM CONTROL IN AN INSURANCE RISK PROCESS
NEEDY, KIM LA SCOLA	PERFORMANCE COMPARISON OF ACTIVITY BASED COSTING VERSUS TRADITIONAL COST ACCOUNTING FOR STRATEGIC DECISION MAKING
ODOM, GARY LYNN	THE EFFECT OF 1981 AND 1982 LEGISLATIVE ACTS ON SMALL CORPORATIONS' SELECTION OF A C OR S CORPORATE FORM
PARK, KYOUNG-HWAN	A SIMULATION MODEL OF TRANSFER PRICING FOR MULTINATIONAL CORPORATIONS BASED ON THE EQUIVALENT ANNUAL COST METHOD
PEEK, LUCIA ELIZABETH	SAS NO. 39 GUIDELINES FOR NONSTATISTICAL SAMPLING: A SIMULATION STUDY
SAGE, JUDITH ANN	SELECTION OF QUALIFIED RETIREMENT PLAN DISTRIBUTION OPTIONS: A SIMULATION
SANDER, JAMES FREDERICK	AN EXAMINATION OF THE RELIABILITY OF VARIOUS INCOME MEASURES FOR ASSESSING THE MAINTENANCE OF OPERATING CAPABILITY
SMITH, W. ROBERT	A STUDY TO INVESTIGATE THE EFFECTS OF STATE TAXATION AND PLAN TYPE ON SMALL EMPLOYER RETIREMENT PLAN COST
SUBRAMANIAM, CHANDRA	MEASURING INFORMATION CONTENT OF CORPORATE ANNOUNCEMENTS
WEISFELDER, CHRISTINE J.	LINKAGES BETWEEN TAX SYSTEMS: AN ANALYSIS OF THE CORPORATE TAX CONSEQUENCES OF TRANSFERRING ROYALTIES, INTEREST AND DIVIDENDS BETWEEN GERMANY, JAPAN AND THE UNITED STATES
WRIGHT, DAVID WILLIAM	THE USE OF EMPIRICAL BAYES ESTIMATION IN AUDIT TESTING
WURST, JOHN CHARLES	AN INVESTIGATION OF THE SIEVE METHOD AND OF RECTIFICATION SAMPLING FOR AUDITING

Survey

ABBASI, NISHAT ULHASAN	IMPLEMENTATION OF DECISION SUPPORT SYSTEMS: A MODEL AND AN INVESTIGATION
ABOUEL-ENIN, MOHAMED A.	AN EMPIRICAL STUDY OF FACTORS INFLUENCING THE SUCCESS OF EGYPT-UNITED STATES OF AMERICA JOINT VENTURES ENGAGING IN BUSINESSES IN EGYPT
ABRAMOVITCH, RAFAEL	A COST-BENEFIT ANALYSIS OF THE ALTERNATIVE FIVE-YEAR ACCOUNTING EDUCATION SYSTEM
ABRAMOWICZ, KENNETH FRANK	AN EMPIRICAL INVESTIGATION OF TAX COMPLIANCE RELATED TO SCHOLARSHIP INCOME
ADEREMI, SYLVESTER OLUYEMISI	AN EMPIRICAL STUDY OF THE IMPORTANCE OF CERTAIN ATTRIBUTES TO ACCOUNTING FIRMS' SELECTION OF NEW PARTNERS

Listing by Research Method 415

AGACER, GILDA MONTEAGUDO	PERCEPTIONS OF THE AUDITOR'S INDEPENDENCE: A CROSS-CULTURAL STUDY
AKERS, MICHAEL DEWAYNE	AN EMPIRICAL INVESTIGATION OF PRODUCT COST METHODS
AL-ERYANI, MOHAMED FADL	POLICIES OF U.S. MULTINATIONAL CORPORATIONS ON PRICING INTRACOMPANY TRANSFERS WITH FOREIGN AFFILIATES IN MORE-DEVELOPED AND LESS-DEVELOPED COUNTRIES
AL-KAZEMI, ALI ABDUL-RAZZAQ	THE UTILIZATION OF MANAGEMENT ACCOUNTING TECHNIQUES WITH EMPHASIS ON QUANTITATIVE ANALYSIS IN THE PUBLIC SECTOR: BUILDING AN EFFECTIVE FINANCIAL MANAGEMENT SYSTEM
AL-NASRULLAH, ABDULAZIZ A.	AN EVALUATION OF INTERNAL CONTROLS OF COMMERCIAL LOANS IN SAUDI ARABIAN BANKS
AL-RASHED, WAEL E. R.	KUWAIT'S TAX REFORMATION, ITS ALTERNATIVES AND IMPACT ON A DEVELOPING ACCOUNTING PROFESSION
ALLEN, PAUL WADE	EXPLAINING CPA PREFERENCES TOWARD ETHICAL ISSUES
AMES, GARY ADNA	EDP AUDITING OF MICROCOMPUTER SYSTEMS: AN EXPERIMENTAL ANALYSIS OF AUDITOR REACTION TO A CHANGED ENVIRONMENT
AMMONS, JANICE LEE	THE IMPACT OF STATE CONTROL OF INDIRECT COST RECOVERIES ON AMERICAN RESEARCH UNIVERSITIES
ANDERSON, JOHN CHARLES	THE SELECTION DECISION FOR MICROCOMPUTER GENERAL LEDGER SOFTWARE: AN INVESTIGATION USING A KNOWLEDGE-BASED SYSTEM
ARMITAGE, JACK LONNIE	EFFECTIVENESS OF AUDIT CONFIRMATIONS FOR TRADE ACCOUNTS RECEIVABLE
BABA, ISLAHUDIN	THE ROLE OF AUDITORS IN INFORMATION SYSTEMS DEVELOPMENT APPLIED TO THE MALAYSIAN PUBLIC SECTOR
BAKER, DONALD R.	RELATIONSHIPS OF INTERNAL ACCOUNTING CONTROLS AND OCCURRENCES OF COMPUTER FRAUD
BARNETT, DONALD JOSEPH	ATTRIBUTION BIASES, COMPETITIVE/COOPERATIVE WORK ENVIRONMENTS, AND THE MANAGEMENT CONTROL PROCESS
BASU, ONKER NATH	MANAGING THE ORGANIZATIONAL ENVIRONMENT: AN INTERPRETIVE FIELD STUDY OF THE UNITED STATES GENERAL ACCOUNTING OFFICE AND THE MAINTENANCE OF PROFESSIONAL INDEPENDENCE
BEAN, LUANN G.	AN EXAMINATION OF STATUS-RISK AND PERSONALITY VARIABLES OF PRACTICING PUBLIC ACCOUNTANTS AND ACCOUNTING ACADEMICIANS AS EXPLANATIONS OF RECEPTIVITY/RESISTANCE TO INNOVATIONS
BEETS, STEPHEN DOUGLAS	EFFECTIVENESS OF THE COMPLAINT-BASED ENFORCEMENT SYSTEM OF THE AICPA CODE OF PROFESSIONAL ETHICS
BENSON, VAUGHN LEON	A STUDY OF THE USEFULNESS OF SELECTED GAAP BASIS ACCOUNTING INFORMATION AND ITS ACTUAL USE IN THE SMALL PRIVATE COMPANY LOAN DECISION PROCESS
BETHEA, PRESTON, JR.	A DESCRIPTIVE EXPLORATORY EXAMINATION OF THE ROLE AND RESPONSIBILITIES OF INTERNAL AUDITORS IN HIGHER EDUCATION
BETTNER, MARK STEVEN	THE EFFECTS OF PERCEIVED ACCOUNTING COMPETENCE, MACHIAVELLIANISM, PAST BUDGETING BEHAVIOR, AND BELIEFS ABOUT THE EFFECTIVENESS OF PAST BUDGETING BEHAVIOR ON BUDGETARY ATTITUDE: AN EMPIRICAL ANALYSIS

BLEDSOE, NANCY LLEWELLYN	AN EMPIRICAL EXAMINATION OF THE EFFECTS OF PERFORMANCE EVALUATION ON GOAL CONGRUENCE WITHIN THE AUTOMOTIVE INDUSTRY
BLESSING, LINDA JANE	REPORTING OF GOVERNMENTAL PERFORMANCE INDICATORS FOR ASSESSMENT OF PUBLIC ACCOUNTABILITY
BLOUCH, WILLIAM EDWARD	EDP CONTROLS TO MAINTAIN DATA INTEGRITY IN DISTRIBUTED PROCESSING SYSTEMS
BOOYSEN, STEFANES FRANCOIS	A FRAMEWORK FOR FINANCIAL REPORTING TO EMPLOYEES IN THE REPUBLIC OF SOUTH AFRICA
BOUILLON, MARVIN L.	ECONOMIC DETERMINANTS OF THE DECISION TO LIQUIDATE LIFO INVENTORY QUANTITIES
BOULEY, JUDITH NOREEN	AN EMPIRICAL INVESTIGATION OF SFAS NO. 52 AND THE IMPLICATIONS FOR PERFORMANCE EVALUATION SYSTEMS
BRADLEY, CASSIE FRANCES	AN EMPIRICAL INVESTIGATION OF FACTORS AFFECTING CORPORATE TAX COMPLIANCE BEHAVIOR
BRANNAN, RODGER LLOYD	THE SINGLE AUDIT ACT OF 1984: AN EXAMINATION OF THE AUDIT PROCESS IN THE GOVERNMENT SECTOR
BROCE, PATRICIA ANN	THE USEFULNESS OF 'PRO FORMA' FINANCIAL STATEMENTS IN DECISION MAKING BY FINANCIAL ANALYSTS
BROWN, KENNETH WAYNE	AN EXAMINATION OF DECISION-RELEVANT FINANCIAL AND NONFINANCIAL INDICATORS IN COLLEGES AND UNIVERSITIES
BROWN, WILLIAM P.	SHARED AND DIFFERING PERCEPTIONS OF COSTS AND BENEFITS ASSOCIATED WITH INTERNAL/EXTERNAL AUDITOR SERVICES AND COOPERATION
BURROWES, ASHLEY WAYNE	A SURVEY OF SOPHISTICATED NEW ZEALAND USERS OF FINANCIAL STATEMENTS AND THEIR INTERIM REPORTING REQUIREMENTS
CALDERON, DARRYL PATRICK	THE USE OF A FORMAL REVIEW PROCESS ON PROSPECTIVE FINANCIAL STATEMENTS BY NONPROFIT ORGANIZATIONS AS A PREDICTOR OF EFFECTIVENESS
CARPENTER, VIVIAN LAVERNE	THE INCENTIVES FOR THE EVOLUTION OF PERFORMANCE-ORIENTED ACCOUNTING INFORMATION SYSTEMS IN THE GOVERNMENTAL SETTING
CARROLL, JAMES J.	CONTROL METHODOLOGIES FOR ACHIEVEMENT OF STRATEGIC OBJECTIVES
CARSTENS, ROBERT HUGO KONRAD	AN ANALYSIS OF THE EXPERT OPINIONS AND EXPERIENCES OF AUDITORS ON THE TOPIC OF INCOME SMOOTHING
CASCINI, KAREN T.	A COMPARATIVE STUDY OF INVESTMENT STRATEGIES OF COLLEGES AND UNIVERSITIES AND COMMERCIAL CORPORATIONS
CASSIDY, JUDITH HELEN	A STUDY OF THE IMPACT OF MEDICARE PROSPECTIVE PAYMENT SYSTEM ON HOSPITAL COST CONTAINMENT ACTIVITIES
CATHEY, JACK M.	CONTINGENT FACTORS AFFECTING BUDGET SYSTEM USEFULNESS: AN INFORMATION PROCESSING PERSPECTIVE
CENKER, WILLIAM JOHN	AN EMPIRICAL ANALYSIS OF THE RESOLUTION OF CONFLICT AND THE PERCEPTIONS OF AUTONOMY AND RESPONSIBILITY OF INDEPENDENT AUDITORS

Listing by Research Method   417

CERULLO, MARGARET VIRGINIA	A STUDY OF INTERNAL AUDITOR PERCEPTIONS OF SELECTED AUDIT ACTIVITIES PERFORMED DURING THE DESIGN PHASE OF SYSTEMS DEVELOPMENT
CHAMBERLAIN, DARNLEY HUGH, JR.	FINANCIAL REPORTING IN THE HIGHER EDUCATION ENVIRONMENT: ASSESSING THE VIEWS OF SELECTED USERS ON THE USEFULNESS AND ACCESSIBILITY OF SPECIFIED OUTCOMES INFORMATION
CHANG, JINNDER	TRANSFER PRICING AND TAX STRATEGIES FOR MULTINATIONAL COMPANIES IN TAIWAN
CHANG, STANLEY YI	A STUDY OF THE BASIC CRITERIA AND STANDARDS BY INTERNAL SERVICE FUNDS
CHASE, BRUCE W.	AN EMPIRICAL INVESTIGATION OF A CHOICE OF ACCOUNTING METHOD FOR INVESTMENTS BY COLLEGES AND UNIVERSITIES: POSITIVE ACCOUNTING THEORY APPLIED IN A NOT-FOR-PROFIT ENVIRONMENT
CHIASSON, MICHAEL ANTHONY	ORGANIZATIONAL-PROFESSIONAL CONFLICT AND THE WHISTLEBLOWING INTENTIONS OF PROFESSIONAL ACCOUNTANTS
CHOU, LING-TAI LYNETTE	A SURVEY EXAMINATION OF THE OBJECTIVE OF ACCOUNTS RECEIVABLE CONFIRMATION AND THE BEHAVIOR PATTERN OF CONFIRMATION RESPONDENTS
CHRISTENSEN, ANNE LESLIE KEENEY	TAX RETURN QUALITY: A CLIENT AND PREPARER PERSPECTIVE
CLAYPOOL, GREGORY ALLEN	AN EXPLORATORY STUDY OF THE COGNITIVE FRAMEWORKS USED BY CPAS AND THEOLOGIANS WHEN CONFRONTED WITH ETHICAL DILEMMAS
CLEVENGER, THOMAS BENTON	THE DEVELOPMENT OF GUIDELINES FOR INTEGRATING MICROCOMPUTERS INTO THE ACCOUNTING CURRICULUM
COLBERT, GARY J.	AN EMPIRICAL INVESTIGATION OF THE TRANSFER PROCESS AND TRANSFER PRICING: A MULTI-CASE RESEARCH DESIGN
COLBERT, PAUL JOSEPH	THE INFLUENCE OF WORK CONTEXT PERCEPTIONS AND EXPERIENCES ON THE ORGANIZATIONAL COMMITMENT OF FIRST-YEAR EMPLOYEES: A LONGITUDINAL STUDY
COLLEY, JAMES RONALD	AN INVESTIGATION OF PERCEPTIONAL DIFFERENCES REGARDING MICROCOMPUTER USE BY CPA FIRMS
COLLINS, KAREN MARIE	A COMPREHENSIVE STUDY OF STRESS ON INDIVIDUALS IN MIDDLE-MANAGEMENT POSITIONS IN PUBLIC ACCOUNTING
COLLINS, MARY KATHERINE	THE BUDGETARY PROCESS: A BEHAVIORAL PERSPECTIVE
COOK, HAROLD BARTLEY	THE RELATIONSHIP BETWEEN MANAGERIAL OWNERSHIP AND THE USE OF ACCOUNTING-BASED BUDGETING SYSTEMS TO MONITOR SUBORDINATES
COOKE, T. E.	AN EMPIRICAL STUDY OF FINANCIAL DISCLOSURE BY SWEDISH COMPANIES
COOMER, SUSAN DARLENE	THE EFFECT OF PRIOR YEAR'S ERRORS AND IRREGULARITIES AND MANAGEMENT'S CHARACTERISTICS ON AUDIT PLANNING: AN EMPIRICAL INVESTIGATION
COOPER-FEDLER, PAMELA ANN	A CHARACTERIZATION AND ANALYSIS OF FACULTY ACTIVITY AND PRODUCTIVITY REPORTING SYSTEMS IN RESEARCH UNIVERSITIES
COPPAGE, RICHARD EDWARD	AN EMPIRICAL DEFINITION OF ETHICS FOR MANAGEMENT ACCOUNTANTS

Listing by Research Method 418

CORY, SUZANNE NELLIE	AN INVESTIGATION OF AUDIT PRACTICE QUALITY
CRAVENS, KAREN SUE	A COMPARATIVE INVESTIGATION OF TRANSFER PRICING PRACTICES IN AN INTERNATIONAL ENVIRONMENT
CZYZEWSKI, ALAN BENJAMIN	THE PRODUCT LIFE CYCLE AND BUDGETING FUNCTIONS: PLANNING, CONTROL, AND MOTIVATION
DANCER, WELDON TERRY	A STUDY OF THE ATTITUDES AND PERCEPTIONS OF MASTER'S LEVEL ACCOUNTING STUDENTS TOWARD A CAREER IN ACCOUNTING EDUCATION
DANIELS, DEANNA KAY	EVALUATING THE QUALITATIVE CHARACTERISTICS OF ACCOUNTING INFORMATION: A DESCRIPTIVE STUDY OF IMPORTANCE WEIGHTS AND LOCATION MEASURES
DANIELS, JANET DELUCA	AN INVESTIGATION OF MUNICIPAL FINANCIAL REPORT FORMAT, USER PREFERENCE, AND DECISION-MAKING
DAVIDSON, RONALD ALLAN	SELECTION-SOCIALIZATION CONTROL IN AUDITING FIRMS: A TEST OF OUCHI'S MODEL OF CONTROL
DEFLORIA, JAMES DALE	THE PERCEPTIONS OF ACCOUNTING STUDENTS AS TO THE IMPORTANCE OF WRITTEN COMMUNICATION SKILLS FOR SUCCESS IN ACCOUNTING CAREERS
DEMIRAG, ISTEMIHAN SEFIK	FOREIGN CURRENCY ACCOUNTING AND MANAGEMENT EVALUATION OF FOREIGN SUBSIDIARY PERFORMANCE
DESAI, SURYAKANT T.	DESIRABLE NON-CONTENT ATTRIBUTES IN PRINCIPLES OF ACCOUNTING MICROCOMPUTER TEST BANKS AMONG TWO-YEAR AND FOUR-YEAR COLLEGE ACCOUNTING INSTRUCTORS: A DELPHI STUDY
DEUTSCH, ROBERT ALLEN	RECRUITING DECISIONS BY SELECTED BIG SIX CPA FIRMS: AN INVESTIGATION OF CHARACTERISTICS THAT INFLUENCE DECISIONS TO SELECT ACCOUNTING STUDENTS FOR OFFICE VISITS
DEXTER, LEE	USAGE OF PROCEDURES AND CONTROLS IN INNOVATIVE MANUFACTURING COMPANIES
DIETZ, DONNA K.	INFORMATION SYSTEMS CONTENT IN UNDERGRADUATE ACCOUNTING PROGRAMS
DOBITZ, CAROL S.	FUND ACCOUNTING PRINCIPLES ADVOCATED BY ACCOUNTING EDUCATORS AND HOSPITAL/MUNICIPAL/COLLEGE CHIEF ACCOUNTANTS
DOBY, VICTORIA JEAN	THE RELATIONSHIP OF JOB STRAIN TO STAFF TURNOVER IN PUBLIC ACCOUNTING FIRMS
DODD, JAMES LEE	ACCOUNTING INFORMATION TIMELINESS: AN EXPLORATORY STUDY OF INTERNAL DELAY
DOUCET, THOMAS ARTHUR	THE DETERMINATION OF THE USEFUL LIFE OF A CLIENT BASE: AN EMPIRICAL STUDY
DREWS-BRYAN, ALISON LUEDTKE	THE PERCEIVED USEFULNESS OF SELECTED INFORMATION CHARACTERISTICS FOR MUNICIPAL BUDGETING
EASON, PATRICIA LEE	AN EMPIRICAL ANALYSIS OF CONSUMPTION SENSITIVITY TO TAX POLICY UNCERTAINTY
EL-REFADI, IDRIS ABDULSALAM	FOREIGN EXCHANGE RISK MANAGEMENT IN U.S. MULTINATIONALS UNDER SFAS NO. 52: CHANGE IN MANAGEMENT DECISION-MAKING IN RESPONSE TO ACCOUNTING POLICY CHANGE

Listing by Research Method

419

ELETR, AMR	A COMPARISON BETWEEN CONTROLLERS AND PRODUCTION MANAGERS IN THE ELECTRONICS MANUFACTURING INDUSTRY OF THE PERCEIVED RELEVANCE AND USE OF MANAGEMENT ACCOUNTING SYSTEMS' CHARACTERISTICS AND PROFITABILITY AS
ELFRINK, JOHN ALBERT	AN EMPIRICAL INVESTIGATION INTO THE UTILITY OF THE UNIFORM CERTIFIED PUBLIC ACCOUNTANT EXAMINATION AS AN ENTRY REQUIREMENT FOR THE ACCOUNTING PROFESSION
ELMORE, ROBERT CLINTON	A CONTINGENCY THEORY APPROACH TO AN EMPIRICAL CLASSIFICATION OF MANAGEMENT ACCOUNTING INFORMATION SYSTEMS
EMIG, JAMES MATTHEW	THE RELATIONSHIP BETWEEN LEADER BEHAVIOR AND SUBORDINATE SATISFACTION IN AN AUDIT ENVIRONMENT: AN EMPIRICAL INVESTIGATION
ENGELBRET, WILLIAM G.	ASSESSING PARTICIPATION BY CERTIFIED PUBLIC ACCOUNTANTS IN CONTINUING PROFESSIONAL EDUCATION AND THE RELATIONSHIP BETWEEN EDUCATION AND CAREER PERFORMANCE
ETHRIDGE, JACK R., JR.	OPERATIONAL AUDITING AND ORGANIZATIONAL PERFORMANCE: SOME PERCEPTIONS OF EXECUTIVES AND INTERNAL AUDITORS
EWER, SID ROY	A STUDY OF THE EFFECT OF TRANSBORDER DATA FLOW RESTRICTIONS ON U.S. MULTINATIONAL CORPORATE ACCOUNTING CONTROL SYSTEMS
FERN, RICHARD HULL	AN INQUIRY INTO THE ROLE OF THE CORPORATE CONTROLLER IN STRATEGIC PLANNING
FERRERI, LINDA BARLOW	UNIVERSITY BUDGET SYSTEMS: A TEST OF CONTINGENCY THEORY AT PRIVATE INSTITUTIONS
FISCHER, CAROL M.	PERCEIVED DETECTION PROBABILITY AND TAXPAYER COMPLIANCE: A CONCEPTUAL AND EMPIRICAL EXAMINATION
FISCHER, MICHAEL J.	'REAL-IZING' THE BENEFITS OF NEW TECHNOLOGIES AS A SOURCE OF AUDIT EVIDENCE: AN INTERPRETIVE FIELD STUDY
FISHER, DANN G.	ASSESSING TAXPAYER MORAL REASONING: THE DEVELOPMENT OF AN OBJECTIVE MEASURE
FOGARTY, TIMOTHY JOSEPH	AUDIT PERFORMANCE: AN EMPIRICAL SYNTHESIS OF THREE THEORETICAL EXPLANATIONS
FRIEDLANDER, PHILIP HOWARD	INFORMATION TECHNOLOGY AND STRATEGIC ATTITUDES IN THE PUBLIC ACCOUNTING PROFESSION: A STRATEGIC GROUP ANALYSIS
FUGLISTER, JAYNE	CORPORATE CAPITAL STRUCTURE AND TAXES: SOME EVIDENCE
FULTS, GAIL JOHNSON	HOW PARTICIPATORY EVALUATION RESEARCH AFFECTS THE MANAGEMENT CONTROL PROCESS OF A MULTINATIONAL NON-PROFIT ORGANIZATION
GABALLA, MAHMOUD A.	PERFORMANCE AND CONTROL OF PUBLIC ENTERPRISE IN EGYPT
GATIAN, AMY ELIZABETH WILLIAMS	USER INFORMATION SATISFACTION (UIS) AND USER PRODUCTIVITY: AN EMPIRICAL EXAMINATION
GERBING, MONICA DIANE	AN EMPIRICAL STUDY OF TAXPAYER PERCEPTIONS OF FAIRNESS
GERSICH, FRANK, III	AN INVESTIGATION OF THE IMPORTANCE OF SELECTED KNOWLEDGE AREAS AND SKILLS FOR A PUBLIC ACCOUNTING AUDITING CAREER AND THE EXTENT OF ACADEMIC PREPARATION AS PERCEIVED BY AUDIT SENIORS AND AUDIT MANAGERS

GIBSON, ANNETTA MAE	AN EMPIRICAL INVESTIGATION INTO ETHICAL DECISION-MAKING IN ACCOUNTING
GIBSON, THOMAS HARRISON, JR.	THE 1985 NCAA FINANCIAL AUDIT LEGISLATION: IS IT WORKING, FROM COLLEGE AND UNIVERSITY PRESIDENTS' PERSPECTIVE?
GLOECK, JUERGEN DIETER	THE EXPECTATION GAP WITH REGARD TO THE AUDITING PROFESSION IN THE REPUBLIC OF SOUTH AFRICA
GLOVER, HUBERT DARNELL	MEASURING AUDIT STRUCTURE AND DETERMINING THE SOURCES OF VARIATION: AN APPLICATION OF ORGANIZATIONAL SCIENCE
GOEDDE, HAROLD	AN EMPIRICAL STUDY OF TAX PRACTITIONERS PERCEPTIONS OF THE EFFECT OF THE 1986 TAX REFORM ACT ON SIMPLIFICATION AND FAIRNESS OF THE FEDERAL INCOME TAX
GONZALEZ CABAN, ARMANDO	FIRE MANAGEMENT COSTS AND SOURCES OF VARIABILITY IN PRESCRIBED BURNING COSTS IN THE FOREST SERVICE'S NORTHERN, INTERMOUNTAIN, AND PACIFIC NORTHWEST REGIONS
GONZALEZ, LUIS	LEVELS OF INFORMATION TECHNOLOGIES INTEGRATION AS FACTORS AFFECTING PERCEPTIONS OF JOB CHARACTERISTICS AND PROFESSIONALISM OF MANAGEMENT ACCOUNTANTS
GORDON, TERESA PEALE	BOUNDED RATIONALITY AND BUDGETING: RESOURCE DEPENDENCE, AGENCY POWER, INDIVIDUAL MOTIVATION AND INCREMENTALISM IN BUDGETARY DECISION-MAKING
GOSSE, DARREL IRVIN	AN EMPIRICAL FIELD STUDY OF THE ROLE OF COST ACCOUNTING IN A COMPUTER-INTEGRATED MANUFACTURING ENVIRONMENT
GOTLOB, DAVID	INVESTOR AND CREDITOR PERCEPTIONS OF CORPORATE PERFORMANCE: A MULTIDIMENSIONAL SCALING APPROACH
GRANGE, EDWARD VANCE, JR.	AN EXAMINATION OF THE IMPACT OF SELECTED FEDERAL INCOME TAX CHANGES ON BIOTECHNOLOGY COMPANIES IN THE UNITED STATES
GRASSO, LAWRENCE PETER	THE ORGANIZATIONAL DETERMINANTS OF THE USE OF INCENTIVES IN COMPENSATING BUSINESS UNIT MANAGERS
GREENLEE, JANET STELLE	THE USE OF ACCOUNTING AND OTHER INFORMATION IN DETERMINING THE ALLOCATION OF RESOURCES TO VOLUNTARY HEALTH AND WELFARE ORGANIZATIONS: AN EMPIRICAL ANALYSIS
GREGSON, TERRY	AN EMPIRICAL INVESTIGATION OF THE RELATIONSHIP BETWEEN COMMUNICATION SATISFACTION, JOB SATISFACTION, TURNOVER, AND PERFORMANCE FOR PUBLIC ACCOUNTANTS
GROSS, NORMA JEAN	CASH FLOW CONCEPTS IN THE FINANCIAL PERFORMANCE EVALUATION OF FOREIGN SUBSIDIARY MANAGERS
GRUCA, STANLEY P.	ADVERTISING BY CPA FIRMS IN THE STATE OF ILLINOIS: AN ANALYSIS OF INCIDENCE, ATTITUDES, AND EFFICACY
GUPTA, PARVEEN PARKASH	THE AUDIT PROCESS AS A FUNCTION OF DIFFERENTIATED ENVIRONMENT: AN EMPIRICAL STUDY
GUTIERREZ, THERESA KAY	THE EFFECTS OF INTERACTIONS WITH IRS EMPLOYEES ON TAX PRACTITIONERS' ATTITUDES TOWARD THE IRS
HABEGGER, JERRELL WAYNE	AN INTERNAL AUDITING INNOVATION DECISION: STATISTICAL SAMPLING
HAMBY, WILLIAM LYLE, JR.	AN INVESTIGATION OF INTERNAL ACCOUNTING CONTROL IN MICROCOMPUTER-BASED SMALL BUSINESS ACCOUNTING SYSTEMS

HAMMER, SETH	THE CPA'S ROLE AS RISK ADVISER
HAMMOND, JOSEPH ANDREW	RISK EXPOSURE AND MANAGEMENT PRACTICES IN RESPONSE TO FLOATING EXCHANGE RATE VOLATILITY IN GHANA
HAMMOND, THERESA ANNE	THE MINORITY RECRUITMENT EFFORTS OF THE MAJOR PUBLIC ACCOUNTING FIRMS IN NEW YORK: A SOCIOLOGICAL ANALYSIS
HARRIS, JUDITH ANN BERMAN	A FIELD STUDY EXAMINING THE STRUCTURE AND SUBSTANCE OF COST ACCOUNTING SYSTEMS
HARRIS, THOMAS DONALD	THE EFFECT OF TYPE OF TAX KNOWLEDGE ON INDIVIDUALS' PERCEPTIONS OF FAIRNESS AND COMPLIANCE WITH THE FEDERAL INCOME TAX SYSTEM: AN EMPIRICAL STUDY
HEAGY, CYNTHIA DONNELL	A NATIONAL STUDY AND EMPIRICAL INVESTIGATION OF THE ACCOUNTING SYSTEMS COURSE: ACADEMIC PRACTICE VERSUS PROFESSIONAL NEEDS
HEBERT, MARCEL G.	AN INVESTIGATION OF THE EFFECT OF ALTERNATIVE PRESENTATION FORMATS ON PREPARERS AND USERS OF CITY FINANCIAL REPORTS
HENRY, LAURIE JANE	A PERSISTENCE-PERFORMANCE MODEL: AN OPERATIONAL MODEL TO ASSIST IN PREDICTING AN INDIVIDUAL'S FUTURE SUCCESS IN ACCOUNTING
HILL, NANCY THORLEY	THE ADOPTION OF COSTING SYSTEMS IN THE HOSPITAL INDUSTRY
HODGE, THOMAS GLEN	THE EMPIRICAL DEVELOPMENT OF ETHICS DECISION MODELS FOR MANAGEMENT ACCOUNTANTS
HOLTER, NORMA C.	AUDITOR-FIRM CONFLICT IN THE DEFENSE CONTRACTING INDUSTRY: AN EMPIRICAL STUDY OF THE CONTRIBUTING FACTORS TO THE PERCEIVED IMBALANCE OF POWER
HOPE, NORMAN PHILLIP	MODES OF CONTINUING PROFESSIONAL EDUCATION: A FACTOR ANALYTIC TEST OF HOULE'S MODES OF LEARNING WITH CERTIFIED PUBLIC ACCOUNTANTS
HOUSTON, CAROL OLSON	U.S. MANAGEMENT HEDGING PRACTICES SUBSEQUENT TO THE ADOPTION OF SFAS NO. 52 'FOREIGN CURRENCY TRANSLATION'
HRNCIR, THERESA JUNE	ACCOUNTANTS IN BUSINESS AND INDUSTRY: DIFFUSION OF INNOVATION WITH REGULATED CHANGE
HUDSON, DENNIS HERSCHEL	AN INQUIRY INTO THE ACCOUNTING PRACTICES AND ATTITUDES OF SELECTED SMALL BUSINESSES: THE IMPACT OF RELEVANCE
HUH, SUNG-KYOO	THE IMPACT OF PERCEIVED ENVIRONMENTAL UNCERTAINTY, COMPENSATION PLANS, AND SIZE ON THE CHOICE OF COST VARIANCE INVESTIGATION SYSTEMS IN LARGE MANUFACTURING FIRMS: AN EMPIRICAL STUDY
HUMAN, WILLEM ADRIAAN FRANS	THE ABILITY OF THE SOUTH AFRICAN AUDIT PROFESSION TO AUDIT IN THE ELECTRONIC DATA INTERCHANGE ERA
HUTTON, MARGUERITE ROACH	PERCEPTUAL DIFFERENTIATION WITH REGARD TO PENALTIES IN PROFESSIONAL TAX PRACTICE
HWANG, HO-CHAN	PROFESSIONAL ACCOUNTANTS' ETHICAL BEHAVIOR: A POSITIVE APPROACH
IBRAHIM, MOHAMED EL HADY M.	AN EXAMINATION OF AN INTEGRATIVE EXPECTANCY MODEL FOR AUDITORS' PERFORMANCE BEHAVIORS UNDER TIME BUDGET PRESSURE

Listing by Research Method

IGWE, VICTOR IHEUKWU	THE IMPACT OF AUDITORS' PERCEPTION OF PERFORMANCE APPRAISAL ON THE EFFORTS EXERTED TOWARDS JOB PERFORMANCE: A STUDY OF AUDITORS THAT AUDIT GOVERNMENTAL ENTITIES, COLLEGES AND UNIVERSITIES IN THE STATE OF FLORIDA
IMOISILI, OLUMHENSE ANTHONY	TASK COMPLEXITY, BUDGET STYLE OF EVALUATING PERFORMANCE AND MANAGERIAL STRESS: AN EMPIRICAL INVESTIGATION
INDRIANTORO, NUR	THE EFFECT OF PARTICIPATIVE BUDGETING ON JOB PERFORMANCE AND JOB SATISFACTION WITH LOCUS-OF-CONTROL AND CULTURAL DIMENSIONS AS MODERATING VARIABLES
ISAACS, PATRICIA COLE	IMA'S CODE OF ETHICS: AN EMPIRICAL EXAMINATION OF VIEWPOINTS OF CERTIFIED MANAGEMENT ACCOUNTANTS
ITTNER, CHRISTOPHER DEAN	THE ECONOMICS AND MEASUREMENT OF QUALITY COSTS: AN EMPIRICAL INVESTIGATION
IYER, VENKATARAMAN MOHAN	FACTORS RELATED TO INCLINATION AND CAPACITY OF CPA FIRM ALUMNI TO BENEFIT THEIR FORMER FIRM: AN EMPIRICAL STUDY
JACKSON, CYNTHIA MAPP	THE INFLUENCE OF USER INVOLVEMENT AND OTHER VARIABLES ON BEHAVIORAL INTENTION TO USE AN INFORMATION SYSTEM
JACKSON, PAMELA GAIL ZIEMER	AN INVESTIGATION OF THE EFFECT OF CONTINGENCY THEORY VARIABLES ON THE DESIGN OF COST ACCOUNTING SYSTEMS IN SERVICE FIRMS
JACKSON-HEARD, MARY FRANCES	THE EFFECT OF THE AUDIT COMMITTEE AND OTHER SELECTED FACTORS ON THE PERCEPTION OF AUDITORS' INDEPENDENCE
JOHNSON, GARY GENE	COMPLIANCE AUDITING IN THE PUBLIC SECTOR: AN EMPIRICAL INVESTIGATION INTO THE EXTENT OF NONCOMPLIANCE WITH STATE LAWS BY COUNTY GOVERNMENTS
JOHNSON, GENE HERBERT	THE RELATIVE USE OF FORMAL AND INFORMAL INFORMATION IN THE EVALUATION OF INDIVIDUAL PERFORMANCE
JOHNSON, JOYCE MARIE	AN EVALUATION OF THE FEDERAL CIVIL TAX PENALTY FOR THE FAILURE TO TIMELY DEPOSIT PAYROLL TAXES: A SURVEY OF GEORGIA TAX PRACTITIONERS
JOHNSON, STEVEN D.	AN EMPIRICAL STUDY OF THE FIDELITY OF ORGANIZATIONAL ACCOUNTING COMMUNICATION AND THE IMPACT OF ORGANIZATIONAL CULTURE
JORDAN, ROBERT EARL	THE INSTITUTE OF MANAGEMENT ACCOUNTANTS' CONTRIBUTION TO ACCOUNTING THOUGHT: A DESCRIPTIVE AND EVALUATIVE STUDY
JOY, ARTHUR C., JR.	AN EMPIRICAL INVESTIGATION INTO TRANSFER PRICING PRACTICES
KALBERS, LAWRENCE PACKARD	THE AUDIT COMMITTEE: A POWER NEXUS FOR FINANCIAL REPORTING AND CORPORATE ACCOUNTABILITY
KAUFFMAN, NORMAN LEROY	PERFORMANCE EVALUATION AND JOB-DIRECTED EFFORT IN THE CPA FIRM: AN INTEGRATION OF EXPECTANCY THEORY, ATTRIBUTION THEORY, AND NEED THEORY
KEASLER, HUBERT LEVERT, JR.	A COMPOSITE PROFILE OF PROPOSED INDIRECT COST RATES APPLICABLE TO ORGANIZED RESEARCH AND DEVELOPMENT AT COLLEGES AND UNIVERSITIES THAT USE MODIFIED TOTAL DIRECT COSTS BASIS FOR FEDERAL IC RATE NEGOTIATIONS
KEMPTON, PETER A.	THE CONTROL OF TAX EVASION--QUESTIONS FOR PRACTISING ACCOUNTANTS
KERCSMAR, JOHN	INDIVIDUAL INVESTORS' INFORMATION CHOICE, INFORMATION PROCESSING, AND JUDGMENT BEHAVIOR: A PROCESS-TRACING STUDY OF THE VERBAL PROTOCOLS ASSOCIATED WITH STOCK SELECTION

Listing by Research Method

KHALSA, JODHA SINGH	CONTEXT EFFECTS IN CERTIFIED PUBLIC ACCOUNTING FIRM SELECTION DECISIONS: THE SMALL BUSINESS ENVIRONMENT
KLEINMAN, GARY BRUCE	CONSTRUCTING THE AUDITOR AND ACCOUNTANT
KLEMSTINE, CHARLES FREDERICK	INTERNAL AND EXTERNAL AUDIT SUBSTITUTION
KWIATKOWSKI, VERNON EVERETT	INFRASTRUCTURE ASSETS: AN ASSESSMENT OF USER NEEDS AND RECOMMENDATIONS FOR FINANCIAL REPORTING
LANDOE, GENE ARLAN	THE IMPACT OF MICROCOMPUTER TECHNOLOGY ON NORTHERN CALIFORNIA CERTIFIED PUBLIC ACCOUNTING FIRMS
LANDRY, RAYMOND MAURICE, JR.	AN EMPIRICAL INVESTIGATION OF EDP AUDIT JUDGMENTS AND CONSENSUS BETWEEN EXTERNAL AND INTERNAL AUDIT EXPERTS
LANGEMEIER, BRIAN LEON	A MODEL OF CHOICE OF BUSINESS ENTITY USING DISCRIMINANT ANALYSIS
LEINICKE, LINDA M.	AN ANALYSIS OF THE BUSINESS ADVISORY SERVICE ACCOUNTANT VERSUS THE TRADITIONAL ACCOUNTING SERVICE ACCOUNTANT, WITH IMPLICATIONS FOR THE ACCOUNTING PROFESSION
LEUNG, VICTOR KWAN LAP	BUDGETING IN RESPECT TO INFORMATION ASYMMETRY, PARTICIPATION AND EVALUATION FROM PERSPECTIVES OF AGENCY THEORY AND SOCIAL BEHAVIOR THEORY
LEWELLYN, PATSY ANN GRANGER	AN INVESTIGATION OF FACTORS RELATED TO TERMINATION IN THE PUBLIC ACCOUNTING PROFESSION AND THE QUALITY OF LIFE OF CERTIFIED PUBLIC ACCOUNTANTS
LI, JUNE FANG	AN EMPIRICAL STUDY OF THE PERCEPTIONS OF FINANCIAL EXECUTIVES AND FINANCIAL ANALYSTS REGARDING SELECTEDASPECTS OF FOREIGN CURRENCY TRANSLATION AS CURRENTLY PROMULGATED BY THE FINANCIAL ACCOUNTING STANDARDS BOARD
LILLIE, RICHARD EUGENE	AN ANALYSIS OF LEARNING STYLES OF PROFESSIONAL PERSONNEL BY LEVEL AND BY FUNCTION WITHIN A NATIONAL PUBLIC ACCOUNTING FIRM (ACCOUNTING EDUCATION)
LOUWERS, TIMOTHY JAMES	AN EMPIRICAL INVESTIGATION OF THE RELATIONSHIP BETWEEN FINANCIAL DISTRESS, EXTERNAL FACTORS, AND THE AUDITOR'S GOING CONCERN OPINION MODIFICATION
LUNDBLAD, HEIDEMARIE	VOLUNTARY FINANCIAL DISCLOSURE: AN INTERNATIONAL COMPARISON OF MANAGERIAL POLICIES
MACQUARRIE, ALLAN JAMES	HEALTH CARE COST CONTAINMENT IN THE NEW ENVIRONMENT OF PROSPECTIVE PRICING OF SERVICES: THE IMPLICATIONS FOR THE ACCOUNTING AND FINANCIAL FUNCTION
MAGNER, NACE RICHARD	A FIELD STUDY OF PROCEDURAL JUSTICE AS AN INTERVENING VARIABLE BETWEEN PARTICIPATION IN BUDGETING AND ORGANIZATIONAL OUTCOMES
MALONE, CHARLES FRANCIS	AN EMPIRICAL INVESTIGATION OF THE RELATIONSHIPS BETWEEN INDIVIDUAL AND FIRM CHARACTERISTICS AND REDUCED AUDIT QUALITY
MALONE, JOHN DAVID, JR.	AN EMPIRICAL INVESTIGATION OF THE EXTENT OF CORPORATE FINANCIAL DISCLOSURE IN THE OIL AND GAS INDUSTRY
MANKO, KENNETH MICHAEL	THE RELATIONSHIP OF MEASURES OF SELF-CONCEPT AND ANXIETY TO ACADEMIC ACHIEVEMENT IN ACCOUNTING
MANN, GARY J.	EFFECTS OF HUMAN NEEDS, GROUP INFLUENCE, AND MANAGEMENT STYLE ON CHANGE-RELATED BEHAVIORAL INTENTIONS IN INFORMATION SYSTEMS

Listing by Research Method   424

MARABELLO, CARMINE F., JR.	A STUDY OF PUBLIC ACCOUNTING INTERNSHIPS IN NEW ENGLAND: AN EVALUATION FROM THE VIEWPOINT OF CPA FIRMS
MARTIN, LISA CLINE	AN EMPIRICAL INVESTIGATION OF THE JOB MOBILITY OF CERTIFIED PUBLIC ACCOUNTANTS WORKING IN INDUSTRY
MATHEWS, MARTIN REGINALD	THE REACTIONS OF ACADEMIC ADMINISTRATORS TO THE ACCOUNTING EDUCATION CHANGE COMMISSION, 1989-1992
MCCARTHY, IRENE N.	PROFESSIONAL ETHICS CODE CONFLICT SITUATIONS: ETHICAL AND VALUE ORIENTATION OF COLLEGIATE ACCOUNTING STUDENTS
MCGOWAN, ANNIE SMITH	AN INVESTIGATION OF THE BEHAVIORAL IMPLICATIONS OF ADOPTING ACTIVITY-BASED COST MANAGEMENT SYSTEMS: AN EXPLORATORY STUDY
MCGREGOR, CALVERT, JR.	AN INVESTIGATION OF ORGANIZATIONAL - PROFESSIONAL CONFLICT IN MANAGEMENT ACCOUNTING
MCKEAN, GERALD WILLIAM	CONGRUENCIES OF COMPUTER COMPETENCIES AS VIEWED BY ACCOUNTING PRACTITIONERS AND ACCOUNTING EDUCATORS
MCKENNA, JOHN N.	ETHICAL DILEMMAS IN FINANCIAL REPORTING SITUATIONS AND THE PREFERRED MODE OF RESOLUTION OF ETHICAL CONFLICTS AS TAKEN BY CERTIFIED AND NONCERTIFIED MANAGEMENT ACCOUNTANTS IN ORGANIZATIONS WITH PERCEIVED DIFFERENT
MCNAIR, CAROL JEAN	THE EFFECTS OF BUDGET PRESSURE ON AUDIT FIRMS: AN EMPIRICAL EXAMINATION OF THE UNDERREPORTING OF CHARGEABLE TIME
MCNAMEE, ALAN HOWARD	THE CONTINGENT EFFECT OF PERFORMANCE EVALUATION CRITERIA ON BUSINESS UNIT PERFORMANCE
MEHAFDI, MESSAOUD	BEHAVIOURAL ASPECTS OF TRANSFER PRICING IN UNITED KINGDOM DECENTRALISED COMPANIES
MEREDITH, VICKI BANET	AN EMPIRICAL EXAMINATION OF BANKERS' PERCEPTIONS OF PROCEDURES PERFORMED BY CPAS IN LIMITED ASSURANCE ENGAGEMENTS
MILLER, GARY ARTHUR	THE COSTS AND BENEFITS OF INTERPERIOD INCOME TAX ALLOCATION
MILLER, GERALD JOHN	AN EMPIRICAL STUDY OF THE IMPROVEMENT IN FINANCIAL MANAGEMENT PRACTICES OF STATE AND LOCAL GOVERNMENTS IN RESPONSE TO THE SINGLE AUDIT ACT
MILLS, SHERRY KAY SNODGRASS	EFFECTS OF THE SERVICE ENCOUNTER ON CPA FIRM RETENTION
MITCHELL, ELIZABETH ANN	AN INTEGRATIVE MODEL FOR THE STUDY OF PUBLIC ACCOUNTING FIRMS
MOHRWEIS, LAWRENCE CHARLES	AN EMPIRICAL INVESTIGATION OF FACTORS AFFECTING THE USE OF CONCURRENT EDP AUDIT TECHNIQUES
MONCADA, SUSAN MARY	A HUMAN FACTORS ANALYSIS OF THE INTERPERSONAL COMMUNICATION EFFECTIVENESS OF PROGRAMMER ANALYSTS
MOONEY, KATHLEEN KAYE BORN	AN INVESTIGATION OF THE ASSOCIATION OF CPAS WITH REAL ESTATE LIMITED PARTNERSHIPS
MOORE, ELMA LEE SCHMIDT	AN ANALYSIS OF LEARNING STYLES, INSTRUCTIONAL STYLES, AND CULTURE AMONG SELECTED ACCOUNTING STUDENTS AND INSTRUCTORS AT THE UNIVERSITY-LEVEL

Listing by Research Method 425

MOORE, PERRY GLEN	EXTERNAL AUDITOR RELIANCE ON INTERNAL AUDITORS: AN EXAMINATION OF THE SIMILARITY OF AUDITOR JUDGMENTS
MOORE, WALTER BURNIS	BUDGETARY SLACK BEHAVIOR IN MUNICIPAL GOVERNMENTS: AN EMPIRICAL BEHAVIORAL STUDY
MOYES, GLEN DAVID	AN ANALYSIS OF THE EFFECTIVENESS OF SPECIFIC AUDITING TECHNIQUES FOR DETECTING FRAUD AS PERCEIVED BY THREE DIFFERENT AUDITOR GROUPS
MUNTORO, RONNY KUSUMA	THE USE OF ORGANIZATION BEHAVIOR METHODS IN THE DEVELOPMENT OF COMPUTERIZED ACCOUNTING SYSTEMS IN INDONESIA: AN ATTITUDINAL SURVEY
MYERS, MARY DOVE	AN EMPIRICAL INVESTIGATION OF POSTAUDIT PROCEDURES FOR CAPITAL EXPENDITURES AND THEIR ASSOCIATION WITH FIRM PERFORMANCE
NANCE, WILLIAM DOUGLAS	TASK/TECHNOLOGY FIT AND KNOWLEDGE WORKER USE OF INFORMATION TECHNOLOGY: A STUDY OF AUDITORS
NICOLAOU, ANDREAS IACOVOU	AN EMPIRICAL EXAMINATION OF INFORMATION SYSTEMS SUCCESS IN RELATION WITH INFORMATION SYSTEMS DEVELOPMENT PHENOMENA
NIKKHAH-AZAD, ALI	PERCEPTIONS OF COLLEGE AND UNIVERSITY AUDITORS CONCERNING THE IMPORTANCE OF SELECTED FACTORS ASSOCIATED WITH OPERATIONAL AUDITING
NORWOOD, CYNTHIA JANE	MENTORING IN PUBLIC ACCOUNTING: AN EMPIRICAL INVESTIGATION
NOURI, HOSSEIN	THE EFFECT OF BUDGETARY PARTICIPATION ON JOB PERFORMANCE: A CONCEPTUAL MODEL AND ITS EMPIRICAL TEST
O'SHAUGHNESSY, JOHN JOSEPH	AN EMPIRICAL STUDY OF THE EXTENT OF IMPLEMENTATION AND EFFECTIVENESS OF THE TREADWAY COMMISSION'S RECOMMENDATIONS AS PERCEIVED BY INTERNAL AUDIT MANAGERS OF CALIFORNIA'S 100 LARGEST PUBLICLY HELD COMPANIES
OLSON, CAROL ANN FELICIA	AN EXAMINATION OF THE FACTORS AFFECTING THE CHOICE OF EMPLOYEE FRINGE BENEFITS AND CAFETERIA PLANS
ONYIRI, SUNNY O. G.	REPLACEMENT OF DEPRECIABLE TANGIBLE ASSETS: A MACRO APPROACH
PAIGE, KENNETH LEE	THE USE OF MANAGEMENT ACCOUNTING PRACTICES BY NONPROFIT ORGANIZATIONS: AN EXPLORATORY STUDY
PANDIT, GANESH MANGESH	THE IMPACT OF CLIENTS' PERCEPTIONS ON AUDITOR SWITCHING
PARK, SEONG WHOE	THE CHARACTERISTICS AND USAGE OF COMPUTERIZED INFORMATION SYSTEMS IN SMALL APPAREL AND TEXTILE COMPANIES
PARKER, DOROTHY JANET	AN EXAMINATION OF A DIFFERENTIAL IN STANDARD COST DETERMINANTS AND ITS IMPACT ON VARIANCE INVESTIGATION PROCEDURES IN MANUFACTURING
PAULEY, PATRICIA ANN	KNOWLEDGE OF THE TAX CONSEQUENCES OF PLAN DISTRIBUTIONS
PENDLEBURY, MAURICE WILSON	AN INVESTIGATION INTO THE ROLE AND NATURE OF MANAGEMENT ACCOUNTING IN LOCAL GOVERNMENT IN ENGLAND AND WALES
PEREIRA, EMILIO ANTHONY	ENVIRONMENTAL UNCERTAINTY AND MANAGERS' BUDGET-RELATED BEHAVIOR: A CROSS-CULTURAL FIELD STUDY

Listing by Research Method

ERKINS, WILLIAM DAVID	THE ASSOCIATION BETWEEN AUDIT STRUCTURE AND AUDITOR SATISFACTION: AN INTEGRATION OF BEHAVIORAL THEORIES
ERRY, SUSAN ELIZABETH	ACCOUNTING INFORMATION IN GOING-PRIVATE TRANSACTIONS
ERSELLIN, MARK BENNETT	AN INVESTIGATION OF THE PLANNING AND POLICY IMPLICATIONS OF THE FOREIGN SALES CORPORATION LEGISLATION
ETERS, JAMES MILTON	A KNOWLEDGE-BASED MODEL OF INHERENT AUDIT RISK ASSESSMENT
EFFER, MARY GRAVES	VENTURE CAPITAL INVESTMENT AND PROTOCOL ANALYSIS
NAC-WARD, SUZANNE RESI	AN EMPIRICAL INVESTIGATION OF THE COMPARABILITY OF REPORTED EARNINGS PER SHARE UNDER ACCOUNTING PRINCIPLES BOARD OPINION NO. 15
OCH Y TORRES, RAMON	THE SYSTEM OF INTERNAL CONTROL OF BUSINESS FIRMS
OE, CLYDE DOUGLAS	AN EXAMINATION OF THE STRENGTH OF THE CONTAGION EFFECT ON EVALUATIVE STYLE IN MANAGERIAL ACCOUNTING
ONEMON, LAWRENCE ANDREW	A COGNITIVE-DEVELOPMENTAL APPROACH TO THE ANALYSIS OF CERTIFIED PUBLIC ACCOUNTANTS' ETHICAL JUDGMENTS
OZNANSKI, PETER JOHN	THE EFFECTS OF ORGANIZATIONAL COMMITMENT, PROFESSIONAL COMMITMENT, LIFE-SPAN CAREER DEVELOPMENT, AND SELF-MONITORING ON JOB SATISFACTION AND JOB PERFORMANCE AMONG STAFF ACCOUNTANTS
URCELL, THOMAS J., III	AN ANALYSIS OF THE FEDERAL INCOME TAX CONCEPT OF EARNINGS AND PROFITS AS COMPARED TO THE FINANCIAL ACCOUNTING CONCEPT OF RETAINED EARNINGS
TAISHAT, MUNIF ABDELRAHMAN	JORDANIAN ACCOUNTING PRACTITIONERS' PERCEPTIONS OF UNDERGRADUATE ACCOUNTING PROGRAM CONTENT
UARLES, NOWLIN ROSS	PROFESSIONAL COMMITMENT, ORGANIZATIONAL COMMITMENT, AND ORGANIZATIONAL - PROFESSIONAL CONFLICT IN THE INTERNAL AUDIT FUNCTION: MODEL DEVELOPMENT AND TEST
AMADAN, SAYEL S.	THE ALLOCATION OF CENTRAL OVERHEAD COSTS FOR THE PURPOSES OF PERFORMANCE EVALUATION: A STUDY OF UK DIVISIONALISED COMPANIES
AMZY, WAFAA ABDEL MAGID	THE DETERMINANTS OF AUDIT FEES: AN ANALYTICAL STUDY
AO, HEMA	AN EMPIRICAL EVALUATION OF THE PRACTICE OF DISCOUNTING INITIAL AUDIT FEES AND THE EFFECT OF THE PRACTICE ON THE APPEARANCE OF AUDIT INDEPENDENCE (FEE DISCOUNTING)
ASTOGI, LOKESH CHANDRA	A COMPARISON OF JOB SATISFACTION OF CERTIFIED MANAGEMENT ACCOUNTANTS (CMAS) WORKING IN CPA FIRMS AND IN INDUSTRY
AY, MANASH RANJAN	TOWARDS A POSITIVE AGENCY THEORY OF CONTROL: AN EMPIRICAL STUDY OF COMPENSATION CONTRACTS IN THE INSURANCE INDUSTRY
EBMANN-HUBER, ZELMA E.	THE INFLUENCE OF VARIOUS GROUPS ON ACCOUNTING STANDARD-SETTING IN SIXTEEN DEVELOPED COUNTRIES: MODEL AND EMPIRICAL INVESTIGATIONS
EDMER, TIMOTHY ALBERT ORAL	BUDGET ACTIVITIES AND THEIR IMPACT ON THE BUDGET PROCESS: AN EXPLORATORY STUDY

REGEL, ROY W.	STAFF PERFORMANCE EVALUATION BY AUDITORS: THE EFFECT OF TRAINING ON ACCURACY AND CONSENSUS
RESCHO, JOYCE ANNE	PUBLIC ACCOUNTING FIRM STRATEGY AND INNOVATIVENESS: A STUDY OF THE ADOPTION OF PRODUCT, TECHNICAL, AND ADMINISTRATIVE INNOVATIONS USING A STRATEGIC TYPOLOGY
REYNOLDS, MARY ANN	AN EXAMINATION OF THE AUDIT FUNCTION IN SOCIETY
RIORDAN, DIANE A.	THE NATURE AND EFFECTIVENESS OF MANAGEMENT CONTROL IN SMALL FAMILY BUSINESSES
RIORDAN, MICHAEL PATRICK	HOW COGNITIVE COMPLEXITY AFFECTS ACCOUNTING CAREER PATHS
ROGERS, LEON REED	COMPARISON AND EVALUATION OF AN INTEGRATED COMPUTERIZED SPREADSHEET ESTIMATING SYSTEM VERSUS MANUAL ESTIMATING FOR RESIDENTIAL CONSTRUCTION PROJECTS
RUSTH, DOUGLAS BRUCE	MULTINATIONAL ENTITIES: PERCEIVED ENVIRONMENTAL UNCERTAINTY AND THE BUDGETARY PLANNING AND CONTROL SYSTEM
SAEMANN, GEORGIA PIERCE	A MODEL OF NYSE FIRM MANAGER POSITION AND PARTICIPATION CHOICE ON THE MARCH 1985 FASB EXPOSURE DRAFT: EMPLOYERS' ACCOUNTING FOR PENSIONS
SAFA MIRHOSSEINY, ALI	CALIFORNIA ACCOUNTING MANAGERS' PERCEPTIONS OF THE EFFECTIVENESS AND RELEVANCY OF DIFFERENT MICROCOMPUTER TRAINING TECHNIQUES FOR GENERAL LEDGER ACCOUNTING PROGRAMS
SALEM, AZIZA ABDEL-RAZIK AHMED	A STUDY OF DETERMINANTS OF TRANSFER PRICING IN MULTINATIONAL CORPORATIONS: THE CASE BETWEEN U.S. PARENTS AND THE EGYPTIAN UNITS
SALLEE, LARRY	AN EMPIRICAL ANALYSIS OF CONTINUING PROFESSIONAL EDUCATION FOR CERTIFIED PUBLIC ACCOUNTANTS EMPLOYED IN NON-PUBLIC OCCUPATIONS
SALTER, STEPHEN BRIAN	CLASSIFICATION OF FINANCIAL REPORTING SYSTEMS AND A TEST OF THEIR ENVIRONMENTAL DETERMINANTS
SAMPSELL, MARTHA EIBERFELD	SURVEY RESPONSES OF DEPARTMENT CHAIRS OF THE ILLINOIS COLLEGIATE ACCOUNTING PROGRAM TO THE REVISED ILLINOIS PUBLIC ACCOUNTING ACT
SANDERS, JOSEPH CASH	A COMPREHENSIVE STUDY OF STRESS IN THE PUBLIC ACCOUNTING PROFESSION
SANDERSON, GEORGE NORMAN	CONTINUING PROFESSIONAL EDUCATION FOR CERTIFIED PUBLIC ACCOUNTANTS: STATE OF THE ART AND PREDICTIONS FOR CHANGE
SAVAGE, KATHRYN S.	THE VALUE-AND-BELIEF STRUCTURES OF TOP FINANCIAL EXECUTIVES
SCARBROUGH, D. PAUL	THE EFFECTS OF ALTERNATIVE GROUPING METHODS ON EMPLOYEE TURNOVER RESEARCH IN CPA FIRMS
SCHAEFER, JAMES CLARK	A STUDY OF THE PROPENSITY OF CERTIFIED PUBLIC ACCOUNTANTS TO ACT UNPROFESSIONALLY
SCHAFERMEYER, KENNETH WILLIAM	AN ANALYSIS OF CHAIN PHARMACIES' COSTS OF DISPENSING A THIRD PARTY PRESCRIPTION
SCHILLER, STEFAN	MANAGEMENT ACCOUNTING SYSTEMS--USE AND DESIGN

SCHLEIFER, LYDIA LANCASTER FOLGER	AN INVESTIGATION OF PERCEPTIONS AND ATTRIBUTES OF THE CONCEPT OF INDEPENDENCE
SCHNEIDER, DOUGLAS KENNETH	RESPONDENT PERCEPTION OF THE CREDIBILITY OF GAAP
SCHNEIDER, WM. BRUCE	CERTIFIED PUBLIC ACCOUNTANTS: A PROFESSION IN CRISIS
SEAY, ROBERT ALAN	AN EMPIRICAL INVESTIGATION INTO HOSPITAL UTILIZATION AND SUPPORT OF THE INTERNAL AUDIT FUNCTION
SENGE, STEPHEN V.	AN ANALYSIS OF THE MBA INTRODUCTORY FINANCIAL ACCOUNTING CURRICULUM
SHAFFER, RAYMOND JAMES	FINANCIAL REPORTING OF DEFERRED MAINTENANCE FOR CAPITAL ASSETS IN GOVERNMENTAL ENTITIES: A SURVEY OF SELECTED USERS
SHAUB, MICHAEL KENNETH	AN EMPIRICAL EXAMINATION OF THE DETERMINANTS OF AUDITORS' ETHICAL SENSITIVITY
SHAVER, JAMES HOWARD	CERTIFICATION OF ACCOUNTING SPECIALISTS: VIEWPOINT OF THE SMALL FIRM PRACTITIONER
SHIM, EUN SUP	COST MANAGEMENT AND ACTIVITY-BASED COST ALLOCATION IN A NEW MANUFACTURING ENVIRONMENT
SHOENTHAL, EDWARD ROBERT	AN INVESTIGATION OF THE HARMONY OF COMPETENCIES FOUND IN CERTIFIED AND CHARTERED ACCOUNTANTS IN THE UNITED STATES AND GREAT BRITAIN
SHREIM, OBEID SAAD	VALUE FOR MONEY AUDITING: ITS DEVELOPMENT AND APPLICATION WITH SPECIAL REFERENCE TO THE U.K. PUBLIC SECTOR
SIEGEL, PHILIP HARRIS	ALTERNATIVE EDUCATIONAL PROGRAMS FOR ENTRY INTO THE PUBLIC ACCOUNTING PROFESSION: AN ANALYSIS
SINGLETON, LARRY G.	A FIELD TEST OF THE PERCEPTIONS OF THE QUALITATIVE CHARACTERISTICS OF STATEMENT OF FINANCIAL ACCOUNTING CONCEPTS NO. 2 BY PRACTICING CPAS
SIPPLE, STANLEY ALFRED	AN EMPIRICAL INVESTIGATION TO DETERMINE IF A PARTNER MAY SERVE THE PARTNERSHIP AS AN EMPLOYEE
SJOBLOM, LEIF MIKAEL	ESSAYS IN SHOP FLOOR QUALITY MANAGEMENT
SMITH, ANNE	AN ASSESSMENT OF THE COGNITIVE LEVELS OF THE UNIFORM CERTIFIED PUBLIC ACCOUNTANT EXAMINATION AND THE CERTIFIED MANAGEMENT ACCOUNTANT EXAMINATION
SMITH, BECKY LYNN	COMPETENCE, INFLUENCE, PROBLEM-SOLVING ABILITY, AND FEAR OF SUCCESS AMONG ACCOUNTANTS
SMITH, CARL STUART	AN ANALYSIS OF THE APPLICATION OF INDIRECT COST ALLOCATION METHODOLOGIES IN HIGHER EDUCATION
SMITH, M. AILEEN	ATTITUDES TOWARD INTERNATIONAL HARMONIZATION EFFORTS: A CROSS-CULTURAL STUDY
SMITH, NANCY E.	THE IMPACT OF THE FASB'S CONCEPTUAL FRAMEWORK PROJECT ON INTERMEDIATE ACCOUNTING

Listing by Research Method

SMITH, SHELDON RAY	ACCOUNTING INFORMATION IN GLOBAL MANUFACTURING NETWORKS: THE INFORMATION EFFECT ON COMPETITIVE POSITION
SOONGSWANG, ORANUJ	THE PERCEIVED IMPORTANCE AND IMPLEMENTATION OF INTERNAL CONTROLS IN A DATABASE ENVIRONMENT
SPIKES, PAMELA ANN	A STUDY OF THE APPLICATION OF THE UNRELATED BUSINESS INCOME TAX PROVISIONS TO COLLEGES AND UNIVERSITIES
STROUD, J. B., JR.	PERCEPTIONS OF CITY MANAGERS CONCERNING MUNICIPAL FINANCIAL STATEMENT USERS, USER IMPORTANCE, AND IMPORTANCE OF SELECTED ITEMS OF DISCLOSURE
SUDIBYO, BAMBANG	THE ADEQUACY OF CPAS' UNDERSTANDING OF THE RELATIVE SERIOUSNESS OF ALPHA AND BETA RISKS IN STATISTICAL AUDIT SAMPLING
SUTTER, MARK D.	A TEST OF FACTORS AFFECTING BUDGETING CHARACTERISTICS OF MUNICIPALITIES
SUTTON, STEVEN GALE	FORMULATING QUALITY MEASURES FOR AUDIT ENGAGEMENTS
SWEENEY, JOHN THOMAS	COGNITIVE MORAL DEVELOPMENT AND AUDITOR INDEPENDENCE: AN EMPIRICAL INVESTIGATION
SWEENEY, MICHAEL PETER	MANAGEMENT ACCOUNTING IN MUNICIPAL GOVERNMENTS
SWENSON, DAN WILLIAM	AN EMPIRICAL INVESTIGATION OF HOW FIRM DIFFERENCES AFFECT MANAGEMENT SATISFACTION WITH ACTIVITY-BASED COSTING
TATUM, KAY WARD	AN EMPIRICAL STUDY OF AUDIT SAMPLING PROBLEMS
TEO, SUSAN PIN PIN	THE DEVELOPMENT OF AN INTERNATIONAL AUDITING HARMONIZATION MODEL AND THE EMPIRICAL TESTING OF ONE OF ITS COMPONENTS: AUDIT QUALITY
TICHICH, MARY CAROL	THE SEC INTERACTION IN THE ACCOUNTING STANDARDS SETTING PROCESS: AN ANALYSIS OF THE FASB STATEMENTS
TOCCO, ANTHONY LEONARD	AN EMPIRICAL INVESTIGATION OF THE OPINIONS OF SELECTED FINANCIAL STATEMENT USERS TOWARD THE ADOPTION OF ADDITIONAL SEGMENT INFORMATION TO 'FINANCIAL ACCOUNTING STANDARD NO. 14'
TOERNER, MICHAEL CHARLES	AN INVESTIGATION OF THE EFFECT OF A FAVORABLE EXTERNAL QUALITY ASSURANCE REVIEW ON THE SCOPE OF THE EXTERNAL AUDITOR'S EXAMINATION OF AN ORGANIZATION'S FINANCIAL STATEMENTS
TROUTMAN, COLEEN S.	MORAL COMMITMENT TO TAX COMPLIANCE AS MEASURED BY THE DEVELOPMENT OF MORAL REASONING AND ATTITUDES TOWARDS THE FAIRNESS OF THE TAX LAWS
TURNER, LESLIE DANIEL	IMPROVED MEASURES OF MANUFACTURING MAINTENANCE IN A CAPITAL BUDGETING CONTEXT: AN APPLICATION OF DATA ENVELOPMENT ANALYSIS EFFICIENCY MEASURES
TURNER, ROBERT M.	AN EXAMINATION OF EXTERNAL FINANCIAL REPORTING BY COLLEGES AND UNIVERSITIES
TYSON, THOMAS N.	FACTORS ASSOCIATED WITH CONTROLLER DEPARTMENT PARTICIPATION IN MEASURING QUALITY COSTS
UENO, SUSUMU	THE INFLUENCE OF CULTURE ON BUDGET CONTROL PRACTICES IN THE U.S.A. AND JAPAN: AN EMPIRICAL STUDY

Listing by Research Method

UGRAS, YUSUF JOSEPH	AN EMPIRICAL EXAMINATION OF THE FACTORS AFFECTING PERFORMANCE EVALUATION USE OF COST ALLOCATION
ULINSKI, MICHAEL	AN ANALYSIS OF THE RELATIONSHIP OF JOB NEED FULFILLMENT AND MICROCOMPUTER TRAINING TO MICROCOMPUTER USER SATISFACTION LEVELS OF PUBLIC ACCOUNTANTS
VANSYCKLE, LARRY D.	A CRITICAL EVALUATION OF THE CPA'S PERFORMANCE OF INTERNAL CONTROL REVIEWS OF EDP SYSTEMS IN COMPLIANCE WITH GENERALLY ACCEPTED AUDITING STANDARDS
VARNON, ANTHONY WAYNE	AN EMPIRICAL EXAMINATION OF FINANCIAL ACCOUNTING PRINCIPLES FOR AGRICULTURAL PRODUCERS: THE CASE OF PREPRODUCTIVE COSTS OF PERENNIAL FRUIT AND NUT CROPS
VENABLE, CAROL FRANCES	AN ANALYSIS OF AUDITOR INDEPENDENCE AND ITS DETERMINANTS
WADHWA, DARSHAN L.	PERCEPTIONS OF CPAS REGARDING THE IMPACT OF THE ECONOMIC RECOVERY TAX ACT OF 1981 AND THE TAX REFORM ACT OF 1986 ON THE DOLLAR-VALUE LIFO INVENTORY METHOD FOR SMALL BUSINESSES
WALKER, LOUELLA	EMPIRICAL TESTS OF AN EXPLANATORY MODEL OF PERFORMANCE IN INTERMEDIATE ACCOUNTING I
WATERS, JOHN MILBOURNE, II	AN EMPIRICAL ASSESSMENT OF ATTITUDES TOWARD AUDIT OPINIONS AND ATTITUDES TOWARD AUDIT REPORTING
WATTERS, MICHAEL PAUL	ACCOUNTING AND REPORTING PRACTICES OF MISSISSIPPI CATFISH PRODUCERS: AN EMPIRICAL STUDY
WEBB, JUDITH L.	TRANSACTION COSTS AND CONTROL SYSTEM CHOICE IN MULTINATIONAL ENTERPRISES: AN EMPIRICAL TEST
WESTBROOK, LESTER CURTIS, JR.	THE USE OF FINANCIAL AND NONFINANCIAL INFORMATION FOR PERFORMANCE EVALUATION OF SEGMENTS AND MANAGERS IN DECENTRALIZED MANUFACTURING COMPANIES: A CONTINGENCY APPROACH
WESTORT, PETER JOSEPH	INVESTMENTS IN HUMAN CAPITAL BY ACCOUNTANTS IN PUBLIC PRACTICE
WHITE, STEVEN DALE	AN EMPIRICAL STUDY OF THE USER SATISFACTION OF ACCOUNTANTS WITH THE SOFTWARE MAINTENANCE FUNCTION
WILLIAMS, LOWELL KIM	ACCOUNTING STANDARDS OVERLOAD: A DESCRIPTIVE MODEL FOR EVALUATING PERCEPTIONS OF ACCOUNTING STANDARDS
WINKLER, LESLIE ANN RICHESON	AN EMPIRICAL ANALYSIS OF THE EFFECTS OF STRUCTURE, BEHAVIOR, AND COMMUNICATION IN A JUST-IN-TIME RELATIONSHIP
WOLK, CAREL MARIE	CAUSAL ATTRIBUTIONS FOR PERFORMANCE: IMPLICATIONS FOR AUDITOR TURNOVER
WOOD, ROYCE WILBURN, JR.	AN ANALYSIS OF SELECTED INTERNAL CONTROLS FOR FINANCIAL ACCOUNTING AT THE CENTRAL OFFICE LEVEL OF ALABAMA BOARDS OF EDUCATION
WULSIN, FREDERICK ROELKER	AN INQUIRY INTO THE CAUSES OF AUDIT FAILURE
YAKHOU, MEHENNA	A COMPARATIVE STUDY OF THE ADOPTION PROCESS OF MANAGEMENT ACCOUNTING INNOVATIONS BY PUBLIC AND PRIVATE MANUFACTURING AND SERVICE ORGANIZATIONS IN FRANCE
YOUNG, GAIL THIBAULT	AN INVESTIGATION OF THE USEFULNESS OF THE FINANCIAL STATEMENTS AS SUPPLEMENTED BY OIL AND GAS PRODUCING ACTIVITIES DISCLOSURES

Listing by Research Method

YOUNG, RONALD MAURICE   THE EFFECTS OF THE METHOD OF ALLOCATING SYSTEM COSTS ON THE INFORMATION SYSTEM

YUEN, ALEXANDER E. C.   THE CALIFORNIA EXPERIENCE: AN EMPIRICAL STUDY OF THE USEFULNESS OF MUNICIPAL FINANCIAL REPORTS FOR NEWSPAPER REPORTERS

ABOUT THE EDITORS

J. David Spiceland, Ph.D., CPA, is Professor of Accounting at the University of Memphis. Dr. Spiceland is the author of a textbook, articles in many academic and professional journals, and the first edition of Directory of Dissertations in Accounting.

Kay E. Zekany, Ph.D., CMA, is Assistant Professor of Accounting at the University of Memphis. Professor Zekany is a recent graduate from the University of South Carolina.

Learning Resources
Centre